THE QURAN

The Quran, a book which brings glad tidings to mankind along with divine admonition, stresses the importance of man's discovery of truth on both spiritual and intellectual planes.

Every book has its objective and the objective of the Quran is to make man aware of the Creation plan of God. That is, to tell man why God created this world; what the purpose is of settling man on earth; what is required from man in his pre-death life span, and what he is going to confront after death. The purpose of the Quran is to make man aware of this reality, thus serving to guide man on his entire journey through life into the after-life.

The main themes of the Quran are enlightenment, closeness to God, peace and spirituality. The Quran uses several terms, tawassum, tadabbur, and tafakkur, which indicate the learning of lessons through reflection, thinking and contemplation on the signs of God scattered across the world. The present translation of the Quran has been done keeping in mind these very themes.

THE QURAN

Translated by
WAHIDUDDIN KHAN
FARIDA KHANAM

تَرْجَمَة
مَعَاني القُرْآن الْكَرِيمِ
بالانْجلِيزِيَّة

GOODWORD BOOKS

This translation of the Quran is copyright free
First published by Goodword Books 2014
Reprinted 2019

Goodword Books
1, Nizamuddin West Market, New Delhi-110013
Tel. +9111-41827083, Mob. +91-8588822672
email: info@goodwordbooks.com
www.goodwordbooks.com

Goodword Books, Chennai
Mob. +91-9790853944, 9600105558

CPS International USA
2665 Byberry Road, Bensalem, PA 19020, USA
Cell: 617-960-7156
email: kkaleemuddin@gmail.com

Printed in India

CONTENTS

THE QURAN

INTRODUCTION

The Quran is the Book of God. It has been preserved in its entirety for all time to come. Although written originally in Arabic, it has been made accessible, thanks to translations, to those who have no knowledge of Arabic. While no substitute for the original, translations serve the signal purpose of spreading the word of God far beyond the Arabic-speaking peoples to a far broader spectrum of humanity.

The Quran is apparently in the Arabic language, but in reality, it is in the language of nature, that is, the language in which God directly addressed all human beings at the time of Creation. This divine invocation of humanity is ever-present in the consciousness of all human beings, that is why the Quran is universally understandable—to some on a conscious plane, and to others at the subconscious level. This reality has been described in the Quran as 'clear revelations in the hearts of those who have been given knowledge.' This verse goes on to say that 'none deny Our revelations save the wrongdoers' (29:49).

This means that the Divine Reality, explained by the Quran on a conscious plane, pre-exists in man at the level of the subconscious. The message of the Quran is not, therefore, something which is alien to man. It is in fact a verbal expression of that same Divine Reality which is in consonance with man's own nature and with which he is already familiar. The Quran explains this by saying that those born in later times were all initially born at the time of the creation of Adam and, at that time, God had directly addressed all these human souls.

This event is thus alluded to in the Quran:

'[Prophet], when your Lord brought forth the offspring from the loins of the Children of Adam and made them bear witness about themselves, He said, 'Am I not your Lord?' and they replied, 'Yes, we bear witness that You are.' So you cannot say on the Day of Resurrection, 'We were not aware of this' (7:172).

In the following verse, the Quran makes further mention of the dialogue between God and man:

'Surely We offered Our trust to the heavens and the earth, and the hills, but they shrank from bearing it and were afraid of it. And man undertook it. But he has proved a tyrant and a fool' (33:72).

The Quran, for man, is in essence already known to him, rather than an entirely unknown entity. In reality, the Quran is the unfolding of the human mind.

When one whose nature is alive—having saved himself from later conditioning—reads the Quran, those brain cells will be activated wherein God's first address lies preserved. If we keep this in mind, it will not be difficult to appreciate that the translation of the Quran is a valid means of understanding it.

If God's address was the First Covenant, the Quran is the Second Covenant. Each testifies to the veracity of the other. If one has little, or even no grasp of the Arabic language, and can read the scriptures only in translation, he should not anticipate that he will be frustrated in his understanding of the Quran, for the Quranic concept of man as the natural recipient of God's word has become a reality in modern times. The science of the genetic code and the findings of anthropology both fully support this viewpoint.

The Creation Plan of God

Every book has its objective and the objective of the Quran is to make man aware of the Creation plan of God. That is, to tell man why God created this world; what the purpose is of settling man on earth; what is required from man in his pre-death life span, and what he is going to confront after death. Man is born as an eternal creature. When God created man as such, He divided his life span into two periods, the pre-death period, which is a time of trial, and the post-death period, which is the time for receiving the rewards or punishment merited by one's actions during one's lifetime. These take the form of eternal paradise or eternal hell. The purpose of the Quran is to make man aware of this reality. This is the theme of this divine Book, which serves to guide man through his entire journey through life into the after-life.

It would be correct to say that man is a seeker by birth. These questions lurk in everyone's mind: Who am I? What is the purpose of my life? What is the reality of life and death? What is the secret of man's success and failure? etc. According to the Quran, the answer to these questions is that the present world is the testing ground and whatever man has been endowed with in his pre-death period is all a part of the test. The Hereafter is the place where the result of the test will be taken into account by the Almighty and whatever man receives in the life after death, by way of reward or punishment, will be commensurate with his deeds in this world. The secret of man's success in this life is to understand God's creation plan and map out his life accordingly.

A Book of Divine Warning

The Quran is a book of divine warning. A combination of lessons and admonitions, it would be even more appropriately called a book of wisdom. The Quran does not follow the pattern of the traditional didactic book. In fact, when the average reader picks up the Quran, it appears to him to be a collection of fragmentary statements. Apparently this feeling is not unreal. But this arrangement of the Quran is not due to any shortcoming, but is rather in conformance with the Quranic plan of retaining its original form in order to fulfill its purpose of conveying the message of truth to the reader who may, in his forays into the scriptures, read only one page, one verse or one line at a time.

One vital aspect of the Quran is that it is a reminder of the blessings granted by the Supreme Benefactor. The most important of these are the exceptional qualities with which God endowed man when He created him. Another great blessing is that He settled him on the earth, a planet where all kinds of support systems existed for his benefit. The purpose of the Quran is to ensure that, while enjoying these blessings of nature, man will keep his Benefactor in mind: he must acknowledge the munificence of his Creator. It is in so doing that man will gain entry into eternal paradise; ignoring his Benefactor, on the other hand, will lead man straight to hell. The Quran is indeed a reminder of this inescapable reality.

The Inner Spirit and God Realization

One important quality of the Quran is that it gives us only basic, but essential principles, often resorting to reiteration to emphasize them. On the contrary, non-basics, or matters relating only to form, constitute only a negligible part of the scriptures. This is in consonance with the Quranic scheme, the importance of form being entirely secondary. To the Quran, only those precepts are important which figure as fundamental guidelines. This aspect of the Quran is so clear that its reader cannot but appreciate it.

The truth is that the inner spirit is of the utmost importance in the building of the Islamic personality. Once the inner spirit is developed, correct form will naturally ensue. But form on its own can never produce the inner spirit. That is why the aim of the Quran is to initiate and bring to fruition an intellectual revolution within man. The expression used by the Quran for this intellectual revolution is *ma'rifah* (realization of truth) (5:83).

The Quran stresses the importance of man's discovery of truth at the level of realization. True faith in God is what one achieves at such a level. Where there is no realization, there is no faith.

The Word of God

When you read the Quran, you will repeatedly find it stated that it is the word of God. Apparently this is a plain fact. But when seen in context, it is an extraordinary statement. There are many books in the world which are believed to be sacred. But, except for the Quran, we do not find any religious book which thus projects itself as the word of God. This kind of statement, appearing uniquely in the Quran, gives a point of departure to the reader. He then studies it as an exceptional book, rather than as a common book written by human beings. We find recurring in the Quran statements worded more or less as follows, 'O man, it is your Lord, who is addressing you. Listen to His words and follow Him.' Even this style of address is quite exceptional. This kind of direct divine invocation is not present in any other book. It leaves a lasting impression on man. He feels his Lord is directly addressing him. This feeling compels man to take the assertions of the Quran with extreme seriousness, rather than treat them like everyday statements in an ordinary book. The style of compilation of the Quran is also unique. Books written by human beings usually have their material arranged in order from

A to Z, according to the topic. But the Quran does not follow a pattern of this kind, so that to the common man it appears to be lacking in order. When looked at in reality, however, it will emerge as an extremely coherent and orderly book, and quite majestic in its style of writing. While reading the Quran, we feel that its writer is on a very high pedestal from where He is looking down and addressing the whole of humanity, which is His special concern. This address focuses on different groups of human beings, while encompassing all of them.

One special aspect of the Quran is that at any moment its reader can consult its Writer, put his questions and receive answers, for the Writer of the Quran is God Himself. He is a living God. As man's Creator, He directly hears and answers man's call.

A Peaceful Ideological Struggle

Those who are introduced to the Quran only through the media, generally have the impression that the Quran is a book of *jihad*, and *jihad* to them is an attempt to achieve one's goal by means of violence. But this idea is based on a misunderstanding. Anyone who reads the Quran for himself will easily appreciate that its message has nothing to do with violence. The Quran is, from beginning to end, a book which promulgates peace and in no way countenances violence. It is true that *jihad* is one of the teachings of the Quran. But *jihad*, taken in its correct sense, is the name of peaceful struggle rather than of any kind of violent action. The Quranic concept of jihad is expressed in the following verse, 'Do greater *jihad* (i.e strive more strenuously) with the help of this [Quran]' (25:52).

Obviously, the Quran is not a weapon, but a book which gives us an introduction to the divine ideology of peaceful struggle. The method of such a struggle, according to the Quran, is 'to speak to them a word to reach their very soul' (4:63).

So, the desired approach, acccording to the Quran, is one which moves man's heart and mind. That is, in addressing people's minds, it satisfies them, convinces them of the veracity of the Quran and, in short, brings about an intellectual revolution within them. This is the mission of the Quran. And this mission can be performed only by means of rational arguments. This target can never be achieved by means of violence or armed action.

It is true that there are certain verses in the Quran, which convey injunctions similar to the following, 'Slay them wherever you find them' (2:191).

Referring to such verses, there are some who attempt to give the impression that Islam is a religion of war and violence. This is totally untrue. Such verses relate, in a restricted sense, to those who have unilaterally attacked the Muslims. The above verse does not convey the general command of Islam.

The truth of the matter is that the Quran was not revealed in the complete form in which it exists today. It was revealed from time to time, according to the circumstances, over a time span of 23 years. If this is divided into years of war and peace, the period of peace amounts to 20 years, while that of state of war amounts only to 3 years. The revelations during these 20 peaceful years were the peaceful teachings of Islam as are conveyed in the verses regarding the realization of God, worship, morality, justice, etc.

This division of commands into different categories is a natural one and is found in all religious books. For instance, the Gita, the holy book of the Hindus, pertains to wisdom and moral values. Yet along with this is the exhortation of Krishna to Arjuna, encouraging him to fight (Bhagavad Gita, 3:30). This does not mean that believers in the Gita should wage wars all the time. Mahatma Gandhi, after all, derived his philosophy of non-violence from the same Gita. The exhortation to wage war in the Gita applies only to exceptional cases where circumstances leave no choice. But for general day-to-day existence it gives the same peaceful commands as derived from it by Mahatma Gandhi.

Similarly, Jesus Christ said, 'Do not think that I came to bring peace on Earth. I did not come to bring peace, but a sword.' (Matthew, 10:34).

It would not be right to conclude that the religion preached by Christ was one of war and violence, for such utterances relate purely to particular occasions. So far as general life is concerned, Christ taught peaceful values, such as the building up of a good character, loving each other, helping the poor and needy, etc.

The same is true of the Quran. When the Prophet Muhammad emigrated from Makkah to Madinah, the idolatrous tribes were aggressive towards him. But the Prophet always averted their attacks by the exercise of patience and the strategy of avoidance. However on certain occasions no other options existed, save that of defence. Therefore, he had to do battle on certain occasions. It was these circumstances, which occasioned those revelations relating to war. These commands, being specific to certain circumstances, had no general application. They were not meant to be valid for all time to come. That is why; the permanent status of the Prophet has been termed a 'mercy for all mankind.' (21:107)

Islam is a religion of peace in the fullest sense of the word. The Quran calls its way 'the paths of peace' (5:16). It describes reconciliation as the best policy (4:128), and states that God abhors any disturbance of the peace (2:205). We can say that it is no exaggeration to say that Islam and violence are contradictory to each other.

A Revealed Book

The Quran is a book of God revealed to the Prophet Muhammad. It did not come to him in the form of a complete book, but in parts over a period of 23 years. The first part was revealed in 610 AD, when the Prophet Muhammad was in Makkah. Subsequently, different parts continued to be revealed regularly, the final part being revealed in 632, when the Prophet was in Madinah.

There are 114 chapters in the Quran, both long and short. The verses number about 6600. To meet the needs of recitation, the Quran was divided into 30 parts. These parts were finally set in order under the guidance of the Angel Gabriel, through whom God had revealed the Quran.

When the Quran was revealed in the first quarter of the 7th century, paper had already been invented. This paper, known as papyrus, was made by hand from the fibres of certain trees. Whenever any part of the Quran was revealed, it was written down on papyrus, or in Arabic, *qirtas* (6:7). During this process, people committed the verses to memory, the Quran being the only Islamic literature which was recited in prayer, as well as being read out for the purposes of *da'wah*. In this way, the Quran continued to be simultaneously memorized as well as written down. This method of preservation continued during the lifetime of the Prophet Muhammad. In this way, the Quran was preserved during the lifetime of the Prophet.

The third caliph, 'Uthman ibn 'Affan, had several copies prepared. He sent these to different cities, where they were kept in the great mosques. People not only recited from these copies, but also prepared more copies from them.

The writing of the Quran by hand continued till the printing press was invented and paper began to be manufactured on a large scale, thanks to the industrial revolution. Then, the Quran began to be printed. Printing methods went on improving and so the printing of the Quran also improved. Now printed copies of the Quran have become so common that they can be found in every home, mosque, library and bookstore. Today anyone can find a beautiful copy of the Quran, wherever he might be, in any part of the globe.

How to Read the Quran?

The Quran says, 'Recite the Quran slowly and distinctly.' (73:4) This means, read the Quran in slow, measured rhythmic tones. That is, read, paying full attention to the import of the content. When read like this, a two-way process between Quran and its reader comes into play. For him, the Quran is an address or speech by God and his heart starts answering this address at every verse. In the Quran where there is any mention of God's majesty, the reader's entire existence is strongly affected by the realisation of His greatness. When God's blessings are enumerated in the Quran, the reader's heart overflows with gratitude; when God's retribution is described in the Quran, the reader trembles on reading it; when an order is laid down in the Quran, the feeling becomes intensified in the reader that he should become the obedient subject of his Lord by carrying out that order.

Wahiduddin Khan, New Delhi, January 2009
skhan@goodwordbooks.com

CHRONOLOGICAL TABLE
OF THE QURAN

570	Birth of the Prophet Muhammad (the Prophet's father died a few months before his birth)
576	Death of the Prophet's mother Aminah, when the Prophet is six year old
578	Death of the Prophet's grandfather, 'Abdul Muttalib
595	The Prophet's marriage to Khadijah
610	The Prophet receives the first revelation of the Quran at Mount al-Nur near Makkah
613	First public preaching.
615	Migration of some of the companions of the Prophet to Abyssinia (Ethiopia) to avoid persecution at the hands of the Makkans
616-619	The Banu Hashim boycotts the Prophet and his family
619	Death of the Prophet's wife Khadijah and uncle Abu Talib
619	The Prophet visits Taif for support, but the people there give him humiliating treatment.
620	The Prophet's Night Journey to Jerusalem and then to the Seven Heavens
622	The Prophet's migration (*hijrah*) from Makkah to Madinah, which marks the beginning of the Islamic calendar
624	Battle of Badr: the pagan Makkans were defeated by the Muslims

625	Battle of Uhud: the Muslims were defeated by the pagan Makkans
628	The Peace Treaty of Hudaybiyyah. Ten year no-war pact with pagan Makkans, allowing peaceful preaching of Islam. As a result many came into the fold of Islam
630	No-war pact broken by the pagan Makkans. Makkah's surrender—the Prophet forgives the Makkans and entire population enters the fold of Islam
631	'The Year of Embassies'—Islam accepted by Arabian tribes. The Prophet enters into peace treaties with the Christians and Jewish tribes
632	The Prophet's Farewell Pilgrimage to Makkah
632	8th June. Death of the Prophet Muhammad at Madinah
633	Quran prepared in one volume by Caliph Abu Bakr
645	Caliph 'Uthman has several copies of the Quran made and distributed in neighbouring countries
1153	First Latin translation of the Quran
1543	First printed edition with preface by Martin Luther
1649	Alexander Ross translates the Quran into English from French
1734	George Sale's translation of the Quran
1930	Muhammad Marmaduke Pickthall's translation of the Quran
1934	'Abdullah Yusuf 'Ali's translation of the Quran
1980	Muhammad Asad's translation of the Quran

Map of Arabian Peninsula showing places at the time of the
revelation of the Quran, 610-632.

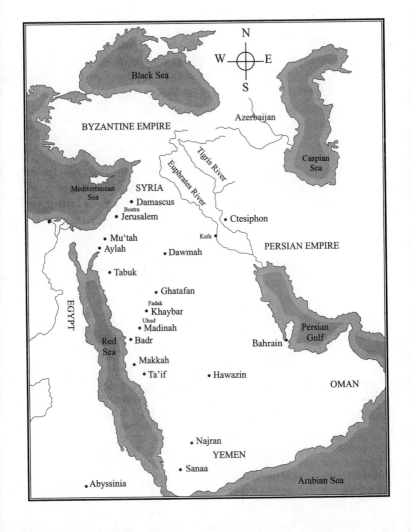

Map of Arabian Peninsula showing places at the time of the revelation of the Quran (610-632)

THE QURAN

1. THE OPENING (*AL-FATIHAH*)

¹In the name of God, the Most Gracious, the Most Merciful*a*

²All praise is due to God, the Lord of the Universe; ³the Beneficent, the Merciful; ⁴Lord of the Day of Judgement. ⁵You alone we worship, and to You alone we turn for help. ⁶Guide us to the straight path: ⁷the path of those You have blessed; not of those who have incurred Your wrath, nor of those who have gone astray.*b*

---

a The best way to begin any task is in the name of God, the Lord, the Being who is the source of all blessings, and whose blessings and mercy are continually pouring upon His creation. To commence any undertaking in His name is to pray that God, in His infinite mercy, should come to one's assistance and bring one's work to a successful conclusion. This is man's acknowledgement of the fact that he is God's servant, and also brings divine assurance of success.

b The Quran has a special and characteristic way of expressing a believer's inner sentiments in the most appropriate words. The invocation of God in the opening chapter of the Quran, constitute a supplication of this nature. The feelings which are naturally aroused in one after discovering the truth are expressed in these lines. When man looks at the world around him, he cannot fail to notice God's power and mercy abundantly in evidence everywhere. Wherever he casts his glance, he finds extraordinary order and supervision. Everything has been extraordinarily and astonishingly adapted to man's needs. This observation shows that the great cosmic machine cannot be in vain. Therefore, one realizes that there must come a day when the grateful and the ungrateful are rewarded for the way they have lived their lives in this world. One spontaneously entreats God in words to this effect, 'Lord, You are the Master of the Day of Judgement. I have submitted to You and humbly seek Your help; have mercy on me. Lord, show us the path that is, to You, the true path. Enable us to tread the path of Your chosen servants. Help us to avoid the path of those who have gone astray, and the path of those who have incurred Your wrath due to their obstinacy.'

God requires His servant to live his life with such feelings and emotions. The opening chapter of the Quran is a miniature portrayal of Islamic belief; the rest of the Quran is an enlargement of this picture.

2. THE HEIFER (*AL-BAQARAH*)

In the name of God, the Most Gracious, the Most Merciful

[1] *Alif Lam Mim*[a]

[2] This is the Book; there is no doubt in it.[b] It is a guide for those who are mindful of God, [3] who believe in the unseen, and are steadfast in prayer, and spend out of what We have provided them with; [4] those who believe in the revelation sent down to you and in what was sent before you, and firmly believe in the life to come—[5] they are the people who are rightly following their Lord and it is they who shall be successful.[c]

[6] As for those who are bent on denying the truth, it makes no difference to them whether you warn them or not, they will not believe. [7] God has sealed their hearts and their ears, and over their eyes there is a covering. They will have a terrible punishment.

---

a Muqatta'at, which in Arabic means abbreviated or shortened letters, are symbolic letter combinations. They appear respectively at the beginning 29 chapters of the Quran in the form of *Alif Lam Mim, Ha Mim, Nun, Ayn Sin, Qaf*, etc. They also appear as chapter names, such as *Ta Ha, Ya Sin, Sad* and *Qaf*.

b There is no doubt that the Quran is a book of guidance. But it guides only those who are sincere in their search for truth, and who are anxious to be guided. The search for truth is inherent in man's nature; one has simply to uncover one's own true nature in order to find it. True searching and true finding are but the initial and the advanced stages of the same journey. One who searches for truth unravels the closed faculties of his own inner self. Thus with God's help, the vague yearnings of his nature begin to receive a definite response.

c The awakening within one of these sincere yearnings is an attempt to discern the world of meanings (the hidden world) behind the world of forms (the present world). When this leads to a discovery, it is transformed into faith in the unseen. That which is initially an urge to submit to some superior power, later takes on the form of bowing to the Almighty. That which is initially a wish to sacrifice oneself for some greater good, later takes the form of spending one's wealth for the cause of God. That which is initially a quest to comprehend the final outcome of life beyond this world, finds an answer in the form of faith in the life to come.

[8] There are some who say, 'We believe in God and the Last Day,' yet they are not believers. [9] They seek to deceive God and the believers, but they only deceive themselves, though they do not realize it. [10] In their hearts is a disease, which God has increased. They will have a painful punishment, because they have been lying. [11] When they are told, 'Do not cause corruption in the land,' they say, 'We are only promoters of peace,' [12] but it is they who are really causing corruption, though they do not realize it. [13] And when they are told, 'Believe as other people have believed,' they say, 'Are we to believe just as fools believe?' Surely they are the fools, even though they do not realize it. [14] When they meet those who believe, they say, 'We believe.' But when they are alone with their evil leaders, they say, 'We are really with you; we were only mocking.' [15] God will requite them for their mockery, and draw them on, for a while, to wander blindly in their insolence. [16] Such are those who have taken misguidance in exchange for guidance; but their bargain does not profit them, nor have they found true guidance.

[17] They are like those who kindled a fire, and when it lighted up all around them, God took away their sight and left them in utter darkness, unable to see—[18] deaf, dumb, and blind: they will never return [to the right path]. [19] Or their case is like that of heavy rain pouring down from the clouds, accompanied by darkness, thunder and lightning; they thrust their fingers in their ears at the sound of thunderclaps for fear of death. God thus encompasses those who deny the truth. [20] The lightning almost takes away their sight: whenever it flashes upon them, they walk on, but as soon as darkness falls around them, they stand still. Indeed, if God pleased, He could take away their hearing and their sight: God has power over all things. [21] People, worship your Lord, who created you and those before you, so that you may become righteous, [22] who made the earth a bed, and the sky a canopy; and it is He who sends down rain from above for the growth of every kind of fruit for your sustenance. And do not knowingly set up rivals to God. [23] If you are in doubt about the revelation We have sent down to Our servant, then produce a single chapter like it, and call upon your helpers besides God, if you are truthful. [24] But if you cannot do it, and you can never do it, then

guard yourselves against the Fire whose fuel is men and stones, prepared for those who deny the truth. ²⁵ Give the good news to those who believe and do good works, that they will have Gardens through which rivers flow: whenever they are given fruit to eat they will say, 'This is what we were provided with before,' because they were given similar things. And there will be pure spouses for them, and they will abide there forever.

²⁶ God does not disdain to give a parable about a gnat or a smaller creature. The faithful know that it is the truth from their Lord, but those who deny the truth ask, 'What could God mean by this parable?' He lets many go astray through it, and guides many by it. But He makes only the disobedient go astray: ²⁷ those who break God's covenant after they have pledged to keep it, and sever whatever God has ordered to be joined, and spread corruption in the land—it is they who are the losers. ²⁸ How can you disbelieve in God when you were dead [lifeless] and He gave you life? He will let you die once more, then bring you back to life again, whereupon you will be returned to Him. ²⁹ It is He who created everything on the earth for you:ᵃ then He turned towards heaven and fashioned it into the seven heavens. He has knowledge of all things.

³⁰ When your Lord said to the angels, 'I am putting a successor on earth,'ᵇ they said, 'Will You place someone there who will cause corruption on it and shed blood, while we glorify You with Your praise and extol Your holiness?' [God] answered, 'Surely, I know that which you do not know.' ³¹ He taught Adam all the names, then He set them before the angels and said, 'Tell Me the names of

---

a God has created man from nothing. This is a favour great enough to make man completely surrender himself to God. But God has not just created man and left it at that: He has given him an earth made to suit his needs perfectly.

But there is more to the matter than merely this. Immediately after his demise, he will be brought before the Lord of the Universe to be judged. This state of affairs demands that he devote himself entirely to God; that he remember and obey God throughout his life, forever remaining His humble servant.

b The literal meaning of the Arabic word, *'khalifah'* is 'one who takes another's place'—a successor. In the age of hereditary rule, it was generally used for a monarch who took the place of his predecessor. See note to 35:39.

these, if what you say be true.' ³²They said, 'Glory be to You; we have no knowledge except whatever You have taught us. You are the All Knowing, the All Wise.' ³³Then He said, 'O Adam, tell them their names.' When Adam had told them the names, God said to the angels, 'Did I not say to you: I know the secrets of the heavens and of the earth, and I know what you reveal and what you conceal?'

³⁴When We said to the angels, 'Bow down before Adam,' they all bowed except for Iblis [Satan].*ᵃ* He refused and acted proudly and became an unbeliever. ³⁵We said, 'O Adam! live with your wife in Paradise and eat freely from it anywhere you may wish. Yet do not approach this tree lest you become wrongdoers.' ³⁶But Satan caused them both to slip through this and thus brought about the loss of their former state. We said, 'Go down from here as enemies to each other; and on earth you shall have your abode and your livelihood for a while!' ³⁷Then Adam received some words [of prayer] from his Lord and He accepted his repentance. He is the Forgiving One, the Merciful. ³⁸We said, 'Go down, all of you, from here: then when guidance comes to you from Me, anyone who follows My guidance will have no fear, nor will they grieve— ³⁹those who deny and reject Our signs shall be the inhabitants of the Fire; therein shall they abide forever.'*ᵇ*

⁴⁰Children of Israel, remember the favours I have bestowed upon you, and fulfil the covenant that you made with Me. I shall fulfil the covenant I made with you. Fear Me alone. ⁴¹And believe in the message I have sent down which fulfils that [predictions about the last prophet in their Scripture] which you already possess and do not be foremost among those who deny its truth. Do not sell My revelations for a paltry price; fear Me alone. ⁴²Do not mix truth with falsehood, or hide the truth when you know it. ⁴³Attend to your prayers, give the *zakat* [prescribed alms] and bow down with

---

a The word literally means one who was far from the truth, and from the mercy of God.

b God does not become plainly visible in this world; He reveals Himself through His signs, thereby testing his creatures. It is only those who can interpret His signs who will discover God Himself.

those who bow down. ⁴⁴ Do you admonish others to do good and forget this yourselves? Yet you read the Book. Will you not then understand? ⁴⁵ Seek help with patience and prayer; this is indeed an exacting discipline, but not to the humble, ⁴⁶ who know for certain that they will meet their Lord, and that they will return to Him.

⁴⁷ Children of Israel, remember My blessing which I have bestowed on you, and how I favoured you above all other people. ⁴⁸ Guard yourselves against the Day on which no soul shall in the least avail another, when neither intercession nor ransom shall be accepted from it nor shall help be given to it. ⁴⁹ Remember when We delivered you from Pharaoh's people, who subjected you to grievous torment, slaying your sons and sparing only your daughters—surely in that there was a great trial for you from your Lord—⁵⁰ and when We divided the sea for you and saved you and drowned Pharaoh's people, while you looked on. ⁵¹ We appointed for Moses forty nights [on Mount Sinai], and in his absence you took to worshipping the calf, and thus became transgressors. ⁵² Yet after that We pardoned you, so that you might be grateful. ⁵³ Remember when We gave Moses the Scripture, and the criterion [to distinguish between right and wrong], so that you might be guided. ⁵⁴ When Moses said to his people, 'O my people, you have indeed wronged yourselves by worshipping the calf; turn in repentance to your Creator and slay [the culprits] among you. That course is best for you in the sight of your Maker.' He relented towards you. He is the Forgiving One, the Merciful. ⁵⁵ Remember when you said, 'Moses, we will not believe in you until we see God with our own eyes,' a thunderbolt struck you while you were looking on. ⁵⁶ Then We brought you back to life after your death, so that you might be grateful. ⁵⁷ Then We caused the clouds to provide shade for you and sent down for you *manna*[a] and quails, saying, 'Eat the good things We have provided for you.' Indeed, they did not wrong Us, but they wronged themselves.

⁵⁸ Remember when We said, 'Enter this land and eat freely wherever you will. Make your way through the gates, bowing down and saying, "God! Forgive us our sins." We shall forgive

---

a A kind of dew; a sweetish liquid.

you your sins and We shall give abundance to those who do good.'
[59] But the wrongdoers changed the words to something other than
what they had been told. So We sent down upon the transgressors
a punishment from heaven, because they were disobedient. [60] When
Moses prayed for water for his people, We said to him, 'Strike the
rock with your staff!' And there gushed out from it twelve springs.
Each tribe knew its drinking-place. [We said], 'Eat and drink what
God has provided and do not act wrongfully in the land, spreading
corruption.' [61] When you said, 'Moses, we cannot bear to eat only
one kind of food, so pray to your Lord to bring forth for us some
of the earth's produce, its herbs and cucumbers, its garlic, lentils,
and onions.' Moses said, 'Would you take a lesser thing in exchange
for what is better? Go to some town and there you will find all that
you demand.' Abasement and destitution were stamped upon them,
and they incurred the wrath of God, for having rejected His signs,
and they killed His prophets unjustly, because they were rebels
and transgressors. [62] The believers, the Jews, the Christians, and the
Sabaeans—all those who believe in God and the Last Day and do
good deeds—will be rewarded by their Lord; they shall have no
fear, nor shall they grieve.

[63] [Children of Israel], We made a covenant with you and raised
the mountain high above you, saying, 'Hold fast to what We have
given you and bear its contents in mind, so that you may guard
yourselves [against evil].' [64] Yet after that you turned away, and but
for God's grace and mercy, you would have surely been among the
losers. [65] You are aware of those who transgressed in the matter of
the Sabbath, whereupon We said to them, 'Be as apes, despised!'
[66] We made their fate an example to their own generation and to
those who followed them and a lesson to those who fear God.

[67] When Moses said to his people, 'God commands you to sacrifice
a heifer,' they said, 'Are you making a mockery of us?' He answered,
'God forbid that I should be so ignorant!' [68] They said, 'Ask your Lord
to make it clear to us what sort of heifer she should be.' He answered,
'God says she should be neither too old nor too young, but in between,
so do as you are commanded.' [69] They said, 'Call on your Lord for
us, to show us what colour she should be.' He answered, 'God says

she should be a bright yellow heifer, pleasing to the eye.' ⁷⁰ They said, 'Ask your Lord to make it clear to us the exact type of heifer she should be, for to us all heifers look alike. If God wills, we shall be rightly guided.' ⁷¹ Moses answered, 'Your Lord says, she should be a heifer which has not been yoked to plough the land or water the fields, a heifer free from any blemish.' 'Now you have told us the truth,' they answered, and they sacrificed it, though they would rather not have done it. ⁷² Then, when you [Israelites] killed someone and started to blame one another—God brought to light what you concealed—⁷³ We said, 'Strike [the corpse] with a part of it.' Thus God restores the dead to life and shows you His signs, so that you may understand.

⁷⁴ Then your hearts became as hard as rock or even harder: for, there are rocks from which streams gush forth; and, there are some that cleave asunder and water flows out from them, while others fall down for fear of God. God is not unaware of what you do.[a]

⁷⁵ Do you then hope that they will believe in you when some of them have already heard the word of God and then, after having understood it, they knowingly perverted it? ⁷⁶ When they meet the faithful, they say, 'We are believers.' But when alone, they say to each other, 'Must you tell them what God has revealed to us? They will only use it to argue against you before your Lord! Have you no sense?' ⁷⁷ Do they not know that God knows all that they conceal and all that they disclose?

⁷⁸ There are among them unlettered people who have no real knowledge of the Scriptures, knowing only their own wishful thinking and following only conjecture. ⁷⁹ Woe to those who write the scripture with their own hands, and then declare, 'This is from God,' in order to sell it for a paltry price. Woe to them because of what their own hands have written, and woe to them for what they

---

a In nature, there is a message in every single thing, for God has created the world as a source of admonition and remembrance for man, to demonstrate to him how to make his life conform to the divine will. While throughout the universe, this message is conveyed in the language of silent examples, in the Quran it has been expressly set forth.

have earned. [80] They say, 'The Fire is not going to touch us, and [even if it does], it will only be for a few days!' Say [to them], 'Have you received a promise from God—for God never breaks His promise—or do you attribute something to God which you do not know?' [81] Truly, those who do evil and are encompassed by their misdeeds, shall be the inmates of the Fire. Therein they shall abide forever, [82] but those who believe and do good works are the heirs of Paradise; there they shall abide forever.

[83] Remember when We made a covenant with the Children of Israel, 'Worship none but God and be good to your parents and to relatives and orphans and the needy. And speak kindly to people.[a] Attend to your prayers and pay the *zakat* [prescribed alms].' But with the exception of a few, you turned away [in aversion] and paid no heed.

[84] When We made a covenant with you, We said, 'You shall not shed each other's blood, nor turn your people out of their homes.' You consented to this and bore witness. [85] Yet, here you are, slaying one another and driving some of your own people from their homelands, aiding one another against them, committing sin and aggression; but if they came to you as captives, you would ransom them. Surely their very expulsion was unlawful for you. Do you believe in one part of the Book and deny another part of it? Those of you who act thus shall be rewarded with disgrace in this world and with a severe punishment on the Day of Resurrection. God is never unaware of what you do. [86] Such are they who buy the life of this world at the price of the Hereafter. Their punishment shall not be lightened for them, nor shall they be helped.

[87] To Moses We gave the Book and sent a succession of messengers after him. We gave Jesus, son of Mary, clear signs and strengthened him with the Holy Spirit. But, whenever a messenger came to you with something which you did not desire, you grew arrogant,

---

a Man's first duty to God is to become His worshipper without ascribing any partners to Him. Secondly, he should show kindness to others. Kindness starts at home, with one's parents and family, extends to one's neighbours and relatives, and finally reaches out to everyone with whom one comes into contact. There is only one proper way to deal with others, and that is with justice and well-wishing.

calling some liars and slaying others. [88] They say, 'Our hearts are impenetrably wrapped [against whatever you say],' but God has rejected them for their denial; they have but little faith.

[89] And now that a Book has come to them from God, fulfilling that [predictions about the final prophet in their scriptures] which is with them, they deny it—whereas previously they used to pray for victory against the disbelievers—yet when there came to them that which they recognized as the truth, they rejected it. God's rejection is the due of all who deny the truth. [90] What they have sold their souls for is evil: to the denial of God's own revelation, grudging that He should reveal His bounty to whom He chooses from among His servants! They have incurred wrath upon wrath. Humiliating punishment awaits those who deny the truth.

[91] When they are told, 'Believe in what God has revealed,' they say, 'We believe in what was revealed to us,' while they deny the truth in what has been sent down after that, even though it is the Truth, confirming that which they already have. Say, 'Why did you kill God's prophets in the past, if you were true believers? [92] Moses came to you with clear signs, but in his absence you worshipped the calf and became wrongdoers.' [93] When We made a covenant with you and raised the mountain above you saying, 'Hold firmly to what We have given you and listen,' you said, 'We hear, but we disobey,' and their hearts were filled with the love of the calf, because of their refusal to acknowledge the truth. Say, 'Evil is that to which your faith enjoins you if you are indeed believers.' [94] Say, 'If God's abode of the Hereafter is for you alone, to the exclusion of all others, then wish for death, if you are truthful.' [95] But they will never wish for death, because of what their own hands have sent on before them; God is fully aware of the wrongdoers. [96] You will find them clinging to life more eagerly than any other people, even the polytheists. Any of them would wish to be given a life of a thousand years, though even such a long life would not save them from [Our] punishment; and God sees all that they do.

[97] Say, 'Anyone who is an enemy of Gabriel—who by God's leave has brought down to your heart [the Quran] fulfilling that [predictions about the last prophet in the earlier revelations] which precedes

it, and is a guidance and good news for the faithful—[98] whoever is an enemy of God, His angels, or His messengers, or of Gabriel or Michael, will surely find that God too is the enemy of those who deny the truth.' [99] We have sent down clear signs to you and no one will reject them except the wicked. [100] Why is it that, whenever they make a covenant, some of them cast it aside? Most of them do not believe. [101] Whenever a messenger from God has come to them, fulfilling that [predictions] which they already had, some of those to whom the Book was given have cast off the Book of God behind their backs as if they had no knowledge.

[102] They pursued what the devils falsely attributed to the kingdom of Solomon. Solomon was not an unbeliever: it is the devils who are unbelievers. They taught people witchcraft, and that which was sent down to Harut and Marut, the two angels in Babylon. But these two taught no one until they had said, 'We are but a trial, therefore, do not disbelieve [in God's guidance].' So men learnt from them that by which they caused discord between man and wife; but they harmed no one thereby, except by the command of God; [on the contrary], these people learned that which would harm them and do them no good, knowing full well that whoever acquired [this knowledge] would have no share in the Hereafter. Evil indeed was the [price] for which they sold their souls, if only they had known it. [103] And had they but believed and been mindful of God, His reward would have been far better for them, if they had but known it.

[104] Believers, do not say to the Prophet, '*Ra'ina*' but say, '*Unzurna*,' and listen to him with attention.[a] For those who deny the truth, there is a painful punishment.[a] [105] They who deny the truth from among the People of the Book, or from among those who associate partners with God, do not desire that any good should be sent down to you from

---

a Some people would sit in the Prophet's company and, by playing on words, make a mockery of his teachings. For instance, instead of using the unambiguous Arabic word for 'May we have your attention'—'*unzurna*'—they would say '*ra'ina*'. '*Ra'ina*', when pronounced properly, has much the same meaning as '*unzurna*', but with the protraction of the second vowel, it becomes '*raeena*', meaning 'our shepherd,' and with the protraction of the first it becomes '*raaina*', which means idiot.

your Lord. But God singles out for His grace whom He wills—for God is limitless in His great bounty. [106] If We abrogate a verse or cause it to be forgotten, We will replace it by a better one or one similar to it. Do you not know that God has power over all things? [107] Do you not know that the kingdom of the heavens and the earth belongs to God alone? And that there is no protector or helper for you besides God? [108] Do you [all] want to question your messenger just as Moses was questioned previously? Anyone who exchanges faith for unbelief has strayed from the right path.

[109] Many among the People of the Book wish, through envy, to lead you back to unbelief, now that you have embraced the faith and the truth has been made plain to them. But you should pardon them and bear with them until God gives His command. Truly, God has power over all things. [110] Attend to your prayers and pay the prescribed alms; any good you store up for yourselves, you will find it with God. Certainly, God sees what you do. [111] They declare, 'None shall ever enter Heaven unless he be a Jew or a Christian.' This is their own wishful thinking. [Prophet], say, 'Produce your evidence if you are telling the truth.' [112] Indeed, those who submit themselves to God and act righteously shall be rewarded by their Lord: they shall have no fear, nor shall they grieve.

[113] The Jews say, 'The Christians have no ground to stand on,' and the Christians say, 'The Jews have no ground to stand on.' Yet they both recite the Book, and those who have no knowledge say the same; God will judge between them on the Day of Resurrection concerning their disputes. [114] Who could be more wicked than someone who prevents God's name from being mentioned in His places of worship, and seeks to bring about their ruin, while it behoves these men to enter them with fear in their hearts? There is disgrace in store for them in this world and a great punishment in the next. [115] The East and the West belong to God. Whichever way you turn, there is the Face of God. God is all pervading and all knowing. [116] They say, 'God has taken a son.' Glory be to Him! Everything in the heavens and the earth belongs to Him; all things are obedient to Him. [117] He is the Originator of the heavens and the earth, and when He decrees something, He says only, 'Be!' and it is.

[118] Those who are devoid of knowledge say, 'Why does God not speak to us or show us a sign?' The same demand was made by those before them; their hearts are all alike. We have made the signs clear to those whose faith is firm. [119] We have sent you with the truth, bearing good news and giving warning. You will not be held accountable for the people of the Fire. [120] Neither the Christians nor the Jews will be pleased with you until you follow their ways. Say, 'God's guidance is the only true guidance.' If you followed their desires after the knowledge which has come to you, you would not have any patron or supporter against God. [121] Those whom We have given this Book follow it as it ought to be followed; it is they who [truly] believe in it; those who deny it will be the losers.

[122] Children of Israel, remember My favour which I have bestowed upon you, and how I preferred you above all other people; [123] and fear a Day when no human being shall avail another. Nor shall ransom be accepted from any of them, nor shall intercession be of any use to them, and none shall be succoured. [124] When his Lord tested Abraham with certain commands and he fulfilled them, He said, 'I will make you a leader of men.' Abraham asked, 'And what of my descendants?' He answered, 'My covenant does not extend to the transgressors.'

[125] And We made the House [the Ka'bah] a place of assembly and a sanctuary for mankind, [saying], 'Make the place where Abraham stood a place of worship.' We commanded Abraham and Ishmael, 'Purify My House for those who walk round it, those who stay there for devotion, and those who bow down and prostrate themselves.' [126] And when Abraham prayed, 'My Lord, make this city a city of peace, and provide its inhabitants with fruits, such of them as believe in God and the Last Day.' God said, 'As for those who deny the truth, I will grant them benefits for a short while and then subject them to the punishment of the Fire—an evil destination.'

[127] And when Abraham and Ishmael were laying the foundations of the House, [they prayed], 'Our Lord, accept this from us; for You are All Hearing, All Knowing. [128] Lord, make us submissive to You; make of our descendants a nation that will submit to You. Teach us our rites of worship and turn to us with mercy; You are

the Forgiving One and the Merciful. ¹²⁹ Our Lord, send forth to them a messenger of their own to recite Your revelations to them, to teach them the Scripture and wisdom, and purify them. You are the Mighty, the Wise One.'

¹³⁰ Who but a foolish man would turn away from the religion of Abraham? We chose him in this world, and in the Hereafter he shall be among the righteous. ¹³¹ When his Lord said to him, 'Surrender!' he responded, 'I have surrendered to the Lord of the Universe,' ¹³² and Abraham enjoined his sons to do the same, as did Jacob, 'My sons, God has chosen this religion for you; so do not let death overtake you, except when you are in a state of submission.' ¹³³ Were you present when Jacob faced the hour of death and he asked his sons, 'Who will you worship after me?' They answered, 'We will worship your God and the God of your fathers, Abraham and Ishmael and Isaac: the one God; we have submitted ourselves to Him.' ¹³⁴ Those were a people that have passed away; what they did is theirs and what you have done is yours. You will not be answerable for their deeds.

¹³⁵ They say, 'Be Jews or Christians, and you shall be rightly guided.' Say, 'By no means! We believe in the faith of Abraham, who was ever inclined [to God]; he was not one of those who set up partners with God.' ¹³⁶ Say, 'We believe in God and what was revealed to us; and what was revealed to Abraham, Ishmael, Isaac, Jacob, and their descendants, and what was given to Moses and Jesus and what was given to the [other] prophets by their Lord. We make no distinction between any of them. It is to Him that we surrender ourselves.' ¹³⁷ If they believe as you have believed, then are they rightly guided; but if they turn back, then know that they are entrenched in hostility. God will surely suffice to defend you against them, for He is All Hearing, All Knowing. ¹³⁸ We take on God's own dye. Who has a better dye than God's? We worship Him alone. ¹³⁹ Say, 'Do you dispute with us about God, while He is our Lord and your Lord? We have our actions and you have your actions. We are devoted to Him alone. ¹⁴⁰ Do you claim that Abraham and Ishmael and Isaac and Jacob and their descendants were all Jews or Christians?' Say, 'Do you know better or does God? And who could be more unjust than one who conceals a testimony given to him by

God? God is not unaware of what you do.' ¹⁴¹ Those were a people that have passed away; theirs is what they did and yours what you have done. You shall not be answerable for their deeds.

¹⁴² The foolish will ask, 'What has made them turn away from their direction of prayer which they used to face?' Say, 'The East and the West belong to God. He guides whom He pleases to the right path.' ¹⁴³ Thus We have made you a middle nation, so that you may act as witnesses for mankind, and the Messenger may be a witness for you. We decreed your former prayer direction towards which you used to face only in order that We might make a clear distinction between the Messenger's true followers and those who were to turn their backs on him. This was indeed a hard test for all but those whom God has guided. God will never let your faith go to waste. God is compassionate and merciful to mankind.

¹⁴⁴ We have frequently seen you turn your face towards heaven. So We will make you turn in a direction for prayer that will please you. So turn your face now towards the Sacred Mosque: and wherever you may be, turn your faces towards it. Those who were given the Book know this to be the truth from their Lord. God is not unaware of what they do. ¹⁴⁵ But even if you should produce every kind of sign for those who have been given the Book, they would never accept your prayer direction, nor would you accept their prayer direction: nor would any of them accept one another's direction. If, after all the knowledge you have been given, you yield to their desires, then, you shall surely become a transgressor. ¹⁴⁶ Those to whom We have given the Book recognize it just as they recognize their own sons. But, some of them knowingly conceal the truth. ¹⁴⁷ Truth is what comes from your Lord; therefore, do not be of those who doubt.

¹⁴⁸ Each community has its own direction in which it turns: vie, then, with one another in doing good works. Wherever you may be, God will bring you all before Him. God has power over all things. ¹⁴⁹ Wherever you set out from, turn your face in the direction of the Sacred Mosque—this is the truth from your Lord: He is not unaware of what you do—¹⁵⁰ wherever you come from, turn your face to the Sacred Mosque; wherever you may be, turn your faces towards it, so that people will not have any argument

against you except for the wrongdoers among them. Do not fear them; fear Me, so that I may perfect My favour to you and you may be rightly guided. ¹⁵¹ Thus We have sent among you a Messenger of your own to recite Our revelations to you, purify you and teach you the Book and wisdom, and to teach you what you did not know. ¹⁵² So remember Me; I will remember you. Be thankful to Me and do not be ungrateful.

¹⁵³ You who believe, seek help through patience and prayer; surely, God is with the steadfast. ¹⁵⁴ Do not say that those who are killed in God's cause are dead; they are alive, but you are not aware of it. ¹⁵⁵ We shall certainly test you with fear and hunger, and loss of property, lives and crops. Give good news to those who endure with fortitude. ¹⁵⁶ Those who say, when afflicted with a calamity, 'We belong to God and to Him we shall return,'*ᵃ* ¹⁵⁷ are the ones who will have blessings and mercy from their Lord: it is they who are on the right path!

¹⁵⁸ Safa and Marwah are among the symbols set up by God; there is nothing wrong if anyone goes on a pilgrimage to the House, or performs a minor pilgrimage, in walking to and fro between them. Of anyone who does good of his own accord, God is appreciative, and aware. ¹⁵⁹ Those who conceal the evidence of the truth and the guidance We have revealed, after We have made them clear to people in the Scripture, will be rejected by God and so do others. ¹⁶⁰ But from those who repent and mend their ways and make known the truth, I will certainly accept their repentance: I am the Ever Relenting, the Most Merciful. ¹⁶¹ Those who deny the truth, and die as deniers, on them shall be the curse of God and of angels

---

a On the death of a loved one, one goes in a state of prayerfulness, deep thinking and contemplation. The experience reminds him that there is very little time at his disposal and that at any moment death can come calling. However, we are so involved in worldly things that we never stop to think about the day which is fast approaching us. The Prophet Muhammad said, 'People are asleep, they will wake up only when they die.' All of a sudden, death will bring you standing face to face with God, at which time you will be held accountable for all your deeds.

and of men altogether. [162] Under it they shall remain forever; their punishment shall not be lightened, nor shall they be granted respite.

[163] Your God is one God. There is no deity save Him. He is the Compassionate, the Merciful. [164] In the creation of the heavens and the earth; in the alternation of night and day; in the ships that sail the ocean bearing cargoes beneficial to man; in the water which God sends down from the sky and with which He revives the earth after its death, scattering over it all kinds of animals; in the courses of the winds, and in the clouds pressed into service between earth and sky, there are indeed signs for people who use their reason.[a]

[165] Yet there are some who set up equals with God and adore them with the adoration due to God, but those who believe love God most. If only the wrongdoers could see—as they will see when they face the punishment—that all power belongs to God, and that God is severe in punishment. [166] When they face their punishment, those who have been followed will disown their followers, and all their ties shall be cut asunder, [167] those who followed will say, 'If we could only return to the world, we would disown them as they have disowned us.' God will thus show them their actions as a cause of bitter regret and remorse. They shall never emerge from the Fire.

---

[a] The vast universe spread out before us serves as a magnificent introduction to God. The existence of a limitless world in the form of the earth and the heavens is a proof that there must be a Creator behind it. Despite apparently different and contrasting elements, all things work together in absolute harmony, showing that their Creator and Sustainer is the one and only God. Then the fact that every single thing benefits the rest of the universe, in some manner or the other, shows that all things have been designed according to a definite and absolutely conscious plan. Apparently lifeless objects are invested with life through a natural process: this shows that death is only a temporary phase in this universe. Here death is always followed by new life. Every variety of animate creature flourishes in this world in huge numbers. All are being sustained by varied forms of the same food and drink, indicating the unfathomable power of God. The atmosphere totally encompassing the earth shows that man's life is entirely in his Creator's hands. Everything in this universe has been tamed to cater to man's needs. This is indicative of the fact that man's Creator is a highly compassionate being. Even before an individual has been born into the world, all his requirements have already been taken care of.

[168] O mankind, eat whatever is lawful and wholesome on the earth; and do not follow in the footsteps of Satan; for he is indeed your avowed enemy. [169] He bids you only to do evil and to commit deeds of abomination and to attribute to God something of which you have no knowledge. [170] But when they are told, 'Follow what God has sent down,' they answer, 'We will follow the ways of our fathers,' even though their fathers did not use their reason, and were devoid of all guidance. [171] Those who deny the truth are like animals which hear nothing in your call but the sound of a voice, without understanding its meaning. They are deaf, dumb and blind. They understand nothing.

[172] Believers, eat the wholesome things which We have provided for you and give thanks to God, if it is Him you worship. [173] He has forbidden you only carrion, blood, and the flesh of swine; also any flesh that is consecrated other than in the name of God. But for one who is driven by necessity, neither craving nor transgressing, it is no sin. For God is forgiving and merciful. [174] Those who conceal any part of the Scriptures which God has revealed in order to gain some paltry end, simply fill their bellies with Fire. On the Day of Resurrection, God will neither speak to them nor purify them. They will have a painful punishment. [175] Those are the ones who have taken error in exchange for guidance and punishment for forgiveness. How little do they seem to fear the Fire! [176] That is because God has sent down the Book with the truth. And those who pursue differences in the Scriptures go much too far in dissension.

[177] Virtue does not consist in whether you face towards the East or the West; virtue means believing in God, the Last Day, the angels, the Book and the prophets; the virtuous are those who, despite their love for it, give away their wealth to their relatives and to orphans and the very poor, and to travellers and those who ask [for charity], and to set slaves free, and who attend to their prayers and pay the alms, and who keep their pledges when they make them, and show patience in hardship and adversity, and in times of distress. Such are the true believers; and such are the God-fearing.[a]

---

a Believing in God is to trust in God in the full sense of the word. Believing

[178] Believers, retribution is prescribed for you in cases of murder: the free man for the free man, the slave for the slave, the female for the female. If the offender is granted some remission by the heir of the slain person, the agreed penalty should be equitably exacted and should be discharged in a handsome manner. This is an alleviation from your Lord and an act of grace. He who transgresses after this shall have a painful punishment. [179] In [this law of] retribution there is life for you, O people of understanding, so that perhaps you will be mindful of God. [180] It is prescribed that when death approaches any of you and he is leaving behind wealth, he shall make a will in favour of his parents and relatives equitably. This is a duty for all who fear God. [181] Anyone who alters it once he has heard it shall be accountable for his crime. Surely, God is all hearing and all knowing. [182] But if anyone apprehends partiality or an injustice on the part of a testator, it shall be no sin for him to bring about a settlement between the parties. God is forgiving and merciful.

[183] Believers, fasting has been prescribed for you, just as it was prescribed for those before you, so that you may guard yourselves against evil. [184] Fast for a specified number of days, but if any one among you is ill or on a journey, let him fast the same number of days later. For those who can fast only with extreme difficulty, there is a way to compensate—the feeding of a needy person. But he who does good of his own accord shall be well rewarded; but to fast is better for you, if you only knew. [185] The month of Ramadan is the month when the Quran was sent down as guidance for mankind with

---

in the Hereafter means giving the utmost importance to the life of the Hereafter instead of to the life of this world. Believing in the angels means believing in God's emissaries who are running this world at the divine command. Believing in the Book means believing that God has sent His guidance for man, which man must follow. Believing in the prophets is to accept these mortals as God's chosen messengers.

The faith in all these matters must so deeply pervade the believer's psyche that he helps the needy and others in distress by spending his wealth, says his prayers by surrendering himself totally to God, and pays the poor due—his only motivation being to earn God's pleasure. One of the characteristics of a true believer is that when he enters into a contract, he fulfils it, treating it as if he has entered into a covenant with God.

clear proofs of guidance and the criterion by which to distinguish right from wrong. Therefore, whoever of you is present in that month, let him fast; but he who is ill or on a journey shall fast a similar number of days later on. God desires ease for you, not hardship. He desires you to fast the whole month, so that you may glorify Him for His having guided you and so that you may be grateful to Him.

¹⁸⁶ When My servants ask you about Me, say that I am near. I respond to the call of one who calls, whenever he calls to Me: let them, then, respond to Me, and believe in Me, so that they may be rightly guided. ¹⁸⁷ It has been made lawful for you to go to your wives on the night of the fast: they are like a garment for you, and you are like a garment for them. God is aware that you were deceiving yourselves and He has turned in mercy towards you and pardoned you. So you may now consort with them and seek what God has ordained for you. Eat and drink until the white thread of dawn becomes distinct from the black. Then resume the fast until nightfall, and do not approach them during the nights of your devotional retreat in the mosques. These are the limits set by God, so do not approach them. Thus He makes clear His commandments to mankind, so that they may guard themselves [against evil].^a ¹⁸⁸ Do not consume one another's property by unjust means, nor offer it as a bribe to the authorities, so that you may deliberately and wrongfully devour a part of other people's wealth.

¹⁸⁹ They ask you about the phases of the moon. Say, 'They are a

---

a Fasting serves as training for two things at the same time—inculcating the spirit of thanksgiving and instilling the fear of God in the heart of the believer. Food and water are great blessings of God, yet man is incapable of attaching due importance to them. While fasting, he goes hungry and thirsty the whole day, then at sunset, in a state of extreme hunger and thirst, he eats and drinks to his fill. He then realizes through his own experience how great are the blessings of God which are present in the form of food and water. This experience produces boundless feelings of gratitude towards his Lord. On the other hand, fasting also serves as a form of training for a God-fearing life, which entails abstaining from all kinds of sins and evil deeds, which God has forbidden. A total abstention from food and drink from dawn until sunset is an exercise in making God one's guardian. The entire life of the believer is a life of fasting.

means of determining time for the regulation of people's affairs and for the pilgrimage.' Piety does not consist in entering your houses from the rear. Indeed, one who guards himself against evil out of fear of God is the truly righteous one. Enter your houses by their doors and be mindful of God, so that you may prosper. [190] And fight in God's cause against those who wage war against you, but do not commit aggression—for surely, God does not love aggressors. [191] Slay them wherever you find them [those who fight against you];*a* a drive them out of the places from which they drove you, for [religious] persecution is worse than killing. Do not fight them at the Sacred Mosque unless they fight you there. If they do fight you, slay them—such is the reward for those who deny the truth—[192] but if they desist, then surely God is most forgiving and merciful. [193] Fight them until there is no more *fitna* [religious persecution] and religion belongs to God alone. If they desist, then let there be no hostility, except towards aggressors.

---

a The Quran was revealed over a 23 year period and, evidently, many commandments were revealed with reference to specific situations, such as when the Prophet and his followers had been assailed by enemies. Certain verses, such as this one, give permission to fight. Many take these verses to mean that the Prophet and his Companions were commanded to wage war against non-Muslims. But the Prophet never engaged in armed aggression. Whenever he fought, it was purely in self-defence. (The Prophet engaged in combat only three times in his lifetime and that too for half a day on each occasion.). These verses obviously use words such as 'jihad', 'fight', etc., as expressions of emphasis rather than legal commands, otherwise the Prophet would certainly have gone on the offensive.

Such commandments can also be found in other religious scriptures, such as the Gita and the Bible. For example, Krishna tells Arjuna in the Mahabharata to go ahead and fight (Bhagavad Gita, 3:30). Similarly, Jesus says in the Bible, 'I did not come to bring peace, but a sword.' (Matthew, 10:34). But these statements were made in quite specific circumstances.

The Quran emphasizes that permission to fight is given only to those under attack (22:39). Clearly, only defensive war is permissible. Guerilla warfare, aggressive attacks, undeclared war, including terrorism and suicide bombings, are all strictly unlawful in Islam and negate the true teachings of the Quran and the Hadith, which are based on peace and non-violence. See pages xiv to xviii of the Introduction. See also notes to 4:1 and 4:102.

¹⁹⁴A sacred month for a sacred month: violation of sanctity calls for fair retribution. Thus you may exact retribution from whoever transgresses against you, in proportion to his transgression. Fear God and know that God is with those who are mindful of Him. ¹⁹⁵Spend for God's cause: do not cast yourselves into destruction by your own hands. Do good, God loves the doers of good.

¹⁹⁶Perform the Hajj and the minor pilgrimage [*umrah*] for the sake of God. If you are prevented from doing so, then make whatever offering you can afford and do not shave your heads until the offering has reached the place of sacrifice. But if any of you is ill, or has an ailment of the head, he should compensate by fasting or almsgiving or sacrifice. In times of peace, if any of you combines the minor pilgrimage with the Hajj, he should make whatever offering he can afford, but if he lacks the means, then let him fast three days during the pilgrimage and for seven days after his return; that is, ten days in all. That is incumbent upon anyone whose family does not live near the Sacred Mosque. Fear God and know that God is severe in punishment. ¹⁹⁷The pilgrimage is in the appointed months. Whoever intends to perform it during them must abstain from indecent speech, from all wicked conduct, and from quarrelling while on the pilgrimage. Whatever good you may do, God is aware of it. Make provision for yourselves—but surely, the best of all provision is God-consciousness. Always be mindful of Me, you that are endowed with understanding.

¹⁹⁸You will be committing no sin if [during the pilgrimage] you seek to obtain any bounty from your Lord. When you return from Arafat, remember God at the sacred place, and remember Him as He has guided you. Before this you were surely astray. ¹⁹⁹Then press on from where the pilgrims stream forth and ask God's forgiveness. God is ever forgiving and most merciful. ²⁰⁰When you have performed the acts of worship prescribed for you,*ᵃ* celebrate the praises of God as

---

a This prayer on the part of the believer is not a request for worldly riches. Material gain and worldly wealth are only parts of a 'test paper'. And no one would like to pray to increase the difficulty of his 'test paper'. This prayer is more like asking God to give him what is best for man in the eyes of God in this

you celebrated the praises of your fathers, or even more fervently than that. There are some who say, 'Our Lord, give us abundance in this world.' These shall have no share in the world to come.[a] [201] But there are others who pray, 'Our Lord, grant us good in this world as well as good in the world to come, and protect us from the torment of the Fire.' [202] They shall have a good share from what they have earned. God is swift in His reckoning. [203] Remember God during the appointed days; for one who hastens to leave in two days, it shall be no sin; and for one who stays on, it shall be no sin for him either. This is for one who fears God. Have fear of God, and know that you shall all be gathered before Him.

[204] There are some men whose views on the affairs of this life may please you. They even call on God to witness whatever is in their heart, yet they are the most contentious of quarrellers. [205] When he turns away, he sets out to spread corruption in the land, destroying crops and cattle. God does not love corruption. [206] When he is told, 'Have fear of God,' he is seized by pride which drives him to wrongdoing. Hell shall be enough for him. A dreadful resting place. [207] But there are others who would dedicate themselves to seeking the pleasure of God. God is compassionate to His servants.

[208] Believers, surrender yourselves totally to God, and do not follow in the footsteps of Satan; surely, he is your sworn enemy. [209] But if you lapse after the clear signs that have come to you, then know that God is mighty and wise. [210] Are they only waiting for God as well as the angels to come down to them under canopies of clouds, so that the matter will be settled? All things return to God. [211] Ask the Children of Israel how many clear signs We have given them. Anyone who changes God's blessing once it has come to him will find God is stern in punishment. [212] The life of this world is made

---

world and what is best for man in the eyes of God in the Hereafter.

a Prayers, especially those offered during the pilgrimage, are an outward manifestation of an inward state. Whatever one cherishes in one's heart, one expresses in prayer. One who has set his mind on worldly riches and grandeur will concentrate on little else when he prays to God, whereas one who seeks the next world, with its infinite happiness and blessings, will make this the central theme of his devotions.

to appear attractive for those who deny the truth and they scoff at those who believe. But those who fear God shall be above them on the Day of Resurrection: God bestows His bounties on whoever He pleases without stinting.

²¹³ Mankind was once a single community, [but then people developed differences], so God sent prophets to them as bearers of good tidings and warning, and sent down with them the Book containing the truth, so that He might judge between their disputes. It was only those to whom it [the scripture] was given who disagreed about it after clear signs had come to them, because of rivalry between them. God by His will guided the believers to the truth about which the others had disputed. God guides whom He will to a straight path. ²¹⁴ Do you think that you will enter Paradise without having suffered like those who passed away before you? Affliction and hardship befell them and so shaken were they that the Messenger and the believers with him would exclaim, 'When will God's help come?' Surely the help of God is near.

²¹⁵ They will ask you what they should spend on others. Say, 'Whatever you give should be for parents, close relatives, orphans, the needy, and travellers. God is well aware of whatever good you do.' ²¹⁶ Fighting [in defence] is ordained for you, abhorrent as it may be to you. You may dislike something although it is good for you, or like something although it is bad for you: God knows but you do not.

²¹⁷ They ask you about fighting in the sacred month. Say, 'To fight [in a sacred month] is a grave matter; but barring people from the path of God, to deny Him, and expelling people from the Sacred Mosque are far graver in His sight; and persecution is worse than killing.' They will not stop fighting you until they make you renounce your faith, if they can. Whoever of you turns back from his faith and dies as a denier of the truth will have his deeds come to nothing in this world and the Hereafter, and he will be an inhabitant of the Fire, to abide therein forever. ²¹⁸ But those who have believed, migrated, and striven for God's cause, can look forward to God's mercy: God is forgiving and merciful.

²¹⁹ They ask you [Prophet] about intoxicants and gambling. Say,

'There is great sin in both, although they have some benefit for people: but their harm is greater than their benefit.' They ask you what they should spend [in God's cause]. Say, 'Whatever is surplus to your needs.' Thus God makes His commandments clear to you so that you may reflect [220] upon this world and the Hereafter. They ask you about orphans. Say, 'Promotion of their welfare is an act of great goodness. There is no harm in your living together with them, for they are your brothers. God knows the mischief-maker from the reformer. If God had so willed, He would have afflicted you with hardship. Surely, God is mighty and wise.'

[221] Do not marry women who associate partners with God until they believe. A believing bondwoman is better than a woman who associates partners with God, however pleasing she may appear to you. Nor give believing women in marriage to men who associate partners with God, till they have believed; a believing bondman is certainly better than a man who associates partners with God, even though he may please you. Such people call you to Hellfire; but God calls you to Paradise and to forgiveness. He makes His messages clear to people, so that they might bear them in mind. [222] They ask you about menstruation. Say, 'It is an impurity, so keep away from women during it and do not approach them until they are cleansed; when they are cleansed you may approach them as God has ordained. God loves those who turn to Him in penitence and He loves those who keep themselves clean. [223] Your wives are your fields. Go, then, into your fields as you will. Send ahead [some good] for yourselves, and fear God, and know that you shall meet Him.' Give good tidings to the believers.

[224] Do not make God a pretext, when you swear by Him, to avoid doing good, being righteous and making peace between people. God is all hearing and all knowing. [225] God will not call you to account for any oaths you uttered unintentionally, but He will take you to task for what is intended in your hearts. God is most forgiving and forbearing. [226] For those who swear that they will not approach their wives, there shall be a waiting period of four months: if they revert to conciliation, surely, God is most forgiving and ever merciful; [227] but if they decide upon divorce, God is all hearing and all knowing.

[228] Divorced women should wait for three menstrual cycles; it is unlawful for them, if they believe in God and the Last Day, to hide what God has created in their wombs. Their husbands have the right to take them back within that time, if they desire to be reconciled. The wives have rights corresponding to those which the husbands have, according to what is recognized to be fair, but men have a rank above them. God is almighty and all wise.

[229] Divorce may be pronounced twice, and then a woman must be retained honourably or released with kindness. It is not lawful for you to take away anything of what you have given your wives, unless both fear that they would not be able to observe the bounds set by God. In such a case it shall be no sin for either of them if the woman opts to give something for her release. These are the bounds set by God; do not transgress them. Those who transgress the bounds of God are wrongdoers. [230] And if man finally divorces his wife, he cannot remarry her until she has married another man. Then if the next husband divorces her, there will be no blame on either of them if the former husband and wife return to one another, provided they think that they can keep within the bounds set by God. These are the bounds prescribed by God, which He makes clear to men of understanding. [231] Once you divorce women, and they have reached the end of their waiting period, then either retain them in all decency or part from them decently. Do not retain them in order to harm them or to wrong them. Whoever does this, wrongs his own soul. Do not make a mockery of God's revelations. Remember the favours God has bestowed upon you, and the Book and the wisdom He has revealed to exhort you. Fear God and know that God is aware of everything.

[232] When you divorce women and they reach the end of their waiting period, do not prevent them from marrying other men, if they have come to an honourable agreement. This is enjoined on every one of you who believes in God and the Last Day; it is more wholesome and purer for you. God knows, but you do not know. [233] And the [divorced] mothers should nurse their children for two whole years, if they wish to complete the period of nursing; and during that period the father of the child shall be responsible for the maintenance of

the mother in a reasonable manner. No soul is charged with more than it can bear. No mother should be made to suffer on account of her child, and no father should be made to suffer on account of his child. The same duties devolve upon the father's heir [in case of the death of the father]. But if, after consultation, they choose by mutual agreement to wean the child, there shall be no blame on them. Nor shall it be any offence for you if you desire to engage a wet-nurse for your children, provided you hand over what you have agreed to pay, in a reasonable manner. Have fear of God and know that God is observant of all your actions.

[234] If any of you die and leave widows, the widows should wait for four months and ten days. When they have reached the end of their waiting period you will not be blamed for what they may reasonably choose to do with themselves: God is aware of what you do. [235] It shall be no offence for you to hint at a proposal of marriage [to divorced or widowed women] or to cherish them in your hearts. God knows that you will bear them in mind. But do not enter into any secret arrangement with them, beyond conveying some indication to them of your inclination. Do not proceed with tying the marriage-knot before the end of their waiting period. Know that God has knowledge of all your thoughts. Therefore, take heed and bear in mind that God is forgiving and forbearing. [236] You will not be blamed [for not paying the dower money] if you divorce women when you have not yet consummated the marriage or fixed a dower money upon them, but make fair provision for them, the affluent according to his means and the straitened according to his means; this is binding on righteous men. [237] If you divorce them before the marriage is consummated, but after their dower money has been settled, give them the half of their dower money, unless they [the women] agree to forego it, or the man [the husband] in whose hand lies the marriage knot foregoes it. To forego is nearer to righteousness. Do not neglect any chance of behaving benevolently towards each other. God is observant of whatever you do.

[238] Be ever mindful of prayers, especially the middle prayer; and stand up before God in submissive devotion. [239] When you are exposed to danger, pray on foot or while riding; when you are safe

again, remember God, for He has taught you what you did not know. 240 If any of you die and leave widows, make a bequest for them of a year's maintenance without causing them to leave their homes; but if they leave of their own accord, you will not be blamed for what they may reasonably choose to do with themselves. God is almighty and wise. 241 For divorced women a provision according to what is fair shall also be made. This is an obligation binding on the righteous. 242 Thus God makes His commandments clear to you, so that you may understand.

243 Have you not seen those who fled their homes in their thousands for fear of death, whereupon God said to them, 'Die!' and later brought them back to life? Surely God is bountiful to mankind, but most of them are ungrateful. 244 Fight [in defence] in God's cause and remember that He is all hearing and all knowing. 245 Who will give God a generous loan?[a] He will multiply it many times over. It is God who withholds, and God who gives abundantly, and it is to Him that you shall all be returned.

246 Have you not heard of what the chiefs of the Children of Israel demanded of one of their prophets after Moses? They said, 'Appoint for us a king, and we will fight for the cause of God.' He replied, 'What if you refuse to fight, when ordered to do so?'[b] 'Why should we not fight for the cause of God,' they replied, 'when we have been driven forth from our homes and our children?' But when at last they were commanded to fight, they all refused, except a few of them. God knows the wrongdoers. 247 Their prophet said to them, 'God has now appointed Talut to be your king.' But they replied, 'How can he be king over us when we are worthier of kingship than he and he has not even been granted an abundance of wealth?' He said, 'God has chosen him over you, and has given him great knowledge and physique. God grants kingship to whoever He pleases: God is

---

a Spending for the cause of God's religion is called giving a 'generous loan'. This spending is purely for God: no other interest is involved. God called for a loan to be given to Him and he called it a 'generous loan' because He would return it many times over.

b See note to 2:191.

magnanimous and all knowing.' [248] Their prophet also said to them, 'The sign of his kingship is that the Ark [of the Covenant] shall come to you. Therein shall be tranquillity from your Lord, and the relics which the House of Moses and the House of Aaron left behind. It will be borne by the angels. There is a sign in this for you, if you believe.'

[249] When Talut set out with his forces, he said to them, 'God will test you with a river: whoever drinks from it is not with me and whoever does not drink is with me. There will, however, be no blame upon one who sips only a handful from it.' But, except for a few of them, they all drank from it. When he and those who believed along with him had crossed the river, they said, 'We have no strength today against Goliath and his warriors.' But those of them who believed that they would meet God replied, 'Many a small group, by God's command has prevailed against a large group. God is indeed with the steadfast.' [250] When they met Goliath and his warriors, they said, 'Our Lord, bestow patience upon us, make us stand firm, and help us against those who deny the truth.' [251] And so by the command of God they defeated them. David killed Goliath, and God gave him kingship and wisdom, and imparted to him the knowledge of whatever He willed. Had it not been for God's repelling some people by means of others, the earth would have been filled with corruption. But God is bountiful to mankind.

[252] These are the revelations of God which We recite to you in all truth, for you are truly one of the messengers. [253] Of these messengers, We have given something additional among them. There are some to whom God spoke directly and others He exalted in rank. We gave Jesus, son of Mary clear signs, and strengthened him with the holy spirit. Had God pleased, those who succeeded them would not have fought against one another after the clear signs had come to them. But they disagreed among themselves; some believed, while others did not. Yet had God willed, they would not have fought against one another; but God does whatever He wills.

[254] Believers, spend out of what We have given you, before the Day comes when there will be neither trading, friendship nor intercession. Truly, it is those who deny the truth who are the wrongdoers. [255] God:

there is no deity save Him, the Living, the Eternal One. Neither slumber nor sleep overtakes Him. To Him belong whatsoever is in the heavens and whatsoever is on the earth. Who can intercede with Him except by His permission? He knows all that is before them and all that is behind them. They can grasp only that part of His knowledge which He wills. His throne extends over the heavens and the earth; and their upholding does not weary Him. He is the Sublime, the Almighty One! [256] There shall be no compulsion in religion: true guidance has become distinct from error. But whoever refuses to be led by Satan and believes in God has grasped the strong handhold that will never break. God is all hearing and all knowing. [257] God is the patron of the faithful. He leads them from darkness to the light. As for those who deny the truth, their supporter is Satan, who brings them out of light into darkness. They are the heirs of the Fire, and there they will remain forever.

[258] Have you not heard of him who argued with Abraham about his Lord because God had bestowed the kingdom upon him? Abraham said, 'My Lord is the one who gives life and brings death.' He answered, 'I [too] give life and bring death!' Abraham said, 'God brings up the sun from the east, so bring it up yourself from the west.' Then the disbeliever was confounded. God does not guide the wrongdoers.

[259] Or of him who, when passing by a town the roofs of which had caved in, exclaimed, 'How will God restore it to life after its destruction?' Thereupon God caused him to die, and after a hundred years, brought him back to life. God asked, 'How long have you remained in this state?' He answered, 'I have remained a day or part of a day.' God said, 'No, you have remained in this state for a hundred years. Now look at your food and your drink; they have not rotted. Look at your ass. We will make you a sign to mankind. Look at the bones—how We set them together, then clothe them with flesh!' When it had all become clear to him, he said, 'Now I know that God has power over all things.' [260] When Abraham said, 'Show me, my Lord, how You revive the dead!' God said, 'Do you not believe?' Abraham answered, 'Yes, indeed I do believe, but just to reassure my heart.' Then God said, 'Take four birds, and train

them to come back to you. Then place them separately on each hilltop, and call them: they will come flying to you. Know that God is almighty and wise.'

²⁶¹ Those who spend their wealth for God's cause may be compared to a grain of corn which sprouts into seven ears, with a hundred grains in each ear: for God grants manifold increase to whom He wills; God is infinite and all knowing. ²⁶² Those who spend their wealth for God's cause and do not follow their almsgiving with taunts and insults shall be rewarded by their Lord; they shall have no fear, nor shall they grieve. ²⁶³ A kind word and forgiveness is better than a charitable deed followed by hurtful words: God is self-sufficient and forbearing. ²⁶⁴ Believers, do not cancel out your charitable deeds with reminders and hurtful words, like one who spends his wealth only to be seen by people, and not believing in God and the Last Day. Such men are like a rock covered with earth: a shower falls upon it and leaves it hard and bare. They will gain nothing from their works. God does not guide those who deny the truth.

²⁶⁵ But those who spend their wealth in order to gain God's approval, and to strengthen their souls are like a garden on elevated ground. When heavy rain falls on it, it doubles its produce; and if heavy rain does not fall, then light rain suffices. God sees what you do. ²⁶⁶ Would any of you, being a man well advanced in age with helpless children to support, like to have a garden of dates and grapes, watered by rivers and containing all kinds of fruits, stricken by a fiery whirlwind and utterly scorched? Thus God makes His signs clear to you, so that you may reflect.

²⁶⁷ Believers, give charitably from the good things which you have earned and what We produce for you from the earth; not worthless things which you yourselves would only reluctantly accept. Know that God is self-sufficient and praiseworthy. ²⁶⁸ Satan threatens you with the prospect of poverty and commands you to do foul deeds. But God promises His forgiveness and His bounty. God is bountiful and all knowing. ²⁶⁹ He grants wisdom to whom He will; and whoever is granted wisdom has indeed been granted abundant wealth. Yet none bear this in mind except those endowed with understanding.

²⁷⁰ Whatever you spend and whatever vows you make are known

to God, but the wrongdoers shall have no helpers. [271] If you give charity openly, it is good, but if you keep it secret and give to the needy in private, that is better for you, and it will atone for some of your bad deeds. God is aware of all that you do. [272] It is not your responsibility to make them follow the right path; God guides whomever He pleases. Whatever wealth you spend is to your own benefit, provided that you spend only to seek the favour of God. Whatever wealth you spend [for God's cause] shall be repaid to you in full and you shall not be wronged. [273] The needy, who are too engrossed in God's cause to be able to travel about the land in search of a livelihood, are considered by those who are unaware of their condition to be free from want, because they refrain from begging. But they can be known from their appearance. They do not make insistent demands upon people. Whatever wealth you spend, God knows it.[a] [274] Those who spend their wealth night and day, both privately and publicly, will receive their reward from their Lord. They shall have no fear, nor shall they grieve.

[275] Those who live on usury[b] shall rise up before God like men whom Satan has demented by his touch; for they say, 'Buying and selling is only a kind of usury.' But God has made trade lawful and made usury unlawful. Therefore, he who desists because of the admonition that has come to him from his Lord may retain what he has received in the past; and it will be for God to judge him. Those who revert to it shall be the inmates of the Fire; they shall abide therein forever.[c] [276] God blights usury and blesses charitable deeds.

---

a There are two ways of spending one's earnings in this world. One is to spend in ways shown by Satan. Another is to spend in ways shown by God. What Satan does is to impress on the minds of human beings the importance of personal requirements, and bring about conviction that all their earnings are best spent on personal comforts and luxuries.

b The Arabic word '*riba*' in the original is translated here as 'usury', which means the practice of lending money to people at unfairly high rates of interest. See also notes to 3:130-134, 102:8.

c A religion which aims at creating a worthwhile social set-up can never accept a money loving society based on usury. In a well-ordered society, mutual exchanges taken place according to the rules of business and not on the principle of usury. Business may be based on the principle of profit-making, but profit

God does not love the ungrateful wrongdoer. [277] Those who believe, do good deeds, attend to their prayers and engage in almsgiving, shall be rewarded by their Lord and shall have no fear, nor shall they grieve.

[278] Believers, have fear of God, and give up what is still due to you from usury, if you are true believers. [279] For, if you do not do so, then know that you are at war with God and His Messenger. But if you repent, you may retain your capital. Do not wrong [others] and you will not be wronged.[a] [280] If the debtor is in straitened circumstances, then grant him respite till a time of ease. If you were to write it off as an act of charity, that would be better for you, if only you knew. [281] Fear the Day when you shall be made to return to God; then every soul shall be paid in full what it has earned; and they shall not be wronged.

[282] Believers, when you contract a debt for a stated term, put it down in writing; have a scribe write it down with fairness between you. No scribe should refuse to write: let him write as God has taught him, let the debtor dictate, and let him fear God, his Lord, and not diminish [the debt] at all. If the debtor is weak in mind or body, or unable to dictate, then in fairness let his guardian dictate for him. Call in two of your men as witnesses. But if two men cannot be found, then call one man and two women out of those you approve of as witnesses, so that if one of the two women should forget the other can remind her. Let the witnesses not refuse when they are summoned. Do not be disinclined to write down your debts, be they small or large, together with the date of payment. This is more just in the sight of God; it is more reliable as testimony, and more likely to prevent doubts arising between you, unless it be ready

---

comes as a result of hard work and at the cost of taking risks. But profit coming from usury betokens selfishness and hoarding.

a Man has not been sent into this world to hoard wealth. All the good things of this life are meant for the next world. Man has been sent into this world so that it may be judged whether or not he has developed those qualities that would qualify him to inherit the world of Paradise in the Hereafter. Those adjudged fit to dwell in Paradise will be separated from the unfit, and the latter will be consigned to hell. See also note to 3:130.

merchandise which you give or take from hand to hand, then it will not be held against you for not writing it down. Have witnesses present whenever you trade with one another, and let no harm be done to either scribe or witness, for if you did cause them harm, it would be a crime on your part. Be mindful of God; He teaches you: He has full knowledge of everything. [283] If you are on a journey and do not find any literate person, something should be handed over as security. If one of you entrusts another with something, let the trustee restore the pledge to its owner; and let him fear God, his Lord. Do not conceal testimony. If someone does conceal it, in his heart he commits a crime. God knows what you do.

[284] All that the heavens and the earth contain belongs to God, whether you disclose what is in your minds or keep it hidden. God will bring you to account for it. He will forgive whom He will and punish whom He pleases: He has power over all things. [285] The Messenger believes in what has been sent down to him from his Lord, and [so do] believers. They all believe in God and His angels, His scriptures, and His messengers. They say, 'We do not differentiate between any of His messengers. We hear and obey. Grant us Your forgiveness, Lord, to You we shall all return!' [286] God does not charge a soul with more than it can bear. It shall be requited for whatever good and whatever evil it has done. [They pray], 'Our Lord, do not take us to task if we forget or make a mistake! Our Lord, do not place on us a burden like the one You placed on those before us! Our Lord, do not place on us a burden we have not the strength to bear! Pardon us; and forgive us; and have mercy on us. You are our Lord and Sustainer, so help us against those who deny the truth.'

3. THE FAMILY OF 'IMRAN (*AL 'IMRAN*)

In the name of God, the Most Gracious, the Most Merciful

[1] *Alif Lam Mim*

[2] God! There is no deity save Him, the Living, the Sustainer. [3] He has sent down the Book to you with truth, which fulfils [the predictions]

in the Scriptures that preceded it: He sent down the Torah and the Gospel [4] in the past as guidance for mankind; He has [also] sent down the Standard by which to discern the true from the false. Surely those who deny God's signs will suffer severe punishment. God is mighty and capable of retribution. [5] Nothing on earth or in the heavens is hidden from God: [6] it is He who shapes you in the womb as He will. There is no deity save Him, the Mighty, the Wise One.

[7] It is He who has sent down the Book to you. Some of its verses are clear and precise in meaning—they are the basis of the Book—while others are allegorical.[a] Those with deviation in their hearts pursue the allegorical, so as to create dissension by seeking to explain it: but no one knows its meaning except God. Those who are firmly grounded in knowledge say, 'We believe in it: it is all from our Lord.' But only the wise take heed. [8] 'Our Lord, do not let our hearts deviate after You have guided us. Bestow upon us Your mercy. Surely You are a Munificent Giver. [9] Our Lord, You will surely gather all mankind on the Day of whose coming there is no doubt. God never fails to fulfil His promise.'

[10] As for those who deny the truth, their wealth and children will not help them against God.[b] They will be fuel for the Fire. [11] Their

---

a There are two kinds of subjects dealt with in the Quran, one pertaining to the known human world, like historical events, signs from the universe and commandments for worldly life; the other pertaining to unseen matters which are not comprehensible by man in this life, for instance, God's attributes, and the states of Heaven and Hell, etc. The first are clear revelations, quite precise in their meaning, since they have been couched in a direct style. The second refer to the unknown world (for man) and cannot, therefore, be expressed in everyday language. That is why they are framed in an allegorical style.

b This world is a place of trial. God, wishing to ascertain which of His creatures are capable of rising above worldly attractions, has so willed it that man should be attracted to and find gratification in the things of this world, but at the same time be faced with the choice of clinging to them or renouncing them in favour of the unseen things of the next world. This is not an easy choice, for he sees that worldly acquisitions lead him to an honourable place in society. By possessing material resources, he can have all that he wants in life. This gives him the impression that it is these things that are of consequence. All his interests and activities centre around his family, his wealth and his property. This presents the greatest obstacle to advancing towards the demands

end will be like Pharaoh's people and those before them; they denied Our signs, so God seized them in their sinfulness: God is stern in punishment. [12] Say to those who deny the truth, 'You shall be overcome and driven into Hell—an evil resting place!' [13] There was a sign for you in the two groups which met face to face [at Badr], one party fighting for the cause of God and the other made up of those who deny the truth. They [unbelievers] saw with their own eyes that the others [believers] were twice their number: but God strengthens with His succour whom He wills. In this, there is indeed a lesson for all who have eyes to see.

[14] The satisfaction of worldly desires through women, and children, and heaped-up treasures of gold and silver, and pedigreed horses, and cattle and lands is attractive to people. All this is the provision of the worldly life; but the most excellent abode is with God. [15] Say, 'Shall I tell you of something better than all of these? For the God-fearing, there are Gardens in nearness to their God with rivers flowing through them where they shall live forever with pure spouses and the goodwill of God. God is watching His servants — [16] those who say, "Lord, we believe in You, forgive us our sins and keep us from the punishment of the Fire," [17] those who are steadfast, truthful, obedient, and those who spend [for God's cause] and who pray before dawn for forgiveness.'

[18] God bears witness that there is no deity save Him, as do the angels and those who possess knowledge. He is the upholder of justice. There is no deity save Him, the Mighty, the Wise One.

---

of the Hereafter. The aura of importance surrounding worldly things makes him oblivious of all that pertains to the next life. He is so engrossed in building the future of his children in this world, that he no longer remembers the fact that there is any 'future' beyond this present life, to which he should give thought. Providing all comforts for his home in this world becomes so dear to him that it never occurs to him that there is any other home save this, to which he should pay heed. Making money, accumulating riches and possessing property in this world seem so estimable to him, that he fails to realize that there is any 'wealth' other than this, to which he should devote his life. However, all these things with the external glitter of this present life will be of no use to him in the next, eternal life. It is only one who makes the permanent life of the Hereafter the focus of his attention who will realize the insignificance of these worldly things.

[19] The only true religion in God's sight is complete submission to God. And those who were given the Book disagreed only out of rivalry, after knowledge had been given to them—he who denies God's signs should know that God is swift in His reckoning. [20] If they dispute with you, say, 'I have submitted my whole being to God and so have those who follow me.' And ask those who have been given the Book, as well as the unlettered, 'Do you submit yourselves to God in the same way?' If they submit themselves to Him, they are on the right path; but if they turn away, your duty is only to convey the message. God is observant of all His servants. [21] Those who deny God's signs and kill the prophets unjustly and kill those who enjoin justice—give them warning of a woeful punishment— [22] their deeds will come to nothing in this world as well as in the hereafter; they will have no supporters.

[23] Have you not seen those who received a portion of the Book? When they are invited to accept the judgement of God's Book, a group of them turns away in aversion. [24] That is because they say, 'The Fire will touch us only for a limited number of days.' Thus the false beliefs which they have invented have deluded them in the matter of their religion. [25] How will it be when We gather them all together upon a Day which is sure to come, when every human being shall be repaid in full for what he has done? They will not be wronged. [26] Say, 'Lord, sovereign of all sovereignty. You bestow sovereignty on whom you will and take it away from whom You please; You exalt whoever You will and abase whoever You will. All that is good lies in Your hands. You have the power to will anything. [27] You cause the night to pass into the day, and the day into the night; You bring forth the living from the lifeless and the lifeless from the living. You give without measure to whom You will.'

[28] Let not the believers take those who deny the truth for their allies in preference to the believers—anyone who does that will isolate himself completely from God—unless it be to protect yourselves against them in this way. God admonishes you to fear Him: for, to God shall all return. [29] Say, 'God knows everything that is in your heart, whether you conceal it or reveal it; He knows everything that the heavens and earth contain; God has power over all things.'

³⁰ On the Day when every human being will find himself faced with all the good that he has done, and with all the evil that he has done, many will wish that there were a long space of time between himself and that [Day]. God admonishes you to fear Him, but God is compassionate towards His servants. ³¹ Say, 'If you love God, follow me and God will love you and forgive you your sins. God is most forgiving, and most merciful.' ³² Say, 'Obey God and the Messenger,' and if they turn away, God does not love those who deny the truth.

³³ God chose Adam and Noah and the family of Abraham and the family of 'Imran above all His creatures. ³⁴ They are the offspring of one another. God hears all and knows all. ³⁵ Remember when the wife of 'Imran said, 'My Lord, I have dedicated what is in my womb entirely to Your service. So accept this from me. You are the One who hears and knows all.' ³⁶ When she gave birth, she said, 'My Lord, I have given birth to a girl'—God knew very well what she had given birth to: a male is not like a female—'I have named her Mary and placed her and her children in Your protection from the rejected Satan.' ³⁷ Her Lord graciously accepted her and made her grow in goodness and entrusted her to the care of Zachariah. Every time Zachariah visited her in her chamber he found some provision with her. He asked, 'Mary, where did this provision come from?' She replied, 'This is from God. God provides for whoever He wills without measure.' ³⁸ Thereupon Zachariah prayed to his Lord, saying, 'Lord, grant me by Your own grace virtuous offspring. You are the hearer of all prayers.' ³⁹ As he stood praying in the chamber, the angels called out to him, saying, 'God gives you the good news of John, who shall confirm the Word from God, and [shall be] outstanding among men, and utterly chaste, and a prophet from among the righteous.' ⁴⁰ 'Lord,' said Zachariah, 'how shall I have a son when I am now overtaken by old age and my wife is barren?' 'Such is the will of God,' replied [the angel], 'He does what He pleases.' ⁴¹ He said, 'My Lord, grant me a sign.' [The angel] said, 'Your sign is that you will not be able to speak to people for three days except by signs. Remember your Lord much and glorify Him morning and evening.' ⁴² The angels said, 'Mary, God has selected

you and purified you. He has selected you over all the women of the world. [43] O Mary! Remain truly devout to your Sustainer, and prostrate yourself in worship, and bow down with those who bow down [before Him].' [44] This is an account of the unseen, which We reveal to you. You were not with them when they drew lots as to which of them should be Mary's guardian and you were not with them when they disputed with one another.

[45] When the angels said, 'O Mary, your Lord gives you good news of a Word from Him. His name is the Messiah, Jesus, son of Mary, honoured in this world and in the next and one of those who are granted nearness to God. [46] And he shall speak to men in his cradle, and as a grown man, and shall be one of the righteous.' [47] 'Lord,' she said, 'how can I have a child when no man has touched me?' [The angel] replied, 'Thus it is: God creates what He wills: when He wills a thing He need only say, "Be," and it is. [48] God will instruct him in the Book and in wisdom and in the Torah and in the Gospel.[a] [49] He will make him a messenger to the Children of Israel. He will say: "I have come to you with a sign from your Lord. I will make the shape of a bird out of clay for you and then breathe into it and, by God's leave, it will become a living bird. And by God's leave I will heal the blind and the leper and bring the dead to life. I will tell you what you eat and what you store up in your homes. Surely in this there is a sign for you, if you are believers. [50] I come to fulfil [the prediction] of the Torah which preceded me and to make lawful for you some of what was forbidden to you and I come to you with a sign from your Lord. So fear God and obey me. [51] God is my Lord and your Lord, so worship Him. That is the straight path."'

[52] When Jesus perceived their denial, he said, 'Who will be my

---

a Jesus Christ was not only given extraordinary signs from God, but he spoke in so effective, persuasive and logical a manner that no one in his time could equal him. When he spoke for the first time in the temple, 'all that heard him were astonished at his understanding and answers.' (Luke 2:47). It was on account of his miraculous personality and his astonishing powers of speech that, although he was born without a father, no one dared to abuse him on this score.

helpers in God's cause?' The disciples said, 'We are God's helpers, we believe in God. Bear witness that we have surrendered ourselves. [53] Our Lord, we believe in what You have sent down and we follow the messenger, so count us among those who bear witness.' [54] And they schemed but God also schemed and God is the Best of Schemers. [55] God said, 'O Jesus, I shall take you to Me and will raise you up to Me and shall clear you [of the calumnies] of the disbelievers, and shall place those who follow you above those who deny the truth, until the Day of Judgement; then to Me shall all return and I will judge between you regarding your disputes. [56] Those who deny the truth shall be sternly punished in this world and in the world to come: there shall be none to help them.' [57] As for those who have believed and do good works, they shall be given their reward in full. God does not love evil-doers. [58] This which We recite to you is a revelation and a wise reminder.

[59] Jesus in the sight of God is like Adam. He created him from dust; then said to him, 'Be!' and he was. [60] This is the truth from your Lord, so do not be among the doubters. [61] And if anyone should argue with you about this [truth] after the knowledge you have received, say to them, 'Come! Let us gather our sons and your sons, our women and your women, and ourselves and yourselves; and then let us pray earnestly and invoke the curse of God upon the liars. [62] This is the true account. There is no deity save Him. God is Mighty and Wise.' [63] And if they turn away, God knows well the evil-doers.

[64] Say, 'People of the Book, let us come to a word common to us that we shall worship none but God and that we shall associate no partner with Him and that none of us shall take others, besides God, for lords.' And if they turn away, say, 'Bear witness that we have submitted to God.' [65] People of the Book, why do you dispute about Abraham when the Torah and Gospel were only sent down after him. Do you not use your reason? [66] You are those who disputed about things of which you had some knowledge. Must you now argue about things of which you have no knowledge? God knows, but you do not know. [67] Abraham was neither a Jew nor a Christian. He was an upright man, one who had surrendered himself to God. He was not

one of those who associate partners with God. [68] Surely, the people who are closest to Abraham are those who followed him and this Prophet [Muhammad], and those who believe in him. God is the guardian of the believers. [69] Some of the People of the Book wish to lead you astray but they only lead themselves astray, though they do not realise it. [70] People of the Book! Why do you deny God's signs, having been witnesses thereof? [71] People of the Book! Why do you mix truth with falsehood and knowingly conceal the truth?

[72] Some of the People of the Book say to one another, 'Believe in what is revealed to the faithful in the morning and deny it in the evening, so that they [the Muslims] may themselves abandon their faith [in confusion]. [73] Believe only in those who follow your own religion.' Say to them, 'Surely, the true guidance is the guidance from God.' [But you think it is impossible that] someone else may be granted [revelation] such as you were granted—or else that they should contend against you before your Lord. Say, 'All grace is in God's hand; He grants it to whom He wills: for God is boundless, and all knowing, [74] He singles out for His mercy whoever He pleases. God is the Lord of exceeding bounty.' [75] Among the people of the Book there are some who, if you entrust them with a heap of gold, will return it to you. But there are others of them who, if you entrust them with a single dinar, will not return it to you, unless you keep demanding it from them. That is because they say, 'We are under no obligation towards the gentiles.' They deliberately tell lies about God. [76] Indeed God loves those who honour their covenants and fear Him. God loves the righteous.

[77] Those who sell out God's covenant and their oaths for a paltry price will have no share in the life to come on the Day of Resurrection. God will neither speak to them nor cast a look upon them on the Day of Judgement, nor will He purify them. For them there shall be a grievous punishment. [78] There are some among them who distort the Book by the way they speak to make you think that what they say is from the Book, whereas it is not. They say it is from God whereas it is not. Thus they tell a lie about God and they know it. [79] No one to whom God has given the Scriptures and on whom He has bestowed wisdom and prophethood would say to men,

'Worship me instead of God.' [He would say rather], 'Be devoted servants of God, for you have taught and studied the Scriptures.' [80] Nor would he enjoin you to take the angels and the prophets as your lords; how could he command you to be disbelievers after you have submitted to God.

[81] When God made a covenant with the prophets, He said, 'Here is the Book and the wisdom which I have given you. When there comes to you a messenger fulfilling that [predictions about him in their Scripture] which is with you, you must believe in him and help him. Do you then affirm this and accept the responsibility I have laid upon you in these terms?' They said, 'We will affirm it.' God said, 'Then bear witness, and I will bear witness with you.' [82] Now whoever turns away after this, are surely transgressors. [83] Do they seek a religion other than the religion of God, when everything in the heavens and the earth has submitted to Him, willingly or unwillingly? To Him they shall all return. [84] Say, 'We believe in God and in what has been sent down to us and to Abraham, Ishmael, Isaac, Jacob and the Tribes. We believe in what has been given to Moses, Jesus and the prophets from their Lord. We make no distinction between any of them.[a] It is to Him that we have surrendered ourselves.' [85] If anyone seeks a religion other than Islam [submission to God], it will not be accepted from him; he will be among the losers in the Hereafter. [86] How would God bestow His guidance upon people who have opted for unbelief after having embraced the faith and having borne witness that this Messenger is true and [after] all evidence of the truth has come to them? For, God does not guide such wrongdoers: [87] such people will be rewarded with rejection by God, by the angels, by all mankind. [88] In this state they shall abide forever; their punishment shall not be lightened nor shall they

---

a Discovering God is to find an eternal reality. It is to become a co-traveller or a travelling companion of the whole universe. Those who find God in this way, can rise above all kinds of prejudices. They recognize truth in all situations, whether the call of truth comes through an 'Israelite prophet' or an 'Ishmaelite prophet'. But those who lead their lives on the level of community-oriented thinking can recognize the truth only when it comes to them from a member of their own community.

be granted respite. ⁸⁹ Except for those who afterwards repent and reform. God is forgiving and merciful; ⁹⁰ but as for those who are bent on denying the truth after accepting the true faith and grow in their refusal to acknowledge the truth, their repentance will not be accepted. They are the ones who have gone far astray. ⁹¹ Those who reject faith and die in the state of rejection will not be saved, even if they offer as ransom enough gold to fill the entire earth. Painful punishment is in store for them and they will have no supporters.

⁹² Never will you attain to righteousness unless you spend for the cause of God out of what you cherish; and whatever you spend is known to God. ⁹³ All food was lawful for the Children of Israel, except whatever Israel had made unlawful for himself before the Torah was sent down. Say to them, 'Bring the Torah then and read it, if you are truthful. ⁹⁴ Those who, after this, persist in making up lies and attributing them to God are transgressors.' ⁹⁵ Say, 'God speaks the Truth, so follow the faith of Abraham. He was an upright man and he was not one of the polytheists.' ⁹⁶ The first House to be built for mankind was the one at Bakkah [Makkah]. It is a blessed place; a source of guidance for the whole world. ⁹⁷ There are clear signs in it; it is the place where Abraham stood. Anyone who enters it will be secure. Pilgrimage to the House is a duty to God for anyone who is able to undertake it. Anyone who disbelieves should remember that God is independent of all creatures. ⁹⁸ Say, 'People of the Book, why do you reject God's revelations when God is witness to all that you do?' ⁹⁹ Say, 'People of the Book, why do you turn the believers away from the path of God, seeking to make it crooked, while you are witnesses thereof? God is not unaware of what you do.'

¹⁰⁰ O believers, if you yield to some of those who were given the Scripture, they will cause you to renounce the truth after you have believed. ¹⁰¹ But how can you deny the truth when God's revelations are being conveyed to you and His own Messenger is in your midst? He who holds fast to God is indeed guided to the straight path. ¹⁰² Believers, fear God as is His due, and when death comes, be in a state of complete submission to Him. ¹⁰³ Hold fast to the cord of God and let nothing divide you. Remember the blessings He has bestowed upon you; you were enemies and then He united your

hearts and by His grace you became brothers; you were on the brink of an abyss of Fire and He rescued you from it. Thus God makes His signs clear to you, so that you may find guidance.

[104] Let there be a group among you who call others to good, and enjoin what is right, and forbid what is wrong: those who do this shall be successful. [105] Do not be like those who, after they had been given clear evidence, split into factions and differed among themselves: a terrible punishment awaits such people. [106] On the Day when some faces are bright and some faces are dark, it will be said to those with darkened faces, 'Did you reject faith after accepting it? Taste, then, this punishment for having denied the truth!' [107] But as for those with shining faces, they shall abide forever in God's grace. [108] These are God's revelations; We recite them to you in all truth. God desires no injustice to mankind. [109] His is all that the heavens and the earth contain. To God shall all things return.

[110] You are indeed the best community that has ever been brought forth for [the good of] mankind. You enjoin what is good, and forbid what is evil, and you believe in God. If the People of the Book had also believed, it would have surely been better for them. Some of them are true believers, but most of them are disobedient. [111] They can do you very little harm; if they come out to fight you, they will show you their backs; then they shall not be helped— [112] abasement shall attend them wherever they are found, unless they make a covenant with God or with man. They have incurred God's wrath and have been utterly humbled, because they have persistently disbelieved in God's signs and killed prophets unjustly. This resulted from their disobedience and their habit of transgression.

[113] Yet they are not all alike. Of the People of the Book there are some who stand by their covenant; they recite the word of God during the night and prostrate themselves before Him, [114] who believe in God and the Last Day, who enjoin justice and forbid evil and vie with each other in good works. These are righteous men [115] and they will not be denied [the reward] for whatever good deeds they do: God knows the righteous. [116] As for those who deny the truth, neither their possessions nor their children shall avail them in the least against God. They will be inmates of the Fire. They will

remain there for ever; [117] that which they spend in pursuit of the life of this world is like a biting frosty blast which smites the harvest of a people who have wronged themselves, and destroys it. God is not unjust to them; they are unjust to their own souls.

[118] Believers, do not take outsiders as your intimate friends, they will spare no effort to harm you. They love to see you suffer; their hatred is evident from the words which fall from their mouths. But what their hearts conceal is far worse. We have made Our signs clear to you; will you not understand? [119] It is you who love them, but they do not love you; you believe in all the revealed Books. When they meet you, they say, 'We believe,' but when they are alone, they bite their fingertips with rage. Say, 'Die of rage!' God is aware of what your hearts contain. [120] Whenever something good happens to you, it grieves them; but when evil befalls you, they rejoice. If you persevere and fear God, their designs will never harm you in the least: God encompasses all that they do.

[121] When you set out at dawn from your home to assign battle positions to the believers—God hears all and knows all. [122] When two groups from among you were about to lose heart, God was their protector. In God let the faithful put their trust. [123] God had already helped you at Badr, when you were weak. Fear God, so that you may be grateful. [124] [And remember] when you said to the believers, 'Does it not suffice that your Lord helps you by sending down three thousand angels? [125] If you remain patient and God-fearing, and the enemy should fall upon you all of a sudden, Your Lord will reinforce you with five thousand angels clearly marked!' [126] and God ordained this only as good news for you so that your hearts might be comforted—help comes only from God, the Powerful, the Wise One—[127] and so that He might cut off a portion of those who are bent on denying the truth or abase them so that they might be turned back frustrated. [128] You have no say in this affair to decide whether He will relent towards them or He will punish them: they are wrongdoers. [129] Whatever is in the heavens and whatever is on the earth belong to God. He forgives whoever He pleases and punishes whoever He pleases. God is most forgiving and ever merciful.

¹³⁰ Believers, do not devour usury multiplied many times over.ᵃ Fear God, so that you may prosper—¹³¹ guard yourself against the Fire prepared for those who deny the truth—¹³² and obey God and the Messenger, so that you may be given mercy. ¹³³ And vie with one another for your Lord's forgiveness and for a Paradise as vast as the heavens and the earth, which has been prepared for the God-fearing, ¹³⁴ for those who spend, both in prosperity and adversity, who restrain their anger and are forgiving towards their fellow men—God loves those who do good works. ¹³⁵ And who, when they have committed an indecency or have wronged their souls, remember God and pray that their sins be forgiven—for who but God can forgive sins?—and do not knowingly persist in their misdeeds, ¹³⁶ their recompense is forgiveness from their Lord, and Gardens with rivers flowing through them, where they will abide forever. How excellent will be the reward of those who do good works. ¹³⁷ There are many examples [of the communities] that have passed away before you: travel through the land, and see what was the end of those who rejected the Truth. ¹³⁸ This Quran is an exposition for the people and a guidance and admonition for those who fear God.

¹³⁹ And do not become faint of heart, nor grieve—you will have the upper hand, if you are believers—¹⁴⁰ if you have suffered a wound, they too have suffered a similar wound. We bring these days to men by turns, so that God may know those who believe, and choose witnesses from among you; and God does not love the unjust, ¹⁴¹ so that God may purge those who believe and wipe out

---

a Engaging in usury is the ultimate in money worship. A usurer thinks day in and day out as to how to double and quadruple his money. But what he ought to pursue relentlessly is not the acquisition of material things but his entry into Paradise in the Hereafter. He ought to be ever eager to attain God's mercy and blessing, but not by increasing his worldly wealth in order to guarantee himself a life of grandeur in this world. Honour and success are of no importance when compared to Paradise, the pleasure and enjoyment of which are immeasurable. Wise is the one who pursues God's Paradise. Hastening towards it means giving away more and more of one's wealth for the cause of God. The way to worldly success is to increase one's riches, while the way to success in the Hereafter is to decrease one's riches. See also notes to 2:275 and 30:39.

those who deny the truth. ¹⁴² Do you suppose that you would enter the Garden, without God knowing those among you who would strive hard for His cause and endure with fortitude? ¹⁴³ You were longing for death, before you met it. Now you have seen it with your own eyes.

¹⁴⁴ Muhammad is only a messenger. Messengers have passed away before him. If he should die, or be killed, will you turn back on your heels? Those who turn on their heels do not harm the Lord in the least. God will reward the grateful. ¹⁴⁵ No soul shall die except with God's permission and at an appointed time. And if one desires the rewards of this world, We shall grant it to him; and if one desires the rewards of the life to come, We shall grant it to him. We will reward the grateful. ¹⁴⁶ How many a prophet has fought with many devout men alongside him! They did not lose heart, despite all that they had to suffer in God's path. They neither weakened nor yielded. God loves the patient! ¹⁴⁷ All they said was, 'Our Lord, forgive us our sins and our excesses. Make our feet firm, and help us against those who deny the truth,' ¹⁴⁸ and so God gave them both the rewards of this life and the excellent recompense of the life to come: God loves those who do good.

¹⁴⁹ Believers, if you yield to those who deny the truth, they will cause you to turn back on your heels and you will turn into losers. ¹⁵⁰ No, indeed! it is God who is your protector: He is the best supporter. ¹⁵¹ We will strike awe into the hearts of those who deny the truth, because they have associated partners with God, for which He has sent down no authority. Their abode shall be the Fire, and evil indeed is the abode of the wrongdoers. ¹⁵² And God made good His promise to you when by His leave you were about to destroy your foes, but then your courage failed you and you disagreed among yourselves [concerning the Prophet's direction] and disobeyed it, after He had brought you within sight of what you wished for—some of you desired the goods of this world and some of you desired the Hereafter—then in order that He might put you to the test, He prevented you from defeating your foes. But now He has pardoned you: God is most gracious to the believers. ¹⁵³ When you were running away and did not look back at anyone, while the

Messenger was calling to you from behind, He paid you back with one sorrow after another, so that you might not grieve for what you lost, nor for what befell you. God is aware of what you do.

¹⁵⁴ Then, after sorrow He sent down peace [of mind] upon you in the shape of drowsiness that overcame some of you, but there were others who were anxious only about themselves. They entertained false notions about God, like the notions of the days of ignorance. 'Have we any say in the matter?' they asked. Say to them, 'All is in the hands of God.' They conceal in their hearts what they would not reveal to you. They say, 'Had we had any say in the matter, none of us would have been killed here.' Say to them, 'Had you stayed in your homes, those whose death had been decreed would nevertheless have gone forth to the places where they were destined to die.' And all this befell you so that God might test what is in your minds. And in order to purify what was in your hearts. For God is aware of your innermost thoughts. ¹⁵⁵ Those of you who turned away on the day the two hosts met [in battle] were made to slip by Satan on account of some of their deeds. But God has pardoned them: God is forgiving and forbearing.

¹⁵⁶ Believers, do not be like those who are bent on denying the truth and who say of their brothers, when they travel about the land or go forth to war, 'Had they but remained with us, they would not have died, or been slain'—for God will cause such thoughts to become a source of bitter regret in their hearts, since it is God who gives life and causes death. And God sees all that you do. ¹⁵⁷ If you are killed or die in God's cause, then surely forgiveness from God and His grace are better than all that one could amass. ¹⁵⁸ For, indeed, if you die or are killed, it is to God that you shall be gathered. ¹⁵⁹ It is by God's grace that you were gentle with them—for if you had been harsh and hard-hearted, they would surely have deserted you—so bear with them and pray for forgiveness for them. Take counsel with them in the conduct of affairs; then, when you have decided upon a course of action, place your trust in God: for God loves those who place their trust in Him. ¹⁶⁰ If God helps you, none can overcome you, but if He withdraws His help from you, who is

there who can help you besides Him? In God, then, let the believers place their trust!

[161] It is not for any Prophet to hold back anything; he who hides anything away shall bring it forth on the Day of Resurrection, when every human being shall be repaid in full for whatever he has done, and none shall be wronged. [162] Can one who seeks the pleasure of God, be like one who incurs the wrath of God and whose abode shall be Hell—an evil destination? [163] All have a different standing in the eyes of God, and God is observant of all their actions. [164] Indeed, God has conferred a great favour on the believers in sending a Messenger from among themselves, to recite His revelations to them, and purify them, and teaches them the Book and wisdom, for, before that they were surely in manifest error.

[165] What! When a misfortune befalls you, after you had yourself inflicted twice as heavy losses, you say, 'How has this come about?' Say, 'It was your own fault.' Truly, God has the power to will anything: [166] the misfortune which befell you on the day when the two armies met happened by God's leave, so that He might mark out the [true] believers [167] and know those who acted hypocritically.' When they were told, 'Come, fight in God's cause and defend yourselves,' they replied, 'If we knew that fighting would take place, we would surely follow you.' They were that day nearer to unbelief than to belief. The words they utter bear no relation to what is in their hearts. God knows well what they conceal. [168] Those who stayed behind, said of their brothers, 'Had they listened to us, they would not have been killed.' Say to them, 'Ward off death from yourselves, then, if what you say be true!'

[169] Do not think of those who have been killed in God's cause as dead. They are alive, and well provided for by their Lord; [170] they are joyful because of what God has bestowed on them of His grace and they rejoice that those they left behind, who have not yet joined them, that they shall have no fear, nor shall they grieve; [171] rejoicing in God's grace and bounty. [They know that] God will not fail to requite the believers. [172] Those who responded to the call of God and the Messenger, despite their having received an injury, and such of them as did good deeds and feared God, shall have a great

reward. [173] Those who, on being told that, 'the enemy has gathered against you a great force, so fear them,' only grew stronger in their faith and replied, 'God is sufficient for us. He is the best guardian.' [174] They returned home with God's favour and blessings, without having been touched by evil; for they pursued God's pleasure. And God's bounty is infinite. [175] It is Satan who instils fear [into you] of his followers; do not fear them. But fear Me, if you are true believers.

[176] And let not those grieve you who vie with one another in denying the truth: they cannot harm God in the least; it is God's will that they will have no share in the life to come—a severe punishment awaits them. [177] Those who have bought a denial of truth at the price of faith can in no way harm God; painful punishment awaits them. [178] Let not those who deny the truth think that Our granting them respite is good for them: Our granting them respite will only cause them to increase in disobedience—shameful punishment awaits them. [179] On no account will God leave the believers in the condition in which they are now, until He separates the evil from the good. Nor will God reveal to you the unseen. But God chooses those of his messengers whom He will. Therefore, believe in God and His messengers, for if you have faith and guard yourselves against evil, you shall have a great reward.

[180] Let not those who are niggardly with what God has granted them out of His bounty think that it is good for them. Indeed, it is evil for them. What they are niggardly about shall be hung about their necks like a collar on the Day of Resurrection. It is God who will inherit the heavens and the earth: God is aware of all that you do. [181] God has indeed heard the words of those who said, 'Behold, God is poor while we are rich!' We shall record what they have said—and their slaying of the prophets unjustly—and We shall say, 'Taste the torment of burning. [182] In return for what your own hands have wrought—for never does God do the least wrong to His creatures!' [183] To those who say, 'God has commanded us not to believe in any messenger unless he brings down to us an offering to be consumed by fire,' say, 'Messengers before me have come to you with clear signs, including the one you demand. Why did you kill them, if you are telling the truth?' [184] If they deny you, so have

other messengers been denied before you, who came with clear signs, scriptures and enlightening book. [185] Every human being is bound to taste death: and you shall receive your rewards in full on the Day of Resurrection. He who is kept away from the Fire and is admitted to Paradise, will surely triumph; for the life of this world is nothing but an illusory enjoyment.

[186] You will surely be tried and tested in your possessions and your persons, and you shall surely hear many hurtful things from those who were given the Book before you and from those who set up partners with God, but if you endure with fortitude and restrain yourselves, that indeed is a matter of strong determination. [187] God made a covenant with those who were given the Book to make it known to people and not conceal it. But they cast it behind their backs and bartered it for a paltry price: what an evil bargain they made! [188] Those who exult in their misdeeds and love to be praised for what they have not done should not suppose that they are secure from punishment; they shall suffer a grievous punishment. [189] The kingdom of the heavens and the earth belongs to God; God has power over all things.

[190] There are signs in the creation of the heavens and the earth, and in the alternation of night and day for people of understanding; [191]who remember God while standing, sitting and [lying] on their sides, and who ponder over the creation of the heavens and the earth, saying, 'Lord, You have not created all this without purpose. Glory be to You! Save us from the torment of the Fire. [192] Lord, those whom You condemn to enter the Fire You have surely brought to disgrace. Wrongdoers will have no supporters. [193] Lord, we have heard a caller calling to the true faith saying, "Believe in your Lord," and we believed. Lord, forgive us our sins and remove from us our bad deeds and make us die with the virtuous. [194] Our Lord! Grant us what You have promised to us through Your messengers, and do not humiliate us on the Day of Resurrection. Surely, You never fail to fulfil Your promise.'

[195] Their Lord accepted their prayer, saying, 'I will deny no man or woman among you the reward of their labours. You are members one of another. I will certainly forgive the sins of those who emigrated

and were expelled from their homes, who suffered persecution in My cause, who fought and were killed.[a] I will certainly admit them to Gardens through which rivers flow, as a reward from God: with God is the best reward.' ¹⁹⁶ Do not be deceived by the actions of those who deny the truth in the land: ¹⁹⁷ this is only a brief enjoyment, after which Hell shall be their abode—what an evil resting place! ¹⁹⁸ Those who fear their Lord shall have gardens through which rivers flow, wherein they will abide forever: and a goodly welcome from their Lord. God's recompense is best for the virtuous. ¹⁹⁹ Some of the People of the Book believe in God, and in what has been revealed to you and what was revealed to them. They humble themselves before God and do not sell God's revelations for a trifling price. These shall be rewarded by their Lord: God is swift in reckoning! ²⁰⁰ Believers, endure, vie with each other in endurance, stand firm in your faith and fear God, so that you may succeed.

4. WOMEN (*AL-NISA'*)

In the name of God, the Most Gracious, the Most Merciful

¹ O mankind! Fear your Lord, who created you from a single soul. He created its mate from it and from the two of them spread countless men and women [throughout the earth]. Fear God, in whose name you appeal to one another, and be mindful of your obligations in respect of ties of kinship. God is always watching over you.[b] ² Give

---

a See note to 2:191.

b All human beings are one and the same by birth. Ultimately, everyone can trace his origin to the same man and woman as father and mother. It is, therefore, necessary that all human beings should have a feeling of affinity with each other and live with fairness and goodwill like the members of one extended family. This racial unity becomes more compact in family relationships and the importance of decent behaviour among kinsfolk becomes further heightened. Good behaviour between fellow human beings is important, not merely from the moral point of view, but rather as a matter of personal concern to man himself. This is so, because everyone is governed by the Great, Almighty God, who as the Reckoner for one and all, will decide the eternal future of all human

the orphans the possessions that belong to them, do not exchange good things with bad and do not consume their property, adding it to your own. Surely, this is a great crime. [3] If you fear that you cannot deal fairly with orphan girls, you may marry women of your choice, two or three or four; but if you fear that you might not be able to treat them with equal fairness, then only one—or [from among] those whom you rightfully possess. That is more likely to keep you from committing an injustice. [4] And give the women their dowers willingly, but if they, of their own accord, remit any part of it to you, you may make use of it with pleasure and goodwill.

[5] Do not give those who are of immature mind your property which God has granted you as a means of support: make provision for them out of it, and clothe them, and give them good advice. [6] Keep a close check on orphans till they attain the age of marriage; then, if you find them to be mature of mind, hand over their property to them. Do not consume it by wasteful spending, before they come of age. If the guardian is affluent, let him abstain altogether, and if he is poor, let him have for himself what is just and reasonable. When you hand over their property to them, call witnesses in their presence; God is sufficient as a Reckoner. [7] Men shall have a share in what parents and relatives leave behind, and women shall have a share in what parents and relatives leave behind, whether it be little or much. This is ordained [by God]. [8] If other relatives, orphans or needy people are present at the time of the division, then provide for them out of it, and speak kindly to them. [9] Those who are concerned about the fate of their own helpless children if they should die and leave them behind should show the same concern for orphans. Let them fear God and uphold justice. [10] Those who consume the property of orphans unjustly are actually swallowing fire into their own bellies; soon they will burn in the blazing Flame.

---

beings in the Hereafter, requiting them according to their actions in this world. Man should, therefore, not consider his dealings with others as a matter between man and man, but as a matter between man and God. He should fear the grip of God and should adhere to the bounds set by God so as to save himself from His wrath.

[11] Concerning your children, God enjoins you that a male shall receive a share equivalent to that of two females. But if there are more than two females, then their share is two thirds of the inheritance. If there is only one, she will receive the half. Each of your parents receives a sixth of what you leave if you have children. If you are childless and your heirs are your parents, your mother receives a third. If you have brothers [or sisters] your mother receives a sixth, after [the deduction of] any bequest you make or the repayment of any debts with regard to your father and your sons. You do not know which of them is going to benefit you more: but this fixing of portions is by God and He is all knowing and all wise. [12] You will inherit half of what your wives leave, provided they have left no children. But if they leave children then you inherit a quarter of what they leave, after payment of any bequests they may have made or any debts they may have incurred. Your wives shall inherit one quarter of what you leave if you are childless. But if you leave children, your wives shall inherit one eighth, after payment of any bequest or debts. If a man or woman has no direct heirs [neither children or parents] but has left a brother or a sister, they shall each inherit one sixth, but if they are more than two, they share one third between them, after payment of any bequests or debts, so that no harm is done to anyone. That is a commandment from God: God is all knowing and forbearing. [13] These are the limits set by God. Anyone who obeys God and His Messenger will be admitted to Gardens through which rivers flow, to live there forever. That will be the supreme achievement. [14] But anyone who disobeys God and His Messenger and transgresses His limits shall be cast into a Fire, wherein he will abide forever. And he shall have a humiliating punishment.

[15] If any of your women commit fornication, call in four male witnesses from among yourselves against them; if they testify to their guilt, confine them to the house until death releases them or until God gives them another way out. [16] If two men commit a like abomination, punish them both. If they repent and mend their ways, leave them alone. God is forgiving and merciful. [17] But God undertakes to accept repentance only from those who do evil out of

ignorance and those who repent soon after. God turns towards such people with mercy; He is all knowing and all wise. [18] Forgiveness is not for those who continue to do evil deeds until, when death comes upon one of them, he says: 'Now I repent!' nor from those who die as deniers of the truth. We have prepared a painful punishment for them.

[19] Believers, it is not lawful for you to inherit women against their will, nor should you detain them wrongfully, so that you may take away a part of what you have given them, unless they are guilty of something clearly outrageous. Live with them in accordance with what is fair and kind; if you dislike them, it may be that you dislike something which God might make a source of abundant good. [20] If you desire to replace one wife with another, do not take any part of her dower back: even if you have given her a treasure. Would you take it by slandering her and with manifest sinfulness? [21] How can you take it when you have been intimate with one another, and she has taken a solemn pledge from you? [22] Do not marry women whom your fathers married, except for what has already taken place in the past. This is indeed a shameful deed, a loathsome thing and an evil practice.

[23] You are forbidden to take as wives your mothers, daughters, sisters, paternal and maternal aunts, your brothers' daughters and your sisters' daughters, your foster mothers and foster sisters, your wives' mothers and stepdaughters in your protection and the daughters of your wives with whom you have consummated your marriage; but if you have not consummated your marriage then you will not be blamed [if you marry their daughters.] You are also forbidden to marry the spouses of your sons or two sisters together, except what has already passed. Surely, God is ever-forgiving and merciful. [24] Also forbidden are married women, except those who have passed into your hands as prisoners of war. This is a commandment of God to you. All women other than these are lawful to you, provided you seek them with your wealth in honest wedlock, not in fornication. When you consummate your marriage with them, give the dowers due to them. And there is no sin for you in what you do by mutual agreement after the fixing of the dower. God is all knowing and wise.

[25] If any of you cannot afford to marry a free believing woman let him marry one of his believing maids whom he possesses. God best knows your faith. You are one of another. So marry them with their owner's permission, and give them their dower according to what is fair, neither committing fornication nor taking secret paramours. And if, after they are married, they commit adultery they shall have half the punishment prescribed for a free woman. This is for those of you who fear lest he should fall into sin. But that it is better for you to practise self-restraint. God is most forgiving and merciful.

[26] God wishes to explain things to you and guide you to the ways of those who have gone before you and to turn to you in mercy. God is all knowing and all wise. [27] He wishes to turn towards you in mercy, but those who follow their own passions want you to drift far away from the right path. [28] God wishes to lighten your burdens, for, man has been created weak.

[29] Believers, do not wrongfully consume each other's wealth, but trade with it by mutual consent. Do not kill one another, for God is most merciful to you. [30] If anyone does these things through transgression and injustice, We shall cast him into the Fire; and that is easy for God. [31] If you shun the great sins you have been forbidden, We shall cancel out your minor misdeeds and admit you to a place of honour. [32] Do not covet the bounties which God has bestowed more abundantly on some of you than on others. Men shall be rewarded according to their deeds, and women shall be rewarded according to their deeds. You should rather ask God for His bounty. God has knowledge of all things. [33] We have appointed heirs for everything that parents and close relatives leave behind. As for those with whom you have entered into agreements, let them, too, have their due. God is witness to all things.

[34] Men are protectors of women, because God has made some of them excel others and because they spend their wealth on them. So virtuous women are obedient and guard in the husband's absence what God would have them guard. As for those from whom you apprehend infidelity, admonish them, then refuse to share their beds, and finally hit them [lightly]. Then if they obey you, take no further action against them. For God is High, Great. [35] If you fear

any breach between a man and his wife, appoint one arbiter from his family and one arbiter from her family. If they both want to set things right, God will bring about a reconciliation between them: He is all knowing and all aware.

³⁶ Worship God: and do not associate partners with Him. Be good to your parents, to relatives, to orphans, to the needy, and the neighbour who is a kinsman, and the neighbour who is not related to you and your companions and the wayfarers and those whom you rightfully possess. God does not like arrogant, boastful people, ³⁷ who are miserly and enjoin others to be the same and conceal the riches which God has given them of His bounty. We have prepared a humiliating punishment for those who deny the truth. ³⁸ And [God does not like] those who spend their wealth for the sake of ostentation, who do not believe in God or the Last Day. Whoever has Satan as his companion has an evil companion. ³⁹ What harm could befall them if they believed in God and the Last Day, and spent out of what God bestowed on them? God knows them well. ⁴⁰ God does not wrong anyone by as much as a grain's weight. If there be a good deed, He will repay twofold, and will bestow out of His own bounty an immense reward.

⁴¹ What will they do when We bring a witness from each community and bring you as a witness against these people? ⁴² On that Day, those who were bent on denying the truth and disobeyed the Messenger will wish that the earth were made level above them. They will not be able to hide anything from God. ⁴³ Believers, do not approach your prayers when you are drunk,ᵃ until you understand what you say, nor when you are in a state of impurity, —except when you are on a journey—till you have bathed. And if you are ill, or on a journey or have relieved yourselves or when you have consorted

---

a This verse appears here to underline the initial prohibition of intoxicants or wine, but it also reveals an important reality about prayer. Prayer does not mean the mere repetition of certain words and motions with accuracy; it must also reflect the concentration of the mind. The individual must say his prayers sincerely. When he is submitting himself to God with his utterances and his body, his mind and intention should also be in submission to Him. Along with his physical obeisance, his consciousness should inhere in his prayer.

with women and you cannot find any water, then find some clean sand and wipe your face and your hands with it. God is gracious and forgiving.

⁴⁴ Do you not know of those who were in possession of a portion of the Book? They buy up error and want you to lose your way. ⁴⁵ God is quite aware as to who your enemies are; God suffices as a patron, and God suffices as a supporter. ⁴⁶ Some Jews take words out of their context and say, 'We have heard, but we disobey,' or 'Hear without listening.' And they say 'Look at us,' twisting the phrase with their tongues so as to disparage religion. But if they had said, 'We hear and we obey,' and 'Listen to us and look at us with favour,' that would have been better and more proper for them. God has rejected them for their defiance so that they shall not believe, except a few of them.

⁴⁷ O People of the Book, believe in what We have sent down, fulfilling [the predictions] that is with you, before We destroy [your sense of] direction, so as to confound or reject you, as We rejected those who broke the Sabbath: God's command is always carried out. ⁴⁸ God will not forgive anyone for associating something with Him, while He will forgive whoever He wishes for anything besides that. Whoever ascribes partners to God is guilty of a monstrous sin. ⁴⁹ Have you not seen those who consider themselves pure? It is indeed God who purifies whoever He pleases and none shall be wronged by as much as a hair's breadth. ⁵⁰ See how they attribute their own lying inventions to God. This is in itself a flagrant sin!

⁵¹ Have you not seen those who were in possession of a portion of the Book? They believe in idols and devils. They say of those who deny the truth, 'They are more rightly guided than the believers.' ⁵² Those are the ones God has rejected: you will not find anyone to help those God has rejected. ⁵³ Have they a share in God's kingdom? If they did, they would not give others so much as the groove of a date stone. ⁵⁴ Do they envy others because of what God has given them out of His bounty? We granted the House of Abraham the Book and wisdom and We granted them a great kingdom. ⁵⁵ Some of them believed in it and some held back from it. Hell will suffice as a blazing Fire. ⁵⁶ We shall send those who reject Our revelations

to the Fire. When their skins are burnt up, We shall replace them with new ones so that they may continue to taste the punishment. God is mighty and wise. [57] As for those who believe and do good works, We shall make them enter Gardens through which rivers flow, to dwell therein forever; therein they shall have pure spouses, and We shall admit them into a dense shade.

[58] God commands you to hand back your trusts to their rightful owners, and when you judge between people, to judge with fairness. God's instructions to you are excellent. God hears and sees all things. [59] Believers, obey God and obey the Messenger and those who have been entrusted with authority among you. If you are in dispute over any matter, refer it to God and the Messenger, if you truly believe in God and the Last Day: this is best, and best in the end. [60] Have you not seen those who profess to believe in what has been revealed to you and [to other prophets] before you? They seek the judgement of evil people, although they were commanded not to obey them. And Satan wants to lead them far astray. [61] When they are told, 'Come to what God has sent down and to the Messenger,' you see the hypocrites turn away from you. [62] How will it be when an affliction befalls them because of what they themselves have done? They will come to you, swearing by God, saying that they were seeking nothing but goodwill and conciliation. [63] But God knows all that is in their hearts; so ignore what they say, admonish them and speak to them in such terms as will address their minds.

[64] All the messengers We sent were meant to be obeyed by God's leave. If they had come to you and sought forgiveness from God whenever they wronged themselves, and the Messenger had prayed for forgiveness for them, they would have found that God is ever-forgiving and merciful. [65] By your Lord, they will not be true believers until they seek your arbitration in their disputes and find within themselves no doubt about what you decide and accept it whole-heartedly.[a] [66] If We had commanded them, 'Lay down your

---

a A prophet is not sent to the world to raise a group of followers who will wax eloquent in his praise and cover him in glory. A prophet comes so that people should learn the code of conduct for their lives and adopt it in practice.

lives or leave your dwellings,' they would have not done it, save a few of them. If they had done what they were instructed to do, it would have been better for them, as well as more strengthening [for their faith], [67] and We would have given them a great reward of Our own, [68] and guided them to a straight path. [69] Whoever obeys God and the Messenger will be among those He has blessed: the messengers, the truthful, the witnesses, and the righteous. What excellent companions these are! [70] That is God's favour. Sufficient is God's infinite knowledge.

[71] You who believe, take your precautions and then go forth in small groups or go forth all together. [72] Among you are some who lag behind and if you encounter a setback, they say, 'God has been gracious to me; I was not present with them.' [73] But if, by God's grace, good fortune should be your lot, they will say, 'If only I had been with them I should have achieved a great success,' as if no affection had existed between you and them. [74] Let those who would exchange the life of this world for the Hereafter, fight for the cause of God;[a] whoever fights for the cause of God, whether he is slain or is victorious, to him We shall give a great reward. [75] And how should you not fight for the cause of God, and for the helpless old men, women, and children who say, 'Deliver us, Lord, from this city of wrongdoers, grant us a protector out of Your grace and grant us a supporter out of Your grace?' [76] The believers fight for the cause of God, while those who reject faith fight for Satan. Then fight the allies of Satan: Satan's scheming is truly weak.

[77] Have you not seen those to whom it was said, 'Restrain your hands, say your prayers and pay the prescribed alms?' And when they have been ordered to fight, some of them have felt afraid of human beings just as they should be afraid of God, or they are even

---

One should be so thoroughly committed to doing so, that even in controversial situations, when conflicting interests have caused strained relations, one will not fail to obey the Prophet's teachings. The true believer will simply suppress his ego and conscientiously follow the guidance of the Prophet. He will willingly accept his ways, even if they are detrimental to his interests and run counter to his way of thinking.

a See note to 2:191.

more afraid. They say, 'Our Lord, why have You ordered us to fight? If You would only postpone it for a little while longer!' Say, 'The benefits of this world are negligible and the Hereafter will be better for one who fears God; and you shall not be wronged in the slightest. [78] Wherever you may be, death will overtake you, even if you be in strongly built towers.' If some good befalls them, they say, 'This is from God,' and if ill befalls them, they say, 'This is from you.' Tell them, 'All is from God.' But what is wrong with these people that they fail to understand anything? [79] Whatever good befalls you, it is from God: and whatever ill befalls you is from yourself. We have sent you forth as a messenger to mankind; and God suffices as a witness.

[80] He who obeys the Messenger obeys God. As for those who turn away, know that We have not sent you to be their keeper. [81] They say: 'We obey you,' but as soon as they leave you, a group of them plan together by night against what you say. God records whatever they scheme. So ignore them, and put your trust in God. God is sufficient as a trustee. [82] Do they not ponder on the Quran? If it had been from anyone other than God, they would have found much inconsistency in it. [83] When they hear any news, whether of peace or of something fearful, they spread it about; whereas if they referred it to the Messenger and to the men in charge, those of them who would have investigated it and could have arrived at the truth of the matter. But for God's grace and mercy, all but a few of you would have followed Satan.

[84] So fight for the cause of God. You are responsible only for yourself. Urge on the believers. God may fend off the power [violence] of those who deny the truth, for He is stronger in might and stronger in inflicting punishment. [85] Whoever rallies to a good cause shall have a share in its blessing; and whoever rallies to an evil cause shall be answerable for his part in it: for, indeed, God watches over everything. [86] When you are greeted by anyone, respond with a better greeting or at least return it; God takes account of all things. [87] He is God: there is no deity other than Him. He will gather you all together on the Day of Resurrection, there is no doubt about it. Whose word can be truer than God's?

[88] How is it that you are divided into two groups regarding the hypocrites, when God Himself cast them back [to disbelief] because of their misdeeds? Do you seek to guide those whom God allows to go astray? You cannot guide those whom God allows to go astray. [89] They want you to deny the Truth, so that you may become all alike. Do not take them as your allies until they emigrate in the way of God. If they turn back (to enmity), seize them and kill them wherever you may find them;[a] and take no friend or helper from among them. [90] But make an exception of those who seek refuge with people with whom you have a treaty, or who come over to you because their hearts forbid them to fight against you or against their own people. Had God pleased, He would have given them power over you, so that they would have taken up arms against you. Therefore, if they keep away from you and cease their hostility and propose peace to you, God does not allow you to harm them. [91] You will find others who wish to be safe from you, and from their own people, yet whenever they find an opportunity of inflicting harm, they plunge into it. So if they neither withdraw, nor offer you peace, nor restrain themselves from fighting you, seize and kill them wherever you encounter them. Over such people We have given you clear authority.

[92] No believer should kill another believer, unless it be by mistake. Anyone who kills a believer by mistake should free a believing slave and pay blood money to the victim's relatives unless they forego it as an act of charity. If the victim belongs to a people at war with you, but is a believer, then the compensation is to free a believing slave. If he belongs to a people with whom you have a treaty, then blood-money should be handed over to his relatives and a believing slave set free. Anyone who lacks the means must fast for two consecutive months. Such is the penance imposed by God. God is all knowing and wise. [93] If anyone kills a believer deliberately, his reward shall be eternal Hell. God will condemn him and reject him, and prepare for him a terrible punishment.[b]

---

a See note to 2:191.

b Killing is a heinous and irreversible crime. One who deliberately kills

[94] Believers, when you go forth in the cause of God, make due investigation and do not say to those who offer you the greeting of peace, 'You are no believer!' because you seek the good things of this life. With God there are good things in plenty. You yourself were in the same position before, but God conferred His special favour on you. Therefore, take care to investigate. Surely God is well-aware of what you do. [95] Those believers who stay behind—apart from those forced by necessity—are not equal to those who strive hard in God's cause with their possessions and their persons. God has given those who strive with their goods and their persons a higher rank than those who stayed behind. God has promised all a good reward; but far greater is the recompense of those who strive for Him—[96] high ranks conferred by Him as well as forgiveness and mercy. God is forgiving and merciful.

[97] When the angels take the souls of those who have wronged themselves, they will ask, 'What was wrong with you?' They will answer, 'We were too weak on earth.' The angels will say, 'Was God's earth not spacious enough for you to have migrated to some other place?' These are the ones whose abode shall be Hell, an evil destination—[98] except such weak ones among men, women and children, as are incapable of adopting any plan or of finding any way out. [99] God may well pardon them. God is ever-pardoning and ever forgiving. [100] Whoever emigrates for the cause of God will find many places of refuge in the land and plentiful provision. Those who leave home for the cause of God and His Messenger; but is then overtaken by death, shall be recompensed by God. God is most forgiving and ever-merciful.

---

another therefore brings down upon himself the wrath of God. Such an act leaves no scope for atonement. God will reject him, and he will be rewarded with eternal hell fire. Accidental killing, however, is more leniently punished. If one unintentionally kills someone, but then, fully realizing the gravity of the crime, sincerely seeks God's forgiveness and makes due monetary compensation, one may hope for divine clemency. One positive development arising from having faced up to the enormity of the crime is the desire for self-reform. To this end God has given man His directives. Self-punishment is a starting point and may be achieved by the observance of a continuous fast.

[101] When you [believers] are travelling in the land, you will not be blamed for shortening your prayers, if you fear the disbelievers may harm you. They are your avowed enemies. [102] When you are among the believers and lead them in prayer, let only part of them stand up along with you, armed with their weapons. After they have prostrated themselves, let them withdraw to the rear to stand guard and then let another party, who have not yet prayed, come forward and pray with you. And let them also be on their guard, armed with their weapons. Those who deny the truth want you to be negligent of your arms and your baggage, so that they may fall upon you suddenly. It is no offence for you to lay aside your arms when overtaken by heavy rain or illness, and always take every precaution for defence. God has prepared a humiliating punishment for those who deny the truth. [103] When you have finished the prayer, remember God while standing, and sitting, and lying on your sides. When you feel secure, say your prayers in the prescribed form. Believers are under the obligation to say their prayers at the appointed hours. [104] Do not relent in the pursuit of the enemy. If you are suffering hardships, they too are suffering similar hardships, but what you can hope for from God, they cannot. God is all knowing and wise.

[105] We have sent the Book down to you with the truth so that you may judge among mankind by means of what God has shown you. And do not be an advocate for the treacherous. [106] Ask God for forgiveness: He is most forgiving and merciful. [107] And do not plead on behalf of those who are dishonest to themselves. Surely God does not love one who is treacherous and sinful. [108] They feel ashamed before men but do not feel ashamed before God, despite His being present with them when they plot at night, uttering things of which He does not approve; and indeed God is fully aware of what they do.

[109] You might argue on their behalf in the life of this world: but who will argue on their behalf with God on the Day of Resurrection and who will be their defender? [110] Yet anyone who does evil or wrongs his own soul and then asks God for forgiveness will find God forgiving and merciful. [111] He who commits sin does so against his own soul. God is all knowing and wise. [112] And anyone who

commits an offence or a sin, then charges an innocent person with it, shall certainly bear the guilt of a calumny and a manifest sin. [113] If it were not for the grace of God and His mercy to you, some of them had resolved to lead you astray but they lead astray no one but themselves. Nor can they do you any harm. God has sent down to you the Book and Wisdom and has taught you what you did not know. God's favour to you has been great indeed.

[114] There is no good in most of their secret talk, except in the case of those who enjoin charity and kindness, or reconciliation between people. If anyone does that, seeking the pleasure of God, We will give him an immense reward. [115] But if anyone opposes the Messenger after his guidance has become clear to him, and follows a path other than that of the faithful, We shall let him pursue his chosen path and shall cast him into Hell: an evil destination.

[116] Surely, God will not forgive the ascribing of partners to Him. He forgives whoever He will for anything other than that. Whoever ascribes partners to God has strayed far indeed. [117] They [the polytheists] call upon female deities, and they invoke none but Satan, the rebellious one, [118] whom God has rejected. He said [to God], 'I will assuredly take a number of Your servants, [119] and shall lead them astray, and fill them with vain desires and order them to slit the ears of cattle. I shall order them to tamper with God's creation. Whoever chooses Satan as a patron instead of God is utterly ruined: [120] he holds out promises to them, and fills them with vain desires: but Satan's promises are nothing but delusion. [121] Hell shall be their home: they shall find no refuge from it.[a] [122] As for those who believe and do good works. We shall admit them to Gardens through which rivers flow; wherein they will abide forever. This is a promise from God; and whose word could be truer than God's?

[123] It is not your desires, nor the desires of the People of the

---

a Man's real challenge in this world is from Satan. Though Satan has no real power, he can lure human beings with fanciful promises to fulfil wishful, imaginary desires and thus manage to make them deviate from the straight path of truth. Satan's way of misguiding is of two main types: one is superstition and the other is interference in God's creation. Faith in superstition means expectation of such results from something as have no relation with that thing.

Book, that shall prevail. Anyone who commits evil will be rewarded accordingly. He will not find any protector or patron for himself besides God. [124] Anyone who performs good deeds, whether it be a man or woman, provided that he is a believer, shall enter Paradise. No one shall suffer the least injustice. [125] Who is better in faith than one who submits himself wholly to God, acts righteously, and follows the religion of Abraham, the upright in faith, whom God chose for a friend? [126] To God belongs all that the heavens and earth contain. God has knowledge of all things.

[127] They consult you concerning women. Say, 'God has given you directions concerning them. The commandment given to you in the Book concerns the orphan girls to whom you do not give what is prescribed for them, and whom you nevertheless desire to marry, and about helpless children. He has instructed you to deal justly with orphans. God has knowledge of all the good you do. [128] If a woman fears ill-treatment or indifference on the part of her husband, it shall be no offence for her to seek a reconciliation, for reconciliation is best. But people are prone to selfish greed. If you do good and fear Him, surely God is aware of what you do. [129] You will never be able to treat your wives with equal fairness, however much you may desire to do so, but do not ignore one wife altogether, leaving her suspended [between marriage and divorce]. And if you make amends and act righteously, surely God is most forgiving and merciful. [130] If they decide to separate, God will compensate both out of His own abundance: God is bountiful and wise.

[131] All that the heavens and the earth contain belongs to God. We have commanded those who were given the Scripture before you, and We command you to fear God. If you deny Him, know that all that the heavens and the earth contain belongs to God. God is self-sufficient and praiseworthy. [132] All that the heavens and the earth contain belongs to God; and none is as worthy of trust as God. [133] If He wanted, He could remove you altogether and replace you with other people: He has the full power to do so. [134] If one desires the rewards of this world [let him remember that] with God are the rewards of [both] this world and the life to come: and God is indeed all hearing, all seeing.

¹³⁵ Believers, be strict in upholding justice and bear witness for the sake of God, even though it be against yourselves, your parents, or your kindred. Be they rich or poor, God knows better about them both. Do not, then, follow your own desires, lest you swerve from justice. If you conceal the truth or evade it, then remember that God is well aware of all that you do.

¹³⁶ Believers, believe in God and His Messenger and in the Scripture He sent down to His Messenger, as well as what He sent down before. He who denies God, His angels, His Scriptures, His messengers and the Last Day has surely gone far astray.^{*a*} ¹³⁷ As for those who come to believe, and then deny the truth, and again come to believe, and again deny the truth, and thereafter grow stubborn in their denial of the truth—God will never forgive them, nor will He guide them. ¹³⁸ Warn the hypocrites that for them there is a painful punishment. ¹³⁹ As for those who take the deniers of the truth for their allies rather than the believers—do they seek honour in their company? Surely all honour belongs to God.

¹⁴⁰ He has instructed you in the Book that, when you hear people deny or ridicule God's revelations, you must not sit with them unless they engage in other talk, or else you yourselves shall become like them. God will gather all the hypocrites and those who deny the truth together in Hell. ¹⁴¹ The hypocrites wait to see what happens to you and, if God grants you a victory, they say, 'Were we not on your side?' And if those who deny the truth have a share of it [victory]

---

a Calling oneself a believer or regarding oneself as such does not suffice for one to be held a believer in the eyes of God. A true believer is only that person who has made God the centre of his life and the source of his trust and confidence. A believer is one who believes in the Prophet and his guidance to the exclusion of all else. A believer is one who adheres to the revealed Scripture in such a manner that his thinking and his feelings become totally subordinated to it. A believer is one to whom belief in the angels means that he is surrounded by God's guardians who are constantly watching him. A believer is one whose belief in the Hereafter is so profound that he begins to examine all his words and deeds in the balance of the Hereafter. One who becomes a believer in this sense is, in the eyes of God, on the right path, on the straight path to success in the Hereafter. One who does not become a believer in this sense has gone astray, however much he may consider himself a true believer.

they say to them, 'Did we not help you win, and protect you from the believers?' God will judge between you [all] on Resurrection Day. And never will God allow those who deny the truth to harm the believers.

¹⁴² The hypocrites seek to outwit God—but it is He who outwits them. And when they stand up for prayer, they do so reluctantly and to be seen by others, and they hardly remember God at all. ¹⁴³ They vacillate between the two, belonging neither to one side nor the other. But for him whom God allows to go astray you can never find the way for him. ¹⁴⁴ Do not take deniers of the truth [who are at war with you] for your allies in preference to believers. Would you give God a clear proof against yourselves? ¹⁴⁵ The hypocrites shall surely be in the lowest depth of the Fire; and you will find no helper for them. ¹⁴⁶ But those who repent and mend their ways, who hold fast to God and are sincere in their worship of God will be joined with the believers; and God will bestow a great reward upon the believers. ¹⁴⁷ Why should God punish you, if you render thanks to Him and believe in Him? God is appreciative and aware.

¹⁴⁸ God does not love the utterance of evil words except in the case of someone who has been wronged. God hears all and knows all. ¹⁴⁹ Whether you reveal any good or hide it, or pardon any evil, God is forgiving and all powerful. ¹⁵⁰ Those who deny God and His messengers and seek to make a distinction between God and His messengers and say, 'We believe in some messengers and disbelieve in others', and desire to adopt a position in between. ¹⁵¹ Those indeed are they who are denying the truth beyond doubt, and We have prepared a humiliating punishment for the deniers. ¹⁵² To those who believe in God and His messengers, and make no distinction between any of them, to those—We shall surely give them their rewards. God is most forgiving and merciful.

¹⁵³ The People of the Book ask you to bring down for them a book from heaven. Of Moses they demanded a greater thing than that. They said to him: 'Show us God face to face.' A thunderbolt struck them for their wickedness. After that, they took to worshipping the [golden] calf, after all evidence of the truth had come to them! Yet We pardoned even that and bestowed on Moses clear authority.

[154] And We raised above them the Mount, while making a covenant with them, and We said to them. 'Enter the gate humbly,' and We also commanded them, 'Transgress not in the matter of the Sabbath.' We took from them a firm covenant.

[155] But they broke their covenant; and they rejected the signs of God; and put the prophets to death without justification, and said, 'Our hearts are sealed.' It is God who has sealed their hearts, on account of their denial of the truth. Except for a few of them, they have no faith. [156] They denied the truth and uttered a monstrous slander against Mary. [157] They declared, 'We have put to death the Messiah, Jesus, son of Mary, the Messenger of God.' They did not kill him, nor did they crucify him, but it only seemed to them [as if it had been so]. And those who differ in this matter are in doubt concerning it. They have no definite knowledge about it, but only follow mere conjecture. But they certainly did not kill him. [158] God raised him towards Himself. God is almighty and wise.

[159] There is none among the People of the Book but will believe in it before his death; and on the Day of Resurrection he shall be a witness against them. [160] Because of the wrongdoings of the Jews, We forbade them certain good things that had been allowed to them before; for having frequently debarred others from God's path; [161] for taking usury, when they had been forbidden to do so. And because of their devouring people's wealth wrongfully. We have prepared a painful punishment for those of them who [continue to] deny the truth. [162] But to those of them, who are firmly grounded in knowledge, and the believers, who truly believe in what is revealed to you, and what was revealed before you. To those who pray regularly and pay the *zakat* [prescribed alms] and believe in God and the Last Day, We will surely give a great reward.

[163] We have sent revelation to you [Prophet] as We did to Noah and the prophets who came after him, to Abraham, Ishmael, Isaac, Jacob, and the Tribes, to Jesus, Job, Jonah, Aaron, and Solomon and David, to whom We gave the Psalms. [164] We have told you about some messengers sent previously, while We have not yet told you about others. God spoke to Moses directly. [165] They were messengers, bearing good news and giving warning, so that mankind would have

no excuse before God, after the coming of the messengers. God is mighty, wise.[a]

[166] But God bears witness to what He has sent down to you. He has sent it down with His knowledge. The angels too bear witness. And God suffices as a witness. [167] Those who are bent on denying the truth and on turning others away from the path of God have strayed far from the right path. [168] God will not forgive those who deny the truth and act wrongfully, nor will He guide them, [169] to any path other than the path of Hell, wherein they shall abide forever. That is easy enough for God. [170] Mankind! The Messenger has brought you the truth from your Lord, so believe for your own good. And if you deny the truth, know that to God belongs all that the heavens and the earth contain. God is all knowing and wise.

[171] People of the Book! Do not go to extremes in your religion. Say nothing but the truth about God. The Christ Jesus, son of Mary, was only a messenger of God and His word, conveyed to Mary, a spirit from Him. So believe in God and His messengers and do not say: 'There are three [gods].' Desist, it will be better for you. Indeed, God is the one and only God. His Holiness is far above having a son. To Him belongs whatever is in the heavens and whatever is on the earth. And God is sufficient as a guardian. [172] Surely, the Messiah would never disdain to be accounted a servant of God. Nor would the angels who are nearest to Him. If any do disdain to worship Him, and grow arrogant, He will in any case gather them all before Him. [173] Those who believe and do good works will be

---

a God created man, and then He created Paradise and Hell. Man was later settled on the earth. Here man has freedom to do as he wishes. But this freedom is not forever. It is temporary and meant for his trial. It is so that good and bad may be distinguished from one another. God is watching those who, despite being granted freedom, can adopt realistic attitudes, and surrender themselves to the will of God, and who are the people who misuse their freedom and prove themselves to be rebels. Both kinds of people have been mixed in this world. Both have equal opportunity to gain fully from the blessings of God. But, after the completion of the appointed time of trial, those groups will be separated from one another. The first group will be lodged in the Gardens of Paradise forever, while the second group will be consigned to Hell for all eternity.

fully recompensed by Him. And He will give them yet more out of His bounty; and as for those who were disdainful and proud, He will punish them with a painful punishment. And they will not find anyone to help or protect them against God. [174] Men, you have received clear evidence from your Lord. We have sent down a clear light to you.

[175] As for those who believe in God and hold fast to Him, He will admit them to His mercy and His grace; He will guide them towards Him on a straight path. [176] They ask you for instruction. Say, 'God instructs you concerning the indirect heirs. If a person dies childless but has a sister, she receives half of what he leaves, and he is her heir if she dies childless. If there are two sisters, they receive two-thirds of what he leaves. If there are brothers and sisters, the share of each male shall be that of two females. God makes things clear to you, so that you will not go astray. God has knowledge of all things.'[a]

5. THE TABLE (*AL-MA'IDAH*)

In the name of God, the Most Gracious, the Most Merciful

[1] Believers, fulfil your obligations. All livestock is lawful for you, other than that which is hereby announced to you. You are forbidden to kill game while you are on a pilgrimage—God commands what He will. [2] Believers, violate neither the sanctity of God's signs, the Sacred Month, the sacrificial animals, the animals wearing garlands [indicating they are to be sacrificed] nor those on their way to the Sacred House seeking the bounty and pleasure of their Lord. When, on completion of your pilgrimage, you take off the garb of the pilgrim, you may hunt. Do not let the enmity of those who barred you from the Sacred Mosque lead you into sin. Help one another in goodness

---

a Giving the injunction regarding inheritance the Quran states, 'God makes things clear to you so that you will not go astray'. This shows that inheritance is not a simple matter. This is one of those areas in which disobeying the divine injunction will lead you astray from the straight and narrow path of guidance.

and in piety. Do not help one another in sin and transgression. Fear God! God is severe in punishment.

³ You are forbidden carrion, blood and pork; and any flesh over which the name of any other than God is invoked; and any creature which has been strangled, or killed by a blow or in a fall, or has been gored to death or half-eaten by a wild animal, saving that which you make lawful [by slaughtering properly while it was still alive] and what has been slaughtered at an altar. You are forbidden to make the division of [meat] by means of divining arrows: that is sinful conduct. Those who deny the truth have this day despaired of ever harming your religion. So do not fear them. Fear Me. Today I have completed your religion for you and completed My blessing upon you. I have chosen for you Islam as your religion. But if anyone is forced by hunger to eat something which is forbidden, not intending to commit a sin, he will find God forgiving and merciful.

⁴ If they ask you what has been made lawful for them, say, 'All good things have been made lawful for you;' and what you have taught your birds and beasts of prey to catch, training them as God has taught you. So eat what they catch for you, but first pronounce God's name over it. Fear God, for God is swift in taking account.

⁵ Today, all good things have been made lawful to you. The food of the People of the Book is lawful to you, and your food is lawful to them. The chaste believing women and the chaste women of the people who were given the Book before you, are lawful to you, provided that you give them their dowers, and marry them, neither committing fornication nor taking them as mistresses. The deeds of anyone who rejects the faith will come to nothing, and in the Hereafter he will be among the losers.

⁶ Believers, when you rise to pray, wash your faces and your hands up to the elbows and wipe your heads and [wash] your feet up to the ankles.ᵃ If you are in a state of impurity, take a full bath.

---

a The purpose of prayers or *salat* is to purify a man of all evils. Ablution or *wudu* is an external preparation for this religious rite. When a man intends to offer prayers, he first goes toward water. Water is a great gift of God which is the best thing for washing out all the impurities from man. Similarly, prayer is a

But if you are sick or on a journey or when you have just relieved yourselves, or you have consorted with your spouses, you can find no water, take some clean sand and rub your faces and hands with it. God does not wish to place any burden on you; He only wishes to purify you and perfect His favour to you, in order that you may be grateful.

[7] Remember God's favour to you, and the covenant, which He made with you when you said, 'We hear and we obey.'[a] Fear God. God has full knowledge of the innermost thoughts of men. [8] Believers, be

---

'divine spring' in which a man bathes and purifies himself of evil emotions and vicious thoughts.

Initiating the process of ablution when a man puts water on his hands, he is, in effect, praying, 'O, God! Save these hands of mine from indulging in evil, and let whatever evil deeds I have indulged in through them be washed off.' Then he rinses his mouth and washes his face. At that time his soul prays silently, 'O, God! Kindly remove the bad effects of any improper food I have put in my mouth; the evil words I have uttered, and the evil things I have seen.' Thereafter, when he takes water in hands and massages his head with his hands, his whole existence is moulded by the prayers, 'O, God! Wash away the bad effects of the evil ideas conceived by my mind and wrong plans devised by me, and cleanse and purify my mind.' When he washes his feet, this action of his becomes the entreaty before his Lord, that He may cleanse his feet of the dust of evil and make them (his feet) never tread any path except the path of righteousness and justice. In this way, the whole process of ablution assumes, so to say, the practical shape of the prayer, 'O, God! Make me a person who turns away from wrongs and one who keeps himself clear of evils.'

a Faith is the vow which binds God and His subject. The subject vows that he will remain God-fearing in his life in this world, and God guarantees that He will be His subject's guardian in this world and in the Hereafter. God's subject has to prove his fulfilment of his vow in two ways. First, he should become steadfast on the path of God. On every occasion his existence should give the response, which is expected of a subject to his Lord. When he observes the universe, his mind should be filled with the realisation of God's glories and powers. When he looks at himself, he should realise that his existence was entirely due to God's grace and His mercy. If his emotions erupt, they should erupt for the sake of God. If his attention is focused on anybody, it should be on God. His love should be for God. His fears should be linked with God. The remembrance to God should be prevalent in his mind. He should be given to prayer and obedience of God. He should spend his assets for the cause of God. He should feel pleasure in devoting his life to God.

steadfast in the cause of God and bear witness with justice. Do not let your enmity for others turn you away from justice. Deal justly; that is nearer to being God-fearing. Fear God. God is aware of all that you do. ⁹ God has promised those who believe and do good deeds forgiveness and a great reward; ¹⁰ but those who deny the truth and deny Our signs are destined for Hell.*a* ¹¹ Believers, remember the blessings which God bestowed upon you when a certain people were about to lay hands on you and He held back their hands from you. Have fear of God and in God let the believers place their trust.

¹² God made a covenant with the Children of Israel; and raised among them twelve leaders. God said, 'Surely, I am with you. If you attend to your prayers and pay the alms and believe in My messengers and support them, and give a generous loan to God, I will certainly forgive you your sins and admit you into Gardens through which rivers flow. Whoever among you denies the truth after this shall go astray from the straight path.' ¹³ Since they broke their solemn pledge, We laid on them Our curse and hardened their hearts. They distorted the meaning of the revealed words, taking them out of their context, and forgot much of what they were enjoined. You will constantly discover treachery on their part, except for a few of them. But pardon them, and bear with them; truly, God loves the doers of good.

¹⁴ We also made a covenant with those who say, 'We are Christians.' But they too have forgotten much of what they were enjoined. So, We have put enmity and hatred between them till the Day of Judgement; and soon God will declare to them what they have been doing.

¹⁵ People of the Book! Our Messenger has come to make clear to you much of what you have hidden of the Scriptures and to forgive you much. A light has now come to you from God and a clear Book, ¹⁶ whereby God guides to the ways of peace all who seek His good

---

a In the world, God makes His appearance felt through symbols, i.e. in the shape of such arguments as cannot be contradicted by man. When an argument of God appears before a man and he indulges in verbal pyrotechnics instead of accepting it, then this amounts to denying the signs of God. Such people will receive severe punishment at God's behest. And those who accept the argument will be held deserving of God's reward.

pleasure, bringing them from darkness to the light, by His will, and guiding them to a straight path. [17] In blasphemy indeed are those who say, 'God is Christ, the son of Mary.' Say, 'Who then could prevent God if He so willed from destroying Christ, son of Mary, and his mother and everyone on earth? The kingdom of the heavens and the earth and everything between them belong to God. He creates what He will and God has power over all things.'

[18] The Jews and the Christians say, 'We are the children of God and His beloved ones.'[a] Say, 'Then why does He punish you for your sins? Indeed, you are but human beings among those He has created. He forgives whom He pleases and punishes whom He pleases. The kingdom of the heavens and the earth and all that is between them, belong to God and all shall return to Him.' [19] People of the Book, Our Messenger has come to you to make things clear to you after an interval between the messengers, lest you say, 'No bearer of glad tidings and no warner has come to us.' So a bearer of glad tidings and a warner has indeed come to you. God has the power to do all things.

[20] Remember when Moses said to his people, 'O my people! Remember God's favour to you, He has raised up prophets among you, made you kings, and granted you [favours] such as He has not granted to anyone else in the world. [21] O my people! Enter the holy land which God has assigned for you. Do not turn back, or you will be the losers.' [22] They said, 'Moses, in that land there is a powerful people. Never shall we enter it until they leave it: if they leave, then we shall certainly enter it.' [23] Thereupon two God-fearing men whom God had blessed said, 'Go into them through the gate—for as soon as you enter, you shall surely be victorious!

---

a Considering any community as a favourite community of God is an absolutely meaningless thought. Before God the reckoning is individual to individual and not community to community. Everybody will get his reward before God according to his deeds. In the eyes of God, every man is a human being irrespective of his belonging to this community or that. Every man's future will be decided on the basis of his performance in this world of test and trial. Paradise is not a place reserved for any particular community; nor is hell a prison for any particular community.

Put your trust in God if you are true believers.' ²⁴ They said, 'We will never enter it, Moses, as long as they are there. Go, you and your Lord, and fight, and we will stay here.'

²⁵ Moses supplicated, 'Lord, I have power over none but myself and my brother; so separate us from the disobedient people.' ²⁶ God said, 'The land is forbidden to them for forty years, while they wander around the earth, bewildered; do not grieve over these wicked people.'

²⁷ Relate to them, the true story of the two sons of Adam.[a] When they both presented an offering, it was accepted from one of them and not from the other. The latter said, 'I shall kill you!' The former said, 'God accepts [things] only from the righteous. ²⁸ If you raise your hand to kill me, I will not raise mine to kill you. I fear God, the Lord of the Universe, ²⁹ and I want you to bear your sins against me as well as your own sins and become an inhabitant of the Fire. Such is the reward of the wrongdoers.'

³⁰ His lower self persuaded him to kill his brother, and he killed him and he became one of the lost. ³¹ Then God sent a raven, which scratched the earth, so that He might show him how to hide the corpse of his brother. 'Alas!' he cried, 'Am I not able even to be like this raven, so that I may hide the corpse of my brother?' And he repented.

³² That was why We laid it down for the Children of Israel that

---

a Whatever a man receives in this world is bestowed by God. Therefore, being jealous of a person on seeing him well situated in life and then inflicting harm on him amounts to trying to nullify God's plan. Such a person is to some extent given the scope to do whatever he likes in this world of trial, but in the eyes of God, he is the worst sinner. Abel drew the attention of his elder brother, Cain, to this fact. This created some hesitation in his mind. He realised that he was bent on killing his younger brother without any justification. But the feeling of jealousy in him did not cool down. He invented excuses to justify his action. Ultimately, his inner struggle resolved itself and rest in his self-devised justification and he proceeded to kill his brother. The voice of conscience is the voice of God. A question arising in a man's conscience about any action of his amounts in fact to his facing a test. A man is successful if he gives a positive response to the voice of his conscience, but if in taking the shelter of false excuses he suppresses the voice of his conscience, then he has failed.

whoever killed a human being—except as a punishment for murder or for spreading corruption in the land— shall be regarded as having killed all mankind, and that whoever saved a human life shall be regarded as having saved all mankind. Our messengers came to them with clear signs, but many of them continued to commit excesses in the land. [33] Those that make war against God and His Messenger and spread disorder in the land shall be put to death or crucified or have their hands and feet cut off on alternate sides, or be banished from the country. They shall be disgraced in this world, and then severely punished in the Hereafter, [34] except for those who repent before you gain power over them: for you must know that God is forgiving and merciful.

[35] Believers, fear God and seek ways to come closer to Him and strive for His cause, so that you may prosper.[a] [36] As for those who reject Faith, if they had everything on earth, and twice as much again and offered it to ransom themselves from the torment of the Day of Resurrection, it shall not be accepted from them—they will have a painful punishment. [37] They will want to get out of the Fire but they will be unable to do so: theirs shall be a lasting punishment. [38] Cut off the hands of thieves, whether they are male or female, as a [deterrent] punishment from God for what they have done. God is almighty and wise. [39] But God will surely turn in mercy to him who repents after his transgression and reforms. Surely, God is most forgiving and ever merciful. [40] Do you not know that the kingdom of the heavens and earth belongs to God? He punishes whom He will and forgives whom He pleases. God has power over all things.

[41] Messenger, do not be grieved by those who vie with one another in denying the truth; those who say with their tongues, 'We believe,' but have no faith in their hearts; from among the Jews also, there are those who listen eagerly to any lies. They listen to you to convey

---

a The greatest achievement for a man is his nearness to God. This nearness in its real and perfect shape will be his in the Hereafter. However, when a man's righteous action brings him nearness to God, he experiences this in this world purely in the form of heavenly feeling. The way to attain this nearness is through becoming a true worshipper of God, and through struggling to make efforts for His cause.

to others [religious leaders] who do not come to you [out of pride and conceit]. They [these leaders] take words out of their context and say, 'If this be given to you, receive it, but if not, then beware!' If anyone's trial is intended by God, you cannot in the least prevail against God on his behalf. Those whose hearts God does not intend to purify shall be subjected to disgrace in this world and a severe punishment in the Hereafter.

42 They listen eagerly to falsehood, and devour forbidden things voraciously. If they come to you, then judge between them or avoid them. If you avoid them, they can in no way harm you, but if you do judge, judge them with fairness: God loves those that deal justly. 43 But why do they come to you for judgement when they have the Torah, which enshrines God's own judgement? Yet, in spite of that, they turn their backs; and certainly they will not believe.

44 We have revealed the Torah, in which there is guidance and light. By it the prophets who were obedient to Us judged the Jews, and so did the rabbis and the priests, according to God's Book which had been entrusted to their care; and to which they were witnesses. Have no fear of man; fear Me, and do not sell My revelations for a paltry sum. Those who do not judge by what God has sent down are deniers of truth. 45 We prescribed for them in [the Torah]: a life for a life, an eye for an eye, a nose for a nose, an ear for an ear, a tooth for a tooth, and a wound for a wound. But, if anyone forgoes it, this shall be for him an expiation. Those who do not judge by what God has sent down are wrongdoers! 46 We caused Jesus, son of Mary to follow in their footsteps, fulfilling what had been revealed before him in the Torah. We gave him the Gospel, which contained guidance and light, fulfilling what was revealed before it in the Torah: a guide and an admonition to the God-fearing. 47 Therefore, let those who follow the Gospel judge according to what God has revealed in it. Those who do not judge by what God has sent down are rebellious.

48 We have sent down the Book to you with the truth, fulfilling [the predictions] revealed in the previous scriptures and determining

what is true therein, and as a guardian over it.[a] Judge, therefore, between them by what God has revealed, and do not follow their vain desires turning away from the truth that has come to you. To every one of you We have ordained a law and a way, and had God so willed, He would have made you all a single community, but He did not so will, in order that He might try you by what He has given you. Vie, then, with one another in doing good works; to God you shall all return; then He will make clear to you about what you have been disputing.

[49] Judge between them by what God has sent down and do not be led by their desires. Beware of them lest they turn you away from a part of that what God has revealed to you. If they reject your judgement, know that God intends to punish them for the sins they have committed. Indeed a large number of the people are disobedient. [50] Is it pagan laws that they wish to be judged by? Who is a better judge than God for men whose faith is firm?

[51] Believers, do not take the Jews and Christians as allies. They are allies with one another. Whoever of you takes them as an ally shall become one of them. God does not guide the wrongdoers.[b] [52] You will see those whose minds are diseased hastening towards them, saying, 'We fear lest a misfortune befall us.' But God may well bring about victory or make a decision which is favourable to you. Then they will repent of the thoughts, which they secretly harboured in their hearts. [53] Then the believers will say, 'Are these the men who swore their strongest oaths by God, that they were with you?' Their works will come to nothing and they will lose all.[c]

---

a The Quran and other Divine Scriptures are not separate books. They are the different editions of a single Book of God which has been named *al-kitab* here. All editions of the Book revealed by God were one and the same as regards content. However, the bearers of the previous scriptures could not in the later periods preserve them in their original form. Therefore, God revealed His Book (*muhaymin*) i.e. the Quran, the authentic expression of His will, — a touch-stone which reveals which sections of the other scriptures have retained their original form and which have been changed.

b See note to 3:28.

c Every test in this world is a test of intention. What man has to do is to

[54] Believers, if any among you renounce the faith, God will replace them by others who love Him and are loved by Him, who will be kind and considerate towards believers and firm and unyielding towards those who deny the truth. They will strive hard for the cause of God and will in no way take to heart the reproaches of the fault finder. Such is God's bounty, which He gives to anyone He wishes. God is bountiful and all-knowing. [55] Your helpers are only God and His Messenger and the believers who say their prayers and pay the alms and bow down in worship. [56] Those who ally themsleves with God, His Messenger, and the believers must know that God's party is sure to triumph.

[57] Believers! Do not seek the friendship of those who were given the Book before you or the disbelievers who ridicule your religion and make a jest of it. Have fear of God, if you are true believers. [58] When you call them to prayer, they treat it as a jest and a diversion. This is because they are devoid of understanding. [59] Say, 'People of the Book! Do you resent us only because we believe in God and in what has been revealed to us and to others before, and because most of you are disobedient?'[a] [60] Say, 'Shall I tell you who will

---

prove his intention by ignoring dangers; in that way he takes the first step on the path towards God. Then God's help comes to him immediately thereafter. But one who does not provide proof of his intention and does not take the first step in the direction of God, is a transgressor in His eyes. Such individuals cannot then expect to be sent God's unilateral help.

Islamic life is a purposeful life and therefore it is a life of struggle. It is the mission of a believer to convey the religion of God to all God's subjects, guiding the world to keep away from the path leading to hell and to tread the path leading to paradise.

a A man's delicate, subtle feelings, such as modesty, broadmindedness, the desire for cleanliness, etc., which function as the watch-guards of God within him and prevent him from evil action, get smothered. The last stage of his downfall comes when his whole life is corroded by satanic ways. When a group reaches this stage, and is distanced from God's grace to the furthest possible extent. Its own humanity becomes distorted and it becomes a curse to itself and to the rest of humanity. Having drifted so far away from the right path of nature, it starts living like the animals.

What prevents a man from following the dictates of his desires is his moral fibre. But when obstinacy and enmity dominate him, his ability to think

receive a worse reward from God? Those whom God has rejected
and with whom He has been angry. They were condemned as apes
and swine and those who worship the evil. These are in the worst
plight and farthest astray from the right path.'

⁶¹ When they come to you they say, 'We believe,' but they come
[with the resolve] to deny the truth and leave in the same state. God
knows best what they are concealing. ⁶² You see many among them
vie with one another in sin and transgression and practice what is
unlawful. It is vile indeed what they have been doing! ⁶³ Why do
their rabbis and scholars not forbid them to utter sinful words or to
consume what is unlawful? Their actions are indeed vile.

⁶⁴ The Jews say, 'The hand of God is tied up.' May their own
hands be tied up and may they be cursed for what they say. No
indeed! His hands are both outstretched: He bestows as He will.
What is revealed to you from your Lord will surely increase in most
of them their obstinate rebellion and denial of truth; and We have
sown among them enmity and hatred till the Day of Resurrection.
Whenever they kindle the fire of war, God puts it out. They spread
evil in the land, but God does not love the evil-doers.

⁶⁵ If only the People of the Book would believe and be mindful
of God, We would surely pardon their sins and We would surely
admit them into the Gardens of Bliss. ⁶⁶ If they had observed the
Torah and the Gospel and what was revealed to them from their
Lord, they would surely have been nourished from above and from
below. There are some among them who are on the right course; but
there are many among them who do nothing but evil.

⁶⁷ O Messenger, deliver whatever has been sent down to you by
your Lord. If you do not do so, you will not have conveyed His
message and God will protect you from the people. For God does
not guide those who deny the truth.

⁶⁸ Say, 'People of the Book, you have no ground to stand on

---

becomes suppressed and then there is nothing to combat the pressure of his
desires. He may be a human being in appearance but, inside he is no better than
an animal; a man with deep insight, just by looking at him, can tell what animal
is hidden inside the human exterior.

until you observe the Torah and the Gospel and what is revealed to you from your Lord.' What is revealed to you from your Lord will surely increase many of them in rebellion and in their denial of the truth. But do not grieve for those who deny the truth. ⁶⁹ Believers, Jews, Sabaeans and Christians—whoever believes in God and the Last Day and does what is right—shall have nothing to fear nor shall they grieve.

⁷⁰ We made a covenant with the Children of Israel and sent forth messengers among them. But whenever a messenger came to them with a message that was not to their liking, some they accused of lying, while others they put to death, ⁷¹ and they imagined that no harm would come to them; and so they became blind and deaf [of heart]. God turned to them in mercy; yet again many of them became blind and deaf. God is fully aware of their actions.

⁷² Indeed, they are deniers of the truth who say, 'God is the Christ, the son of Mary.' For the Christ himself said, 'Children of Israel, serve God, my Lord and your Lord.' If anyone associates anything with God, God will forbid him the Garden and the Fire will be his home. The wrongdoers shall have no helpers. ⁷³ They are deniers of the truth who say, 'God is one of three.' There is only One God. If they do not desist from so saying, a painful punishment is bound to befall such of them as are bent on denying the truth. ⁷⁴ Why do they not turn to God and ask for His forgiveness? God is forgiving and merciful. ⁷⁵ Christ, son of Mary, was no more than a messenger. Many messengers passed away before him. His mother was a virtuous woman; and they both ate food [like other mortals]. See how We make the signs clear to them! See how they turn away! ⁷⁶ Say, 'Do you worship something other than God, that has no power to do you harm or good? God alone is the All Hearing and All Knowing.'

⁷⁷ Say, 'People of the Book! Do not go to extremes in your religion and do not follow the whims of those who went astray before you—they caused many to go astray and themselves strayed away from the right path.'

⁷⁸ Those of the Children of Israel who were bent on denying the truth were cursed by David and Jesus, the son of Mary. That was because they disobeyed and were given to transgression; ⁷⁹ they

would not prevent one another from doing the wrong things they did. Evil indeed were their deeds. [80] You see many among them allying themselves with those who deny the truth. Evil is that which their souls have sent on ahead for them. They have incurred the wrath of God and shall suffer eternal punishment. [81] Had they believed in God and the Prophet and what was revealed to him, they would not have taken those who deny the truth as their allies, but many of them are disobedient.

[82] You will find that the bitterest in their enmity to the faithful are the Jews and the polytheists; the nearest in affection to them are those who say, 'We are Christians.' That is because there are priests and monks among them; and because they are free from pride. [83] When they listen to what has been sent down to the Messenger, you see their eyes overflowing with tears, because of the Truth they recognize. They say, 'Our Lord, we believe, so count us among those who bear witness. [84] Why should we not believe in God and in the truth that has come down to us? We yearn for our Lord to admit us among the righteous.' [85] And for their words God will reward them with Gardens through which rivers flow, wherein they shall abide forever. That is the reward of those who do good. [86] But those who deny the truth and deny Our signs will become the inmates of Hell.[a]

[87] Believers, do not forbid the wholesome good things, which God made lawful to you. Do not transgress; God does not love the transgressors. [88] Eat the lawful and wholesome things, which God has given you. Fear God, in whom you believe. [89] God will not call you to account for your meaningless oaths, but He will call you to account for the oaths, which you swear in earnest. The expiation

---

a In this verse paradise is declared the reward for certain 'words' uttered by people (*fa athabahumullah bima qalu*). But what were these 'words' which made the speakers of them entitled to eternal paradise? What they said represented and gave expression to their entire being. They heard God's message in such a way that they found the whole truth enshrined in it. It penetrated their hearts and minds. It caused in them a revolution which changed the entire focus of their wishes and aspirations—to the extent that all barriers of prejudice and interests broke down. The Quran was not a mere book for them but a living sign of the Lord of the Universe.

for a broken oath is the feeding of ten needy men with such food as you normally offer to your own people; or the clothing of ten needy men; or the freeing of one slave. Anyone who lacks the means shall fast for three days. That is the expiation of your breaking the oaths that you have sworn. Do keep your oaths. Thus God explains to you His commandments, so that you may be grateful.

⁹⁰ Believers, intoxicants and gambling*a* and [occult dedication of] stones and divining arrows are abominations devised by Satan. Avoid them, so that you may prosper. ⁹¹ Satan seeks to sow enmity and hatred among you by means of wine and gambling, and to keep you from the remembrance of God and from your prayers. Will you not then abstain? ⁹² Obey God and obey the Messenger, and be ever on your guard [against evil]. But if you turn away, then know that Our Messenger's duty is only to deliver the message clearly. ⁹³ Those who believe and do good deeds will not be blamed for what they may have consumed [in the past], so long as they fear God and believe in Him and do good works; so long as they fear God and believe in Him, so long as they fear God and do good deeds. For God loves those who do good.

⁹⁴ Believers, God will test you with game which come within the

---

a Islam wants man to become a rememberer and worshipper of God; making himself completely obedient to God and His Prophet. For this purpose, a man's being serious is absolutely necessary. But the above mentioned misdeeds are the greatest destroyers of seriousness. Islam wants to create a man who recognizes and understands realities, who in living his life, rises above materialism, whereas intoxicants make a man forgetful of realities. Arrows and the drawing of lots plunge a man into the dark abyss of superstition, while gambling leads man into materialism to an extent which is criminal. Islam wants to create a man who elevates himself on the basis of facts and realities, but intoxicants promote an excessive lack of awareness of what is proper and gambling promotes excessive selfishness.

Similarly, gambling is the worst form of exploitation and selfishness in that it enables a man to rob many people, thus enriching himself and achieving great material success. A drunkard is devoid of any awareness of others' trouble or grief, while for a gambler, others are only subjects of exploitation. A society where such people exist will be vitiated by clashes and enmity, and its members will live in an atmosphere of mutual mistrust and recrimination.

reach of your hands and spears, so that He may know those who fear Him, even if they cannot see Him. Anyone who oversteps the limits after this will have a painful punishment. ⁹⁵ Believers, do not kill any game while you are on a pilgrimage. Anyone of you who kills game deliberately shall make compensation with an animal which is the equivalent of what he has killed, to be determined by two just men from among you, as an offering brought to the Ka'bah; or he shall, in expiation, either feed the poor or do the equivalent of that in fasting, so that he may taste the consequence of his deeds. God forgives what is past, but if anyone relapses into wrongdoing, God will exact His retribution. God is mighty, the Lord of retribution.

⁹⁶ To hunt and to eat the fish of the sea is made lawful for you, a provision made for you and for seafarers. But you are forbidden the game of the land while you are on a pilgrimage. Have fear of God, before whom you shall all be gathered. ⁹⁷ God has made the Ka'bah, the Sacred House, a means of support as well as the sacred month and the sacrificial animals with their garlands. That is so that you may know that God has knowledge of whatever is in the heavens and on the earth and that He is fully aware of all things. ⁹⁸ Know that God is severe in punishment, yet most forgiving and merciful. ⁹⁹ The Messenger's sole duty is to convey the message. God knows what you reveal and what you hide. ¹⁰⁰ Say, 'The bad and the good are not alike, even though the abundance of the bad may appear pleasing to you. So fear God, O men of understanding, so that you may prosper.'

¹⁰¹ Believers, do not ask questions about things which, if they were made known to you, would only become burdensome for you; but if you ask them when the Quran is being revealed, they shall be made plain to you—God has kept silent about them: God is most forgiving and forbearing. ¹⁰² Other people before you enquired about such things, but when they were disclosed to them, they refused to carry them out. ¹⁰³ God has ordained no sanctity about animals described as *bahirah*, or *sa'ibah*, or *wasilah* or *ham.ᵃ* Those who

---

a These are different categories of domestic animals which the pre-Islamic Arabs used to dedicate to their deities.

deny the truth invent falsehoods about God. Most of them do not use their reason: [104] when it is said to them, 'Come to what God has sent down and to the Messenger.' They reply, 'The faith we have inherited from our fathers is sufficient for us.' Even though their forefathers knew nothing and were not guided! [105] Believers, take care of your own souls. The misguided cannot harm you as long as you are guided. All of you will return to God. Then He will make you realize that which you used to do.

[106] Believers, when death approaches you, let two just men from among you act as witnesses when you make your testaments; or two men from another tribe, if the calamity of death overtakes you while you are travelling in the land. Detain them after prayers, and if you doubt their honesty, let them swear by God, 'We will not sell our testimony for any price, even to a kinsman. And we will not conceal the testimony of God. If we did, we would indeed be guilty of sin.' [107] If it turns out that both prove dishonest, two others should take their place from amongst those whose rights have been usurped and let them swear by God, saying, 'Our testimony is indeed truer than the testimony of these two. And we have not been guilty of any misstatement for then indeed we would be transgressors.' [108] That makes it more likely that people will bear true witness, or else they will fear that their oaths will be contradicted by the oaths of others. Heed God and listen; God does not guide a rebellious, disobedient people.

[109] The Day when God assembles the messengers and asks them, 'What was the response you received [from the people]?' they will reply, 'We have no knowledge of it. You alone know what is hidden.' [110] Then God will say, 'Jesus, son of Mary, remember My favour to you and to your mother: how I strengthened you with the holy spirit, so that you could speak to people in childhood and in maturity; and how I taught you the Book, and wisdom, the Torah and the Gospel; how by My leave you fashioned from clay the shape of a bird and blew upon it, so that, by My leave, it became a bird, and healed the blind and the leper by My permission, and when you brought forth the dead by My permission; and how I prevented the Children of

Israel from harming you when you came to them with clear signs, when those of them who denied the truth said, "This is sheer magic."

[111] [Remember the time], when I inspired the disciples to believe in Me and in My messenger, they replied, "We believe, bear witness that we have submitted."' [112] When the disciples said, 'O Jesus, son of Mary! Can your Lord send down to us from heaven a table spread with food?' He replied, 'Have fear of God, if you are true believers.' [113] They said, 'We want to eat from it, so that we may satisfy our hearts and know that you have told us the truth, and that we should be witnesses of it.' [114] Jesus, son of Mary, said, 'O God, our Lord! Send down for us a table spread with food from heaven,[a] so that it may be a feast for us, for the first of us and for the last of us: a sign from You. Give us our sustenance, for You are the best of sustainers.' [115] God replied, 'I will certainly send it down to you, but whosoever of you deny the truth thereafter will be punished with a punishment such as I have never meted out to anyone else in the world.'

[116] When God says, 'Jesus, son of Mary, did you say to people, "Take me and my mother as two deities besides God"?' He will answer, 'Glory be to You! How could I ever say that to which I have no right? If I had ever said so, You would surely have known it. You know what is in my mind, while I do not know anything that is within Yours. You alone are the knower of unseen things— [117] I told them only what You commanded me to, "Worship God, my Lord and your Lord." I was a witness to what they did as long as I remained among them, and when You took my soul, You were the watcher over them. You are the witness of all things, [118] and if

---

a Man is constantly being provided with the provisions for his life by God. In fact, the whole earth has become a table laid with provisions for man. But the demand made by the believers in Jesus for food to be sent down from the sky caused a severe warning to be given to them. The reason for this is that the provisions we receive under normal conditions are routed through a veil of cause and effect, while the demand of the believers involved the removal of that veil. This is again the way of God, because if this veil is removed, the very purpose of test will be defeated.

You punish them, they are surely Your servants; and if You forgive them, You are surely the Mighty and Wise.'

[119] God will say, 'This is the Day when the truthful will benefit from their truthfulness. They shall forever dwell in Gardens through which rivers flow. God is pleased with them and they with Him: that is the supreme triumph. [120] The kingdom of the heavens and the earth and everything in them belongs to God: He has power over all things.

6. THE CATTLE (*AL-AN'AM*)

In the name of God, the Most Gracious, the Most Merciful

[1] Praise be to God, who has created the heavens and the earth and brought into being darkness and light. Yet those who deny the truth set up equals to their Lord![a] [2] It is He who has created you out of clay, and then has decreed a term [for you]—a term known [only] to Him. Yet you are still in doubt— [3] He is God both in the heavens and on earth. He has knowledge of all that you hide and all that you reveal. He knows what you do; [4] yet every time a sign comes to them from their Lord, they turn away from it. [5] They have rejected truth whenever it came to them, yet [more] news will reach them concerning what they have been making a mockery of. [6] Have they not seen how many generations We destroyed before them? We established them on the earth more firmly than you, and We sent the clouds over them, pouring down abundant rain; and made the rivers flow at their feet. Yet We destroyed them for their sins, and raised up other generations after them.

---

a The system inherent in the governance of heaven and earth is so perfect in its coordination and its unitary nature—despite the magnitude of the task—that it proclaims aloud the fact that its Creator and Organiser can be none other than the one and only God. Witness how unimaginably great is this universe in its vastness, wisdom and meaningfulness. The flawlessly regulated revolution of the earth in space around the bright sphere of the Sun and, hence the coming into existence of light and darkness and day and night are events beyond human comprehension.

[7] But even if We had sent down to you a Book written on parchment, and they had touched it with their own hands—those who deny the truth would still have said, 'This is mere magic.' [8] They ask, 'Why has an angel not been sent down to him?' If We did send down an angel, the matter would be settled and they would not have been granted any respite. [9] Indeed, if We had sent an angel as messenger, We would have made him in the form of a man as well, and would have thus added to their confusion. [10] Messengers have been mocked before you, but those who scoffed were overtaken by the very thing they scoffed at. [11] Say, 'Travel about the land and see what was the end of the deniers.'

[12] Say, 'To whom belongs all that is in the heavens and earth?' Say, 'To God. He has taken it upon Himself to be merciful. That He will gather you on the Day of Resurrection is beyond all doubt. Those who have forfeited their souls will never have faith.' [13] To Him belongs all that dwells in the night and the day. He is the All Hearing and the All Knowing. [14] Say, 'Shall I take as my protector someone other than God, Creator of the heavens and the earth, who feeds all and is fed by none?' Say, 'I have been commanded to be the first of those who submit. Do not be one of the polytheists.' [15] Say, 'I will never disobey my Lord, for I fear the punishment of a dreadful Day.' [16] Anyone from whom punishment is averted on that Day has been shown great mercy by God. That is a supreme achievement.[a]

[17] If God should let any harm touch you, no one could remove it except He; while if He should let some good touch you, know that He has the power to do all that He wills. [18] He reigns Supreme

---

[a] Man is a creature with a will of his own and that is why voluntary worship is required of him. Those who do not choose to exercise their will rightly, do not deserve a share in God's bounties, not having fulfilled the purpose of their creation. After the period of trial is over, all human beings will be gathered in a new world. On that Day God will take into His hands the direct control of the rest of the world. On that Day God's scale of justice will be operative. On that Day those who admitted the reality and surrendered themselves to God will come to the fore and those who did not, having lead a life of arrogance and obstinacy in the world, will be the losers.

over His servants; and He is the All Wise, the All Aware. ¹⁹ Ask them, 'What carries the most weight as a witness?' Tell them it is God. He is a witness between you and me. Say, 'This Quran has been revealed to me so that through it I may warn you and whoever it reaches. Do you really bear witness that there are other deities beside God?' Say, 'I do not bear witness to this.' Say, 'He is only one God, and I disown whatever you associate with Him.'

²⁰ Those to whom We have given the Scriptures know this as they know their own sons. But those who have ruined their souls will not believe. ²¹ Who does greater wrong than he who invents a lie against God and denies His signs? Assuredly, the wrongdoers will not succeed. ²² On the Day when We gather them all together, We will say to those who associated [others with Us], 'Where are those partners that you claimed?' ²³ Then they will have no excuse but to say, 'By God our Lord, we have never been polytheists.' ²⁴ See how they lie to themselves, and how those [the deities] they invented have deserted them.

²⁵ Among them are some who listen to you, but We have placed veils over their hearts and deafness in their ears which prevent them from understanding what you say. Even if they saw all the signs, they would still not believe in them. When those who deny the truth come to dispute with you, they will say, 'This is nothing but ancient fables,' ²⁶ and they bar others from believing and themselves keep away. But they ruin no one but themselves, though they fail to realize this. ²⁷ If you could only see when they are set before the Fire. They will say, 'If only we could be sent back. Then we would not deny the signs of our Lord and we would be of the believers.' ²⁸ The truth they used to hide will become all too clear to them. But if they were sent back, they would return to what they had been forbidden. For they are indeed liars.

²⁹ They say, 'There is nothing beyond our life in this world: we shall not be raised up again from the dead.' ³⁰ If you could only see when they are made to stand before their Lord! He will ask them, 'Is this [second life] not the truth?' They will say, 'Yes, by our

Lord!' He will say, 'Then, taste the punishment that comes from your having refused to acknowledge the truth!'[a]

³¹ Those indeed are the losers who deny the meeting with God. When the Hour comes on them suddenly, they cry, 'Alas for us, that we neglected it!' They shall bear their burdens on their backs. Evil are the burdens they shall bear. ³² The life of this world is but a sport and a pastime. Surely the Home of the Hereafter is best for those who fear God. Will you not understand?

³³ We know that what they say grieves you. It is not you that the wrongdoers are rejecting, rather it is the signs of God that they reject. ³⁴ Other messengers have been denied before you, and they bore their rejection and persecution steadfastly, until Our help came to them. There is no one who can change the words of God. You have already received some account of those messengers. ³⁵ If you find their rejection hard to bear, then seek a tunnel into the ground or a ladder into the sky, if you can, and bring them a sign. Had God so willed, He would indeed have given them all [His] guidance. So do not be among the ignorant. ³⁶ Only they who listen can respond to a call; and as for the dead, God will raise them up, and then they will all return to Him.

³⁷ They ask, 'Why has no sign been sent down to him from his Lord?' Say, 'God alone has the power to send down a sign.' But most of them do not understand: ³⁸ there is not an animal that moves about on the earth, nor a bird that flies on its two wings, but are creatures like you. We have left out nothing in the Book—they shall all be

---

a Whenever a man denies the Truth or follows the desires of his self, it is because he does not live his life in this world on the understanding that he will be resurrected after death and made to stand before the Lord of the universe to give an account of himself in everyday life. Man has been given a certain power which he uses unhesitatingly. He has the material prop of wealth, and friends and companions on whom he relies. He has been given a brain, which he uses to think out arrogant strategies and find clever pretexts for his transgressions. The success of his initiatives deceives him; he starts placing false reliance on things other than God, and imagines that the position he enjoys today is of a perennial nature. He forgets that whatever he has been given in this world is only by way of trial and is not a matter of entitlement.

gathered before their Lord. ³⁹ Those who reject Our signs are deaf and dumb, [groping along] in darkness. God lets anyone He wishes go astray and sets whoever He will on a straight path.

⁴⁰ Say, 'Tell me if the punishment of God came upon you or the Hour overtook you, would you call upon any other than God, if you are truthful?' ⁴¹ Indeed, it is on Him that you would call, and He could remove that [affliction] which made you call on Him, if He will, and then you would forget [the false deities] which you associate with Him!'

⁴² We sent messengers before you [Prophet] to many communities and afflicted their people with suffering and hardship, so that they might humble themselves. ⁴³ When the affliction decreed by Us befell them, they did not humble themselves, but rather their hearts hardened, for Satan had made all their doings seem fair to them. ⁴⁴ When they had forgotten Our admonition, We granted them all that they desired; but just as they were rejoicing in what they were given, We seized them suddenly and they were plunged into despair.^a ⁴⁵ The wrongdoers were thus annihilated. All praise be to God, the Lord of the Worlds.

⁴⁶ Say, 'If God should take away your hearing and your sight and seal your hearts, who is the deity who could restore it to you save God?' See how We explain the signs to them in diverse ways, yet they turn away. ⁴⁷ Ask them, 'Tell me, if the punishment of God came upon you suddenly or predictably, would any but the wrongdoers be destroyed?'^b ⁴⁸ We send the messengers only to give good news

---

a When a man is faced with the truth and he does not accept it, God does not seize him immediately, but gives him some jolts by way of monetary loss or physical trouble, so that he should review his way of life, and his thinking should be revolutionised. Life's events are not mere happenings but vibrant messages from God sent to wake a man up from his sleep of forgetfulness. But man learns nothing from these things. He consoles himself by saying that these are normal ups and downs and that such ups and downs do occur in life.

b The granting of ears, eyes and heart to man indicates what his Creator wants from him. The Creator wants man to hear and see His signs and accept them using rational arguments. If a man does not utilise these God-given capabilities for the purpose they are meant, then he is running the risk that he may be declared incapable and his capabilities may be snatched from him.

and to warn, so those who believe and reform themselves need have no fear, nor will they grieve. ⁴⁹ Chastisement will befall those who reject Our signs because of their disobedience. ⁵⁰ Say, 'I do not say to you that I possess the treasures of God, nor do I know the unseen, nor do I say to you that I am an angel. I follow only that which is revealed to me.' Say, 'Are the blind and the seeing alike? Can you not then think?'

⁵¹ Warn by it those who fear to be gathered before their Lord, when they have no guardian or intercessor besides God, so that they may become God-fearing. ⁵² Do not send away those who call upon their Lord in the morning and in the evening, seeking only His grace. You are not by any means accountable for them, nor are they accountable for you. If you turn them away, you yourself will become one of the unjust. ⁵³ In this way We try some of them by means of others, so that they may ask, 'Are these [lowly ones] whom God has singled out for His favours from among us? Does God not know best who are the grateful ones?'

⁵⁴ When those who believe in Our revelations come to you, say, 'Peace be upon you. Your Lord has taken it upon Himself to be merciful. So that if any one among you does evil in ignorance and repents thereafter and makes amends, then He is most forgiving and ever merciful.' ⁵⁵ Thus We make plain Our signs, so that the path of the evil-doers might be laid bare.^a

⁵⁶ Say, 'I am forbidden to worship those you call upon besides God.' Say, 'I do not follow your whims and desires. If I did, I would go astray and cease to be rightly guided.' ⁵⁷ Say, 'I stand by the clear evidence from my Lord, yet you deny it. What you seek to hasten is not within my power. Judgement is for God alone. He declares the truth. He is the best of judges.' ⁵⁸ Say, 'If what you seek to hasten were within my power, the matter would be settled between you and me. God best knows the evil-doers.' ⁵⁹ He holds the keys to the

---

    a God expresses Himself in the language of 'symbols'. Symbols are useful only to one who has the desire to read or interpret them. Similarly, guidance will be available only to one who is eager to have it. One who shows no interest in guidance has no other option but to go astray.

unseen; none knows them but He. He has knowledge of all that land and sea contain. No leaf falls without His knowledge, nor is there a single grain in the darkness of the earth, or anything, wet or dry, but is recorded in a clear Record.

⁶⁰ It is He who gathers you in at night and knows all that you do by day; then He raises you up during the day so that an appointed term may be completed. Then to Him you shall return and He will declare to you all that you used to do.*[a]* ⁶¹ He is the Absolute Master over His servants. He sends forth guardians [angels] who watch over you until, when death approaches one of you, Our angels take his soul, and they never fail in their duty. ⁶² Then they will all be returned to God, their true Lord. The Judgement is His alone. He is the swiftest reckoner.

⁶³ Say, 'Who is it who delivers you from the dark depths of land and sea when you call out to Him humbly and in secret, saying, "If He rescues us from this, we shall most certainly be among the grateful."?' ⁶⁴ Say, 'It is God who delivers you from it and from every other distress, yet you associate partners with Him.' ⁶⁵ Say, 'He has the power to send punishment on you from above your heads or from beneath your feet, or to divide you in sects and make you taste one another's violence.' See how We explain Our revelations in various ways, so that they may understand. ⁶⁶ Your people have rejected the message We have sent through you, though it is the truth. Say 'I am not your keeper. ⁶⁷ Every prophecy has its fixed time to be fulfilled: and soon you will come to know.'

⁶⁸ When you see people engaged in finding fault with Our revelations, withdraw from them until they turn to some other topic. Should Satan cause you to forget this, take leave of the wrongdoers

---

a Sleep is a wonderful thing. Man roams about here and there; he sees and speaks; but when he sleeps all his senses become suspended, just as if life had oozed out of them. When he has had his full sleep and wakes up, he becomes as active as before. This is, so to say, an example of life and death. This event demonstrates how a man will die and how he will be resurrected, i.e. be brought back to life. These events prove that all men are in the power of God and soon that Day will come when God will take fateful decisions about them in the exercise of His powers.

as soon as you remember. [69] The God-fearing are not in any way held accountable for the wrongdoers; their only duty is to remind them, so that they may fear God. [70] Leave alone those for whom religion is only a sport and pastime and are deceived by the life of this world, but continue to remind them with the Quran, lest a soul be held in pledge because of what it has wrought, having no helper or intercessor besides God. Whatever ransom they may offer, it will not be accepted. Such are those that are damned by their own actions: they will have boiling water to drink and a painful punishment for their denial of truth.

[71] Say, 'Instead of God, shall we call upon that which can neither benefit us nor harm us? Are we to turn upon our heels after God has guided us, like one who, beguiled by devils in the land, wanders bewildered, his companions calling him to the right path, saying, "Come to us"?' Say, 'God's guidance is the only guidance. We are commanded to surrender ourselves to the Lord of the Universe, [72] say our prayers regularly and to fear God.' He it is to whom you will be gathered.' [73] It was He who created the heavens and the earth for a true purpose. On the Day when He says, 'Be,' it shall be: His word is the truth. All sovereignty shall be His on the Day when the trumpet is sounded. The Knower of the unseen and the visible, He is the Wise, the Aware One. [74] Remember when Abraham said to his father, Azar, 'Do you take idols as your gods? I see that you and your people have clearly gone astray.'

[75] In this way We showed Abraham Our kingdom of the heavens and the earth, so that he might have certainty of faith. [76] When night descended on him, he saw a star. He said, 'This is my Lord!' Then when it set he said, 'I do not love things that set.' [77] When he saw the moon rise and spread its light, he said, 'This is my Lord.' But when it set, he said, 'If my Lord does not guide me, I will be one of the misguided people.' [78] Then, when he saw the sun shining, he said, 'This is my Lord! This is the greatest of all!' Then when it set, he said, 'My people, I disown all that you worship besides God. [79] I have set my face with single-minded devotion, towards Him who has created the heavens and the earth, and I am not one of the polytheists.' [80] His people argued with him. He said, 'Are

you arguing with me about God, while He has guided me? I have no fear of any partner you ascribe to Him, unless my Lord should wish otherwise. My Lord encompasses all things in His knowledge, so will you not pay heed? ⁸¹ Why should I fear what you associate with Him, while you do not fear to associate with God that for which He has sent down to you no authority? Tell me, if you know the truth, which side has more right to feel secure. ⁸² It is those who have faith, and do not mix their faith with wrongdoing, who will be secure, and it is they who are rightly guided.' ⁸³ This is the reasoning We gave to Abraham against his people—We raise in rank anyone We please—your Lord is wise and aware. ⁸⁴ We gave him Isaac and Jacob, each of whom We guided as We had guided Noah before. Among his descendants were David and Solomon, and Job, Joseph, Moses and Aaron. Thus do We reward the righteous.

⁸⁵ Zachariah, John, Jesus, and Elijah—every one of them was righteous—⁸⁶ Ishmael, Elisha, Jonah, and Lot—We favoured each one of them above other people, ⁸⁷ and also some of their forefathers, their offspring, and their brothers: We chose them and guided them to a straight path. ⁸⁸ This is the guidance of God: He gives that guidance to whichever of His servants He pleases. If they had associated other deities with Him, surely all they did would have been of no avail. ⁸⁹ Those are the ones to whom We gave the Scripture, wisdom, and prophethood. If these people [the Makkans] reject it, We shall entrust it to a people who will never refuse to acknowledge it. ⁹⁰ Those [the previous prophets] were the people whom God guided. Follow their guidance then and say, 'I ask no reward for this from you: it is only a reminder for all mankind.' ⁹¹ They do not make a just estimate of God, when they say, 'God has not revealed anything to any human being.' Say, 'Who revealed the Book which Moses brought, a light and guidance for the people, which you made into separate sheets, showing some but hiding many? You have been taught things that neither you nor your forefathers had known before.' Say, 'God has sent it;' then leave them toying away with their speculation.

⁹² This is a blessed Book which We have revealed, confirming what came before it, so that you may warn the Mother of Cities [Makkah] and the people around it. Those who believe in the Hereafter do

believe in it, and they are ever-mindful of their prayers. ⁹³ Who could do greater wrong than someone who invents a lie against God or who says, 'It has been revealed to me,' while nothing has been revealed to him, or someone who says, 'I will send down the like of what God has sent down'? If you could only see the wrongdoers in the throes of death when the angels are stretching out their hands, saying, 'Give up your souls. Today you will be repaid with a humiliating punishment for saying false things about God and being arrogant about His signs.'

⁹⁴ And now you have returned to Us, alone as We created you at first, leaving behind all that We gave you. Nor do We see with you your intercessors, those you claimed were your partners with God. The link between you is cut and that which you presumed has failed you. ⁹⁵ It is God who splits the seed and the fruit-stone. He brings forth the living from the dead, and the dead from the living. That is God. How then can you, deluded, turn away from the truth?

⁹⁶ He causes the break of day, and has made the night for rest and He made the sun and the moon to a precise measure. That is the measure determined by the Almighty and the All Knowing.ᵃ ⁹⁷ It is He who has set up for you the stars so that you might be guided by them in the midst of the darkness of land and sea. We have made the signs clear for people who want to understand. ⁹⁸ It is He who first produced you from a single soul, then gave you a place to stay [in

---

a The volume of the sun is 1.2 million times that of the earth, and the earth itself is four times larger than the moon. The moon is about two hundred and fifty thousand miles away from the earth and revolves around it. The earth is at a distance of about 95 million miles from the sun and is moving round the latter in two ways—one in rotation on its axis and the other in orbit around the sun. Similarly, there is the revolution of other stars which are at vast distances from us and each other but all moving with extreme regularity. Due to this system of the universe, day and night come into existence; systems based on the measurement of time take shape; in turn, it becomes possible for man to regulate his life on land and sea. This gigantic system runs with such exactitude that no discrepancy has crept into it even after millions of years. This proves the immanence of a Being whose powers are of unlimited greatness.

life] and a resting place [after death]. We have made Our revelations clear to those who are men of understanding.[a]

[99] It is He who sends down water from the sky. With it We produce vegetation of all kinds; out of green foliage, We produce clustered grain; and from the date-palm, out of its sheath, We produce bunches of dates hanging low. We produce vineyards and olive groves and pomegranates, alike yet different. Look at their fruit as He causes it to grow and ripen. In this are signs for people who believe. [100] They have set up jinns as associates with God, even though He created them! They have even dared, in their ignorance, to attribute sons and daughters to Him. Hallowed be He and exalted far above what they ascribe to Him, [101] the Originator of the heavens and the earth. How could He have a son when He has no consort? He created everything and is aware of everything! [102] This is God, your Lord, there is no God but Him, the Creator of all things, so worship Him; He is the guardian of all things. [103] No vision can grasp Him, but He takes in over all vision; He is the Subtle and Aware One.[b] [104] Clear insights

---

a Man, in the beginning, is nurtured in the womb of his mother and thereafter makes his entry into the present world. The grave is also, so to say, a sort of 'womb', to which man is ultimately consigned. Thereafter, he opens his eyes in another, future world, so that he may be sent to Heaven or Hell according to his deeds. Glimpses of and arguments in favour of the unseen hidden world, which man must necessarily accept, are already there in the present tangible and visible world. But only that person will accept it who is already mentally prepared to do so. It is only when a man has travelled half the distance along the path towards Faith (*iman*) that it is possible for the call to the faith to enter freely into his mind and to be acceptable to him.

b Man wants to see God in a tangible shape and when God does not manifest Himself in this way, he presumes other tangible things to be gods and thus satisfies his appearance-loving instinct. But this shows a very poor appreciation of God's Being. After all, how can God, who is so great as to have created this gigantic universe with its highly regulated systems, be so ordinary as to present Himself to a weak human creature in a form that will be visible to his eyes and touchable with his hands? Man must rather discover God through his heart and see Him with the eye of his faith. Only one who is satisfied with observation through insight will discover God. One who insists on His being visible to the naked eye will never truly find God, just like the person who

have come to you from your Lord. Whoever, therefore, chooses to see, does so for his own good; and whoever chooses to remain blind, does so to his own loss. Say, 'I am not here as your keeper.' [105] This is how We explain Our revelations in various ways—so that they might come to the point of saying, 'You have read this out to us,' and that We might make it clear [that this is the truth] to those who are eager to know.

[106] Follow what has been revealed to you from your Lord: there is no deity but Him; and ignore the polytheists. [107] If God had willed, they would not have associated anything with Him. We did not appoint you over them as their keeper, nor are you their guardian. [108] Do not revile those [beings] whom they invoke instead of God, lest they, in their hostility, revile God out of ignorance. Thus to every people We have caused their actions to seem fair. To their Lord they shall all return, and He will declare to them all that they have done. [109] They swear a solemn oath by God that if there should come to them a sign, they will believe in it. Say, 'Signs are granted only by God.' How can you tell that if a sign be given to them, they will indeed believe in it?

[110] We will turn away their hearts and eyes from the Truth, since they refused to believe in it in the first instance. We will let them wander blindly in their insolence. [111] Even if We sent down angels to them, and caused the dead to speak to them, and We gathered together everything in front of them, they would still not believe, unless God had so willed. But most of them behave ignorantly. [112] In like manner We have assigned for every prophet an opponent, Satans from among men and jinn, who make evil suggestions to each other by means of specious words in order to deceive—had it been your Lord's will, they would not have done so; so leave them alone to their fabrication, [113] in order that the hearts of those who do not believe in the life to come might incline towards those suggestions and, being pleased, persist in their sinful ways. [114] Should I seek a judge other than God, when it is He who has revealed the Book,

---

fails to recognise a flower by its fragrance and insists on referring to chemical standards.

clearly explained. Those to whom We gave the Book earlier know that it is the truth revealed by your Lord. Therefore, have no doubts.

¹¹⁵ The Word of your Lord is perfected in truth and justice. None can change His words. He is the All Hearing, the All Knowing. ¹¹⁶ If you obey the majority of those on earth, they will lead you astray from God's way. They follow nothing but conjecture. They are only guessing. ¹¹⁷ Your Lord knows best who has strayed from His Way and He knows best those who are guided. ¹¹⁸ Eat then, only that over which God's name has been pronounced, if you truly believe in His revelations.

¹¹⁹ Why should you not eat what has been consecrated in God's name, when He has already explained to you what He has forbidden you, unless you are compelled by necessity? Surely, many mislead others by their desires through lack of knowledge. But your Lord best knows the transgressors. ¹²⁰ Eschew all sin, open or secret: Those who commit sin will receive due punishment for their sins, ¹²¹ and do not eat anything over which God's name has not been pronounced, for that surely is disobedience. The devils inspire their followers to argue with you. If you obey them, you will become of those who associate partners with God. ¹²² Can he who was dead, to whom We gave life, and a light whereby he could walk among people be like him who is in utter darkness from which he can never emerge? Thus the deeds of those who deny the truth have been made fair-seeming to them.

¹²³ Thus We have placed leaders of the wicked in every town to plot therein. Yet it is only against themselves that they scheme, though they may not perceive it. ¹²⁴ When a sign comes to them, they say, 'We will not believe in it until we are given what God's messengers have been given. But God knows best whom to appoint as His Messenger. Humiliation before God and severe torment will befall the evil-doers for their scheming. ¹²⁵ When God desires to guide someone, He opens his breast to Islam; and whoever He wills to let go astray, He causes his breast to be constricted as if he had to climb up to the skies. That is how God heaps ignominy upon those who refuse to believe.

¹²⁶ This is the straight path leading to your Lord. We have made

the signs clear for thinking men. [127] They shall dwell in the Home of Peace with their Lord; He will be their Protector as a recompense for what they have been doing. [128] On the day when He gathers them all together, He will say, 'Company of jinn, you took away many followers among mankind.' And their adherents among mankind will say, 'Our Lord, we benefited from one another, but now we have reached the end of the term which You determined for us.' He will say, 'The Fire shall be your home, and there you shall remain forever, except as God wills. Surely your Lord is wise and all knowing.

[129] And in like manner We shall keep the wrongdoers close to others as a punishment for their misdeeds. [130] Company of jinn and mankind! Did messengers not come from among you to recite My revelations to you, and warn you of the meeting of this Day?' They will say, 'We bear witness against ourselves.' It was the life of this world that deceived them and so they will bear witness against themselves, that they rejected the truth. [131] Your Lord would not destroy a community for its wrongdoing, so long as its people were still unaware. [132] For all are degrees of rank according to their deeds; your Lord is not unaware of anything they do.

[133] Your Lord is the self-sufficient One, the merciful. If He wills, He can take you away and replace you by anyone He pleases, just as He raised you from the offspring of other people. [134] That which you are promised shall surely come to pass and you cannot prevent it. [135] Say, 'O my people! Go on acting in your way; indeed I am going to act in my way; soon you will know whose end will be best in the Hereafter.' Surely, the wrongdoers shall not prosper. [136] They set aside for God a share in what He has produced, such as crops and livestock, and they say, 'This is for God'—so they claim!—and 'this is for our associate-gods? Their associate-gods' share does not reach God, whereas God's share reaches their associate-gods. How ill they judge!

[137] And in like manner, their associate gods have made killing their children seem fair to many pagans, so that they may ruin them and cause confusion in their religion. Had God pleased, they would not have done so; so leave them to their false inventions. [138] They also say, 'These animals and these crops are forbidden. None may

eat them except those we permit.' So they claim! There are some animals they exempt from labour and some over which they do not pronounce God's name, thus committing a sin against Him. He will requite them for the falsehoods they invent.

139 They say, 'What is in the wombs of such and such cattle is exclusively for our males and is forbidden to our females. But if it is stillborn, they may have a share of it.' God will soon punish them for their [false] attribution. He is wise, and all-knowing. 140 Losers indeed are they who kill their children foolishly and without knowledge and declare as forbidden what God has provided for them as sustenance—a fabrication against God: they have gone astray and have not chosen to be rightly guided. 141 It is He who has produced gardens, both trellised and untrellised, and date palms and field crops, all varying in taste, and the olive and the pomegranate, both similar and dissimilar. Eat their fruits when they bear fruit and give away what is due of them on the day of their harvest. Do not waste anything. He does not love the wasteful!

142 Of the cattle there are some for carrying burdens and some for food. Eat what God has provided for you and do not follow in Satan's footsteps, for he is a declared enemy of yours. 143 God has created four kinds of livestock of either sex: two of sheep and two of goats. Ask them, 'Is it the two males He has forbidden or the two females or what the wombs of the two females contain? Tell me on the basis of knowledge, if you are truthful.'

144 Again, of the camels there are two, and of the oxen two. Ask them, 'Is it the two males He has forbidden, or the two females or what the wombs of the two females contain? Were you present when God enjoined this on you?' Who is more unjust than one who, without knowledge, fabricates a lie against God, so that he may lead people astray without knowledge? Surely, God does not guide the wrongdoers. 145 Say [O Prophet], 'In all that has been revealed to me, I do not find a ban on anything to eat, except for carrion, flowing blood and pork, all these being unclean or profane, on which the name of someone other than God has been invoked.' But if anyone is forced by necessity, being neither disobedient nor exceeding the limit, then surely your Lord is most forgiving and merciful. 146 We

forbade the Jews all animals with claws and the fat of sheep [and goats] and oxen, except what is on their backs and in their intestines and what adheres to their bones. That is the penalty We imposed on them for their disobedience. And We assuredly are true to Our word.

[147] So, if they accuse you of lying, say, 'The mercy of your Lord is all-encompassing. His punishment cannot be averted from sinful men.' [148] Those who associate partners with God will surely say, 'Had God pleased, neither we nor our fathers would have served other gods besides Him; nor would we have made anything unlawful.' Likewise those who lived before them argued falsely until they came to taste Our punishment! Say, 'Have you any knowledge? If so, produce it before us. You follow nothing but conjecture. You are merely guessing.'

[149] Say, 'God alone has the conclusive proof. If He had willed, He could have guided every one of you.' [150] Say, 'Come, bring your witnesses, who can testify that God forbade [all] this.' If they bear witness [falsely], do not bear witness with them; nor yield to the wishes of those who deny Our signs, nor of those who do not believe in the life to come and set up others as equals with their Lord. [151] Say, 'Come! I will tell you what your Lord has really forbidden you! Do not associate anything with Him; be good to your parents;[a] and do not kill your children for fear of poverty—We shall provide sustenance for you as well as for them—refrain from committing indecent deeds, whether openly or in secret; and do not kill the life which God has made sacred, save by right. That is what He has enjoined upon you, so that you may understand.[b]

---

a If an individual's parents are weak and needy, while he is strong, and if he treats them well, this is not the outcome of self-interest but of righteousness. In this way, the question of discharging the rights of parents becomes the first test of a man's adoption of God's religion, not just at the level of mere talk but as a matter of practical action. If he places emphasis on the parents' rights rather than on their weakness, if his love for his friends and his wife and children does not take him away from his parents, he has, as it were given the first proof that his behaviour will be subject to principles and regard for rights and not to self-interest and self-consideration.

b With the advent of the explosion of Doomsday, all hidden realities will

¹⁵² Stay well away from an orphan's property, except with the best intentions, before he comes of age. Give full measure and weight, according to justice—We never charge a soul with more than it can bear—when you speak, observe justice, even though it concerns a close relative; and fulfil the covenants of God. That is what He has enjoined upon you so that you may take heed.

¹⁵³ [He has enjoined], 'This is My straight path; so follow it, and do not follow other ways: that will lead you away from His path.' That is what He enjoins upon you, so that you may guard yourselves. ¹⁵⁴ Then We gave Moses the Book, completing [Our favour] to the righteous, explaining everything clearly, as guidance and mercy, so that they might believe in meeting their Lord.

¹⁵⁵ This is a Book which We have revealed as a blessing—follow it and fear your Lord, so that you may receive mercy—¹⁵⁶ and not say, 'The Book was only sent down to the two groups before us and we were indeed unaware of their teachings,' ¹⁵⁷ or you may say, 'If the Book had been sent down to us, we would surely have followed its guidance better than they did.' There has now come to you clear evidence from your Lord, and guidance and mercy. Who, then, is more unjust than one who rejects the signs of God and turns away from them? We shall requite those who turn away from Our signs with a painful punishment, for their turning away. ¹⁵⁸ Are they waiting for the angels or your Lord to come down to them, or for some of your Lord's signs to come? The day when some of the signs of your Lord shall come, it shall not profit any human being who did not believe before, or who did not do any good by his faith. Say to them, 'Wait then, we too are waiting.' ¹⁵⁹ Have nothing to do with those who have split up their religion into sects. Their case rests with God; He will tell them about what they used to do.

¹⁶⁰ Whoever does a good deed will be repaid tenfold, but those

---

reveal themselves to the people. At that time, man will be compelled to accept God and act only at His behest, but acceptance at that time will have no value. Only that acceptance is real acceptance which takes place at the stage of the Almighty still being unseen. True faith lies in accepting, without seeing, that which one is compelled to accept after seeing. One who accepts after seeing has, as it were, not accepted at all.

who do a bad deed will only be repaid with its equivalent and they shall not be wronged. [161] Say, 'My Lord has guided me to a straight path, and to an upright religion, the religion of Abraham the upright, who was not of those who associate partners with God.'

[162] Say, 'My prayer and my sacrifice and my life and my death are all for God, the Lord of the worlds; [163] He has no partner. So am I commanded, and I am the first of those who submit.' [164] Say, 'Shall I seek a lord other than God, while He is the Lord of all things?' Everyone must bear the consequence of what he does, and no bearer of a burden can bear the burden of another. Then to your Lord you will return, and He will inform you of what you used to dispute about. [165] It is He who has made you successors [of others] on the earth and has exalted some of you over the others in degrees of rank, so that He may test you by that which He has given you. Your Lord is swift in punishment; yet surely He is forgiving, and merciful.[a]

7. THE HEIGHTS (*AL-A 'RAF*)

In the name of God, the Most Gracious, the Most Merciful

[1] *Alif Lam Mim Sad*

[2] This Book has been sent down to you—let there be no heaviness in your heart about it—so that you may warn by means of it and it is a reminder to the believers. [3] Follow what has been sent down to you by your Lord and do not follow any protector other than Him. How seldom you take heed. [4] How many towns We have destroyed. Our scourge fell upon them by night or at midday when they were

---

a The reason for man's arrogance in this world is that he thinks of the good things of this life as God's reward. The fact is that whatever a man receives in this life is meant to be a test and not a reward. If a man considers the good things available to him in this life as his due, this will cause him to be proud, but if he considers them as a means of testing him, this will develop a sense of humility in him. While a proud mentality is marked by haughtiness, a humble attitude is marked by the willingness to obey God.

resting: [5] and when Our scourge fell upon them, their only cry was, 'We were indeed wrongdoers!' [6] Then shall We question those to whom Our message was sent and those through whom We sent it [7] with full knowledge, We shall tell them what they did, for We have never been away from them. [8] Truth alone will be of weight that Day. Those whose scales are heavy shall be successful, [9] and those whose good deeds are light [in the balance] will be the ones who have lost themselves because they wrongfully rejected Our signs.

[10] We established you in the land and provided you with a means of livelihood there: yet you are seldom thankful. [11] We created you, then We shaped you and then We said to the angels, 'Prostrate yourselves before Adam,' and they all prostrated themselves, except Satan. He was not among those who prostrated themselves. [12] God asked, 'What prevented you from prostrating yourself when I commanded you to?' He replied, 'I am better than he is; You created me from fire, while You created him from clay.' [13] God said, 'Get down from here! This is no place for your arrogance. Get out! You are contemptible!' [14] Satan said, 'Give me respite until the Day of Resurrection,' [15] and God replied, 'You are granted respite.' [16] Then Satan said, 'Because You have put me in the wrong, I will lie in ambush for them on Your straight path: [17] then I will surely come upon them from before them and from behind them and from their right and from their left, and then You will find most of them ungrateful.' [18] He said, 'Get out of here, despised, and rejected! I shall fill Hell with all of those who follow you.'

[19] To Adam He said, 'You and your wife, dwell in the Garden and eat and drink there from wherever you wish, but do not approach this tree, lest you become wrongdoers.' [20] But Satan tempted them so that he might reveal to them their nakedness which had been hidden from them. He said, 'Your Lord has forbidden you to approach this tree lest you should become angels or become of the immortals,' [21] and he swore to them, 'Surely, I am your well-wisher.'

[22] Thus he cunningly seduced them. When they tasted the tree's fruit, their nakedness became exposed to them and they started covering themselves with the leaves of the garden. Their Lord called out to them, 'Did I not forbid you to approach that tree, and did I not say

to you that Satan was surely your open enemy?' [23] They replied, 'Our Lord, we have wronged our souls: if You do not forgive us and have mercy on us, we shall be among the lost.' [24] He said, 'Go down from here as enemies to each other. For a while, there is an abode for you and a provision on earth. [25] There you will live; there you will die; from there you will be raised up again.'

[26] O children of Adam! We have sent down to you clothes to cover your nakedness, and to be pleasing to the eye; but the raiment of righteousness is the best. That is one of the signs of God. So that people may take heed. [27] Children of Adam, do not let Satan seduce you, just as he turned your parents out of the Garden: he deprived them of their garment in order to make them aware of their nakedness. He and his forces watch you from where you do not see them! We have made the devils friends of those who do not believe.[a]

[28] And when they commit an indecency, they say, 'This is what our fathers used to do and God has enjoined it on us.' Say, 'God does not enjoin what is indecent. Would you attribute to God something of which you have no knowledge?' [29] Say, 'My Lord has commanded you to act justly. Turn your faces up toward Him at every time and place of worship, and call upon Him, making yourselves sincere towards Him in religion. As He brought you into being, so shall you return.' [30] Some He has guided and some have earned misguidance:

---

a God has given clothes to man which protect him as well as being a means of improving his looks and prestige. This is indicative of the fact that a form of clothing is necessary for man's spiritual existence as well. This clothing is righteousness born of the fear of God (*taqwa*), which represents the inner personality of a man. This vestment of *taqwa* on the one hand protects man from the attacks of Satan and, on the other, enhances his inner self and makes him capable of inhabiting the fine and aesthetic world of Paradise. What is this righteousness, or *taqwa*? It is fear of God, acknowledging of the Truth, adhering to uniform criteria for oneself and others, considering oneself a subject of God, behaving with modesty and humility, leading a Hereafter-oriented life instead of going astray in the world. When a man develops these virtues he 'dresses' his inner self. While the outer body is covered by a garment made of cloth, the inner self, the soul, is clad in *taqwa*. But if his behaviour is the opposite, he is, as it were, laying his inner self bare.

they have taken devils rather than God as their patrons, thinking that they are rightly guided.

³¹ O Children of Adam, dress yourself properly whenever you are at worship: and eat and drink but exceed not the bounds: God does not love those who exceed the bounds. ³² Say, 'Who has forbidden the adornment of God, which He has brought forth for His servants and good things, clean and pure, which God has provided for His servants?' Say, 'They are [lawful] for the believers in the present life but they shall be exclusively for them on the Day of Resurrection.' Thus We explain Our signs for a people who understand. ³³ Say, 'My Lord has forbidden indecency, both open and hidden, sin and wrongful oppression and that, without His sanction, you associate things with Him, and that you say things about Him without knowledge.'

³⁴ For all people a term has been set: and when [the end of] their term approaches, they can neither delay it by a single moment, nor can they advance it. ³⁵ Children of Adam! If messengers come to you from among yourselves, reciting My revelations to you, then those that take warning and mend their ways, on such shall come no fear nor shall they grieve. ³⁶ But those who deny and scorn Our revelations shall be the inmates of Hell, where they shall remain forever. ³⁷ Who does a greater wrong than he who invents lies against God or rejects His revelations? Such people will have what has been decreed for them. And when Our messengers come to them to take away their souls, they shall ask them, 'Where are those you used to call upon besides God?' They will answer, 'They have deserted us;' and they will bear witness against themselves that they were disbelievers?

³⁸ God will say, 'Enter the Fire and join the bands of jinn and men that have gone before you.' Every time a host enters [the fire], it will curse its fellow-host, then, when they are all gathered there, the last of them will say of the first, 'Our Lord, it was they who led us astray: give them double punishment in the Fire,'—God will say, 'Every one of you will have double punishment, though you do not know it'—³⁹ then the preceding one will say to the succeeding one, 'You are no better than us: so taste the punishment you have earned.'

⁴⁰ The gates of Heaven shall not be opened for those who rejected

Our signs and arrogantly spurned them; nor shall they enter Paradise until a camel shall pass through the eye of a needle. That is how We repay the evil-doers—[41] Hell shall be their bed, and over them will be coverings of fire—thus shall We reward the wrongdoers. [42] But those who believed and did good deeds—and We do not burden any soul with more than it can bear—such are the heirs of the Garden and there they will remain forever. [43] And We shall remove whatever rancour may be in their hearts. At their feet shall flow rivers. And they shall say, 'All praise belongs to God who has guided us to this. Had God not guided us, we would never have found the way. The messengers of our Lord brought the Truth.' A voice will call out to them, 'This is the Garden which you have inherited by your labours.'

[44] The people of the Garden will call out to the people of the Fire, 'We have found that what our Lord promised us is true. Have you, too, found that what your Lord promised you is true?' They will say, 'Yes, we have!' Then a crier shall call out among them saying, 'The curse of God is upon the wrongdoers— [45] who turned people away from the path of God and sought to make it appear crooked, and who denied the Hereafter.'

[46] A barrier will divide the two groups, and on the heights there will be men who recognize each group by their marks. They will call out to the people of the Garden, 'Peace be with you.' They will not have yet entered, but they will be hoping [to do so], [47] and when they turn their eyes towards the inmates of the Fire, they will say, 'Our Lord, do not include us among the wrongdoers!' [48] And the people of the heights will call out to men they recognize by their marks, 'What use have your great numbers and your false pride been? [49] See! are these not the people you swore would never earn God's mercy? "Enter the Garden! No fear shall come upon you nor shall you grieve."'

[50] The people of the Fire shall call out to the people of heaven, 'Pour out some water on us, or give us something out of that which God has bestowed upon you.' But the blessed will reply, 'God has forbidden all that to those who denied the truth. [51] Who treated religion as a pastime and an idle sport and whom the life of the

world had beguiled.' On that Day We shall forget them, as they forgot their meeting of that Day with Us, for they denied Our revelations.

⁵² And surely We have brought them a Book which We have expounded with knowledge, a guide and a mercy for those who believe. ⁵³ Do they wait for the fulfilment of that of which it warns? On the Day when that fulfilment comes, those who had neglected it before will say, 'The messengers of our Lord did indeed bring the truth. Have we then any intercessors who would intercede for us? Or, could we be sent back so that we might act differently from the way we used to?' They have indeed ruined their souls and what they invented has forsaken them.

⁵⁴ Your Lord is God, who created the heavens and the earth in six Days [periods] and then settled Himself firmly on the throne. He throws the veil of night over the day, each seeking the other in rapid succession. It was He who created the sun, the moon and the stars, and made them subservient to His will. His is the creation, His the command. Blessed be God, Lord of the universe!ᵃ ⁵⁵ Call on your Lord with humility and in secret—He does not love the transgressors: ⁵⁶ do not spread corruption on the earth after it has been set in order—pray to Him with fear and hope, God's mercy is close to those who do good.

⁵⁷ It is God who sends forth the winds as harbingers of His mercy, and when they have gathered up the heavy clouds, We drive them on to a dead land where We cause rain to fall, bringing out all kinds of fruit, just as We will raise the dead to life. Perhaps you will take heed. ⁵⁸ Vegetation comes out of good land in abundance by the will

---

a God is the Creator of the earth, the sky and all things. This creation could have been haphazard, i.e. all things could have been created, then left in confusion. But He did not do so. He linked all things in an absolutely perfect, well-organised and wisely regulated system, and activated them in such a way that everything kept working exactly in the manner in which it ought to, if it had to serve the collective interest. Man is also a small part of this world. Then, what should be his role in this well-formed environment? His role should be the same as that of all other things. He should devote himself to the Creator's plan, in the way that the whole Universe has surrendered itself to this plan in all obedience.

of its Lord, but out of bad land only scantily. Thus We explain Our signs in diverse ways for those who give thanks.[a]

⁵⁹ We sent Noah to his people. He said, 'O my people, worship God; you have no other god but He. I fear for you the punishment of a dreadful Day,' ⁶⁰ but the leading men of his people said, 'Truly, we see that you are obviously lost in error!' ⁶¹ Said [Noah], 'O my people! I am not in error. Indeed, I am a messenger from the Lord of the Worlds, ⁶² I am conveying my Lord's messages to you and giving you sincere advice. I know things from God that you do not. ⁶³ Do you find it so strange that a message should come from your Lord through a man from among yourselves, so that he may warn you and so that you may fear God and be shown mercy?' ⁶⁴ But they denied him, so We saved him and those with him in the Ark, and We drowned those who rejected Our signs. They were indeed a blind people.

⁶⁵ To the people of 'Ad We sent their brother, Hud. He said, 'O my people, worship God, you have no other god but He. Then will you not be God-fearing?' ⁶⁶ The leading men of his people who refused to acknowledge the truth, said, 'We can see you are a foolish man, and we think you are lying.' ⁶⁷ He said, 'My people, I am by no means a fool, but rather am a messenger from the Lord of the Universe, ⁶⁸ I am conveying my Lord's messages to you and I am your sincere and honest adviser. ⁶⁹ Do you find it strange that a Message should come from your Lord, through one of your own men, to warn you? Remember how He made you successors

---

a God has made the world in such a way that its material occurrences symbolize its spiritual aspects. When rain falls anywhere, the water reaches every part of that place. But in respect of its use, conditions in different lands vary. The same is the position of that spiritual rainfall which comes down on behalf of God in the shape of His guidance. The message of this guidance reaches the ears of every man but its benefits accrue to everybody according to his receptivity. One who is receptive to accepting the Truth, derives full advantage from it; he gets a new lease of life from it; his nature is suddenly activated. His contact with his Almighty Lord is established. His parched soul blooms with divine inspiration.

of Noah's people, and increased you greatly in stature. Remember the favours of God, so that you may prosper.'

⁷⁰ They said, 'Have you come to tell us to serve God alone and to forsake the gods our forefathers served? Bring us then what you threaten us with, if you are truthful.' ⁷¹ He said, 'Your Lord's wrath and indignation have already fallen upon you. Would you dispute with me about mere names, which you and your fathers have invented, and for which God has revealed no authority? Wait then if you will: I am waiting alongside you.' ⁷² Then We saved him and those who were with him, by Our mercy; We annihilated those who denied Our signs and would not believe.

⁷³ To the Thamud We sent their brother Salih. He said, 'O my people, worship God; you have no other god but Him. A veritable proof has come to you from your Lord: this is God's she-camel, a sign for you, so let her feed in God's land and do not harm her in any way, or you will be overwhelmed by a painful punishment. ⁷⁴ Remember when He made you successors to the 'Ad and settled you in the land. You built palaces on its plains and carved houses out of the mountains. Remember God's blessings and do not spread corruption in the land,' ⁷⁵ but the arrogant leaders of his people said to the believers who were deemed weak, 'Do you know for certain that Salih is one sent from his Lord?' They replied, 'We believe in the message which has been sent through him.' ⁷⁶ The arrogant leaders said, 'We reject what you believe in.' ⁷⁷ So they hamstrung the she-camel, and insolently defied the commandment of their Lord, saying, 'O Salih! Bring upon us what you threaten us with if you are indeed a messenger.' ⁷⁸ So the earthquake overwhelmed them, and morning found them prostrate in their dwelling places. ⁷⁹ He left them, saying, 'My people, I delivered my Lord's messages to you and counselled you sincerely, but you do not like sincere advisors.'

⁸⁰ We sent Lot, who said to his people, 'How can you commit an abomination such as no one in the world has ever done before you? ⁸¹ You lust after men rather than women! You transgress all bounds!' ⁸² The only answer given by his people was, 'Turn them out of your town. They are people who regard themselves to be pure.' ⁸³ So We saved him and his family—except for his wife. She

was one of those who stayed behind. [84] We rained down on them a shower [of brimstone]. Then see what was the end of the evil-doers.

[85] To Midian We sent their brother Shu'ayb. He said, 'O my people, worship God; you have no other god but Him. A clear Sign has indeed come to you from your Lord. So give full measure and full weight, and do not deliver short. Do not corrupt the land after it has been set in order. This is for your own good, if you are true believers. [86] Do not lie in ambush on every pathway, threatening people, barring those who believe from the Way of God, seeking to make it appear crooked. Remember when you were few in number and He multiplied you. Consider the fate of those who used to spread corruption. [87] And if there is a group of you which believes in My message and others who disbelieve it, be patient until God shall judge between us. He is the best of judges.'

[88] The arrogant leaders of his people said, 'Shu'ayb, we will expel you and your fellow believers from our town unless you return to our faith.' He said, 'Even though we detest it? [89] We would be inventing lies against God if we returned to your faith after God has delivered us from it. It is not for us to return to it unless God our Lord so willed. Our Lord encompasses all things in His knowledge. We have put our trust in God. Our Lord, expose the truth [and judge] between us and our people, You are the best judge.' [90] The leading men of his people who were bent on denying the truth, said, 'If you follow Shu'ayb, you will certainly be the losers.' [91] Thereupon an earthquake overtook them and morning found them lying flattened in their homes; [92] those who had denied Shu'ayb became as though they had never lived there. Those who denied Shu'ayb, were themselves the losers. [93] So he turned away from them, saying, 'My people, I delivered my Lord's messages to you and gave you sincere advice, so why should I grieve for people who refused to believe?'

[94] Whenever We sent a prophet to a town, We afflicted its people with suffering and adversity, so that they might humble themselves [before God], [95] and then We changed their hardship into ease until they grew affluent and said, 'Our fathers had also experienced adversity and prosperity,' then We seized them suddenly, unawares. [96] Had the people of those towns believed in and feared God, We

would have showered upon them blessings from heaven and earth, but they rejected the truth. So We seized them on account of their misdeeds. ⁹⁷ Do the people of these towns now feel secure against the coming of Our punishment upon them by night while they are asleep? ⁹⁸ Or, do they feel secure against the coming of Our punishment upon them in the forenoon while they are at play? ⁹⁹ Do they feel secure against God's devising? No one feels secure against God's devising except for those doomed to ruin.

¹⁰⁰ Does it not guide the people who inherit the land from former people that We can punish them for their sins if We will? And seal up their hearts so that they would not be able to lend an ear to words of guidance? ¹⁰¹ We have told you the stories of those towns: their messengers came to them with clear signs, but they were never going to believe in something they had already rejected. Thus God seals up the hearts of those who deny the truth. ¹⁰² We found most of them untrue to their covenants, indeed We found most of them to be defiant.

¹⁰³ After them We sent Moses with Our signs to Pharaoh and his chiefs. But they wilfully rejected them. Consider the end of the evil-doers. ¹⁰⁴ Moses said, 'Pharaoh, I am a messenger from the Lord of the Universe, ¹⁰⁵ duty-bound to say nothing about God but the truth, and I have brought you a clear sign from your Lord. Let the Children of Israel go with me.' ¹⁰⁶ [Pharaoh] said, 'If you come with a sign, then produce it, if you are telling the truth.' ¹⁰⁷ Then Moses threw down his staff and suddenly, unmistakably, it appeared as a serpent, ¹⁰⁸ and he drew forth his hand, and it appeared [shining] white to the beholders. ¹⁰⁹ The chiefs of Pharaoh's people said, 'This is most surely a skilful magician, ¹¹⁰ who seeks to drive you from your land!' Pharaoh said, 'What then do you advise?' ¹¹¹ They said, 'Let him and his brother wait awhile, and send into the cities summoners, ¹¹² who should bring to you every skilful magician.'

¹¹³ And the magicians came to Pharaoh and asked, 'Shall we have a reward, if we should prevail?' ¹¹⁴ Pharaoh replied, 'Certainly, and you shall also become my courtiers.' ¹¹⁵ They said, 'Moses, will you first throw, or shall we?' ¹¹⁶ He said, 'You throw [first]!' When they made their cast, they bewitched the eyes of the people and struck

them with awe, for they showed a great [feat of] magic. [117] Then We inspired Moses, saying, 'Throw down your staff.' And it immediately swallowed up their false devices. [118] Thus the truth prevailed and what they had produced came to nothing: [119] Pharaoh and his men were defeated and utterly humiliated. [120] And the sorcerers prostrated themselves [121] and said, 'We believe in the Lord of the Universe, [122] the Lord of Moses and Aaron!'

[123] Pharaoh said, 'You dare believe in Him before I have given you permission? Behold, this is indeed a plot which you have devised in this city in order to drive its people out. But you shall soon know the consequences, [124] I will cut off your hands and feet on alternate sides and then crucify you all!' [125] They replied, 'We shall surely return to our Lord. [126] You would punish us only because we believed in the signs of our Lord when they were shown to us. Our Lord, pour patience upon us, and cause us to die in a state of submission to You.'

[127] The chiefs of Pharaoh's people said, 'Will you allow Moses and his people to spread corruption in the land, and to forsake you and your gods?' He replied, 'We shall kill their male children and spare only the females. We have complete power over them.' [128] Moses said to his people, 'Turn to God for help and be patient. The earth belongs to God. He gives it to those of His servants whom He chooses, and the future belongs to the God-fearing.' [129] They replied, 'We were being persecuted before you came to us, and we are still being persecuted.' He said, 'Your Lord may well destroy your enemy and make you successors to the land. Then He will see how you conduct yourselves.'

[130] We afflicted Pharaoh's people with shortages of food and famine so that they might take heed, [131] then when something good came to them, they said, 'It is our due!'—but when something bad came, they ascribed it as an ill-omen to Moses and those with him. Surely their [evil] fortune had been decreed by God, but most of them did not know this. [132] They said, 'Whatever miracles you work to bewitch us, we will not believe in you.'

[133] Then We afflicted them with storms, and locusts, and lice, and frogs, and blood: so many clear signs. But they were steeped

in arrogance, for they were a people given to sin. [134] Whenever a plague struck them, they would say, 'Moses, pray to your Lord for us by virtue of the promise He has made to you: if you remove this plague from us, we will surely believe in you and let the Children of Israel go with you,' [135] but whenever We removed the plague from them, giving them time to make good their promise, they would break their word.

[136] So We exacted retribution from them and drowned them in the sea, because they rejected Our signs and paid no heed to them; [137] We made the people who were considered weak inheritors of the eastern parts and western parts of the land which We had blessed. Thus your Lord's good promise to the Children of Israel was fulfilled, because of their patience, and We destroyed all that Pharaoh and his people had built and all that they had raised high.

[138] We brought the Children of Israel across the sea and they came upon a people who were devoted to their idols. They said, 'Moses, give us a god just like the gods these people have.' He said, 'You are indeed an ignorant people: [139] what they are engaged in is doomed to destruction and all their works are in vain.' [140] He said, 'Shall I seek a deity for you other than God, while it is He who has exalted you above all peoples? [141] We delivered you from Pharaoh's people, who afflicted you with dreadful torment, slaying your male children and sparing only your daughters. That was surely a great trial for you by your Lord.'

[142] We appointed thirty nights for Moses, then added ten more: the term set by his Lord was fulfilled in forty nights. Moses said to his brother Aaron, 'Take my place among my people: act rightly and do not follow the way of those who spread corruption.' [143] And when Moses came at Our appointed time and his Lord spoke to him, he said, 'My Lord, show Yourself to me so that I may look at You.' He replied, 'You cannot see Me, but look at the mountain; if it remains firmly in its place, then only will you see Me.' And when his Lord manifested Himself on the mountain, He broke it into pieces and Moses fell down unconscious. And when he recovered, he said, 'Glory be to You, I turn towards You, and I am the first to believe.'

[144] He replied, 'Moses, I have chosen you of all mankind for My

messages and My Words. Hold fast to what I have given you, and be among the grateful!' [145] And We wrote for him upon the Tablets an admonition and details of all things, then [bade him], 'Hold fast to them; and command your people to follow them in their best sense. Soon I shall show you the home of the wicked. [146] I will turn away from My signs all those who are arrogant in the land without any right, so that even if they see all the signs they will not believe in them. If they see the right path, they shall not walk upon it: but if they see the path of error, they shall choose it for their path, because they have given the lie to Our signs and paid no heed to them. [147] The actions of those who denied Our signs and the Meeting of the Hereafter will come to nothing—they shall be requited only, according to their deeds.'

[148] In his absence, the people of Moses made a calf from their ornaments, an image which made a lowing sound. Could they not see that it did not speak to them or guide them in any way? Yet they took to worshipping it: they were evil-doers. [149] When they were afflicted with remorse, and realized that they had indeed gone astray, they said, 'If our Lord does not have mercy on us and forgive us, we shall be among the lost.' [150] When Moses returned to his people in anger and great sorrow, he said, 'What an awful sin you have committed in my absence. Did you want to hasten your Lord's command?' He threw down the Tablets and seized his brother by the head, pulling him towards himself. Aaron said, 'Son of my mother, the people oppressed me and almost killed me. Do not give my enemies cause to gloat over me. Do not number me among the wrongdoers.' [151] He said, 'My Lord, forgive me and my brother and admit us to Your mercy. You are the Most Merciful of the merciful.'

[152] Those who took to worshipping the calf will be afflicted by their Lord's wrath, and be disgraced in the life of this world. This is the way We requite those who invent falsehoods. [153] As for those who committed evils, and thereafter repented and believed, they shall find your Lord forgiving and merciful.

[154] When his anger had subsided, Moses took up the Tablets upon which was inscribed a pledge of guidance and mercy for those who

fear their Lord. ¹⁵⁵ And Moses chose from his people seventy men for Our appointment. When they were seized with violent quaking, he prayed, 'O my Lord! If it had been Your will, You could have destroyed both them and me long ago. But would You destroy us for the deeds of the foolish ones among us? This is no more than Your trial: by it You cause whom You will to stray, and You lead whom You will to the right path. You are our Protector. Forgive us, therefore, and have mercy on us, for You are the best of those who forgive. ¹⁵⁶ Grant us good things, both in this life and in the hereafter. To You alone we turn.' He replied, 'As for My punishment, I smite with it anyone I will. But My mercy encompasses all things. I shall prescribe it for those who do their duty, pay the *zakat* and who believe in Our signs. ¹⁵⁷ Also for those who follow the Messenger—the unlettered prophet they find described in the Torah that is with them, and in the Gospel—who commands them to do right and forbids them to do wrong, who makes good things lawful to them and bad things unlawful, who will relieve them of their burdens and of the shackles that weigh upon them. Those that believe in him and honour him, those that aid him and follow the light sent down with him, shall surely triumph.'

¹⁵⁸ Say, 'People, I am God's Messenger to you all, He has sovereignty over the heavens and the earth. There is no god but Him. He ordains life and death, so believe in God and His Messenger, the unlettered prophet who believes in God and His words. Follow him so that you may be rightly guided.' ¹⁵⁹ Yet there is a group among the people of Moses who guide with truth and act justly in accordance with it.

¹⁶⁰ We divided them up into twelve tribes, each a whole community, and We revealed Our will to Moses, when his people asked for water, saying, 'Strike the rock with your staff.' Twelve springs gushed from it and each tribe knew its drinking place. We caused the clouds to draw their shadow over them and sent down for them manna and quails, saying, 'Eat the good things We have given you.' They did not wrong Us; rather it was themselves they wronged. ¹⁶¹ When they were told, 'Settle down in the town and eat wherever you wish in it, and pray for forgiveness and enter the gate in humility: We shall forgive you your sins and shall bestow further favours upon

those who do good,' ¹⁶² the transgressors among them substituted something else for the word they had been given. So We sent them a punishment from heaven for their wrongdoing.

¹⁶³ Ask them about the town which was by the sea and what befell its people when they broke the Sabbath. On their Sabbath the fish came to them near the surface, but on week-days they never came near them—thus We tried them because of their disobedience. ¹⁶⁴ When some of them asked, 'Why do you admonish a people whom God is going to destroy or to afflict with a severe punishment?' They answered, 'In order to be free from blame before your Lord, and that they may perhaps fear Him.'

¹⁶⁵ Therefore when they forgot what they had been reminded of, We saved those who had tried to prevent the doing of evil. And We meted out a severe punishment to the transgressors because they were rebellious. ¹⁶⁶ And then, when they disdainfully persisted in doing what they had been forbidden to do, We said to them, 'Be as apes, despised!'

¹⁶⁷ Then your Lord declared that, until the Day of Resurrection, He would send others against them to inflict terrible suffering on them. Your Lord is swift in retribution; yet surely He is most forgiving and merciful. ¹⁶⁸ We split them up into sections on the earth. Some of them are righteous while some of them are otherwise, and We tested them with blessings and misfortunes, so that they might return to the right path.

¹⁶⁹ They were succeeded by generations who inherited the Scripture and took to the fleeting gains of this world, saying, 'We shall certainly be forgiven.' If there came to them similar fleeting gains again, they would take them. Was a pledge not taken from them, written in the Scripture, that they would not say anything but the truth about God? And they have studied whatever is in it. Surely the Home of the Hereafter is better for those who fear Him. Will you not understand? ¹⁷⁰ As for those who hold fast to the Book and are steadfast in prayer, We shall not deny the righteous their reward. ¹⁷¹ When We suspended the mountain over them as if it were a canopy, and they thought it was going to fall down on them, We

said, 'Hold on firmly to what We have given you and remember what is in it, so that you may remain conscious of God.'

172 When your Lord brought forth offspring from the loins of the Children of Adam and made them bear witness about themselves, He said, 'Am I not your Lord?' They replied, 'We bear witness that You are.' This He did, lest you should say on the Day of Resurrection, 'We had no knowledge of that.' 173 Or lest you say, 'Our forefathers associated others with God before our time, and we are only the descendants who came after them. So are You going to destroy us for what those inventors of falsehood did?' 174 We explain Our signs in detail thus, so that perhaps they may return to Us.*a*

175 Recite to them the tale of the man to whom We gave Our signs, but who then cast them to one side and Satan overtook him. And he became one of those who went astray—176 if it had been Our will, We could have used these signs to exalt him, but instead he clung to the earth and followed his own desires—he was like a dog that pants whether you chase it away or leave it alone. Such are those who reject Our signs. Tell them this story so that they may reflect.

---

a If an animal is separated from its father and mother and it is brought up in a strange atmosphere, even then after growing up it retains the characteristics of its species. It adopts the same ways as are rooted in its instinct in all its dealings. The same is true of the human being as regards his 'God-consciousness'. In the soul of a human being the consciousness of a Creator and Lord has been instilled so deep-rootedly that he never loses it. However, there is one difference between animals and human beings. Animals are not capable of going against their nature. They are compelled to do whatever their inner nature urges them to do. But the case of a human being is different. This awareness is embedded in his nature, but he is completely free in the matter of action, even although his mind and his conscience start pointing out to him what is right and what is wrong. A human being has therefore the power and the option either to follow his inner voice, or to ignore it and start doing whatever he likes. It is on such occasions of moral choice that man is on trial and on the basis of its result, decisions regarding heaven or hell are taken. The person who lends his ears to the voice of God and does whatever He tells him to do through the silent language of 'Nature', passes the test. The doors of heaven (Paradise) will be thrown open for him after death, whereas one who ignores the voice of God speaking at Nature's level, will be held guilty in the eyes of God and He will ignore him as he ignored God's voice.

¹⁷⁷ How evil is the case of those who deny Our signs. They only wrong themselves: ¹⁷⁸ anyone whom God guides has been rightly guided; while those He lets go astray will surely be the losers.

¹⁷⁹ We created many of the jinn and mankind for hell. They have hearts they do not understand with; they have eyes they do not see with; and they have ears they do not hear with. Such people are like cattle—no, they are even more misguided. Such are the heedless. ¹⁸⁰ God has the Most Excellent Names. Call on Him by His Names and keep away from those who distort them. They shall be requited for what they do. ¹⁸¹ Of those We have created there are some who give true guidance and act justly. ¹⁸² We shall gradually seize those who reject Our signs from a place they do not recognize. ¹⁸³ For though I give them rein for a while, My strategy is sure.

¹⁸⁴ Have they not reflected that their companion is not mad? He is only a plain warner. ¹⁸⁵ Have they not looked into the realms of the heavens and the earth and all that God created, and seen that the end of their time might be near? What will they believe in if they do not believe in this? ¹⁸⁶ No one can guide those whom God lets go astray: He leaves them blundering about in their arrogance. ¹⁸⁷ They ask you [Prophet] about the Last Hour, 'When will it come?' Say, 'Knowledge about it rests only with my Lord; He alone will reveal when its time will come, it lies heavy on the heavens and the earth: it will suddenly overtake you.' They will put questions to you as though you had full knowledge of it. Say, 'Knowledge about it rests only with God, though most people do not realize it.' ¹⁸⁸ Say, 'I myself have no power to benefit or do harm, save as God pleases. If I had knowledge of the unseen, I would have availed myself of an abundance of good, and no harm would have touched me. I am but a warner and a bearer of good tidings for those who will believe.'

¹⁸⁹ It was He who created you from a single soul, and from it made its mate so that he may find comfort in her. Once he has covered her, she conceives and goes about with a light burden. When it grows heavy, they both call to God, their Lord, 'If You bestow on us a healthy child, we will surely be grateful,' ¹⁹⁰ yet when He grants them a healthy child, they begin to ascribe to others a share in the gift they have received. But God is far above what they associate

with Him! [191] Do they associate with Him those who create nothing and are themselves created? [192] They can give them no help, nor can they help themselves. [193] It makes no difference whether you call on them or remain silent. If you call them to the right path, they will not follow you. [194] Those whom you call on besides God are but creatures like yourselves. Call upon them, then, and let them respond to you, if what you say is true.[a]

[195] Have they feet to walk with? Have they hands to hold with? Have they eyes to see with? Have they ears to hear with? Say, 'Call upon those you associate with God as partners, then all of you contrive against me and give me no respite. [196] My protector is God who sent down the Book, for it is He who protects the righteous. [197] Those whom you call on besides Him have no power to help you, nor can they help themselves.' [198] If you call them to the right path, they will not hear you. You find them looking towards you, but they do not see you.

[199] Be tolerant; enjoin what is right; and avoid the ignorant. [200] If an evil impulse from Satan provokes you, seek refuge with God; He is all hearing, and all knowing. [201] When any evil suggestion from Satan touches those who fear God, they are instantly alerted and become watchful; [202] but the followers of devils are led relentlessly into error by them. They never desist.

[203] When you do not bring them a sign, they say, 'Why do you not invent one?' Say, 'I follow only what is revealed to me by my Lord. This Book is an enlightenment from your Lord and a guide and mercy to true believers. [204] When the Quran is read, listen to it with attention, and hold your peace, so that you may receive mercy. [205] Remember your Lord deep in your very soul, in all humility and awe, without raising your voice, morning and evening—do not be one of the heedless—[206] [even] the ones [angels] who live in the

---

a This vast universe itself introduces its Creator. This introduction in no case admits of the concept of polytheism. In the universe countless items or parts are found separately; but all these parts combine and become a harmonious whole. There is no contradiction or clash among them. This perfect harmony could not be possible unless the Creator and Lord of this universe were one and in control of its functioning.

presence of your Lord are not too proud to worship Him: they glorify Him and prostrate themselves before Him.

8. THE SPOILS OF WAR (*AL-ANFAL*)

In the name of God, the Most Gracious, the Most Merciful

[1] They ask you about the spoils of war. Say, 'They belong to God and His Messenger. So fear God, and set things right among yourselves, and obey God and His Messenger, if you are true believers: [2] true believers are those whose hearts tremble with awe at the mention of God, and whose faith grows stronger as they listen to His revelations. They are those who put their trust in their Lord, [3] who pray regularly and give in alms out of what We have provided for them.[4] Such are the true believers. They have a high standing with their Lord, His forgiveness and an honourable provision made for them.

[5] As it was your Lord who rightfully brought you forth from your house, even though some of the believers disliked it, [6] and they disputed with you concerning the truth after it had become manifest, as though they were being driven to their death with open eyes. [7] God promised you that one of the two parties would fall to you, and you wished that the one without sting should be yours, but God wanted to establish the truth by His words and cut off the root of those who denied the truth—[8] so that He might prove the truth to be true and the false to be false, however much the wrongdoers might dislike it.

[9] When you prayed to your Lord for help, He answered, 'I am sending to your aid a thousand angels in succession.' [10] God only did this to give you good news, and so that your hearts might be set at rest, for help comes from God alone. Surely, God is Mighty and Wise. [11] He brought drowsiness upon you to give you His reassurance and sent down water from the sky upon you, so that He might thereby purify you and remove Satan's pollution from you, and make your hearts strong and your feet firm. [12] When your Lord commanded the angels, saying, 'I am with you, so make those who believe stand firm. I will instil fear in the hearts of those who deny

the truth: so strike their necks and strike all their finger joints!'[a]
[13] That was because they defied God and His Messenger. He who defies God and His Messenger shall be severely punished by God. [14] That is your punishment, taste it then; and know that for those who deny the truth there is the punishment of the Fire.

[15] Believers, when you meet in battle those who deny the truth, never turn your backs on them: [16] whoever turns his back on such an occasion, unless it be as a stratagem of war, or in an endeavour to join another group [of the believers] will indeed draw down upon himself the wrath of God, and Hell shall be his abode and the worst indeed is that destination.

[17] You did not kill them; it was God who killed them; and when you [Prophet] threw [sand] at them it was not you, but God who threw it so that He might confer on the believers a great favour from Himself. Surely, God is all hearing, all-knowing—[18] that is what happened—and God will surely undermine the design of those who deny the truth. [19] If you were seeking a judgement, a judgement has now come to you. If you desist, it will be the better for you. But if you return [to hostility] We too will return. And your host will avail you naught, however numerous it may be, and [know] that surely God is with the believers.

[20] Believers, obey God and His Messenger, and do not turn away from him now that you have heard all. [21] Do not be like those who say, 'We hear,' but pay no heed to what they hear—[22] the worst creatures in God's eyes are those who are deaf and dumb, and who possess no understanding. [23] If God had found any good in them, He would certainly have made them hear; but being as they are, even if He makes them hear, they will turn away in aversion.

[24] Believers, obey God and the Messenger when he calls you to that which gives you life. Know that God stands between man and his heart, and you shall all be gathered in His presence. [25] And beware of an affliction that will not smite exclusively those among you who have done wrong. Know that God is severe in exacting retribution. [26] Remember when you were few in number and were accounted

---

a See note to 2:191.

weak in the land, ever fearing the onslaught of your enemies, but He provided you with shelter, and supported you with His help and provided you with good things, so that you might be grateful. [27] Do not betray God and His Messenger, and do not knowingly violate your trusts. [28] Know that your wealth and children are a trial and that there is an immense reward with God.

[29] Believers, if you fear God, He will grant you the ability to discriminate between right and wrong, and will forgive you your sins: for God is limitless in His great bounty.*a* [30] Remember how those who bent on denying the truth plotted against you to imprison you or kill you or expel you: they schemed—but God also schemed. God is the best of schemers.

[31] Whenever Our revelations are recited to them, they say, 'We have heard them. If we wished, we could produce the like. They are nothing but the fables of the ancients.' [32] They also said, 'God, if this really is the truth from You, then rain down upon us stones from heaven, or send us some other painful punishment.' [33] But God would not punish them while you [Prophet] were in their midst, nor would He punish them so long as they sought forgiveness. [34] Yet why should God not punish them when they debar people from the Sacred Mosque, although they are not its guardians? Its rightful guardians are those who fear God, though most of them do not realize it. [35] Their prayers at the Sacred House are nothing but whistling and clapping of hands. 'So taste the punishment because of your denial.'

---

a This ability to tell right from wrong (*furqan*) is almost the same as inner realisation (*ma'rifah*) or insight (*basirah*). The last mentioned creating an inner light in a man which enables him to see everything in its reality without his being deceived by its outward aspects. Whenever a man involves himself in anything to the point of always being careful about it, a particular sort of sensitivity develops in him which makes him recognise the favourable and unfavourable aspects of that matter. This applies to everyone, whether he be a religious man, a trader, a doctor or an engineer. If a man becomes totally devoted to his work, his inner realisation attains a degree when, without being entangled in this or that confusion, he straightway reaches the reality of the matter.

Development of this divine insight (*furqan*) in a man is the greatest guarantee that he will be safe from evils; he will regularise his relations with God, and he finally will become entitled to the grace of God.

³⁶ Those who are bent on denying the truth are spending their wealth in debarring others from the path of God. They will continue to spend it in this way till, in the end, this spending will become a source of intense regret for them, and then they will be overcome. And those who denied the truth will be gathered together in Hell. ³⁷ So that God may separate the bad from the good, He will heap the wicked one upon another and then cast them into Hell. These will surely be the losers.

³⁸ Tell those who are bent on denying the truth that if they desist, their past shall be forgiven, but if they persist in sin, they have an example in the fate of those who went before.*ᵃ* ³⁹ Fight them until there is no more [religious] persecution,*ᵇ* and religion belongs wholly to God: if they desist, then surely God is watchful of what they do, ⁴⁰ but if they turn away, know that God is your Protector; the Best of Protectors and the Best of Helpers!

⁴¹ Know that one-fifth of your battle gains belongs to God and the Messenger, to his close relatives and orphans, to the needy and travellers, if you believe in God and the revelation We sent down to Our servant on the Decisive Day, the day when the two forces met. God has power over all things.

⁴² You were on the nearer side of the valley, and they were on the farther side, and the caravan was below you. Had you wished to set a time by mutual agreement, you would certainly have disagreed on the timing. However, the encounter took place, so that God might settle a matter which had already been ordained, so that he who was to perish might perish after clear evidence of the truth, and he who was to live might live in clear evidence of the truth. Surely, God is all hearing and all-knowing. ⁴³ God showed them to you in your

---

a It is the principle of Islam that the individual is rewarded according to his deeds. However, by His grace the Almighty God has made special exemptions to this general principle: when a man is truly repentant, he will not be punished thereafter for his earlier deeds. Suppose a man spent his life in ungodliness, then he received the light of guidance, became a true believer and adopted the righteous life, in this case, he will be forgiven for the evil deeds done by him earlier; he will not be seized on the basis of his earlier sins.

b See note to 2:191.

dream as small in number. If He had shown them to you as many, you would have lost heart and disputed about the matter; but God saved you. He has full knowledge of what is in the human heart. [44] When at the time of your encounter He made them appear few in your eyes, and made you appear few in their eyes, it was so that God might bring about that which had been decreed. Everything returns to God.

[45] Believers! When you encounter a party, remain firm and remember God much, so that you may succeed. [46] Obey God and His Messenger, and avoid dissension, lest you falter and are no longer held in awe. Have patience: God is with those who are patient. [47] Do not be like those who left their homes full of conceit and showing off to others. They debar others from the path of God: but God has knowledge of all their actions.

[48] Satan made their deeds seem fair to them and said, 'None of the people shall prevail against you this day; I shall be your protector!' But when the two forces came in sight of each other, he turned on his heels, saying, 'This is where I leave you: I see what you do not, and I fear God—God is severe in His punishment.' [49] The hypocrites and those whose hearts were perverted said, 'These people [the believers] must be deluded by their religion.' But he who places his trust in God [knows that], God is Almighty and Wise.

[50] If you could see, when the angels take the souls of those who are bent on denying the truth [at death], how they strike their faces and backs: saying 'Taste the punishment of the Burning! [51] This is the punishment for what your hands committed—for, God never does the least wrong to His servants.' [52] Like Pharaoh's people and those that have gone before them, they rejected God's signs and God seized them for their sins. God is strong, and severe in punishment! [53] God would never withdraw a favour that He had conferred upon a people unless they change what is in their hearts. God is all hearing and all-knowing. [54] Like Pharaoh's people and those who went before them, they denied their Lord's signs: We destroyed them for their sins, and We drowned Pharaoh's people—they were all evil-doers.

[55] The worst creatures in the sight of God are those who reject Him and will not believe; [56] those with whom you have made a covenant,

and who break their covenant on every occasion and have no fear [of God]. ⁵⁷ Should you encounter them in war, then deal with them in such a manner that those that follow them should abandon their designs and may take warning. ⁵⁸ And if you learn of treachery on the part of any people, throw their treaty back at them, so as to be on equal terms, for God does not love the treacherous.

⁵⁹ Let not the deniers think that they will ever get away. They cannot frustrate [God's purpose]. They have not the power to do so. ⁶⁰ Prepare any strength you can muster against them, and any cavalry with which you can overawe God's enemy and your own enemy as well, and others besides them whom you do not know, but who are known to God. Anything you spend in the way of God will be repaid to you in full. You will not be wronged. ⁶¹ Then if they should be inclined to make peace, make peace with them, and put your trust in God. Surely, it is He who is All Hearing and All Knowing. ⁶² Should they seek to deceive you, God is enough for you: it was He who strengthened you with His help, and rallied the faithful around you, and bound their hearts together. ⁶³ Even if you had spent all that is on the earth, you could

not have bound their hearts together, but God has bound them together. Surely, He is Mighty and Wise.

⁶⁴ O Prophet! God is sufficient for you and the believers who follow you. ⁶⁵ Prophet, urge the believers to fight;^{*a*} if there are twenty of you who are steadfast, they will overcome two hundred, and if there are a hundred of you, they will overcome a thousand of those who deny the truth, for they are devoid of understanding. ⁶⁶ God has now lightened your burden, for He knows that there is weakness in you. If there are a hundred of you who are steadfast, they will overcome two hundred; and if there are a thousand of you, they will overcome two thousand by God's will. God is with the steadfast.

⁶⁷ It is not right for a Prophet to keep captives unless he has battled strenuously in the land. You desire the gain of this world, while God desires for you the Hereafter—God is mighty and wise. ⁶⁸ Had it not been for a writ from God that had already gone forth,

---

a See note to 2:191.

you would have been severely punished on account of what you took. [69] So eat of that which you have gained in war as lawful and good, and fear God. Surely, God is most forgiving and merciful.

[70] Prophet, tell those you have taken captive: 'If God knows of any good in your hearts, He will give you something better than what has been taken from you, and He will forgive you: God is Forgiving and Merciful.' [71] And if they would betray you, they betrayed God before, and He gave [you] power over them. God is aware and wise.

[72] Those who have believed and migrated and struggled for God's cause with their possessions and persons, and those who have given refuge and help, are the friends and protectors of one another. But as for those who have come to believe without having migrated —you are in no way responsible for their protection until they migrate. If they seek your help in the matter of religion, it is incumbent on you to help them, except against a people with whom you have a pact. God sees what you do. [73] Those who deny the truth support one another. If you fail to do likewise, there will be great disorder and corruption in the land.

[74] Those who have believed and migrated and striven for the cause of God, as well as those who have given them refuge and support, are the true believers; they shall have forgiveness and an honourable provision. [75] And those who have believed later on, and emigrated and struggled for God's sake alongside you are also a part of you. But as to blood relations, they are nearer one to another in the Book of God. God has full knowledge of all things.

9. REPENTANCE (*AL-TAWBAH*)

[1] This is a declaration of immunity from God and His Messenger to the polytheists, with whom you had made agreements. [2] So go about in the land for four months, but know that you cannot frustrate the plan of God and that God will disgrace those who deny the truth. [3] This is a proclamation from God and His Messenger to the people on the day of the Pilgrimage, that God is free of all obligation to the polytheists, and so is His Messenger. If you repent, it will be better for you, but if you turn away, then know that you cannot frustrate the

plan of God. Proclaim a grievous punishment to those who are bent on denying the truth. [4] As for those who have honoured the treaty you made with them and who have not supported anyone against you: fulfil your agreement with them to the end of their term. God loves those who are righteous.

[5] When the forbidden months have passed, kill the polytheists [who are at war with you] wherever you find them.[a] Take them captive, and besiege them, and lie in wait for them at every place of ambush. But if they repent, and take to prayer regularly and pay the alms, then let them go their way. God is forgiving and merciful. [6] If any one of the polytheists seeks asylum with you, grant him asylum so that he may hear the word of God; then convey him to a place of safety. That is because they are a people who have no knowledge.

[7] How can there be a treaty with the polytheists on the part of God and His Messenger, except for those with whom you entered into a treaty at the Sacred Mosque? As long as they act straight with you, act straight with them. God loves those who are righteous. [8] How [can there be a treaty] for, if they get the upper hand over you, they will respect neither kinship nor covenant. They [try to] please you with their tongues but their hearts reject you; most of them are perfidious. [9] They have sold God's revelations for a paltry price, and barred others from His path. How evil is what they have been doing! [10] Where believers are concerned, they respect no tie of kinship or treaty. They are people who overstep the limits. [11] If they repent and keep up their prayers and pay the alms, then they are your brethren in faith. We make Our messages clear for people who are willing to learn.

[12] But if they break faith after pledging it and revile your religion, then fight these leaders of unbelief, so that they may desist, for they have no regard for their pledged word. [13] Will you not fight against those who have broken their oaths and conspired to banish the Messenger? They were the first to attack you. Do you fear them? Surely God is more deserving of your fear, if you are true believers.[b]

---

a See note to 2:191.

b The root of all wisdom is fear of God. The fear of God develops in man

[14] Fight them: God will punish them at your hands, and will disgrace them. He will help you to overcome them and heal the hearts of the faithful; [15] He will remove the rage from their hearts. God will turn in His mercy to whom He wills. God is all knowing and wise.

[16] Do you [O believers] think that you will be spared without God identifying which of you have struggled and did not take anyone for friends and protectors except God, His Messenger, and the believers? God is fully aware of all your actions.

[17] It is not right that the polytheists should frequent God's places of worship while they are self-confessed unbelievers. It is they whose works shall come to nothing and they shall abide in Hell. [18] Only he should tend God's houses of worship who believes in God and the Last Day, and is constant in prayer, and spends in charity, and stands in awe of none but God: such people may hope to be among the rightly guided. [19] Do you regard giving water to pilgrims and tending the Sacred Mosque as being equal to the deeds of those who believe in God and the Last Day and who strive in God's path? They are not equal in the sight of God. God does not guide such unjust people.[a] [20] Those who have believed and have migrated, and have striven for God's sake with their possessions and persons, stand much higher in God's esteem. It is they who will triumph; [21] their Lord gives them the good news of His mercy and His pleasure and gardens of eternal bliss. [22] There they will dwell for ever. Truly there is an immense reward with God.

---

the readiness to accept the Truth; it awakens in man a certain consciousness that enables him to see realities in their original form. That is why it does not take the God-fearing man long to understand the Divine plan. He comes to know the will of God and dedicates himself to it with full confidence. He starts moving on that right path which ultimately leads to success. The fear of God makes a man's eye tearful, and before God, it is only the tearful eye which is destined to be cooled in this world as well as in the Hereafter.

[a] There are two types of attachment: one is to ritual, in which a man performs deeds of a showy nature, but does not offer himself or his wealth for the cause of God. The other is one in which a man is so serious about his faith that if he is required to renounce anything for its sake, he does so willingly, and whatever he is required to give, he gives willingly. One who evinces the second kind of attachment will, after death, be blessed by God with great munificence.

²³ Believers, do not take your fathers and your brothers for allies if they choose denial of truth in preference to faith. Those among you who ally themselves with them are wrongdoers. ²⁴ Say, 'If your fathers and your sons and your brothers and your spouses and your tribe, and the worldly goods which you have acquired, and the commerce which you fear will decline, and the homes you love are dearer to you than God and His Messenger and the struggle for His cause, then wait until God fulfils His decree. God does not guide the disobedient people.'ᵃ

²⁵ Indeed, God has helped you on many occasions. On the day of Hunayn, when you took pride in your great numbers, they proved of no avail to you—for the earth, despite all its vastness, became [too] narrow for you and you turned back, in retreat.ᵇ ²⁶ God caused His tranquillity to descend upon His Messenger and the faithful: and sent down forces which you did not see: He punished those who denied the truth—for such is the recompense of all who deny the truth— ²⁷ then after that, God will turn in His mercy to whom He wills: God is forgiving and merciful. ²⁸ Believers, know that the polytheists are impure, so they should not approach the Sacred Mosque after this

---

a For human beings, their families, their wealth and their economic interests have the greatest value. They consider these things the most important. They prefer these things to all other things and sacrifice their all for them. This sort of life is of the worldly type, and whatever the worldly person receives, he receives only in this world. There is nothing for him in the eternal life after death. As opposed to this, the other type of life is that in which a man gives the greatest importance to God, His Prophet and to efforts for the cause of God and for the sake of these things he is ready to leave everything else. It is the latter which is the God-worshipping life and for God's worshippers, the doors of eternal paradise will remain open in the Hereafter.

b Reliance on oneself develops sort of a haughtiness in a man which results in carelessness of external facts. He falls short in carrying out disciplinary regulations. Due to overweening self-confidence, he starts acting in an unrealistic manner, the result of which is necessarily defeat in this world of cause and effect. As opposed to this, having confidence in God is reliance on the greatest power. This develops humility in a man; he becomes extremely realistic; and realism is the key to all success.

year onwards. If you should fear destitution, God will enrich you out of His bounty, if He so wishes. God is aware and wise.

²⁹ Fight those from among the People of the Book who believe neither in God, nor in the Last Day, nor hold as unlawful what God and His Messenger have declared to be unlawful, nor follow the true religion, until they pay the tax willingly and agree to submit.*

³⁰ The [ancient] Jews [used to] say, 'Ezra is the son of God,' and the Christians say, 'The Messiah is the son of God.' These are but their baseless utterances. They imitate the assertions made in earlier times by those who deny the truth. May God destroy them! How far astray they have been led!

³¹ They have taken their learned men and their monks for their lords besides God. So have they taken the Messiah, son of Mary, although they were commanded to worship only the One God. There is no deity but He. He is far above whatever they set up as His partners!

³² They want to extinguish God's light with their mouths, but God seeks only to perfect His light, no matter how those who deny the truth may abhor it. ³³ It is He who has sent His Messenger with guidance and the religion of Truth, so that He may make it prevail [ideologically] over every other religion, however much the polytheists may hate this.

³⁴ Believers, many religious scholars and monks wrongfully appropriate people's possessions and turn people away from God's path! Tell those who hoard gold and silver instead of giving in God's cause that they will have a painful punishment: ³⁵ on the Day their treasure is heated up in the fire of hell, their foreheads and their sides and their backs shall be branded with it, and they will be told,

---

a If faith is active and alive, man attributes every event to God. He is able to understand a thing only when he forms an opinion about it with reference to God. He appreciates and understands the sweet smell of a flower when he finds the fragrance of God in it. He discovers the sun only when he comes to know of its Creator. Every greatness seems to him the blessing of God. Every good reminds him of God's Grace. Contrary to this, if man's relation with God is reduced to the stage of a feeble belief, then God will become an unknown entity in the sphere of his active consciousness; he will start imagining God on the pattern of the visible things of the world.

'This is what you hoarded up for yourselves. Taste then what you were hoarding.'

36 On the Day God created heaven and earth, He decreed that the number of months should be twelve in number. Out of these, four are sacred. That is the true religion. Do not wrong your souls in these months. Fight the polytheists all together, as they fight you all together, and know that God is with the righteous.[a] 37 The postponing of [sacred months] is but one more instance of [their] refusal to acknowledge the truth—by which those who are bent on denying the truth are led astray. They declare this to be permissible in one year and forbidden in another year, so that they may adjust the months which God has sanctified, thus making lawful what God has forbidden. Their evil deed seems fair to them: God does not guide those who deny the truth.

38 Believers, what is the matter with you that when you are asked to go forth in the cause of God, you cling slothfully to the land? Do you prefer the life of this world to the Hereafter? But little is the comfort of this life, compared to that of the Hereafter. 39 If you do not go forth, He will punish you sternly and replace you by other people. You will not harm Him in the least. God has power over all things. 40 If you do not support him [Muhammad], know that God did support him when those who denied the truth expelled him when the two of them were in the cave, he [Muhammad] told his companion, 'Do not worry; for God is with us.' So God sent His tranquillity down on him and aided him with forces invisible to you and placed the word of those who disbelieved lowest, while God's word remained supreme. God is powerful and wise.

41 Go forth, whether lightly or heavily equipped, and strive and struggle, with your goods and your persons, for the cause of God. That is better for you, if you only knew. 42 Had the gain been immediate and the journey shorter, they would have followed you: but the distance seemed too great for them. Yet they will swear by God, 'Had we been able, we would have gone out with you.' They bring ruin upon themselves. God knows that they are surely lying.

---

a See note to 2:191.

[43] May God pardon you! Why did you permit them to do so before it had become clear to you which ones were truthful, so that you might recognize the liars? [44] Those who believe in God and the Last Day will never ask you to exempt them from striving with their wealth and their lives—God best knows the righteous[a]—[45] only those seek exemption who do not truly believe in God and the Last Day, and whose hearts have become a prey to doubt. Because they doubt, they waver. [46] If they had wished to go forth, they would surely have made some preparation for it, but God disliked their setting out [and being raised high in God's eyes] and held them back. They were told to stay behind with those who stay behind.

[47] Had they gone forth with you, they would only have proved a source of evil for you, and would have run back and forth among you, seeking to sow discord among you: and among you there were some who would have willingly listened to them. God knows the evil-doers. [48] They have already tried to sow dissension, and hatched plots against you, until the truth became manifest and God's will prevailed, much to their disgust.

[49] Some of them say, 'Give us leave to stay behind and do not put us to trial.' Surely, they have already fallen into trial. Surely, Hell shall engulf those who deny the truth. [50] If good befalls you, it grieves them, but if a misfortune befalls you, they say, 'We took our precautions beforehand!' They turn away rejoicing. [51] Say, 'Nothing can befall us, except what God has ordained for us. He is

---

a If a son is ill or if there is a daughter's marriage, at such a time nobody spares himself or his money. If such an occasion arises, he will sacrifice his life and his wealth for the sole purpose if being of use to his kinsfolk. This is the time to do one's utmost rather than sheltering behind excuses. The truly religious individual, however, will never put forward excuses, when some occasion arises which demands sacrifice for religion. The restless emotions of faith in his heart await such a crucial moment when he will have the occasion to sacrifice himself and prove his loyalty before God. Then, such an occasion having arisen, how would such a person try to hide behind an excuse? The benefits of the Hereafter not being present before a human being, he entertains doubts about undertaking any sacrifices for it. But to tear off this veil of doubt is the real test of man in this world.

our Supreme Lord. In God let the faithful put their trust.'[a] 52 Say, 'Are you waiting for anything to befall us except one of the two best things [Victory in this world or Paradise in the next]? But we expect that God will send His punishment to you either directly from Himself, or by our hands. So wait, if you will; we too, are waiting with you.'

53 Say, 'Whether you give willingly or unwillingly, your offerings shall not be accepted by God, for you are indeed a disobedient people.' 54 The only reason their contributions are not accepted is that they have denied God and His Messenger, they come to the prayer half-heartedly, and they offer contributions unwillingly. 55 Do not let their wealth and children impress you. For God seeks to punish them through these things in the life of this world, so that their souls shall depart while they are still denying the truth.[b] 56 They swear by God that they are believers like you; but they are not. They are afraid [to appear in their true colours]: 57 if they could find a place of refuge, or a cave or any hiding-place, they would run there with frantic haste.

58 Among them there are some who find fault with you concerning the distribution of alms. If a share is given to them, they are pleased, but if they receive nothing, they grow resentful. 59 If only they had been content with what God and His Messenger had given them and had said, 'God is sufficient for us. God will give us out of His bounty, and so will His Messenger. To God alone do we turn with hope!' 60 Alms are only for: the poor and the destitute, for those who collect

---

a For true men of faith, there is no question of failure in this world. Their success lies in God being pleased with them and this is a certainty, in both good times and bad. If any trouble befalls a believer, this increases his inclination towards God. If he receives some benefit, this creates the feeling of obligation and gratitude in him and, by being grateful to God, he becomes entitled to further blessings from Him.

b If a man basks in the glories of wealth and has many minions constantly in attendance, the general public will envy him. But the fact is that such people are the most unlucky. Their condition is such that their wealth and status become fetters, rendering them unable to proceed fully towards God's religion; they forget God and busy themselves with worldly affairs until they meet with death, which mercilessly divests them of their wealth and high position.

zakat, for conciliating people's hearts, for freeing slaves, for those in debt, for spending for God's cause, and for travellers in need. It is a legal obligation enjoined by God. God is all-knowing and wise.

⁶¹ Among them are those who vex the Prophet by saying, 'He listens to everyone.' Say, 'His listening to everyone is good for you; he believes in God and puts his trust in the faithful, and is a mercy to those of you who believe. Those who annoy God's Messenger shall have a painful punishment.' ⁶² They swear by God in order to please you [believers]: but it would be more fitting for them to please God and His Messenger, if they are believers. ⁶³ Do they not know that whoever opposes God and His Messenger shall abide forever in the fire of Hell? That is the supreme humiliation.

⁶⁴ The hypocrites are afraid lest a chapter [of the Quran] be sent down about them, telling them what is in their hearts—say, 'Go on mocking. God will surely bring to light what you are dreading.' ⁶⁵If you ask them, they will say, 'We were only joking and playing with words.' Say, 'Would you make a mockery of God and of His Revelations and of His Messenger? ⁶⁶ Make no excuses; you rejected the faith after you accepted it.' If We pardon some of you, We will punish others amongst you, for they are guilty.'

⁶⁷ The hypocrites, both men and women, are all alike. They enjoin what is evil, forbid what is right and they are niggardly when it comes to spending for the cause of God. They have forgotten God, so He has forgotten them. The hypocrites are the disobedient ones. ⁶⁸ God has promised the hypocrites, both men and women, and those who deny the truth, the Fire of Hell. They shall abide in it forever. That is a sufficient recompense for them. God has rejected them. They shall have everlasting punishment. ⁶⁹ Like those before you who were stronger than you, possessed more wealth and children; they enjoyed their share in this life as you have enjoyed yours; like them, you have indulged in idle talk. It is they whose works shall come to nothing in this world and in the life to come—and it is they who shall be the losers. ⁷⁰ Have they never heard the stories about their predecessors, the peoples of Noah, 'Ad, Thamud, Abraham, Midian, and of the ruined cities? Their messengers brought them

clear evidence of the truth. It was not God who wronged them; they wronged themselves.

⁷¹ The believers, both men and women, are friends to each other; they enjoin what is good and forbid evil, they attend to their prayers and pay the alms and obey God and His Messenger. On these God will have mercy, for God is almighty and wise.*ᵃ* ⁷² God has promised the believers, both men and women, Gardens through which rivers flow, wherein they will abide, and fine dwelling places in Gardens of eternity. But the good pleasure of God is greater still. That is the supreme achievement.

⁷³ O Prophet, strive against those who deny the truth and the hypocrites, and be firm against them. Their abode shall be Hell: an evil destination.*ᵇ* ⁷⁴ They swear by God that they did not, yet they uttered the words of denial of truth after they had accepted Islam. They meditated a plot which they were unable to carry out, and being spiteful was their only response to God, who had enriched them out of His bounty, and to His Messenger. If they repent, it will indeed be better for them. If they turn away, God will punish them with grievous suffering in this world and the Hereafter, and there will be no one on earth to protect or help them.

⁷⁵ There are some among them who pledged themselves to God, saying, 'If God gives us something out of His bounty, we shall certainly give alms and be righteous,'*ᶜ* ⁷⁶ but when He bestowed His

---

a The life of the people of Faith in this world is symbolic of their life in the Hereafter. In this world, the people of faith live like so many flourishing trees standing in a lush green garden; everyone adds to the beauty of the other. Every believer is the well-wisher and companion of other believers, so much so, that the whole atmosphere becomes that of an abode of peace and tranquillity. This godly life will turn into the heavenly life in the Hereafter. There, the believer will not only reap the harvest sown by him, but will also receive such bounty by the special grace of God as he had never hitherto imagined.

b According to a tradition, during the period of the Prophet Muhammad, there were about eighty hypocrites in Madinah. This indicates that the jihad ordered here against hypocrites did not mean waging war on them. Had it been so, the Prophet would have had them eliminated. According to a hadith narrated by Ibn 'Abbas, here jihad meant striving by word of mouth.

c That person is a hypocrite in the eyes of God who prays to God for the

favours on them they grew niggardly, and turned away in aversion. [77] So He caused hypocrisy to settle in their hearts until the Day of their meeting with Him, because they broke their word to God, and because they lied. [78] Do they not know that God knows what they conceal and what they talk about in secret? That God knows all that is hidden?

[79] As for those who ridicule such believers as give alms freely for the sake of God and taunt those who find nothing to give save that which they earn through their toil, God will cause their ridicule to rebound on them: they shall have a painful punishment. [80] It is the same whether or not you ask forgiveness for them. Even if you ask forgiveness for them seventy times, God will not forgive them, for they have denied God and His Messenger. God does not guide the evil-doers.

[81] Those who stayed at home were glad that they were left behind by God's Messenger. They hated the thought of striving for God's cause with their possessions and their persons. They said, 'Do not go forth in this heat.' Say, 'The Fire of Hell is far hotter.' If only they could understand. [82] Let them laugh a little and weep much in return for their misdeeds. [83] So [Prophet], if God brings you back to a group of them, and should they ask your leave to go forth with you, say, 'You shall never go forth with me and shall never fight an enemy with me. You chose to sit at home the first time, so sit now with those who remain behind.' [84] And never [O Muhammad] pray for one of them who dies, nor stand by his grave. For they denied God and His Messenger, and died rebellious.

[85] Do not let their wealth and their children dazzle you. God only wants to punish them through these things in this world, and let

---

blessing of wealth and when God makes him wealthy, forgets to keep aside God's share. When a man has no wealth, he finds fault with wealthy persons, saying that they are wasting wealth in improper ways; and that if he were to be blessed with wealth by God, he would spend it on good and charitable causes. But when he receives wealth, his mentality changes. He forgets what he had said earlier and what feelings he had expressed. Now, he thinks that his wealth is the result of his own diligence and talents, which gives him the right to sole possession of it. He forgets to set aside God's share in his wealth.

their souls depart while they deny the truth. [86] When a chapter is revealed enjoining, 'Believe in God and strive for the cause of God along with His Messenger,' the wealthy among them ask you to exempt them saying, 'Let us stay with those who are to stay behind.' [87] They preferred to be with [the women], who remained behind [at home]: their hearts are sealed and so they do not understand. [88] But the Messenger and those who shared his faith strove hard with their possessions and their lives. It is they who shall have all kinds of good, and it is they who shall surely prosper. [89] God has prepared for them Gardens through which rivers flow, in which they shall abide forever. That is the supreme triumph.

[90] Some of the desert Arabs, too, came to make excuses, asking to be granted exemption. Those who lied to God and His Messenger stayed behind at home. Those who denied the truth among them will be afflicted with a painful chastisement, [91] but no blame shall attach to the weak, the sick, and those who have no means to spend, provided they are sincere to God and His Messenger. There is no reason to reproach those who do good deeds; God is most forgiving and merciful. [92] Nor [does any blame] attach to those who came to you to be provided with mounts, and when you said, 'I can find no mounts for you,' they went back, and tears welled up in their eyes with sadness, since they could not find any way to contribute.[a] [93] The blameworthy are those who are men of wealth and yet ask for exemption. They are content to be with those [women] who stay behind. God has sealed their hearts: they do not understand.

[94] They will make excuses to you when you return to them. Say, 'Do not make excuses, we will not believe you. God has already informed us about you. God will see your actions, as will His Messenger. Then you will be returned to the One who knows the

---

a Now, who are those fortunate people whose inaction is regarded as action and who are therefore rewarded for it? They are those who, while not physically participating because of some incapacity, give proof of three things—heartfelt solidarity with the participants (*nush*); doing at least by word of mouth whatever is possible for them to do (*ihsan*); and, sorrowfulness about their shortcomings that is so intense that it gushes out in the form of tears (*huzn*).

seen and the unseen and He will tell you all that you used to do.'
⁹⁵ When you return, they will swear to you by God so that you may
leave them alone, so leave them alone. They are unclean, and Hell
will be their home as a reward for their actions—⁹⁶ they will swear
to you, so that you may be pleased with them. But [even] if you
are pleased with them, God is not pleased with rebellious people.[a]

⁹⁷ The desert Arabs are more stubborn in their denial of truth and
hypocrisy, and are the least likely to be aware of the limits which
God has revealed to His Messenger. God is all knowing and wise.
⁹⁸ Some desert Arabs regard what they give for the cause of God as
a fine and wait for some misfortune to befall you. May ill-fortune
befall them! God hears all and knows all.

⁹⁹ There are also those among them who believe in God and the
Last Day and regard what they spend for the cause of God as a means
of bringing them nearer to God and of deserving the prayers of the
Messenger. This shall certainly be for them a means of drawing
near to God. God will admit them into His mercy; God is indeed
most forgiving and merciful.

¹⁰⁰ As for those who led the way, the first of the emigrants and
the supporters, as well as those who nobly followed them, God is
well pleased with them, and they are well pleased with Him; He
has prepared for them Gardens through which rivers flow, where
they shall dwell forever. That is the supreme achievement. ¹⁰¹ Some
of the desert Arabs around you are hypocrites as are some of the
people of Madinah—they are obdurate in their hypocrisy. You do
not know them, but We know them. We shall cause them to suffer
doubly and then they will be subjected to a great punishment.

¹⁰² There are others who have confessed their wrongdoing, who
have done some good deeds and some bad ones. It is likely that God
will turn to them in mercy. Surely, God is most forgiving, merciful.[b]

---

a Paradise is attainable on the basis of personal deeds and not on the basis
of having joined any class or group of Muslims. All the hypocrites were a part
of the Muslim *ummah*; they used to offer prayers and observe the ritual of
fasting along with the Muslims, but in spite of that, God decalred them to be
bound for Hell.

b Doing wrong is not the real evil in the eyes of God; persistence in that

[103] Take alms out of their wealth to cleanse them and purify them, and pray for them; your prayer will be a comfort to them. God is all hearing, all knowing. [104] Do they not know that God accepts the repentance of His servants and receives their alms, and that God is the Forgiving, the Merciful One? [105] Say, 'Do as you will. God will watch your conduct and so will His Messenger and the believers. Soon you will be brought back to Him who knows what is hidden and what is manifest: then He will show you the truth of all that you have done.' [106] [There are yet] others whose cases are deferred until it is God's will to judge them. He will either punish them, or turn in mercy to them; God is all knowing and wise.

[107] Then there are those who built a mosque to cause harm, to spread apostasy and disunity among the believers—as an outpost for those who from the outset warred on God and His Messenger. They swear, 'Our intentions were nothing but good,' but God bears witness that they are lying. [108] Do not set foot in it. Only a house of worship, founded from the very first day upon piety, is worthy of your setting foot therein. In it are men who love to be purified and God loves those who purify themselves. [109] Who is better, he who founds his building on the fear of God and His good pleasure, or he who builds on the brink of a crumbling precipice, so that his house is ready to fall with him into the Fire of Hell? God does not guide the wrongdoers: [110] the building which they have built will never cease to be a source of deep disquiet in their hearts, until their hearts are cut to pieces. God is all knowing and wise.

[111] God has bought from the believers their lives and their wealth in return for the Garden. They fight for the cause of God and they kill and are killed.[a] It is a promise binding on Him in the Torah, the Gospel and the Quran, and who is truer to his promise than God? Rejoice then in the bargain you have made. That is the supreme achievement. [112] [The believers are] those who turn to God in

---

wrong is the real evil. One who begins to justify his wrongs ruins himself, while one who admits his mistakes and tries his best to atone for them with good deeds is worthy of being pardoned by God.

a See note to 2:191.

repentance; who worship and praise Him; who go about in the land serving His cause, who bow down, who prostrate themselves, who enjoin good and forbid evil, and who observe the limits set by God. Give good news to the believers!

[113] It is not proper for the Prophet and those who believe to seek forgiveness for polytheists, even though they are close relatives, after it has become clear to them that they have earned the punishment of Hell. [114] Abraham's asking forgiveness for his father was only because of a promise he had made to him, but when it became clear to him, that he was God's enemy, he disassociated himself from him. Surely, Abraham was most tender-hearted and forbearing. [115] God would never lead a people astray after He has guided them and until He has made clear to them what they should guard against. God has knowledge of all things; [116] surely to God belongs the kingdom of the heavens and of the earth. He gives life and death. You have none besides God to protect or help you.

[117] God turned in mercy to the Prophet, and the emigrants and the helpers who followed him in the hour of hardship. After the hearts of a group of them had almost faltered, He turned towards them, for He was compassionate and merciful towards them. [118] He has turned with mercy to the three whose case was deferred, when the earth, for all its spaciousness, closed in upon them, and their own souls seemed straitened to them and they realised that there was no refuge from God except in Him. He turned to them so that they might turn to Him. God is the Ever Forgiving, the Most Merciful.

[119] Believers, fear God and stand with the truthful. [120] It was not proper for the people of Madinah and those desert Arabs around them to hold back from following God's Messenger, and to prefer their own lives to his life. This is because whenever they suffer from thirst or weariness or hunger for God's cause, and whenever they take any step which provokes those who deny the truth, or inflicts any loss upon the enemy, it shall be counted as a good deed in the sight of God—God will not deny the righteous their reward—[121] and whenever they spend anything [for the sake of God], be it little or much, and whenever they traverse the land [in God's cause]—it is

recorded to their credit, and God will grant them the best reward for all that they have been doing.

¹²² It is not right that all the believers should go out [in time of war] all together. Why, then, does not a party from every group come to [the Prophet] in order to acquire a deeper knowledge of religion and to warn their people, so that they can guard themselves against evil?

¹²³ Believers! Fight against those deniers of the truth who are near you.*ᵃ* Deal firmly with them. Know that God is with those who fear Him. ¹²⁴ Whenever a chapter is sent down, there are some of them who say, 'Which of you has had his faith increased by it?' But, as for those who believe, it increases their faith and they rejoice, ¹²⁵ but as for those with sickness in their hearts, it adds defilement to their defilement and they die in a state of denial of truth. ¹²⁶ Do they not see that they are tried every year once or twice? Yet they do not repent, nor would they be admonished. ¹²⁷ Whenever a chapter is revealed, they glance at each other, asking, 'Is anyone watching?' Then they turn away. God has turned their hearts away, because they are people who do not understand.

¹²⁸ There has come to you a Messenger of your own. Your suffering distresses him: he is deeply concerned for your welfare and full of kindness and mercy towards the believers.*ᵇ* ¹²⁹ But if they turn away, say, 'God suffices me: there is no deity but He: in Him I have put my trust. He is the Lord of the Glorious Throne.'

---

a See note to 2:191.

b The Quran tells us that God's messenger is extremely kind and affectionate towards people. He is so perturbed by others' suffering that it is as if he himself were affected by it. He is extremely anxious to give guidance to others. What moves him to convey the message of truth to the people is nothing but his great desire for their welfare—far from his having any personal ambition or there being any national problem.

According to a tradition narrated by 'Abdullah ibn Mas'ud, the Prophet Muhammad said, 'People are falling into the fire like flies and I am trying to keep them away from it by holding on to their waists.' (*Musnad Ahmad*).

10. JONAH (*YUNUS*)

In the name of God, the Most Gracious, the Most Merciful

¹ *Alif Lam Ra*

These are the verses of the Book of Wisdom. ² Does it seem strange to people that We have sent revelation to a man from among themselves, saying, 'Warn mankind and give glad tidings to the believers that they have a true rank [of honour] with their Lord?' Those who deny the truth say, 'This man is clearly a sorcerer.'*ª*

³ Truly, your Lord is God who created the heavens and the earth in six days [periods], then He ascended the Throne, disposing the whole affair. No one may intercede with Him save with His permission. Such is God, your Lord, so worship Him alone. Will you not take heed? ⁴ To Him you shall all return. God's promise is true; He originates Creation, then He restores it, so that He may reward with justice those who believe and do good works. Those who have denied the truth shall have boiling water to drink, and a painful punishment, because of their denial.

⁵ It is He who made the sun radiate a brilliant light and the moon shed its lustre, and ordained for it stages so that you may learn to count out the years and [to make other such] reckoning of time. God has not created all these without a purpose. He makes plain His revelations to men of understanding. ⁶ In the alternation of night and day, and in all that God has created in the heavens and the earth,

---

a The real mission of a prophet is warning others (*inzar*) and giving good news (*tabshir*). That is, warning people of God's retribution and giving good news of Paradise to those who are ready to live in the world in fear of God. The prophet appears in the world in order to make people aware of the fact that man is not free and all-powerful in this world and that the story of his life is not going to end with his death. Indeed, there is eternal life after death and man should take the utmost care to prepare for this. One who is unmindful of this or adopts an attitude of insolence, will reach the world after death in such a condition that nothing will await him there except agony and misery.

there are signs for a God-fearing people.*a* *7* Those who entertain no hope of meeting Us, being pleased and contented with the life of this world, and those who give no heed to Our signs, *8* shall have their abode in the Fire in requital for their deeds. *9* Those who believe and do good deeds will be guided by their Lord because of their faith. Rivers shall flow at their feet in the Gardens of Bliss. *10* In that [state of happiness] they will call out; 'Glory be to You, O God!', while their greeting in it will be: 'Peace!' And the close of their call will be, 'All praise is due to God, the Lord of the Universe!'

11 Had God hastened the punishment of men as He hastens the good, the end of their term of life would already have been reached. We leave those who do not hope to meet Us groping along in their arrogance. *12* Whenever any trouble befalls a person, he prays to Us all the time, lying on his side, sitting or standing; but when We remove his trouble, he goes on his way as if he had never prayed to Us for the removal of his trouble. Thus it is that the doings of the transgressors are made to look fair to them.

13 And indeed, before your time We destroyed [whole] generations when they [persistently] did evil; their messengers came to them with clear signs, but they would not believe. Thus We requite the guilty. *14* Then We made you their successors in the land, so that We might observe how you would conduct yourselves.

15 When Our clear revelations are recited to them, those who do not expect to meet Us say, 'Bring us a different Quran, or make some changes in it.' Say, 'It is not for me to change it of my own

---

a In the heavens and on the earth, there are countless signs, but they serve as a lesson only for those who are God-fearing. Fear, or apprehension, is a thing which makes a man serious. Unless a man is serious, he will not pay full attention to matters of importance and will not understand their various aspects.

The whole universe is held together in a creative balance. This is a clear indication of the fact that the Lord of the universe is One who has the power to seize hold of man. Similarly, the initial life which we are now experiencing provides clear proof of the fact that a second life is also possible. The appearance of material results in the present world and the non-appearance of moral results warrants the taking shape of another world where the moral results will appear to the fullest extent. This is an unassailable truth, but this can be grasped only by one who looks at life in fear and apprehension.

accord. I follow only what is revealed to me. I fear, if I were to disobey my Lord, the punishment on a Dreadful Day.' ¹⁶ Say, 'If God had so wished, I would not have recited it to you, nor would He have brought it to your knowledge. Indeed, I have spent a whole lifetime among you before it came to me. How can you not use your reason?' ¹⁷ Who is more unjust than the man who invents a falsehood about God or denies His signs? Surely, the guilty shall never prosper.

¹⁸ Instead of God they worship what neither harms nor benefits them, and they say: 'These are our intercessors with God.' Say, 'Do you inform God about something in heavens and on earth that He does not know? Glory be to Him; may He be Exalted over whatever they associate [with Him]!' ¹⁹ Mankind was only one community, but then they differed, and had it not been for a prior word from your Lord, their differences would have been settled for them.

²⁰ They ask, 'Why has no sign been sent down to him from his Lord?' Tell them, 'God alone has knowledge of the unseen. So wait; I too will wait with you.' ²¹ Whenever We let mankind taste mercy after some adversity has afflicted them, they forthwith turn to devising false arguments against Our signs. Say, 'God is swifter in His devising! Our angels are recording your intrigues.'

²² It is God who enables you to travel on land and sea. And when you are sailing on ships and rejoicing in the favourable wind, a storm arrives, and the waves surge upon those on board from every side and they think they are encompassed, then they make a fervent appeal to God, saying in all sincerity, 'If You deliver us from this, we will surely be of the thankful.' ²³ But when He has delivered them, they begin, wrongfully to commit excesses in the land. O you men, your excesses only affect your own selves. Have the enjoyment of the present life. Then to Us you shall return; and We will inform you of all that you have done.

²⁴ The life of the world is like the water which We send down from the sky, and which is absorbed by the plants of the earth, from which men and cattle eat. But when the earth has taken on its finest appearance, and looks beautiful, and its people think they have it under their control, then by day or by night, Our command comes

to it and We convert it into a field of stubble, as if nothing had existed there the day before. Thus We make plain Our revelations for those who reflect.*a*

25 God calls man to the home of peace and He guides whom He wills to a straight path. 26 Those who do good works shall have a good reward and more besides. No darkness and no ignominy shall cover their faces. They are destined for Paradise wherein they shall dwell forever. 27 But as for those who have done evil deeds, the recompense shall be in proportion. They will have none to defend them against God. Ignominy shall cover them, as though their faces were veiled by the night's own darkness. It is they who are destined for the fire, where they will live forever.

28 On the Day when We gather them all together, We shall say to those who ascribed partners to God, 'Keep to your places, you and your partners!' Then We shall separate them from one another and their partner-gods will say, 'It was not us that you worshipped. 29 God suffices as a witness between us and you. We were entirely unaware that you worshipped us.' 30 Then every soul shall realize what it has done. They shall be returned to God, their true Master, and anything they had invented will forsake them.

31 Say, 'Who provides [sustenance] for you from heaven and earth? Who is it who controls the ears and the eyes? Who brings forth the living from the dead, and the dead from the living? And who governs all affairs?' They will say, 'God'. Then say, 'Will

---

a The life of this world is for the purpose of putting man to the test. Therefore, here man has been given complete freedom and all sorts of opportunities. Apparently, a man is free to do whatever he likes and to shape his own future in whatever way he likes. But in the midst of these preoccupations, certain events unfold which teach lessons to thoughtful persons and which indicate the fact that all this is temporary and will very soon be taken away from them. One such example is that of green vegetation on the earth. When there is rain, the earth becomes lush green with different kinds of vegetation. Man is pleased with this; he starts thinking that things are completely under his control and very soon he will be the owner of a rich crop. Exactly at the same time, some calamity suddenly befalls him, for example, a tornado strikes, there is snowfall or there is a plague of locusts and in this way the whole crop is destroyed in a moment.

you not then fear Him? [32] That is God, your true Lord. What is there, besides the truth, but error? How then can you turn away?' [33] Thus the Word of your Lord is proved true against those who are disobedient. They will not believe.[a]

[34] Ask then, 'Can any of your partner-gods originate creation, and then reproduce it?' Say, 'It is God who originates creation and then restores it: how then are you so misled?' [35] Say, 'Does any of your partner-gods guide one to the Truth?' Say, 'It is God who guides to the truth. Then, is He who guides to the truth more worthy to be followed or one who cannot find the way himself unless he be guided? What is the matter with you? How ill you judge!' [36] Most of them follow nothing but mere conjecture. But conjecture is of no use against the Truth. God is well aware of what they do.

[37] This Quran is not such as could have been produced by anyone but God. It fulfills that [the predictions] which came before it and gives a fuller explanation of the [earlier] Revelations. There is no doubt about it: it is from the Lord of the Universe. [38] Do they say, 'He has fabricated it?' Say, 'Bring me one chapter like it. Call on whom you may besides God to help you, if what you say be true!' [39] Indeed, they are denying something which they cannot comprehend; the reality not yet having dawned on them. Likewise those before them rejected the truth. But see what was the end of the wrongdoers.

[40] Some of them will believe in it [the Quran], while others will not. And your Lord is fully aware of the evil-doers. [41] If they should reject you, say, 'My deeds are mine and your deeds are yours. You

---

a Man needs sustenance. How does he receive it? It is through the coordinated action of the universe. The whole universe, with the utmost harmony, acts in a particular direction. Then only is it possible to make available to man that provision without which it would not be possible for him to survive on this earth. Studies show that every phenomenon in the universe is a product of a great and harmonious coordination among numerous elements of different and opposite nature. The polytheists' stand makes this universal coordination of such a high degree unexplainable. For these supposed partners in godhood are responsible for only one small part of the functioning of the universe. And a 'god' of one part can never cause an event which comes into existence through harmonious coordination of all parts.

are not accountable for my actions, nor am I accountable for what you do.' 42 Some of them appear to be listening to you; but can you make the deaf hear, incapable as they are of understanding? 43 Some of them look fixedly at you; but can you make the blind see, bereft as they are of sight? 44 Surely, God does not wrong people at all, but people wrong themselves.

45 And on the Day when He shall gather them together, it will seem to them as if they had not tarried in the world longer than an hour of a day. They will recognize one another; lost indeed will be those who considered it a lie that they were destined to meet God, and did not follow the right path. 46 Whether We show you something of what We have promised them or cause you to die [before that], to Us they shall return. God is Witness to all that they do.

47 Every nation has a messenger. Once their messenger has come, judgement will be passed upon them in all fairness and they will not be wronged.

48 They say, 'When will this promise come to pass—if you speak the truth?' 49 Say, 'I have no control over any harm or benefit to myself, except by the will of God. For every people, however, there is an appointed term. When the end of their term arrives, they cannot postpone it for an hour, nor can they advance it.' 50 Say, 'If His punishment comes upon you in the dead of night, or by the light of day, how will the guilty escape it? 51 Will you believe in it only after it has overtaken you, although it was your wish to hurry it on?' 52 Then the evil-doers will be told, 'Taste the everlasting punishment. Have you not been rewarded according to your deeds?'

53 They enquire of you if this will really happen. Tell them, 'Yes, by my Lord. Most certainly it will happen, and you cannot avert it.' 54 If every wrongdoer possessed all that was on the earth, he would seek to ransom himself with it: when they see the punishment, they will repent in secret. But judgement will be passed upon them in all fairness, and they will not be wronged. 55 Assuredly, everything that is in the heavens and on the earth belongs to God. Assuredly, God's promise is true. Yet most of them do not realize it. 56 He gives life and brings about death, and to Him you shall all return.

57 O mankind! There has come to you an admonition from your

Lord, a cure for what is in the hearts, and a guide and a blessing to true believers. [58] Say, 'In the grace and mercy of God let them rejoice, for these are better than the worldly riches which they hoard.' [59] Say, 'Have you considered the provision God has sent down for you, and have you made some of it unlawful and some lawful?' Say, 'Has God given you permission [to do this], or are you inventing falsehoods about God?' [60] What will they think, those who invent falsehoods about God, on the Day of Resurrection? God is bountiful to men: yet most of them are not grateful.[a]

[61] In whatever activity you may be engaged, and whichever part of the Quran you recite, and whatever deed you do, We are witness to it when you are engaged in it. Not the smallest particle on the earth or in heaven is hidden from your Lord; and there is nothing smaller or bigger but is recorded in a clear Book. [62] Those who are close to God shall certainly have no fear, nor shall they grieve. [63] For those who believe and are mindful of God, [64] there is good news in this life and in the Hereafter: the Word of God shall never change. That is the supreme triumph. [65] Do not let their words grieve you. Surely, all might and glory belongs to God alone; He is the all-hearing, the all-knowing. [66] Surely, all who are in the heavens and on the earth belong to Him. What do those follow, who appeal to associates instead of to God? They merely follow conjecture and they are only guessing. [67] It is He who has made the night dark for you so that you may rest in it, and the day a source of light. Surely, there are signs in this for a people who listen.

---

a Whatever God has given to man—whether in the form of agricultural produce or in some other form—everything is divine provision (*rizq*). If a man treats them as gifts of God and utilizes them in the way shown by God, then a feeling of gratitude to God will develop in him. But Satan wants man to fail to remember God while making use of divine provisions. In ancient times Satan fixed the rites of certain imaginary false gods and goddesses in the produce so that man should not remember God but those false gods and goddesses while availing of the produce. In the present age Satan is achieving this purpose by advancing material explanations for things. God-gifted things are being shown to people as resulting from certain material factors, so that when they receive these things, they will not treat these bounties as the provision (*rizq*) of God but as the outcome of worldly events.

⁶⁸ They say, 'God has begotten a son.' Glory be to Him. He is the Self-Sufficient One; everything in the heavens and on the earth belongs to Him. Do you have any authority for this? Would you ascribe to God something which you do not know? ⁶⁹ Say, 'Those who invent falsehoods about God shall not prosper.' ⁷⁰ Their portion is short-lived enjoyment in this world; but to Us they shall return. Then We shall make them taste a severe punishment, because of their denial of truth.

⁷¹ Tell them the story of Noah. He said to his people, 'My people, if my presence among you and my preaching to you of God's revelations offends you, know that I put my trust in God, so agree on your course of action, along with your partner-gods, and let no hesitation deflect you from it, then put it into effect against me, and give me no respite. ⁷² If you turn away from me, remember I demand no recompense from you. Only God will reward me and I have been commanded to submit completely to Him.' ⁷³ Then they rejected him; then We delivered him and those with him in the Ark, and We made them successors; while We drowned the others who belied Our signs. Observe then the fate of those who had been forewarned.*ᵃ*

⁷⁴ After him We sent other messengers to their respective peoples, and they brought them clear proofs. But they would not believe in the truth, because they had rejected it before. Thus We seal up the hearts of the transgressors.

⁷⁵ Then We sent forth Moses and Aaron with Our signs to Pharaoh and his nobles, but they behaved arrogantly, for they were wicked people. ⁷⁶ When the truth came to them from Us, they said, 'This is plain sorcery.' ⁷⁷ Moses replied, 'Do you speak thus of the truth

---

a When Noah had finally delivered his message in its entirety to his community, and still his community was adamant about being arrogant, the latter were drowned in turbulent flood waters so that the earth was rid of them, while the Faithful (adherents of Noah) were given the opportunity to live in the world as inheritors of the earth. This, in Quranic terminology, is described as '*khalifah.*' Before the flood, the community of Noah was the *khalifah* of the earth; after the flood those faithful to Noah were made the successors of the earth.

after it has been brought to you? Can this be sorcery? Sorcerers never prosper.' [78] They said, 'Have you come to turn us away from what we found our forefathers following, so that the two of you might become supreme in this land? We will never believe in you.'

[79] Then Pharaoh said, 'Bring me every skilled magician!' [80] When the magicians came, Moses said to them, 'Cast down whatever you are going to cast down.' [81] And when they had done so, Moses said, 'What you have wrought is mere sorcery. Surely, God will bring it to nothing. Truly, God does not support the work of mischief-makers; [82] God establishes the truth by His words, however much the sinners may dislike it.'

[83] But none save a few youths declared their faith in Moses, [while others held back] for fear that Pharaoh and his nobles would persecute them. Pharaoh was high and mighty in the land. And one who transgressed all bounds. [84] Moses said, 'O my people; if you believe in God, [and] if you have surrendered yourselves to Him, then in Him alone put your trust.' [85] They said, 'In God we put our trust. Our Lord, make us not a trial [the subject of persecution] for the oppressors. [86] And deliver us by Your mercy from the people who deny the truth.'

[87] We revealed [Our will] to Moses and his brother, saying, 'Set aside for your people some houses in the city and turn them into places of worship, and be constant in prayer! And give [O Moses] the good news to the believers.'

[88] Moses prayed, 'Our Lord, You have bestowed upon Pharaoh and his nobles pomp and wealth in the present life, whereby they lead people astray from Your path. Our Lord, destroy their riches and harden their hearts, so that they shall not believe until they are faced with grievous punishment.'

[89] God said, 'Your prayer is granted, so continue, then, both of you, steadfastly on the right path, and do not follow the path of those who have no knowledge.'

[90] So We brought the Children of Israel across the sea. Pharaoh and his troops pursued them arrogantly and aggressively. When he was about to drown, [Pharaoh] exclaimed, 'I believe that there is no deity save Him in whom the Children of Israel believe, and I am

of those who surrender themselves to Him!' ⁹¹ 'Only now? When you had always been a rebel, and a wrongdoer. ⁹² So We shall save your body this day, so that you may serve as a sign for those who come after you: for many people are indeed heedless of Our signs.'

⁹³ We settled the Children of Israel in a blessed land, and We provided them with good things. And it was not until knowledge [of God's revelation] was granted to them that they began to hold divergent views. Your Lord will judge between them on the Day of Resurrection concerning that in which they differed.

⁹⁴ If you are in any doubt concerning what We have sent down to you, then question those who have read the Book before you: the Truth has come to you from your Lord, so do not be one of the doubters—⁹⁵do not be one who rejects God's signs, for then you would become one of the losers.

⁹⁶ Those against whom your Lord's word has been confirmed will never believe; ⁹⁷ not even if every Sign were to come to them—until they see the painful punishment. ⁹⁸ Why was there no other people, save the people of Jonah, who should have believed so that their belief would have benefited them. Once they believed, We lifted the torment of shame from them during their worldly life and let them enjoy Our provision for a while.

⁹⁹ Had your Lord pleased, all the people on earth would have believed in Him, without exception. So will you compel people to become believers? ¹⁰⁰ No soul can believe except by the will of God. He will place the filth [of doubt] upon those who do not use their reason.

¹⁰¹ Say, 'Look at whatever [exists] in heavens and on earth.' But signs and warnings do not benefit the unbelievers. ¹⁰² What can they be waiting for but the punishment that came to those before them? Say, 'So wait; I am one of those waiting with you.' ¹⁰³ Then We shall save Our messengers and those who believe. Thus We have made it incumbent upon Ourself to save the believers.

¹⁰⁴ Say, 'O people, if you are in doubt concerning my religion, then [know that] I do not worship those whom you worship instead of God, but rather I worship God who will cause you to die, for I am commanded to be one of the believers.' ¹⁰⁵ And set your face towards

the [true] faith in all uprightness, and do not be one of those who ascribe partners to God; [106] and do not invoke besides God what can neither help nor harm you. If you do, you will be one of the wrongdoers. [107] If God inflicts harm on you, no one can remove it but He, and if He intends good for you, no one can withhold His bounty; He grants His bounty to any of His servants whom He will. He is the Most Forgiving, and the Most Merciful.

[108] Say, 'Mankind, Truth has come to you from your Lord! Anyone who accepts guidance is guided only for his own sake; and he who goes astray does so at his own peril. I am not appointed as your keeper.' [109] Follow what is revealed to you, [O Prophet], and be steadfast until God gives His judgement. He is the Best of Judges.

11. HUD

In the name of God, the Most Gracious, the Most Merciful

[1] *Alif Lam Ra*

[This is] a Book, with verses which are fundamental [in nature], and then expounded in detail by One who is all wise and all aware. [2] [It teaches] that you should worship none but God. I am sent to you from Him to warn you and to give you good tidings. [3] Seek forgiveness from your Lord; then turn towards Him [in repentance]. He will make generous provision for you for an appointed term and will bestow His grace on all who merit it! But if you turn away, then I fear for you the torment of a dreadful Day: [4] to God you shall all return; and He has power over all things.*a*

[5] See how they cover themselves up to hide [their thoughts] from

---

a The message of the Quran is that man should not worship anyone except the one and only God. He should make the one and only God his everything; he should fear Him alone and repose his hopes in Him alone; his mind and heart should obey Him alone. In the affairs of his life, he should give prior consideration to His will and pleasure. He should be willing to place himself in the position of a worshipper and give God the status of the worshipped one.

Him. But when they cover themselves up with their garments, He knows what they hide and what they reveal. He knows their innermost thoughts. ⁶ There is not a living creature on the earth but it is for God to provide its sustenance. He knows its dwelling and its [final] resting place. All this is recorded in a clear book.

⁷ Enthroned above the waters, it was He who created the heavens and the earth in six Days [periods], in order to test which of you is best in conduct. If you say, 'You will [all] be raised up after death,' those who deny the truth will say, 'This is just sheer sorcery!' ⁸ If We defer their punishment till an appointed time, they ask, 'What is holding it back?' On the Day when it overtakes them, there will be nothing to avert it from them; and what they used to mock at shall encompass them.*ᵃ*

⁹ When We bestow upon man a measure of Our grace and then take it away from him, he yields to despair and becomes ungrateful. ¹⁰ And if, after adversity, We let him taste good fortune he says, 'All my ills are gone.' He becomes exultant and boastful. ¹¹ Not so those who are patient and do good deeds. They shall have forgiveness and a great reward.*ᵇ*

¹² You may [feel the inclination] to leave aside a part of what is revealed to you and you may be distressed because they say, 'Why has no treasure been sent down to him, why has no angel come with him?' But you are only to give warning. God is the guardian of all things. ¹³ If they say, 'He has invented it himself.' Say, 'If you are truthful, produce ten invented chapters like it, and

---

a The present world was created by God in six days, that is, in six stages or six periods. There was a period when its surface was covered with water. In this part of God's domain, only water was seen everywhere at that time. Then, at God's behest, patches of land emerged and water filled the great hollows which became the seas and the oceans. In this way it was possible for various species of life to come into existence on the earth.

b In the present world, man is given ease and hardship by turns. But here, neither is comfort given as a reward nor is hardship imposed as a punishment. The purpose of both is to put human beings to the test. This world is a great examination hall. The purpose of whatever happens to man here is to see what sort of responses he offers to different testing conditions.

call on whom you can besides God, to help you.' ¹⁴ But if they do not respond to you, then know that this [Quran] is sent down with God's knowledge and that there is no deity but Him. Will you then surrender yourselves to Him?

¹⁵ Those who desire the life of this world and all its finery shall be repaid in full in this life for their deeds—nothing shall be denied them. ¹⁶ These are the people who, in the world to come, shall have nothing but Hellfire and all that they used to do shall be in vain.

¹⁷ Can they be compared to those who possess a clear proof from their Lord, followed up by a witness from Him, preceded by the Book of Moses, as a guide and a mercy? These people believe in it; whereas those groups that deny its truth are promised the Fire. Therefore, have no doubt about it. It is the truth from your Lord, but most people do not believe it.

¹⁸ Who does greater wrong than the one who fabricates a lie against God? Such people shall be brought before their Lord, and the witnesses will say, 'These are the ones who lied about their Lord.' Surely God's rejection is merited by such wrongdoers. ¹⁹ Such as those who turn others away from the path of God and seek to make it appear crooked: these are the ones who deny the Hereafter. ²⁰ They can never frustrate God on earth, nor have they any protectors besides God. They will be subjected to double punishment, for they could neither hear nor see. ²¹ It is such as these who have ruined their souls, and that which they fabricated shall fail them. ²² In the Hereafter, it is they who shall be the greatest losers.[a]

²³ Those who have believed and done good deeds and humbled themselves before their Lord are destined for Paradise, and they will live in it forever. ²⁴ These two groups are like the blind and the

---

a God has blessed man with fine capabilities and talents. If he utilises them, he can understand any subject in depth. In his worldly matters, he actually utilises these talents, but when it comes to the Hereafter, he becomes deaf, in spite of having ears. He becomes blind, in spite of having eyes.

Man's success depends entirely upon his sincerity. Those who are sincere in worldly matters are successful in them. Similarly, those who are sincere in matters of the Hereafter will be successful in the Hereafter.

deaf as compared with those who can see and hear. Can the two be equal? Will you not then understand?[a]

²⁵ We sent Noah to his people. He said, 'I have come to you with a clear warning: ²⁶ worship none but God. I fear lest punishment befall you on a woeful Day.' ²⁷ The leaders of his people, who refused to acknowledge the truth, said, 'We regard you only as a human being like ourselves. We do not see that anyone follows you but the lowliest of us, those of immature judgement. We see no superior merit in you; in fact we believe you are a liar.'

²⁸ He said, 'O my people, tell me: if I have clear evidence from my Lord and He has favoured me with grace from Himself, which you have been unable to recognize, can we force it on you against your will? ²⁹ O my people, I do not ask you for any money for this; my reward comes only from God. I will not drive away those who believe; they shall surely meet their Lord. Yet I see that you are a people who act out of ignorance. ³⁰ My people, who would support me against God if I were to drive them off? Will you not take heed? ³¹ I do not say to you that I possess God's treasures, or that I have knowledge of the unseen, or that I am an angel. Nor do I say concerning those upon whom you look with contempt, that God will not bestow any good upon them—God knows best what is in their hearts. If I did, I would certainly be one of the wrongdoers.'[b]

---

a Faith, humility and righteous deeds—all three are different aspects of the same reality. Faith is the conscious discovery of God and His perfect attributes. Humility is the state of the heart which necessarily develops in man as a result of the discovery of God. When man thinks in godly terms, when his heart is full of godly feelings, the natural result is that the external aspect of his life becomes moulded in the shape of godly, or righteous deeds. One who is the embodiment of Faith, humility and righteous deeds is the very person desired by God and as such will find his abode in the eternal gardens of paradise.

b The task of calling upon people to bow to God relates purely to the Hereafter. In order to ensure its success, it is absolutely necessary that there should be no disputes relating to money, land or property between the call-giver and his addressees. The missionary himself has to shoulder the responsibility of maintaining a normal atmosphere between himself and his addressees, and for that purpose, he should unilaterally put an end to all types of material and economic disputes. That preacher who, on the one hand, makes a plea for

³² 'Noah,' they replied, 'you have argued with us, and argued to excess. Now bring down upon us what you threaten us with, if you speak the truth!?' ³³ He said, 'It is God who will bring it down upon you, if He wishes, and you will not be able to escape. ³⁴ My advice will not benefit you, no matter how sincerely I want to advise you, if God lets you go astray. He is your Lord and you will all return to Him.'

³⁵ If they say, 'He has invented it himself,' say to them, 'If I have indeed invented this myself, then may I be punished for my sin; I am innocent of the crimes that you commit.'

³⁶ God's will was revealed to Noah, 'No more of your people will believe in you than those who already believe; do not grieve, therefore, over what they have been doing. ³⁷ Build the Ark under Our eyes and in accordance with Our revelation. Do not plead with Me concerning the evil-doers. They shall certainly be drowned.' ³⁸ So he began to build the Ark, and whenever leaders of his people passed by, they scoffed at him. He said, 'If you are scoffing at us, we shall scoff at you [and your ignorance], just as you scoff at us: ³⁹ you will soon come to know who will receive a humiliating punishment, and find unleashed against him an everlasting punishment.'

⁴⁰ When Our command came, and water gushed forth in torrents, We said to Noah, 'Take into the Ark a pair from every species, and your own family—except those on whom the sentence has already been passed, and all the true believers.' But only a few believed along with him. ⁴¹ Noah said, 'Embark on it. In the name of God, be its sailing and its anchoring. Truly, my Lord is forgiving and merciful.'ᵃ ⁴² The Ark sailed along with them through mountainous

---

the acceptance of Truth and, on the other, agitates and makes demands about worldly things is not a preacher in the real sense but a charlatan. He can have no value in the eyes either of his addressees or of God.

a When the Ark was ready, stormy winds started blowing at God's behest. Torrents of water started gushing out of the ground and there was continuous rainfall. So much so that there was water everywhere and all the people were drowned. The only survivors were a few human beings and some animals who had boarded Noah's Ark. Even Noah's son was drowned. In the eyes of God a man's worth is judged according to his deeds and not according to relationship,

waves. Noah called out to his son who stood apart, 'O my son! Embark with us and do not be among the deniers!' ⁴³ He replied, 'I shall seek refuge on a mountain, which will save me from the water.' Noah cried, 'Today there is no refuge for anyone from God's command except for those to whom He shows mercy!' Thereupon, a wave swept in between them, and Noah's son was among those who were drowned. ⁴⁴ A voice cried out, 'Earth, swallow up your waters. O sky, cease your rain.' The waters receded. The command was fulfilled. The Ark came to rest on Mount Judi. It was said, 'Away with the wrong-doing people.'ᵃ

⁴⁵ Noah called out to his Lord, saying, 'My Lord, my son was a part of my family. Your promise was surely true. You are the most just of all judges.' ⁴⁶ God said, 'Noah, he was not one of your family. For, indeed, he was unrighteous in his conduct. Do not question Me about something of which you have no knowledge; I admonish you lest you become like an ignorant man.' ⁴⁷ He said, 'My Lord, I take refuge with You from asking You something of which I have no knowledge. If You do not forgive me and show me mercy, I shall be one of the losers.'ᵇ

⁴⁸ God said, 'Noah, go ashore in peace; Our blessings upon you and upon the people who are with you and upon some of the descendants of those who are with you. [As for the unrighteous] We shall grant provision for a time, then a grievous punishment from Us shall afflict them.' ⁴⁹ These are tidings of the unseen that We

---

even if the relationship is with a prophet.

a The system of 'cause and effect' in this world is only a veil; otherwise, whatever is happening does so by the direct orders of God. It is the test of a human being that he should be able to tear asunder the outward veil and see the reality; he should discover the divine godly powers working behind the screen of cause and effect.

b In this world, ancestral relationship are of great importance, unlike, in the Hereafter, where moral relationships outweigh all else. Noah's flood had occurred in order that all divisions of human beings other than moral ones be abolished, and all doers of righteous deeds be saved by accommodating them in the Divine Ark, while the unrighteous were consigned to the merciless waves. There will be a repetition of such an event on Doomsday, only on a larger scale and to a greater degree of perfection.

reveal to you, [O Prophet], which you did not know before, nor did your people, so be patient: the future belongs to the God-fearing.*a*

⁵⁰ To 'Ad We sent their brother Hud. He said, 'O my people, worship God alone; you have no god but Him. You do nothing but fabricate lies. ⁵¹ I ask of you nothing in return for this [Message]. My recompense is with Him who has created me. Why do you not use your reason? ⁵² My people, seek forgiveness of your Lord and turn to Him in repentance. He will send from the sky abundant rain upon you; He will add strength to your strength. Do not turn away from Him as evil-doers.'

⁵³ They replied, 'Hud, you have not brought us any clear evidence and we shall not forsake our deities merely at your behest, nor will we believe in you. ⁵⁴ We can only say that some of our gods have stricken you with evil.' He said, 'I call God to witness, and you also bear witness, that I disown those which you associate [with God], ⁵⁵ instead of Him. So scheme against me, all of you together, and then grant me no respite. ⁵⁶ I have put my trust in God, my Lord and your Lord. For there is no living creature which He does not hold by its forelock. My Lord is on the straight path.*b*

⁵⁷ 'If you turn away, I have conveyed to you the message with which

---

a The history of Noah teaches the lesson that lovers of falsehood may appear to be all-powerful and they may be very long-lived, but they are nevertheless destined to face destruction. On the contrary, men of Faith may be very few in number and may appear to be quite powerless, but by God's will, these are the very people who will ultimately share His grace in the present world, in the beginning and, finally, in the Hereafter.

b In the light of these verses, the straight path shown by Hud comprises the following: belief in the unity of God, worship of God, seeking God's pardon, repentance, turning towards God (*tawbah*), gratitude for God's grace, placing trust in God, treating God as our Sustainer, treating God as the only possessor of all power, accepting God's watchfulness over oneself, and remaining humble. All these are the basic teachings of religion. Following these teachings and making them the centre of one's attention amounts to treading the highway of religion. One who treads this path straightaway reaches God. On the contrary, if a man gives importance to other things, it is as if he is taking the side paths to the right or the left of the highway and hastening along them. Such a course takes a man away from God, not closer to God.

I was sent. My Lord will make another people your successors and you cannot harm Him in the least. For my Lord is guardian over all things.' [58] When Our command came, We delivered Hud and those who believed with him by Our special mercy. We saved them from a severe punishment. [59] Such were the 'Ad who denied the signs of their Lord and disobeyed His messengers and followed the bidding of every headstrong enemy of truth. [60] They were pursued by a curse in this world as they will be on the Day of Resurrection. Indeed, the 'Ad denied their Lord. So away with the 'Ad, the people of Hud![a]

[61] To the Thamud We sent their brother Salih. He said, 'My people, worship God! You have no god but Him. It was He who brought you into being from the earth and settled you upon it and so ask His forgiveness. Turn to Him in repentance. My Lord is near and responsive.' [62] They said, 'O Salih! We had great hopes in you. Do you forbid us to worship what our fathers worshipped? We are in grave doubt, amounting to suspicion, concerning that to which you call us.' [63] He said, 'O my people, tell me: if I have clear evidence from my Lord, and He has granted His mercy, who then will support me against God, if I disobey Him? You would only make my loss greater.

[64] My people! This she-camel of God is a sign for you. So leave her alone to graze on God's earth. And do her no harm, lest you should be instantly afflicted with a torment.' [65] But they hamstrung her. He [Salih] said, 'Enjoy yourselves in your homes for three more days. This warning will not prove false.' [66] Then when Our command came by Our grace, We saved Salih and those who believed along with him from the disgrace of that day. Surely, your Lord is powerful and mighty. [67] The wrongdoers were overtaken by a dreadful blast

---

a God has introduced the principle of succession (*istikhlaf*) in this world, that is, the removal of a community from its position of prominence and the installing of another community in its place. This temporary prominence in the world is for the purpose of putting people to the test. In the Hereafter, in the perfect world of God, such prominence will be granted only to people of true Faith as an everlasting reward.

and they lay dead in their homes, [68] as if they had never dwelt there. The Thamud denied their Lord; cursed are the tribe of Thamud.[a]

[69] Our messengers came to Abraham with good news and greeted him with, 'Peace.' He too said, 'Peace be on you,' and hastened to bring a roasted calf. [70] But when he saw that they made no move to eat,[b] he found this strange and became afraid of them. They said, 'Do not be afraid, for we have been sent to the people of Lot.' [71] His wife, who was standing nearby, laughed when We gave her the good news of Isaac, and after Isaac, Jacob. [72] She said, 'Alas! Shall I bear a child in this old age, while my husband here is also old? This is indeed a strange thing!' [73] They said, 'Are you astonished at God's command? May the mercy of God and His blessings be upon you, O people of this house. Surely, He is praiseworthy and glorious.'

[74] When the fear had left Abraham, and the glad tidings had been conveyed to him, he began to plead with Us for Lot's people, [75] for Abraham was forbearing, tender-hearted and oft-returning to God. [76] We said, 'Abraham, cease your pleading: the command of

---

a When Salih's community were not ready to bow to his word, at their demand a tangible miracle was performed as a final sign. This was a she-camel which came out of a solid rock before their very eyes. It is the law of God that the appearance of such a sign indicates that the period of testing is coming to an end. Salih thereupon announced that they should repent and accept his word: otherwise all of them would be destroyed. But those who are not impressed by theoretical arguments, fail to learn a lesson even from tangible signs. So, even then, Salih's community did not refrain from arrogance and they even went to the extent of slaying the she-camel. Thereafter, there being no question of any further respite for them, Salih was commanded to leave his community which, at that time, was settled in Western Arabia. Accompanied by his sincere companions, he therefore left for Syria. Subsequently, a horrible earthquake swallowed up the entire community, killing everyone.

b One person should certainly pray for another; in every period, prophets and righteous people have prayed for others. But this is, in fact, an expression of the forbearance, kind-heartedness and the inclination towards God of the person who prays. A servant of God has fear of God at heart, starts trembling when he sees God's punishment, and starts praying for himself and for others. However, prayer by others will be effective only when the affected person himself fears God and invokes His grace.

your Lord has gone forth. There shall fall upon them a punishment which none can avert!'

⁷⁷ When Our messengers came to Lot, he was uneasy on this account and felt powerless to protect them. He said, 'This is a dreadful day.' ⁷⁸ His people, who were used to committing foul deeds, came running to him. He said, 'My people, here are my daughters. They are purer for you, [if you marry] so have some fear of God and do not disgrace me before my guests. Is there not a single right-minded man among you?' ⁷⁹ They replied, 'You know we have no need of your daughters. You know very well what we are seeking.'

⁸⁰ He said, 'If only I had the strength to stop you or could take refuge in some powerful support!' ⁸¹ They said, 'Lot, we are your Lord's messengers. By no means shall they reach you! So depart with your family while it is yet night and let none of you look back. But your wife will suffer the fate that befalls the others. Their appointed time is the morning: is the morning not near?' ⁸² When Our command came, We turned that town upside down and We rained upon it stones of clay, layer upon layer, ⁸³ marked for them by the decree of your Lord. The punishment of the unjust was not far off.

⁸⁴ To the people of Midian, We sent their brother Shu'ayb. He said, 'My people, worship God. You have no deity other than Him. Do not give short measure and short weight. I see you are prospering. I fear for you the punishment of a fateful Day. ⁸⁵ O my people, [always] give full measure and weight, in all fairness and do not defraud people by making short delivery, and do not spread corruption in the land. ⁸⁶ What God leaves with you is the best for you, if you are believers. I have not been appointed as your keeper.'ᵃ

---

a He said that their faith demanded that they worship the one and only God, adhere to justice and fair play in their transactions and choose for others what they liked for themselves. Every one of them had to discharge his obligations fully to others and there should be no shortcoming in this. They should live on the earth as God wanted His subjects to live, remaining contented with their legitimately gained earnings and not try to gain more through disobedience. If they did all this, they would be treated as believers in the eyes of God. Otherwise, there was the likelihood of their being smitten by God's punishment.

Prophets come for the guidance of everyone, but their words are especially

⁸⁷ They said, 'Shu'ayb, does your prayer tell you that we should abandon what our forefathers worshipped and that we should stop disposing of our belongings as we please? You are indeed the only wise and rightly-guided man!'

⁸⁸ [Shu'ayb] said, 'O my people! What do you think? If I have clear evidence from my Lord, and He has sustained me with fair sustenance from Himself [should I not guide you?]. I have no desire to do, out of opposition to you, what I am asking you not to do. I only want to reform you as far as I can. Nor can I succeed without God's help. In Him I have put my trust and to Him I turn. ⁸⁹ O my people, do not let your opposition to me bring upon you a fate similar to the peoples of Noah or Hud or Salih; nor is it long since the people of Lot were punished! ⁹⁰ Seek forgiveness of your Lord and turn to Him in repentance. For my Lord is indeed merciful and loving.'

⁹¹ They replied, 'Shu'ayb, we do not understand much of what you say. In fact, we see that you are powerless among us. Were it not for your clan, we would have stoned you,ᵃ for you are not strong against us.' ⁹² He said, 'My people, is my tribe mightier to you than God? You put Him behind you, turning your backs on Him! Surely, my Lord encompasses all that you do. ⁹³ My people,

---

directed towards the upper echelons of the community, as defined by their wealth and intellect, because the general public goes along with them. Mostly they follow in the footsteps of their 'great ones,' so that, the addressing of a missionary call to the elite amounts to reaching the general public also.

a The community was engrossed in obeisance to human beings whereas Shu'ayb called upon them to do obeisance to the one and only God. They were under the impression that belief in saints or great ones was enough for their salvation. But Shu'ayb's dictum was that salvation can be attained only through the performance of good deeds. The community members thought that since they considered themselves believers, they really were believers. Shu'ayb said however, that a believer was one who was so by God's assessment. In the eyes of the community *salat* (prayer) was merely a sort of ineffective formal supplement. Shu'ayb declared, on the contrary, that *salat* was a reckoner of man's life, his income and expenditure. The community thought that Faith was merely a spiritless acceptance, whereas he said that faith was that which was acquired by a live consciousness.

do what you will and so shall I. You will certainly come to know who will receive a punishment to disgrace him, and who is a liar. Wait on; I shall wait on with you.'

⁹⁴ When Our command came, We saved Shu'ayb and those who believed with him as a mercy from Ourself, while the blast overtook the wrongdoers, so that they lay dead in their homes, ⁹⁵ as though they had never dwelt therein. Oh, away with the people of Midian, just as happened with the Thamud!

⁹⁶ We sent forth Moses with Our signs and with manifest authority, ⁹⁷ to Pharaoh and his nobles. But they followed the command of Pharaoh and the command of Pharaoh was not rightly directed. ⁹⁸ He shall stand at the head of his people on the Day of Resurrection, and shall lead them into the Fire. Evil is the place to which they shall be led. ⁹⁹ A curse followed them in this world, and shall follow them on the Day of Resurrection. What a foul gift to be given!

¹⁰⁰ We relate to you such accounts of earlier towns: some of them are still standing; while others have ceased to exist; ¹⁰¹ We did not wrong them; they wronged themselves; the deities they called on besides God availed them nothing: when God's command came upon them, they only added to their ruin.

¹⁰² Such is the punishment of your Lord when He seizes the towns in the midst of their sins: His punishing grip is terrible and severe. ¹⁰³ In that is a sign for him who fears the punishment of the Hereafter. That is a Day for which mankind shall be gathered together, a Day when all will be present. ¹⁰⁴ We will only postpone it until a predetermined time, ¹⁰⁵ and when that Day arrives, no soul shall speak but by His leave. Among those some shall be damned, and others shall be blessed.

¹⁰⁶ The wretched ones will be in the Fire sighing and groaning, ¹⁰⁷ remaining in it timelessly, for ever, as long as the heavens and earth endure, except as your Lord wills. Your Lord carries out whatever He wills. ¹⁰⁸ Those who are blessed shall abide in the Garden; they will dwell therein as long as the heavens and the earth endure, except as your Lord wills. Such bounty shall be unending. ¹⁰⁹ Have no doubt as to what they worship. They worship nothing

but what their fathers worshipped before [them]. We shall certainly give them their share in full, without diminishing anything.

¹¹⁰ We certainly gave the Book to Moses, but differences arose about it: had it not been that a word had gone forth before from your Lord, Judgement would indeed have been passed on them: yet they are in grave doubt about it. ¹¹¹ Your Lord will reward each one of them in full for their deeds. He is well-aware of all their actions.

¹¹² Therefore stand firm [in the straight path] as you are commanded, along with those who have turned to God with you, and do not exceed the bounds, for He sees everything you do. ¹¹³ Do not incline toward those who do wrong, lest the Fire touch you. For [then] you would have none to protect you from God, and you will not be helped. ¹¹⁴ Say your prayers morning and evening, and during parts of the night; surely good makes amends for evil. This is a reminder for people who pay heed. ¹¹⁵ Be steadfast; for surely, God does not let the wages of the righteous be wasted.

¹¹⁶ Why, then, were there not among the generations before you upright men who would speak out against the [spread of] corruption on earth—except for the few whom We saved? But the wrongdoers pursued their worldly pleasures and thus became guilty. ¹¹⁷ Your Lord would never unjustly destroy communities while their people were trying to reform.

¹¹⁸ If your Lord had wished, He would have made mankind into one community. As it is, they will not cease to dispute,—¹¹⁹ and to this end He has created them [all], except for those to whom your Lord has shown mercy. The word of your Lord shall be fulfilled, 'I will fill Hell with jinn and men all together.'

¹²⁰ We have told you the stories of the prophets to make your heart firm and in these accounts truth has come to you, with an exhortation and a reminder for the believers. ¹²¹ Say to those who do not believe, 'You do things in your way and we are doing things in our way, ¹²² and wait, we too are waiting.' ¹²³ The knowledge of the secret of the heavens and the earth belongs to God alone, and to Him shall

all affairs be referred. So worship Him and put your trust in Him alone. Your Lord is not unaware of what you do.[a]

12. JOSEPH (*YUSUF*)

In the name of God, the Most Gracious, the Most Merciful

[1] *Alif Lam Ra*

These are verses from the clear Book. [2] We have sent down the Quran in Arabic, so that you may understand. [3] We recount to you the best of narratives in revealing this Quran to you, even though you were unaware of it before it came.[b]

---

a In our world, there are innumerable creatures besides human beings. All these creatures follow the one fixed path of nature at all times. Similarly, God could have created human beings as compulsory followers of the straight path too. But this is in no way God's scheme with regard to human beings. God's plan was that they would be so created that they should, of their own accord, be able independently to make correct moral choices. The difference in the world of human beings (i.e. some of them adopting one way and others adopting another way) is, in fact, due to this special plan of God.

This plan was certainly a risky one, because it meant that many people had the opportunity to misuse their freedom and thus make themselves liable to be cast into hell. But, with the help of this very plan, such noble souls could be chosen as could be treated as deserving the special grace of God. God has blessed the entire universe with His bounties. Now, God devised this plan so that he might give His creatures the benefit of His grace, saying, 'You are entitled to this.'

God's grace will be granted to that person whose consciousness is so alert that he recognizes in the power given to him by way of testing him his real powerlessness. Such a person will be able to see through the veil of human power and have a glimpse of God's power behind it. Such perceptiveness takes away the capacity for arrogance in a man. So much so that, when God grants him His Grace saying, 'This is your entitlement,' in his awareness of reality he cries out, 'O God! This is also a manifestation of your grace, otherwise my deeds have no value.'

b In this chapter, people of Faith are told, by means of a prophet's story, that God is all-powerful. He helps those who come forward to promote the cause of Truth, finally making them successful in spite of the intrigues of opponents, on

⁴ When Joseph told his father, 'My father, I dreamt of eleven stars, and the sun and moon: I saw them prostrate themselves before me,' ⁵ he replied, 'My son, do not relate your dream to your brothers, lest they plot evil against you—Satan is the sworn enemy of man.*a* ⁶ You shall be chosen by your Lord and He will impart to you some understanding of the inner meaning of events. He will bestow the full measure of His blessings upon you and upon the House of Jacob—even as He formerly bestowed it in full measure upon your forefathers, Abraham and Isaac. Truly, your Sustainer is all-knowing and wise!'

⁷ Surely, in Joseph and his brothers there are signs for the inquirers. ⁸ They said [to each other], 'Surely Joseph and his brother [Benjamin] are dearer to our father than ourselves, although we are a band. Truly, our father is clearly mistaken. ⁹ Therefore, let us put Joseph to death or cast him away to some [far-off] land, so that our father's attention should turn only to us, and you can thereafter become a righteous people.' ¹⁰ One of them said, 'Do not kill Joseph, but if you must do something, cast him into the bottom of a well; some of the travellers will pick him up.'

¹¹ They said to their father, 'Why do you not trust us with Joseph? We are indeed his well-wishers. ¹² Send him with us tomorrow, so that he may play and enjoy himself. We will look after him.' ¹³ [Jacob] said, 'It would indeed grieve me if you took him away with you, and I fear lest the wolf should devour him while you are

---

the condition that the people should be God-fearing and should have the quality of patience; they should have the fear of God in their hearts and regardless of the circumstances, should persevere on the path of Truth.

a According to a hadith of the Prophet Muhammad, there are three kinds of dreams—those of wish fulfilment, fear of Satan and good tidings from God. A common man's dream may be of any of these kinds, but a Prophet's dream is always from God. Sometimes it is direct in meaning and sometimes it is purely symbolic.

Feeling jealous of a person on account of his greatness shows an evil nature. One who has this trait in him ought to turn to God in repentance, because this is a proof that he is not reconciled to God's will; he is following the lead of Satan rather than God's guidance.

off your guard.' ¹⁴ They said, 'Surely, if the wolf devoured him while we were a strong party, we should indeed be great losers.'

¹⁵ And so, when they went away with him, they decided to cast him into the dark depths of a well. Then We revealed to him Our will, 'You shall [one day] tell them of this deed of theirs, when they do not realize who you are.' ¹⁶ And at nightfall they came to their father, weeping. ¹⁷ They said, 'Father, we went off racing and left Joseph with our belongings, and the wolf devoured him. But you will not believe us, even though we are telling the truth.' ¹⁸ And they showed him their brother's shirt, stained with false blood. 'No!' he cried. 'Your souls have tempted you to do something evil! But it is best to be patient: God alone can help me bear the loss you speak of.'^{*a*}

¹⁹ And there came a caravan of travellers and they sent their water-drawer to draw water from the well. He let down his bucket into the well and he exclaimed, 'Oh, what a lucky find, here is a boy!' They hid him like a piece of merchandise, but God knew well what they did. ²⁰ Later they sold him for a paltry sum, a few pieces of silver [dirhams]: So little did they value him.^{*b*}

²¹ The Egyptian who bought him said to his wife, 'Lodge him honourably, he may prove of benefit to us, or we may even adopt him as our son.' Thus We established Joseph in the land, so that We might teach him the true meaning of events. God has power over all things. However, most people do not know this. ²² And

---

a What Joseph's brothers did was an act of extreme provocation. Unlike them, Joseph entrusted his fate to God and, sitting quietly in the dry well at a deserted place, waited for God's help to arrive. Joseph's father, Jacob, for his part, took the course of noble patience. According to some commentaries he is reported to have told his sons that had a wolf devoured Joseph, it would certainly have torn his shirt. He meant, what a noble wolf it was who took away Joseph and removed his blood-stained shirt to hand it over to them undamaged.

b Joseph's brothers exiled him and pushed him into a well. The people of the caravan had sold him as a slave. Thereafter the wife of a highly-placed officer of Egypt (Zulaykha) had him imprisoned. But God Almighty made all these stages stepping stones of honour and glory for him. What a tremendous difference there is between human knowledge and the divine knowledge of God!

when he reached maturity, We bestowed on him right judgement and knowledge. Thus We reward those who do good.*ᵃ*

²³ However, the woman in whose house he lived, wanted to seduce him. One day she bolted the doors and said, 'Come!' He replied, 'God forbid! Truly [your husband] is my master and has treated me honourably. Wrongdoers certainly never prosper.' ²⁴ She started towards him, and he would have succumbed to her, if he had not seen a sign from his Lord—We did this in order to keep evil and indecency away from him, for he was truly one of Our chosen servants.

²⁵ They both ran to the door and, in the struggle, she tore his shirt at the back. They found her husband at the door. She cried, 'Shall not the man who wished to violate your wife be thrown into prison or sternly punished?' ²⁶ Joseph said, 'It was she who sought to seduce me.' One of her household testified, 'If his shirt is torn at the front then she is speaking the truth, and he is lying. ²⁷ But if it is torn from behind then she is lying, and he speaks the truth.' ²⁸ So when he saw his shirt torn from behind [her husband] said, 'This is the guile of you women. Your guile is great indeed. ²⁹ Joseph, overlook this: but you [wife], ask forgiveness for your sin, for you have done wrong.'*ᵇ*

---

a When Joseph was about forty years old, God blessed him with prophethood on the one hand and with power and authority on the other. He received this reward owing to his righteous deeds. The door of God's blessings is always open for righteous people! The only difference is that during the age of prophethood, a deserving person could have been given prophethood as a result of his righteous deeds but, in later periods, (after the Prophet Muhammad, the last messenger of God) he may receive all bounties except that of prophethood.

b Zulaykha, the wife of the nobleman, was charmed by the beauty of Joseph. She constantly tried to seduce him and one day, finding the opportunity, she closed the door of the room. This was a very critical occasion for an unmarried youth, but Joseph had preserved his godly nature and this nature came to his rescue on this occasion. The capacity to distinguish between truth and untruth, right and wrong, is ingrained in every human being by birth and this serves as a warning on all such occasions. To ignore it amounts to ignoring the voice of God. One who does so is deprived of God's succour so that his moral strength gradually ebbs away. On the contrary, one who immediately

³⁰ Women in the town began to gossip, 'The nobleman's wife is trying to seduce her slave! Love for him consumes her heart! Indeed! We see her in manifest error.' ³¹ When she heard of their intrigues, she sent for them and prepared a party for them. She gave a knife to each of them [to cut fruits, etc.] and then asked Joseph to appear before them. When the women saw him, they were greatly amazed [at his beauty], and they cut their hands, exclaiming, 'God preserve us! This is no human being but a noble angel!' ³² She said, 'This is he about whom you have been blaming me! And, indeed, I did try to make him yield to me, but he was unyielding. Now, however, if he does not do as I bid him, he shall certainly be put in prison and be humiliated.' ³³ Joseph said, 'O my Lord! I would prefer prison to what these women are inviting me to do. And if You do not avert their guile from me, I may yield to them and so become one of the ignorant.' ³⁴ So his Lord answered him and warded off their guile. He is All Hearing and All Knowing.

³⁵ Yet, even after all the evidence they had seen, they thought it right to jail him for a time. ³⁶ Two young men entered the prison along with him. One of them said, 'I saw myself [in a dream] I was pressing wine.' The other said, 'I dreamed I was carrying bread on my head from which the birds were eating. Tell us their meaning; for we see that you are one who does good [to all].'

³⁷ Joseph said to them, 'I shall inform you of the interpretation of your dreams before your meal is brought to you. This is a part of the knowledge that my Lord has taught me. I have renounced the religion of the people who do not believe in God and who deny

bows down before the divine call, as soon as it is given, can count on God's help; this improves his moral fibre and on future occasions he becomes stronger in the face of evil.

What prevented Joseph from indulging in evil was in fact the fear of God but, at that time, invoking God before Zulaykha would have been ineffective. This was not an occasion for a declaration of Truth but an occasion when he had to save himself in a critical situation. In view of this situation he referred to Zulaykha's husband. He said that 'her husband was his master and he had maintained him in his house with due honour. Therefore, it was not possible for him to besmirch the honour of his benefactor.'

the Hereafter. [38] I follow the religion of my fathers, Abraham, Isaac and Jacob; and it is not for us to associate anyone with God as a partner. This is of God's grace upon us and upon mankind; even though most men are not grateful. [39] O my two fellow-prisoners! Are many diverse lords better, or God, the One, the Almighty? [40] All those you worship instead of Him are mere names you and your forefathers have invented, names for which God has sent down no authority: all power belongs to God alone, and He orders you to worship none but Him: this is the true faith, though most people do not realize it.

[41] O my two fellow-prisoners, one of you will serve wine to his lord, the other of you will be crucified and birds will feed off his head. The matter about which you have been seeking my opinion has been so decreed.' [42] He said to the one he thought would be saved, 'Mention me to your master.' However Satan made him forget to mention him to his master, and so Joseph remained in prison for a number of years.

[43] The king said, 'I saw [in a dream] seven fat cows which seven lean ones were eating, also seven green ears of corn and seven others which were dry. Tell me the meaning of this vision, my nobles, if you can interpret visions.' [44] They said, 'These are confusing dreams and we do not know the interpretation of such dreams.' [45] Then one of the two men who had been released and who, after a long time, remembered, said, 'I shall tell you its interpretation; therefore, give me leave to go [to Joseph in prison].'

[46] 'O truthful Joseph!' he said, 'Tell us the meaning of a dream in which seven fat cows are being eaten by seven lean ones, and there are seven green ears of corn and seven others which are dry, so that I may return to my people and inform them.' [47] Joseph said, 'You shall sow for seven consecutive years as usual, but leave in the ear the harvest that you reap, except for a little which you may eat. [48] Then there will follow seven years of great hardship which will consume all but a little of what you stored. [49] Then a year will come after that when people will have abundant rain and when once more they will press [wine and oil].'

[50] The king said, 'Bring him to me.' When the king's messenger

came to Joseph, he said, 'Go back to your master and ask him about the women who cut their hands: my Lord knows well their guile.' [51] The king asked the women, 'What was the truth of the affair in which you tried to seduce Joseph?' The women said, 'God forbid! We know no evil of him.' The wife of the nobleman said, 'The truth has now come to light. It was I who tried to seduce him; he is surely an honest man.'[a]

[52] 'From this,' said Joseph, '[The nobleman] should know that I did not betray him in his absence, and that God does not guide the plotting of the treacherous. [53] I am not trying to absolve myself: for man's very soul incites him to evil unless my Lord bestows His mercy. Indeed, my Lord is forgiving and merciful.'

[54] The king said, 'Bring him to me. I will take him for my special service.' And when he had spoken to him, he said, 'From now on you will dwell with us, honoured and trusted.' [55] Joseph said, 'Place in my charge the storehouses of the land; for I am a good and knowledgeable custodian.' [56] Thus We caused Joseph to be established in a position of authority in the land. He could dwell therein wherever he pleased. We bestow Our mercy on whomever We please, and We do not allow the reward of the righteous to go to waste. [57] Yet the reward of the hereafter is best for those who believe and are mindful of God.

[58] Joseph's brothers arrived and presented themselves before him. He recognized them, but they did not know him. [59] When he had made provision for them, he told them, 'Bring me your brother on your father's side. Do you not see that I give you full measure and that I am the best of hosts? [60] But if you do not bring him to me, you shall have no grain from me, nor shall you ever approach me

---

a After hearing the whole history of Joseph's imprisonment, the king made inquiries of the concerned women. All of them unanimously declared him to be innocent. The wife of the nobleman of Egypt (Zulaykha) did not spare herself in the admission of truth. She declared in clear terms that they were telling the truth. She said that she had been entirely to blame in this matter and that Joseph was totally innocent. This admission on the part of the wife of the nobleman was such a noble action that it would not have been surprising if she had been guided towards the true faith thereafter.

again.' [61] They replied, 'We shall try to persuade his father to send him with us. We shall do [our utmost]!'

[62] Joseph said to his servants, 'Put their money back into their saddlebags, so that they will recognize it when they return home to their family; thus they may come back.' [63] When they returned to their father, they said, 'Our father, any [further] measure of grain has been denied us, so send our brother [Benjamin] along with us, so that we may obtain our measure [of grain]; and, we shall guard him well.' [64] He replied, 'Am I to trust you with him as I once trusted you with his brother? But God is the best of guardians, the Most Merciful of all.'

[65] When they opened their packs, they discovered that their money had been returned to them. They said, 'Our father, what more do we desire than this? This money of ours has been returned to us, so we shall [again] buy food for our family and we shall guard our brother, and we shall obtain an additional camel-load of grain. This [that we bring now] is a small quantity.' [66] He [Jacob] said, 'I will never send him with you until you give me a solemn pledge, before God, that you will indeed bring him back to me, unless you yourselves are trapped [in a compulsive situation].' And when they had given him their solemn pledge, [Jacob] said, 'God shall be witness to all that we say.'

[67] 'O my sons! Do not all of you enter [the city] by one gate; enter by separate gates. I cannot help you in any way against God; judgement is His alone. In Him I have put my trust. In Him let the faithful put their trust.' [68] They entered [safely] as their father had told them. However, he had no power to guard them against God's decree. It was only a wish in Jacob's soul which he had thus fulfilled. He was possessed of knowledge which We had given him. But most people have no knowledge.

[69] When they presented themselves before Joseph, he took his brother [Benjamin] aside. He said, 'I am your brother, so do not feel distressed about whatever they have been doing.' [70] And when he had given them their provisions, he placed a drinking-cup in his brother's pack. Then a crier called out after them, 'Men of the caravan! You have committed theft!' [71] They said, turning towards

him, 'What is it that you have lost?' [72] 'We miss the royal measuring bowl,' he replied. 'He who brings it shall have a camel-load of corn. I pledge my word for it.' [73] They said, 'By God, you [ought to] know we have not come here to cause any trouble in the land. We are not thieves!' [74] The Egyptians asked them, 'And if we find that you are lying, what penalty shall we mete out to you?' [75] They replied, 'The penalty should be that he in whose saddlebag it is found, should be held [as bondman] to atone for the crime. That is how we punish the wrongdoers.' [76] He [the herald] searched their bags before his brother's and then took out the cup from his brother's bag.[a] In this way, We devised a plan on behalf of Joseph. He could not have detained his brother under the King's law, unless God so willed. We exalt whoever We please: but above those who have knowledge there is One all knowing.

[77] They said, 'If he is a thief, a brother of his had [also] committed theft before him.' But Joseph kept his secret and revealed nothing to them. He said [to himself], 'Your deed was worse. God best knows the things you speak of.' [78] They said, 'O exalted one, he has a very aged father, take one of us in his place. We can see that you are a very good man.' [79] He replied, 'God forbid that we should take anyone other than the person on whom we found our property. In that case, we would clearly be wrongdoers.'

---

a Joseph did not want his younger brother to depart. When Benjamin's packs were being readied, Joseph put his drinking cup in his younger brother's packs. This was no malicious subterfuge on the part of Joseph, but was done out of great affection for his younger brother. Previously Joseph had done something similar when he put all the money which they had brought to buy grain in his brothers' packs. In the meantime, the weighing bowl of the king had been misplaced and the courtiers suspected Joseph's brothers of stealing it. When they opened their packs, they found Joseph's drinking cup in Benjamin's bag. This was not the cup they were looking for, but it was a similar one. The difference in these two cups can be understood by the two different words used for them in the Quran. The drinking cup belonging to Joseph is called *siqayah*, while the royal measuring bowl is called *suwa'* (verse 72). The cup which was recovered from Benjamin's bag was a *siqayah* not a *suwa'*, as a feminine pronoun, '*ha*' (*istakhrajaha*) used for the cup here refers to the drinking cup of Joseph, and not the lost measuring bowl of the king.

[80] When they had lost all hope of [persuading] him, they withdrew, conferring among themselves. The eldest said, 'Do you not know that your father took from you a pledge in God's name. You have already failed with regard to Joseph, so I shall never leave the land until my father permits me to, or God decides [things] for me. He is the best judge! [81] Return to your father and say, "Father, your son has committed a theft. We testify only to what we know. How could we guard against the unforeseen? [82] Inquire of [the people of] the city where we lodged, and of the caravan with which we travelled. We are telling you the truth."'

[83] Jacob said, 'No, but you have yourselves contrived a story. But it is best to be patient. God may well bring them all back to me [in the end]. For He is indeed full of knowledge and wisdom.' [84] And he turned away from them, crying, 'Alas for Joseph!' His eyes went white with grief, and he was filled with sorrow. [85] They said, 'By God, will you keep on remembering Joseph until your health is ruined, and you die?' [86] He said 'I only complain of my anguish and my sorrow to God. God has made known to me things that you do not know. [87] Go, my sons, and seek news of Joseph and his brother. Do not despair of God's mercy; none but those who deny the truth despair of God's mercy.'

[88] When his brothers presented themselves before Joseph, they pleaded, 'Exalted one, distress has afflicted us and our family and we have brought only a paltry sum; but give us full measure. Be charitable to us. Truly, God rewards the charitable.' [89] He said, 'Are you aware of what you did to Joseph and his brother in ignorance?' [90] They exclaimed, 'Are you indeed Joseph?' He replied, 'I am Joseph and this is my brother. God has indeed been gracious to us. The truth is that God does not waste the reward of those who do good, who are righteous and steadfast.'[a]

---

a 'God does not waste the reward of those who do good, who are righteous and steadfast'. This is the moral lesson and substance of the whole story of Joseph. Almighty God wanted to set a clear example showing that one who adopts the God-fearing way in his worldly dealings and who avoids the ways of impatience will ultimately achieve success with His help. Joseph's story was made a tangible example of this reality.

[91] [The brothers] said, 'By God! Most certainly God has raised you high above us, and we have indeed been guilty!' [92] He said, 'No blame [shall fall] on you this day; may God forgive you! And He is the Most Merciful of those who show mercy. [93] Go with this shirt of mine and cast it upon my father's face. He will recover his sight; thereupon come [back] to me with all your family.'[a]

[94] When the caravan set out from Egypt, their father [in Canaan] said, 'You may think I am senile, but I certainly perceive the breath of Joseph.' [95] They said, 'By God, you still persist in your illusions!' [96] But when the bearer of the good news arrived and cast the shirt on Jacob's face, his eyesight returned and he said, 'Did I not tell you that I know from God what you do not know?' [97] They said, 'O our father! Ask forgiveness for our sins—we were truly in the wrong.' [98] He said, 'I shall certainly ask my Lord to forgive you. Surely, He is the Most Forgiving and Merciful.'

[99] Then, when they presented themselves before Joseph, he drew his parents to him and said, 'Welcome to Egypt, in safety, if God wills!' [100] He helped his parents to a couch and they all fell down on their knees before him. He said, 'My father, this is the interpretation of my dream. My Lord has made it come true! He was kind to me when He let me out of prison and brought you from the desert after Satan had brought about discord between me and my brethren. My Lord is the best planner in achieving what He will; He is All Knowing, and Truly Wise.'

[101] Then Joseph prayed, 'My Lord, You have given me power and taught me the interpretation of dreams. Creator of the heavens and the earth, You are my patron in this world and the Hereafter! Make me die in submission to You and admit me among the righteous.'[b]

---

a When the truth came out into the open, Joseph's brothers acknowledged Joseph's greatness and freely admitted their guilt. In the same way, Joseph also showed such broadmindedness as a true God-worshipper is expected to show on such occasions. He did not condemn his brothers. He completely forgot and forgave the bitter experiences of the past and once again entered into fraternal relations with his brothers.

b His sense of the majesty of God had obliterated all feelings of personal superiority. Even on reaching the zenith of worldly glory, he uttered these

¹⁰² These are tidings of the unseen that We reveal to you, [O Prophet], though you were not present with them when they plotted and agreed upon a plan. ¹⁰³ Yet most men will not become believers, no matter how eager you may be. ¹⁰⁴ You shall not ask them for any reward for this. It is but a reminder for all mankind.

¹⁰⁵ And there are many signs in the heavens and the earth that they pass by and give no heed to—¹⁰⁶ and most of them, even when they profess belief in God, attribute partners to Him. ¹⁰⁷ Do they feel secure that the all-encompassing punishment of God will not come upon them, or that the Last Hour will not come upon them suddenly when they least expect it? ¹⁰⁸ Say, 'This is my way; on the basis of sure knowledge, I call on you to have faith in God, I and those who follow me. God is Holy; I am not one of those who associate partners with God.'

¹⁰⁹ All the messengers We sent before you [Muhammad] were human beings to whom We made revelations; they were men chosen from the people of their towns. Did they not travel across the earth and see the end of those before them? Those who are mindful of God prefer the life to come. Will you not then understand? ¹¹⁰ When the messengers lost all hopes and thought that they had been told lies, Our help came to them: We saved whoever We pleased, but Our punishment will not be averted from the guilty.

¹¹¹ In their stories there is a lesson for men of understanding. This [Quran] is no invented tale, but a confirmation of the previous [scripture] and a detailed explanation of all things as well as guidance and mercy to true believers.

---

words, 'O, God! Your being is all-powerful. It is You who fulfill all my needs. Kindly help me in the world as well as in the Hereafter. Include me among those people who have had the inspiration to submit to Your will in the world and in the Hereafter and are worthy of Your eternal reward.'

13. THUNDER (*AL-RA'D*)

In the name of God, the Most Gracious, the Most Merciful

¹ *Alif Lam Mim Ra*

These are the verses of the Book. What is sent down to you from your Lord is the truth, yet most men do not believe in it. ² It was God who raised the heavens with no visible supports, and then established Himself on the throne; He has regulated the sun and the moon, so that each will pursue its course for an appointed time; He ordains all things and makes plain His revelations, so that you may be certain of meeting your Lord; ³ it was He who spread out the earth and placed upon it mountains and rivers, and fruits of every kind in male and female pairs. He drew the veil of night over the day. In all this, truly, there are signs for people who reflect.

⁴ On the earth are diverse tracts, adjoining one another: vineyards and cornfields and groves of palm, the single and the clustered. Their fruits are nourished by the same water; yet We make the taste of some excel that of others. In this also are signs for people who understand.

⁵ If anything can astonish you, you should surely be astonished at their asking, 'What? When we become dust, shall we be created anew?' These are the ones who deny their Lord: around their necks there shall be fetters. They are the inheritors of the Fire, and shall abide therein forever.

⁶ They demand that you hasten on the evil rather than the good, although there have been many examples of punishment before them—your Lord is full of forgiveness for mankind, despite their wrongdoings, but He is truly severe in punishment.

⁷ Those who deny the truth ask, 'Why has no sign been sent down to him by His Lord?' But you are only a warner; every people has its guide.

⁸ God knows what every female bears. He knows of every change within the womb. For everything He has a proper measure; ⁹ He is the knower of the unseen and the visible, the Great, the Most-

Exalted. [10] It makes no difference whether you converse in secret or aloud, whether you hide under the cloak of night or walk about freely in the light of day.

[11] Each has guardian angels before him and behind him, who watch him at God's command. God does not change the condition of a people's lot, unless they change what is in their hearts. But when God decrees punishment for a people, none can ward it off. Besides Him, they have no protector.

[12] It is He who shows you the lightning, inspiring fear and hope, and gathers up the heavy clouds; [13] and the thunder glorifies Him with His praise and the angels do so too in awe of Him, and He sends His thunderbolts to strike anyone He pleases, yet they dispute about God, who is inexorable in His power.

[14] The only true appeal is to God alone; those they appeal to instead of Him will never respond to them in any way. They are like a man who stretches forth his hands toward the water, so that it may reach his mouth, but it never does. The calls of those who deny the truth are all in vain.[a]

[15] All who dwell in heavens and on the earth submit to God alone, willingly or unwillingly, as do their shadows in the mornings and in the evenings. [16] Say, 'Who is Lord of the heavens and the earth?' Say, 'God.' Say, 'Why do you take protectors other than Him, who can neither benefit nor harm even themselves?' Say, 'Are the blind and the seeing equal? Is darkness equal to the light? Or have they assigned partners to God who create as He creates, so that both

---

a If you spread your hands and call upon the ocean, it will never happen that it responds to your call and its waters come out of the depths to quench your thirst and irrigate your fields and gardens. But by the laws of nature the waters of that same ocean rise into space, leaving behind the salt. Then under the influence of heat, gravitational pull and the blowing winds, it spreads over town and country and pours down in the shape of fresh, sweet water and irrigates the land. This shows that the ocean, in spite of being gigantic, is really helpless. It has no innate power either to act on its own, or to respond to another's call.

This is the condition of all the things of this world. As such, the wise person is one who worships the Creator and not the creations—one who concentrates on the Lord of the things and not on the things themselves.

creations appear to them alike?' Say, 'God is the Creator of all things. He is the One, the Almighty.'

¹⁷ He sends down water from the sky that fills riverbeds to overflowing, each according to its measure. The torrent carries along swelling foam, akin to what rises from smelted ore from which man makes ornaments and tools. God thus depicts truth and falsehood. The scum is cast away, but whatever is of use to man remains behind. God thus speaks in parables.[a]

¹⁸ There will be the best of rewards for those who respond to their Lord: while those who do not respond to Him—if they possessed all that is on earth and twice as much, they would surely offer it as ransom [on the Day of Judgement];—will have the worst reckoning and their goal is Hell: and how evil a resting-place!

¹⁹ Can one who knows that whatever has been sent down to you from your Lord is the Truth, be equal to one who is blind? It is only those who are endowed with insight who pay heed; ²⁰ they who are true to their bond with God and never break their covenant; ²¹ and those who join together what God has commanded to be joined, and fear their Lord and dread the harshness of the reckoning; ²² those who are steadfast in seeking the favour of their Lord, and pray regularly and spend secretly and openly out of what We have provided them with, and ward off evil with good. Theirs shall be the final abode. ²³ They shall enter the eternal Gardens of Eden, along with the righteous from among their fathers, wives and descendants. From every gate the angels will come to them, saying, ²⁴ 'Peace be upon you for all that you have steadfastly endured. How excellent is the final abode!'

²⁵ As for those who break the covenant of God, after having confirmed it, who cut asunder what God has commanded to be joined and spread corruption in the land, a curse shall be laid on

---

a These are the events of nature through which God shows symbolically what principles He has fixed for the success or failure of life. Our principle is that in this world only that person or that community has a place who proves useful to others. The individual or the group which has lost its capacity to benefit others has no place in this world created by God.

them; they shall have an evil abode.*a* [26] God gives abundantly to whom He will and sparingly to whom He pleases—[those who deny the truth] rejoice in the life of this world; yet the life of this world is but a fleeting pleasure compared with the life to come.

[27] Those who deny the truth ask, 'Why has no Sign been sent down to him by his Lord?' Say, 'God lets go astray those whom He wills and guides to Himself those who turn to Him, [28] those who believe and whose hearts find comfort in the remembrance of God—surely in the remembrance of God hearts can find comfort. [29] 'As for those who believe and do righteous deeds—blissful is their end.'

[30] Thus We have sent you to a people, before whom other peoples have passed away, so that you may recite to them what We have revealed to you. Yet they deny the Gracious God. Say, 'He is my Lord; there is no god but He. In Him I put my trust and to Him I shall return.'

[31] Even if there were a Quran by which mountains could be set in motion, by which the earth could be rent asunder, or by which the dead could be made to speak [they would not believe in it]. Surely all things are subject to God's will. Are the faithful unaware that, had He pleased, God could have guided all mankind? Calamity shall not cease to strike those who deny the truth because of their misdeeds or to strike near their homes, until God's promise be fulfilled. God will not fail to keep His promise. [32] Other messengers were also mocked before you; but though I granted respite to those who denied the truth, at last I seized them, and how awful was My punishment.

[33] Is then He who watches over every soul and its actions [like any other]? Yet they ascribe partners to God. Say, 'Name them!

---

a Man is bound to God by the bond of nature and to his fellow beings by the bond of humanity. Breaking both bonds leads to creating an imbalance on God's earth. Loving a balanced, peaceful life while on God's earth means making his life subject to the above-mentioned bonds. In liberating himself from these bonds – caring nothing for the rights of God or men—he only creates mischief.

Those who act thus incur the curse of God. Such as these will not share in the Grace of God. They have fouled God's earth, so they deserve to be pushed into the foulest of places—Hell.

Or do you presume to inform Him of something on the earth of which He does not know? Or, is all this only your verbal assertion?' Indeed, their devices seem fair to those who deny the truth, and they are kept back from the right path. There can be no guide for those whom God lets go astray. [34] Punishment awaits them in the present life: but harsher is the punishment of the Hereafter—no one will defend them against God.

[35] Such is the Paradise which the righteous have been promised: it is watered by running streams: eternal is its fruit, and eternal is its shade. That is the recompense of those who are righteous, but the recompense of those who deny the truth is the Fire.

[36] Those to whom We sent the Scriptures rejoice in what has been revealed to you, while some factions deny parts of it. Say to them, 'I have been commanded only to worship God and not to associate partners with Him: to Him I pray and to Him I shall return.' [37] Thus We have revealed it as a [clear] commandment in Arabic. If you followed their desires after all the knowledge which has come to you, you would have no protector or shield against God. [38] We sent down messengers before you and gave them wives and children. Yet it was not possible for a messenger to bring a sign, save by the command of God. Every age has had its revelation. [39] God abrogates or confirms what He pleases; with Him is the source of all commandments.

[40] Whether We show you part of what We have promised them or cause you to pass away [before that], your mission is only to give warning; it is for Us to do the reckoning. [41] Do they not see how We come to [their] land and shrink its borders? God decides—no one can reverse His decision—and He is swift in reckoning. [42] Those before them did also devise plots; but in all things the master planning is God's. He knows what each soul does. Those who deny the truth shall soon know for whom is the final abode.

[43] Those who deny the truth say, 'You are not God's messenger.' Say, 'Sufficient is God as my witness between me and you, and those who have knowledge of the Book.'

14. ABRAHAM (*IBRAHIM*)

In the name of God, the Most Gracious, the Most Merciful

¹ *Alif Lam Ra*

We have revealed to you this Book so that, by their Lord's command, you may lead men from darkness to the light: to the path of the Mighty, the Praiseworthy One, ² to God, who possesses whatever is in the heavens and whatever is on earth. Woe to those who deny the truth, for they shall be sternly punished!ᵃ ³ Woe to those who love this life more than the Hereafter; who turn others away from the path of God and seek to make it crooked. They have gone far astray.

⁴ Each messenger We have sent has spoken in the language of his own people, so that he might make the message clear to them. But God lets go astray whom He will and guides whom He pleases. He is the Almighty, the All Wise.

⁵ We sent Moses with Our signs, saying, 'Lead your people out of the darkness into the light, and remind them of God's Days. In that there are signs for every patient, grateful person.'

⁶ Moses said to his people, 'Remember God's goodness to you when He delivered you from Pharaoh's people who were treating you cruelly, putting your sons to death and sparing only your daughters. Surely that was a great trial from your Lord. ⁷ Remember also the time when your Lord declared, "If you are grateful, I will surely bestow more favours on you; but if you are ungrateful, then know that My punishment is severe indeed."' ⁸ Moses said, 'Even if you

---

a Faith enables man to discover God as a Being who is all powerful and possessed of all the good attributes. Such a mental state is not merely a formal belief. It, in fact, signals the emergence of a man from the darkness of ignorance and his entering into the light of knowledge. It amounts to passing through the curtain of unseen-ness to the stage of the glory of actual observation; this is the observation and realization of the Hereafter, while actually remaining in this world. Faith in reality is a conscious attainment and not the spiritless repetition of certain combinations of words. The Book of God came into existence to take man to this stage of consciousness.

should deny the truth, and all who dwell on earth together, God is self-sufficient, praiseworthy.'

⁹ Has not news come to you concerning those who preceded you, such as Noah's people, and the 'Ad and Thamud, as well as those who came after them? Only God knows who they were. The messengers came to them with clear signs, but they put their hands to their mouths saying, 'We deny the message you have been sent with. We have grave doubts about what you are inviting us to do.'

¹⁰ Their messengers said, 'Is there any doubt about God, the Originator of the heavens and earth? He calls you to Him in order to forgive you some of your offences and to reprieve you for a specific period.' They said, 'You are only human beings like ourselves! You want to divert us from what our forefathers have been worshipping, so bring us some clear authority.'[a]

¹¹ Their messengers replied, 'We are indeed mortals like yourselves. But God bestows His grace on such of His servants as He chooses. We cannot give you miracles, except by God's leave. In God let true believers put their trust—¹² and why should we not put our trust in God when He has already guided us to our paths? We will, surely, bear with patience all the harm you do us. So in God let those who trust put their trust.'

¹³ Those who deny the truth said to their messengers, 'We shall banish you from our land unless you return to our ways.' But their Lord inspired the messengers, saying, 'We shall destroy the evil-doers,

---

a Modern research shows that the matter constituting heaven and earth was initially in the shape of the solid ball known as the super atom. According to the known laws of nature, all its parts were attracted towards its centre with extreme intensity. The present extensive universe came into existence due to the explosion of this super atom. In this verse the word *fatir* (the Tearer) refers to this universal event—an absolute proof of the existence of a Creator, because the parts of the super atom which were completely attracted inside could not move in an outward direction by themselves. If one accepts that they did so (the Big Bang) then one must also accept the theory of external intervention. The other name for this intervening power is God.

¹⁴ and settle you on the land to succeed them. That is [in store] for anyone who is in awe of meeting Me, and who heeds My warnings.'

¹⁵ When they sought Our Judgement, every stubborn oppressor was frustrated. ¹⁶ Beyond him is Hell, and he shall drink putrid water; ¹⁷ he will sip and will not find it easy to swallow it. Death will approach him from every quarter, yet he will not die. More intense suffering will lie ahead of him.

¹⁸ The works of those who deny their Lord are like ashes which the wind scatters on a stormy day: they shall gain nothing from what they do. To act thus is to stray far into error. ¹⁹ Do you not see that God has created the heavens and the earth for a purpose? He can eliminate you if He wills and bring into being a new creation: ²⁰ that is no difficult thing for God.

²¹ They shall all appear before God and the weak will say to those who behaved proudly, 'We were your followers. Can you protect us from God's punishment?' They will reply, 'Had God given us guidance, we would have guided you. It is all the same whether we are patient or impatient; there is no escape for us.'

²² When the Judgement has been passed, Satan will say to them, 'God made you a true promise; I too made you promises, but I failed you. I had no authority over you, except that I called you and you responded to me. Do not now blame me, but blame yourselves! I cannot help you, nor can you help me. I reject your former act in associating me with God.' The wrongdoers will have a painful punishment.

²³ But those who believed and did good deeds will be brought into Gardens with rivers flowing through them. They shall abide there forever by their Lord's permission, and will be welcomed with the greeting, 'Peace'!

²⁴ Do you not see how God compares a good word to a good tree?^a Its root is firm and its branches are in the sky, ²⁵ it yields

---

a It is the special characteristic of a tree that it makes the whole world its 'dining table', and in this way develops from the stage of a seed to establish itself on the earth as a majestic tree. The tree absorbs from the earth water, minerals and salts in order to grow: at the same time it obtains nourishment

its fruit each season with its Lord's permission—God makes such comparisons for people, in order that they may take heed—²⁶ but an evil word is like an evil tree torn out of the earth; it has no foothold.

²⁷ God will strengthen the believers with His steadfast word, both in the present life and in the Hereafter. God lets the wrongdoers go astray. He does what He wills.

²⁸ Do you not see those who, in exchange for God's favour, offer only ingratitude and cause their people to descend into the Abode of Ruin? ²⁹ In Hell shall they burn; an evil place to stay. ³⁰ They have set up rivals to God to lead people away from His path. Say, 'Enjoy yourselves awhile: you will then proceed to the Fire.'

³¹ Tell My servants, those who are true believers, to keep up prayer and to give alms secretly and openly out of what We have given them, before the Day comes when there will be neither trading nor befriending.

³² It was God who created the heavens and the earth. He sends down water from the sky with which He brings forth fruits for your sustenance; He has made ships subservient to you, so that they may sail across the sea by His command; and has subjected the rivers to you. ³³ He has also subjected to you the sun and the moon, both steadfastly pursuing their courses. He has subjected to you the night as well as the day; ³⁴ He has given you all that you asked of Him; and if you try to reckon up God's favours, you will not be able to count them. Truly man is very unjust, very ungrateful.

³⁵ [Remember] when Abraham said, 'My Lord, make this a city of peace and help me and my children to keep away from worshipping idols. ³⁶ My Lord, they have led so many men astray! Anyone who follows me is with me, but if anyone turns against me, You are surely forgiving and merciful.

---

from the air and the sun. It takes nourishment from below as well as from above. This is also true of the believer (*mu'min*). While the common tree is materially a tree, the believer is a conscious tree. The believer observes in the world God's creation and, looking to the system governing it, derives from it a proper lesson and guidance. Moreover, he continuously receives God's blessing from 'above'. He receives the nourishment of enhancement in faith from God's creatures, as well as the Creator.

³⁷ O Lord! I have settled some of my offspring in an uncultivable valley near Your Sacred House, Lord, so that they might establish their prayers. So, make people's hearts incline towards them and provide them with fruits so that they may be grateful.ᵃ

³⁸ Lord, You have knowledge of all that we hide and all that we reveal: nothing in heaven or on earth is hidden from God.ᵇ ³⁹ Praise be to God who has bestowed upon me, despite my old age, Ishmael and Isaac. Surely my Lord is the hearer of prayer. ⁴⁰ Lord, grant that I may keep up the prayer, and so may my offspring. My Lord, accept my prayer. ⁴¹ Forgive me, Lord, and forgive my parents and all the believers on the Day of Reckoning.'

⁴² Do not think God is unaware of the wrongdoers' actions. He only gives them respite till the Day on which all eyes will stare fixedly in horror. ⁴³ They will hurry on in fright, their heads lifted up, their gaze directed forward, their minds utterly void.

⁴⁴ Warn men of the Day when the punishment will come upon them, and when the wrongdoers will say, 'Our Lord, grant us respite for a short while. We will respond to Your call and will follow the messengers.' [But God will answer], are you not those who swore that you would never suffer any decline? ⁴⁵ You lived in the dwellings of those who wronged themselves, and it was made clear to you how We had dealt with them and We gave you many examples. ⁴⁶ They hatched their plots; but these plots were all within God's knowledge.

---

a The hilly and desert world of ancient Makkah was a natural training ground for the realization of God; the entire panorama of nature was an encouragement to man to remember Him. The only considerable sign of human construction here, which claimed man's attention, was the stone mosque, the Ka'bah, built by Abraham and Ishmael. This he could enter and engage in the remembrance of God.

b In this prayer of Abraham, one sees the glimpses of all those emotions which emerge in the heart of a true subject of God while addressing a prayer to Him. His submissive attitude compels him to admit his humility before God; whatever he requests is on the basis of his being needy and not on the basis of any entitlement; on the one hand, he admits to the bounties already available to him and, on the other, presents his request, fulfilling all the requirements of respectfulness. He admits that God is the Giver and man the beneficiary.

Though their plots were such as to shake the mountains, [God will bring their plots to nothing.]

[47] Never think that God will fail in His promise to His messengers. God is mighty and capable of retribution. [48] On the Day when the earth shall be changed into another earth, as shall be the heavens, they will all appear before God, the One, the Most Supreme. [49] On that Day you shall see the guilty bound in chains, [50] their garments shall be of pitch and the fire shall envelop their faces. [51] God will requite each soul according to its deeds. Swift is God's reckoning.

[52] This is a message for mankind. Let them take warning from it and know that He is but one God. Let those possessed of understanding may take heed.

15. THE ROCKY TRACT (*AL-HIJR*)

In the name of God, the Most Gracious, the Most Merciful

[1] *Alif Lam Ra*

These are the verses of a clear Book, the Quran. [2] A time will surely come when those who are bent on denying the truth will wish that they had surrendered themselves to God, [3] so leave them to eat and enjoy themselves and let them be beguiled by vain hopes; for soon they will realise [the truth]. [4] We have never destroyed a township without a definite decree having been issued; [5] no people can forestall their doom, nor can they delay it.

[6] They say, 'You to whom the Reminder [the Quran] has been sent down, you are surely possessed. [7] Why do you not bring down the angels upon us, if you are truthful?' [8] But We send down the angels only to bring justice and then they will not be reprieved.

[9] It is We who have sent down the Reminder and We will, most surely, safeguard it.

[10] We sent messengers before you to the previous peoples, [11] but there was never a messenger who came to them but they mocked him: [12] thus We cause this [habit of mocking] to enter into the hearts of the sinful. [13] They will not believe in it, though they have before

them the example of former peoples, [14] and even if We opened to them a door from heaven, and they began ascending through it, [15] they would still say, 'Our eyes have been dazzled. We are bewitched.'

[16] We have placed constellations in heaven and have beautified it for beholders, [17] and We have guarded it from every accursed devil: [18] but if anyone eavesdrops, he is pursued by a bright flaming fire.

[19] We have spread out the earth, and set upon it firm mountains and caused everything to grow in due proportion. [20] We have provided therein a means of livelihood for you and for all those creatures for whom you do not provide.[a]

[21] There is not a thing but its storehouses are with Us. But We only send down each thing in an appropriate measure: [22] We let loose fertilizing winds, and bring water from the sky for you to drink; and you could not have stored it up for yourselves.[b]

[23] Truly, it is We who bring to life and We who cause death and We are the inheritor of all things. [24] We know those who lived before you and those who will come after you. [25] It is your Lord who will gather them. He is all wise and all knowing.

---

a Human beings require innumerable things for their sustenance and for civilization to develop. All these things have been made available on earth in exact accordance with human needs. The provision for all these things and the assurance of their continued existence is of God's devising. If we were required to provide sustenance for ourselves, we would find it well-nigh impossible to do so.

b The life of man and all living things on earth depend on water. From the underground reservoirs of water to the clouds spread throughout the atmosphere, the system of providing water is so complex and functions on such a large scale that its establishment could never be within the powers of man. This wonderful and gigantic arrangement is continuously maintained by God exactly according to human needs (*nunazziluhu illa biqadarim ma'lum*).

The human being is an extremely delicate creature. Any difference in atmospheric pressure and composition would be enough to upset his existence. The atmosphere, in spite of having innumerable possibilities, is stable as regards that particular measure which is suitable for a creature like a human being. This balance and this proportion could not have been accidental. Certainly, this is so thanks to the earth's most Majestic Creator and Sustainer. In view of this, one who does not accept God, or believes God to have partners, proves merely his own lack of reason and not the unreasonableness of the concept of the one God.

²⁶ We created man out of dry clay, from moulded mud, ²⁷ and the jinn We had created before from flaming fire.

²⁸ Your Lord said to the angels, 'I am about to bring into being a man wrought from mud. ²⁹ When I have formed him and breathed My spirit into him, fall down in prostration before him,' ³⁰ then the angels all prostrated themselves together. ³¹ But Satan did not; he refused to join those who prostrated themselves. ³² God asked him, 'What is the matter with you, that you are not among those who have prostrated themselves?' ³³ He replied, 'I am not one to prostrate myself to a man whom You have created out of a clay of moulded mud.'

³⁴ God said, 'Then get out of here; for you are accursed, ³⁵ and the curse shall be on you till the Day of Judgement!' ³⁶ Satan said, 'O my Lord! Grant me respite till the Day of Resurrection.' ³⁷ He said, 'You are granted respite ³⁸ till that Appointed Day.'

³⁹ He said, 'My Lord, since You have let me go astray. I shall make the path of error seem alluring to them on the earth and shall mislead them all, ⁴⁰ except for Your chosen servants.'

⁴¹ God said, 'This is the path which leads straight to Me. ⁴² Surely, you shall have no power over My true servants, except those misguided ones who choose to follow you. ⁴³ Surely, Hell is the place to which they are destined, ⁴⁴ it has seven gates: and each gate has a portion of them allotted to it.

⁴⁵ Truly, the God-fearing shall dwell amid gardens and fountains— ⁴⁶ "Enter therein in peace and security!"—⁴⁷ We shall cleanse their hearts of all traces of ill-will; they will be like brethren seated on couches facing one another.*a* ⁴⁸ They will not be affected by any weariness there, and they will never be made to leave.' ⁴⁹ Tell My

---

a A man may accumulate all kinds of pleasure-giving things and luxuries in the world; but even then, various kinds of unpleasantness make all his accumulation meaningless. Paradise, however, is a place where pleasures and luxuries will be free of all unpleasantness. It is recorded in a tradition of the Prophet Muhammad that the people of Paradise will be told, 'Now, you will always be healthy and will never be ill; now, you will be alive for ever and will never die; now you will always be young and you will never grow old; now you will always be here and you will never have to leave this place.'

servants that I alone am the Forgiving, the Merciful One, ⁵⁰ and that My punishment is a painful punishment.

⁵¹ Tell them about Abraham's guests: ⁵² when they came to him they greeted him with: 'Peace.' He said, 'We feel afraid of you.' ⁵³ They said, 'Do not be afraid. We come to you with good news. You shall have a son who shall be endowed with great knowledge.' ⁵⁴ He said, 'Do you bring me such news despite my old age? What kind of good news are you bringing me?'

⁵⁵ They said, 'We have, indeed, given you glad tidings in truth; do not therefore despair.' ⁵⁶ He said, 'Who but the misguided despair of the mercy of their Lord?'*a*

⁵⁷ Then he asked, 'What then is your business, O messengers?' ⁵⁸ They said, 'We have been sent forth to a guilty people.' ⁵⁹ Except for Lot's household, all of whom we shall rescue, ⁶⁰ except his wife. We have decreed that she will be among those who remain behind [and will be lost].

⁶¹ When the messengers came to Lot and his family, ⁶² he said, 'You are strangers [to me].' ⁶³ They said, 'No, but we bring you news about what they disputed, ⁶⁴ and we have come to you with the truth, and surely we are truthful, ⁶⁵ so leave with your family some time in the latter part of the night, and walk behind them. Let none of you look back. Go where you are commanded.' ⁶⁶ We communicated to him Our decree that the guilty ones would be destroyed by the morning.

⁶⁷ The people of the town came along, revelling, ⁶⁸ and he told them, 'These are my guests, so do not disgrace me. ⁶⁹ Fear God and do not shame me.' ⁷⁰ They said, 'Did we not forbid you to extend hospitality to strangers?' ⁷¹ He said, 'Here are my daughters,*b* if you must act in this way.'

---

a Angels of this kind come to prophets as well as to ordinary mortals. The difference is that when a prophet is visited by angels, he sees them and consciously grasps that those are angels, but ordinary men do not have this kind of certain knowledge or consciousness. However, the close proximity of angels may evoke unusual feelings in him. Such feelings can convey hints of the fact that at that time he is possibly in the company of the special angels sent by God.

b This means that 'here are the young girls of the city for you to marry'.

⁷² By your life, they wandered on in their wild intoxication ⁷³ and thereupon the blast [of Our punishment] overtook them at sunrise. ⁷⁴ We turned the town upside down and rained upon them stones of clay. ⁷⁵ There are certainly signs in that for those who can learn a lesson—⁷⁶ it is still there on the highway—⁷⁷ surely in this there is a sign for those who believe.

⁷⁸ The people of the Wood were also surely wrongdoers. ⁷⁹ So We took vengeance on them. Both are still there on the highway, plain for all to see. ⁸⁰ The people of al-Hijr also rejected Our messengers: ⁸¹ We gave them Our signs, but they turned away from them. ⁸² They carved out dwellings in the mountains, and lived in security—⁸³ the blast overtook them early one morning. ⁸⁴ All that they had acquired was of no avail to them.

⁸⁵ We have created the heavens and the earth and all that is between the two in accordance with the requirements of truth and wisdom. The Hour is surely coming. So overlook [their faults] with gracious forgiveness. ⁸⁶ Surely your Lord is the All Knowing Creator!

⁸⁷ We have given you the seven oft-recited verses and the great Quran. ⁸⁸ Do not strain your eyes towards the worldly benefits We have bestowed on some of them, nor grieve on their account. Lower your wing of mercy for the believers ⁸⁹ and say, 'I am, indeed, a plain warner,' ⁹⁰ such as We send down for those who are divisive, ⁹¹ and who have broken the Scripture into fragments—⁹² by your Lord, We shall question them all ⁹³ about whatever they had been doing!

⁹⁴ Proclaim openly what you are commanded, and avoid the polytheists. ⁹⁵ We will, surely, suffice you against those who mock, ⁹⁶ who set up another god with God, but they shall soon learn. ⁹⁷ We do indeed know how your heart is distressed at what they say. ⁹⁸ But glorify your Lord with His praise, and prostrate yourself: ⁹⁹ and worship your Lord until what is certain [death] comes to you.

16. BEES (*AL-NAHL*)

In the name of God, the Most Gracious, the Most Merciful

¹ The decree of God is at hand, so do not seek to hasten it. Holy is He, and exalted far above what they associate with Him. ² He sends down the angels with revelations by His command to whoever of His servants He pleases, saying, 'Warn mankind that there is no god save Me, so fear Me.' ³ He created the heavens and the earth for a true purpose. He is exalted above anything they associate with Him.[a]

⁴ He created man out of a [mere] drop of sperm: yet he shows himself to be openly contentious! ⁵ He has created cattle for you: from them you derive food and clothing and numerous other benefits; ⁶ how pleasant they look when you bring them home in the evenings and when you take them out to pasture in the mornings. ⁷ They carry your loads to places which you could otherwise not reach without great hardship—surely, your Lord is compassionate and merciful—⁸ He has created horses, mules and donkeys, so that you may ride them, and also so that they may be put on show, and He creates other things beyond your knowledge.

⁹ The straight way leads to God and there are ways which deviate from the right course. If He so wished, He would guide you all.

¹⁰ It is He who sends down water from the sky. From it you drink and with it trees grow on which you pasture your cattle. ¹¹ And with it He grows for you corn, and the olive and the date-palm and the

---

a The reality of religion is that man should apprehend the Being of God and His workmanship in the universe so intensely and realistically that the Being of the one God should become everything for him; only Him should he (man) fear and on Him only, should he build up his hopes. The one God should be the entire focus of his heart and mind.

This is what constitutes the act of making God the object of worship (*ilah*) and amounts to praying to Him. All the prophets came into the world in order to bring about this condition. Those who prove to have this sense of submission to God will be treated as successful on Judgement Day, but those who go against this will be left without hope.

grape, and all kinds of fruits. Surely, in that is a sign for a people who reflect.[a]

[12] He has made the night and the day and the sun and the moon subservient to you; and all the stars are subservient to His command. Surely in this there are signs for men of understanding. [13] On the earth He has fashioned for you objects of various hues: there is certainly a sign in that for people who pay heed.[b]

[14] It is He who subjected to you the sea, so that you may eat its fresh seafood and bring forth from it ornaments to wear. You see the ships cleaving through it. All this, so that you may seek His bounty and feel grateful.

[15] He has set up on the earth firm mountains, lest it shake under you, and rivers and tracks, so that you may find your way, [16] and He has set up other landmarks. By these and by the stars people set their course.

[17] Is He, then, who creates like him who does not create? Will you not, then, take heed? [18] If you tried to count God's blessings, you would never be able to number them. God is ever forgiving and most merciful. [19] God knows all that you conceal and all that you reveal.[c]

---

a There is perfect harmony among the different parts of the universe. This harmony is definite proof of the fact that the Creator and Lord of the whole universe is only one. In the present structure of the universe, there is no scope for more than one God, and when the real Creator and Lord is one God, making any thing other than Him an object of worship will be absolutely indefensible.

b The sun, the moon and the stars all revolve continuously in the vastness of space with total precision. These scenes are so wonderful that the keen-eyed observer cannot remain unaffected by them. In these things, he will see God's majesty and His role as Sustainer; he will discover unseen realities hidden in external occurrences; by looking at God's creations, he will be immersed in the realization of the Creator.

c Whatever things there are in the world, none of them has the power of creating (i.e. bringing non-existent things into existence). It stands proved therefore that this world is not its own creator. Only that being can be its creator who has the inherent power in it to bring a thing into existence which does not already exist. Therefore the belief in one God is absolutely natural. There can be no rational explanation of the universe without accepting the existence of God who possesses the perfect capability to create.

²⁰ Those you call on besides God cannot create anything. They are themselves created. ²¹ They are dead, not living; nor do they know when they will be raised to life. ²² Your God is the One God. As for those who do not believe in the Hereafter, their hearts refuse to admit the truth and they are arrogant. ²³ God surely knows what they conceal and what they reveal. He does not love the arrogant.

²⁴ When they are asked, 'What is it that your Lord has sent down?' they say, 'Stories of the ancients.' ²⁵ Let them bear all their own burdens on Resurrection Day as well as some of the burdens of those whom they lead astray without any knowledge. How evil the load with which they shall be burdened!

²⁶ Those who went before them also plotted. But God struck at the foundations of their building, and the roof fell down upon them from above. The punishment came upon them from where they did not expect. ²⁷ Then on the Day of Resurrection He will disgrace them, and say, 'Where are My partners for whose sake you opposed [My guidance]?' Those given knowledge will say, 'This Day humiliation and affliction will surely befall those who have been denying the truth.'

²⁸ Those whose lives the angels take while they are wronging their own souls will offer submission saying, 'We were not doing anything evil!' 'Indeed!' the angels will reply, 'God is aware of what you have been doing, ²⁹ so enter the gates of Hell. There you shall abide forever.' Evil indeed is the abode of the arrogant.

³⁰ When those who fear God are asked, 'What has your Lord sent down?' Their reply is, 'Goodness!' The reward of those who do good works in this world is good, but the abode of the Hereafter is even better. The home of the righteous is indeed excellent. ³¹ They will enter Gardens of Eternity, where rivers will flow at their feet. There they will have all that they wish for. Thus God rewards the righteous, ³² those whose lives the angels take in a state of purity, saying [to them], 'Peace be on you; enter the Garden, because of [the good] which you did [in the world].'

³³ Are they waiting for the angels to come to them, or the fulfilment of your Lord's will? Those who went before them did the same. God did not wrong them; rather they wronged themselves. ³⁴ The

evil results of their deeds overtook them, and that which they used to mock at encompassed them.

³⁵ Those who associate [others with God] say, 'If God had so willed we would not have worshipped anything besides Him, neither we nor our fathers, nor would we have forbidden anything without His sanction.' So did those who went before them. The duty of the messengers is only to convey the message clearly.

³⁶ We raised among every people a messenger who enjoined, 'Worship God alone and shun the evil one.' Then among them were some whom God guided and among them were others who became deserving of ruin. So travel across the earth and observe what was the end of those who rejected the messengers. ³⁷ Though you [Prophet] may be eager to guide them, God does not guide those whom He lets go astray, [because of their refusal to give a positive response to the truth]. They will have no supporters.

³⁸ They swear their strongest oaths by God that God will never raise the dead to life—nonetheless, it is a promise truly binding on Him, even though most people do not realize it—³⁹ this is so that He may make clear to them what they have differed about and so that those who are bent on denying the truth may realize that they were lying. ⁴⁰ When We will something to happen, all that We say is, 'Be!' and it is.

⁴¹ As for those who, after persecution, migrated from their homes for the cause of God, We will provide them with a goodly abode in this life: but truly the reward of the Hereafter will be greater, if they only knew it. ⁴² They are the ones who are steadfast and put their trust in their Lord.

⁴³ Before you also the messengers We sent were but [mortal] men to whom We vouchsafed revelation. Ask the People of the Book, if you do not know. ⁴⁴ [We sent them] with clear signs and scriptures. We have sent down the Reminder to you, to enable you to make clear to mankind what has been sent down to them, so that they may reflect upon it.

⁴⁵ Do those who devise evil plans feel secure that God will not make them sink into the land, or that a punishment will not come upon them from where they least expect? ⁴⁶ Or that He will not seize

them suddenly in their daily activities and they will not be able to frustrate Him? [47] Or that He will not punish them by giving them a fright? Indeed, your Lord is kind and merciful.

[48] Have they not observed the things God has created, casting their shadows right and left, prostrating themselves before God in all humility? [49] Everything in the heavens and all the creatures on the earth prostrate themselves before God, as do the angels, and they do not behave proudly: [50] they fear their Lord above them, and do what they are commanded.

[51] God says, 'Do not take two gods. He is only One God. So fear Me alone.' [52] To Him belongs whatsoever is in the heavens and on the earth, and obedience is due to Him alone. Will you then fear anyone other than God?

[53] Whatever blessing you have is from God, and to Him you turn for help when distress befalls you, [54] yet no sooner does He relieve your distress than some among you set up other partners besides their Lord, [55] showing no gratitude for what We have given them. Enjoy yourselves awhile; but soon you will know! [56] They even appoint a share of what We have provided for them [to false gods] they know nothing of. You shall surely be questioned about the lies you have been fabricating.

[57] They assign daughters to God—glory be to Him!—but for themselves [sons] that they desire to have. [58] When the birth of a girl is announced to any of them, his face darkens and he is filled with gloom. [59] In his shame he hides himself away from his people, because of the bad news he has been given. Should he keep her and feel disgraced or bury her in the dust? How ill they judge! [60] The attribute of evil applies to those who do not believe in the Hereafter, while to God applies the highest attribute, for He is Mighty, the Wise.

[61] If God were to take people to task for their wrongdoing, He would not leave even one living creature on earth, but He gives them respite till an appointed time: when their time comes they cannot delay it for an hour, nor can they bring it forward.

[62] They attribute to God what they themselves dislike and their tongues utter the lie that all good things are for themselves. Without doubt, the Fire awaits them, and they shall be hastened on into it.

⁶³ By God! We have sent messengers before you to other nations. But Satan made their [foul] deeds seem fair to them and today he is their patron. They shall have a painful punishment. ⁶⁴ We have only sent down the Book to you so that you can make clear to them that concerning which they differ, and as a guidance and a mercy to people who believe.

⁶⁵ God sends down water from the sky and with it revives the earth when it is dead. There is truly a sign in this for people who listen.

⁶⁶ There is also a lesson for you in cattle. From the contents of their bellies, from between the dung and blood, We give you pure milk to drink, pleasant for those who drink it.ᵃ ⁶⁷ From the fruit of the date palm and the grapes you derive intoxicants as well as wholesome food. Surely in this there is a sign for men of understanding.

⁶⁸ Your Lord inspired the bee, saying, 'Make your homes in the mountains, in the trees, and also in the structures which men erect. ⁶⁹ Then feed on every kind of fruit, and follow the trodden paths of your Lord.' From its belly comes a drink with different colours which provides healing for mankind. Indeed, in this there is a sign for people who give thought.ᵇ

---

a A characteristic peculiar to milch animals is that whatever they eat is converted into dung and blood yet there emerges along with these a liquid, milk, which is the most valuable food for man. This is true of the trees. Mud, water and other such things enter them and under the influence of their internal system, they take the shape of juicy fruits which hang from the branches.

These occurrences are meant to remind people of God. Through them man should start seeing glimpses of His Majesty. This realization should be so intense that he should spontaneously exclaim, 'Oh God! You cause milk to come out from between dung and blood. Pray, let favourable results emerge from the fruits, please turn my valueless life into a valuable one.'

b The honey-bee is the most wonderful masterpiece of God's creation. It constructs its beehive to a standard pattern, strictly following the relevant mathematical principles. Then, in the best planned manner, sucks the juice from the flowers, brings it back and, in a perfectly systematic manner, stores it in the hive. Then, in accordance with hygienic principles prepares honey, which serves as a valuable food as well as a remedy for human ailments. All this takes place in such an amazingly regulated manner that voluminous books have been written on it and still the description is not complete.

Anyone who observes the bees, will have a live example of God's

70 God created you; then He shall cause you to die: and some shall have their lives prolonged to abject old age, ceasing to know anything after once having had knowledge. God is all knowing and powerful.

71 God has given some of you more provision than others. Those who have been given more are unwilling to pass their provision to the servants they possess so that they become their equals. Will they then deny the favour of God?

72 God has given you wives from among yourselves, and given you children and grandchildren from your wives, and provided wholesome things for you. Will they then believe in falsehood and deny God's favours? 73 They worship, instead of God, things that have no control over their provision from the heavens or the earth in any way, nor do they have any power [to do so]. 74 Do not compare God with anyone. God has knowledge, but you have not.

75 God makes a comparison between an owned slave possessing no power over anything, and someone to whom We have given plentiful provision, who gives out from it privately and openly. Are they equal? Praise be to God! But most people do not know it.

76 God makes another comparison between two men, one of whom is dumb and cannot do a thing, and is a burden on his master. Wherever he sends him on an errand, he brings [him] no good. Is he equal to someone who commands justice and is on a straight path?

77 God alone has knowledge of the hidden reality of the heavens and the earth; and the coming of the Hour [of Judgement] is like the twinkling of an eye, or even quicker. Surely God has full power over everything.

78 God brought you forth from the wombs of your mothers while you knew nothing, and gave you hearing and sight and hearts, so that you might be grateful.

79 Do they not see the birds held poised in the vault of heaven? Nothing holds them up except God. Truly, there are signs in this for those who believe. 80 God has made your houses places of rest for you and made tents for you out of cattle hides, which are light

---

workmanship and will see a glimpse of God in their wonderfully meaningful activities.

for you to carry, both when you are travelling and when you are staying in one place. He provides for you from the wool and fur and hair of cattle, household goods and articles for use for a time.[a]

[81] God has granted you shade out of what He has created, places of shelter in the mountains, garments with which to protect yourselves from the heat and coats of mail to shield you in battle. Thus He completes His favour to you, so that you may submit wholly to Him. [82] But if they turn away, you are responsible only for conveying the message clearly. [83] They recognize the favour of God, yet they deny it; and most of them are ungrateful.

[84] On the Day when We raise up a witness from every people, those who were bent on denying the truth will not be permitted to put forward excuses, or to make amends. [85] When the wrongdoers face their punishment, it shall not be lightened for them, nor shall they be granted any reprieve.

[86] When those who associate partners with God see their associate gods, they will say, 'Our Lord, these are our associate gods whom we used to call upon instead of You.' But they will throw back their words at them, [saying], 'Indeed you are liars,' [87] and on that Day they will offer total submission to God: and all that they used to devise will fail them. [88] Upon all who were bent on denying the truth and who turned others away from the path of God, We will heap punishment upon punishment, in return for all the corruption that they brought about.

[89] The Day will come when We raise up in every people a witness against them from amongst themselves, and We will bring you as a witness against these people. We have sent down the Book to you

---

a The flight of birds in the atmosphere is possible thanks to the magnificent planning of nature. (The shape of birds, most suitable for the purpose of flight is imitated in the shape of aeroplanes). Just as ships could not have sailed without the existence of water on the surface of the earth, birds would not have been able to fly if there had not been the superior arrangement of continuously maintaining air on the earth's surface by means of the earth's gravity.

If man reflects deeply upon these phenomena, he will feel as if he is seeing God in action in His universe; he will discover the Creator in the creative system; he will see the glory of the Manufacturer in the artefacts.

to make everything clear, a guidance, and a mercy, and glad tidings for those who submit to God.

⁹⁰ God commands justice, kindness and giving their [due to] near relatives, and He forbids all shameful deeds, and injustice and transgression. He admonishes you so that you may take heed! ⁹¹ Fulfill the covenant of God when you have made one; and do not break your pledges after their confirmation. Indeed you have made God your surety; for God knows all that you do. ⁹² Do not, like the woman who unravels her yarn after its strands have been firmly spun, use your oaths as a means of deceiving one another, just because one community could become bigger than another. God is only testing you by means of this. On the Day of Resurrection He will make it clear to you what you differed about.

⁹³ Had God pleased, He would have united you in one community; but He lets go astray whoever He will, and guides whoever He will, and you will surely be called upon to account for all your actions.

⁹⁴ Do not use your oaths to deceive each other lest any foot should slip after being firmly placed and lest you should taste the penalty for having hindered others from the path of God, for then you will have a terrible punishment. ⁹⁵ Do not sell God's covenant for a paltry price. What is with God is better for you if you only knew.*a*

⁹⁶ What you have shall pass away, but what is with God is lasting. We will certainly give those who are patient their reward according to the best of their actions. ⁹⁷ To whoever does good deeds, man or woman, and is a believer, We shall assuredly give a good life; and We will bestow upon them their reward according to the best of their works.

⁹⁸ When you read the Quran, seek God's protection from Satan, the rejected one. ⁹⁹ Surely, he has no power over those who believe

---

a The act of breaking an agreement against the principles of Islamic law inevitably occurs when one partner to it sees that he will receive certain worldly benefits by doing so. But a believer's view is Hereafter-oriented. Whenever it is the self which makes a move to break the agreement, the person concerned curbs his self by saying that there may be some worldly benefit in breaking it, but he will gain no advantage thereby in the Hereafter. And the advantage of the Hereafter is definitely greater than any worldly benefit.

and put their trust in their Lord; [100] he has power only over those who are willing to follow him and associate others with God.

[101] When We substitute one revelation for another—and God knows best what He reveals—they say, 'You are but a fabricator.' Indeed, most of them have no knowledge. [102] Say, 'The Holy Spirit has brought it down as truth from your Lord, so that He may strengthen those who believe, and also as guidance and as good tidings for those who submit.'

[103] Indeed, We know what they say, 'It is only a human being who imparts [all] this to him!' But the tongue of him to whom they point is foreign, whereas this is plain Arabic speech. [104] God will not guide those who will not believe in the signs of God; and theirs will be a painful punishment. [105] Only those fabricate lies concerning God who do not believe in the signs of God, and these are the liars.

[106] As for one who denies God after he has believed, with the exception of one who is forced to do it, while his heart rests securely in faith, but one who opens his heart to a denial of truth shall incur the wrath of God; such as these will have a terrible punishment. [107] This is because they prefer the life of this world to the Hereafter and because God does not guide those who deny the truth. [108] These are the ones upon whose hearts and hearing and sight God has set a seal. It is they who are heedless, [109] and in the life to come, they will surely be the losers.

[110] Surely, your Lord will be forgiving and merciful towards those who migrated after persecution and strove hard for the cause of God and remained steadfast. [111] On the Day each soul will come pleading for itself, and every soul will be repaid according to whatever it has done, and they will not be wronged.

[112] God makes an example of a town that was secure and at ease, with provisions coming to it abundantly from every quarter. Then it showed ingratitude for God's blessings and God afflicted it with hunger and fear because of what they did. [113] There came to them a messenger from among themselves, but they rejected him as false, so punishment overtook them, as they were wrongdoers.

[114] So eat the lawful and good things which God has provided for you, and be thankful for the blessing of God, if it is Him you

worship.*a* [115] He has forbidden you only carrion, blood and the flesh of swine; also any [flesh] consecrated in the name of any but God. But if anyone is forced by dire necessity, not desiring it or exceeding his immediate need, God is forgiving and merciful towards him.

[116] Do not falsely declare, 'This is lawful, and this is forbidden,' so as to invent a lie against God. Surely, those who invent a lie against God do not prosper—[117] their enjoyment of this life is brief, and they shall have a painful punishment.

[118] We forbade the Jews those things We told you about before. We did not wrong them; rather they wronged themselves. [119] Surely, your Lord is most forgiving and ever merciful towards those who do evil in ignorance and truly repent thereafter and make amends.

[120] Abraham was a community*b* in himself devoted to God and true in faith, He was not one of the polytheists; [121] he was thankful for His blessings. God chose him and guided him to a straight path. [122] We gave him blessings in this world, and in the Hereafter he shall be among the righteous. [123] Then We revealed Our will to you [O Muhammad], saying, 'Follow the religion of Abraham, the upright in faith; he was not one of the polytheists.'

[124] The Sabbath was only enjoined on those who differed about it. Your Lord will judge between them on the Day of Resurrection regarding the things about which they differed.

[125] Call to the way of your Lord with wisdom and fair exhortation and reason with them in a way that is best. Your Lord knows best those who have strayed away from His path, and He knows best those who are rightly guided.

[126] If you want to retaliate, retaliate to the same degree as the injury done to you. But if you are patient, it is better to be so. [127] Endure with patience; truly, your patience is possible only with the help of God. Do not grieve for them, or feel distressed because

---

a Food is the most important of all man's needs. It is a need which is experienced morning and evening. God desires that, whenever a man uses food, he should eat it considering it, as a gift from God and he should be grateful to Him for it. But man has reversed the whole matter.

b This means that Abraham combined within himself all virtues.

of their plottings, [128] for God is with those who are righteous and those who do good.

17. THE NIGHT JOURNEY (*AL-ISRA'*)

In the name of God, the Most Gracious, the Most Merciful

[1] Holy is He who took His servant by night from the sacred place of worship [at Makkah] to the remote house of worship [at Jerusalem]—the precincts of which We have blessed, so that We might show him some of Our signs. Surely, it is He who is All Hearing, and All Seeing.

[2] We gave Moses the Book and made it a guide for the Children of Israel saying, 'Do not take anyone besides Me as a guardian, [3] you who are the descendants of those whom We carried in the Ark with Noah. He was a truly thankful servant.'[a]

[4] We forewarned the Children of Israel in the Scripture, 'Twice you shall commit evil in the land. You shall become great transgressors.' [5] When the time of the first of these warnings came, We sent against you servants of Ours, of great might, who ravaged your homes. So the warning was fulfilled, [6] and after a time We allowed you to prevail over them once again and aided you with wealth and offspring and made you greater in number.

[7] [We said], 'If you persevere in doing good, you will be doing good to yourselves; but if you do evil, it will go against you.' When the time of the second warning came, [We roused against you others] to disgrace you utterly and to enter the place of worship as they had entered it before, utterly destroying all that they laid their hands on. [8] We said, 'Your Lord may yet have mercy on you, but if you do

---

a When man discovers God in all His majesty and power, it is but natural that he should make God his Caretaker (*wakil*). One who attains the true realization of God (*ma'rifah*) will make God his everything, and will lead the life of a true believer in the present world. In order to lead such a life, man has to do so, and only that person will be able to rise above all creation who has found the greatest thing, that is, the Creator and Lord of all creation.

the same again, so shall We: We have made Hell a prison for those who deny the truth.'

⁹ Surely, this Quran guides to the most upright way and gives good news to the believers who do good deeds, so that they will have a great reward ¹⁰ and warns those who deny the life to come with grievous punishment.

¹¹Yet man asks for evil as eagerly as he should ask for good. Truly, man is indeed hasty.a ¹² We have made the night and the day as two signs. We blotted out the sign of night and made the sign of the day illuminating, so that you may seek the bounty of your Lord and learn to compute the seasons and the years. We have set everything forth in detail.*a*

¹³ We have tied the fate of every man about his neck; and We shall produce a book for him on Resurrection Day that he will find spread open. ¹⁴ It will say, 'Read your record, today there will be none but yourself to call you to account!' ¹⁵ Whoever chooses to follow the right path, follows it for his own good; and whoever goes astray, goes astray at his own peril; no bearer of burdens shall bear the burdens of another. Nor do We punish until We have sent forth a messenger to forewarn them.*b*

¹⁶ When We decide to destroy a town, We command the affluent section of its people, but they transgress therein; thus the word [sentence of punishment] is justified, then We destroy the town utterly. ¹⁷ How many generations have We destroyed since Noah's

---

a God wants man to be patient about acquiring the immediate luxuries of the world, so that he should keep to the right path on his journey towards the Hereafter. But man, due to his hasty nature, rushes to acquire ephemeral worldly luxuries, which prove to be impediments to his continuing his onward journey. Man's desire for instant gratification is the greatest reason for his being deprived of the bounties of the Hereafter.

b God raised prophets among the various communities and revealed the scriptures to them. He did this so that people should be aware in advance of the Day of Reckoning. Now it is for every man to decide what fate he wants to face in the future: eternal paradise as a result of his following the path of guidance, or an eternity in hell as a result of his straying from the path of guidance.

time. Your Lord is well aware of the sins of His servants and observes them all.

¹⁸ We give whatever We will to whoever desires immediate gains; but then We have prepared Hell for him which he will enter, disgraced and rejected. ¹⁹ Anyone who desires the Hereafter and makes a proper effort to achieve it, being a true believer, shall find favour with God for his endeavours.

²⁰ Upon all, both these [who desire the world] and those [who desire the Hereafter] We bestow the bounty of your Lord: none shall be denied the bounty of your Lord—²¹ see how We have exalted some above others [in the present life]. Yet the Hereafter shall be greater in degrees of rank and greater in excellence.

²² Do not set up any other deity beside God, lest you incur disgrace, and be forsaken. ²³ Your Lord has commanded that you should worship none but Him, and show kindness to your parents. If either or both of them attain old age with you, say no word of contempt to them and do not rebuke them, but always speak gently to them ²⁴ and treat them with humility and tenderness and say, 'Lord, be merciful to them both, as they raised me up when I was little.' ²⁵ Your Lord knows best what is in your hearts; if you are righteous, He is most forgiving to those who constantly turn to Him.

²⁶ Give to your relatives their due, and also to the needy and the wayfarer. Yet do not spend extravagantly; ²⁷ spendthrifts are the brothers of Satan, and Satan is ever ungrateful to his Lord—²⁸ but if, while waiting for your Lord's bounty which you are expecting, you turn them down, then at least speak to them kindly.

²⁹ Be neither miserly, nor so open-handed that you suffer reproach and become destitute. ³⁰ Your Lord gives abundantly to whom He will and sparingly to whom He pleases. He is informed and observant about His servants.

³¹ You shall not kill your offspring for fear of want. It is We who provide for them, and for you. Indeed, killing them is a great sin. ³² Do not commit adultery,ᵃ for it is an indecent thing and an evil course.

---

a Literally 'do not go near adultery'. One of the evils, which God wants

³³ Do not take life which God has made inviolate—except by right. If anyone is killed wrongfully, We have given authority to his heirs to demand retribution, but let them not transgress the prescribed limits in exacting retribution; for then he will be assisted [by the law].

³⁴ Do not go near the orphans' property, except with the best of intentions, until they reach maturity. Keep your promises;ᵃ you will be called to account for every promise which you have made! ³⁵ Give full measure, when you measure, and weigh with accurate scales.ᵇ That is fair, and better in the end.

³⁶ Do not follow what you do not know; for the ear and the eye and the heart shall all be called to account. ³⁷ Do not walk proudly on the earth. You cannot cleave the earth, nor can you rival the mountains in height. ³⁸ All that is evil in the sight of your Lord, and is detestable.ᶜ

---

to root out completely, is adultery, or *zina*. That is, adultery is such a great evil and is proof of such shamelessness, that man should abstain even from its initial stages. Here, only a basic command has been given on this subject. Detailed orders have been given in chapter 24.

a Literally 'a pledge must be accounted for to God'. These words make it quite clear that if one man makes a promise to another, it does not concern just the two of them: God actively participates in the capacity of the third party. One who breaks his pledge to someone weaker than himself should fear God—who is also present—for it is quite impossible to escape His wrath.

b Every kind of business in the world is based on weights and measures. Therefore, it has been ordained that weights and measures should be accurate.

c Qatada, one of the early commentators of the Quran, said, 'Don't say, "I have seen" when you have not seen, don't say, "I have heard" when you have not heard, and don't say "I know" when you do not know.' One who fears to be called to account before God, will never say anything without first verifying it. Man should use his eyes, ears and brain for the purpose they were designed and should talk of and act only upon such matters for which there is adequate evidence to warrant this. He should eschew all that is baseless, for example, bearing false witness, making false allegations, condemning someone on the basis of hearsay, justifying falsehoods merely on account of envy, placing credence on things that man does not know for sure because of his limitations. The ears, eyes and mind are apparently under man's control. But these are, as it were, entrusted to him by God, and so it is a must for a man to utilize them according to God's will, otherwise he will be taken strictly to task for their misuse.

³⁹ This is part of the wisdom that your Lord has revealed to you. Do not set up any other deity with God, lest you be cast into Hell, condemned and rejected.

⁴⁰ What! Has your Lord then favoured you with sons and Himself adopted females from among the angels? What you say is monstrous.
⁴¹ We have explained [the truth] in this Quran in various ways, so that they may take heed, but it has only increased their aversion.
⁴² Say, 'If there were [other] deities along with Him, as they claim, then they would surely have tried to find a way to the Lord of the Throne. ⁴³ Glory be to Him! Exalted above all that they say! ⁴⁴ The seven heavens and the earth and all who dwell therein glorify Him. There is not a single thing but glorifies Him with His praise; but you do not understand their glorification. Truly, He is forbearing and most forgiving.'

⁴⁵ When you recite the Quran, We place an invisible barrier between you and those who do not believe in the Hereafter. ⁴⁶ We put veils over their hearts to prevent them from comprehending it, and We afflict their ears with deafness. When you mention your one and only Lord in your recitation of the Quran, they turn their backs in aversion.

⁴⁷ We are fully aware of what they wish to hear when they listen to you; and what they say when they converse in private; and when the wrongdoers say, 'You are only following a man who is bewitched!' ⁴⁸ See to what they liken you! But they are lost and cannot find the right path.

⁴⁹ 'What!' they say, 'When we are turned to bones and dust, shall we be restored to life?' ⁵⁰ Say, '[yes] even if you turned to stones or iron, ⁵¹ or any other substance which you think unlikely to be given life.' Then they will ask, 'Who is it that shall restore us to life?' Answer them, 'He who created you the first time.' They will then shake their heads at you and say, 'When will that be?' Say, 'It may well be very soon.' ⁵² On that Day He will call you, and you will answer by praising Him, thinking that you have stayed for only a little while.'

⁵³ Tell My servants that they should always say what is best.

Satan stirs up discord among them. Surely, Satan is an outright enemy to man.

⁵⁴ Your Lord is fully aware of you. He may show you mercy if He will, or punish you if He will. We have not sent you as their guardian. ⁵⁵ Your Lord knows best about everyone in the heavens and on the earth. We gave some prophets more than others: We gave David the Psalms.

⁵⁶ Call upon those you claim to be deities besides God and you will know that they have no power to remove affliction from you or to bring about any change [that you may desire]. ⁵⁷ Those whom they invoke are themselves seeking a way of approach to their Lord, vying with each other to be near Him. They hope for His mercy and fear His punishment. Surely, the punishment of your Lord is to be feared: ⁵⁸ there is not a town [community] but We shall destroy or sternly punish it before the Day of Judgement. That is recorded in the Book.

⁵⁹ Nothing has prevented Us from sending signs, except the fact that previous peoples denied them. We gave the people of Thamud the she-camel as a clear sign, yet they mistreated her. We give signs only by way of warning.

⁶⁰ We told you that your Lord encompasses mankind. We granted the vision which We showed you, as well as the tree that is cursed in the Quran, only as a test for mankind. We warn them, but this only increases their insolence.

⁶¹ When We said to the angels, 'Prostrate yourselves before Adam,' they all prostrated themselves except Iblis. He said, 'Am I to prostrate myself to someone You have created out of clay?' ⁶² and [further] said, 'Do you see this being whom You have exalted above me? If You reprieve me until the Day of Resurrection, I will bring all but a few of his descendants under my sway.'

⁶³ God said, 'Go away! Hell will be your reward and the reward of any of them who follow you—an ample recompense. ⁶⁴ Go ahead and entice whomsoever of them you can, with your voice, and mount assaults against them with your cavalry and infantry and be their partner in wealth and offspring, and make promises to them—Satan

promises nothing but delusion—⁶⁵ but over My true servants you shall have no power. Your Lord will be their all-sufficient guardian.'

⁶⁶ Your Lord is He who causes the ships to move onward for you across the sea, so that you may go in quest of His bounty: He is most merciful towards you. ⁶⁷ When danger threatens you at sea, you call upon Him, and forget all others you are wont to invoke. But when He brings you safe to land, you turn away from Him. Man is ever ungrateful.

⁶⁸ Do you then feel secure against His causing you to be swallowed up by the earth when you are back on land, or His sending a deadly sand storm upon you? Then you will find none to protect you. ⁶⁹ Or do you feel secure against His sending you back to sea once again, and raising a fierce gale against you and causing you to drown in requital for your ingratitude? You will find no helper against Us there.

⁷⁰ We have honoured the children of Adam, and have borne them on the land and the sea, given them for sustenance things which are good and pure; and exalted them above many of Our creatures.

⁷¹ The Day will surely come when We shall summon every people with their leader. Then those who are given their records in their right hands will read their records [eagerly] and shall not in the least be wronged: ⁷² but whoever has been blind in this life will be blind in the life to come, and still farther astray from the path [of truth].

⁷³ They indeed sought to entice you away from what We revealed to you, hoping that you might invent something else in Our name; and then they would have accepted you as a close friend. ⁷⁴ If We had not made you stand firm, you would almost have inclined towards them a little. ⁷⁵ In that case, We should have inflicted a double punishment in this life, and a double punishment after death. Then you would have found no one to help you against Us.

⁷⁶ Indeed they came near to unsettling you, so that they might expel you from the land, but in that case they themselves would not have stayed on for very long after you. ⁷⁷ Such was Our way with the messengers We sent before you, and you will find no change in Our ways.

⁷⁸ Say your prayers from the decline of the sun, until nightfall; and at dawn—the recitation at dawn is indeed witnessed. ⁷⁹ And during

the night wake up and pray, as an additional prayer: it may well be that your Lord will raise you to a station of praise and glory.'

80 Say, 'Lord, grant me an honourable entrance and an honourable exit, and sustain me with Your power.' 81 Say, 'Truth has come and falsehood has disappeared. Falsehood is always bound to wither away.'

82 We send down in the Quran that which is healing and a mercy to those who believe; as for the evil-doers, it only increases their loss.

83 When We bestow a favour upon a person, he turns his back and draws aside; and when evil afflicts him he gives himself up to despair. 84 Say to them, 'Everyone acts in his own way, and your Lord knows best who is rightly guided.'

85 They question you about the Spirit. Say, 'The Spirit is at my Lord's command, and you have been granted but little knowledge.'

86 If We pleased, We would certainly take away that which We have revealed to you—then you would find no guardian for you against Us—87 except through the special mercy of your Lord. His favours towards you has been great indeed.

88 Say, 'If all men and jinn gathered together to produce the like of this Quran, they could not produce one like it, however much they helped one another.'

89 In this Quran, We have set out all kinds of examples for people, yet most of them persist in denying the truth. 90 They declare, 'We will never believe in you until you cause a spring to flow for us from the earth; 91 or you have a garden of date palms and vines, and cause streams to flow plentifully in the midst of them; 92 or you cause the heavens to fall down on us in pieces, as you have claimed; or you bring God and the angels before us face to face; 93 or you have a house made of gold; or you ascend to heaven; and we will not believe in your ascension until you send down to us a Book that we can read.' Tell them, 'Holy is my Lord. I am but a human being sent as a messenger.'

94 Nothing has prevented men from believing whenever guidance came to them, save their query, 'Has God sent a human being as a messenger?' 95 Say, 'If there had been angels walking around on earth, We would have sent an angel down from Heaven as a

messenger for them.' ⁹⁶ Say, 'God suffices as a witness between me and you [all]. He is informed about and observant of His servants.'

⁹⁷ Those whom God guides are the truly guided, and for those whom He lets go astray, you will find no helper besides Him, on the Day of Judgement. We shall gather them together, lying upon their faces, blind, dumb and deaf. Their abode shall be Hell. Every time the fire dies down, We will make it blaze up again for them. ⁹⁸ That is their recompense, because they rejected Our signs and asked, 'When we are reduced to bones and dust, shall we indeed be raised up as a new creation?'

⁹⁹ Do they not see that God, who has created heavens and earth, is able to create the like of them? He has appointed a definite term for them; there is no doubt about it, but the wrongdoers persist in denying the truth. ¹⁰⁰ Say, 'Even if you possessed the treasures of the mercy of my Lord, you would surely hold them back for fear of spending. Man is indeed niggardly!'

¹⁰¹ We did indeed give Moses nine manifest signs; you can enquire from the Children of Israel. When he came to them, Pharaoh said to him, 'Moses, I can see that you are bewitched.' ¹⁰² He said, 'You know full well that none has sent down these signs but the Lord of the heavens and the earth as eye-opening evidence. Indeed, Pharaoh, I can see that you are doomed.' ¹⁰³ So he resolved to scare them out of the land: but We drowned him along with all those who were with him. ¹⁰⁴ Thereafter, We said to the Israelites, 'Dwell in the land. When the promise of the Hereafter comes to be fulfilled, We shall assemble you all together.'

¹⁰⁵ We have revealed the Quran with the truth, and with the truth it has come down. We have sent you forth only to give good news and to give warning—¹⁰⁶ We have revealed the Quran bit by bit so that you may recite it to the people slowly and with deliberation. We have imparted it by gradual revelation.

¹⁰⁷ Say to them, 'You may believe in it or not. Those to whom knowledge had been revealed, fall on their faces in prostration when it is recited, ¹⁰⁸ and say, "Glory to our Lord! Our Lord's promise is bound to be fulfilled." ¹⁰⁹ They fall down upon their faces weeping, and [the Quran] increases their humility.'

¹¹⁰ Say, 'Whether you call on God or on the Merciful One: His are the finest names.' Pray neither in too loud a voice nor in silence, but between these two extremes. Seek a middle way ¹¹¹ and say, 'All praise is due to God who has never begotten a son and who has no partner in His kingdom; nor does anyone aid Him because of any weakness of His. Proclaim His greatness.'

18. THE CAVE (*AL-KAHF*)

In the name of God, the Most Gracious, the Most Merciful

¹ Praise be to God who has sent down to His servant—the Book, which is free from any ambiguity ² and which rightly directs, to give warning of stern punishment from Him, and to proclaim to the believers who do righteous deeds that they shall have an excellent recompense, ³ wherein they will remain [in a state of bliss] forever. ⁴ And to warn those who say, 'God has taken to Himself a son.' ⁵ They have no knowledge of this, nor did their forefathers have any either. What they say is monstrous: they are merely uttering falsehoods!ᵃ

⁶ Perhaps you may destroy yourself with grief if they do not believe in this message. ⁷ We have adorned the earth with attractive things, so that We may test mankind as to which one is best in conduct, ⁸ but We shall reduce all this to barren waste.

⁹ Do you think that the Men of the Caveᵇ and the Inscription were

---

a Why is it that God has arranged for the revelation of scriptures to the people of the world? The purpose of this is to acquaint them with His divine scheme. God has created man in this world for the purpose of trial. Thereafter, He will take a reckoning of everybody, and according to his deeds, will send him to hell or settle him in the eternal gardens of heaven. God wants everybody to be aware of this before death, so that nobody should have any excuse for wrongdoing.

b The incident of the Men of the Cave shows symbolically the stages through which true believers have to pass in their lives and the hurdles which they have to surmount. We learn from this incident that true believers sometimes, by force of circumstances, are compelled to take refuge in a 'cave'.

one of Our wondrous signs? [10] When the young men sought refuge in the cave, they said, 'Our Lord, grant us Your special mercy and give us right guidance in our affair.' [11] Then We caused them to fall into a deep sleep for many years inside the cave. [12] Then We woke them up again so that We might see which of the two groups would better calculate the time they had stayed there.

[13] We shall tell you their story as it really was. They were young men who believed in their Lord, and on whom We bestowed further guidance. [14] We strengthened their hearts, when they rose up and declared, 'Our Lord is the Lord of the heavens and the earth. Never shall we call upon any deity other than Him: for that would be an outrageous thing to do. [15] These people of ours have taken deities other than Him. Why do they not produce clear evidence about them? Who is more wicked than the man who invents a falsehood against God?

[16] 'Now that you have withdrawn from them and from all that they worship instead of God, take refuge in that cave; your Lord will extend His mercy to you and will make fitting provision for you in your situation.'[a]

[17] The sun could be observed to incline away from their cave on the right, as it rose, and to turn away from them on the left, when it set, while they lay in the wide space inside the cave. This is one of the signs of God. He whom God guides is rightly guided; but for him whom He lets go astray, you will find no helper or guide.[b]

But, from this cave which, to all appearances, was a grave for them, emerged a flood of life and vitality. Where their opponents had planned to end the lives of these young men, a new history began for them from that very same place.

a When a man, on account of his devotion to truth, becomes isolated from his fellow-beings, he comes closer to God. He comes so close to his Lord that he can converse with God. He talks with his Lord and receives a response from Him.

The new faith of the 'Men of the Cave', their fearless preaching, their willingness to forego everything rather than forego the right path, had all bestowed upon them the high status of nearness to God.

b Furthermore, God had chosen them for His special plan. The spiritual heights that they had attained had entitled them, in the eyes of God, to be seen as objective evidence of life after death. The Men of the Cave sleeping for such

[18] You would have thought they were awake, though they lay asleep. We turned them over, to the right and the left, while their dog lay at the cave's entrance with legs outstretched. Had you looked down and seen them, you would have surely turned your back and fled in terror.

[19] In the course of time, We raised them up again so that they might question one another. One of them asked, 'How long have you stayed [here]?' They said, 'We have stayed a day, or part of a day.' But others said, 'Your Lord knows best how long you have stayed here. Let one of you go then with these silver coins to the town, and let him find out what food is purest there, and bring you back a supply of it. Let him conduct himself with caution and not disclose your whereabouts to anyone: [20] for if they find you out, they will stone you to death, or force you back into their faith. In that case you would never prosper.'

[21] Thus We disclosed things to them so that they might know that God's promise was true and there was no doubt about the Hour [Judgement Day]. The people argued about them among themselves. They said, 'Build a monument over them. Their Lord knows best concerning them.' Those who prevailed in their affair said, 'Let us surely build a place of worship over them.'[a]

[22] Some will say, 'They were three, the fourth was their dog,' and others will say, 'They were five, the sixth was their dog,' guessing

---

a long period of time, and their awakening at the end of this period serves as a proof of life after death.

a The span of a man's life in this world is hardly a hundred years or even much less than that. After he dies, to all appearances it seems that he is finished once and for all, but the fact is that he exists even after death and rises again in a new world where he receives perpetual comfort or perpetual punishment.

This is a very serious human problem and has always been the subject of discussion. In view of its importance, God arranged for tangible evidence in addition to logical arguments so that there should be no scope for doubt about 'life after death'. Such tangible evidence has been presented in different forms in different periods. In the fifth century A.D., the emergence of 'the Men of the Cave' from the cave after 'death' is an extraordinary incident of this kind. In the present age, the researches of meta-science are perhaps the instances of a similar nature which establish the veracity of the theory of life after death.

at random. And yet others say, 'They were seven, the eighth was their dog.' Say, 'My Lord knows best their number.' Only a few know anything about them. Therefore, do not enter into controversies over them, nor seek information about them from any of them; ²³ never say of anything, 'I shall certainly do this tomorrow,' ²⁴ without [adding], "if God so wills." Remember your Lord whenever you might forget and say, 'I trust my Lord will guide me to that which is even nearer to the right path than this.'

²⁵ [Some say], 'They stayed in their cave three hundred years,' and to that some have added another nine years. ²⁶ Say, 'God knows best how long they stayed in it.' Only God has knowledge of the unseen in the heavens and on the earth. How well He sees and how well He hears! Man has no other guardian besides Him. He allows none to share His sovereignty.

²⁷ Proclaim what has been revealed to you from your Lord's Book. None can change His words. You shall find no refuge besides Him. ²⁸ Keep yourself attached to those who call on their Lord, morning and evening, seeking His pleasure; and do not let your eyes turn away from them, desiring the attraction of worldly life; and do not obey one whose heart We have made heedless of Our remembrance, one who pursues his own whims and becomes dissolute.

²⁹ Say, 'This is the truth from your Lord. Let him who will, believe in it, and him who will, deny it.' For the wrongdoers We have prepared a Fire which will cover them like a canopy, and if they beg for water, they will be given water as hot as molten lead, which will scald their faces: how dreadful a drink, and how evil a resting place!

³⁰ As for those who believe and do good deeds—We do not let the reward of anyone who does a good deed go to waste— ³¹ they shall dwell in the Gardens of eternity where rivers flow at their feet. Reclining upon raised couches, they will be adorned with bracelets of gold, and will wear green robes of fine silk and heavy brocade. An excellent reward and an excellent resting place!

³² Recite to them the parable of two men! One of them We provided with two vineyards which We surrounded with date-palms, and placed a field of grain in between; ³³ each garden produced its fruit and did

not fail to yield its best; We even caused a river to gush forth in the midst of them, [34] and so he had fruit in abundance. While conversing with his companion, he said, 'I am wealthier than you are, and have a bigger following!' [35] Having thus harmed his own soul, he entered his garden saying, 'I do not think this will ever perish, [36] and I do not believe that the Hour will ever come. Even if I am returned to my Lord, I shall surely find a better place than this.'[a]

[37] His companion replied, in the course of their discussion, 'Do you deny Him who created you from dust, from a small drop of fluid, then formed you into a man? [38] But as far as I am concerned, God alone is my Lord and I set up no partners with Him. [39] When you entered your garden, why did you not say, "That which God wills [will surely come to pass], there is no power save with God?" Although you see I have less wealth and offspring than you, [40] my Lord may well give me a garden better than yours and send down thunderbolts from heaven upon your vineyard, turning it into a barren waste; [41] or its water may sink into the earth, so that you will never be able to find it again!'[b]

[42] So it was, and all his fruit was destroyed. The vines had all fallen down on their trellises, and their owner wrung his hands, bewailing

---

a Take the example of a lush green garden which, due to a sudden natural calamity, is completely destroyed. This, figuratively speaking, will be the fate of one who achieves wealth and position in this world and becomes proud as a result.

Whatever share of wealth and position a man receives in this world is, in fact, a test from God. But an unjust and transgressing man takes it to be the result of his own efforts. Consequently, develops an attitude of arrogance. He looks down upon a person whose share of wealth and position in this world is comparatively inferior. He develops a certain type of mindset by which he thinks that his world will never come to an end, and that even if this world ends and another world comes into existence, there is no reason why he should not enjoy the same comfortable conditions as he is enjoying here.

He fails to differentiate between the world of trial and the world of reward.

b If God showers His blessings on a man, he should always remain grateful to Him. But, if he does not possess the right mentality, prosperity becomes the cause of arrogance and vanity developing in him. On the contrary, one who possesses the right mentality does not forget God, even in poverty. He is content with whatever he has, while entertaining the hope that God will give him more.

all that he had spent on his garden. He said, 'Would that I had not associated anyone with my Lord!' ⁴³ He had no party to help him against God, nor was he able to defend himself. ⁴⁴ The only support is from God, the True God. He is the best in rewarding and the best in respect of the final outcome.ᵃ

⁴⁵ Give them an example about worldly life. It is like the vegetation of the earth that thrives when watered by the rain, which We send down from the sky, and then it all becomes stubble which the wind blows away. God has power over all things. ⁴⁶ Wealth and children are an ornament of the life of this world. But deeds of lasting merit are better rewarded by your Lord and a far better source of hope.ᵇ

⁴⁷ The Day We shall make the mountains move and you will see the earth laid bare, and We shall gather all mankind together and shall not leave any one of them behind. ⁴⁸ They will be ranged before your Lord, standing in rows and He will say to them, 'Now you have come to Us as We created you at first. But you supposed that We would not appoint the time for the fulfilment of Our promise to you.'

---

a An individual may invest his money in a venture and also apply his talents to it, hoping that his investment and his talents will lead to a successful result and will bring him good returns. But, different types of untoward incidents occur and his hopes are dashed to pieces. No human device or human talent is able to save him.

In this world, time and time again God creates such situations, so that people should learn a lesson from them and should not commit the mistake of giving importance to anything except God.

b Things in this present world make the world hereafter understandable to us. When the earth, after getting water, becomes fresh and green, it appears as if it will remain like this forever. But thereafter the weather changes and all the greenery dries up and withers away.

The glamour of this world is no different. The charms of the world attract a man, but they are all quite ephemeral. Doomsday (the Day of Judgement) will soon destroy them in such a manner that it will appear as if they never existed.

The attraction of the world will not last, but here there is one thing that is going to endure forever and that is the good and pious deeds of a man. Just as plants in the garden grow by seeds being sown in the earth, so also there is a garden which flourishes by God being remembered and obeyed. This garden never has a winter season. Unlike the garden of the world, this garden grows in the life hereafter but it will be available there only to the sower of seeds.

⁴⁹ The Book [of deeds] will be placed before them and you will see the guilty apprehensive about its contents. They will say, 'Woe to us! What a record this is! It does not leave any deed, small or large, unaccounted for!' They will find everything they ever did laid in front of them: your Lord will not be unjust to anyone.

⁵⁰ When We said to the angels, 'Prostrate yourselves before Adam,' all prostrated themselves except Satan. He was one of the jinn and he disobeyed his Lord's command. Do you then take him and his offspring as protectors instead of Me, despite their enmity towards you? This is an evil exchange for the wrongdoers!

⁵¹ I did not call them to witness at the creation of the heavens and the earth, nor at their own creation; I do not take as My helpers those who lead others astray.

⁵² On that Day He will say to them, 'Call on those whom you thought to be My partners.' And they will call on them, but their prayer will not be heard; and We shall place a barrier [of enmity] between them. ⁵³ The guilty shall see the Fire and realize that they are going to fall into it: they shall find no way of escape from it.

⁵⁴ We have explained in various ways in this Quran, for the benefit of mankind, all kinds of examples, but man is most contentious. ⁵⁵ Nothing prevents people from believing when they are given guidance or from asking forgiveness of their Lord, but the fact that the fate of the previous peoples should befall them or to have the punishment come upon them face to face.

⁵⁶ We only send the messengers to bring good news and to give warning. Those who deny use fallacious arguments to nullify the truth, treating My revelations and My warnings as a jest. ⁵⁷ Who is more wicked than he who has been reminded of the revelations of his Lord, then turns away from them and forgets what his own hands have done? We have cast veils over their hearts lest they understand Our words, and made them hard of hearing. Call them as you may to the right path, they shall never be guided.

⁵⁸ Your Lord is the Forgiving One, the possessor of mercy. If He had to take them to task for the wrongs they have done, He would have hastened their punishment. They have an appointed time beyond which there will be no escape for them. ⁵⁹ We destroyed these

communities when they went on doing wrong, and We appointed a time for their destruction.

⁶⁰ Recall how Moses said to his servant, 'I shall not give up until I reach the place where both seas meet, even if it takes me years!' ⁶¹ But when at last they came to the land where the two seas met, they forgot their fish and it swiftly made its way into the sea. ⁶² After they had passed the place, Moses said to his young companion, 'Bring us our morning meal; we have indeed been fatigued by this journey.'

⁶³ He replied, 'Did you see when we were resting by the rock, that I forgot the fish? Satan made me forget it, so I did not mention it. It made its way to the sea in a miraculous way!' ⁶⁴ Moses said, 'That is just what we were looking for.' So they went back the way they had come, ⁶⁵ and they found one of Our servants to whom We had granted Our mercy and had given a knowledge from Ourself.

⁶⁶ Moses said to him, 'May I follow you, so that you may guide me by what you have been taught?' ⁶⁷ He replied, 'You will not be able to bear with me patiently. ⁶⁸ How could you be patient in matters beyond your knowledge?' ⁶⁹ Moses said, 'God willing, you will find me patient, and I will not disobey you in any thing.' ⁷⁰ He said, 'Well then, if you would follow me, do not ask me about anything till I speak of it to you.'

⁷¹ So they set out, but, when they got into a boat, the man made a hole in it. Moses exclaimed, 'Have you made a hole in the boat to drown the people in it? You have indeed done a dreadful thing!' ⁷² He replied, 'Did I not tell you that you would never be able to bear with me patiently?' ⁷³ He said, 'Do not take me to task for what I have forgotten, and do not be hard on me on account of what I have done!' ⁷⁴ So they travelled on. Then they met a young boy and the man killed him. Moses said, 'Have you slain an innocent person without his having slain anyone? Indeed, you have done a terrible thing!'ᵃ

---

a To damage a good boat and to kill a child do not appear to be good deeds. But, as the ensuing verses show, a profound sagacity was hidden in these deeds. These apparently wrong deeds were in reality correct and useful acts. This also provides an answer to what is known as the 'problem of evil'. In this world of

⁷⁵ The man said, 'Did I not tell you that you would not be able to have any patience with me?' ⁷⁶ Moses replied, 'If I ever ask you about anything after this, do not let me accompany you. I will have given you sufficient excuse.' ⁷⁷ So they went on until they came to a town. They asked its people for food, but were refused hospitality. They found a wall in the town which was about to fall down. His companion buttressed it and Moses said, 'Had you wished, you could have demanded payment for your labours.' ⁷⁸ He answered, 'This is where you and I must part company. But first I will tell you the meaning of the things you could not bear with patiently.*a*

⁷⁹ 'The boat belonged to some poor people who made their living from the sea. I wanted to damage it because there was a king coming behind them who was seizing every boat by force.

⁸⁰ As for the youth, his parents were believers and we feared that he would trouble them by rebellion and denial of truth. ⁸¹ We wanted their Lord to replace him with someone purer than him and more compassionate.*b*

⁸² 'The wall belonged to two young orphans in the town whose father had been a righteous man, and a treasure of theirs lay

---

human beings, there are many things which at first sight appear to be evils in the system. Yet, they are based on deep wisdom. It is true that in the present world this wisdom is hidden behind a veil. But, in the life hereafter, this veil will not be there. At that time, man will come to know that whatever happened did so according to the highest standards of justice.

a In spite of this inhospitable treatment, Khidr set right a crumbling wall belonging to the local people. The behaviour of God's true and pious subjects with others is not retaliatory, but is always in accordance with the norms of justice and righteousness.

b Khidr had not rendered the boat completely useless; he had only made it defective for the time being. The wisdom behind it was that, farther up the river where the boat was going, there was a king who, perhaps in connection with a war campaign, was forcibly confiscating good boats. So, the boat was made defective so that when the king's agents saw it, they should treat is as undeserving of attention and leave it.

This teaches us that a man should not lose heart if he has to face some untoward incident. He should reconcile with it, hoping that there should be some advantage hidden in whatever God has done, though man is not at that time fully aware of it.

underneath it. So your Lord wanted them to come of age and then to dig up their treasure as a mercy from Him. I did not do [it] of my own accord. That is the explanation of the things about which you were not able to restrain yourself.'[a]

83 They will ask you about Dhu'l-Qarnayn. Say, 'I will give you an account of him.' 84 We established him in the land, and gave him the means to achieve all things.

85 He travelled on a certain road; 86 until, when he reached the setting of the sun, he found it setting in a spring of murky water and near it he found some people. We said, 'Dhu'l-Qarnayn! You can either punish them or else you can treat them with gentleness.' 87 He said, 'We shall certainly punish him who does wrong; then he shall be brought back to his Lord who will punish him with a grievous punishment, 88 but whoever believes and does good works shall have a good reward and We shall facilitate his matter by Our command.'

89 Then he followed yet another path, 90 until he came to the rising-place of the sun, where he found it rising on a people for whom We had provided no shelter from it. 91 Thus indeed it was. We had full knowledge of him.

92 Then he followed still another path, 93 until he came between two mountains. He found beside them a people who could scarcely understand a word [of his language]. 94 They said, 'O Dhu'l-Qarnayn! Gog and Magog are causing corruption in the land, so may we pay you tribute on condition that you set a barrier between us and them?'[b]

---

a This incident of the child indicates the different ways in which God helps his subjects. He even helps them in matters of which they are not even aware and, not being aware of them, cannot pray to their Lord seeking a solution. Man should always demonstrate patience and gratitude to God. He should always hope for good from God in all circumstances. God is all knowing and that is why He knows best. God knows better what is good for his subject while the subject himself cannot be aware of this due to his limited knowledge.

b The 'two mountains' probably lay between the Caspian Sea and the Black Sea. Here savage tribes used to invade from other places and would then flee through mountain passes after indulging in plunder. Dhu'l-Qarnayn constructed an iron wall between the two mountains.

[95] He said, 'What My Lord has given me is better [than any tribute]. Help me with a force of labourers and I will erect a barrier between you and them: [96] bring me blocks of iron.' Then, when he had filled the gap between the mountain sides [he said], 'Now blow on the fire with your bellows.' When the iron blocks were red with heat, he said, 'Bring me molten brass to pour on them.' [97] So they [Gog and Magog] were not able to scale it, nor were they able to bore through it, [98] and he said, 'This is a mercy from my Lord. But when the promise of my Lord comes to pass, He will level it to dust. My Lord's promise is ever true!'[a]

[99] On that Day, We shall let them surge against each other like waves and then the Trumpet will be blown and We shall gather them all together. [100] On that Day We shall lay Hell bare before those who deny the truth,

[101] who have turned a blind eye to My reminder and a deaf ear to My warning.

[102] Do those who deny the truth, think that they can make My servants patrons instead of Me? We have reserved Hell as a lodging for those who deny the truth.

[103] Say, 'Shall I tell you of those who will lose the most through their actions? [104] They are those whose efforts have been wasted in the life of the world while they thought they were doing good. [105] They are those who deny their Lord's signs and the meeting with Him.' So their works are in vain, and We shall give them no weight on the Day of Resurrection. [106] Hell will be their reward, because they denied the truth, and made a jest of My signs and My messengers.

[107] Those who believe and do good works shall have the gardens of Paradise for their abode. [108] They shall forever dwell in the Gardens of Paradise, desiring no change.

[109] Tell them, 'If the ocean became ink for writing the words of my

---

a To erect an 'Iron Wall' to ward off enemies is a feat which generally generates a sense of pride in people. But even after constructing such an invincible wall, Dhu'l- Qarnayn did not lose his modesty and humility. He had set his eyes not on his own creations but on God's mighty powers, and a human being's power is nothing as compared to God's might.

Lord, surely the ocean would be exhausted before the words of my Lord came to an end—even if We were to add another ocean to it.'

¹¹⁰ Say, 'I am only a human being like yourselves. It is revealed to me that your God is One God. So let him who hopes to meet his Lord do good deeds and let him associate no one else in the worship of his Lord.'*a*

19. MARY (*MARYAM*)

In the name of God, the Most Gracious, the Most Merciful

¹ *Kaf Ha Ya 'Ayn Sad*

² This is an account of your Lord's mercy bestowed upon His servant Zachariah, ³ when he called upon his Lord in low tones, saying,*b* ⁴ 'Lord, my bones have weakened and my head has turned hoary with age, but never, Lord, have I been disappointed in my prayer to you: ⁵ now I fear my kinsmen when I am gone. [I have no hope of their continuing my mission] for my wife is barren, so grant me a successor from Yourself, ⁶ to be my heir and to be the heir [of

---

a To lead a life of faith and piety in this world is to give proof of tremendous sacrifice. It amounts to renouncing an apparent and visible heaven for the sake of a hidden, invisible heaven. This also means succeeding in the most difficult of tests, i.e. when man recognises the Truth on the strength of abstract arguments and then he turns his life in that direction, though there is no pressure on him to do so.

Those who exhibit such awareness (of truth) and perform such actions truly deserve to be admitted to gardens of eternal comfort and pleasure.

b Zachariah silently prayed to God and the prayer was granted in an astonishing and wonderful manner. This shows what real prayer is. True prayer is a spontaneous expression of the firm belief that all powers vest in God. Man receives every single thing only on His giving it to him, and no one can own a thing if He does not confer it on him. True prayer needs to be directed solely towards the one and only God. That is why true prayer gushes forth when one is alone—when there is nobody present except God and oneself.

the blessings] of the House of Jacob; and make him, O my Lord, acceptable to you.'

7 'Zachariah, We bring you good news of a son whose name shall be John. We have not given such a name to anyone before.' 8 'My Lord!' [said Zachariah], 'How shall I have a son when my wife is barren and I have reached such extreme old age?'

9 He said, 'It will be so! Your Lord says, "It is easy for Me for I created you when you were nothing before."' 10 He said, 'My Lord, grant me a sign!' He said, 'Your sign will be that you will not speak to anyone for three successive days and nights, although sound in body.' 11 Then Zachariah came forth from the shrine to his people and told them by signs to glorify the Lord morning and evening.*a*

12 To John We said, 'Hold fast the Book,' and while he was still a child, We bestowed upon him wisdom, 13 and tenderness [of heart] and purity. He was pious, 14 and dutiful towards his parents and was not haughty or disobedient. 15 Peace be on him on the day of his birth, and on the day of his death, and peace will be on him on the day he is raised up to life again.

16 Recount in the Book how Mary withdrew from her people to an eastern place 17 and kept herself in seclusion from them. We sent her Our angel, who presented himself to her as a full-grown human being. 18 When she saw him, she said, 'I seek refuge in the compassionate God from you; [do not come near] if you fear the Lord.' 19 'I am only the messenger of your Lord,' he replied. 'I shall bestow upon you the gift of a son endowed with purity.' 20 She said, 'How can I have a son when no man has touched me; and neither have I been unchaste?' 21 [The angel] replied, 'So shall it be; your Lord says, "This is easy for Me; and We shall make him a sign to people and a blessing, from Us. This has been decreed."'

22 So she conceived him and withdrew with him to a distant place.

---

a Just as the creation of the first human being, without a father or a mother, was a miracle of God, the birth of a child through a father and a mother is also God's miracle, irrespective of whether the father and mother are old or young. The fact is that it is God who creates man. He created him in the first instance and He creates man even today. The seeming cause is not the real reason, though appearances would suggest otherwise.

²³ The pains of labour drove her to the trunk of a date-palm. She said, 'Oh, if only I had died before this and passed into oblivion!'

²⁴ But a voice called out to her from below, 'Do not despair. Your Lord has provided a brook that runs at your feet, ²⁵ and if you shake the trunk of this palm-tree, it will drop fresh ripe dates on you. ²⁶ Eat and drink and rejoice. And if you see any human being say, "I have vowed a fast [of silence] to the Gracious God, and will not speak with any human being today."'

²⁷ Carrying her child, she brought him to her people. They said, 'O Mary, you have indeed done something terrible! ²⁸ Sister of Aaron, your father was not an evil man, nor was your mother an unchaste woman!'

²⁹ She pointed to the child. They said, 'How shall we talk to someone who is a child in the cradle?' ³⁰ [But] he said, 'I am God's servant. He has given me the Book and made me a prophet; ³¹ He has made me blessed wherever I may be, and has enjoined upon me prayer and almsgiving throughout my life. ³² He has made me dutiful toward my mother, and He has not made me arrogant or wicked. ³³ Blessed was I on the day I was born, and blessed I shall be on the day I die and on the day I am raised to life again.'

³⁴ Such was Jesus, the son of Mary. That is the whole truth, about which they still dispute: ³⁵ it does not befit the majesty of God that He should beget a son. Glory be to Him! He is far above that: when He decrees something, He says only, 'Be!' and it is.

³⁶ God is my Lord and your Lord, so worship Him alone. That is the right path. ³⁷ Yet different groups differed among themselves. How awful it will be for those who have rejected the truth when a dreadful Day arrives! ³⁸ How sharp of hearing, how sharp of sight they will be when they come to Us. But today, these evil-doers are obviously lost in error.

³⁹ Warn them of [the coming of] the Day of Remorse, when everything will have been decided, while they are heedless and do not believe. ⁴⁰ It is We who will inherit the earth and all who dwell upon it: they shall all return to Us.

⁴¹ Also recount the story of Abraham in the Book. He was a man of truth, and a prophet. ⁴² He said to his father, 'Why do you worship

something that can neither hear nor see nor benefit you in any way? [43] Father, I have been given some knowledge which has not come to you, so follow me: I shall guide you along a straight path. [44] Father! Do not worship Satan—for, truly, Satan is a rebel against the Most Gracious One! [45] Father, indeed I fear lest a punishment from the Gracious One afflict you, and you become a friend of Satan.'

[46] [His father] said, 'Do you reject my deities, Abraham? If you do not desist, I shall surely stone you to death. Keep out of my way!' [47] Abraham replied, 'Peace be on you: I will pray to my Lord for your forgiveness—He has indeed been gracious to me—[48] I will separate myself from you and from whatever you call upon besides God, and I will pray only to my Lord. It may well be that, in calling on my Lord, I will not be disappointed.'

[49] So when he had separated himself from them and from what they worshipped besides God, We bestowed on him Isaac and Jacob, and We made each of them a prophet. [50] We granted them Our mercy and bestowed on them true and high renown.

[51] Tell also of Moses in the Book. He was indeed a chosen one, and was a messenger and a prophet. [52] We called out to him from the right side of the mount and made him draw near to be in close communion with Us; [53] and We gave him as his helper, out of Our mercy, his brother Aaron, having made him a prophet.

[54] Tell also of Ishmael in the Book. He was true to his promise and was a messenger and a prophet. [55] He exhorted his people to prayer and almsgiving, and his Lord was pleased with him. [56] Tell also of Idris in the Book. He was a man of truth and a prophet. [57] We raised him to a high position.

[58] These are the ones whom God has favoured: the prophets from among the descendants of Adam and of those whom We carried in the Ark with Noah; the descendants of Abraham, of Israel, and of those whom We have guided and chosen. For when the revelations of the Merciful were recited to them, they fell down, prostrating themselves and weeping.

[59] But then they were succeeded by generations who neglected their prayers and were driven by their own desires. They will assuredly meet with destruction, [60] except for those who repent and believe

and do good deeds. These will enter Heaven, and they will not be wronged in the least.

⁶¹ Theirs shall be the Gardens of Eden, which the All Merciful has promised to His servants without their having seen them, and most surely His promise shall be fulfilled. ⁶² They will not hear therein anything vain, only greetings of peace. They will receive their provision there morning and evening. ⁶³ That is the Garden which We will grant to those of Our servants who have been God-fearing.*

⁶⁴ We never descend except at your Lord's command. What is before us and behind us and all that lies between belong to Him. Your Lord is not forgetful. ⁶⁵ He is the Lord of the heavens and of the earth and of all that is between the two. So worship Him alone and be steadfast in His worship. Do you know of anyone equal to Him in His attributes?

⁶⁶ Man asks, 'When I am once dead, shall I be raised to life?' ⁶⁷ But does man not remember that We created him when he was nothing before? ⁶⁸ By your Lord, We shall most surely gather them and the devils too; and bring them close to hell on their knees.

⁶⁹ Then We shall carry off from every group those who were most stubborn in their opposition to the Gracious One—⁷⁰ We surely know best those most deserving of the fires of hell—⁷¹ and there is not one of you but shall pass through it: a decree from your Lord which must be fulfilled. ⁷² Then We shall save those who feared God, but the wrongdoers shall be left there on their knees.

⁷³ When Our clear revelations are recited to them, those who deny the truth say to the faithful, 'Which of the two sides is better in respect of position and makes a more impressive assembly?' ⁷⁴ We have destroyed so many generations before them, who surpassed them in material power and splendour.

⁷⁵ Say, 'The Gracious One grants respite for a time to those who

---

a In this world, the hardest task is to abstain from vain pursuits and to lead one's life as an embodiment of peace. To this end, one has to willingly change a life of freedom into a life full of limitations. This is the most difficult sacrifice, which can be offered only by one who is truly God-fearing. Only those who fear God in this world can live here as people destined for paradise. They are the only ones who will be admitted to the eternal paradise of the Hereafter.

are in error until, when they are confronted with what they are promised, either in punishment [in the world] or in [the approach of] the Hour, they will realize who is worse in respect of position and who is weaker in resources.'

⁷⁶ God increases His guidance to those who follow guidance; and lasting good works are better in the sight of your Lord and are most rewarding.ᵃ

⁷⁷ Have you seen him who denies the truth in Our revelations and says, 'I shall certainly be given wealth and children.' ⁷⁸ Has he looked to the unseen, or has he made a pledge to the Merciful One? ⁷⁹ Indeed not. We shall record what he says and shall prolong the punishment for him. ⁸⁰ We shall inherit all that he boasts of, and he will come to Us all alone. ⁸¹ They have taken other deities besides God, so that they may be a source of strength for them. ⁸² But they shall reject their worship and turn against them.

⁸³ Do you not see that We have appointed devils to incite those who deny the truth to disobedience? ⁸⁴ So take no hasty action against them; their days are numbered. ⁸⁵ The Day will surely come when We shall gather the God-fearing like [honoured] guests before the Compassionate God ⁸⁶ and We shall drive the sinful like a thirsty herd into Hell. ⁸⁷ No one will have power to intercede, except for those who have permission from the Lord of Mercy.

⁸⁸ They say, 'The Gracious One has begotten a son.' ⁸⁹ Assuredly, you have uttered a monstrous falsehood: ⁹⁰ the heavens might well-

---

a To be rightly guided means the arousal of one's consciousness and the turning of it in the right direction. Whatever the circumstances, and whatever events befall such a rightly guided man, he interprets them correctly and his soul derives nourishment from them. In this way there is a constant increase in the guidance he receives in terms of faith and quality of life. The guidance received by him is not like a stagnant pool or a lifeless rock: it is like a living and ever growing tree.

Just as one who keeps worldly interests in view progresses in this world, similarly, one who acts with the Hereafter in view keeps on accumulating his good deeds. But as they are being amassed and stored in the Hereafter, their build-up is not visible in this world. However, when Doomsday tears apart the veil, everybody will see how the guidance of the guided one was being enhanced and how, along with this, his righteous deeds were also accruing.

nigh burst thereat, and the earth break asunder, and the mountains fall down in pieces, ⁹¹ because they ascribe a son to the Gracious One. ⁹² It does not become the majesty of the Compassionate God to take to Himself a son: ⁹³ there is none in the heavens or on the earth but shall return to the Merciful in utter submission— ⁹⁴ He has counted them and numbered them precisely— ⁹⁵ each one of them shall come to Him one by one on the Day of Judgement. ⁹⁶ The Lord of Mercy will bestow affection upon those who believe and perform righteous deeds.

⁹⁷ We have made it [the Quran] easy, in your own language [Prophet], so that you may convey glad news to the righteous and give warning to a stubborn people. ⁹⁸ How many generations We have destroyed before them! Can you find a single one of them alive now, or hear so much as a whisper from them?

20. TA HA

In the name of God, the Most Gracious, the Most Merciful

¹ *Ta Ha*

² We have not sent the Quran down to you to distress you, ³ but only as an exhortation for him who fears God; ⁴ it is a revelation from Him who has created the earth and the high heavens, ⁵ the All Merciful settled on the throne. ⁶ To Him belongs whatever is in the heavens and whatever is on the earth, and whatever lies in between them, and all that lies under the ground.

⁷ Whether you speak aloud [or in a low voice], He hears all, for He knows your secrets and what is even more hidden. ⁸ God, there is no deity but Him. His are the most excellent names.

⁹ Have you heard the story of Moses? ¹⁰ When he saw a fire, he said to his family, 'Wait here. I can see a fire. Perhaps I can bring you a brand from it, or find some guidance at the fire.'

¹¹ When he came close to it, a voice called out, 'Moses, ¹² I am your Lord! Take off your sandals, for you are in the sacred valley of Tuwa. ¹³ I have chosen you. So listen to what is being revealed.

¹⁴ I am God. There is no deity save Me; so worship Me alone, and say your prayers in My remembrance. ¹⁵ The Hour is coming. But I choose to keep it hidden, so that every human being may be recompensed in accordance with his labours. ¹⁶ Do not let anyone who does not believe in it and follows his own desires turn you away from it and so bring you to ruin.'

¹⁷ 'What do you have in your right hand, Moses?' ¹⁸ He replied, 'It is my staff. I lean on it, and with it, I beat down the leaves for my flock; I also have other uses for it.' ¹⁹ God said, 'Moses, cast it down.' ²⁰ So he threw it down, and all of a sudden, it turned into a fast-moving serpent. ²¹ God said, 'Take hold of it, and have no fear: We shall return it to its former state. ²² Put your hand under your armpit: it will come out [shining] white, without any blemish. This shall be another sign.ᵃ ²³ We shall show you some of Our greatest signs. ²⁴ Go to Pharaoh; he has transgressed all bounds.'

²⁵ Moses said, 'My Lord! open up my heart, ²⁶ and make my task easy for me. ²⁷ Loosen the knot in my tongue, ²⁸ so that they may understand my speech, ²⁹ and appoint for me a helper from among my family, ³⁰ Aaron, my brother. ³¹ Strengthen me through him, ³² and let him share my task, ³³ so that we may glorify You much ³⁴ and remember You much: ³⁵ You are surely watching over us.' ³⁶ God said, 'You have been granted your request, Moses.ᵇ

³⁷ 'Indeed, We showed Our favour to you before also, ³⁸ when We revealed Our will to your mother, saying, ³⁹ "Put him into a chest, then cast it into the river. The river will cast it on to the bank, and there he shall be taken up by an enemy of Mine and his." I

---

a The fact is that whatever there is in this world, or whatever the events, all are 'miracles' of God, be it the emerging of a sapling from the earth or a stick becoming a snake. 'Extraordinary' miracles are shown through prophets to make man take notice of the everyday miracles wrought by God.

b Remembrance of God's Grace is the real purpose of religion. But, remembrance does not mean the mere oral repetition of certain words. It indicates rather that state which is quite naturally engendered by the discovery of Truth. At that time, a man experiences the perfection of God's attributes to the point of being quite swept away by them. He becomes so intoxicated with godly feeling that he dedicates himself unstintingly to the divine cause.

showered My love on you so that you might be reared under My watchful eye. ⁴⁰ Recall when your sister walked along and said, "Shall I guide you to one who will take care of him?" Thus We returned you to your mother, so that her eyes might be cooled and that she might not grieve. And you killed a man and We delivered you from sorrow. We tested you with various trials. You stayed for a number of years among the people of Midian, then you came upto the standard, Moses.

⁴¹ I have chosen you for Myself. ⁴² Go, you and your brother, with My signs, and do not be remiss in remembering Me. ⁴³ Go, both of you to Pharaoh, for he has transgressed all bounds. ⁴⁴ But speak gently to him; perhaps he may yet take heed or even feel afraid.'

⁴⁵ They both said, 'Our Lord, We fear that he may commit some excess against us, or exceed all bounds in transgression.' ⁴⁶ God said, 'Do not fear; I am with you both. I hear and I see. ⁴⁷ Go to him and say, "We are both messengers from your Lord. Let the Children of Israel go with us, and do not oppress them. We have brought you a Sign from your Lord, and may peace be upon whoever follows the right guidance; ⁴⁸ it has been revealed to us that punishment shall overtake him who rejects it and turns away!"'

⁴⁹ Pharaoh said, 'Who then is the Lord of you both, Moses?' ⁵⁰ Moses replied, 'Our Lord is He who has given everything its form, then guided it.' ⁵¹ Pharaoh asked, 'What about the previous generations?' ⁵² Moses said, 'My Lord alone has knowledge of that, recorded in a Book. My Lord neither errs nor forgets.'

⁵³ It is He who has laid out the earth for you and traced routes in it and sent down water from the sky. We have brought forth every sort of plant with it, ⁵⁴ so eat and graze your cattle. In this there are signs for men of understanding. ⁵⁵ From the earth We have created you and We will return you to it, and from it We shall bring you forth a second time.*^a*

---

a The creation of the earth, the institution of the system of rainfall, the growth of plants and greenery and other natural phenomena that have made the present world habitable for living things, are astonishingly great and wonderful manifestations.

⁵⁶ We showed Pharaoh all Our signs but he rejected them and refused to believe in them. ⁵⁷ He said, 'Have you come to us to turn us out of our land by means of your magic, Moses? ⁵⁸ We will certainly bring you magic to match it. So appoint a time between us and you, in an open space, which neither we nor you will fail to keep.'

⁵⁹ Moses said, 'The day of the encounter will be the day of the festival, and let the people assemble when the sun has risen high.' ⁶⁰ So Pharaoh withdrew, devised his stratagem and returned. ⁶¹ Moses said to them, 'Woe to you! Do not invent lies against God, lest He destroy you by some calamity: whoever invents lies is bound to fail.'

⁶² Then they [the magicians] conferred among themselves, whispering to one another. ⁶³ They said, 'Certainly they are both magicians who want to drive you out of your land by their magic, and destroy your best traditions. ⁶⁴ Therefore, decide upon your plan and then come forward in ranks. Whoever gains the upper hand today shall surely triumph.'

⁶⁵ They said, 'Moses, will you throw down first, or shall we be the first to throw down?' ⁶⁶ Moses said, 'You throw down first.' Suddenly their ropes and staffs appeared to him, by their magic, to be moving about rapidly, ⁶⁷ and in his heart Moses became apprehensive, ⁶⁸ but We said, 'Do not be afraid. It is you who shall prevail.' ⁶⁹ Throw down that [staff] which is in your right hand—it shall swallow up what they have wrought, for what they have wrought is only a magician's trick. A magician shall never thrive, come whence he may. ⁷⁰ The magicians then prostrated themselves. They said, 'We believe in the Lord of Aaron and Moses.'

⁷¹ Pharaoh said, 'Have you believed in him before I permit you? He must be your master who has taught you magic. I will cut your hands and feet off on opposite sides, and have you crucified on the

---

They are 'signs' which prove that the Creator and Lord of this world can be none other than Almighty God. In order to bring into existence such a world as the present one, extraordinary power is required, which is available neither to any 'Sun' nor to any 'King'. This being so, there is no alternative but to admit that the One who has created our world and the One who controls it is a Superior Being, namely God.

trunks of palm-trees. You shall know whose punishment is more severe and more lasting.'

⁷² They said, 'Never shall we prefer you to all the evidence of the truth that has come to us. Nor to Him who has brought us into being. So decide whatever you will. Your jurisdiction only covers the life of this world—⁷³ we have believed in our Lord so that He may forgive us our sins and forgive us the sorcery that you have forced us to practice. God is the best and the most abiding.'

⁷⁴ Indeed, he who comes to his Lord a sinner shall be consigned to Hell; he shall neither die therein nor live. ⁷⁵ But he who comes to Him as a believer, having done good deeds, shall be exalted to the highest ranks, ⁷⁶ he will abide forever in the Gardens of eternity, through which rivers flow. That is the recompense for those who purify themselves.

⁷⁷ We sent a revelation to Moses saying, 'Take away My servants by night and strike for them a dry path through the sea. Have no fear of being overtaken and do not be afraid.' ⁷⁸ Pharaoh pursued them with his hosts, but they were submerged by the sea, which was destined to overwhelm them. ⁷⁹ For Pharaoh had led his people astray and did not guide them.

⁸⁰ Children of Israel! We delivered you from your enemies and We made a covenant with you on the right side of the Mount. We sent down manna and quails for you, ⁸¹ 'Eat from the wholesome things with which We have provided you but do not transgress, lest you should incur My wrath.' [We said], 'He that incurs My wrath shall surely be ruined. ⁸² But I am most forgiving towards him who turns in repentance and believes and acts righteously and follows the right path.'

⁸³ [When Moses was upon the Mount, God said,] 'O Moses, why have you come with such haste from your people?' ⁸⁴ He said, 'They are following in my footsteps, while I have hastened to You, my Lord, to please You.' ⁸⁵ But God said, 'We have tested your people in your absence. The Samiri has led them astray.'

⁸⁶ Moses returned to his people in anger and great sorrow. He said, 'My people, did your Lord not make you a handsome promise? Was

my absence too long for you? Did you desire that your Lord's wrath should descend upon you, when you broke your promise to me?'

⁸⁷ They answered, 'We did not break our promise to you of our own accord, but we had to carry loads of the people's ornaments and so we threw them [into the fire] for that was what the Samiri suggested,' ⁸⁸ then he forged a calf for them—an image producing a lowing sound. They said, 'This is your deity, the deity of Moses; he has forgotten it.' ⁸⁹ Why did they not see that it could not give them any response and had no power to harm or benefit them?

⁹⁰ Aaron had already told them, 'O my people! You are only being tested by this. Your Lord is the All Merciful, so follow me and obey my command.' ⁹¹ They replied, 'We shall not cease to worship it until Moses returns to us.'

⁹² Moses said to Aaron, 'What prevented you, when you saw that they had gone astray, ⁹³ from following me? Why did you disobey my command?' ⁹⁴ Aaron said, 'Son of my mother! Do not seize me by my beard nor by my head. I was afraid that you would say, "You have caused dissension among the Children of Israel and did not pay heed to my words."'

⁹⁵ Moses said, 'What was the matter with you, Samiri?' ⁹⁶ He said, 'I perceived what they did not see. So I took a handful [of dust] from the footprint of the Messenger and threw it in [the calf]. That is what my inner self prompted me to do.' ⁹⁷ Moses said, 'Begone! It shall be your lot to say throughout your life, "Do not touch me," and you will be faced with a fate from which there will be no escape. Now look at your deity to which you have become so devoted: we shall burn it up, and then scatter it into the sea. ⁹⁸ Your only deity is God, there is no deity but Him. His knowledge encompasses all things.'

⁹⁹ Thus We relate to you the history of past events, and We have given you a reminder [the Quran] from Us. ¹⁰⁰ Whoever turns away from it will bear a heavy burden on the Day of Judgement, ¹⁰¹ which they shall bear forever. It will be a grievous burden for them on the Day of Judgement, ¹⁰² the Day when the trumpet shall be blown: We shall gather all the sinners on that Day. Their eyes will turn blue with terror ¹⁰³ and they shall murmur to one another, 'You stayed

only ten days on the earth'—[104] We know best what they will say. The most perceptive of them will say, 'You stayed only one day.'

[105] They ask you about the mountains. Say, 'My Lord will scatter them as dust [106] and leave the earth level and bare, [107] with neither hollows nor upthrust mounds to be seen. [108] On that Day all will follow the summoning voice from which there is no escape; and all voices will be hushed before the Lord of Mercy, and nothing will be heard except a subdued murmur.

[109] On that Day no intercession will avail, except from one who has received the sanction of the Merciful and of whose words He approves—[110] He knows what is before them and what is behind them, but they cannot encompass Him with their knowledge—[111] on that Day all faces shall be humbled before the Living, Self-Subsisting One. Those burdened with evil deeds will come to grief, [112] but he who does good works, being a believer, shall fear no harm nor any injustice.'[a]

[113] We have thus sent down the Quran in Arabic and given all kinds of warnings in it, so that they may fear God, or may take heed—[114] exalted is God, the True King. Do not be impatient with the Quran before its revelation is completed, and say, 'My Lord, increase my knowledge.'

[115] We made a covenant with Adam before you, but he forgot, and We found him lacking in constancy. [116] When We said to the angels, 'Prostrate yourselves before Adam,' they all prostrated themselves, except for Satan, who refused, [117] We said, 'Adam, [Satan] is an enemy to you and to your wife. Let him not turn you both out of Paradise and thus make you come to grief.

[118] 'Here you shall not go hungry or be naked, [119] you shall not thirst, nor feel the sun's heat.' [120] But Satan whispered evil to him, saying, 'Adam, shall I lead you to the tree of immortality and to a

---

a On the Day of Judgement, real importance will be attached to what the individual has brought with him in terms of his piety, his good deeds and his personal virtues. One who has founded his life on untruth is bound to meet with failure in the Hereafter. There, only those will be successful who recognised their Lord—who remained invisible in this world—and who shaped their lives in accordance with His will and pleasure.

kingdom that never declines?' [121] They both ate the fruit of this tree, and so they became conscious of their nakedness and began to cover themselves with the leaves of the Garden. Thus Adam disobeyed his Lord and fell into error. [122] Then his Lord had mercy on him, accepted his repentance and guided him.

[123] God said, 'Go down, both of you, from here, as enemies to one another.' If there comes to you guidance from Me, then whoever follows My guidance will not lose his way, nor will he come to grief, [124] but whoever turns away from My reminder, will lead a straitened existence and on the Day of Judgement We shall raise him up blind [125] and he will ask, 'Lord, why have You raised me up blind, while I possessed sight before?' [126] God will say, 'Just as Our signs came to you and you ignored them, so will you on this Day be ignored.' [127] Thus We shall reward the transgressor who denies the signs of his Lord. But the suffering of the life to come is more terrible and more lasting.[a]

[128] Do they not learn a lesson from Our destruction of many generations before them in whose dwelling-places they walk about? Surely in this are signs for men of understanding. [129] But for a pre-ordained Word from your Lord, and a term [of respite] already fixed, immediate punishment would inevitably have taken place. [130] So be patient with anything they may say and glorify your Lord with His praise before the rising of the sun and before its setting; and glorify Him in the hours of the night and at the beginning and end of the day, so that you may find comfort.

[131] Do not regard with envy the worldly benefits We have given some of them, for with these We seek only to test them. The provision of your Lord is better and more lasting. [132] Bid your people say their prayers, and be constant in their observance. We demand nothing

---

a Those who turn away from God's guidance will be reduced in the Hereafter to blindness, being deprived of both the eyes. The reason for this is that such people are given eyes in the world in order to be able to see and recognise God's signs. But they live in such a manner that when they encounter God's signs, they fail to recognise them. Thus, they prove that, in spite of having eyes, they are really blind. So God will ask on that Day, what use it had been to give eyes to those who were determined to be blind.

from you. It is We who provide for you, and the best end is that of righteousness.

¹³³ They say, 'Why does he not bring us a sign from his Lord?' Have they not been given sufficient proof in previous scriptures? ¹³⁴ If We had destroyed them with a punishment before this, they would have surely said, 'Our Lord, why did you not send to us a messenger so that we might have followed Your commandment before we were humiliated and disgraced?' ¹³⁵ Say, 'Everyone is waiting; so wait if you will. You shall know who has followed the right path, and who has found guidance.'

21. THE PROPHETS (*AL-ANBIYA'*)

In the name of God, the Most Gracious, the Most Merciful

¹ The time of reckoning has drawn near for mankind, yet they are heedless and turn away. ² Whenever any fresh admonition comes to them from their Lord, they listen to it, but do not take it seriously; ³ their hearts are distracted and forgetful. The wrongdoers confer together secretly, saying, 'Is not this man a mortal like you? Will you succumb to magic with your eyes open?' ⁴ Say, 'My Lord knows every word spoken in the heavens and on the earth. He is All Hearing, All Knowing.'

⁵ Some say, 'These are his confused dreams.' Others say, 'He has invented it himself,' and yet others say, 'He is a poet. Let him bring us a sign as previous messengers did.' ⁶ Before them, not one of the communities which We destroyed believed either. Will these believe?

⁷ The messengers We sent before you were but men whom We had sent revelations. Ask the People of the Book if you do not know this—⁸ We did not give them bodies that needed no food, nor were they to live forever. ⁹ Then We fulfilled Our promise to them and We saved them and those with them whom We pleased, and We destroyed those who exceeded all bounds.

¹⁰ We have revealed a Book to you which is admonition for you. Will you not then understand? ¹¹ How many communities of evil-doers We have destroyed, raising up other people after them. ¹² When they

felt Our punishment coming upon them, they began to flee from it.
[13] They were told, 'Do not try to flee, but return to the comfort and luxuries in which you exulted and to the places where you lived, so that you may be questioned.' [14] They said, 'Woe to us! We were indeed wrongdoers,' [15] and this they kept repeating until We caused them to become like a field mowed down, and reduced to ashes.

[16] It was not in play that We created the heavens and the earth and all that lies between them. [17] Had We wished to find a pastime, We would surely have found it in that which is with Us, if such had been Our will. [18] We will hurl the truth at falsehood, the falsehood shall be crushed and will disappear. Woe to you for what you utter.

[19] To Him belongs whosoever is in the heavens and on the earth and those that are with Him are never too proud to worship Him, nor do they grow weary; [20] they glorify Him night and day without tiring.

[21] Have they taken deities from the earth who can bring the dead to life? [22] If there had been in the heavens and on the earth, other deities besides God, both the heavens and earth would be ruined. God, Lord of the throne, is far above that which they ascribe to Him. [23] None shall question Him about His works, but they shall be questioned.

[24] Have they taken other deities besides Him? Say to them, 'Bring your proofs. This is the reminder of those who are with me and the reminder of those who were before me.' But most of them do not know the truth, and so they turn away from it. [25] We sent all messengers before you with this revelation: 'There is no deity save Me, so worship Me alone.'

[26] They say, 'The All Merciful has taken a son!' Glory be to Him! They are only His honoured servants: [27] they do not try to speak ahead of Him, and they act at His command. [28] He knows what is before them and what is behind them, and they cannot intercede without His permission. Indeed they themselves stand in awe of Him. [29] Whoever of them should say, 'I am a deity besides Him,' shall be requited with Hell. Thus do We reward the wrongdoers.

[30] Do not those who deny the truth see that the heavens and the earth were joined together and that We then split them asunder?

And that We have made every living thing out of water? Will they still not believe?[a]

³¹ We set firm mountains upon the earth lest it should sway under them, and We placed therein passages for paths so that they might find their way. ³² We have made the heaven a well-secured canopy; yet still they turn away from Our signs. ³³ It is He who created the night and the day, and the sun and the moon, each gliding in its orbit.

³⁴ We have not granted everlasting life to any human being before you; then if you [Muhammad] should die, will they live forever? ³⁵ Every soul shall taste death; We test you with both good and evil [circumstances] as a trial. To Us you shall return.

³⁶ When those who deny the truth see you, they laugh at you, saying, 'Is this the one who talks of your deities?' Yet it is they who deny all mention of the Gracious One.

³⁷ Man is a creature of haste. Soon I will show you My signs, but do not ask Me to hasten them. ³⁸ They ask, 'When will this promise be fulfilled, if what you say be true?' ³⁹ If only those who deny the truth knew the time when they would not be able to ward off the fire neither from their faces nor from their backs. They will not be helped! ⁴⁰ Indeed, it will come upon them suddenly and confound them; and they will not be able to ward it off, nor shall they be reprieved. ⁴¹ Other messengers have been mocked before you, but those who scoffed were overwhelmed by the very thing they had mocked.

⁴² Say, 'Who will save you from the wrath of the Most Gracious,

---

a The solid mass which God 'tore asunder' probably refers to the earliest state of the earth and skies which, in this modern age is explained in terms of the 'Big Bang' theory. According to modern scientific calculations, the entire matter of the Universe was originally in the shape of a very big ball (a super atom). In obedience to known physical laws, all its parts were attracted towards its centre and were bound together very strongly. At some point, there was a huge explosion in this ball and its parts suddenly started hurtling outwards. In this way, finally the vast universe, which now extends before us, came into being. Innumerable such signs are found on the earth. If man examines them in depth, he will be overwhelmed by the realisation of God's blessings and His powers. But he ignores them. Even after seeing clear events and signs, he continues to turn a deaf ear and a blind eye to them.

by night and by day?' Yet they turn away from the remembrance of their Lord. ⁴³ Do they have other deities who can defend them against Us? They cannot even help themselves, neither can they be aided against Us.

⁴⁴ Yet We bestowed the good things [of life] upon their fathers for a great length of time. But do they not see how We are shrinking their borders? Is it they who will prevail?

⁴⁵ Say, 'I warn you only through the Revelation.' But the deaf can hear nothing when they are warned, ⁴⁶ yet if even a breath of your Lord's punishment touched them, they would say, 'Woe to us! We were indeed wrongdoers.'

⁴⁷ We shall set up scales of justice on the Day of Resurrection, so that no soul can be in the least wronged. Actions as small as a grain of mustard seed shall be weighed. We are sufficient as a reckoner.

⁴⁸ We gave Moses and Aaron the criterion of right and wrong and a light and reminder for the righteous,ᵃ ⁴⁹ those who fear their Lord in the unseen, also dread the Hour of Judgement. ⁵⁰ This is a blessed reminder that We have revealed to you. Will you then reject it?

⁵¹ Before this We gave Abraham his guidance. We knew him well. ⁵² When he asked his father and his people, 'What are these images to which you are so devoted?' ⁵³ They replied, 'We found our fathers worshipping them.' ⁵⁴ Abraham said, 'Indeed, you and your fathers have been clearly misguided.'

⁵⁵ They said, 'Have you brought us the truth or are you jesting?' ⁵⁶ Abraham replied, 'Your Lord is the Lord of the heavens and the

---

a The criterion or discernment (*furqan*) light and reminder or remembrance, which were given to Moses, were the very things which all the prophets received from God. The criterion means that ideological standard which enables a man to distinguish between Truth and falsehood. Light means divine guidance which pulls a man out of the darkness of the wrong path and puts him in the light of the straight path. Remembrance highlight the latent educative aspect of things, so that things do not figure simply as things, but as treasure chests of knowledge for the recognition and realisation of God and His Divine guidance. In this way God has arranged for the guidance of man. But, it is possible for God's Guide Book to provide guidance in the real sense only when a man is anxious about his fate in the Hereafter, and this anxiety makes him so serious that he attaches more importance to Truth and righteousness than to all other things.

earth, who created them, and I bear witness to that. ⁵⁷ By the Lord, I will devise a plan against your deities after you have gone away and turned your backs!' ⁵⁸ He broke them all into pieces, except for the biggest one of them, so that they might return to it [for enquiry].

⁵⁹ 'Who has done this to our deities? He must be a wrongdoer.' ⁶⁰ Some said, 'We heard a young man, called Abraham, talking about them.' ⁶¹ They said, 'Then bring him here in the sight of all the people, so that they may act as witnesses.' ⁶² They said, 'Abraham, was it you who did this to our deities?' ⁶³ He answered, 'Rather this biggest one of them did it. Ask them, if they can speak.'

⁶⁴ Then they turned to one another and said, 'It is you yourselves who are in the wrong,' ⁶⁵ then they hung their heads, and said, 'O Abraham! You know they cannot speak.' ⁶⁶ Abraham said, 'So, do you worship something instead of God that can neither benefit you nor harm you? ⁶⁷Shame on you and on whatever you worship instead of God. Can you not understand?'

⁶⁸ They said, 'Burn him and help your deities, if you are resolved to do something.' ⁶⁹ But We said, 'Fire! Be cool and a means of safety for Abraham.' ⁷⁰ They had sought to do him harm, but We frustrated them.

⁷¹ And We saved him and Lot [and brought them] to a land which We had blessed for all people, ⁷² We bestowed Isaac and then Jacob on him as an additional boon and We made all of them righteous. ⁷³ We made them leaders who guided people by Our command. We revealed to them the doing of good, observance of prayer and the giving of alms and Us alone did they worship.

⁷⁴ To Lot We gave wisdom and knowledge and delivered him from the city which practiced abomination. They were indeed a wicked people. ⁷⁵ We admitted him to Our mercy; he was a righteous man.

⁷⁶ Before him Noah cried out to Us, and We heard his prayer. We saved him and all his household from a great distress. ⁷⁷ We helped him against his people who rejected Our revelations. They were surely a wicked people, so We drowned them all.

⁷⁸ Tell of David and Solomon who both passed judgement on the field into which some people's sheep had strayed [and grazed] at night. We bore witness to their judgement. ⁷⁹ We gave Solomon the

right understanding of the matter, and We bestowed wisdom and knowledge on both of them. We caused the mountains and the birds to celebrate Our praises along with David. We had the power to do this— [80] We taught him the art of making coats of mail for you, to protect you in battle. Will you then give thanks?

[81] We subjected to Solomon the stormy wind, which blew at his behest towards the land which We had blessed. For it is We who have knowledge of all things—[82] We also subjected to him some of the jinn who dived for him in the sea and performed other tasks; We kept a watch over them.

[83] Remember Job when he called on his Lord saying, 'I have been afflicted with great distress: but You are the most merciful of the merciful.' [84] We heard his prayer and relieved his suffering, We restored to him his family, doubling their number as an act of Our grace, and as a reminder for the worshippers.

[85] Remember Ishmael and Idris and Dhul Kifl: they were all patient and steadfast. [86] We admitted them to Our mercy. They were all righteous men.

[87] Remember the man in the whale [Jonah] when he went away in anger, thinking We had no power over him. But he cried out in the darkness, 'There is no deity but You. Glory be to You! I was indeed wrong.' [88] So We heard his prayer and delivered him from sorrow. Thus shall We deliver the true believers.

[89] Remember Zachariah, when he called out to his Lord, 'Do not leave me heirless Lord, You are the best of heirs.' [90] So We heard his prayer and bestowed John upon him and made his wife fit to bear him a child. They used to hasten to do good and they called on Us in hope and fear, and they were always humble towards Us.

[91] Remember the one who guarded her chastity; so We breathed Our Spirit into her, and made her and her son a sign for all people.[a]

---

[a] The special quality of Mary (Maryam) is said to be that she guarded her chastity. By way of a reward for this, she was made the mother of a prophet who was born of a direct miracle of God.

This is true of common men and women also. Everybody is being tried in this world by being required to keep his urges and desires under control. The more an individual shows self-discipline on this score, the more will be his

⁹² This community of yours is one community and I am your Lord, so worship Me. ⁹³ But they divided themselves into factions, but to Us they shall all return. ⁹⁴ He who does good works while he is a believer, shall not see his efforts disregarded: We record them all.

⁹⁵ It is ordained that no nation We have destroyed shall ever rise again, ⁹⁶ but when Gog and Magog are let loose and swarm down from every hillside and they spread out, [leaping across every barrier of land and sea], ⁹⁷ when the true promise of God draws near, those who denied the truth will stare in amazement, crying, 'Woe to us! We have been so heedless of this. Indeed, we were wrongdoers.'

⁹⁸ You and what you worship instead of God will be fuel for hell: to it you shall all come— ⁹⁹ if those had really been deities, they would not have been led there; but there they will remain forever. ¹⁰⁰ They shall groan. They will not hear therein anything else. ¹⁰¹ But those who have been promised a good reward by Us will be kept far away from Hell—¹⁰² they will not hear the slightest sound of it, and they shall forever abide in a state of bliss, among everything their souls longed for. ¹⁰³ The great Horror [of the Day of Judgement] shall not grieve them, and the angels will welcome them, saying, 'This is your Day which you have been promised.'

¹⁰⁴ On that Day We shall roll up the heavens like a scroll of parchment. As We originated the first creation, so shall We repeat it. This is a promise binding on Us. Truly, We shall fulfill it. ¹⁰⁵ We have already written in the Psalms following the Reminder, 'My righteous servants shall inherit the earth.' ¹⁰⁶ Herein, surely is a message for true worshippers.

¹⁰⁷ We have sent you forth as a mercy to all mankind. ¹⁰⁸ Say, 'It has been revealed to me that your God is but One God. Will you then submit to Him?' ¹⁰⁹ If they turn away, say, 'I have warned you all alike, though I do not know whether [the scourge] which you are promised is near at hand or far off. ¹¹⁰ God surely knows what you say openly and also knows what you conceal. ¹¹¹ Nor do I know whether it may mean a trial for you and a short reprieve.' ¹¹² Say,

share in God's special blessings.

'My Lord, judge with truth. Our Lord is the Gracious One whose help we seek against what you utter.'

22. THE PILGRIMAGE (*AL-HAJJ*)

In the name of God, the Most Gracious, the Most Merciful

[1] O People! Fear your Lord. The catastrophe of the Last Hour shall be terrible indeed: [2] when that Day comes, every suckling mother shall forsake her infant and every pregnant woman shall cast her burden and everyone will appear intoxicated, although they are not: the punishment of God will be severe indeed.[a] [3] Yet there are some who dispute about God without having any knowledge and they follow every rebellious devil, [4] it has been decreed concerning anyone whom he befriends, that he shall mislead him and guide him to the punishment of the Fire.

[5] O people! If you are in doubt about the Resurrection, remember that We first created you from dust, then from a sperm drop, then from clotted blood, then a lump of flesh, both shaped and unshaped, so that We might manifest to you [Our power]. We cause what We will to stay in the womb for an appointed time, then We bring you forth as infants and then We cause you to grow and reach full growth. Then, some of you will pass away early in life, while some of you will reach extreme old age in which they will know nothing of what they once knew. You see the earth, dead and barren, but no sooner do We send down rain upon it than it begins to stir and swell, and produce every kind of luxuriant vegetation: [6] that is because God is the truth. It is He who gives life to the dead and He has the

---

a This is a literal description of some of the horrors of Doomsday, a day which will throw people into a state of sheer horror which will cause the mother to forget the baby at her breast and the pregnant woman to miscarry.

The earthquakes occurring in our present world give only a slight foretaste of the events of Doomsday. The onset of the great earthquake of Doomsday will make man forget everything he had considered important and due to which he had forgotten Doomsday—so much so that on that Day he will forget even his most cherished possessions and his near and dear ones.

power to will anything. [7] The Last Hour is bound to come. There is no doubt about it. God will raise up those who are in their graves.

[8] There are some who dispute about God without having any knowledge or guidance, or any enlightening Book. [9] They turn away arrogantly, leading people astray from God's path. Such men shall incur disgrace in this life and taste the punishment of the Fire on the Day of Judgement. [10] [God will say],'This is the reward of your misdeeds. God is not unjust to His servants.'

[11] There are some who worship God half-heartedly, then, if some good befalls them, they are content with it, but if an ordeal befalls them, they revert to their former ways. They lose in this world as well in the Hereafter. That is a clear loss.

[12] He calls on, instead of God, something that can neither harm him, nor benefit him. That is indeed straying far away—[13] he calls on that which would sooner harm than help. Such a patron is indeed evil and such a companion is indeed evil. [14] God will admit those who believe and act righteously into Gardens watered by flowing rivers. God does whatever He wills.

[15] Anyone who thinks that God will not help him [His messenger] in this world and the Hereafter, let him stretch a rope up to the sky; then let him cut it off and see if his plan can help to remove the cause of his anger. [16] We have sent down the Quran as clear evidence, and surely God guides whom He will.

[17] God will judge between the believers, the Jews, the Sabaeans, the Christians, the Magians and the polytheists on the Day of Judgement. Surely God is witness to everything.

[18] Do you not see that whoever is in the heavens and whoever is on the earth, as well as the sun and the moon, and the stars and the mountains, and the trees and the beasts and many human beings—all submit to God? But there are many who have become deserving of punishment. Whoever God disgraces, will have no one to honour him. Surely, God does what He wills.

[19] These two groups, [the believers and those who deny the truth], dispute concerning their Lord. Those who deny the truth will have garments of fire cut out for them; and boiling water will be poured down over their heads, [20] anything in their stomachs as well as

their skins will be melted by it. [21] There will be maces of iron for them; [22] whenever, in their anguish they seek to escape from Hell, they will be driven back into it, and they will be told, 'Taste the punishment of Hell.'

[23] God will admit those who believe and do good deeds to Gardens watered by flowing rivers; there they will be given bracelets of gold and pearls to wear and their clothing will be of silk. [24] For they were guided to purity of speech. And they were guided to the path of the Glorious Lord.

[25] As for those who deny the truth and debar others from God's path and from the Sacred Mosque which We set up for all people, natives and strangers alike, and all who seek to profane it by evil-doing—We shall make them taste a painful punishment.

[26] We assigned to Abraham the site of the House, saying, 'Do not associate with Me anything and purify My House for those who circumambulate [the Kabah] and those who stand upright, and those who bow and prostrate themselves.'

[27] Call mankind to the Pilgrimage. They will come to you, on foot, and on every kind of lean camel, by every distant track [28] so that they may witness its benefit for them and, on the appointed days may utter the name of God over the cattle He has provided for them. Then eat their flesh, and feed the distressed and the needy—[29] then let the pilgrims purify themselves and fulfil their vows and perform the circumambulation of the Ancient House.

[30] Such is God's commandment. Whoever honours that which is declared sacred by God may be sure that it counts for good in the sight of his Lord. Livestock is lawful for you, except that which has already been explicitly forbidden. Then shun the abomination of the deities and shun all falsehood.

[31] Devote yourselves to God, not associating any partners with Him. Whoever associates anything with God is like one who falls from heaven and is snatched by the birds or carried away by the wind to a distant place.

[32] Thus it is. He who honours the symbols set up by God shows

the piety of his heart.[a] 33 You may benefit from the animals for an appointed time. Then they must be sacrificed at the Ancient House.

34 For every people We have appointed rites of sacrifice, so that they may pronounce the name of God over the cattle which He has provided for them. Your God is One God; surrender yourselves to Him; and give good news to the humble 35 whose hearts are filled with awe at the mention of God; who endure adversity with fortitude, say their prayers regularly and spend out of what We have given them.

36 We have appointed for you the sacrificial camels as one of the symbols set up by God, in which there is much good for you. So invoke God's name over them as you line them up for slaughter, and when they have fallen down dead, feed yourselves and feed the needy—those who do not ask as well as those who do. We have thus subjected them to you so that you may be grateful. 37 Their flesh and blood do not reach God: it is your piety that reaches Him. Thus God has subjected them to you, so that you may glorify Him for the guidance He has given you. Give glad tidings to those who do good.

38 God will surely defend the believers. God does not love the perfidious and the ungrateful. 39 Permission to fight is granted to those who are attacked, because they have been wronged—God indeed has the power to help them—40 they are those who have been driven out of their homes unjustly, only because they said, 'Our Lord is God.' If God did not repel the aggression of some people by means of others, cloisters and churches and synagogues and mosques, wherein the name of God is much invoked, would surely be destroyed. God will surely help him who helps His cause—God is indeed powerful and mighty.

41 [They are] those who, if We established them in the land, would say their prayers regularly and pay the *zakat* and enjoin good and forbid evil. The final outcome of all affairs rests with God.

---

a The rites of worship or prayer in Islam have two aspects—the outward and the inward. The inward aspect is the real essence of worship. The outward aspect serves as a symbol (*sha'irah*, pl. *sha'a'ir*) of this inward aspect. The rites specified by God cannot be treated as being carried out properly if they are simply observed outwardly. In order to be properly observed, these deserve to be performed with a pure and God-fearing heart.

⁴² If your opponents deny you, remember that, before them, the people of Noah and the tribes of 'Ad and Thamud denied their messengers likewise. ⁴³ So did the people of Abraham and the people of Lot, ⁴⁴ and the inhabitants of Midian also charged their prophets with falsehood. Moses was also rejected. I gave respite to those who denied the truth, but then I seized them. Consider then, how terrible My repudiation of them was.

⁴⁵ How many a town We destroyed which was given to wrongdoing, so that its roofs fell down, and how many a well is deserted and how many a lofty castle is in ruins. ⁴⁶ Have these people not travelled through the land to make their hearts understand and let their ears hear; the truth is that it is not the eyes that are blind but the hearts that are in the bosoms that are blinded.

⁴⁷ They ask you to hasten the punishment; God will never go back on His promise. A Day with your Lord is like a thousand years in your reckoning. ⁴⁸ To how many a town We gave respite while it was given to wrongdoing. Then I seized it. To Me all things shall return.

⁴⁹ Say, 'O people, I am sent only to give you clear warning.' ⁵⁰ Those who believe and do good deeds shall be forgiven and shall receive an honourable provision. ⁵¹ Whereas those who strive against Our signs, seeking to defeat their purpose, shall be the inmates of the Fire.

⁵² Whenever We sent any messenger or prophet before you, and he recited anything [of Our revelation], Satan tampered with it. But God abrogates Satan's interjections and then He firmly reaffirms His revelations. God is all knowing and all wise. ⁵³ He makes Satan's suggestions a trial for those whose hearts are diseased or hardened—and, surely, the wrongdoers are far gone in error— ⁵⁴ so that those who are given knowledge may realize that this is the truth from your Lord and thus believe in it, and so that in their hearts they may humbly submit to Him. God will surely guide the faithful to a straight path.

⁵⁵ Those who deny the truth will continue in doubt until the [Last] Hour suddenly comes upon them or the scourge of the woeful Day descends upon them. ⁵⁶ On that Day all control will belong to God. He will judge between them. Those who believe and do good deeds

shall enter the Gardens of Bliss, [57] but those who deny the truth and deny Our signs will receive a humiliating punishment.

[58] As for those who left their homes for the cause of God and then were slain or died, God will give them a generous provision. Surely God is the Best of Providers. [59] He will admit them to a place with which they shall be well-pleased. For God is all knowing and most forbearing.

[60] Thus it shall be. As for one who retaliates to the same extent as he has suffered and then is again wronged, God will surely come to his aid. God is merciful and forgiving.

[61] That is because God makes the night pass into the day and makes the day pass into the night. God is all hearing and all seeing. [62] That is because God is the Truth while anything they invoke besides God is sheer falsehood. God is the Sublime, the Great One.

[63] Have you not seen how God sends down water from sky, whereupon the earth becomes green? God is unfathomable, and all aware; [64] all that is in the heavens and on the earth belongs to Him. Surely, God is self-sufficient and praiseworthy.

[65] Do you not see, how God has subjected everything on the earth to you, and the ships that sail on the sea by His command. He holds back the sky from falling down on the earth, except with His permission. God is most compassionate and most merciful to mankind—[66] it is He who gave you life. Then He will cause you to die. Then He will give you life again. Surely, man is most ungrateful.

[67] We have appointed for every community ways of worship to observe. Let them not dispute with you on this matter. Call them to the path of your Lord—for surely, you are rightly guided— [68] if they should dispute with you, then say, 'God is well aware of what you do.' [69] On the Day of Resurrection, God will judge between you regarding your differences. [70] Do you not know that God has knowledge of what the heavens and the earth contain? All is recorded in a Book; all this is easy for God.

[71] Yet instead of God, they worship something for which God has sent no authority and about which they have no knowledge. The wrongdoers will have no helper. [72] Whenever Our clear revelations are recited to them, you will recognize the disgust on the faces of

those who deny the truth. It is almost as if they are going to attack those who recite Our message to them. Say, 'Shall I tell you of something worse than this? It is the Fire that God has promised to those who are bent on denying the truth. What an evil destination!'

⁷³ People, here is an illustration. So listen carefully. Surely, those whom you invoke other than God cannot create even a fly, even if they were all to combine together to do it, and if a fly should snatch anything away from them, they cannot recover it from it. Both are indeed weak, the seeker and the sought. ⁷⁴ No just estimate have they made of God. Surely God is powerful and mighty.

⁷⁵ God selects messengers from both angels and from mankind; God is all hearing and all seeing: ⁷⁶ He knows what lies ahead of them and what is behind them. All things shall return to God.

⁷⁷ You who are true believers, kneel and prostrate yourselves, worship your Lord and do good works, so that you may succeed. ⁷⁸ Strive for the cause of God as it behoves you to strive for it. He has chosen you and laid on you no burden in the matter of your religion, the faith of Abraham your forefather. In this, as in former scriptures He has given you the name of Muslims, so that the Messenger may be a witness over you, and so that you may be witnesses over mankind. Therefore, say your prayers regularly and pay the *zakat* and hold fast to God. He is your master. An excellent master and an excellent helper!

23. THE BELIEVERS (*AL-MU'MINUN*)

In the name of God, the Most Gracious, the Most Merciful

¹ Successful indeed are the believers; ² those who are humble in their prayer; ³ those who turn away from all that is frivolous; ⁴ those who pay the *zakat*; ⁵ those who safeguard their chastity ⁶ except with their wives, and what their right hands possess—for then they are free from blame, ⁷ but those who seek to go beyond that are transgressors—⁸ those who are faithful to their trusts and

promises; [9] and those who attend to their prayers; [10] these are the heirs of Paradise [11] they shall abide in it forever.[a]

[12] We created man from an essence of clay, [13] then We placed him as a drop of fluid in a safe place, [14] then We developed that drop into a clinging form, and We developed that form into a lump of flesh, and We developed that lump into bones, and clothed the bones with flesh. Then We brought him into being as a new creation[b]—glory be to God, the best of creators—[15] after this you shall surely die. [16] Then you will be raised up again on the Resurrection Day.

[17] We have created seven paths above you; We have never been unmindful of Our creation. [18] We sent down water from the sky in due measure and lodged it in the earth—but if We please, We have the power to take it away—[19] We have produced palm-groves and vineyards for you, in which there are abundant fruits for you; and you eat these, [20] also a tree growing on Mount Sinai which produces oil and a condiment for those who eat it. [21] You have a lesson in livestock. We provide you with drink from what is in their bellies, and you have many other benefits from them; some of them you eat, [22] and you ride on them as you do in ships.

[23] We sent Noah to his people, and he said, 'My people, worship God; you have no other deity except Him. Will you not fear Him?' [24] The leaders of his people who denied the truth, said, 'He is only

---

a When faith comes to a man, it is not a simple matter. It brings about a revolution in his life. He becomes a worshipper of God and one who bows down before Him. His sincerity and seriousness increase to the extent that wasting time in useless pursuits appears fatal to him. He sets aside a portion of his earnings in the name of God and with that he helps the needy. He exercises control over his sexual desires and enjoys them within the limit prescribed by God for the purpose. He lives his life in this world as a responsible person. He never misappropriates whatever is entrusted to him. He never dishonours any pledge undertaken by him.

b The vivid Quranic description of the various developmental stages of the formation and birth of human beings, is surprisingly identical with modern scientific findings. This provides a clear proof of the fact that the Quran is the Book of God. Had it not been so, such similarity between the findings of modern research and the statements of the Quran, made fourteen hundred years ago, would not have been possible. Cf. 39:6 and the corresponding note.

a human being like yourselves who wants to make himself superior to you. If God had wished, He would have sent down angels. We never heard about this from our forefathers. [25] He is only a madman, so, as far as he is concerned wait for a while.'

[26] Noah said, 'My Lord, help me! for they have rejected me,' [27] then We revealed Our will to him: 'Build the Ark under Our watchful eye according to Our instructions. When Our command comes, and waters gush up out of the earth, take on board pairs of every species and members of your household, except for any of them on whom sentence has already been passed—do not plead with Me for those who have done wrong: they shall be drowned.

[28] When you and all your followers have settled in the Ark, say, "Praise be to God who has delivered us from a wicked people," [29] and say, "My Lord, let me land with Your blessing in a blessed landing place. You alone can provide the best landings".' [30] Surely there are clear signs in that. In this way We put people to the test.

[31] Then We raised another generation after them, [32] and sent a messenger to them from among themselves: 'Worship God alone. You have no deity other than Him. Will you not then fear God?' [33] But the leaders of his people who denied the truth and denied the Meeting in the Hereafter, because We had granted them ease and plenty in their worldly life, said, 'This is only a human being like yourselves—he eats what you eat, and drinks what you drink—[34] if you obey a human being just like yourselves, then you will surely be lost.

[35] Does he promise you that when you die and have become dust and bones, that you will be brought forth again? [36] What you are promised is indeed far-fetched. [37] There exists only our present life: we die and we live [but once], and shall never be raised up again. [38] He is only a man who has invented a lie about God, and we are not going to believe him!'

[39] The messenger said, 'My Lord, help me, for they have rejected me.' [40] God said, 'Before long they will be filled with regret.' [41] The blast justly struck them and We reduced them to rubble. Away with such wicked people!

[42] Then We raised up other generations after them—[43] no community

can advance or postpone its appointed time—⁴⁴ then We sent Our messengers in succession. Every time their messenger came to a people, they rejected him. So We destroyed them one after the other, and let them become mere tales. So away with the people who will not believe!

⁴⁵ Then We sent Moses and his brother Aaron with Our signs and clear authority ⁴⁶ to Pharaoh and his courtiers, but they behaved insolently, for they were an arrogant people. ⁴⁷ They said, 'Are we to believe in two human beings like ourselves, while their people are subject to us?'*ᵃ* ⁴⁸ So they rejected them both, and became those who were destroyed. ⁴⁹ We gave Moses the Book so that they might be guided.

⁵⁰ We made the son of Mary and his mother a sign and gave them shelter on a peaceful hillside watered by a fresh spring.

⁵¹ Messengers, eat what is wholesome and do good deeds: I am well aware of what you do. ⁵² Your religion is but one religion—and I am your only Lord, therefore, fear Me.

⁵³ Yet they divided themselves into factions, each rejoicing in what they had. ⁵⁴ So leave them in their bewilderment for a while. ⁵⁵ Do they imagine that the wealth and children We have provided ⁵⁶ have no other purpose except to help them in acquiring material benefits? No indeed. But they do not understand.

⁵⁷ Those who tremble with fear of their Lord; ⁵⁸ and believe in His messages ⁵⁹ and do not ascribe partners to Him; ⁶⁰ and those who give to others what has been bestowed upon them with their hearts trembling at the thought that they must return to their Lord; ⁶¹ it is they who vie with one another in doing good works and shall be the foremost in doing so. ⁶² We charge no soul with more than it can bear. We have a record which clearly shows the truth and they will not be wronged.

⁶³ But their hearts are heedless of this. Moreover, there are other

---

a They observed that the Prophet was not surrounded by heaps of wealth, nor was he seated upon a throne of power. So they considered him to be a lowly person. On account of their being worshippers of externals, they failed to fathom the Prophet's inner greatness.

deeds besides this which they do. ⁶⁴ But then when We seize the affluent among them, they will cry out for help. ⁶⁵ Do not cry out for help this day, for surely you shall not be helped by Us. ⁶⁶ My revelations were recited to you, but you turned your backs ⁶⁷ in arrogance, as if you were abandoning a story-teller.

⁶⁸ Have they not pondered over the word of God? Has something come to them that did not come to their forefathers? ⁶⁹ Or do they not recognize their Messenger, and so deny him? ⁷⁰ Do they say he is possessed? Rather he has brought them the truth, but most of them are averse to the truth. ⁷¹ If truth had followed their whims and desires, heavens and earth and all that lives in them would have been brought to ruin. Rather We have brought them their Reminder. Yet they keep avoiding their Reminder.

⁷² Or are you asking them for any reward? But the reward of your Lord is the best, for He is the Best of Providers, ⁷³ and, most surely, you are calling them to a straight path. ⁷⁴ But those who do not believe in the Hereafter have indeed deviated from that path.

⁷⁵ Even if We showed them mercy and relieved them of their afflictions, they would still persist in their transgression, wandering blindly. ⁷⁶ We seized them with the punishment, but they did not surrender to their Lord, nor will they humble themselves ⁷⁷ until We open before them a gate of harsh punishment and then they will be dumbfounded.

⁷⁸ It is He who gave you ears, eyes and hearts, yet how seldom you are grateful!ᵃ ⁷⁹ He it is who has multiplied you on the earth

---

a In this universe the human being is a special creation who has been given the exceptional powers of hearing, seeing and thinking. These capacities have been given to man for a special purpose, namely, to understand the reality of life. He should use his ears to hear the voice of Truth. With his eyes he should see the signs of God that are spread all around him. He should use his thinking powers for an in-depth study of all these things. This, in reality, is the way of thankfulness of the ears, the eyes and the heart. Those who do not give evidence of such thankfulness in this world risk losing their entitlement to these gifts forever.

b Among the attributes of God that are prominently visible in this world are His powers to make a living thing die and to make a dead one come alive. Finally, God will cause all the dead people to assemble again. Thereafter, just

and to Him you shall all be gathered: [80] He is the One who gives life and causes death and He controls the alternation of night and day. Will you not then understand?

[81] But they say the same as the ancients said, [82] 'When we have died and become dust and bones, will we be raised up again? [83] We and our forefathers were promised this before. This is nothing but fables of the ancients.'

[84] Say, 'To whom do the earth and all therein belong? Tell me, if you have any knowledge?' [85] They will say, 'To God.' Say, 'So will you not pay heed? [86] Say, 'Who is the Lord of the seven heavens, and of the Glorious Throne?' [87] They will say, 'They belong to God.' Say, 'So do you not fear Him?' [88] Say, 'In whose hands lies sovereignty over all things, protecting all, while none can seek protection against Him? Tell me, if you have any knowledge.' [89] They will say, 'All this belongs to God.' Say to them, 'How are you then deluded?'

[90] We have revealed to them the truth. But they are certainly liars. [91] God has not taken to Himself a son, nor is there any other deity besides Him; otherwise, each god would have walked away with what he had created. They would surely have tried to overcome one another. Glory be to God, above all that they ascribe to Him. [92] Knower of the unseen and the visible; He is exalted above all that which they associate with Him.

[93] Pray, 'Lord, if you would show me that [the punishment] of which they have been warned, [94] then do not place me, Lord, with the wrongdoers.' [95] We certainly have the power to show you what they have been warned about.

[96] Repel evil with what is best—We are well aware of the things they say—[97] and say, 'My Lord, I seek refuge with You from the prompting of the devils. [98] I seek refuge with You, Lord, lest they should come near me.'

[99] When death comes to any of them, he says, 'My Lord, send

---

as He turns night into day, similarly He will remove the veils of ignorance that had been covering the eyes of the people. Then, the reality of things will stand fully revealed.

me back [100] so that I may do good works in the world I have left behind.' Never! It is indeed but a meaningless word that he utters. A barrier shall stand behind such people till the Day they are raised up again. [101] When the trumpet is blown, on that Day there will be no ties of relationship between them; neither will they ask about one another: [102] then those whose scales weigh heavy with good works will be successful. [103] But those whose scales weigh light will have ruined their souls; in Hell will they abide. [104] The Fire will scorch their faces and they will abide therein with their faces distorted.

[105] Were not My messages recited to you and did you not reject them? [106] They will answer, 'Lord, misfortune overcame us and we became an erring people. [107] Lord, deliver us from Hell. Then, if we revert again, we shall definitely be wrongdoers.' [108] God will say, 'Stay there and do not speak to Me. [109] Among My servants, there were those who said, "Lord, We believe, so forgive us and have mercy on us. You are the best one to show mercy." [110] But you made a laughing stock of them to the point where it made you forget My remembrance; and you went on laughing at them. [111] I have rewarded them this Day for their steadfastness, and it is they who have triumphed.'

[112] He will ask, 'How many years did you stay on earth?' [113] They will say, 'We stayed a day or part of a day. Ask those who have kept count.' [114] He will say, 'You only stayed for a little while, if only you knew.

[115] 'Do you imagine that We created you without any purpose and that you would not be brought back to Us?' [116] Then, exalted be God, the true King, there is no deity except Him, the Lord of the Glorious Throne. [117] He, who invokes another deity along with God—a deity of whose divinity he has no proof—will be brought to account by his Lord. Certainly, those who deny the truth shall never prosper. [118] Say, 'Lord, forgive us and have mercy. You are the best of those who show mercy.'

24. LIGHT (*AL-NUR*)

In the name of God, the Most Gracious, the Most Merciful

¹ This is a chapter which We have revealed and which We have made obligatory; We have sent down clear revelations in it, so that you may take heed. ² Flog the adulteress and the adulterer, each one of them, with a hundred lashes. Let no pity for them cause you to disobey God, if you truly believe in God and the Last Day; and let their punishment be witnessed by a number of believers. ³ The adulterer shall marry only an adulteress or a polytheist woman, and an adulteress shall marry only an adulterer or a polytheist man; such marriages are forbidden for believers.

⁴ Those who defame chaste women, but cannot produce four witnesses, shall be given eighty lashes. Do not accept their testimony ever after, for they are transgressors,ᵃ ⁵ save those who afterwards repent and make amends, for truly God is forgiving and merciful.

⁶ One who accuses his wife and has no witnesses except himself shall swear four times by God that his charge is true, ⁷ and the fifth time, that God's curse may be upon him if he is telling a lie. ⁸ The wife shall receive no punishment, if she bears witness four times in the name of God that her husband has lied ⁹ and, a fifth time that God's wrath will be upon her if he is telling the truth. ¹⁰ Were it not for God's grace and His mercy upon you, [you would have come to grief] and God is wise, acceptor of repentance.

¹¹ Those who brought up that slander were a band from among you. Do not regard it as a misfortune, for it is good for you. Every one of them shall be held to account for the sin he has committed; and he who took the greater part in it shall have a terrible punishment.

¹² When you heard of it, why did not the believing men and

---

a Levelling false allegations against anyone is, in fact, an attempt at moral assassination. Severe punishments are prescribed in Islam for such an offence. Even if a wrongdoer escapes punishment in this world, he cannot in any case escape punishment in the life Hereafter, unless he repents and seeks God's pardon.

believing women think well of their own people, and say, 'This is a manifest slander?' [13] Why did they not produce four witnesses? If they could not produce any witnesses, they were indeed liars in the sight of God![a]

[14] Had it not been for the grace of God and His mercy on you in this world and the Hereafter, a terrible punishment would have afflicted you for your plunging headlong into slander. [15] When you were spreading it with your tongues and saying with your mouths things of which you had no knowledge, you considered it to be a trivial matter, but, in God's sight, it was very serious. [16] When you heard it, why did you not say, 'It is not right for us to speak of this. God forbid! This is a monstrous slander.' [17] God warns you never to repeat the like of it again, if you are true believers. [18] God explains the commandments to you. God is all knowing and wise.

[19] Those who desire that indecencies should spread among the believers, will have a painful chastisement in this world and the Hereafter. God knows, and you do not know. [20] But for the grace of God and His mercy upon you, and were not God compassionate and merciful, [you would have come to grief].

[21] O you who believe, do not follow in the footsteps of Satan, and whoever follows in the footsteps of Satan should know that he enjoins only indecency and evil. But for the grace of God and His mercy upon you, not one of you would ever be purified; but God purifies whom He pleases. God is all hearing and all knowing.

[22] Let not those who are possessed of means and plenty among you resolve to withhold their bounty from their kindred and the needy and those who have migrated from their homes in the cause

---

a Every right-minded believer must think well of his fellow believer. Entertaining bad opinions about others is actually exposing one's own evil nature and, conversely, holding a good opinion about others is a proof of one's own righteous nature.

The correct procedure is that whenever anyone speaks ill of any other person, proof should immediately be demanded of him. One who hears such an allegation should not simply start repeating it to others.

of God. Let them forgive and overlook. Do you not wish God to forgive you? God is forgiving and merciful.*a*

²³ Truly, those who accuse chaste, unwary, believing women are cursed in this world and the Hereafter. For them awaits a terrible chastisement. ²⁴ On the Day when their own tongues, hands and feet shall bear witness against them about what they did—²⁵ on that Day God will justly requite them—and they will realize that God is the truth, that makes all things manifest.*b*

²⁶ Corrupt women are for corrupt men, and corrupt men are for corrupt women; good women are for good men and good men are for good women. The latter are absolved from anything they may say; forgiveness and an honourable provision await them.

²⁷ Believers, do not enter other people's houses until you have asked their owners' permission and greeted them. That will be the better for you, so that you may be heedful. ²⁸ If you find no one at home, do not go in until permission has been granted you. If you are told to go away, then go away. That is more proper for you. God knows well what you do. ²⁹ There is nothing wrong in your entering uninhabited houses if that serves a useful purpose: God knows all that you do openly, and all that you would conceal.

---

a In Islam, help is to be given to needy persons on account of their being needy and not on any other grounds. Therefore, the Quranic verses were revealed ordering that the 'haves' should not stop giving monetary help to the 'have-nots' on account of their personal grudges. They were asked whether they did not want to be pardoned by God and told that if they expected God's forgiveness, they too should adopt a forgiving attitude towards others.

b Man often denigrates others. But he does not know that the words uttered by him reach God before reaching others. Man uses his limbs, that is, his hands and legs to harm and oppress others. But, he remains unaware of the fact that when the Day of Judgement arrives, his own hands and legs, being his no longer, will turn against him and act as God's witnesses. This unawareness is the real root of all evils. If a man were to come to grips with the reality that he lives in a world where the eyes of God do not lose sight of him even for a single moment, and where every single action of his is being recorded by a divinely established system, his whole life would change. He would weigh every word before uttering it, and he would use the powers of his hands and legs with extreme caution.

³⁰ Tell believing men to lower their gaze and remain chaste. That is purer for them. God is aware of what they do.

³¹ Say to believing women that they should lower their gaze and remain chaste and not to reveal their adornments—save what is normally apparent thereof, and they should fold their shawls over their bosoms. They can only reveal their adornments to their husbands or their fathers or their husbands' fathers, or their sons or their husbands' sons or their brothers or their brothers' sons or their sisters' sons or maidservants or those whom their right hands possess or their male attendants who have no sexual desire or children who still have no carnal knowledge of women. Nor should they swing their legs to draw attention to their hidden ornaments. Believers, turn to God, every one of you, so that you may prosper.^{*a*}

³² Marry those among you who are single, and those of your male and female slaves who are fit [for marriage]. If they are poor, God will provide for them from His bounty, for God's bounty is infinite and He is all knowing. ³³ Those who do not have the means to marry should keep themselves chaste until God grants them enough out of His bounty. If any of your slaves desire a deed of freedom, write it out for them, if you find any promise in them, and give them some of the wealth God has given you. Do not force your [slave] maids into prostitution, in order to enrich yourself, when they wish to preserve their chastity. Yet if anyone forces them, once they have been forced, God will be forgiving and merciful to them. ³⁴ We have

---

a In the period when Islam came into existence, the system of owning slaves was prevalent in Arabia and, indeed, throughout the whole world. Islam, following its basic principles, started abolishing slavery in a very systematic though gradual manner. One of the methods followed was known as *makatibah*. The literal meaning of *kitab* or *makatibah* is 'writing'. Here this term denotes a bond by which a male or female slave promises his or her owner to earn a specified amount within a specified period and give it to the owner, after which he or she will be free. Both male and female slaves were thus being set free either by *makatibah* or by other methods, so much so, that by the end of the period of early Islamic history known as the 'four rightly guided caliphates' this institution was almost completely abolished.

sent down clear revelations to you and the example of those who passed away before you and an admonition for the God-fearing.

[35] God is the light of the heavens and the earth. His light may be compared to a niche containing a lamp, the lamp inside a crystal of star-like brilliance lit from a blessed olive tree, neither of the east nor of the west.a The [luminous] oil is as if ready to burn without even the fire touching it. Light upon light; God guides to His light whom He will. God draws such comparisons for mankind; God has full knowledge of everything.*a*

[36] [They worship] in the houses which God has allowed to be raised for the remembrance of His name, morning and evening, [37] people who are not distracted by trade or commerce from the remembrance of God and the observance of prayer and the payment of the *zakat*—fearing a Day when hearts and eyes will be convulsed, [38] so that God may reward them according to the best of their deeds and give them more out of His bounty. God provides for whoever He wills without measure.

[39] As for those who deny the truth, their works are like a mirage in a desert. The thirsty traveller thinks it to be water, but when he comes near, he finds it to be nothing. He finds God there, who pays him his account in full. God is swift in His reckoning. [40] Or like darkness on a deep ocean covered by waves billowing over waves and overcast with clouds: darkness upon darkness. If he stretches out his hand, he can scarcely see it. Indeed, the man from whom God withholds His light shall find no light at all.

[41] [Prophet], do you not see that all those who are in the heavens

---

a This is a metaphor with many layers of meaning. 'Light' symbolizes the guidance of God Almighty. 'Niche' is man's heart and 'lamp' is faith (*iman*), sheltered in that niche. The image is elaborated by yet two more points of reference: 'crystal of star-like brilliance' and 'luminous oil'. Faith, already compared to a 'lamp' standing in the 'niche' of the human heart, is safe and well protected from any external influence by the 'crystal' or the walls of the niche, which is, as already mentioned, the human heart. The 'luminous oil' filling the lamp and ready to be lit at any moment, speaks of the eagerness with which faith waits for the Truth to appear before it, so that it may accept it without the slightest delay and set itself ablaze with it.

and on earth praise God, as do the birds with wings outstretched? Each knows his own mode of prayer and glorification: God has full knowledge of all that they do. ⁴² To God belongs the kingdom of the heavens and the earth, and to God shall all things return.

⁴³ Do you not see how God drives the clouds, then joins them together, then piles them into layers and then you see the rain pour from their midst? He

sends down from the skies mountainous masses [of clouds] charged with hail, and He makes it fall on whom He will, and turns it away from whom He pleases. The flash of His lightning may well-nigh take away the sight. ⁴⁴ God alternates the night and the day—truly, in this there is a lesson for men of insight.

⁴⁵ God created every creature from water. Some crawl upon their bellies, others walk on two legs, and others walk on four. God creates what He pleases. He has power over all things. ⁴⁶ We have sent down revelations clearly showing the truth. God guides whom He wills to the straight path.

⁴⁷ They say, 'We believe in God and in the Messenger, and we obey.' But then, even after that a group of them will turn away. Those are surely not believers ⁴⁸ and when they are called to God and His Messenger so that he may judge between them, some of them turn away. ⁴⁹ But if the truth happens to be to their liking, they are quite willing to accept it! ⁵⁰ Is there a sickness in their hearts, or are they full of doubt? Or do they fear that God and His Messenger will be unjust to them? The truth is that they themselves are wrongdoers.

⁵¹ The response of the believers, when they are called to God and His Messenger in order that he may judge between them, is only, 'We hear and we obey.' It is they who will prosper: ⁵² those who obey God and His Messenger, and fear God, and are mindful of their duty to Him, are the ones who will triumph.

⁵³ They swear firm oaths by God that if you command them to march forth, they will obey you. Say, 'Do not swear: your obedience, not your oaths, will count. God is well aware of all your actions.' ⁵⁴ Obey God and obey the Messenger. If you turn away, then he is responsible for what he is charged with and you are responsible

for what you are charged with. If you obey him, you will be rightly guided. The Messenger is responsible only for delivering the message clearly.

⁵⁵ God has promised to those among you who believe and do good works that He will surely grant them power in the land as He granted to those who were before them; and that He will surely establish for them their religion which He has chosen for them. He will cause their state of fear to be replaced by a sense of security. Let them worship Me and associate no other with Me. Whoever still chooses to deny the truth is truly rebellious.

⁵⁶ Attend to your prayers and pay the *zakat* and obey the Messenger, so that you may be shown mercy. ⁵⁷ Do not think that those who deny the truth can frustrate Our plan on earth; their abode shall be Hell; and it is indeed an evil resort.

⁵⁸ Believers, let [even] those whom you rightfully possess, and those who are under age ask your leave on three occasions when they come in to see you: before the morning prayer, when you have taken off your garments in the heat of noon, and after the evening prayer. These are the three occasions for your privacy. At other times, there is nothing blameworthy if you or they go around visiting one another. Thus God makes clear to you His revelations: God is all knowing and wise. ⁵⁹ When your children have reached the age of puberty, let them still ask permission as their elders do. Thus God expounds to you His revelations: God is all knowing and wise. ⁶⁰ There is no blame on elderly women who are past the age of marriage, if they take off their outer clothing, without revealing their adornments. But it would be better for them to guard themselves. God is all hearing, all knowing.

⁶¹ There is no harm if the blind, the lame, the sick or you yourselves eat in your own houses, or in the houses of your fathers, or mothers, or brothers, or sisters, or paternal uncles, or paternal aunts, or maternal uncles, or maternal aunts, or in those that you are in charge of or in the house of a friend. There is no objection to your eating together or separately. But when you enter houses, salute one another with a greeting of peace, a greeting from your Lord full of blessings and

purity. Thus does God expound to you His commandments, so that you may understand.

⁶² They only are true believers who believe in God and His Messenger. When they are with him on some matter of common concern, they should not depart until they have asked him for permission to do so. Those who ask you for such permission are the ones who truly believe in God and His Messenger. When they ask you for permission to attend to some affair of their own, then grant it to whoever you please and seek forgiveness from God for them. God is forgiving and merciful.

⁶³ Do not treat being called by the Messenger like being called by one another. God knows those of you who slip away on some pretext. Let those who go against his order beware lest some affliction befall them or they receive a painful punishment. ⁶⁴ Surely, whatever is in the heavens and on the earth belongs to God. God knows well what condition you are in. On the Day when they return to Him, He will declare to them all that they have done. God has full knowledge of all things.

25. THE CRITERION (*AL-FURQAN*)

In the name of God, the Most Gracious, the Most Merciful

¹ Blessed be He who has revealed the criterion [the Quran] to His servant that he may warn the nations. ² Sovereign of the heavens and the earth, who has begotten no children and who has no partner in His sovereignty, it is He who has created all things and measured them out precisely. ³ Yet they have taken, besides Him, deities who create nothing and are themselves created, and who have no power to harm, or benefit themselves and who control neither death, nor life, nor resurrection.

⁴ Those who deny the truth say, 'This is only a forgery of his own invention in which others have helped him.' What they say is unjust and false. ⁵ They say, 'It is just fables of the ancients, which he has had written down. They are dictated to him morning and evening.' ⁶ Say to them, 'It has been revealed by Him who knows every secret

that is in the heavens and on the earth. Truly, He is most forgiving and most merciful.'

⁷ They say, 'What kind of a messenger is this who eats food and walks about in the market-places? Why has no angel been sent down with him to warn us?' ⁸ Or a treasure should have been sent down to him, or he should have had a garden from which to eat.' The wrongdoers say, 'You are surely following a man who is bewitched.' ⁹ Observe what kind of things they attribute to you. They have surely gone astray and cannot find the right way again.

¹⁰ Blessed is He who, if He please, can give you better things than that; gardens watered by flowing streams, and palaces too. ¹¹ They deny the Hour. For those who deny that Hour, We have prepared a blazing fire. ¹² When it sees them from afar, they will hear its raging and roaring. ¹³ When they are thrown into a narrow space, chained together, they will plead for death. ¹⁴ But they will be told, 'Do not call today for one death, call for many deaths!' ¹⁵ Say, 'Which is better, this or the Paradise of immortality which the righteous have been promised? It is their recompense and their destination.' ¹⁶ Abiding there forever, they shall find in it all that they desire. This is a binding promise which your Lord has made.

¹⁷ On the Day He gathers them all together with those they worship besides Him, He will say, 'Was it you who misled My servants, or did they stray away by themselves?' ¹⁸ They will answer, 'Hallowed be You! It was not proper for us to choose any guardian other than You. But You gave them and their fathers the comforts of this life, so that they forgot Your reminder and thus brought destruction upon themselves.' ¹⁹ [God will say], 'Now, they have given the lie to all your assertions, and you can neither ward off [your punishment] nor obtain any help.' For, whoever of you has committed evil, shall be caused by Us to taste great suffering!'

²⁰ We never sent any messengers before you who did not eat food and walk in the market-place. We make some of you a means of trial for others, to see whether you are steadfast. Your Lord is all seeing.

²¹ Those who do not expect a meeting with Us say, 'Why are angels not sent down to us?' Or 'Why do we not see our Lord?' Surely, they are too proud of themselves and have greatly exceeded

all bounds. 22 There will be no good tidings for the guilty on the day they see the angels; and they will cry out, 'Keep away, keep away!' 23 and We shall take all that they did and turn it into scattered dust. 24 The inhabitants of the Garden will have the best residence and the finest lodging on that Day.

25 On a Day when the sky will split open with its clouds and the angels are sent down rank upon rank, 26 true sovereignty on that Day will belong to the Gracious One, and it will be a hard Day for those who deny the truth. 27 On that Day, the wrongdoer will bite his hands and say, 'Would that I had walked in the Messenger's path! 28 Oh, would that I had never chosen such a one for my companion—29 he made me forgetful of the warning after it had reached me. Satan is man's great betrayer.' 30 The Messenger will say, 'Lord, my people did indeed discard the Quran,' 31 thus did We assign to every prophet an enemy from among the sinners; your Lord is sufficient as a guide and a helper.

32 Those who deny the truth say, 'Why was the Quran not sent down to him in a single revelation?' We sent it in this manner, so that We might strengthen your heart. We gave it to you in gradual revelation. 33 Every time they raise an objection, We will bring you the truth and the best of explanations. 34 Those who will be dragged headlong into Hell shall have an evil place to dwell in, for they have strayed far from the right path.

35 We gave Moses the Book, and appointed his brother Aaron as his supporter. 36 Then We said, 'Go together to the people who have denied Our signs.' We utterly destroyed them! 37 We drowned the people of Noah also when they rejected their messengers and We made them an example to all mankind. We have prepared a painful punishment for the wrongdoers, 38 to 'Ad, and Thamud, and the people of al-Rass, and as We did for the many a generation between them. 39 To each of them We gave warnings and each of them We destroyed completely. 40 Indeed they must have come upon the town on which an evil rain had poured down. Did they not see it? Yet they have no faith in the Resurrection.

41 Whenever they see you they only make a mockery of you—'Is this the one God has sent as His Messenger? 42 Indeed, he would

well-nigh have led us astray from our deities, had we not been [so] steadfastly attached to them!' When they behold the punishment, they shall realize who strayed furthest from the right path.

⁴³ Have you seen him who has taken his own desire to be his god? Can you be a guardian over him? ⁴⁴ Do you think most of them can hear or understand? They are like cattle. Indeed, they are even more astray.

⁴⁵ Have you not seen how your Lord lengthens the shadows? Had He pleased, He could have made them constant; then We placed the sun as an indicator for them, ⁴⁶ then We withdrew it to Us, a gradual withdrawal.*a* ⁴⁷ It is He who made the night a mantle for you, and sleep for repose; and made the day a time for rising.a ⁴⁸ It is He who sends the winds as heralds of His mercy and We send down pure water from the sky, ⁴⁹ so that We may bring life to a dead land; and slake the thirst of Our creation; cattle and men, in great numbers.

⁵⁰ We have explained it to them in diverse ways, so that they may take heed, but most persist in their ingratitude. ⁵¹ If We had so wished, We might have sent a warner into every town, ⁵² so do not yield to those who deny the truth, but strive with the utmost strenuousness by means of this [Quran, to convey its message to them].

⁵³ It is He who released the two bodies of flowing water, one sweet and fresh and the other salty and bitter, and set up an insurmountable barrier between them. ⁵⁴ It is He who has created human beings from water and He has granted them the ties of blood as well as marriage. Your Lord is all powerful.

---

a The phenomenon which in the present age is known as the axial rotation of the earth has been set down here in layman's language. The earth rotates on its axis once in twenty-four hours, due to which day and night follow upon each other. This is a wonderful miracle of Almighty God's power. Had there been no axial rotation of the earth, half of it would have been continuously under the blazing sun, while the other half would have been continuously enveloped by night. Thus it would have been extremely difficult to live on the earth.

There are many lessons in this system of the earth. As the light of day necessarily follows the darkness of night, so also is it necessary that untruth be followed by Truth. While waking up in the morning after sleeping at night symbolizes resurrection in the life after death.

⁵⁵ Yet they worship besides God that which can neither benefit them nor harm them. One who denies the truth is a helper [of evil] against his Lord. ⁵⁶ We have sent you only as a bearer of glad tidings and as a warner. ⁵⁷ Say, 'I do not ask you for any recompense for this except that anyone who so wishes should take the right path to his Lord.'

⁵⁸ Put your trust in the One who is the Ever-Living [God], who never dies, and glorify Him with His praise. He is fully aware of the sins of His servants; ⁵⁹ it is He who created the heavens and the earth and all that is between them in six Days [periods], then settled Himself on the throne—the Gracious One. Ask any informed person about Him.ᵃ ⁶⁰ When they are told, 'Prostrate yourselves before the Gracious One,' they ask, 'Who is this Gracious One? Shall we prostrate ourselves before whatever you will?' This increases their aversion.

⁶¹ Exalted is He who put constellations in the heavens, a radiant lamp and an illuminating moon—⁶² it is He who has made night and day succeed each other, a sign for those who would take heed and would be grateful.ᵇ

⁶³ The true servants of the Gracious One are those who walk upon the earth with humility and when they are addressed by the ignorant ones, their response is, 'Peace'; ⁶⁴ and those who spend the night prostrating themselves, and standing before their Lord, ⁶⁵ who say, 'Our Lord, ward off from us the punishment of Hell, for

---

a Here 'six Days' means six Days of God. In the language of human beings it may be called six stages or six periods. The Creation of the Universe in six stages indicates that it was done in a well planned manner. Whatever is brought into existence on the basis of a plan and a specific arrangement cannot be futile.

b The result of realisation-oriented knowledge (*ma'rifah*) is also that a sort of ending unrest enters their lives. In their state of unrest, they not only call God upon during the daytime; but they solitude also fill the of their nights with the remembrance of God. Similarly, realisation of God makes them extremely prudent. They earn with a sense of responsibility and spend with a sense of responsibility. It is their sense of accountability to God which makes them moderate and cautious in the matter of income and expenditure. A tradition of the Prophet says, 'It will be one of the wise actions of man if he adopts a via media where his life is concerned.'

its punishment is a dreadful torment to suffer. [66] Indeed, it is an evil abode and evil dwelling-place.' [67] They are those who are neither extravagant nor niggardly, but keep a balance between the two; [68] those who never invoke any other deity besides God, nor take a life which God has made sacred, except with the right to do so, nor commit adultery. Anyone who does that shall face punishment: [69] he shall have his suffering doubled on the Day of Resurrection and he will abide forever in disgrace, [70] except for those who repent and believe and do good deeds. God will change the evil deeds of such people into good ones: He is most forgiving and most merciful. [71] He who repents and does good deeds has truly turned to God.

[72] And those who do not bear false witness, and when they pass by frivolity, they pass by with dignity; [73] who do not turn a blind eye and a deaf ear to the signs of their Lord when they are reminded of them; [74] who say, 'Lord, grant us joy in our wives and children and make us a model for the righteous.'[a]

[75] These are the ones who will be rewarded with lofty mansions in Paradise, for their steadfastness. They will be received therein with greetings of welcome and salutations of peace.[b] [76] There they shall abide forever: a blessed dwelling and a blessed resting place. [77] Say, 'What would my Lord care for you, if you do not call on Him. Because you have indeed rejected the truth and His punishment is bound to overtake you.

---

a Every man with a family is the leader (imam) of his family. If his family members are God-fearing, he is the imam of God-fearing people. But and if his family members are forgetful of God, he is at the head of those who are oblivious of God.

b Those who had humbled themselves in this world for the sake of Truth, will be lodged in the loftiest dwellings of paradise. They lived with humility in this world, so in the Hereafter God will reward them with high status. This was expressed by Jesus Christ as follows: 'Blessed are those who are poor in this world. It is they who will enter the Kingdom of Heaven.'

26. THE POETS (*AL-SHU'ARA'*)

In the name of God, the Most Gracious, the Most Merciful

¹ *Ta Sin Mim*

² These are the verses of the Book that makes things clear. ³ It may be that you will destroy yourself with grief because they will not believe. ⁴ But if We had so willed, We could have sent down to them a sign from the heavens so that their heads would be bowed down before it in utter humility. ⁵ Whenever there comes to them any fresh warning from the Merciful, they always turn their backs on it: ⁶ they have indeed rejected the message. But the truth of what they laughed to scorn will dawn upon them before long.

⁷ Do they not see the earth, and what beneficial kinds of things We have caused to grow in it?*ᵃ* ⁸ Surely in this there is a sign, yet most of them would not believe: ⁹ truly, your Lord is the Mighty One, the Merciful.

¹⁰ When your Lord called out to Moses, saying, 'Go to the wrongdoing people, ¹¹ the people of Pharaoh, will they not fear God?' ¹² Moses replied, 'My Lord, I fear they will reject me, ¹³ and my breast is straitened and my tongue is not fluent; so send Aaron as well; ¹⁴ besides, they accuse me of a crime, and I fear that they may put me to death.'*ᵇ*

---

a The sprouting of a green and flourishing tree from the earth is as wonderful an event as the sudden emergence of a camel from the earth and its starting to walk on its surface. People are wonder-struck by the second type of incident, though the more wonderful incidents are always happening on the earth without their learning any lesson from it.

Almighty God wants man to notice the extraordinary but hidden aspects of ordinary events. In the events happening in the chain of cause and effect, he should be able to observe the direct role of God. Those who display this high degree of insight are the ones who will be treated as having faith in God and the ones who will be blessed with the eternal grace of God.

b The fact is that God looks at the inner self of a man rather than at his visible condition. If someone has inner strength, God chooses him on the basis of that inner talent to carry out the tasks of His religion. But man has first

[15] God said, 'Indeed not; go both of you with Our signs, We shall be with you, listening [to your call]. [16] Go to Pharaoh, both of you, and say, "We are messengers from the Lord of the Worlds: [17] let the Children of Israel go with us!"' [18] Pharaoh said to Moses, 'Did we not bring you up among us as a child? And you spent several years of your life with us. [19] Yet you committed the deed you did, surely you are one of the ingrates.'

[20] Moses replied, 'I did that when I was one of the misguided, [21] and I fled from you because I feared you. Then my Lord granted me wisdom and made me one of the messengers.

[22] And this is the favour with which you taunt me—that you have enslaved the Children of Israel?' [23] Pharaoh said, 'What is this: Lord of the Universe?' [24] Moses said, 'Lord of the heavens and the earth and all that is between them, if only you would be convinced.' [25] Pharaoh said to those around him, 'Did you hear?' [26] Moses went on, 'He is your Lord and the Lord of your forefathers.' [27] Pharaoh said, 'This messenger who has been sent to you is surely possessed!' [28] Moses said, 'He is the Lord of the East and the West, and all that lies between them, if only you could understand.' [29] Pharaoh said, 'If you take any deity other than myself, I will throw you into prison,' [30] and Moses asked, 'Even if I show you a clear sign?' [31] Pharaoh said, 'Show it then, if you are telling the truth!' [32] So Moses threw down his staff and suddenly it appeared as a serpent, plainly visible. [33] And he drew out his hand, and it appeared [shining] white to the beholders. [34] Pharaoh said to the chiefs around him, 'Surely this man is a skilful sorcerer. [35] Who wants to drive you out of your land by his sorcery. Now what do you advise?'

[36] They said, 'Let him and his brother wait a while, and send heralds into the cities, [37] who shall bring to you every skilful sorcerer.' [38] So the sorcerers were gathered on the appointed day [39] and the people were told, 'Will you also gather together, [40] so that we may follow the magicians, if they be the winners.' [41] When the magicians came,

---

to reveal his inner capabilties himself. Thereafter, if there are any outward shortcomings, they are compensated for by God.

they asked Pharaoh, 'Shall we have a reward, if we are the winners?' ⁴² He replied, 'Certainly, in that case you will join my inner circle.'

⁴³ Moses said to the magicians, 'Throw down whatever you are going to throw.' ⁴⁴ So they cast down their ropes and staffs, and said, 'By Pharaoh's honour, we shall surely win.' ⁴⁵ Then Moses threw down his staff, and it swallowed up all that they had conjured into being. ⁴⁶ The magicians fell down prostrate, ⁴⁷ saying, 'We believe in the Lord of the Worlds, ⁴⁸ the Lord of Moses and Aaron.'

⁴⁹ Pharaoh said, 'Have you come to believe in him, before I have given you permission? He is surely your master who has taught you magic. But you shall see. I will cut off your hands and feet on alternate sides and crucify you all.' ⁵⁰ They said, 'There is no harm. To our Lord we shall return. ⁵¹We hope our Lord will forgive us, as we are the first of the believers.'

⁵² Then We revealed Our will to Moses, saying, 'Set forth with My servants, in the night, for you will surely be pursued.' ⁵³ And Pharaoh sent forth heralds to all the cities. ⁵⁴ 'These,' they said, 'are only a small band— ⁵⁵ and they have enraged us— ⁵⁶ we are a large and watchful force.' ⁵⁷ So We made them leave their gardens and springs, ⁵⁸ their treasures and their noble dwellings—⁵⁹ and We made the Children of Israel inheritors of these bounties.

⁶⁰ Pharaoh and his people pursued them at sunrise, ⁶¹ and when the two groups saw each other, Moses' companions said, 'We are sure to be overtaken.' ⁶² Moses replied, 'No, My Lord is with me, and He will guide me.' ⁶³ Then We bade Moses strike the sea with his staff. And it parted, and each part was like a huge mountain.⁶⁴ In the meantime We made the others approach that place. ⁶⁵ We delivered Moses and all those who were with him, ⁶⁶ then We drowned the others. ⁶⁷ Surely in that there is a sign; yet most of them do not believe: ⁶⁸ truly, your Lord is the Mighty One, the Merciful.

⁶⁹ Tell them the story of Abraham, ⁷⁰ when he asked his father and his people, 'What is that which you worship?' ⁷¹ They said, 'We worship idols and will continue to cling to them.' ⁷² He asked, 'Do they hear you when you call to them? ⁷³ Do they help or harm you?' ⁷⁴ They replied, 'But we found our fathers doing the same.'

⁷⁵ Abraham said, 'Have you really thought about what you have

been worshipping, ⁷⁶ you and your forefathers—⁷⁷ they are all my enemies, not so the Lord of the Universe, ⁷⁸ who created me. It is He who guides me; ⁷⁹ He who gives me food and drink; ⁸⁰ He who cures me when I am ill; ⁸¹ He who will cause me to die and bring me back to life; ⁸² and He who will, I hope, forgive me my faults on the Day of the Judgement.

⁸³ My Lord, bestow wisdom upon me; unite me with the righteous; ⁸⁴ give me a good name among later generations; ⁸⁵ and make me one of the inheritors of the Garden of Bliss; ⁸⁶ and forgive my father; for he is one of the misguided; ⁸⁷ and do not disgrace me on the Day when all people are resurrected, ⁸⁸ the Day when wealth and sons will be of no avail, ⁸⁹ and when he alone will be saved who comes to God with a sound heart.'

⁹⁰ When Paradise shall be brought near to the God-fearing ⁹¹ and Hell shall be revealed to the misguided, ⁹² they will be asked, 'Where are those whom you worshipped ⁹³ besides God? Can they help you or even help themselves?' ⁹⁴ Then they will be thrown headlong into Hell, both they and the misguided ones, ⁹⁵ and Satan's legions, all together. ⁹⁶ They will dispute between themselves therein, and will say, ⁹⁷ 'We were clearly misguided ⁹⁸ when we made you equal with the Lord of the Universe. ⁹⁹ It was the evildoers who led us astray, ¹⁰⁰ and we have no intercessors now, ¹⁰¹ and no sincere friend. ¹⁰² If we could only return to the world and be among the believers.' ¹⁰³ There is certainly a sign in that, but most of them would not believe: ¹⁰⁴ surely, your Lord is the Mighty One, the Merciful.

¹⁰⁵ The people of Noah also rejected the messengers. ¹⁰⁶ When their brother Noah said to them, 'Will you have no fear of God? ¹⁰⁷ I am a trustworthy messenger for you: ¹⁰⁸ fear God, and obey me. ¹⁰⁹ I ask of you no recompense for it, for my only reward is with the Lord of the Universe, ¹¹⁰ so fear God and obey me.' ¹¹¹ They replied, 'Are we to believe in you when your followers are but the lowest of the low?' ¹¹² He said, 'What knowledge do I have of their doings? ¹¹³ My Lord alone can bring them to account—if only you could understand—¹¹⁴ I am not going to drive away any believers. ¹¹⁵ I am only a plain warner.'

¹¹⁶ They said, 'Noah, if you do not desist, you will be stoned.'

[117] Noah said, 'My Lord, my people have rejected me, [118] therefore, judge decisively between me and them; and save me and the believers who are with me.' [119] So We saved him, and those who were with him in the laden ark, [120] and drowned the rest. [121] There is certainly a sign in that; but most of them do not believe: [122] surely your Lord is the Mighty One, the Merciful.

[123] The people of 'Ad, too, rejected the messengers. [124] Their brother Hud said to them, 'Will you not fear God? [125] I am a trustworthy messenger for you: [126] fear God, then, and obey me. [127] I ask no recompense of you; my reward is only with the Lord of the Universe. [128] Do you build monuments on every high place in vanity, [129] and erect castles hoping that you will live forever. [130] When you lay hands upon anyone, you do so as tyrants. [131] So fear God, and obey me; [132] fear Him who has aided you with all that you know—[133] He has bestowed on you cattle, and sons, [134] and gardens, and springs—[135] indeed, I fear for you the torment of an awful day.'

[136] They replied, 'It makes no difference to us whether you preach or do not preach, [137] this is nothing but a habit of the ancients: [138] and we shall not be punished.' [139] So they rejected him; and We destroyed them. There is certainly a sign in that; but most of them would not believe. [140] Surely your Lord is the Mighty One, the Merciful.

[141] The tribe of Thamud
also rejected the messengers. [142] When their brother Salih said to them, 'Will you not fear God? [143] Truly, I am a trustworthy messenger for you, [144] so fear God and obey me. [145] For this I demand no recompense from you; my reward is only with the Lord of the Universe. [146] Do you think that you will be left secure [forever]—[147] in the midst of gardens and fountains, [148] and cornfields, and palm-trees laden with fruit—[149] hewing out houses in the mountains and taking pride in your skill? [150] So fear God and obey me: [151] do not obey the bidding of those who are given to excesses, [152] those who spread corruption in the land instead of putting things right.'

[153] They replied, 'Surely you are bewitched. [154] You are only a human being like ourselves. Show us a sign, if you are telling the truth.' [155] He said, 'Here is a she-camel. She shall have her turn of drinking, as you have yours, each on an appointed day, [156] so do

her no harm, or the punishment of an awful day will befall you.' ¹⁵⁷ Yet they hamstrung her, and then they became regretful: ¹⁵⁸ so the punishment came down upon them. Surely in that there is a sign, but most of them would not believe. ¹⁵⁹ Your Lord is the Mighty One, the Merciful.

¹⁶⁰ Then the people of Lot rejected the messengers. ¹⁶¹ When their brother Lot said to them, 'Will you not fear God? ¹⁶² I am a trustworthy messenger to you: ¹⁶³ so fear God and obey me. ¹⁶⁴ I ask of you no recompense for this; my reward is only with the Lord of the Universe. ¹⁶⁵ Do you, of all people, approach males, ¹⁶⁶ and leave your wives whom your Lord has created for you? You are a people who transgress all bounds.'

¹⁶⁷ They said, 'If you do not desist, Lot, you will surely be banished.' ¹⁶⁸ He said, 'I am one of those who abhors your ways. ¹⁶⁹ My Lord, save me and my family from their evil doings.' ¹⁷⁰ We saved him and all of his family, ¹⁷¹ except for an old woman who stayed behind, ¹⁷² then We totally destroyed the rest, ¹⁷³ and We poured a rain [of destruction] down upon them—and how evil was the rain which fell on those who were forewarned. ¹⁷⁴ Surely in this there is a sign: but most of them would not believe: ¹⁷⁵ your Lord is the Mighty One, the Merciful.

¹⁷⁶ The dwellers of the forest also rejected the messengers. ¹⁷⁷ Shu'ayb said to them, 'Will you not fear God? ¹⁷⁸ I am a trustworthy messenger to you: ¹⁷⁹ so fear God, and obey me. ¹⁸⁰ I ask of you no recompense for this; my reward is only with the Lord of the Universe. ¹⁸¹ Give full measure, and cause no loss to others.^a ¹⁸² Weigh with correct scales: ¹⁸³ do not defraud people of what is rightfully theirs; and do not spread corruption in the land. ¹⁸⁴ Fear Him who created you and those who have gone before you.'

---

a The root cause of all moral and social evils is disturbing the 'balance' (*mizan*). The real 'balance' (weighing scale) is man giving to others whatever they have to receive as a matter of right, and taking for himself only what he can rightfully take. This is the Divine 'balance'. When this is upset, disturbance occurs in collective social life. The secret of maintaining this balance is the fear of God. If the fear of God goes out of the heart, nothing can make a man keep his moral equilibrium.

[185] They replied, 'You are bewitched. [186] You are only a human being like ourselves. Indeed we think you are a liar. [187] So cause a fragment of the sky to fall on us, if you are truthful.' [188] He said, 'My Lord has full knowledge of all your actions.' [189] They rejected him, and then had to suffer the punishment of a day of overshadowing gloom: That was indeed the punishment of an awful day. [190] Surely, in this is indeed a sign; but most of them would not believe: [191] your Lord is the Mighty One, the Merciful.

[192] This surely is a revelation from the Lord of the Universe: [193] the Faithful Spirit has brought it down [194] into your heart, so that you may be a warner, [195] in clear Arabic speech. [196] Surely, it is foretold in the ancient scriptures. [197] Is it not evidence enough for them that the learned among the Children of Israel have recognized this [as true]?

[198] Had We revealed it to any one of the non-Arabs, [199] and he had recited it to them, they would not have believed in it. [200] We have thus caused denial of truth to enter into the hearts of the sinners: [201] they will not believe in it until they see the grievous punishment. [202] It will come upon them suddenly when they are not expecting it. [203] Then they will exclaim, 'Could we have some respite?'

[204] Do they want to hasten Our punishment? [205] Think! If We let them enjoy life for some years, [206] and then the promised punishment fell upon them, [207] of what avail would their past enjoyment be to them? [208] Never have We destroyed a town without sending down messengers to warn it, [209] as a reminder from Us: We are never unjust. [210] It was not the devils who brought down the Quran: [211] neither are they worthy of it, nor are they capable of it, [212] indeed they are debarred from overhearing it.

[213] So do not call on any deity besides God, lest you incur His punishment. [214] Warn your nearest kinsmen, [215] and extend kindness and affection to those of the believers who follow you. [216] If they disobey you, say, 'I bear no responsibility for what you do.' [217] Put your trust in the Mighty One, the Merciful, [218] who sees you when you stand up [for prayer], [219] and sees your movements among those who prostrate themselves: [220] He is the All Hearing, the All Knowing. [221] Shall I tell you upon whom the devils descend? [222] They descend

on every lying sinner, ²²³ who lends an ear to them, and most of them are liars. ²²⁴ And as for the poets—it is the misled who follow them.^a ²²⁵ Do you not see how they wander aimlessly in every valley, ²²⁶ preaching what they do not practice. ²²⁷ Not so the true believers who do good works and remember God with fervour and defend themselves only after they are wronged. The wrongdoers will soon know how evil a turn their affairs will take.

27. THE ANTS (*AL-NAML*)

In the name of God, the Most Gracious, the Most Merciful

¹ *Ta Sin*

These are verses from the Quran, a book that makes things clear; ² it is guidance and good news for the believers ³ who pray regularly and pay obligatory alms and have firm faith in the Hereafter. ⁴ We have made those who do not believe in the Hereafter feel their actions appear good to them, so they wander blindly: ⁵ they are the ones who will have the worst of punishment, and in the Hereafter they will be the greatest losers. ⁶ You have received this Quran from One who is all-wise, all-knowing.

⁷ Tell of Moses who said to his family, 'I have seen a fire. I will bring you news from there, or a burning brand for you to warm yourselves.' ⁸ When he came up to it, a voice called out, 'Blessed

---

a The basis of poetry is imagination and not facts and realities. That is why poets have flights of fancy, allowing their ideas to go hither and thither. Unlike the poets, the prophet and his companions focussed their entire attention upon God—the greatest Reality. Their lives were ideal examples of harmony between preaching and practice. Deep knowledge of God (*ma'rifah*) made them rememberers of their Creator. They were extremely cautious and if they took action against anyone, it was only when his behaviour towards them was clearly oppressive. The expected critical nature of the future makes a man serious about his present. One who is not sensitive about the future cannot be sensitive about the present either.

be whoever is near this fire, and whoever is around it! Glory be to God, Lord of the Universe!

⁹ O Moses, I am God, the Powerful, the Wise. ¹⁰ Throw down your staff.' But when he saw it moving like a snake, he turned and fled. 'Moses, do not be afraid! The messengers need have no fear in My presence; ¹¹ as for those who do wrong and then do good after evil, I am most forgiving, most merciful. ¹² Now put your hand inside your cloak next to your bosom and it will come out [shining] white, without any blemish. This will be one of the nine signs for Pharaoh and his people: for truly they are a rebellious people.' ¹³ But when Our signs came to them in all their clarity they said, 'This is clearly sorcery!' ¹⁴ And they persisted in rejecting them wrongfully and arrogantly, while in their hearts they were convinced of their truth. Observe, then, how evil was the fate of the evil-doers.

¹⁵ We bestowed knowledge on David and Solomon and they both said, 'Praise be to God who has exalted us above many of His believing servants.' ¹⁶ Solomon succeeded David. He said, 'Know, my people, that we have been taught the speech of birds and endowed with all good things. Surely this is God's manifest grace.'

¹⁷ Solomon's hosts of jinn and men and birds, were all gathered together in his presence and were ranged in battle order, ¹⁸ and when they came to the Valley of the Ants, one ant said, 'Ants! Go into your dwellings, in case Solomon and his hosts inadvertently crush you.' ¹⁹ Solomon smiled broadly at its words and said, 'Lord, inspire me to be thankful for the blessings You have granted me and my parents, and to do good deeds that please You; and include me, by Your grace, among Your righteous servants!'ᵃ

²⁰ Then Solomon inspected the birds, and said, 'How is it that I

---

a In Solomon's army there were not only human beings but also genies and birds. Once Solomon's army passed through a valley where there was a large number of ants. On this occasion Solomon understood what the ants were saying to each other.

Such an incident would be enough to give rise to conceit and pride in an ordinary man. But, Solomon became the embodiment of gratitude on this account. He fully attributed to God whatever appeared to be his—and this is the way of a pious and righteous man.

do not see the hoopoe? Is he absent then? ²¹ I shall surely punish him severely or order him to be executed, unless he gives me a good reason for his absence.' ²² But he was not long in coming, and said, 'I have learnt something you did not know. I have come to you from Sheba with reliable news. ²³ I found a woman ruling over them, who has been given everything and she has a mighty throne. ²⁴ I found her and her people worshipping the sun, instead of God. Satan has made their conduct appear good to them, and has thus diverted them from the right path, so that they might not be guided. ²⁵ Should they not worship God who brings forth what is hidden in the heavens and earth and knows both what you conceal and what you make known? ²⁶ He is God: there is no deity but He, the Lord of the mighty throne.'

²⁷ Solomon said, 'We shall soon see whether you have spoken the truth, or whether you are a liar. ²⁸ Go with this letter of mine and lay it before them, then withdraw from them and see how they respond.' ²⁹ The Queen of Sheba said, 'O Counsellors, an honourable letter has been delivered to me. ³⁰ It is from Solomon. It reads, "In the name of God, Most Gracious, Most Merciful, ³¹ do not exalt yourselves above me, but come to me in all submission." ³² Now advise me in this, Counsellors. I never decide any affair till I have conferred with you.' ³³ They said, 'We are strong and our prowess in battle is great, but the decision is in your hands, so consider what you will command.' ³⁴ She said, 'Surely, when mighty kings invade a country, they despoil it and humiliate its noblest inhabitants—these men will do the same—³⁵ but I shall send them a present and see with what reply my envoys will return.'

³⁶ So when [the envoy] came to Solomon he said, 'What! Are you offering me wealth? But that which God has given me is better than that which He has given you. Yet you rejoice in your gift. ³⁷ Go back to them: we shall most certainly come upon them with forces which they will never be able to withstand, and shall most certainly cause them to be driven from their lands, disgraced and humbled!'

³⁸ Solomon then said, 'O Counsellors, which of you can bring me her throne before they come to me in submission? ³⁹ A demon from among the jinn said, 'I will bring it to you before you get up from

your seat. I am strong and trustworthy enough to do it.' ⁴⁰ But one of them who had some knowledge of the Book said, 'I will bring it to you in the twinkling of an eye.' When Solomon saw it placed before him, he exclaimed, 'This is by the grace of my Lord, to test whether I am grateful or ungrateful. Whosoever is grateful, it is for the good of his own self; and whosoever is ungrateful, then surely my Lord is self-sufficient and generous.'ᵃ

⁴¹ He said, 'Disguise her throne. We shall see whether or not she will recognize it.' ⁴² When she came to Solomon, she was asked, 'Is your throne like this?' She replied, 'It looks as though it were the same, and we had been given knowledge [of your power] before this, and we have already submitted.' ⁴³ And that which she used to worship beside God had stopped her [from believing]; for she came of a disbelieving people. ⁴⁴ Then she was bidden to enter the palace; but when she saw it, she thought it was a deep pool of water, and bared her legs. But Solomon explained, 'It is just a palace paved with glass,' and she said, 'My Lord, I have wronged myself: now I submit myself along with Solomon, to God, the Lord of the Universe.'

⁴⁵ To Thamud We sent their brother Salih. He said, 'Serve none but God.' But they divided themselves into two factions contending with one another. ⁴⁶ He urged them, 'O my people, why do you wish to hasten on the evil rather than the good? Why do you not ask forgiveness of God, so that you may be shown mercy?' ⁴⁷ They said, 'We see you and your followers as an evil omen.' He replied, 'No, your evil omen is with God; the truth is that you are a people being put to the test.'

⁴⁸ There were in the city nine men who spread corruption in the land, and would not reform. ⁴⁹ They said, 'Let us bind ourselves by an oath sworn in the name of God that we shall attack Salih and his family by night, and to his protector [who demands retribution], we

---

a The distance between Ma'rib and Jerusalem is about fifteen hundred miles. This long distance was covered in such a way that no sooner had the words of command fallen from Solomon's lips than the jewel-studded throne was there before him. In spite of this extraordinary power, feelings of pride did not arise in him. He remained the embodiment of modesty and kept bowing down before God.

shall say, 'We were not present when they were slain. We are telling the truth.' ⁵⁰ Thus they devised a plan, and We also devised a plan, but they were not aware of it. ⁵¹ See, then, what the consequences of their plan were. We destroyed them and their people utterly, all together. ⁵² Because of their wrongdoing, their houses are in ruins—in that surely there is a sign for people who have knowledge*a*—⁵³ and We saved those who believed in and feared God.

⁵⁴ And tell of Lot. He said to his people, 'Will you commit evil knowingly? ⁵⁵ Must you go lustfully to men instead of women? Indeed, you are a people who are deeply ignorant.' ⁵⁶ The only answer of his people was, 'Drive out Lot and his family from the city. They are a people who make themselves out to be pure.' ⁵⁷ So We delivered him and his family—except his wife: We ordained her to be one of those who stayed behind— ⁵⁸ and We pelted them with torrential rain. How dreadful that rain was for those who had been warned! ⁵⁹ Say, 'All praise be to God, and peace be upon those servants of His whom He has chosen. Is God better, or what they associate with Him?

⁶⁰ Who created the heavens and the earth and sends down water for you from the sky, by which We make luxuriant gardens grow— you could never make such trees grow in them—is it another deity besides God? No indeed, but they are a people who equate others with Him. ⁶¹ Who is it that made the earth a stable place to live in? Who made rivers flow through it? Who set mountains upon it and placed a barrier between the two seas? Is there another deity besides God? Indeed, most of them have no knowledge.

⁶² Who responds to the oppressed when he calls out to Him, and relieves his suffering and who will make you inheritors of the earth? Then, is there a god besides God? How little you pay heed! ⁶³ Who guides you in the darkness of the land and sea? Who sends the breezes as heralds of His mercy? Then, is there a deity besides

---

a A great lesson is hidden in such historical events. But, this lesson may be learnt only by one who is capable of connecting such events with the eternal laws of God. Conversely, those who attribute such events to physical causes, cannot learn any lesson from them.

God? Exalted is God above what they associate with Him. [64] Who originates creation, then regenerates it, and who gives you sustenance from heaven and earth? Then, is there a deity besides God?' Say, 'Bring forward your proofs, if you are telling the truth.'

[65] Say, 'No one in the heavens and the earth has knowledge of the unseen except God.' They do not know when they will be raised up again. [66] Indeed, their knowledge of the life to come stops short of the truth: they are [often] in doubt as to its reality: in fact, they are blind to it. [67] Those who deny the truth say, 'When we have turned to dust like our fathers, shall we be brought back to life again? [68] We and our fathers were promised this before; these are but old stories.' [69] Say, 'Roam across the earth and observe what was the end of the sinful ones.'

[70] Do not grieve over them, nor feel distressed at their schemes. [71] They ask, 'When will this promise be fulfilled, if what you say be true?' [72] Say, 'It may be that a part of what you would hasten on is close behind you.' [73] Truly, your Lord is bountiful to mankind, but most of them are not grateful. [74] The Lord knows full well what they conceal in their hearts and what they disclose: [75] there is nothing hidden in heaven and on earth, but is recorded in a clear Book.

[76] This Quran explains to the children of Israel much of what they differ over, [77] certainly it is guidance and a blessing for the believers. [78] Certainly your Lord will decide between them in His wisdom—He is the Almighty, the All Knowing—[79] so put your trust in God. Surely you are on the path of manifest truth. [80] You cannot make the dead hear, nor can you make the deaf hear your call, when they turn their backs on it, [81] nor can you guide the blind out of their error. You can make only those hear you who believe in Our revelations and surrender themselves to Us.

[82] When God's word is justly carried out against them, We will produce a *dabbaha*[a] from the earth which will tell them that mankind

---

a At the time when Almighty God takes the decision to bring to an end the present history of the earth, some extraordinary signs will appear to usher in the last phase. Among these signs will be the appearance of a *daabbah*. The message, which was brought through human beings and which was not

had no real faith in Our signs. [83] On that Day We shall assemble together a host from every community of those who cried lies to Our revelations and they will be grouped [84] then, when they have arrived, He will say, 'Did you deny My revelations, even though you did not have proper knowledge of them? Or what was it that you were doing?' [85] The verdict will be given against them, because they did wrong, and they will be speechless. [86] Do they not see that We have made the night for them to rest in and the day to give them light? There are certainly signs in that for people who believe.

[87] On the Day when the trumpet is blown, whoever is in the heavens and whoever is on the earth will be struck with terror, except for those whom God wishes to spare. All shall come to Him in utter humility. [88] You see the mountains and think them firmly fixed. But they shall pass away as the clouds pass away. Such is the work of God, who has ordered all things to perfection: He is fully aware of what you do. [89] Whoever does a good deed, shall be rewarded with what is better, and will be secure from fear of that Day, [90] and those who do evil will be flung down on their faces in the Fire. Are you not rewarded according to your deeds?

[91] Say, 'I am commanded to serve the Lord of this town, which He has made inviolable and to whom everything belongs; I am commanded to be one of those devoted to Him;

[92] to recite the Quran.' Whoever follows its guidance, follows it only for the good of his own soul; and as for him who goes astray, just say, 'I am only a warner.' [93] Then say, 'Praise be to God! He will show you His signs and you will recognize them. Your Lord is not unaware of what you do.'

---

accepted by the people, will be announced by *daabbah*. Modern systems of communication, particularly the internet and multimedia are probably what is alluded to here as *daabbah*. This will be the bell announcing the end of the examination period and not its beginning.

28. THE STORY (*AL-QASAS*)

In the name of God, the Most Gracious, the Most Merciful

¹ *Ta Sin Mim*

² These are verses from the Book that makes things clear. ³ We shall narrate to you some of the story of Moses and Pharaoh, with truth, for people who would believe. ⁴ Pharaoh behaved arrogantly in the land, and divided the people into groups, seeking to weaken one section, slaying their sons and sparing their daughters—he was one of those who spread corruption— ⁵ We wished to favour those who were oppressed in the land, and to make them leaders and make them inheritors [of Our bounties], ⁶ and to give them power in the land; and to show Pharaoh and Haman and their hosts that very thing which they feared.

⁷ We inspired Moses' mother saying, 'Suckle him, and then, when you fear for him, cast him into the river, and have no fear and do not grieve, for We shall return him to you, and shall make him one of the Messengers.' ⁸ Then Pharaoh's household picked him up—later to become for them an enemy and a source of grief for them: Pharaoh and Haman and their hosts were wrongdoers—⁹ and Pharaoh's wife said, 'He will be a joy to the eye for me and you! Do not slay him: he may well be of use to us, or we may adopt him as a son.' They did not realize what they were doing.

¹⁰ Moses' mother's heart was full of anxiety—she would have disclosed his identity had We not strengthened her heart so that she might be a firm believer [in Our promise]. ¹¹ She said to Moses' sister, 'Go, and follow him.' So she watched him from a distance, like a stranger, without anyone noticing her. ¹² We had already made him refuse all wet nurses. So his sister said to them, 'Shall I tell you of a family who will bring him up for you and take good care of him?' ¹³ Thus We restored him to his mother, so that she might be comforted and not grieve any more, and so that she would know

that God's promise was true. But most of them do not realize this.*ᵃ*
¹⁴ When Moses reached full manhood and maturity, We bestowed upon him wisdom and knowledge: this is how We reward those who do good.

¹⁵ He entered the city unnoticed by its people, and there he encountered two men fighting with one another—one of his own people and the other one of his enemies. The one who belonged to his own people cried out to him for help against his foe—whereupon Moses struck him down with his fist, thereby causing his death. Moses said, 'This is Satan's doing; he is an open foe, leading man astray.' ¹⁶ He prayed, 'Forgive me Lord, for I have sinned against my soul.' God forgave him; for He is the Forgiving One, the Merciful. ¹⁷ He said, 'My Lord, because of the favour that You have shown me, I vow that I will never be a helper of the guilty.'

¹⁸ The next morning, when he was walking in the city, apprehensive, and watchful, and the man who had sought his help the day before cried out to him again for help. Moses said to him, 'You are clearly a misguided man.' ¹⁹ When he wanted to catch the one who was an enemy to them both, the man said, 'Moses, do you want to kill me just as you killed a man yesterday? You only want to become a tyrant in the land; you do not want to set things right.' ²⁰ A man came running from the far side of the city, and said, 'Moses, the authorities are conspiring to kill you, so leave the city. I am one of your well-wishers.' ²¹ So Moses departed from the city, fearful and vigilant, and prayed, 'My Lord, save me from these unjust people.'

²² When he made his way towards Midian, he said, 'I am sure, my Lord will guide me to the right way.' ²³ And when he arrived at the well of Midian, he found around it a group of men watering their

---

a Moses was set afloat in the river in a state of helplessness, but he reached the bank safe and sound. The king ruling at the time planned to kill him, but God ordained that he be brought up by that very king. He was born in an ordinary family, but Almighty God so arranged matters that he became connected with the royal palace and became acquainted with the learning and etiquette of the time at the highest level. This is an example which shows that Almighty God's powers are unlimited and there is nobody who can prevent His plans from coming into effect.

flocks, and he saw two women standing apart from them, who were holding back their flocks, so he asked, 'What is the matter with you?' They replied, 'We cannot draw water until the shepherds take away their sheep. Our father is a very old man.' 24 So Moses watered their flocks for them; and returned into the shade and prayed, 'Lord, I am truly in need of whatever blessing You may send down for me,'*a* 25 and then one of the two women came walking shyly up to him and said, 'My father is asking you to come so that he may reward you for watering our flocks for us.' When Moses came to their father and gave him an account of himself, he said: 'Don't be afraid! You have escaped from those wrongdoing people.' 26 One of the girls said, 'Father, hire him! For the best man to hire is someone strong and trustworthy.' 27 The father said, 'I would like to marry you to one of these two daughters of mine on the condition that you stay eight years in my service. But if you wish it, you may stay ten. I do not want to impose any hardship on you. God willing, you will find me a fair person.' 28 Moses said, 'That is agreed between me and you; whichever of the two terms I fulfil, there will be no blame on me. God is witness to what we say.'

29 When Moses completed the term and set out with his family, he noticed a fire in the direction of Mount Tur. He said to his family: 'Stay here, I can see a fire. Perhaps I can bring you news, or a burning brand from the fire with which you may warm yourself.' 30 And when he came to it, he was called by a voice from a bush in a blessed spot, on the right side of the valley: 'O Moses, I am God, Lord of the Universe. 31 Throw down your staff.' And when he saw it move as though it were a serpent, he turned his back and fled, and did not look back. 'O Moses,' said the voice, 'come forward and have no fear; you are quite safe. 32 Put your hand into your bosom; it will come out [shining] white, without blemish; now

---

a At that time, this prayer spontaneously fell from Moses's lips, 'Lord, I am truly in need of whatever blessing You may send down for me.' This prayer shows the condition of a believer in such circumstances. He entrusts all his affairs to the care of God. He has the firm belief that whatever a man receives comes from God, and that whatever is received from God is 'good'.

draw your arm close to your body to calm your fears. These are two credentials from your Lord for Pharaoh and his nobles. Surely, they are a rebellious people.'

³³ Moses said, 'My Lord, I have killed one of their people and fear that they may kill me. ³⁴ My brother Aaron is more eloquent than I am. Send him with me to support me and back me up. For I fear that they will reject me.' ³⁵ God said: 'We shall strengthen your arm through your brother, We shall give you both power, so that they shall not be able to harm you. Set forth with Our signs. You, and those who follow you, will surely prevail.'

³⁶ When Moses came to them with Our clear signs, they said, 'This is nothing but contrived magic. We never heard of this among our forefathers.' ³⁷ And Moses replied, 'My Lord knows best who comes with guidance from Him and who will attain the heavenly abode in the hereafter. The wrongdoers shall never prosper.' ³⁸ Pharaoh said, 'O nobles, I know of no god for you other than myself. So, Haman, burn me bricks of clay, and build me a high tower, so that I may have a look at the God of Moses, though I consider him to be one of the liars.'

³⁹ He and his hosts behaved arrogantly in the land without any justification—thinking that they would not be recalled to Us— ⁴⁰ so We seized him and his hosts and cast them into the sea. Consider the fate of the wrongdoers. ⁴¹ We had made them leaders, but they called people to the Fire; and on the Day of Judgement they will not be helped. ⁴² We have caused a curse to follow them in this world and, on the Day of Judgement, they will be among the wretched. ⁴³ After We had destroyed the earlier generations, We gave Moses the Book to give men insight, and as guidance and a blessing for people, so that they might take heed.

⁴⁴ You were not present on the western side of the Mount when We gave Our Command to Moses: nor were you among the witnesses— ⁴⁵ We brought into being many generations who lived long lives—nor did you live among the people of Midian and recite our revelations to them—it is We who send messengers—⁴⁶ you were not on the side of the Mount when We called out to Moses, but We have sent you as a mercy from your Lord, so that you may warn people to whom

no warner has been sent before you, so that they may take heed,
⁴⁷ and may not say, if an affliction should befall them on account
of their misdeeds: 'Lord, if only You had sent us a messenger, we
might have followed Your message and become believers.' ⁴⁸ But
when the truth came to them from Us, they said, 'Why has he not
been given the like of what Moses was given?' But did they not
reject what Moses was given before? They said, 'Both [Moses and
Muhammad] are kinds of sorcery, each assisting the other.' And
they add, 'We reject both of them.'

⁴⁹ Say to them, 'Bring down from God a scripture that is a better
guide than these two and I will follow it, if what you say be true.'
⁵⁰ If they do not respond to you, then know that they follow only
their own desires. Who could be more astray than he who follows
his own likes and dislikes with no guidance from God? God does
not guide the evil-doers. ⁵¹ We have conveyed Our Word to them,
in succession, so that they may give heed.

⁵² Those to whom We gave the Book before this believe in it [the
Quran], ⁵³ and, when it is recited to them, they say, 'We believe in
it. Indeed it is the truth from our Lord. Even before it came, we had
submitted ourselves.' ⁵⁴ Such people as these will receive a double
reward, because they are steadfast and repel evil with good, and
give alms out of what We have given them, ⁵⁵ and when they hear
vain talk, they turn away from it and say, 'We have our actions and
you have yours. We wish you peace. We will have nothing to do
with the ignorant.' ⁵⁶ You cannot guide whoever you please: it is
God who guides whom He will. He best knows those who would
accept guidance.

⁵⁷ They say, 'If we were to follow your guidance, we should be
uprooted from our land.' But have We not established for them a
safe haven to which fruits of every kind are brought as a provision
from Ourself? But most of them have no knowledge.

⁵⁸ How many townships have We destroyed where the people had
become arrogant on account of their affluence? Since then their
dwelling-places have scarcely been inhabited—We became their
inheritors. ⁵⁹ Your Lord would never destroy a people until He had

sent messengers to their capital cities, reciting to them Our revelations. Nor did We destroy a town unless their people became wrongdoers.

⁶⁰ Whatever you are given in this life is nothing but a temporary provision of this life and its glitter; what God has is better and more lasting. Will you not then understand?*ᵃ* ⁶¹ Can someone to whom We have made a gracious promise and who will see it fulfilled, be compared to someone We have allowed to enjoy a worldly life, awhile, and who will be brought up [before God] for his accounting on the Day of Resurrection?

⁶² On that Day He will call to them, and say, 'Where are those whom you claimed to be My partners?' ⁶³ And those on whom sentence has been passed, will say, 'Our Lord, these are the ones who led us astray. We led them astray as we ourselves were led astray. We now dissociate ourselves from them before You; it was not us that they worshipped.'

⁶⁴ Then they will be told, 'Call upon your partners.' And they will call upon them, but will receive no answer. They shall witness the punishment. If only they had allowed themselves to be guided. ⁶⁵ On that Day God will call out to them, saying, 'What answer did you give to Our messengers?' ⁶⁶ They will be left speechless on that Day, and they will not be able to consult each other. ⁶⁷ But as for him who repents and believes and does good deeds, he can hope to find himself among the successful.

⁶⁸ Your Lord creates whatsoever He wills and chooses whomsoever He pleases. They have no choice. Praise be to God—exalted is He over anything they may associate with Him! ⁶⁹ Your Lord knows what they conceal in their hearts and what they disclose. ⁷⁰ He is God: there is no god but Him. All Praise is due to Him in this world and the hereafter. His is the Judgement and to Him you shall be returned.

⁷¹ Ask them, 'Tell me, if God were to extend perpetual night over

---

a At the time of death, a man, however great, finally parts with his possessions. After death, the things which go along with him are his righteous deeds and not his worldly honours or his material possessions. In these circumstances, wise counsel demands that a man give preference to eternal success over temporary worldly success—he should take care to build up his Hereafter rather than build up his worldly position.

you till the Day of Judgement, is there any deity other than God that could bring you light? Will you not listen?' ⁷² Say, 'Tell me, if God were to extend perpetual day over you till the Day of Judgement—is there any deity other than God that could bring you night, in which to rest? Will you not then see?' ⁷³ In His mercy He has made for you the night and the day, during which you may rest, and seek His bounty and be grateful.

⁷⁴ And on the Day He shall call out to them and say, 'Where are those whom you alleged were My partners.' ⁷⁵ And We shall bring forth from every people a witness and We shall say to them: 'Bring your proof.' Then they will know that truth belongs to God alone, and that which they used to invent will fall away from them.

⁷⁶ Korah was one of Moses' people, but he behaved arrogantly towards them. We had given him such treasures that their very keys would have weighed down a band of strong men. His people said to him, 'Do not exult in your riches, for God does not love the exultant. ⁷⁷ But seek the Home of the Hereafter by means of that which God has bestowed on you; do not forget to take your portion [of the Hereafter] in this world. Be good to others as God has been good to you and do not strive for evil in the land, for God does not love the evil-doers.'ᵃ

⁷⁸ But he said, 'I have been given it only because of the knowledge I possess.' Did he not know that God had destroyed before him people who were stronger than he and possessed even greater resources? The guilty are not required to offer explanations of their sins.

⁷⁹ Then he went forth before his people in all his pomp. Those who

---

a What is meant by creating 'evil in the land?' According to verse 77, one of the ways of creating a disturbance on earth is for a man acquiring a lot of wealth, to spend it only on himself. Water from various parts of land gathers in a sea. The sea again scatters the water back over the whole land after turning it into vapour. This is an example of peaceful activity (*islah*) which is the opposite of creating discord (*fasad*) in this world of God. The very same approach is required of man. If, for any reason, wealth is accumulated by someone, he should by different methods, return it to those less favoured in the distribution of wealth. In other words, circulating accumulated wealth promotes *islah*, while hoarding accumulated wealth brings about *fasad*.

were eager for the life of this world said, 'If only we had the like of Korah's fortune! He really is a very fortunate man,' [80] but those who had been given knowledge said, 'Woe to you, God's reward is better for those who believe and do good deeds: and it is awarded only to those who are steadfast.'[a]

[81] Then We caused the earth to swallow up him and his home: there was no one to help him against God, nor could he defend himself. [82] Those who had coveted his position the day before now began to say, 'Ah! It is indeed God alone who gives abundantly to whom He will and sparingly to whom He pleases. Had not God been gracious to us, He would have caused us to be swallowed up also.' Alas indeed! Those who deny the truth will never prosper.

[83] As for the abode of the Hereafter, We shall assign it to those who seek neither self-aggrandisement on the earth nor corruption. The righteous shall have a blessed end. [84] He who does good shall be rewarded with something better. But he who does evil shall be requited according to his deeds.

[85] He who has entrusted you with the responsibility of the Quran, will surely lead you to a successful end. Say, 'My Lord knows best who is rightly guided and who is in gross error.' [86] You never expected that this Book would be revealed to you. Yet, by the grace of your Lord, you have received it. So do not support those who reject the truth. [87] And let no one divert you from God's revelations, once they have been sent down to you. Call people to your Lord. Never be of those who ascribe partners to God. [88] Invoke no god other than God, for there is no god but Him. All things are bound to perish except Himself. His is the judgement, and to Him you shall be returned.

---

a The character of Korah described here is the same as is invariably found in men of wealth. A wealthy man thinks that whatever he has acquired is thanks to his own talents. But with all his knowledge, the rich man never stops to wonder how his wealth is going to save him in this ephemeral world from the same fate as all his rich predecessors met with—namely death and destruction. All the glamour of the world gathers around a person who possesses wealth. Seeing this, many foolish persons envy his lot. But those who possess real knowledge are quick to realize that this glamour is ephemeral, and that something so unenduring has no value.

29. THE SPIDER (*AL-'ANKABUT*)

In the name of God, the Most Gracious, the Most Merciful

¹ *Alif Lam Mim*

² Do people think that once they say, 'We believe,' they will be left alone and not be put to the test? ³ We certainly tried those who have gone before them, so God will certainly distinguish between those who are truthful and those who are lying.*ᵃ*

⁴ Do those who do evil imagine that they will escape Us? How ill they judge! ⁵ He who hopes to meet God should know that God's appointed hour is sure to come. He is the All Hearing, the All Knowing. ⁶ And whoever strives, strives only for himself—God is independent of all His creation—⁷ as for those who have faith and do good works, We shall certainly cleanse them of their evil deeds and reward them according to the best of their actions.

⁸ We have enjoined man to show kindness to his parents. But if they bid you associate with Me something about which you have no

---

a The question of whether a man is a true believer is decided on the basis of how he conducts himself in extraordinary rather than in ordinary circumstances. It becomes clear, on such occasions through a man's overt actions whether he is in actual fact what he claims to be. Those who prove to be steadfast in their belief and convictions under extraordinary circumstances, will be treated by God as believers in the true sense.

To pass the divine test means to become a man of faith by adopting the way of sacrifice, that is to say, to accept and confirm the Truth when people in general reject it; to be staunch in one's beliefs when people harbour doubts; to be a believer even at the cost of curbing one's ego; to accept the Truth even when rejection of it does not entail any loss; to spend when restraint would appear to be more prudent; to be steadfast and firm when circumstances warrant fleeing; to surrender when the occasion demands that one save one's skin; to bow down in submission when there is an occasion for arrogance; to support and co-operate when it amounts to surrendering and sacrificing everything.

The inner man is revealed on such extraordinary occasions. Thereafter, no one is left with the opportunity to make fictitious claims about what in actual fact one is not.

knowledge, do not obey them. To Me you shall all return, and I shall tell you about all that you have done. ⁹ We shall surely admit those who believe and do good deeds to the company of the righteous.

¹⁰ Some profess to believe in God, but when they suffer for God's cause they mistake the persecution of man for the punishment of God. But when help comes to you from God, they will say, 'We have always been with you.' Is not God fully aware of what is in the hearts of all creatures? ¹¹ Most certainly God will mark out those who believe and mark out those who are hypocrites.

¹² Those who deny the truth say to the faithful, 'Follow our way, and we will bear the burden of your sins.' But they will bear none of their sins. They are surely lying. ¹³ They shall bear their own burdens, and other burdens besides. On the Day of Resurrection they shall be questioned about their false assertions.

¹⁴ We sent Noah to his people and he lived among them for fifty short of a thousand years; then the deluge overtook them, for they were wrongdoers. ¹⁵ But We saved him and those who were with him in the Ark and made the event a sign for mankind.

¹⁶ Tell of Abraham. He said to his people, 'Worship God and fear Him, that would be best for you, if only you knew. ¹⁷ You worship idols besides God and fabricate falsehoods. Those whom you worship besides God have no power to provide sustenance for you. So seek your sustenance from God and worship Him and be grateful to Him, for to Him you shall return. ¹⁸ If you reject the truth, other communities before you also rejected the truth. The messenger's responsibility is only to convey the message clearly.'

¹⁹ Do they not see how God originates creation, then reproduces it? That surely is easy for God.*a* ²⁰ Tell them, 'Roam the earth and

---

a Man was non-existent and came into being only at a certain point in time. In view of this, why should it not be possible for the creation which occurred once, to take place once again? Shah Abdul Qadir Dehlavi has written this meaningful observation, 'You have seen the beginning, you can now guess that it can be repeated in future.'

Each man himself is an example of the First Creation. If he needs further examples, he should observe and study this wide world of God. He will see that the whole world is replete with living examples of this event. God has provided

see how He originated creation. Then God will bring into being your second life. God has power over all things. [21] He punishes whom He will and shows mercy to whom He pleases. And to Him you shall be returned. [22] You cannot defeat His purpose on earth or in heaven; nor have you any friend or helper besides God.' [23] Those who deny God's revelations and the meeting with Him—it is they who have despaired of My mercy. They will suffer a grievous punishment.

[24] The only response of Abraham's people was, 'Kill him or burn him!' But God saved him from the fire. Surely in this there are signs for people who believe. [25] Abraham said, 'You have taken up the worship of idols, instead of God, to promote friendship between yourselves in the present life. But on the Day of Judgement, you will disown and curse one another. Your abode will be the Fire and you will have no helpers.' [26] Lot was the one who believed in him and said, 'I shall migrate to another land for the sake of my Lord. He is the Mighty One, the Wise One.' [27] We gave him Isaac and Jacob and granted prophethood and the Book to his descendants. We gave him his reward in this life and in the Hereafter he shall dwell among the righteous.

[28] We sent Lot to his people and he said to them, 'Indeed you commit obscenity such as no people before you have ever committed. [29] You approach men and waylay them on the road and commit depravities within your gatherings.' But his people's only reply was, 'Bring down God's punishment upon us, if what you say be true.' [30] Lot prayed, 'Lord, help me against this wicked people.'

[31] When Our messengers brought Abraham the good news [of the birth of Isaac] they [also] said, 'We are indeed going to destroy the people of this city, for the people of this city are truly wrongdoers.' [32] Abraham said, 'But, Lot lives here.' They answered, 'We well know who lives here. We shall surely save him and his whole family, except his wife, who will be among those who stay behind.' [33] When Our messengers came to Lot, he was troubled and distressed on their

---

these examples in this world so that man may understand what the Second Creation means and then perform such deeds as will be of avail to him in the next stage of existence.

account. They said, 'Have no fear or grief. We shall certainly save you and your household, except your wife—who will be among those who stay behind— [34] We are surely going to bring down a punishment from heaven on the people of this town because of their depravities.' [35] Surely the ruins We left of that city are a clear sign for a people who use their reason.

[36] To the people of Midian We sent their brother Shu'ayb. He said, 'My people, worship God, and look forward to the Last Day, and do not commit evil and spread corruption in the land.' [37] But they rejected him, so the earthquake overwhelmed them and they were left lying prostrate on the ground in their homes.

[38] The same happened to the tribes of 'Ad and Thamud: this must be clear to you from their ruins. Satan made their actions seem good to them, and turned them away from the straight path, even though they were intelligent people.[a]

[39] Korah, Pharaoh, and Haman: Moses came to them with clear signs but they were arrogant in the land. They could not escape Us. [40] So We seized each one for his sins; some We struck with a violent storm; some of them were overcome by a sudden blast, some were swallowed up by the earth and some We drowned. God did not wrong them: they wronged themselves.

[41] Those who take protectors other than God can be compared to the spider which builds itself a cobweb, but the frailest of all structures is the house of the spider, if they but knew it.[b] [42] God surely knows what they invoke besides Him. He is the Mighty,

---

a In ancient times the 'Ad people inhabited the area of southern Arabia, which is now known as Yemen, Ahqaf and Hadramouth. Similarly, the Thamud people inhabited the areas located in the northern part of Hijaz stretching from Rabegh to Aquaba and from Madinah and Khyber to Tyma and Tabuk.

b It is shown here that one who sees a spider's web and learns a lesson about reality from it, is a learned person in the true sense. This clearly demonstrates who are the truly learned in the eyes of God. They are not those who have become expert in bookish discourses, but individuals who are capable of imbibing the sound advice given by God's signs scattered throughout His world, and whose minds are capable of magnifying small events into great lessons. When this very learning reaches the final stage of *ma'rifah* or 'knowledge with intense realization of God,' then it is called by its other name: faith or *iman*.

the Wise One. ⁴³ Such are the comparisons We make for people, but only those understand them who have knowledge. ⁴⁴ God has created the heavens and the earth for a purpose; surely in this there is a sign for true believers.

⁴⁵ Recite what has been revealed to you of the Book, and pray regularly. Surely prayer restrains one from indecency and evil and remembrance of God is greater. God has knowledge of all your actions.^{*a*}

⁴⁶ Believers, argue only in the best way with the People of the Book, [but contend not at all] with such of them as are unjust. Say, 'We believe in what has been revealed to us, and what has been revealed to you; our God and your God are one; and to Him we submit.'

⁴⁷ Likewise We have sent down the Book to you. Those to whom We gave the scripture believe in it, and so do some of your own people. Only those who deny the truth reject Our revelations. ⁴⁸ You were not able to read any book before this, nor did you write one down with your hand. If you had done so, the followers of falsehood would have had cause to doubt it. ⁴⁹ But the Quran is a revelation that is clear to the hearts of those endowed with knowledge. Only the evil-doers refuse to acknowledge Our revelations.

⁵⁰ They say, 'Why has no sign been given to him by his Lord?' Say, 'The signs are in the hands of God. I am but a plain warner.' ⁵¹ Is it not sufficient for them that We have sent you down the Book to be recited to them? In this surely there is a blessing and an admonition for a people who believe. ⁵² Say, 'God is sufficient as a witness between you and me. He knows all that is in the heavens and the earth. Those who believe in falsehood and reject God will surely be the losers.'

⁵³ They ask you to hasten the punishment. Had there not been an appointed time for it, the punishment would already have come to

---

a When a man attains perfect knowledge through intense realization of God, or *ma'rifah*, the result is that the thought of God permeates his very existence. This is what is meant by remembrance of God (*dhikr*). This spring of God's remembrance, or *dhikr*, wells up and flows through his body and soul. Reaching this height of spirituality, man begins uttering noble words in praise of God, and this is undoubtedly the highest form of prayer or worship.

them. Indeed it will come down upon them suddenly and catch them unawares. ⁵⁴ They ask you to hasten the punishment, but surely, Hell is [already] encompassing those who deny the truth. ⁵⁵ On the Day the punishment envelops them from above them and from underneath their feet, they will be told, 'Taste [the punishment] for what you used to do!'

⁵⁶ My servants who believe, My earth is vast, so worship Me alone. ⁵⁷ Every soul shall taste death and then to Us you shall return. ⁵⁸ We shall lodge forever those who believe and do good works in the mansions of Paradise beside which rivers flow. How excellent is the reward of those who labour, ⁵⁹ and who are steadfast and put their trust in their Lord. ⁶⁰ How many creatures cannot fend for themselves!ᵃ God provides for them and for you. He is the All Hearing, the All Knowing.

⁶¹ If you ask them who it is that has created the heavens and the earth and subjugated the sun and the moon, they will say, 'God.' How then are they turned away? ⁶² God gives abundantly to whom He will and sparingly to whom He pleases. God has full knowledge of all things. ⁶³ And if you ask them who it is that sends down water from the sky and revives the earth with it after its death, they will surely answer, 'God.' Then praise be to God. But most of them do not understand.

⁶⁴ The life of this world is nothing but sport and a diversion. It is the life of the Hereafter which is the only true life, if they but knew it. ⁶⁵ When they board a vessel, they call on God, sincere in their faith for Him alone; but when He brings them safe to land, they begin to ascribe partners to Him. ⁶⁶ And thus they may show utter ingratitude for Our favours; let them enjoy themselves for a time. But they will soon come to know.

⁶⁷ Have they not seen how We have granted them a safe sanctuary, though all around them people are snatched away? Would they still believe in falsehood, and deny the favour of God? ⁶⁸ Who does greater wrong than he who invents a lie about God or rejects the truth when it comes to him? Is Hell not the home for those who

---

a i.e. they do not carry their provision with them.

deny the truth. [69] We will surely guide in Our ways those who strive hard for Our cause, God is surely with the righteous.

30. THE ROMANS (*AL-RUM*)

In the name of God, the Most Gracious, the Most Merciful

[1] *Alif Lam Mim*

[2] The Romans have been defeated [3] in a nearby land. They will reverse their defeat with a victory [4] within a few years: [for] with God rests all power of decision, first and last. On that day the believers too will have cause to rejoice, [5] with the help of God. He helps whom He pleases: He is the Mighty, and the Merciful. [6] [This is] God's promise. Never does God fail to fulfil His promise—but most people do not know this; [7] they only know the outward appearance of the life of this world, and they are neglectful of the Hereafter.

[8] Do they not ponder about their own selves? God has created the heavens and the earth and all that is between them for a purpose and for an appointed time? Yet many deny they will ever meet with their Lord. [9] Have they not travelled through the land and seen what end their predecessors met? They were mightier than them: they cultivated the earth more and built more upon it than these have ever built. Their own messengers also came to them with clear signs: God did not wrong them; they wronged themselves. [10] Then the end of those who committed evil was evil, for they belied the signs of God, and they derided them.

[11] God originates the creation, and shall repeat it, then to Him you shall be returned. [12] On the Day the Hour arrives, the guilty will be struck dumb with despair, [13] and they will have no intercessors among those partners they ascribed to God. They will deny these partners. [14] When the Last Hour dawns—on that Day they will be sorted out: [15] those who believed and did good deeds will rejoice in a Garden, [16] and as for those who denied the truth and belied Our signs and the meeting in the Hereafter—they shall be brought to the torment. [17] So glorify God in the evening and in the morning—

[18] and praise be to Him in the heavens and on the earth—and glorify Him in the late afternoon, and at midday.[a]

[19] He brings forth the living from the dead and the dead from the living. He gives life to the earth after its death, and you shall be raised to life in the same way. [20] One of His signs is that He created you from dust and, behold, you became human beings and multiplied yourselves throughout the earth.[b] [21] Another of His signs is that He created for you from among yourselves spouses, so that you might find repose in them, and He created between you affection and kindness. Truly there are signs in this for people who reflect.

[22] Another of His signs is that He created the heavens and earth, and the diversity of your languages and colours. There truly are signs in this for those who know. [23] Among His signs are your sleep, at night or in daytime, and your seeking His bounty. There truly are signs in this for people who hear. [24] Among His signs is this: He shows you the lightning, giving rise to [both] fear and hope, and sends down water from the sky, giving life thereby to the earth after it had been lifeless: in this, behold, there are signs indeed for people who use their reason!

[25] Another of His signs is this: the heavens and the earth stand firm by His command and afterwards when He calls you, behold,

---

a On the Day of Judgement, human beings will be divided into two groups—one consisting of those who glorify God and offer praises to Him, and the other consisting of those who do quite the reverse. The people of the first group are those who realize God to such a degree that He becomes the sole topic of their conversation.

b A wonderful miracle of the present world is growth and development. Here, one finds an inert, non-growing material turning into a material which is capable of growing and increasing. Here, lifeless earth, in other words, earth's elements, undergo a change and take the shape of moving and talking human beings. On account of this, human civilization has survived for thousands of years now. This change, and that too a well-organized, proportionate and harmonious change, would not be at all possible unless it were the work of an all-powerful God.

The fact is that if a man gives deep consideration to God's creations, he will feel that the Might of God is reflected in everything and that God is peeping out from all things.

from the earth you will come forth.[a] 26 All those in the heavens and on the earth belong to Him. All are obedient to Him. 27 He is the One who originates creation, then repeats it, and it is very easy for Him. His is the most exalted state in the heavens and on the earth; He is the Mighty, the Wise One.

28 He sets forth for you an example taken from your own lives. Do you make your servants full partners with an equal share in the wealth We have bestowed upon you? Do you fear them as you fear each other? In this way We explain the signs to people who use their reason. 29 And still those who are unjust follow their own desires without having any knowledge. Then who can guide those whom God has let go astray? There shall be none to help them.

30 Devote yourself single-mindedly to the Religion. And follow the nature [constitution] as made by God, that nature in which He has created mankind. There is no altering the creation of God. That is the right religion. But most people do not realize it. 31 Turn to Him and fear Him, and be steadfast in prayer, and do not be one of those who associate partners with God, 32 those who split up their religion and became divided into sects; each one exulting in what they have.

33 When an affliction befalls men, they cry out to their Lord, turning to Him in repentance; but then, when He has made them taste His mercy, a section of them associate partners with their Lord,[b] 34 and

---

a In the vastness of space, the earth, the sun, the planets and stars—all wonderfully rare phenomena—proclaim by their very existence that they are maintained by the power of a Maintainer and continue to function by deriving their strength from a Supreme Being. If this extraordinary help were taken away from the cosmos even for a moment, the whole system would be scattered helter-skelter. In this world, even an ordinary aeroplane will be destroyed if the pilot loses control. Then, how can the huge system of the Universe be run without the control of a Controller?

b Under ordinary circumstances man finds himself possessed of certain powers. Therefore, he assumes an air of arrogance. But, when critical conditions make him feel his helplessness, the veils are removed from his mind. At that time he is cut down to size, and realizing his helplessness, he starts calling upon God for help.

This is the psychological proof of the Oneness of God. In this way, the reality is mirrored in the personal experience of the individual. But man is so

are ungrateful for what We have given them. So enjoy yourselves for a while, but soon you will come to know. ³⁵ Have We sent down to them any authority which speaks in favour of what they associate with Him?

³⁶ When We give mankind a taste of Our blessing, they rejoice therein: but if they encounter tribulation because of their own actions—they fall into despair. ³⁷ Do they not see that God gives abundantly to whoever He pleases, and sparingly to whoever He pleases? In that truly there are signs for those who believe. ³⁸ So give the near relative, the needy, and the wayfarer their due—that is best for those who seek God's pleasure: such men are the ones who will surely prosper. ³⁹ Whatever you lend out in usury to gain in value through other people's wealth will not increase in God's eyes, but whatever you give in alms in your desire for God's pleasure will be multiplied.

⁴⁰ God is He who created you, then provides for you, then will cause you to die and then bring you back to life. Can any of your 'partners' do any one of these things? Glory be to Him and exalted be He above anything they associate with Him! ⁴¹ Corruption has appeared on land and sea because of the evil which men's hands have done: and so He will make them taste the fruit of some of their doings, so that they may turn back from evil.ᵃ ⁴² Say, 'Journey through the land, and see how those before you met their end—most of them, ascribed partners with God.'

---

foolish that, as soon as the circumstances become favourable, he reverts to his neglectfulness and arrogance.

a Man deviated from God's scheme and completely ignored His creation plan, in that he single-mindedly pursued worldly comforts. He very soon realized that modern civilization, which he had thought would fulfil his limitless hidden desires and ambitions, was only a source of utter destruction and chaos.

The present global warming is an apt illustration of this point: the modern culture of consumerism and greed for more and more has given an immense boost to industrialization, which has resulted in global climate change. Scientists now believe that the modern industrial age spells total catastrophe and that the world is careering head on to its doom. The damage is so severe and irreversible that, very soon, life on this earth will be impossible.

[43] [Prophet], set your face to the right religion, before that Day comes from God which cannot be averted. On that Day, mankind will be parted in two. [44] Those who rejected the truth will bear the burden of that rejection, and those who did good deeds will have made good provision for themselves. [45] For then He will reward out of His bounty those who believe and do good deeds; He does not love those who reject the truth.

[46] Among His signs is this: He sends out the winds bearing good news so that He may make you taste His mercy, and ships sail at His command, so that you may seek His bounty, and be grateful. [47] Surely, We sent messengers before you to their own people, and they brought them clear signs. Then We took vengeance on the guilty. It was certainly Our duty to help the believers.

[48] It is God who sends out the winds so that they raise the clouds. Then He spreads them in the sky as He wills and places them layer upon layer and you see the rain issuing forth from their midst. When He causes it to fall on whichever of His servants He pleases, behold! they rejoice; [49] though before that—before it was sent down upon them—they were in despair. [50] Look, therefore, at the signs of God's mercy; how He resurrects the earth after its death. Truly, the same God will resurrect the dead; for He has power over all things. [51] Yet if We send a wind and they see their harvest turn yellow, they will then begin to deny [Our favours]. [52] You [Prophet] cannot make the dead hear and you cannot make the deaf hear your call when they turn their backs and leave; [53] just as you cannot lead the blind [of heart] out of their error, you cannot make anyone hear your call save those who are willing to believe in Our revelations, and thus surrender themselves to Us and are submissive to Our will.

[54] God is the One who has created you in a state of weakness; then He has granted you strength following [your] weakness; later on He has given you infirmity and grey hairs in place of strength. He creates whatever He wishes; He is the All Knowing and All Powerful.[a] [55] On the Day the Last Hour arrives, the evil-doers will

---

a When a man is born, he is but a weak child. Then after experiencing the strength of youth, followed by middle age, he again faces the weakness of old

swear they have not even tarried for an hour—they have always been deluded—[56] but those endowed with knowledge and faith will say, 'Indeed, you did tarry, as God ordained, till the Day of Resurrection, and this is the Day of Resurrection: but you were not aware of it.' [57] So on that Day their pleas shall be of no avail, nor will they be allowed to make amends.

[58] Truly, We have set forth for men in this Quran every kind of parable and indeed, if you bring them a sign, those who are bent on denying the truth are sure to say, 'You are only making false claims!' [59] In this way God seals the hearts of those who do not [want to] know [the truth], [60] so have patience [O Muhammad]! God's promise is true; let not those who will not be convinced make you discouraged.

31. LUQMAN

In the name of God, the Most Gracious, the Most Merciful

[1] *Alif Lam Mim*

[2] These are the verses of the Book of wisdom, [3] a guide and a mercy for those who do good, [4] for those who attend to their prayers and pay the *zakat* and who have firm faith in the Hereafter: [5] these are rightly guided by their Lord: and these are the ones who will prosper.

[6] But among men there are some who spend their time in idle diversions only to lead people astray from the path of God, and without knowledge, hold it up to ridicule: for such there is a humiliating punishment in store. [7] Whenever Our messages are conveyed to

---

age. This means that a man's strength is not his own. He receives it when it is given to him. It is in the power of the Giver to give when He likes and take away when He likes.

In the life of this world, man cares nothing for the Hereafter, because the Day of Judgement appears to be very far away. But, this is only due to his ignorance. When the Day of Judgement arrives, —the stage for the next world to arrive—he will feel as if he had lived in the previous world for only a moment.

such a person, he turns away in his arrogance, as though he had not heard them—as though his ears were sealed: give him, then, the tidings of grievous suffering [in the life to come]. [8] Surely, those who believe and do good works shall enter gardens of bliss, [9] wherein they will abide forever. That is God's true promise; He is the Mighty, the Wise One.

[10] He has created the skies without any support that you could see,[a] and has placed firm mountains upon the earth, lest it sway with you, and has caused all manner of living creatures to multiply thereon. And We sent down water from the skies, and thus We made every kind of excellent plant grow there: [11] this is God's creation. Show me then what those besides Him have created! The wrongdoers are in manifest error.

[12] We bestowed wisdom on Luqman, saying, 'Be grateful to God: he who is grateful, is grateful only for the good of his own soul. But if anyone is ungrateful, then surely God is self-sufficient and praiseworthy.' [13] Luqman said to his son, counselling him, 'My son, do not associate anything with God. Associating others with Him is a terrible wrong.'[b]

[14] We have enjoined man to show kindness to his parents—for his mother bears him, in hardship upon hardship, and his weaning takes two years. [We said] Give thanks to Me and to your parents; all will return to Me. [15] But if they press you to associate something

---

a The universe exists in infinite space. In it the continuous revolving of innumerable large stellar bodies is a great and awe-inspiring feature. In this universe, the earth is an extremely exceptional sphere, upon which numerous factors and arrangements have made human life possible. Among these arrangements are the maintenance of balance by the rising mountains on the earth, and also the plentiful existence of valuable things like water, greenery, etc. There is nobody except Almighty God who can manage this huge system. As such, is it legitimate for man to worship things other than God?

b The Quran says that Luqman was a man who was a grateful subject of God and who advised his son to save himself from polytheism. The belief in the oneness of God stems from the intense realization that God is the sole benefactor, whereas polytheism holds that beings other than God are man's benefactors and that man should direct his feelings of gratitude towards them. If the Benefactor is One, then all gratitude should be shown only to that One.

with Me about which you have no knowledge, do not obey them. Yet be kind to them in this world and follow the path of those who turn to Me. You will all return to Me in the end, and I will tell you everything that you have done.

¹⁶ [Luqman further said,] 'O my son! Though it be but the weight of a grain of mustard seed and though it be hidden in a rock, or in the heavens or on the earth, God will bring it forth. Truly, God is the knower of all subtleties and He is aware. ¹⁷ O my dear son! Say your prayers regularly, and enjoin good, and forbid evil, and endure patiently whatever may befall you. Surely, this is something which requires firm resolve. ¹⁸ Do not avert your face from people out of haughtiness and do not walk with pride on the earth: for, behold, God does not love arrogant and boastful people. ¹⁹ Walk modestly and lower your voice, for the ugliest of all voices is the braying of the ass.'

²⁰ Have you not seen that God has subjected to you whatever is in the heavens and whatever is on the earth, and has completed His favours to you, both seen and unseen? Yet there are some who dispute concerning God, without knowledge or guidance or an enlightening Book. ²¹ When they are told to follow the [Revelations] that God has sent down, they say, 'No, we shall follow the ways that we found our fathers [following].' Yes! Even though Satan is inviting them to the punishment of the burning Fire?

²² He who submits himself completely to God, and is a doer of good, has surely grasped a strong handle, for the final outcome of all events rests with God. ²³ But if any reject the Faith, let not his rejection grieve you: for to Us they shall return, and We shall tell them the truth about their deeds: for God knows well all that is in the human hearts—²⁴ We shall let them enjoy themselves for a little while, but then We shall drive them to a harsh punishment.

²⁵ If you should ask them, 'Who created the heavens and the earth?' They will surely answer, 'God.' Say, 'Praise be to God!' But most of them do not understand. ²⁶ Whatever is in the heavens and the earth belongs to God. Assuredly, God is self-sufficient and praiseworthy. ²⁷ If all the trees on earth were pens, and the sea [were]

ink, with seven [more] seas added to it, the words of God would not be exhausted: for, truly, God is Almighty and Wise.*a*

²⁸ Creating and resurrecting all of you is just like creating and resurrecting a single soul. Truly, God hears all and observes all. ²⁹ Have you not seen that God makes the night pass into the day, and makes the day pass into the night, and that He has pressed the sun and the moon into His service, each pursuing its course for an appointed term, and that God is well aware of what you do? ³⁰ That is because God is the Truth, and what they call upon besides Him is falsehood. God is the Most High, the Supreme One.

³¹ Have you not seen how the ships sail on the sea by God's grace so that He may show you some of His signs? Surely therein are signs for every steadfast, thankful person. ³² When the waves engulf them like shadows [of death], they call to God, sincere [at that moment] in their faith in Him alone: but as soon as He has brought them safe ashore, only some of them take the right course. And none denies Our signs save the perfidious and ungrateful person.

³³ O men, seek protection with your Lord and fear the Day when neither will the father be of any avail to his son, nor will the son be of any avail to his father. God's promise is surely true. So let not worldly life beguile you, nor let the Deceiver deceive you concerning God. ³⁴ Truly, God alone has knowledge of the Hour. He sends down the rain, and He knows what is in the wombs. No soul knows what it will earn tomorrow, and no soul knows in what land it will die. Surely, God is all knowing, all-aware.*b*

---

a The Majesty of God is too great to be expressed in words. The history of physical sciences is spread over thousands of years. But, in spite of innumerable researches, there are still many things about which it has not been possible to obtain complete information. For example man does not know even today how many stars there are in space, how many species of animals and vegetation there are on the earth, what are the true nature and composition of the leaf of a tree or a grain of sand or how many wonders are hidden in the sea. In short, there are few things, big or small, in this world, about which man has obtained full information. This in itself is enough to prove that all the trees of the world chiselled into pens and all the seas changed into ink will not be enough to record the innumerable feats of God.

b In the present world people have been given a certain amount of liberty

32. PROSTRATION (*AL-SAJDAH*)

In the name of God, the Most Gracious, the Most Merciful

¹ *Alif Lam Mim*

² This Book has beyond all doubt been revealed by the Lord of the Universe. ³ Do they say, 'He has invented it himself.'? No indeed! It is the truth from your Lord to warn a people to whom, before you, no warner came, so that hopefully they may be rightly guided.

⁴ It was God who created the heavens and the earth and whatsoever is in between in six Days,*ᵃ* and then He established Himself on the throne. You have no patron nor any intercessor besides Him. So will you not pay heed? ⁵ He directs all affairs from heaven to earth. Then all will again ascend to Him on a Day whose length is a thousand years by the way you measure. ⁶ Such is the Knower of the unseen and the visible, the Powerful, the Merciful, ⁷ who gave everything its perfect form. He originated the creation of man from clay, ⁸ then He made his progeny from an extract of a humble fluid. ⁹ Then He

---

as a means of putting them to the test. Man takes this trial-oriented freedom as the real freedom. This is the greatest illusion. All human evils are born out of this illusion. Apparently it seems that a man is free here to do whatever he likes and there is nobody to check him. But the fact remains that a very difficult period is awaiting him, when father and son will not be able to help each other.

a The gradual creation of the universe, in six days or six stages, along with and the system full of wisdom governing it, indicative of the fact that the Creator has some special purpose behind this creation. Moreover, numerous processes are incessantly going on in the universe. This further proves that its Creator is running it in a well-planned manner. The human being is a wonderful living organism, but if his body is analysed, it will be found that it is composed of earth elements. Then this creation does not end there, but continues eternally through the process of procreation and regeneration.

If the individual gives deep and serious consideration to these facts, his mind will be free of feelings of awe for anything except the Majesty of God. He will become a grateful subject of God. But there are very few who give deep consideration to anything. That is why there are very few people who offer praises to God, or are grateful to Him, in the true sense.

moulded him; He breathed His Spirit into him; He gave you hearing, sight, and hearts. How seldom you are grateful![a]

[10] They say, 'When we are lost in the earth, how can we then be recreated?' Indeed, they deny they will ever meet their Lord. [11] Say, 'The Angel of Death who has been given charge of you will gather in your souls. Then you will [all] be returned to your Lord.' [12] If only you could see the evil-doers hanging their heads in shame before their Lord, 'Our Lord, we have seen and we have heard, so send us back again and we will act rightly. For we do indeed now believe.' [13] Yet had We so willed, We could indeed have imposed Our guidance upon every human being: but My word shall come true: 'I will fill Hell with jinns and men all together.' [14] We shall say to them, 'Taste this—for you forgot you would ever meet this Day. We too will forget you—taste the chastisement of Eternity for your [evil] deeds!' [15] The people who truly believe in Our messages are those who fall to the ground in prostration when they are reminded of them, and glorify their Lord with praise and are not arrogant. [16] They forsake their beds, calling upon their Lord in fear and in hope, and spend out of what We have provided them with. [17] No soul knows what joy is kept hidden in store for them as a reward for their labours.

[18] So, is someone who believes equal to someone who defies God? No, they are not equal. [19] Those who believe and do good deeds shall be lodged in the Gardens of Paradise as a reward for what they have done. [20] As for those who defy God, their home shall be the Fire. Whenever they try to escape it, they shall be driven back into it, and they shall be told, 'Taste the torment of the Fire, which you have persistently denied.' [21] And most surely We will make them taste a lesser punishment before the greater punishment, so that perhaps they may return to Us in repentance. [22] Who does greater wrong

---

[a] Man's creation for the first time is enough to convince mankind of the possibility of creation for the second time. But when a man does not believe in his accountability before God, he ridicules the possibility of a second creation, and he talks flippantly of it.

than someone who, when revelations of his Lord are recited to him, turns away from them? We shall inflict retribution on the guilty.

²³ We gave Moses the Scripture—so [Muhammad] do not doubt that you are receiving it—just as We made it a guide for the Children of Israel. ²⁴ We appointed leaders from among them, guiding by Our command when they were steadfast and when they had firm faith in Our signs. ²⁵ Surely your Lord will judge between them on the Day of Resurrection concerning that wherein they used to differ. ²⁶ Does it not guide them [to see] how many generations We destroyed before them, among whose ruined dwellings they now walk about? There truly are signs in this—will they not listen?

²⁷ Have they not seen that We drive the water to the barren land and produce thereby crops of which their cattle and they themselves eat? Will they not then see? ²⁸ And they say, 'When will this judgement come, if you are telling the truth?' ²⁹ Say, 'On the Day of Judgement it will be of no benefit to those who were bent on denying the truth, if they [then] believe! They will be granted no respite.' ³⁰ So turn away from them and wait. They too are waiting.

33. THE CONFEDERATES (*AL-AHZAB*)

In the name of God, the Most Gracious, the Most Merciful

¹ O Prophet, have fear of God and do not yield to those who deny the truth and the hypocrites. God is all-knowing and all-wise. ² Follow what is revealed to you from your Lord. God is aware of all that you do. ³ Put your trust in God; God is sufficient as a Guardian.

⁴ God has not placed two hearts in any man's body, nor has He made your wives—from whom you keep away by saying, 'Be as my mother's back'—your [real] mothers, neither He has made your adopted sons as your own sons. These are merely words which you utter with your mouths: but God speaks the truth and gives guidance to the right path. ⁵ Call them after their own fathers; that is closer to justice in the sight of God. If you do not know their fathers, regard them as your brothers in faith and your protégés. You will not be blamed if you make a mistake, you will be held accountable

only for what in your hearts you have done intentionally. God is forgiving and merciful.

⁶ The Prophet has a higher claim on the believers than [they have on] their own selves, and his wives are their mothers. Blood relatives are closer to one another in God's Book than are believers and the Emigrants except that you want to show your friends a kindness. That is decreed in the Book.

⁷ We took a solemn pledge from the prophets, from you and Noah, Abraham, Moses and Jesus, the son of Mary—We took a solemn pledge from all of them. ⁸ So that God might ask those men of truth as to [what response] their truthfulness [had received on earth]. But for those who deny the truth, He has prepared a woeful punishment.

⁹ You who have attained to faith, remember God's blessings upon you when mighty armies massed against you. We sent a violent wind against them and hosts that you could not see. God sees all that you do. ¹⁰ When they came against you both from above you and from below you, your eyes rolled [with fear] and your hearts leapt up to your throats, and you entertained [ill] thoughts about God. ¹¹ There the faithful were put to the proof and they were shaken as if by an earthquake.

¹² The hypocrites and people with sickness in their hearts said, 'God and His Messenger have promised us nothing but delusions.' ¹³ Others said, 'People of Yathrib, you cannot withstand [the enemy] here: so go back!' Yet others asked leave of the Prophet, saying, 'Our houses are exposed and [defenceless].' They were in truth not exposed: they only wished to flee. ¹⁴ If their town had been stormed, and they had been incited to sedition, they would have rebelled with little hesitation. ¹⁵ They had already vowed before God that they would never turn their backs: and a vow made to God must be answered for. ¹⁶ Say, 'Flight shall not avail you: if you manage to escape from death or killing, you will enjoy life only for a short while.'ᵃ ¹⁷ Say, 'Who is there to shield you from God if He wishes to harm you? If God wishes to show you mercy, who can prevent

---

a See note to 2:191.

Him.' Besides God they shall find none to protect them, and none to bring them succour.

¹⁸ God knows exactly who among you hold the others back, who say to their brethren, 'Come over to our side,' and they seldom take part in the fighting. ¹⁹ Begrudging you all help, but when danger comes, you can see them looking at you with rolling eyes as if in their death throes; but once their fear has passed, they come to you and do glib-talking in their greed for wealth. Such men have no faith, so God has foiled their actions. This is indeed easy for God. ²⁰ They thought the confederate tribes would never withdraw. Indeed, if the confederates should come again, they would prefer to be in the desert, among the Bedouins. There they would ask news of you [from a distance]. But if they were with you, they would take very little part in the fighting.

²¹ You have indeed in the Prophet of God a good example for those of you who look to God and the Last Day, and remember God always. ²² When the believers saw the confederates, they said, 'This is what God and His Messenger have promised us. Surely the promise of God and His Messenger has come true.' It served to increase them in faith and submission. ²³ Among the believers there are men who have been true to the pledge they made with God. Among them are such as have fulfilled their vow, and some who [still] wait, without having changed [their resolve] in the least. ²⁴ God will surely reward the truthful for their truthfulness and punish the hypocrites, if He so wishes, or He may accept their repentance, for God is forgiving and merciful.

²⁵ God turned back those who denied the truth in their rage, without their having gained any advantage. God was enough to [protect] the believers in battle. God is strong and all-powerful.^a ²⁶ He brought down from their strongholds those People of the Book who supported the aggressors and filled their hearts with terror. Some of them you

---

a At the Battle of Ahzab or the Trenches conditions were very severe. But, in this battle the stage of regular fighting was never reached. Almighty God sent stormy winds and an army of angels against the enemies and terrified them to such an extent that they themselves fled the battlefield.

killed and others you took captive. [27] He made you heirs to their lands, and their houses, and their possessions and lands on which you had not set foot before. God has power over all things.

[28] O Prophet, say to your wives, 'If you seek the life of this world and all its finery then come, I will make provision for you, and release you honourably. [29] But if you seek God and His Messenger and the abode of the Hereafter, then know that God has prepared a great reward for those of you who do good deeds.' [30] Wives of the Prophet! Any one of you who commits a flagrant act of misconduct shall be doubly punished. That is easy enough for God.

[31] But those of you who obey God and His Messenger and do good deeds, shall be doubly rewarded. For them We have made an excellent provision. [32] Wives of the Prophet, you are not like any other women. If you fear God, do not be too soft-spoken in case the ill-intentioned should feel tempted. Speak in an appropriate manner.

[33] Stay in your homes and do not flaunt your charms as in the former times of ignorance. Attend to your prayers, pay the *zakat* and obey God and His Messenger. Women of the [Prophet's] Household, God seeks only to remove all impurity from you, and to make you completely pure.[a] [34] Bear in mind all that is recited in your homes of the revelations of God and of wisdom. God is all pervading and all aware.

[35] Surely, for men and women who have surrendered [to God]— believing men and believing women, obedient men and obedient women, truthful men and truthful women, patient men and patient

---

a Here, by recording the guidance given to the Prophet's consorts about correct behaviour, instruction is indirectly given to Muslim women as to how they should conduct themselves. Strictly speaking, they should stay at home and, unlike worldly women, it should not be their aim to show off their charms and finery. Their attention should be entirely directed towards the worship of God. They should spend their wealth for the cause of God. Whatever instructions they receive from God and his Prophet concerning daily affairs should be acted upon immediately. They should spend their time in hearing about God and His Prophet and understanding what they are told.

This style of life makes one pure and righteous and it is only such a person who is approved of by Almighty God.

women, humble men and humble women, charitable men and charitable women, fasting men and fasting women, men and women who guard their chastity, men and women who are ever mindful of God—God is ready with forgiveness and an immense reward. ³⁶ It is not fitting for a believing man or woman to exercise any choice in his or her own affairs once God and His Messenger have reached a decision upon them. Anyone who disobeys God and His Messenger is in manifest error.

³⁷ You said to the man who had been favoured by God and by you, 'Keep your wife to yourself and have fear of God.' You sought to hide in your heart what God wished to reveal. You were afraid of people, whereas it would have been more proper to fear God. When Zayd divorced his wife, We gave her to you in marriage, so that there should be no restriction on believers marrying the spouses of their adopted sons when they have divorced them. The commandment of God must be fulfilled. ³⁸ No blame shall be attached to the Prophet for doing what is sanctioned for him by God. This was God's way with those who went before him—and the command of God is a decree determined. ³⁹ Those who conveyed God's messages and feared Him, and feared none but God: God suffices as a Reckoner. ⁴⁰ Muhammad is not the father of any of your men, but is God's Messenger and the seal of the Prophets. God has knowledge of all things.[a]

⁴¹ Believers, remember God often. ⁴² Glorify Him morning and evening. ⁴³ It is He who sends blessings to you, as do His angels, so that He may bring you out of the darkness into the light. He is most merciful to the believers. ⁴⁴ On the Day they meet Him, they will be welcomed with the greeting, 'Peace!' He has prepared an honourable reward for them.

---

a The Prophet Muhammad was the seal of the prophets. The word '*khatam*' is used for 'seal', i.e. the last action. To seal an envelop means closing it finally, after which nothing can come out of it and nothing can enter it. That is why in Arabic, the '*khatam*' of a community means the last person of that community.

The announcement that the Prophet Muhammad was the '*khataman-Nabiyyin*' means that no prophet was going to come after him and as such was necessary that all godly matters be revealed through him.

[45] O Prophet, We have sent forth you as a witness, as a bearer of good news and a warner.[a] [46] As one who calls people to God by His leave, and guides them like a shining light. [47] Convey to the believers the good news that God has bounteous blessings in store for them. [48] Do not yield to those who deny the truth and the hypocrites: ignore their hurtful talk. Put your trust in God; God is your all sufficient guardian.

[49] Believers, if you marry believing women, and divorce them before the marriage is consummated, you are not required to observe a waiting period: make provision for them and release them in an honourable way.

[50] Prophet, We have made lawful for you the wives to whom you have given their dowers, as well as those whom your right hand possesses from among the captives of war whom God has bestowed upon you. and [We have made lawful to you] the daughters of your paternal uncles and aunts, and the daughters of your maternal uncles and aunts, who have migrated with you; and any believing woman who gives herself to the Prophet, provided the Prophet wants to marry her. This applies only to you and not to the rest of the believers. We know what We have prescribed for them concerning their wives and those whom their right hands may possess, in order that there may be no blame on you. God is most forgiving, most merciful.

---

a The witness (*shahid*), the bearer of good news (*mubashshir*), the warner, (*nadhir*) and the giver of the call for Truth (*da'i*) all represent different aspects of the same reality. It is the Prophet's mission to make people aware of the realities of life and inform them about heaven and hell. This is an action related to the missionary call of the Prophet and on this basis only, will the Prophet give evidence in the Court of the Hereafter about the people to whom he conveyed the message of Truth, upon which some accepted while others rejected it.

The Prophet's mission is also the mission of the followers of Islam. While treading this path, one has to face trouble from the people: for give support; while some give timely support but later desert, uttering falsehoods. Under these circumstances, it was Trust in God alone which kept the Prophet (or his follower-missionaries) firmly on the way both missionary work. To be tolerant of whatever comes from the people, to ignore it and under all circumstances to keep one's eyes fixed on God: these are the real assets of one who performs Islamic missionary work.

⁵¹ You may defer [the turn of] any of them that you please, and you may receive any you please: and there is no blame on you if you invite one whose [turn] you have set aside. That is more proper, so that their eyes may be cooled, and so that they may not grieve, and so that they will be satisfied with what you have given them. God knows what is in your hearts; and God is all knowing, and forbearing. ⁵² It is not lawful for you to marry more women after this, nor to change them for other wives, even though their beauty may please you, except any that your right hand possesses. God is watchful over all things.

⁵³ Believers, do not enter the houses of the Prophet, unless you are invited for a meal. Do not linger until a meal is ready. When you are invited enter and when you have taken your meal, depart. Do not stay on, indulging in conversation. Doing that causes annoyance to the Prophet, though he is too reticent to tell you so, but God is not reticent with the truth. When you ask [the wives of the Prophet] for anything, ask them from behind a curtain. That will be purer for your hearts as well as their hearts. It is not right for you to cause annoyance to the Messenger of God or for you ever to marry his wives after him. Indeed that would be an enormity in the sight of God. ⁵⁴ Whether you reveal anything or hide it, God is aware of everything.

⁵⁵ There shall be no blame on them for appearing before their fathers, their sons, their brothers, their brothers' sons, their sisters' sons, their women or those whom their right hands may possess. Women, fear God. God observes all things.ᵃ

⁵⁶ God and His angels bestow blessings on the Prophet. O believers, you also should invoke blessings on him and give him greetings of peace. ⁵⁷ Those who annoy God and His Messenger shall be cursed by God in this world and in the Hereafter. God has prepared for them a humiliating punishment. ⁵⁸ Those who affront believing men

---

a The sum and substance of all these instructions is that men and women should have the fear of God in their hearts. They should lead their lives keeping in mind that God is keeping a watch on them at all times.

and believing women without their having deserved it [done any wrong] shall bear the weight of slander and flagrant sin.

⁵⁹ O Prophet! Tell your wives and your daughters and believing women that they should draw over themselves some of their outer garments [when in public], so as to be recognized and not harmed. God is most forgiving and most merciful.*ᵃ* ⁶⁰ If the hypocrites and those who have tainted hearts and the scandal mongers of Madinah do not desist, We shall surely give you authority over them and their days in that city will be numbered. ⁶¹ Accursed, wherever they are found, they will be seized and killed.*ᵇ* ⁶² Such has been God's way with those who have gone before them. You shall find no change in the ways of God.

⁶³ People will ask you about the Hour. Say, 'God alone has knowledge of it. Who knows? The Hour may well be near at hand.' ⁶⁴ God has rejected those who deny the truth and prepared for them a blazing Fire. ⁶⁵ There they will live forever, and they will find therein neither friend nor helper. ⁶⁶ On the Day when their faces are turned over in the Fire, they shall say: 'Oh, would that we had obeyed God, and obeyed the Messenger!' ⁶⁷ They shall say, 'Our Lord, we paid heed to our leaders and our elders, but they led us away from the right path. ⁶⁸ Our Lord, give them double punishment and curse them with a mighty curse.'

⁶⁹ Believers, do not behave like those who slandered Moses. God cleared him of their allegations. He was honourable in the sight of God. ⁷⁰ Believers, fear God, and say the right word. ⁷¹ He will bless your works for you and forgive you your sins. Whoever obeys God and His Messenger has indeed achieved a great success.

⁷² We offered the Trust to the heavens and the earth and the mountains, but they refused to bear it, because they were afraid of

---

a When a Muslim woman leaves her house on an errand, she should be so clad as to silently announce that she is a well-bred, respectable and modest woman, and that she has left her home for some pressing and serious need and not to make merry or to go in search of entertainment.

Simple apparel, modest gait, body properly covered, etc.—these are the symbols of that approach.

b See note to 2: 191.

it. But man bore it: he surely proved unjust and ignorant. [73] God will punish the hypocrites, both men and women, and polytheists, both men and women, but God will turn in His mercy to believing men and believing women; God is most forgiving and most merciful.

34. SHEBA (*SABA'*)

In the name of God, the Most Gracious, the Most Merciful

[1] Praise be to God, to whom belongs all that the heavens and the earth contain and praise be to Him in the Hereafter. He is the All Wise, the All Aware. [2] He knows whatever goes into the earth and whatever comes forth from it, and whatever descends from heaven and whatever ascends into it. He is the Merciful, the Forgiving.[a]

[3] Those who deny the truth declare, 'The Hour will never come upon us.' Say, 'Yes, by my Lord, it will surely come upon you! Who knows the unseen. Not the smallest particle in the heavens or the earth, or anything less or greater than that escapes Him; all is recorded in an open Book. [4] He will surely reward those who believe and do good deeds: they shall have forgiveness and an honourable provision.' [5] But those who strive against Our signs, trying to defeat them, will suffer a painful torment. [6] Those who have been given knowledge know that what has been revealed to you from your Lord is the truth, and that it guides to the path of the Almighty, the Praiseworthy.

---

a This Universe is an introduction to its Creator. Its terrifying vastness reveals the majesty of its Creator. The utter perfection of its harmony indicates that its Creator is a perfect and complete being. The perfect co-ordination between its various parts proves that the Being who controls it is extremely wise and all-knowing. The fact of the Universe being extremely congenial and conducive to the nourishment of human life clearly shows that its Creator is extremely kind and merciful towards His creation.

One who ponders over the mysteries of the Universe will be totally absorbed in the realization of God's majesty and perfection. He will be convinced that from the beginning of time till the end of eternity, all majesty pertains to the one and only God and to no other than Him.

⁷ Those who deny the truth say, 'Shall we point out to you a man who will tell you that when you are broken up into particles, you will be put together again in a new creation? ⁸ Has he invented a lie about God, or is he afflicted with madness?' Indeed no. It is those who do not believe in the Hereafter who will suffer torment, for they have strayed far into error. ⁹ Do they not observe how they are encompassed by what is before them and what is behind them in heaven and on earth? We could, if We pleased, cause the earth to swallow them up, or cause a piece of the sky to fall upon them. In that certainly there is a sign for every servant of Ours who turns to us.

¹⁰ We bestowed upon David great favour. We said, 'O mountains and birds! Join with him in celebrating Our praise.' We softened iron for him, saying, ¹¹ 'Make full-length coats of mail, measuring the links well. And do righteous deeds. Surely, I see all that you do.'

¹² We subjected the wind to Solomon; its morning course was a month and its evening course a month; and We caused a fount of molten copper to flow for him. And of the jinn there were some who worked under him, by the command of his Lord. If any one of them turned away from Our command, We would make him taste the punishment of the burning fire. ¹³ They made for him whatever he desired: palaces and statues, basins like reservoirs, and large cooking vessels fixed in their places. We said, 'Give thanks, house of David, for few of My servants are truly grateful.'ᵃ

¹⁴ When We decreed Solomon's death, nothing indicated his death to them except a worm from the earth, which was eating away at his cane. When he fell down, the jinn plainly realized that if they

---

a The entire existence of man is the gift of God. From head to foot he is the manifestation of the Grace of God. Therefore, he should have in him feelings of the utmost gratefulness and indebtedness towards God. But, this is the very feeling with which a human being is least imbued. The reason for this is that whatever a man may receive in this world is in the guise of the result of the cause and effect chain. Therefore, he considers it as such—the result of some cause. But this is the real test of man. It is expected that he should see the hand of God in whatever he ostensibly receives through cause and effect. Whatever he obtains, apparently on account of his talents and diligence, should be treated by him as direct gifts from God.

had known what was unseen, they would not have had to continue with such humiliating labour.

¹⁵ For the people of Sheba there was a sign in their homeland: two gardens, one on the right hand and the other on the left. We said to them: 'Eat what your Lord has provided for you, and be grateful. You have a good land and a Lord most forgiving.' ¹⁶ Yet they turned away [from the truth]. So We let loose on them a flood from the dam and replaced their two gardens by two others bearing bitter fruits, tamarisks, and a few lote trees. ¹⁷ We requited them in that way because of their ingratitude.ᵃ We requite no one in that way but the ungrateful.

¹⁸ We had placed between them and the towns that We had blessed, other towns situated close to each other, and We fixed the stages [of journey] between them, saying, 'Travel between them in safety by night and day,' ¹⁹ but they said, 'Our Lord! Make the stages of our journeys longer.' Thus they wronged themselves and We made them bygone tales and scattered them throughout the land. There are certainly signs in that for everyone who is steadfast and thankful.

²⁰ Satan was correct in his assessment of them and they all followed him—except for a band of true believers—²¹ but he had no authority over them; We only desired to distinguish those who believed in the Hereafter from those who were in doubt concerning it. Your Lord is watchful over all things.

²² Call upon those whom you set up beside God! They possess not an atom's weight either in the heavens or on the earth, nor have

---

a Sheba (Saba') was a very developed community of ancient times. It was spread over the area at present known as Yemen. Its centre was the city of Ma'rib. All these developments had been possible thanks to the provision made by God. Therefore, the people of Sheba should have been grateful to their Lord. But, instead, they became neglectful and arrogant, as generally happens in the case of prosperous communities. Thereafter, the Ma'rib Dam started developing cracks. This was an initial warning, but they did not come to their senses. An earthquake shattered the dam irreparably in the seventh century A.D., as a result of which there were devastating floods and the whole area was destroyed. Moreover, due to the destruction of fertile soil, only wild bushes would grow in this area. (The Encyclopaedia Britannica).

they any share in either, nor has He any helpers among them. ²³ No intercession avails with Him, except on the part of one to whom He grants permission. When their hearts are relieved of fear, they will enquire from those to whom permission is granted, 'What has your Lord said?' They will answer, 'The truth. He is the Most High, the Supreme One.'

²⁴ Ask them, 'Who provides sustenance for you from the heavens and the earth?' Say, 'It is God'; either you or we are rightly guided or in manifest error. ²⁵ Say to them, 'You will not be called to account for our sins and we shall not be called to account for what you do.' ²⁶ Tell them, 'Our Lord will gather us together; then He will judge between us with truth and justice. He is the Just Decider, the All Knowing.' ²⁷ Say to them, 'Show me those whom you have joined with Him as partners. No indeed! For He alone is God, the Mighty One, the Wise One.'

²⁸ We have sent you as a bearer of glad tidings and a warner for the whole of mankind, but most people have no knowledge. ²⁹ They ask, 'When will this promise be fulfilled, if you are truthful?' ³⁰ Say, 'A Day has already been appointed for you which you can neither delay nor advance by a single moment.'

³¹ Those who deny the truth say, 'We shall believe neither in this scripture nor in [any] that [came] before it.' Could you but see when the wrongdoers will be made to stand before their Lord, casting blame on one another! Those who had been weak will say to the arrogant ones, 'Had it not been for you, we should certainly have been believers!' ³² The haughty ones will then reply to the weak ones, 'Did we keep you away from the guidance when it came to you? Indeed not. You yourselves were the guilty ones.' ³³ Those deemed weak will say to those deemed great, 'No, it was your scheming night and day when you commanded us to reject God and assign equals to Him.' But they will show their remorse when they see the punishment. We will put iron collars round the necks of those who had been bent on denying the truth. They will be requited only in proportion to their misdeeds.

³⁴ For it has been thus whenever We sent a warner to any community. Its affluent ones said, 'We reject what you have been sent with.'

³⁵ They say, 'We have more wealth and children; and we are surely not going to be punished.' ³⁶ Say to them, 'My Lord increases the provision for whoever He pleases and decreases it for whoever He pleases; but most people do not know it.' ³⁷ It is not your wealth or your children that will confer on you nearness to Us. It is those who believe and act righteously who will be doubly rewarded for their good deeds, and will dwell in peace in the high pavilions [of paradise], ³⁸ while those who strive to thwart Our messages, seeking to defeat their purpose, shall be summoned to punishment. ³⁹ Say to them, 'It is my Lord who increases the provision for such of His servants as He pleases, and decreases it for such of them as He pleases. Whatever you spend, He will recompense you for it. He is the best of providers.'ᵃ

⁴⁰ On the Day when He gathers them all together, He will ask the angels, 'Was it you that these people worshipped?' ⁴¹ They will say, 'Glory be to You! You are our protector, not them. Indeed no! They worshipped the jinn; it was in them that most of them believed.' ⁴² Today you possess no power to benefit or harm one another. We shall say to the wrongdoers, 'Suffer the punishment of the Fire that you persistently denied.'

⁴³ Whenever Our messages are conveyed to them in all their clarity, they say, 'This [Muhammad] is nothing but a man who wants to turn you away from what your forefathers worshipped.' And they say, 'This [Quran] is nothing but an invented falsehood.' And they who are bent on denying the truth speak thus of the truth when it comes to them, 'This is clearly nothing but plain sorcery!' ⁴⁴ We had not given them books to study, nor have We sent them a warner before you. ⁴⁵ Their predecessors also rejected the truth. These have not attained to one tenth of the power that We had bestowed upon the earlier people. But they rejected My messengers. Then how terrible, was My chastisement!

---

a The wealth and other material things of this world are for the purpose of putting human beings to the test and are not meant as rewards. A surfeit of worldly effects is not a sign of nearness to God; nor does their shortage indicate being at a distance from Him.

⁴⁶ Say to them, 'I exhort you to do one thing: and that is to stand up before God in pairs, or singly, and then reflect. You will thus realize that your companion is not afflicted with madness. He is only a warner, warning you of an impending severe chastisement.' ⁴⁷ Say, 'If I have asked you for any recompense, you can keep it. It is God alone who will reward me: He is the witness of all things.'

⁴⁸ Say to them, 'My Lord hurls forth the Truth [at falsehood] and He is the knower of hidden things.' ⁴⁹ Say to them, 'The Truth has come and will endure. Falsehood has no power to originate any good, nor to reproduce it.' ⁵⁰ Affirm, 'If I am in error, I shall carry the burden thereof; and if I am rightly guided, it is because of what my Lord has revealed to me. Truly, He is all-hearing and near at hand.'

⁵¹ If you could only see when those who denied the truth are terrified, and there is no way out, and they are seized from a place nearby; ⁵² then they will say, 'We now believe in Him.' But how will they attain to faith, having gone so far away from it? ⁵³ They had rejected it before, while they indulged in conjectures from far away. ⁵⁴ And between them and their desires a barrier shall be placed as was done in the past with people of their ilk; for they were indeed in disquieting doubt.

35. THE CREATOR (*FATIR*)

In the name of God, the Most Gracious, the Most Merciful

¹ All praise be to God, Creator of the heavens and the earth, who made the angels His messengers, with wings—two, or three, or four pairs. He adds to His creation whatever He wills; for God has the power to will anything. ² No one can withhold the blessings God bestows upon people, nor can anyone apart from Him bestow whatever He withholds: He is the Almighty, the Wise One.

³ People, remember God's favour to you. Is there any creator other than God who provides for you from the heavens and the earth? There is no God save Him. How then are you turned away from

the truth.[a] [4] If they reject you, other messengers have been rejected before you. To God all affairs will be returned.

[5] O Men. The promise of God is true.a Let not the life of this world deceive you, nor let the Deceiver deceive you about God.[b] [6] Surely Satan is your enemy: so treat him as an enemy: he calls on his followers only so that they should become inmates of the burning Fire. [7] Those who are bent on denying the truth will have a severe punishment, while those who believe and do good deeds will have forgiveness and a great reward.

[8] Is he whose evil deeds are made alluring to him so that he looks upon them as good, [equal to the man who is rightly guided]? God leaves to stray whom He wills, and guides whom He wills. Do not destroy yourself with grief for them. God has full knowledge of all their actions.

[9] It is God who sends forth the winds so that they raise up the clouds. We drive them to a dead land, and by them bring the earth to life after its death. Such is the Resurrection. [10] If anyone seeks glory, let him know that glory belongs to God alone. Good words ascend to Him and righteous deeds are exalted by Him. Those who plot evil deeds shall be sternly punished and their plotting will come

---

a Man is in need of innumerable things to sustain his life, for example, light, water, air, food, minerals, etc., and each one of them requires for its coming into existence the combined and concerted actions of universal forces. Who else except the one God is capable of bringing about such a big event? Even polytheists and atheists cannot claim that anybody other than the one God can provide these essentials of life. When the Creator and Organiser of all these things is the one God, then how could it be reasonable for people to worship any entity other than Him?

b Sudden death, the upheaval of earthquakes and other such incidents shake a man's composure. These, in fact, remind one of Doomsday, before its actual occurrence. But, Satan immediately diverts the attention of the people by saying that these events have natural causes and are not due to any divine intervention. But, this way of thinking results from Satan's falsity. That day is bound to come when a distinction is drawn between the true and the false; righteous people will be rewarded for their virtue and wrongdoers will be punished for their evil deeds.

to nothing.[a] [11] God has created you from dust, then from a drop of semen and then divided you into pairs; no female conceives or gives birth without His knowledge; and no one's life is prolonged or shortened, but it is recorded in a Book. That surely is easy for God.[b]

[12] The two seas are not alike. The one is sweet, thirst-quenching, and pleasant to drink from, while the other is salty and bitter. Yet from each you eat fresh fish and extract ornaments to wear, and in each you see the ships ploughing through the waves so that you may seek His bounty and so that you may feel thankful.[c] [13] He

---

a The present world is a testing ground. Therefore, here even an undeserving person may temporarily receive honour, but in the Hereafter all the honours will fall to the lot of those who are really deserving of them. The criteria for judging worthiness will be righteous words and pious deeds, that is, man's expression—in thought, word and deed—of his discovery of God and his devotion of all his strength to the service of the Almighty. Those who build their lives in piety are bound to secure God's help, and those who are supported by God, cannot be oppressed by anybody.

b Man was first created by God out of the elements of the earth, then from a seed within a drop. Then by dividing human beings into men and women, God caused the human race to multiply. This shows the tremendous power of our Creator.

Then, at the time when a child starts developing in his mother's womb, he finds that all the factors essential to his growth are provided without asking. This shows that the Creator of the child knew his requirements beforehand, otherwise how could He have made such perfect arrangements in advance?

c There is a large store of water on the earth—salt water—in the oceans and seas, and fresh water in rivers, lakes and springs. This water is the source of innumerable advantages for man. It is used for drinking and irrigation. The creatures which live in water provide valuable food for man. The oceans and seas, spread over three-fourths of the earth, are virtually watery roads and highways that have made travelling and transportation very easy. Then, pearls, mineral ores and other such valuable things are obtained from the oceans, and so on and so forth.

Then, in the vastness of space, the sun and the moon being at God's command results in many advantages. He causes the earth to revolve around the sun and rotate on its axis in a regulated manner, thereby causing the seasons, and the alternation of day and night. There are similar innumerable arrangements which have been brought into being by God alone. As such, who else is there other than God who deserves man's utmost gratitude? It is God with His unfathomable powers who can fulfil the needs of man, and not those

makes the night pass into the day and He makes the day pass into the night. He has subjected the sun and the moon, each running for an appointed term. Such is God, your Lord: His is the kingdom. Those whom you invoke besides Him do not own so much as the skin of a date stone; [14] if you invoke them, they do not hear your call; and even if they could hear, they would not respond to you. And on the Day of Resurrection they will disown your having associated them with God. No one can tell you [the Truth] like the One who is all knowing.

[15] O men! It is you who stand in need of God—God is self-sufficient, and praiseworthy— [16] if He so wished, He could take you away and replace you with a new creation; [17] that is not difficult for God. [18] No burden-bearer shall bear another's burden, and if some over-laden soul should call out for someone else to carry his load, not the least portion of it will be borne for him, even though he were a near relative. You can only warn those who fear their Lord in the unseen, and pray regularly. Anyone who purifies himself will benefit greatly from doing so. To God all shall return.

[19] The blind and the sighted are not equal, [20] nor are the darkness and the light; [21] shade and heat are not alike, [22] nor are the living and the dead. God causes whom He will to hear Him, but you cannot make those who are in their graves hear you. [23] You are but a warner— [24] We have sent you with the truth as a bearer of good news and a warner—there is no community to which a warner has not come. [25] If they reject you, so did their predecessors. Messengers came to them with clear signs, with scriptures, and with the enlightening Book, [26] but in the end I seized those who were bent on denying the truth and how terrible was My punishment.

[27] Did you not see how God sent down water from the sky with which We bring forth fruit of diverse colours. In the mountains there are streaks of various shades of white and red, and jet-black rocks; [28] in like manner, men, beasts, and cattle have their diverse hues too. Only those of His servants, who possess knowledge, fear God. God is almighty and most forgiving.

---

imaginary gods who have absolutely no powers.

²⁹ Those who read the Book of God and attend to their prayers and spend in charity in private and in public out of what We have provided them, may hope for a commerce that suffers no loss. ³⁰ He will give them their full rewards and give them more out of His bounty. He is forgiving and appreciative. ³¹ The Book which We have revealed to you is the truth confirming previous scriptures. God knows and observes His servants.

³² We have bestowed the Book on those of Our servants whom We have chosen. Some wrong their own souls, some keep half-way [between right and wrong]; some, by God's leave, excel others in good deeds. This is a great bounty of God: ³³ they shall enter the Gardens of Eternity, where they shall be adorned with bracelets of gold and pearls, and wear silk garments. ³⁴ They will say, 'Praise be to God who has taken away all sorrow from us.

Our Lord is forgiving and appreciative. ³⁵ Through His grace He has admitted us to the everlasting Abode, where neither toil nor weariness affects us.'

³⁶ Those who deny the truth shall remain in the fire of Hell. Death will not be decreed for them, so that they could escape by way of death, nor will its torment ever be eased for them. Thus do We requite every ungrateful person. ³⁷ There they will cry out, 'Lord, take us out! We shall do good deeds, and behave differently from the way we used to.' But He will answer, 'Did We not make your life long enough to take warning if you were going to? The warner did come to you. So now have a taste of the punishment.' Wrongdoers will have no supporter.

³⁸ God knows the hidden reality of the heavens and the earth. He has full knowledge of what is in the hearts of men; ³⁹ it is He who has made you inherit the earth. He who denies Him shall bear the burden of his denial. God's displeasure with the deniers will only be increased by their denial of the truth, it will only increase their loss.ᵃ

---

a In this verse, being given 'the earth to inherit' (*khalifah*) means that 'after the advent of the previous nations, you were settled on the earth in their place'. It is the way of Almighty God that He allows a nation the opportunity to settle and make progress on the earth. Then, when it proves itself incapable, He

⁴⁰ Say, 'Have you ever considered your associate gods whom you call on besides God? Show me what it is that they have created on earth. Or have they a share in the creation of the heavens?' Or have We given them a book so that they may act on evidence from it? Indeed, the wrongdoers' promises to one another are nothing but deception. ⁴¹ Surely, God holds the heavens and the earth, lest they should deviate [from their orbits]. Were they to deviate, none could hold them after Him. Surely, He is forbearing and most forgiving.

⁴² They swore their most solemn oaths that if a warner should ever come to them, they would be better guided than any other community. But when a warner did come to them, it only increased their aversion, ⁴³ and they behaved arrogantly in the land and plotted evil. But the plotting of evil only rebounds on those who plot. Are they but looking for the way the previous peoples [sinners] were dealt with? You will never find any change in the ways of God; nor will you ever find God's decree averted. ⁴⁴ Have they not travelled around the earth and seen the fate of those who preceded them? And they were far superior to them in strength. Nothing in the heavens or the earth can ever frustrate God's [plans]. He is all-knowing and all powerful.

⁴⁵ If God were to take men to task for their misdeeds, He would not leave a single living creature on the surface of the earth; but He grants them respite until an appointed time; and when their appointed time comes, then they will know that God is indeed observant of all His servants.

---

replaces it by another nation. In this way, the process of settling the nations one by one will go on until the arrival of Doomsday. See note to 2:30.

36. YA SIN

In the name of God, the Most Gracious, the Most Merciful

[1] *Ya Sin*

[2] By the Quran, full of wisdom, [3] you are indeed one of the messengers [4] on a straight path, [5] with a revelation sent down by the Mighty One, the Merciful, [6] so that you may warn a people whose fathers were not warned and so they are unaware.

[7] The word has been proved true against the greater part of them: they will not believe. [8] We have put yokes round their necks right up to their chins, so that they cannot bow their heads [9] and We have set a barrier before them and a barrier behind them, and We have covered them up so that they cannot see. [10] It makes no difference to them whether you warn them or do not warn them: they will not believe. [11] You can warn only those who would follow the Reminder and fear the Gracious God, unseen. Give them the good news of forgiveness and a noble reward.

[12] We shall surely bring the dead back to life and We record what they send ahead and what they leave behind. We have recorded everything in a clear book.[a]

[13] Recount to them the example of the people to whose town Our messengers came. [14] When We sent them two messengers, they rejected them both, so We strengthened them with a third. They said, 'Truly, we have been sent to you [by God] as messengers.' [15] They replied, 'You are nothing but mortal men like us and the Merciful God has not revealed anything. You are surely lying.' [16] They said,

---

a Modern research has established that whatever a man utters remains preserved in the atmosphere in the shape of vibrations or waves. Similarly, the image of the actions which a man performs remains preserved in this world permanently in the shape of light waves. In other words, there is constant video-recording of every individual going on in this world. It should be borne in mind that in this world, without a man's knowledge and quite independent of his will, his utterances and actions, being completely recorded and preserved, could be replayed at any moment.

'Our Lord knows that we have been sent to you. ¹⁷ And our duty is only to convey the message to you clearly,' ¹⁸ but they answered, 'We see an evil omen in you. If you do not stop, we shall certainly stone you, and you will suffer a painful punishment at our hands.' ¹⁹ They said, 'Your evil augury be with you! Is it because you are admonished about the truth? Surely, you are a people transgressing all bounds!'

²⁰ Then, from the furthest part of the city, a man came running. He said, 'My people, follow the messengers. ²¹ Follow those who ask no recompense of you and are rightly guided.

²² 'Why should I not worship Him who has brought me into being, and to whom you shall all be recalled? ²³ Shall I take others besides Him as gods? If the Gracious God should intend me any harm, their intercession will be of no avail, nor can they deliver me. ²⁴ In that case I should indeed be in manifest error. ²⁵ Indeed, I have believed in your Lord, so listen to me.' ²⁶ We said to him, 'Enter paradise,' and he exclaimed: 'Would that my people knew ²⁷ how my Lord has forgiven me and placed me among the honoured ones!'

²⁸ After him We did not send down against his people a host from heaven, nor do We send down such hosts: ²⁹ it was but one great blast and they fell down lifeless. ³⁰ Alas for human beings! They ridicule every messenger that comes to them.*ᵃ* ³¹ Do they not see how many generations We have destroyed before them? Never shall they return to them. ³² All of them, gathered together, will certainly be brought before Us.

³³ There is a sign for them in the lifeless earth. We revive it and We produce grain from it of which they eat. ³⁴ We have placed in it gardens of date palms and vines, and caused springs to gush [forth] from it, ³⁵ so that they may eat its fruit, though it was not

---

a Why were the prophets ridiculed? The answer to this is found in the word 'ridicule' (*istihza*) itself. People always mock or ridicule one who appears to them to be of a low status. This was the case with the prophets. The prophets' personalities were underestimated by the people and they were considered of too low a standing to represent Divine Truths. That is why they refused to accept them.

their hands that made this. Will they not then be grateful?[a] 36 Holy is He who created all things in pairs; of what the earth grows, and of themselves, and other things which they do not know.

37 They have a sign in the night: We withdraw from it the [light of] day—and they are left in darkness. 38 The sun, too, follows its determined course laid down for it by the Almighty, the All Knowing. 39 We have ordained phases for the moon until finally it becomes like an old date-stalk. 40 The sun cannot overtake the moon, nor can the night outpace the day: each floats in [its own] orbit.[b]

41 Another sign for them is that We carried their offspring in the laden Ark. 42 We have created for them the like of it in which they ride. 43 If it were Our will, We could drown them: then there would be no helper [to hear their cry], nor could they be saved. 44 It is only by Our mercy that they are granted provision for a time.

45 When they are told, 'guard yourselves against what is before you and what is behind you, in order that you may be shown mercy,' [they turn away]. 46 Indeed, not one of your Lord's signs comes to them without their turning away from it, 47 and when they are told, 'Give to others out of what God has provided for you,' those who are bent on denying the truth say to the believers, 'Why should we

---

a The accumulation of fertile soil on the surface of the earth; the provision of water, sun and air; then the potentiality in the seed to germinate and grow—these and other such innumerable known and unknown factors combine to produce the food-grains, fruits and vegetables which become the food for human beings. This entire system, however, is not the handiwork of human beings. Its coming into existence and its maintenance are entirely thanks to the Grace of God. If its beneficiaries ponder over these facts, they will be filled with gratitude.

b The earth, the moon and the sun have their fixed orbits, in which they move with the utmost precision, and due to which different phenomena take place: for instance, the occurrence of day and night on the earth and the waxing and waning of the moon, serve as a heavenly calendar. This system has been in existence for millions of years now and, and there is still no deviation of any kind in it.

This observation is purely an introduction to the fathomless and unlimited powers of God. If man learns lessons from these phenomena, the majesty of the one God will prevail over his mind to such an extent that all other impressions of greatness will be automatically erased from it.

feed those whom God could feed if He wanted? You are clearly in error!'[a]

⁴⁸ They say, 'When will this promise be fulfilled, if you are truthful?' ⁴⁹ They must be waiting for but one single blast, which will overtake them while they are still disputing.[b] ⁵⁰ They will have no time to make a will, nor shall they return to their own people. ⁵¹ The trumpet will be blown and, at once, they will rise up from their graves, and hasten to their Lord. ⁵² 'Woe betide us!' they will say, 'Who has roused us from our sleep?' This is what the Lord of Mercy promised: the messengers spoke the truth! ⁵³ It will be but one blast, and they will all be brought before Us together.

⁵⁴ On that Day no soul shall suffer the least injustice. You shall be rewarded only according to your deeds. ⁵⁵ The people of Paradise shall be happily occupied on that Day—⁵⁶ they and their wives—shall recline on couches in the shade. ⁵⁷ They shall have fruits therein, and all that they ask for. ⁵⁸ 'Peace!' shall be the greeting from the Merciful Lord.

⁵⁹ [And God will say], 'Separate yourselves from the righteous this Day, you criminals. ⁶⁰ Did I not enjoin you, sons of Adam, not to worship Satan—for he is your sworn enemy, ⁶¹ but to worship Me? Surely, that is a straight path. ⁶² Yet he led astray a great multitude of you. Why did you not then understand? ⁶³ This is the Hell you were promised. ⁶⁴ Enter it this Day on account of your denial of

---

a Behind a man are his actions and before him is the Day of Reckoning. Life, in other words, is a journey from the world of actions towards the world of results. This is a very crucial state of affairs. If a man actually realises this position, he will start trembling. But he does not consider this; nor does any sign open his eyes. He tries to justify his actions by false interpretations until the day he dies.

b It has been recorded in the Hadith that the Angel Israfil is looking towards the throne (*'arsh*) of God with the trumpet (*sur*) in his mouth awaiting His orders and ready to blow the trumpet instantly. The blowing of the trumpet will be just like the ringing of a bell which signals the end of the examination. Immediately thereafter, the system of the world will change: the stage of the appearance of results will commence, while at present we are still at the stage of actions.

the truth.' [65] Today We shall seal up their mouths and their hands will speak to Us, and their feet will bear witness to their misdeeds.[a]

[66] If it had been Our will, We could have put out their eyes. They would have struggled to find the way, but how could they have seen it? [67] If it had been Our will, We could have paralysed them where they stood, so that they would not be able to go forward or turn back. [68] If We extend anyone's life, We reverse his development. Can they not use their reason? [69] We have not taught him any poetry nor would it be fitting for him. This is merely a Reminder and a clear Quran [70] to warn all who are truly alive, and to justify the word [God's verdict] against the deniers.

[71] Do they not see that, among the things which Our hands have fashioned, We have created for them cattle of which they are the masters, [72] We have subjected these to them, so that some may be used for riding and some for food, [73] some for milk to drink and some from which other benefits may be received? Will they not be grateful? [74] They have set up other gods besides God, hoping to be helped by them, [75] but they are not able to help them: rather they will be brought before God as their allied host. [76] Let not their words grieve you. We have knowledge of all that they conceal and all that they reveal.

[77] Does not man see that We created him from a drop. Yet there he is, flagrantly contentious, [78] producing arguments against Us, and forgetting his own creation. He asks, 'Who can give life back to bones after they have rotted away?' [79] Say, 'He who brought them into being in the first instance will give them life again: He has knowledge of every type of creation:[b] [80] He who produces fire for

---

a Modern research has proved that a man's skin is a form of record on which his utterances are recorded and from which they can be reproduced. This is a sign which makes it understandable that in the Hereafter man's hands and legs will give reports about him.

b The creation of man and the universe for the first time itself furnishes ample proof of the fact that such creation for the second time is also possible. But ignoring this, man argues about how a dead man can come back to life. The changing of a dead man into a living one will no doubt occur on the Day of Judgement, but this possibility is seen in other things even today. One may take

you from green trees and from this you kindle fire.' ⁸¹ Is He who created the heavens and earth not able to create others like these people? Of course He is! He is indeed the Supreme Creator, the All Knowing: ⁸² when He decrees a thing, He need only say, 'Be!' and it is. ⁸³ So glory be to Him who has control over all things. It is to Him that you will all be brought back.

37. THE RANKS (*AL-SAFFAT*)

In the name of God, the Most Gracious, the Most Merciful

¹ By those [angels] who range themselves in close ranks*ᵃ* ² and those who drive away [the wicked] with reproof ³ and by the reciters of the Reminder: ⁴ your God is One, ⁵ Lord of the heavens and the earth and everything between them; Lord of the Easts.

⁶ We have adorned the lowest heaven with the beauty of the planets; ⁷ and guarded it against all rebellious devils: ⁸ they cannot overhear the Higher Assembly for they are pelted from every side, ⁹ driven away, and will suffer eternal punishment. ¹⁰ But if anyone does succeed in snatching a glimpse [of such knowledge], he shall be pursued by a piercing flame.

¹¹ So, ask those who deny the truth if it was harder to create them than all the other things We have created? We created them from sticky clay.*ᵇ* ¹² No wonder you are surprised as they laugh with scorn.

---

the example of a tree. The tree is apparently green and fresh, but when it is cut up and burnt as sticks, it takes on a completely different shape, that of fire.

a One of the secrets revealed through the Prophet is the existence of angels. Here, three special aspects of the angels have been mentioned. First, they are completely obedient to God. Without the slightest hesitation or objection, they stand by in rows ready to carry out His orders. Then there is a group of angels which implements the punishments imposed by God on human beings, either in the shape of calamities or untoward incidents or in any other manner dictated by Him. Then the angels bring God's advice to His subjects, i.e. to the common man in the shape of inspiration or intuition (*ilham*) and as revelation (*wahi*) to the prophets.

b On analysing the human body, it appears that it is a combination of all the earthly materials. Man is made up of substances found on earth, such as

¹³ When they are reminded, they do not pay heed, ¹⁴ and whenever they see some sign, they ridicule it, ¹⁵ saying, 'This is plain sorcery!' ¹⁶ 'What! When we have died and become dust and bones, will we be brought back to life again, ¹⁷ along with our forefathers?' ¹⁸ Say, 'Yes indeed, and you will be brought low.'

¹⁹ There will be but a single blast and then their eyes will open. ²⁰ They will say, 'Woe to us! This is the Day of Reckoning.' ²¹ [It will be said], 'This is the Day of Judgement which you have been denying.' ²² But We shall say, 'Assemble those who did wrong together with their associates and what they worshipped ²³ besides God, and lead them to the path of the Fire; ²⁴ and stop them there for questioning: ²⁵ "But what is the matter with you that you cannot help one another?"'—²⁶ indeed, on that Day they will surrender themselves.

²⁷ They will turn upon one another, and question one another. ²⁸ They will say, 'You used to come at us from the right.' ²⁹ They will say, 'No! It was you who would not believe—³⁰ we had no power over you; but you yourselves were a rebellious people. ³¹ But now our Lord's word has come true against us: truly, we are bound to taste [the punishment]. ³² We led you astray as we were ourselves astray.' ³³ On that Day they will all share the punishment: ³⁴ that is how We deal with evil-doers. ³⁵ When they were told, 'There is no deity but God,' they turned away with disdain, ³⁶ and replied, 'Shall we then give up our deities at the bidding of a mad poet?' ³⁷ 'Surely, he has brought the truth, confirming those who were sent before; ³⁸ you shall surely taste the painful punishment, ³⁹ and be rewarded only according to your deeds.'

⁴⁰ But the chosen servants of God; ⁴¹ shall have a known provision—⁴² fruits of various kinds; and they shall be honoured, ⁴³ in the Gardens of Bliss, ⁴⁴ seated on couches, facing one another.ᵃ

---

water, calcium, iron, sodium, tungsten, etc. All these are found in our world in abundance. Then by utilising the same elements from which He once created human beings, can He not do so once again?

a Paradise will be a world of aesthetic and noble activity. There will be interesting meetings; there will be enjoyable experiences; conversation will be of a high level there, and all kinds of limitations and unpleasantness will have

⁴⁵ A drink will be passed round among them from a flowing spring: ⁴⁶ white and delicious to those who drink it, ⁴⁷ causing no headiness or intoxication. ⁴⁸ With them will be spouses—modest of gaze and beautiful of eye—⁴⁹ like closely guarded pearls.

⁵⁰ They will turn to one another with questions: ⁵¹ one of them will say, 'I had a friend, ⁵² who used to ask, "Do you really believe that ⁵³ after we die and become dust and bones, we shall be brought to judgement?"' ⁵⁴ Then he will say, 'Shall we look for him?' ⁵⁵ Then he will look and see him in the midst of the Fire. ⁵⁶ He will say, 'By God! You almost brought me to ruin! ⁵⁷ If it had not been for the blessing of my Lord, I would also have been taken to Hell.' ⁵⁸ Then he will say [to his blessed companions], 'Are we not going to die, ⁵⁹ except for our first death? Are we not going to be punished? ⁶⁰ Truly, this is a great victory!' ⁶¹ It is for the like of this that all should strive.

⁶² Is that better by way of hospitality or the Zaqqum tree,*ᵃ* ⁶³ which We have made as a test for the wrongdoers. ⁶⁴ For it is a tree that springs out of the bottom of Hellfire: ⁶⁵ and its fruits are like devils' heads. ⁶⁶ They will eat from it and fill their bellies with it; ⁶⁷ then in addition to it they shall have a draught of boiling water to drink; ⁶⁸ then surely they shall return to Hell. ⁶⁹ They found their fathers had gone astray; ⁷⁰ so they are rushing to follow in their footsteps. ⁷¹ And assuredly many of the ancients went astray before them, ⁷² though We had sent warners among them. ⁷³ See how those who were warned met their end! ⁷⁴ Not so the chosen servants of God.

⁷⁵ Noah cried to Us, and how excellent was Our response! ⁷⁶ We saved him and his people from great distress, ⁷⁷ and We made his offspring the only survivors. ⁷⁸ We left mention of him among later generations. ⁷⁹ Peace be upon Noah among all the peoples! ⁸⁰ That is how We recompense the righteous: ⁸¹ he was truly one of Our faithful servants. ⁸² We drowned the rest.

---

come to an end.

a It is stated in the Quran that there will be a Zaqqum tree in hell and that its fruits will be eaten by the inmates of hell when they are overwhelmed by hunger. (See 56: 52).

[83] Abraham was of the same faith: [84] he came to his Lord with a sound heart. [85] 'Behold!' he said to his father and to his people, 'What are these that you worship? [86] Would you serve false deities instead of God? [87] What do you think of the Lord of the Worlds?'

[88] He looked up at the stars. [89] And said, 'I am sick,' [90] so they turned their backs on him and went off. [91] He turned to their gods and said, 'Do you not eat? [92] What is the matter with you that you do not speak?' [93] then he turned on them, striking them down with his right hand. [94] His people came rushing towards him, [95] but he said, 'How can you worship things you carve with your own hands, [96] when it is God who has created you and all your handiwork?' [97] They said, 'Build a pyre for him and throw him into the blaze!' [98] They wanted to harm him, but We humiliated them all. [99] He said, 'I will go to my Lord: He is sure to guide me. [100] Lord, grant me a righteous son.' [101] We gave him the good news that he would have a patient, forbearing son.

[102] And when he reached the age when he could work with him, he said, 'O my son, I have seen in a dream that I am sacrificing you. So tell me what you think of it!' He replied, 'O my father, do as you are commanded; and God willing, you will find me steadfast.' [103] When they had both submitted to God, and he had laid his son down on his face, [104] We called out to him, 'Abraham, [105] you have fulfilled the dream.' It is thus indeed that We reward those who do good—[106] that surely was a manifest trial—[107] We ransomed him with a great sacrifice, [108] and left him thus to be succeeded by a group [of followers] among later generations: [109] 'Peace and salutation to Abraham!' [110] That is how We recompense the righteous: [111] truly, he was one of Our faithful servants. [112] We gave Abraham the good news of Isaac—a prophet and a righteous man—[113] and blessed him and Isaac too: some of their offspring were good, but some clearly sinned against their souls.

[114] We also bestowed Our favour on Moses and Aaron: [115] We saved them and their people from great distress; [116] and We helped them, so that they were victorious; [117] and We gave them the Book which helps to make things clear; [118] and guided them to the straight path; [119] and We left them thus to be succeeded by a group [of followers]

among later generations: ¹²⁰ 'Peace be upon Moses and Aaron!' ¹²¹ This is how We reward those who do good: ¹²² truly they were among Our faithful servants.

¹²³ Elijah too was one of the messengers. ¹²⁴ He said to his people, 'Have you no fear [of God?] ¹²⁵ Do you call on Baal and abandon the Best of Creators, ¹²⁶ God your Lord and Lord of your forefathers?' ¹²⁷ but they rejected him, and thus will certainly be called to account; ¹²⁸ except the chosen servants of God. ¹²⁹ We left him thus to be succeeded by a group [of followers] among the following generations—¹³⁰ 'Peace be on Elijah and his people!' ¹³¹ It is thus indeed that We reward those who do good: ¹³² surely he was one of Our believing servants.

¹³³ Lot was also one of the messengers. ¹³⁴ We saved him and all his people—¹³⁵ except for an old woman who stayed behind—¹³⁶ and We destroyed the rest. ¹³⁷ You pass by their ruins morning ¹³⁸ and night: will you not take heed?

¹³⁹ Jonah too was one of the messengers.ᵃ ¹⁴⁰ He fled to the overloaded ship. ¹⁴¹ And then they cast lots and he was the one who lost, ¹⁴² and the fish swallowed him while he was blaming himself. ¹⁴³ Had he not been one of those who acknowledge the glory of God, ¹⁴⁴ he would certainly have remained inside the fish till the

---

a Jonah (Yunus) lived in the eighth century B.C. when he was sent as a prophet to the ancient city of Nineveh in Iraq. After performing his mission for a certain period of time, he came to the conclusion that his people were not going to embrace the true faith, and then he left the city. To proceed with his journey, he boarded a boat, perhaps on the bank of the River Tigris (Dajlah). The boat was overloaded; and halfway to its destination it was feared that it would sink. Therefore, in order to lighten the burden of the boat, lots were drawn to decide who should be thrown out of the boat. The name of Jonah was drawn and so the seamen threw him over board. At that time, at God's behest, a huge fish swallowed him, took him to the river bank and cast him up on the bank. Jonah had left his people before time. Therefore, God ordered him to go back to his people. He went back and once again started preaching, with the result that all the one hundred and twenty five thousand inhabitants of the area became believers. This incident shows that it is absolutely essential for a missionary to have patience, even at a time when people's behaviour has clearly become frustrating.

Day of Resurrection. ¹⁴⁵ But We caused him to be cast forth on to the beach, sick as he was, ¹⁴⁶ and We caused a gourd tree to grow over him. ¹⁴⁷ We sent him as a messenger to a hundred thousand people or more, ¹⁴⁸ and they believed in him: so We let them live in ease for a while.

¹⁴⁹ Now ask them whether your Lord has daughters, whereas they have sons. ¹⁵⁰ Did We create the angels females, to which they were witnesses? ¹⁵¹ No indeed! It is one of their fabrications when they say: ¹⁵² 'God has begotten children.' They are truly liars. ¹⁵³ Has He chosen daughters over sons? ¹⁵⁴ What is the matter with you? How do you form your judgement? ¹⁵⁵ Will you not then reflect? ¹⁵⁶ Or have you clear evidence? ¹⁵⁷ Then produce your scriptures, if you are telling the truth.

¹⁵⁸ They claim that He has kinship with the jinn, yet the jinn themselves know that they will be produced before Him [for judgement]. ¹⁵⁹ God is far above what they attribute to Him— ¹⁶⁰ but not so the true servants of God—¹⁶¹ neither you nor what you worship ¹⁶² can lure away from God any ¹⁶³ except those who will burn in Hell. ¹⁶⁴ [The angels say], 'Every single one of us has his place assigned: ¹⁶⁵ we are those who stand ranged in ranks. ¹⁶⁶ We glorify God.'

¹⁶⁷ They used to say, ¹⁶⁸ 'If we had had with us a Book like that of the people of old, ¹⁶⁹ we would surely have been God's chosen servants,' ¹⁷⁰ but they have rejected it, [the Quran] and they shall soon learn! ¹⁷¹ And surely Our word has gone forth respecting Our servants, the messengers: ¹⁷² that it is certainly they who will be helped; ¹⁷³ and that it is Our host that would certainly triumph. ¹⁷⁴ So turn away from them for a while. ¹⁷⁵ Watch them: they will soon see.

¹⁷⁶ Do they really wish to hasten Our punishment? ¹⁷⁷ When it descends on their courtyards, how terrible that morning will be for those who were warned! ¹⁷⁸ So turn away from them for a while. ¹⁷⁹ And watch, for they will soon see. ¹⁸⁰ Glory be to your Lord: the Lord of Glory is far above what they attribute to Him. ¹⁸¹ Peace be upon the Messengers ¹⁸² and praise be to God, the Lord of all the Worlds.

38. SAD

In the name of God, the Most Gracious, the Most Merciful

¹ *Sad*

By the Quran, full of admonition! ² Those who deny the truth are steeped in arrogance and hostility. ³ How many generations We have destroyed before them! And they cried out when it was too late to escape.

⁴ They are surprised that a warner should come to them from among themselves. They say, 'This is a magician, a great liar. ⁵ Does he make all the deities out to be one God? This is indeed a strange thing.' ⁶ Their leaders departed, saying, 'Walk away! Hold fast to your deities. This is clearly a conspiracy. ⁷ We have not heard of any such thing in the old religion. This is nothing but a fabrication. ⁸ Was the message sent only to him out of all of us?' In fact, they doubt My warning; in fact, they have not yet tasted My punishment.

⁹ Do they possess the treasures of the mercy of your Lord, the Mighty, the Great Bestower? ¹⁰ Have they control over heavens and earth and whatever [lies] between them? Then let them climb up to heaven by ropes: ¹¹ this host too, among other hosts, is bound to suffer defeat. ¹² Before them the people of Noah denied the truth, as did the 'Ad and Pharaoh of the Stakes, ¹³ and the tribe of Thamud, and the people of Lot, and the dwellers of the Wood—these were the confederates. ¹⁴ There was not one of them but treated their messengers as liars, so My punishment rightly overtook them: ¹⁵ they have only to wait for one single blast [of punishment]: it shall not be delayed by one whit. ¹⁶ They say: 'Our Lord! Hasten on for us our fate before the Day of Reckoning.'

¹⁷ Bear with their words patiently. Remember Our servant David, a man of strength who always turned to Us: ¹⁸ We made the mountains join him in glorifying Us at sunset and sunrise; ¹⁹ and the birds, too, in flocks, all turned to Him. ²⁰ We made his kingdom strong, and bestowed upon him wisdom and sagacity in judgement.

²¹ Have you heard the story of the disputants who entered his

chamber*ª* by climbing over the wall? ²² When they reached David, he took fright, but they said, 'Do not be afraid. We are two disputants, one of whom has wronged the other: judge between us fairly—do not be unjust—and guide us to the right path.

²³ 'This brother of mine has ninety-nine ewes and I have only one. He said, "Let me have charge of it," and got the better of me with his words.' ²⁴ David said, 'He has certainly wronged you by demanding that your ewe be added to his ewes! Thus many partners wrong one another—[all] save those who believe [in God] and do righteous deeds: but how few are they!' And [suddenly] David understood that We were only putting him to the test, and so he asked his Lord to forgive him his sins; he fell to his knees, and turned to Him in repentance. ²⁵ We forgave him his sins. His reward will be nearness to Us, a good place to return to.

²⁶ We said, 'David, We have given you mastery over the land. Judge fairly between people. Do not follow your desires, lest they divert you from God's path: those who wander from His path will have a severe punishment, because they ignore the Day of Reckoning.'

²⁷ We did not create heaven and earth and all that is between them in vain. That is the opinion of those who deny the truth. Woe betide those who deny the truth, when they are cast into the Fire— ²⁸ shall We treat those who believe and do good works the same as those who spread corruption in the land; shall We treat the pious the same as the wicked? ²⁹ This is a blessed Book which We sent down to you [Muhammad], for people to ponder over its messages, and for those with understanding to take heed.

³⁰ We gave David Solomon. He was an excellent servant who always turned to God. ³¹ When well-bred horses, which were fleet of foot were paraded before him near the close of day, ³² he said, 'I have put the love of good things above the remembrance of my Lord'—until [the sun] disappeared behind its veil and the horses disappeared from sight—³³ 'Bring them back to me!'—[he said] and began to stroke their legs and their necks.

³⁴ We tried Solomon by placing upon his throne a [lifeless] body;

---

a i.e. the sanctuary in which David prayed.

and thereupon he turned towards Us. [35] He prayed, 'Lord forgive me! Grant me such power as no one after me will have—You are the Most Generous Provider.'[a] [36] Then We subjected the wind to his power, so that it blew gently, at his behest, wherever he willed— [37] and also the jinn—every kind of builder and diver [38] and others chained in fetters. [39] We said: 'This is Our gift, so give or withhold as you wish without reckoning.' [40] His reward will be nearness to Us, a good place to return to.

[41] Bring to mind Our servant Job who cried to his Lord, 'Satan has afflicted me with distress and suffering.' [42] We said, 'Stamp your foot! Here is cool water for you to wash in and drink,' [43] We restored his family to him, doubling their number as an act of grace from Us, and as a reminder to all who are endowed with insight. [44] We said to Him, 'Take a handful of twigs in your hand and strike with that but do not break your oath.' We found him steadfast. What an excellent servant! He turned constantly to his Lord.[b]

---

a Every human being is liable to err. But, for the pious and righteous subjects of God, a wrongful act leads to great virtue, because after the misdeed, they turn towards their Lord with much more devotion and thus become entitled to a much better reward.

On one occasion, Solomon made an error in judgement which required an interpretation and making a decision. When the truth dawned on him, he turned towards God with the utmost devotion. Almighty God forgave him and in addition gave him the reward of a great empire; He also gave him such extraordinary powers as no other man had ever enjoyed.

b Job (Ayyub) was an Israeli prophet probably some time in the ninth century B.C. According to the Bible, he was initially very rich. He was blessed with farms, cattle, houses, children, etc., to such an extent that it was said that nobody was his peer in the entire East. In spite of this, however, Job was a very grateful and faithful person. His life set an example of how a person may remain humble and modest, in spite of being blessed with great wealth and honour.

God thereupon set another example through him. Job's cattle died, his farms were destroyed, his children died and even his body was afflicted with a disease. All his friends and relatives left him, except his wife who remained with him. But Job reconciled himself with God's decision. He exercised the utmost patience. In the words of the Bible, 'Then Job, tore his robe and shaved his head; and he fell to the ground and worshipped. And he said: Naked I came

[45] Remember Our servants Abraham, Isaac, and Jacob—possessors of strength and vision.*a* [46] We chose them for a special [purpose]—proclaiming the message of the Hereafter: [47] and, in Our sight they were indeed among the select, the truly good! [48] Remember [Our servants] Ishmael, Elisha, and Dhu'l-Kifl. Each of them was among the just.

[49] This is a Reminder. The righteous shall have a good place to return to: [50] the Gardens of eternity with gates thrown wide open to them. [51] They will be comfortably seated; reclining, they will call for abundant fruit and drink; [52] with them, they will have pure, modest women of an equal age. [53] This is what you were promised on the Day of Reckoning: [54] Our provision for you will never be exhausted.

[55] But the arrogant will have the worst return: [56] they will burn, in Hell, an evil resting place—[57] all this will be theirs; let them taste it—a scalding, dark, foul fluid, [58] and other such torments. [59] [And they will say to one another: 'Do you see] this crowd of people rushing headlong to join you?' 'No welcome to them! Indeed, they are headed for the fire!' [60] They will say to them, 'You are not welcome! It was you who brought this on us, an evil place to stay,' [61] adding, 'Our Lord, give double punishment to those who brought this upon us.' [62] And they will say, 'How is it that we do not see [here any of the] men whom we used to count among the wicked, [63] [and] whom we made the target of our derision? Or are they here, and our eyes have missed them?' [64] All this is certainly true—the inhabitants of the Fire will blame one another in this way.

[65] Say, [Prophet], 'I am only a warner. There is no god but God, the One, the All-Powerful, [66] Lord of the heavens and earth and

---

from my mother's womb, and naked shall I return there. The Lord gave and the Lord has taken away; blessed be the name of the Lord. In all this Job did not sin, nor did he charge God with wrongdoing' (Job, 1:20-22).

a What is that special assignment of God for which He chooses messengers from amongst human beings? That assignment is reminding people of the abode of the Hereafter. It has always been the special mission of prophets to make people aware of the fact that the real destination of a human being is the Hereafter, and that they should prepare themselves for it. This is the most crucial problem for man. The greatest task is to warn him of its seriousness.

everything between them, the Almighty, the Most Forgiving.' [67] Say, 'This is momentous news, [68] yet you ignore it. [69] I had no knowledge of the Exalted Assembly when they argued [against the creation of man]: [70] it has only been revealed to me that I am a plain warner.'

[71] Your Lord said to the angels, 'I am about to create a human being out of clay; [72] and when I have formed him fully and breathed My spirit into him, prostrate yourselves before him.' [73] Thereupon the angels prostrated themselves, all of them together, [74] but not Satan, who was too proud. He became one of those who deny the truth.[a] [75] God said, 'Satan, what prevented you from prostrating yourself to what I created with My own Hands? Were you overcome by arrogance, or are you of those who think [only] of themselves as exalted?' [76] Satan replied, 'I am better than him. You created me from fire, but You created him from clay.' [77] 'Begone! You are accursed: [78] My curse will remain upon you till the Day of Judgement!'

[79] But Satan said, 'My Lord, grant me respite until the Day of Resurrection,' [80] so He said, 'You are granted respite [81] till the Appointed Day.' [82] He said, 'By Your Honour, I will lead all of them astray, [83] except for those among them who are Your chosen servants.' [84] God said, 'This is the truth—I speak only the truth— [85] I will fill up Hell with you and every one of them who follows you.'

[86] Say, 'I do not ask you for any recompense for this, nor am I a man of false pretentions: [87] this is simply an admonition to mankind, [88] you shall before long know its truth.'

---

a The most important piece of information that one can give to anyone in life is that, Satan is pursuing him at all times. He surreptitiously enters his thoughts and feelings and misguides him. Man should save himself from this danger. The prophets came into this world in order to warn man of this crucial danger.

39. THE CROWDS (*AL-ZUMAR*)

In the name of God, the Most Gracious, the Most Merciful

¹ This Book is sent down by God the Mighty, the Wise. ² It is We who sent down the Book to you [Prophet] with the Truth, so worship God with your total devotion: ³ it is to God alone that sincere obedience is due. And those who take other guardians besides Him say, 'We serve them only that they may bring us nearer to God.' Surely, God will judge between them concerning that wherein they differ. God does not guide anyone who is bent on lying and is a disbelieving liar.

⁴ If God had willed to take a son He could have chosen anyone He pleased out of His creation: but Glory be to Him! [He is above such things.] He is God, the One, the Omnipotent. ⁵ He created the heavens and the earth for a true purpose; He causes the night to succeed the day and the day to succeed the night; He has subjected the sun and moon, so that they run their courses for an appointed time; He is truly the Mighty, the Forgiving.

⁶ He created you from a single soul, then produced its spouse from it, and He has provided for you eight heads of cattle in pairs. He creates you stage by stage in your mothers' wombs in a threefold darkness. Such is God, your Lord. Sovereignty is His. There is no god but Him. So what has made you turn away?*ᵃ*

⁷ If you are ungrateful, remember that God has no need of you. He is not pleased by ingratitude in His servants; if you are grateful, He is pleased [to see] it in you. No soul shall bear another's burden. You will return to your Lord in the end and He will declare to you what you have done: He knows well what is in the hearts of men.

⁸ When man suffers some affliction, he prays to his Lord and turns

---

a The three kinds of darknesses mentioned in connection with human birth refer to three membranes, namely the mother's abdominal wall, the wall of the uterus and the aminochorionic membrane. This whole system is so wonderfully complicated as to be quite awesome: nobody except the Creator of the universe could have brought it into existence. Then, who else except God can be treated as worthy of worship? See 23:12 and the corresponding note.

to Him in penitence, but once he has been granted a favour from God, he forgets the One he had been praying to and sets up rivals to God, to make others stray from His path. Say, 'Enjoy your unbelief for a little while: you will be one of the inmates of the Fire.' [9] Is he who prays devoutly to God in the hours of the night, prostrating himself and standing in prayer, who is ever mindful of the life to come and hopes for the mercy of his Lord [like one who does not]? Say, 'Are those who know equal to those who do not know?' Truly, only those endowed with understanding will take heed.

[10] Say, '[God says] O My servants who have believed, fear your Lord. For those who do good in this world will have a good reward—and God's earth is spacious. Truly, those who persevere patiently will be requited without measure.'

[11] Say, 'I have been commanded to serve God, dedicating my worship entirely to Him. [12] I have been commanded to be the first to submit.' [13] Say, 'I fear, if I disobey my Lord, the punishment of a Terrible Day.' [14] Say, 'It is God I serve, sincere in my faith in Him alone—[15] as for yourselves, worship anything you please besides Him!' Say, 'The real losers will be those who lose themselves and all their kith and kin on the Day of Resurrection. That is the [most] obvious loss. [16] They will have sheets of fire above them and sheets of fire beneath them.' That is how God puts fear into the hearts of His servants. Fear me, then, My servants.

[17] There is good news for those who shun the worship of false deities and turn to God, so give good news to My servants, [18] who listen to what is said and follow what is best in it. These are the ones God has guided; these are the people endowed with understanding.

[19] But what of him against whom the sentence of punishment is justified? Can you rescue one who is already in the Fire? [20] But for those who truly feared their Lord, there will be tall mansions, built up storey upon storey, beneath which there will be rivers flowing. This is God's promise: God never fails in His promise.

[21] Have you not seen that God sends down water from the sky, guides it to form springs in the earth, and then, with it, brings forth vegetation of various colours, which later withers, turns yellow before your eyes, and then He makes it crumble away? There is truly a

reminder in this for those who possess understanding.*a* 22 Anyone whose heart God has opened up to Islam possesses a light from his Lord. But woe betide those whose hearts have been hardened against the remembrance of God! Such people are in obvious error.

23 God has sent down the best Message: a Scripture that is consimilar and oft-repeated: that causes the skins of those in awe of their Lord to creep. Then their skins and their hearts soften at the mention of God: such is God's guidance. He bestows it upon whoever He will; but no one can guide those whom God leaves to stray.

24 What about the one who will have only his bare face to protect him from his terrible punishment on the Day of Resurrection? The evil-doers will be told, 'Taste what you have earned.' 25 Those before them also denied the truth, and the punishment fell on them from where they did not expect. 26 God gave them a taste of humiliation in the life of this world, but the punishment of the Hereafter is greater, if they only knew it.

27 We have set forth to men all kinds of parables in this Quran so that they may take heed: 28 a Quran in Arabic, free from any ambiguity—so that people may be mindful. 29 God sets forth a parable: there are two men—one belonging to many masters, all disagreeing with one another, and the other belonging entirely to one master: are those two equal in comparison? Praise be to God! But most of them have no knowledge. 30 You will die and they too

---

a The wonderful system of rains on the earth, the resulting growth of greenery and the preparations for harvesting, all these events have countless meaningful lessons in them. But, these lessons are available only to those who by nature go deep into things.

On the one hand, God has created the external world in a way that everything in it has become a sign of great realities, and, on the other, He has endowed man with the ability to read these signs and understand them. Those who keep their natural capabilities alive and by utilising them give deep consideration to the things of the world, will have their minds filled with the deep realisation (*ma'rifah*) of God, while those who do not keep these capabilities alive, will be unable to learn anything, even though surrounded by countless lessons. They will not be able to see, even after seeing and will not be able to hear, even after hearing.

will die, ³¹ and, then on the Day of Resurrection you shall place your dispute before your Sustainer.

³² Who, then, is more unjust than he who lies about God and rejects the truth when it comes to him? Is not Hell an abode for those who deny the truth? ³³ He who brings the truth, and he who testifies to it as such—those are surely the people who are God-fearing: ³⁴ they will have everything they wish for from their Lord. Such is the reward of those who do good: ³⁵ God will efface their worst deeds from their record and give them their reward in accordance with the best of their actions.

³⁶ Is God not enough for His servant? Yet they try to frighten you with other [deities] besides Him! For such as God lets go astray, there will be no guide; ³⁷ but he whom God guides cannot be led astray by anyone. Is God not mighty and capable of retribution?

³⁸ If you ask them who created the heavens and the earth, they will surely reply, 'God.' Say, 'Consider those you invoke besides Him: if God wished to harm me, could they undo that harm? Or if God wished to show me mercy, could they withhold that mercy?' Say, 'God is sufficient for me. In Him let the faithful put their trust.' ³⁹ Say, 'My people, do whatever is in your power—and so will I. Soon you shall come to know ⁴⁰ who will suffer a humiliating torment and on whom will descend an everlasting punishment.' ⁴¹ [O Prophet!] We have sent down to you the Book for mankind with the truth. Then whoever adopts the right way, will do so for his own soul, and whoever goes astray, injures his own soul. You are not their custodian.

⁴² It is God who takes away men's souls upon their death and the souls of the living during their sleep. Then He withholds those for whom He has ordained death and restores the souls of others for an appointed term. There are certainly signs in this for those who reflect.*ᵃ*

---

a While sleeping a man loses consciousness. In this way sleep is similar to death. When he wakes up from sleep, he regains consciousness. This is an image of resurrection after death.

Through this system of nature a man is shown today itself in an elementary manner how he will die and how he will rise up again. If man gives serious consideration to the matter, he will find in this very mundane event the lesson

[43] Have they taken others for intercessors besides God? Say, 'Even though they have no power nor understanding?' [44] Say, 'Intercession is entirely in the hands of God. He controls the heavens and the earth; you will all return to Him.' [45] When God alone is named, the hearts of those who do not believe in the Hereafter shrink with aversion, but when others are named instead of Him, they are filled with joy. [46] Say, 'O God! Originator of the heavens and earth! Knower of all that is hidden and all that is manifest, You will judge between Your servants regarding their differences.' [47] If the wrongdoers possessed all that is on earth, and twice as much, they would offer it to redeem themselves from the awful suffering on the Day of Resurrection. For God will show them what they had never anticipated, [48] the evil of their deeds will become apparent to them, and they will be overwhelmed by that which they used to mock.

[49] When affliction befalls man, he appeals to Us; but when We bestow a favour upon him he says, 'All this has been given to me because of my own knowledge.' By no means! It is a trial: yet most of them do not realize it. [50] Those who preceded them said the same thing but they gained nothing from what they did; [51] the very evil of their deeds recoiled upon them; today's wrongdoers shall also have the evil of their deeds recoil upon them: they will never be able to frustrate [Our plan]. [52] Do they not know that God grants abundant sustenance to anyone He wishes and gives sparingly to anyone He pleases? Surely there are signs in this for those who believe. [53] Say, [God says] 'O My servants, who have committed excesses against their own souls, do not despair of God's mercy, for God surely forgives all sins. He is truly the Most Forgiving, the Most Merciful. [54] Turn to your Lord and submit to Him before His scourge overtakes you, for then you shall not be helped.

[55] Follow the best aspect of what is sent down to you from your Lord, before the scourge comes upon you unawares, [56] lest anyone should say, "Alas for me, for having neglected what is due to God, and having been one of those who scoffed!" [57] Or, "If only God had guided me, I would surely have joined the God-fearing." [58] Or,

---

of the Hereafter.

he may say as he sees the punishment, "Would that I had a second chance, so that I could be among the doers of good." ⁵⁹ No indeed! My revelations did come to you, but you rejected them: you showed arrogance, and were among those who deny the truth.' ⁶⁰ On the Day of Resurrection you will see those who uttered falsehoods about God with their faces blackened. Is there not enough room in Hell for the arrogant? ⁶¹ But God will deliver them who feared Him to their place of salvation. No evil shall touch them, nor shall they grieve.

⁶² God is the Creator of all things, He has charge of everything; ⁶³ the keys of the heavens and the earth belong to Him. Those who deny God's revelations will surely be the losers. ⁶⁴ Say, 'Ignorant men! Would you bid me worship someone other than God?' ⁶⁵ It has already been revealed to you and to those who have gone before you that if you ascribe any partner to God, all your works will come to nothing, and you will surely be among the losers. ⁶⁶ Therefore, you should worship God alone and be among the thankful.

⁶⁷ No just estimate have they made of God, such as is due to Him. But on the Day of Resurrection, the whole earth will lie within His grasp, while heaven will be folded up in His right hand—Glory be to Him! Exalted is He above all that they associate with Him—⁶⁸ the Trumpet shall be blown and whoever is in heaven and whoever is on earth will fall down in a swoon, except those who shall be spared by God. Then the Trumpet will be blown again and they shall rise and gaze around them. ⁶⁹ The earth will shine with the light of its Lord, and the Book will be laid open; the prophets and witnesses will be brought in; and judgement will be passed on them with fairness. And none shall be wronged. ⁷⁰ Every soul will be repaid in full for what it has done. He is fully aware of all that they did.

⁷¹ Those who rejected the truth will be led to Hell in throngs. When they reach it, its gates will be opened and its keepers will say to them, 'Have messengers not come to you from among yourselves, who conveyed to you the revelations of your Lord and warned you about meeting [Him] on this Day?' They will answer, 'Yes, they did come.' But the decree of punishment has proved true against the deniers of the truth. ⁷² They will be told, 'Enter the gates of Hell, to stay therein forever.' What an evil dwelling place for the haughty.

[73] But those who fear their Lord will be led in groups towards Paradise. When they reach it, its gate will be opened, and its keepers will say to them, 'Peace be upon you. You have done well, enter Paradise and dwell in it forever,' [74] and they will say, 'Praise be to God who has fulfilled His promise to us and made us the inheritors of this land, letting us settle in the Garden wherever we want.' How excellent is the reward of those who labour! [75] You shall see the angels circling about the throne, glorifying their Lord with praise. And judgement will have been passed in justice on all and it will be said, 'Praise be to God, Lord of the Universe!'

40. THE FORGIVER (*GHAFIR*)

In the name of God, the Most Gracious, the Most Merciful

[1] *Ha Mim*

[2] This Book is revealed by God, the Almighty, the All Knowing. [3] The Forgiver of sin and the Accepter of repentance, who is severe in punishment and Infinite in His Bounty. There is no God but Him. All shall return to Him.

[4] Only those who deny the truth dispute God's signs. Do not let their activity in the land deceive you. [5] The people of Noah and later factions also rejected the truth and every community plotted against the messenger sent to them, aiming to lay hands on him, and they contended [against his message] with fallacious arguments, so that they might defeat the truth, therefore I seized them. How terrible was My punishment. [6] Thus has the word of your Lord come true against the deniers; they shall be the inmates of the Fire.

[7] Those who bear the Throne, and those who are around it, glorify their Lord with His praise, and believe in Him. They ask forgiveness for those who believe, saying, 'Our Lord, You embrace all things in mercy and knowledge. Forgive those who turn to You and follow Your path. Save them from the punishment of Hell [8] and admit them, Lord, to the Eternal Garden You have promised to them, together with their righteous ancestors, spouses, and offspring: You alone

are the Almighty; the All Wise. ⁹ Protect them from all evil deeds: those You protect from [the punishment for] evil deeds will receive Your mercy—that is the supreme success.'

¹⁰ Those who deny the truth will be told, 'God's abhorrence of you is greater than your hatred of yourselves. You were called to the faith but you denied it.' ¹¹ They will say, 'Our Lord! Twice You have made us die, and twice You have given us life! Now we have confessed our sins: is there any way out [of this]?' ¹² [They will be told], 'This is because when God alone was invoked you denied the truth, yet when others were associated with Him you believed in them.' Judgement rests with God, the Most High, the Most Great.

¹³ It is He who shows you His signs, and sends down provision for you from heaven; but none pays heed except the repentant.ᵃ ¹⁴ Therefore call upon God, making faith pure for Him, averse as the deniers of the truth may be to it: ¹⁵ Exalted and throned on high, He lets the Spirit descend at His behest upon whichever of His servants He will, so that he may warn of the Day of Meeting, ¹⁶ the Day when they shall rise up [from their graves] and nothing about them will be hidden from God. 'To whom shall the kingdom belong that Day?' It shall belong to God, the One, the All Powerful. ¹⁷ That Day every soul shall be requited for what it has earned. On that Day none shall be wronged. And God is swift in reckoning.

¹⁸ [O Prophet] forewarn them of the approaching Day, when hearts will leap up to the throats and choke them; when the wrongdoers will have no friend, nor any intercessor who will be listened to, ¹⁹ [for] He is aware of the [most] stealthy glance, and of all that the hearts conceal. ²⁰ God will judge with [justice and] truth: but

---

a There are countless signs in the universe which teach us lessons in symbolic language. One of these is the system of rains. This material phenomenon depicts allegorically the reality of Revelation. Just as rains are useful for fertile land and useless for barren land, similarly Revelation, God's shower of wisdom, brings forth fruit in some but not in others. This 'rain' enters the souls of those who have kept their hearts open and makes their existence a flourishing lush green. On the contrary, those whose hearts are full of the greatness of beings other than God are like barren lands. They will be deprived of the benefit of the Revelation.

those whom they invoke besides Him, have no power to judge at all. Surely, God is all hearing, all seeing.

²¹ Have they not travelled through the land and seen what was the end of those who have gone before them? They were stronger than them and made a more impressive mark upon the land, yet God destroyed them for their sins—they had no one to defend them against Him—²² that was because their messengers came to them with clear signs but they rejected them. So God seized them: He is powerful, severe in punishment.

²³ We sent Moses with Our signs and clear authority ²⁴ to Pharaoh, Haman and Korah. But they said, 'A magician, a liar.' ²⁵ When he came to them with the truth from Us, they said, 'Slay the sons of those who believe with him and spare only their daughters'—the schemes of those who denied the truth were futile.

²⁶ Pharaoh said, 'Let me kill Moses—let him call upon his Lord—I fear that he may cause you to change your religion, or that he may cause disorder in the land.' ²⁷ Moses replied, 'I seek refuge with my Lord and your Lord from every arrogant person who does not believe in the Day of Reckoning.'

²⁸ A believer, a man from among the people of Pharaoh, who had concealed his faith, said, 'Would you slay a man merely because he says, "My Lord is God." He has brought you clear signs from your Lord, and if he is lying, the sin of his will be on his own head; but if he is truthful, a part of that of which he warns you will surely befall you. Certainly, God does not guide one who is a transgressor and a liar. ²⁹ My people! Yours is the kingdom today, you have dominion in the land; but who will help us against the scourge of God if it befalls us?' But Pharaoh said, 'I point out to you only that which I consider right; and I guide you to the right path.'

³⁰ The believer said, 'My people! I fear for you a fate like that of the people of old: ³¹ like the fate of the people of Noah, 'Ad, Thamud, and those who came after them—God never wills injustice on His creatures. ³² My people, I fear for you the Day you will cry out to one another, ³³ the Day when you will [wish to] turn your backs and flee, having none to defend you against God: for he whom God lets go astray can never find any guide.

³⁴ Joseph came to you before with clear signs, but you never ceased to doubt the message he brought you. When he died, you said, "God will not send another messenger."' In this way God leaves the transgressors and doubters to go astray—³⁵ those who dispute God's revelations without any authority are doing something that is greatly abhorrent to God and to the believers. That is how God seals up the heart of every arrogant oppressor.

³⁶ Pharaoh said, 'O Haman, build for me a lofty building so that I may gain access ³⁷ to the heavens, so that I may look upon the God of Moses: I am convinced that he is a liar!' That is how Pharaoh's evil actions were made to look fair in the eyes of Pharaoh, and he was turned away from the path [of truth]. Pharaoh's scheming led to nothing but ruin.

³⁸ The believer said, 'My people, follow me! I will guide you to the right path. ³⁹ O my people, the life of this world is only a temporary provision; and the Hereafter is the permanent abode. ⁴⁰ Whoever does evil will be requited with evil; but whoever does good, whether male or female, and is a believer, will enter the Garden; where they will be provided for without measure. ⁴¹ My people! How is it that I call you to salvation, while you call me to the Fire? ⁴² You call upon me to deny God and to serve other deities about which I have no knowledge, while I call you to the Almighty, the Forgiver. ⁴³ Surely that to which you call me has no say in this world or in the life to come, that our return is to God alone, and that the transgressors shall be the inmates of the Fire. ⁴⁴ Soon you will remember what I say to you! I shall entrust my affair to God, for God is observant of all [His] servants.'

⁴⁵ Thus, God delivered him from the evils which they plotted, and the companions of Pharaoh themselves were encompassed by a dreadful scourge; ⁴⁶ they will be brought before the Fire morning and evening. On the Day the Hour comes, [a voice will cry], 'Mete out to Pharaoh's people the harshest punishment!'

⁴⁷ When they dispute with one another in the Fire, the weak will say to those who deemed themselves mighty, 'We were your followers; will you then relieve us of some of the Fire?' ⁴⁸ But those who had been arrogant will say, 'We are all in this together. God has judged

between His servants.' [49] Those in the Fire will say to its keepers, 'Implore your Lord to relieve our torment for one day,' [50] but they will say, 'Did not your messengers come to you with clear signs?' They will say, 'Yes.' The keepers will say, 'Then pray [for help] yourselves.' But the prayer of those who deny the truth is of no avail.

[51] Most surely We help our messengers, and those who believe, in the life of this world and on the Day when all the witnesses will stand up. [52] The Day when their excuses will be of no avail to the wrongdoers, the curse shall be their lot and they will have the most evil abode. [53] We gave Moses Our guidance, and made the Children of Israel the inheritors of the Book—[54] a guide and an admonition to men of understanding. [55] So be patient, for what God has promised is sure to come. Ask forgiveness for your sins; praise your Lord morning and evening.

[56] As for those who, with no authority to do so, dispute God's messages, there is nothing in their hearts but a feeling of greatness which they will never attain. Seek refuge in God, for He is the All Hearing, the All Seeing. [57] Certainly, the creation of the heavens and the earth is greater than the creation of mankind; but most people do not know this. [58] The blind and the sighted are not equal, just as those who believe and do good works and those who do evil are not equal: how seldom you reflect! [59] The Final Hour is sure to come, without doubt, but most people do not believe.

[60] Your Lord has said, 'Call on Me, and I will answer your prayers.' But those who are too arrogant to worship Me will certainly enter Hell, in disgrace. [61] It is God who has given you the night in which to rest and the day in which to see. God is truly bountiful to people, but most people do not give thanks. [62] Such is God, your Lord, the Creator of all things. There is no god but He. How then are you being turned away [from Him]? [63] Thus, indeed, those who deny the signs of God turn away from Him.[a]

---

a The regular night and day system operating on the earth and other life-nurturing systems are too perfect and too great to have been brought into existence by any human being or even by all God's creatures put together. This is a clear argument which urges that the Creator is the only one who is worthy of

⁶⁴ It is God who has given you the earth for a resting place and the heavens for a canopy.*a* He shaped you, formed you well, and provided you with good things. Such is God, your Lord, so glory be to Him, the Lord of the Universe. ⁶⁵ He is the Living One. There is no deity save Him. So pray to Him, making religion pure for Him [only]. Praise be to God, the Lord of the Universe!

⁶⁶ Say, 'I have been forbidden to invoke those whom you invoke besides God—seeing that clear signs have come to me from my Lord; and I have been commanded to submit to the Lord of the Universe.' ⁶⁷ It is He who created you from dust, then from a drop of fluid, then from a tiny, clinging form, then He brought you forth as infants, then He allowed you to reach maturity, then He let you grow old—though some of you die sooner—and reach your appointed term so that you may reflect. ⁶⁸ It is He who gives life and death, and when He ordains a thing, He says only, 'Be!' and it is.*b*

---

being worshipped. Man should bow down only before Him and entertain hopes solely of Him.

a The earth has been endowed with countless physical resources. On this basis it has been possible for creatures like human beings to build up their civilization in the world. Similarly, in the atmosphere above the earth there are countless favourable arrangements in which if there occurred even the slightest of disturbances, the whole system of human life would go topsy-turvy. Then, the constitution of man has been framed in such a sublime manner that he has become the most superior creature in the world, both in respect of his mind as well as his physique. So, who can be worthy of man's devotion and worship except the Creator who has done all this?

b These verses give details of certain phenomena of nature of which it is said, 'So that you may reflect', in other words, 'All these exist so that you may give them deep consideration'. That is, these material happenings of nature have some inner lessons in them, and it is expected of man that he should ponder deeply upon them, so that he may uncover their hidden lessons.

The events of nature that have been mentioned here are—the conversion of lifeless matter into living objects; the development of the human being in a gradual manner; man's passing through the stages of youth to old age; living man's becoming dead again, sometimes in old age and sometimes at a young age. All these events introduce us to various attributes of the Creator. It is revealed by these events that the Being who brought this universe into existence is the All Powerful and Wise God. He is Supreme and Dominant.

[69] Do you not see how those who dispute God's signs, are turned away from the right path—[70] those who reject the Book and that with which We sent Our messengers shall soon know—[71] when, with iron collars and chains around their necks, they are dragged [72] into the boiling water and then are thrown into the Fire, [73] and then they will be asked, 'Where are those whom you associated [with God]?' [74] They will say, 'They have been lost to us; nay, we did not invoke anything before [that had real existence].' Thus God leaves the deniers of the truth to stray; [75] that is because you exulted in the land without justification and because you behaved insolently. [76] Enter the gates of Hell to stay therein forever. The abode of the arrogant is evil.

[77] So be patient [Prophet], for God's promise is true: whether We show you part of what We have promised them in this life, or cause you to die first, it is to Us that they will be recalled.

[78] Before your time We sent other messengers: of them there are some whose story We have related to you, and some whose story We have not related to you. It was not [possible] for any messenger to bring a sign except by the leave of God: but when the command of God was issued, the matter was decided in truth and justice. There and then, those who stood on falsehoods perished.

[79] It is God who provides livestock for you, some for riding and some for your food: [80] you have other benefits in them too. You can reach any destination you wish on them: they carry you by land, as ships carry you on the sea. [81] He shows you His signs; which then of the signs of God will you deny?

[82] Have they not travelled in the land to see the fate of those who went before them? They were more numerous and mightier and left greater traces of their power on the earth; yet all that they accomplished was of no avail to them. [83] When messengers came to them with clear signs, they revelled in whatever knowledge they had, and so they were engulfed by the very punishment they mocked: [84] but when they saw Our punishment, they said, 'We believe in God—the One God—and we reject the partners we used to associate with Him,' [85] but believing after seeing Our punishment

did not benefit them at all: this is the law of God to deal with His creatures, and thus the disbelievers were the losers.

41. REVELATIONS WELL EXPOUNDED (*FUSSILAT*)

In the name of God, the Most Gracious, the Most Merciful

¹ *Ha Mim*

² A revelation from [God], the Most Gracious, the Most Merciful— ³ a Book whose revelations are well expounded, an Arabic Quran for people who possess knowledge, ⁴ proclaiming good news and a warning. Yet most of them turn away and so do not listen. ⁵ And they say, 'Our hearts are encased against that to which you call us, and there is a heaviness in our ears, and there is a barrier between us, so do as you will and so shall we.'*a*

⁶ Say, 'I am only a human being like yourselves. It has been revealed to me that your God is One God. So take the straight path to Him and ask His forgiveness.' Woe to those who associate others with Him, ⁷ who do not pay the *zakat*, and who deny the Hereafter. ⁸ 'The ones who believe and perform good deeds shall have a reward which will never be withheld from them.'*b*

---

a The call of a prophet is the pure call of religion. However, people mostly follow the religion of their forebears. Their thinking is dominated by their national traditions and contemporary mores. For this reason, the prophet's unadulterated religion does not fit the pattern or mould of their thought. He appears a stranger to them. This difference acts as a mental barrier between the prophet and the common people. Unable to see the prophet's call in its proper perspective, they are not prepared to accept it. The prophet's call is in itself extremely rational. It is in itself a proof that it has come from God. But the aforesaid mental barrier proves so impregnable that a man is unable to penetrate it in order to grasp the meaning of the prophet's call. Thus God opens the doors of his Grace to man, but he does not pass through them.

b 'So take the straight path to Him' means 'keep your worship purely for God', i.e. your whole attention should be directed towards God; the sole object of your prayers and worship should be the one and only God; your

⁹ Say, 'What! Do you indeed deny Him who created the earth in two Days [periods] and do you set up equals with Him? He is the Lord of the Universe.' ¹⁰ He placed firm mountains on the earth, and blessed it. He measured out its means of sustenance all in four Days; this is for those who ask for it. ¹¹ Then He turned to heaven when it was vapour and said to it and to the earth, 'Come willingly or unwillingly.' They both said, 'We come willingly,' ¹² and in two Days He formed seven heavens, and revealed to each heaven its functions; and We adorned the lower heaven with brilliant lamps [stars] and guarded it. That is the decree of the Almighty, the All Knowing.*ᵃ*

¹³ If they turn away, then say, 'I warn you of a lightning-bolt like the one which struck the 'Ad and the Thamud: ¹⁴ when the messengers came to them from before them and behind them, saying, "Worship none but God!" They said, "If our Lord had willed, He would have sent down angels [to us]. Therefore, we shall never believe in your message."'

¹⁵ As for the tribe of 'Ad, they behaved arrogantly in the land without any justification and said, 'Who is mightier than we in power?' Did they not see that God, who created them, was mightier than they in power? Still they continued to deny Our signs, ¹⁶ so We

---

entire thinking should become God-oriented. God's perpetual blessings will be showered on those who conduct themselves in this way.

a A study of the universe reveals that its creation has been effected gradually in a phased manner. Creation in this way—in other words by stages, means planned creation; and when the creation of the universe has been so carried out, it essentially follows that it has a Planner who has purposefully created it according to a set plan. Similarly, there are mountains on this earth at various places that maintain the balance of the earth. There are millions of species of living organisms on this earth and every species requires different types of sustenance, which are found in its environs. Similarly, a study of the universe also shows that initially all things were in the shape of divided atoms. Then they combined to form different entities. It is further evident from such a study that all the things in this immense universe are uniformly governed by a universal law of nature. These observations clearly establish that the Creator of the universe is all-knowing and all-aware. He is all-powerful and dominant. So, who else can be there whom a man can treat as being worthy of worship?

let loose upon them a raging wind over several inauspicious days,*a* so that We might make them taste the torment of humiliation in the life of this world, and surely the torment of the Hereafter will be more humiliating. They shall have none to help them. [17] As for the Thamud We offered them Our guidance, but they preferred blindness to guidance. So the lightning-bolt of the punishment of humiliation seized them on account of their misdeeds. [18] We saved those who had attained to faith and were God-fearing.

[19] On the Day that the enemies of God shall be gathered together and driven to the Fire, they shall be formed into groups, and [20] when they come close to it, their ears, eyes and skins will testify against them for their misdeeds. [21] And they will ask their skins, 'Why did you bear witness against us?' and their skins will reply, 'God, who gives speech to all things, has given speech to us [as well]—it was He who created you in the first instance and to Him you are [now] brought back—[22] you could not hide yourselves from your ears and your eyes and your skins to prevent them from testifying against you, and you thought that God would never know much of what you did, [23] but these thoughts which you entertained concerning your Lord, have brought you to destruction, and [now] you are among the utterly lost!' [24] Even if they are patient, the Fire will still be their homes. And if they pray to be allowed to make amends, they will not be allowed to do so.*b*

---

a By inauspicious days is meant winters, for the Arabs regarded winter as inauspicious.

b It is stated in the Quran that on the Day of Judgement a man's skin and limbs will testify to his deeds. The theory of 'skin speech' of modern times has established the feasibility of such a happening. It has now been discovered that every utterance a man makes is recorded on the skin of his body and that it can be heard once again, just like a voice recorded by mechanical devices. Since God is not visible, man carries the impression that God does not see him. This misunderstanding gives rise to arrogance in man. But if a man realises that he is being observed by God at all times, his whole behaviour will change.

In the Hereafter, when he finally stands before God, man will express sentiments of obedience, but this will be of no avail, because obedience or submission has value or credibility only if it is practised at the 'unseen stage' and not after reality has been unveiled for all to see.

²⁵ We assigned to them companions who made their doings appear fair to them. But the same decree [of punishment] proved true against them, which had proved true against nations of jinn and mankind who passed away before them. Surely they were the losers.

²⁶ Those who deny the truth say, 'Do not listen to this Quran. Drown it out with noise, so that you may gain the upper hand.' ²⁷ Therefore, We will most certainly make those who are bent on denying the truth taste a severe punishment and We will most certainly requite them according to the worst of their deeds—²⁸ that is the reward of the enemies of God—the Fire will be their everlasting home, a reward for their rejection of Our revelations.

²⁹ Those who deny the truth will say, 'Our Lord, show us those jinn and men who misled us and we shall trample them underfoot, so that they may be among the lowest of the low.' ³⁰ As for those who affirm, 'Our Lord is God,' and then remain steadfast, the angels will descend on them, saying, 'Have no fear and do not grieve. Rejoice in the [good news of the] Garden that you have been promised. ³¹ 'We are your companions in this life and in the Hereafter. Therein you shall have all that your souls desire, and therein you shall have all that you ask for ³² as a rich provision from One who is ever forgiving and most merciful.'

³³ Who speaks better than one who calls to God and does good works and says, 'I am surely of those who submit'? ³⁴ Good and evil deeds are not equal. Repel evil with what is better; then you will see that one who was once your enemy has become your dearest friend, ³⁵ but no one will be granted such goodness except those who exercise patience and self-restraint—no one is granted it save those who are truly fortunate. ³⁶ If a prompting from Satan should stir you, seek refuge with God: He is the All Hearing and the All Knowing.*ᵃ*

³⁷ Among His signs are the night and the day, and the sun and the

---

a The call of the Quran is one inviting people to unite with God. Joining man with his Lord and Sustainer; making him spend his whole life in remembrance of God; developing a feeling in man that he should make the one and only God the centre of his attention—these are the real aims of the Quranic call and undoubtedly there is no call better than this.

moon. Do not prostrate yourselves before the sun and the moon, but prostrate yourselves before God who created them all, if it is truly Him that you worship. ³⁸ If they grow arrogant, [remember that] those who are with your Lord glorify Him night and day and never grow tired.*a*

³⁹ Among His signs is this: you see the earth dry and barren, but when We send down on it water, it stirs and swells: most surely He who gives it life is the giver of life to the dead; surely He has power over all things. ⁴⁰ Those who distort the meaning of Our message are not concealed from Us.*b* Who is better—someone who will be thrown into the Fire or someone who will arrive in safety on the Day of Resurrection? Do as you will, He sees whatever you do.

⁴¹ Those who reject the Reminder [the Quran] when it comes to them [are the losers]—truly it is a mighty Book: ⁴² falsehood shall not reach from before or from behind. It is a revelation from the Wise, the One worthy of all praise. ⁴³ Nothing is said to you but what was said indeed to the messengers before you; surely your Lord is the Lord of forgiveness but also the Lord of painful retribution.

⁴⁴ Had We sent this as a Quran [in a language] other than Arabic, they would have said, 'Why are its verses not clearly explained? What! An Arab Prophet, and a scripture in a foreign tongue?' Say, 'It is a guide and a healing to those who believe; but for those who do

---

a The greatest human blunder is having regard for outward appearances. In ancient times, the sun, the moon and stars appeared quite dazzling to man, so he took them as deities and started worshipping them. In the present age, it is the glamour of the material side of civilization which appears dazzling. So, materialism has now been given the same status as was enjoyed in former times by the sun and the moon, though the sun, the moon and other phenomena are all creations of God. A man should worship the Creator and not his creatures.

b The rains soaking dry land and thereafter greenery sprouting from it are phenomena generally witnessed again and again. This is in material form an allegorical reference to an inner reality. In this way man is informed that God has made extensive and elaborate arrangements here to refresh and invigorate this dry existence. The soil absorbs the water and allows it to percolate downwards, and that is why it is possible for the rains to become a source of revitalization for it. Similarly, if man allows God's guidance to permeate his existence, he too will become reanimated upon receiving it.

not believe, there is a deafness in their ears, and a covering over their eyes: they are [as it were] being called from a very distant place.'

⁴⁵ We gave Moses the Book, but differences were created concerning it: and had it not been for a word that had already gone forth from your Lord, the matter would have been decided between them; and certainly they are in grave doubt about it. ⁴⁶ Whoever does what is just and right, does so for his own good; and whoever does evil, does so to his own detriment: and God is never in the least unjust to His creatures.

⁴⁷ He alone has knowledge of the Hour [of Judgment]. And no fruit emerges from its husk, nor does any female become pregnant or give birth, without His knowledge.ᵃ On the Day He will call out to them, 'Where are My associates?' They will reply, 'We declare to You that none of us can bear witness to them:' ⁴⁸ [the deities] they invoked before will have vanished; they will know that there is no escape.

⁴⁹ Man never tires of asking for the good things of life; but if evil fortune befalls him, he abandons all hope, giving himself up to despair. ⁵⁰ When We give him a taste of some of Our mercy, after some adversity has touched him, he is sure to say, 'This is my due. I do not think that the Hour is going to come. And even if I return to my Lord, He will surely reward me well.' But truly We shall tell those who deny the truth [all] that they did, and shall make them suffer a hard punishment.

⁵¹ When We grant a blessing to a man, he turns away and draws

---

a The springing of a fruit from a tree or the emerging of a live being from the womb of a mother is in essence the same as the emergence of the world of the Hereafter from the present world.

What is fruit? It is the change of the fruitless into the fruitful. What is a human being? It is a non-human entity turning into a human being. The Hereafter, too, in fact, is the change of present existence into the Hereafter. The first type of change occurs before us every day. Then why should another, but greater change of a similar nature (i.e. the change of the present world into the world of the Hereafter) be incredible?

The Day of the Hereafter will be the day of the final appearance of realities. When that Day arrives, all false bases on which human beings had built their lives will be demolished.

aside, but when any evil touches him, he is full of endless prayers! [52] Say to them, 'Have you considered, if this Quran is really from God and you still reject it, then who could be more astray than someone who has drifted far away from the truth?'

[53] We shall show them Our signs in the universe and within themselves, until it becomes clear to them that this is the Truth. Is it not enough that your Lord is the witness of all things? [54] Yet they still doubt that they will ever meet their Lord. Surely, He encompasses all things.

42. MUTUAL CONSULTATION (*AL-SHURA*)

In the name of God, the Most Gracious, the Most Merciful

[1] *Ha Mim* [2] *'Ayn Sin Qaf*

[3] Thus God, the Powerful, the Wise, sends revelation to you as He did to those before you. [4] All that is in the heavens and earth belongs to Him: He is the Exalted, the Almighty. [5] The heavens are almost split asunder from above as the angels sing their Lord's praise and seek forgiveness for those on earth. God is indeed the Most Forgiving, the Most Merciful.[a] [6] And [as for] those who take protectors besides Him, God is watching them and you are not a guardian over them.

[7] Thus We revealed to you, this Arabic Quran so that you may warn the mother of cities [Makkah] and those around it, and warn

---

a If man were to be blessed with boundless vision, he would see with his own eye that there is one God who is the Lord of the heavens and the earth in their entirety. His Power is so immense that the Universe, so to say, dreads it and bursts with fear. The angels, who are directly aware of God's omnipotence are awe-struck and continue to recite His praises at all times. Then man will also see that God, in exercise of His special powers, selects certain individuals as His messengers and sends them directly to mankind so that they may inform all God's creatures of the truth.

them of the Day of Gathering which is sure to come: when some group will be in the Garden, and some will be in the Fire.

⁸ Had God so willed, He could have made all of them one community, but He admits into His mercy whom He wills; and the wrongdoers have neither protector, nor helper. ⁹ Have they taken for themselves protectors other than Him? But it is God who is the real Protector. He resurrects the dead, and He has power over all things. ¹⁰ In whatever you may differ, [O believers] the verdict thereon rests with God. [Say, therefore], 'Such is God, my Lord: in Him I have placed my trust, and to Him I always turn.'

¹¹ Creator of the Heavens and the Earth, He has made spouses for you from among yourselves, as well as pairs of livestock by means of which He multiplies His creatures. Nothing can be compared with Him! He is the All Hearing, the All Seeing. ¹² To Him belongs the keys of the heavens and the earth; He gives abundantly to whoever He wills and gives sparingly to whoever He wills. He has full knowledge of all things.[a]

¹³ God has ordained for you the same religion which He enjoined on Noah, and which We have revealed to you, and which We enjoined upon Abraham and Moses and Jesus, so that you should remain steadfast in religion and not become divided in it. What you call upon the polytheists to do is hard for them; God chooses for Himself whoever He pleases and guides towards Himself those who turn to Him.

¹⁴ They became divided only after knowledge had reached them, out of mutual jealousy. Had it not been for a decree already passed by your Lord, [to reprieve them] till a specified period, the matter would surely have been decided between them. Those who inherited the Book after them are indeed in grave doubt, amounting to suspicion about it.

---

a The attributes of the Creator which come to our knowledge through observation of His creations are sufficient to prove how great the Creator is. He is All Knowing and All Observing. Most High and Almighty, He possesses all powers. Whatever one receives, is due to His Grace and whatever is taken away, is taken away by Him. He is Unique. There is nobody like Him.

¹⁵ So call people to that faith and hold fast to it yourself as you are commanded, and do not be led by their desires, but say, 'I believe in the Book which God has sent down, and I am commanded to do justice between you: God is our Lord and your Lord; we are responsible for what we do and you are responsible for what you do. There is no contention between us and you. God will gather us together, for to Him we shall return.' ¹⁶ As for those who argue about God after He has been accepted, their arguments will carry no weight with their Lord, and His wrath will fall upon them. Severe punishment awaits them.

¹⁷ It is God who has sent down the Book with the truth and the scales of justice. What will make you realize that the Hour might well have drawn near?ᵃ ¹⁸ Those who do not believe in it seek to hasten it, but those who believe in it dread it, and know it to be the truth. Those who dispute the Hour have gone far astray.

¹⁹ God is most Gracious to His creatures: He provides sustenance for whoever He wills—for He alone is the Powerful One, the Almighty. ²⁰ To him who desires a harvest in the life to come, We shall grant an increase in his harvest; whereas to him who desires [but] a harvest in this world, We [may] give something thereof—but he will have no share in [the blessings of] the life to come.

²¹ Do they have associate gods who have laid down for them a religion without the permission of God? Had it not been for God's decree on the final Judgement, the matter would have been decided between them. Surely the wrongdoers shall have a painful punishment. ²² You will see the wrongdoers fearful of the consequences of their deeds, which will be inescapable. Whereas, those who have believed and done righteous deeds, will be in the meadows of the Garden and shall have whatever they desire from their Lord. That will be the supreme favour. ²³ These are the glad tidings which God gives

---

a Just as a balance is meant for weighing material things, so in order to weigh intangible ethereal realities has God revealed His book. God's book is the touch-stone for distinguishing the Truth and separating it from falsehood. Every thing will be tested by the standards set by God's book, instead of God's book being tested by the standards of other things.

to His servants who believe and do righteous deeds. Say, 'I do not ask of you any reward for it, except [that I am inviting you to God because of] love of kinship.' Whoever earns a good deed, We shall increase its good for him; God is most forgiving, most appreciative.

²⁴ Do they say, 'He has invented a lie about God'? If God so willed, He could seal your heart. God wipes out falsehood and vindicates the truth by His words. He has full knowledge of what is in men's hearts—²⁵ He accepts repentance from His servants and pardons their sins. He knows everything you do. ²⁶ He responds to those who believe and do good deeds, and gives them more of His bounty; agonizing torment awaits the deniers of the truth.

²⁷ If God were to grant His abundant provision to [all] His creatures, they would act insolently on earth, but He sends down in due measure whatever He will, for He is well aware of His servants and watchful over them: ²⁸ it is He who sends rain after they have despaired and spreads His mercy far and wide. He is the Protector, Worthy of All Praise. ²⁹ Among His signs is the creation of the heavens and earth and all the living creatures He has dispersed throughout them: He has the power to gather them all together whenever He will.

³⁰ Whatever misfortune befalls you is of your own doing—God forgives much—³¹ you cannot escape Him anywhere on earth. You have no protector or helper other than God.

³² Among His signs are the ships sailing like mountains on the sea: ³³ if He willed, He could bring the wind to a standstill and they would lie motionless on the surface of the sea—truly there are signs in this for anyone who is steadfast and grateful—³⁴ or He may cause them to founder because of people's misdeeds—He pardons many of them—³⁵ those who dispute Our signs shall learn that they have no escape.

³⁶ Whatever you have been given is only a temporary provision of this life, but that which is with God is better and more lasting for those who believe and put their trust in their Lord; ³⁷ who refrain from heinous sins and gross indecencies; who forgive when they are angry; ³⁸ who respond to their Lord and attend to their prayers; who conduct their affairs by mutual consultation and spend out of what We have provided for them; ³⁹ who, when they are attacked,

defend themselves. ⁴⁰ Let harm be requited by an equal harm. But whoever pardons and amends will find his reward with God. He does not love the wrongdoers. ⁴¹ Those who defend themselves after they have been wronged cannot be held blameworthy, ⁴² blame falls only on those who wrong men and transgress on this earth without justification—such will have a painful punishment— ⁴³ whoever is patient and forgiving, acts with great courage and resolution.

⁴⁴ Anyone whom God lets go astray will thereafter have no protector whatsoever: you will see the wrongdoers, when they face the punishment, exclaiming, 'Is there no way back?' ⁴⁵ You will see them exposed to the Fire, abject in humiliation, glancing furtively at it, while those who believed will say, 'The losers are those ones who have forfeited their souls and their people on the Day of Resurrection.' Truly, the wrongdoers will remain in everlasting torment; ⁴⁶ they will have no allies to help them against God; there is no way [forward] for those whom God lets go astray.

⁴⁷ Respond to your Lord before a Day arrives that will not be averted [against God's will]. You will not find any refuge from God on that Day, nor will you have [any opportunity] to deny your sins. ⁴⁸ Now if they turn away, We have not sent you [O Prophet] as their keeper: your responsibility is only to convey the message. Man is such that when We let him taste Our mercy, he exults in it, but if an evil befalls him which is his own doing, he becomes utterly ungrateful.

⁴⁹ God has control of the heavens and the earth; He creates whatever He will—He grants female offspring to whoever He will, male to whoever He will, ⁵⁰ or both male and female, and He leaves whoever He will barren; He is all-knowing and all powerful.

⁵¹ It is not granted to any human being that God should speak to him other than by revelation or from behind a veil, or by sending him a messenger, so that the messenger may reveal, by His command, whatsoever He will. Truly, He is exalted and wise.ᵃ ⁵² We have thus

---

a In the present world no human being can directly talk to God. Man's humble position is the hindrance to such dialogue. Therefore the revelation of God's words to the prophets was made in an indirect manner. There are many

revealed a Spirit to you [Prophet] by Our command: you knew neither the Scripture nor the faith, but We made it a light, guiding with it whoever We will of Our servants. You are indeed guiding to the straight path, ⁵³ the path of God, to whom belongs all that is in the heavens and on the earth. Indeed all matters return eventually to God.

43. ORNAMENTS OF GOLD
(*AL-ZUKHRUF*)

In the name of God, the Most Gracious, the Most Merciful

¹ *Ha Mim*

² By the Book that makes things clear, ³ We have made it an Arabic Quran so that you may understand. ⁴ Truly, it is inscribed in the Original Book, in Our keeping; it is sublime and full of wisdom.

⁵ Should We withdraw the admonition from you because you are a people far gone in transgression? ⁶ We have sent many a prophet to earlier peoples ⁷ but whenever a prophet came to them, they mocked him, ⁸ so We destroyed those who were mightier than these; such was the example of the earlier peoples.

⁹ If you ask them, 'Who has created the heavens and the earth?', they will surely answer, 'The Almighty, the All Knowing One has created them.' ¹⁰ Who has made the earth a cradle for you and made thereon paths for you so that, hopefully, you may find your way. ¹¹ It is He who sends water down from the sky in due measure— We revive dead land with it and likewise you will be resurrected from the grave—¹² it is He who created all living things in pairs and gave you ships to sail in and beasts to ride upon ¹³ so that you may sit firmly on their backs. Then once you have mounted them, remember your Lord's favour and say, 'Glory be to Him who has subjected these creatures to us; we would never on our own have subdued them. ¹⁴ And to our Lord we shall surely return.'

---

methods of indirect revelation. Examples of these are found in the lives of the various prophets.

¹⁵ Yet they make some of His servants partners in His divinity. Man is clearly ungrateful! ¹⁶ Has He then taken daughters out of His own creation and chosen sons for you? ¹⁷ When any of them is given the news of the very thing [i.e. a female child] which he himself has ascribed to the All Merciful, his face darkens and he is filled with grief—

¹⁸ ['Do you ascribe to God] one who is brought up among ornaments and who cannot produce a cogent argument?' ¹⁹ They consider the angels—God's servants—to be female. Did they witness their creation? Their claim will be put on record and they will be questioned about it.

²⁰ They say, 'If the All Merciful had so willed, we would not have worshipped them.' They have no knowledge of that. They are only conjecturing. ²¹ Have We given them a Book before this, to which they are holding fast? ²² No indeed! They say, 'We have found our fathers following a certain course, and we are guided by their footsteps.' ²³ Whenever We sent a messenger before you to warn a township, the affluent among them said, in the same way, 'We saw our fathers following this tradition; we are only following in their footsteps.' ²⁴ Each messenger said, 'What if I should bring you better guidance than what you found your forefathers had?' They replied, 'We reject any message you have been sent with!' ²⁵ So We wreaked Our vengeance on them: now see what was the end of those who rejected [the Truth]!

²⁶ Call to mind when Abraham said to his father and his people, 'I disown utterly that which you worship. ²⁷ [I worship] only Him who created me, and He will certainly guide me,' ²⁸ and he left these words to endure among his descendants, so that they might return [to God]. ²⁹ Yes, I gave the good things of this life to these [men] and their fathers, until the truth came to them, and a messenger expounding things clearly, ³⁰ but when the truth came to them, they said, 'This is sorcery, and we reject it.'

³¹ They said, 'Why was this Quran not sent down to one of the great men of the two cities?' ³² Is it they who apportion the mercy of your Lord? It is We who distribute among them their livelihood in the life of this world, and raise some of them above others in

rank, so that they may take one another into service; and the mercy of your Lord is better than [the wealth] which they amass. [33] If it were not that all mankind might have become one community [of disbelievers], We could have given all those who deny the Lord of Mercy, houses with roofs of silver, silver staircases to ascend, [34] and silver doors to their houses and silver couches on which to recline, [35] and ornaments of gold. But all of these are but the provision of this present life; it is the life to come that the Lord reserves for those who fear Him.

[36] As for one who turns away from the remembrance of the Gracious God, We appoint for him a devil, who will become his intimate companion. [37] Devils divert men from the [right] way, while they think that they are rightly guided. [38] When such a person comes to Us, he will say [to his comrade], 'If only you had been as far away from me as east is from west. What an evil comrade!' [39] It will be said [to such a person], 'You have done wrong. Having partners in punishment will be of no avail to you today.'

[40] Can you [Prophet] make the deaf hear? Or guide either the blind or those who are in manifest error? [41] Even if We take you away from the world, We shall surely take vengeance on them [42] or We shall show you what We have promised them; for surely We have complete power over them. [43] So, hold fast to the Book that has been revealed to you—you are surely on the right path— [44] it is certainly a reminder to you and to your people and you will soon be called to account. [45] Ask those of Our messengers whom We sent before you, 'Did We ever appoint gods to be worshipped besides the Beneficent One?'

[46] We sent Moses with Our signs to Pharaoh and his nobles. He said, 'I am the messenger of the Lord of the Universe,' [47] but when he came to them with Our signs, they ridiculed them, [48] even though each sign We showed them was greater than the previous one. We afflicted them with torment so that they might return [to the right path]. [49] They said, 'Sorcerer, call on your Lord for us, by virtue of His pledge to you: we shall certainly accept guidance,' [50] but when We relieved them of the torment, they broke their word.

[51] Pharaoh called to his people, 'My people, is the Kingdom of

Egypt not mine? And these rivers that flow at my feet, are they not mine? Do you not see? [52] Am I not better than this contemptible man who can hardly make his meaning clear: [53] and why have not armlets of gold been bestowed on him and why is there not a train of angels accompanying him?' [54] In this way he fooled his people and they obeyed him: they were a rebellious people. [55] Then when they provoked Our wrath, We took revenge on them and drowned every one of them. [56] We made them a precedent, an example for later peoples.

[57] When [Jesus] the son of Mary is held up as an example, your people raise an outcry on this, [58] saying, 'Are our gods better or him?'—they cite him only to challenge you: they are a contentious people—[59] but he was only a servant We favoured and made an example for the Children of Israel: [60] if We had so wished, We could have appointed angels in exchange for you to succeed you on the earth. [61] He is a sign of the Hour. Have no doubt about it. But follow me. This is a straight path; [62] do not let Satan bar your way. He is truly your sworn enemy.

[63] When Jesus came with clear signs, he said, 'Now I have come to you with wisdom, in order to make clear to you some of the things about which you dispute: therefore fear God and obey me. [64] For God, He is my Lord and your Lord: so worship Him: that is a straight path.' [65] The various factions among them differed—woe then to those who did wrong: they will suffer the punishment of a painful Day.

[66] Are they merely waiting for the Hour, which will come upon them suddenly and take them unawares? [67] On that Day, friends will become each other's enemies, except the righteous—[68] 'O My servants, you need not fear this Day, nor shall you grieve'—[69] those who believed in Our revelations and surrendered themselves to Us. [70] 'Enter the Garden rejoicing, both you and your spouses!' [71] Dishes and goblets of gold will be passed around them with all that their souls desire and their eyes delight in. 'There you will remain forever: [72] this is the Garden which you will inherit by virtue of your past deeds, [73] and there is abundant fruit in it for you to eat.'

[74] As for the evil-doers, they shall endure forever the torment of

Hell, [75] from which there is no relief: they will remain there in utter despair. [76] We have not wronged them; it was they who were the wrongdoers. [77] They will cry, 'Master, if only your Lord would put an end to us!' But he [the angel] will answer, 'No! You are here to stay.' [78] We have certainly brought the truth to you: but most of you have an aversion for the truth. [79] Have they determined upon a course? Then We too are determined. [80] Do they imagine We do not hear their secret talk and their private counsels? On the contrary, Our messengers [angels] are at their sides, recording everything.

[81] Say, 'If the All Merciful had a son, I would be the first to worship him.' [82] But—exalted be the Lord of the heavens and earth, the Lord of the Throne[a]—He is far above their [false] descriptions. [83] So leave them alone to indulge in vain discourse and amuse themselves until they come face to face with that Day which they have been promised.

[84] It is He who is God in heaven, and God on earth: He is the Wise One, the All Knowing; [85] blessed be He who has sovereignty over the kingdom of the heavens and the earth and all that lies between them. He alone has knowledge of the Hour, and to Him you shall be returned.

[86] Those whom they invoke besides God have no power of intercession, only those who bear witness to the truth and they know.[b]

---

a Heaven and earth are continuously at work in perfect harmony. Perfect unity of wisdom and unity of knowledge are found in them. This proves that there is only one God Who is alone running the systems of both heaven and earth.

The universe introduces us to God's unlimited power and at the same time His unlimited mercy. These facts call for man to fear God most of all, and at the same time entertain the greatest hopes of Him. Those who prove to have this consciousness and this character in this world are the only individuals upon whom—when they reach God—He will shower his infinite Mercy.

b Jesus Christ was blessed with the miraculous power to bring a dead man back to life. He used to bring earthen statues to life by blowing his breath into them. This was in fact a sign of God which was displayed in order to demonstrate the possibility of life after death. But the people did not learn a lesson from this; on the contrary, they treated Jesus as a superhuman and started worshipping him. The signs of God appear before us in different ways. If they

[87] And if you ask them who created them, they will surely say, God. How then are they turned away? [88] The Prophet has said, 'Lord! Truly they are a people who do not believe.' [89] Then bear with them [O Muhammad] and say, 'Peace.' They will soon come to know.

44. SMOKE (*AL-DUKHAN*)

In the name of God, the Most Gracious, the Most Merciful

[1] *Ha Mim*

[2] By the Book that makes things clear, [3] surely We sent it down on a blessed night—We have always sent warnings—[4] on that night every wise decree is specified [5] by Our own command—We have been sending messages, [6] as a mercy from your Lord, He hears all and knows all, [7] He is the Lord of heaven and earth and all that is between them—if only you would really believe—[8] there is no deity save Him: It is He who gives both life and death—He is your Lord, and the Lord of your forefathers, [9] yet, they toy with their doubts. [10] Wait, then, for the Day when the sky brings forth plainly visible clouds of smoke. [11] That will envelop the people. This will be a painful punishment. [12] Then they will say, 'Lord, relieve us from this torment, for truly we are now believers in You.' [13] How can they benefit from admonition, seeing that a messenger had already come to them explaining things clearly? [14] Then they turned away from him and said, 'He is a madman, taught by others!' [15] Were We to ease the torment for a while, you would still revert to denial of the truth. [16] On the Day We inflict the direst scourge upon all sinners, We will certainly exact retribution.

[17] We tried the people of Pharaoh before them: a noble messenger was sent to them, [18] saying, 'Hand over God's servants to me. I am a trustworthy messenger for you. [19] Do not set yourselves above

---

are treated as such they are a tremendous source of guidance. But if they are considered something other than divine portents, they may become the cause of man's going astray.

God: I bring you clear authority. [20] I have sought refuge with my Lord and your Lord lest you stone me [to death]. [21] If you do not believe in me, at least keep away from me.'

[22] Then he cried out to his Lord, 'These are sinful people.' [23] God said, 'Set out with My servants by night, for you will certainly be pursued. [24] Leave the sea behind you parted; they are a host destined to be drowned.' [25] How many gardens and fountains they left behind them, [26] and cornfields and splendid buildings, [27] and pleasant things in which they delighted! [28] Such was their end, and what had been theirs We gave to other people to inherit. [29] Neither heaven nor earth wept for them, nor were they allowed any respite.

[30] We saved the Children of Israel from their humiliating torment [31] at the hands of Pharaoh: he was a tyrant who exceeded all bounds. [32] We knowingly chose them above all other people [33] and showed them signs in which there was a clear test.

[34] Yet those who deny the truth say, [35] there is nothing beyond our first death; we shall not be raised again. [36] So bring our fathers [back], if what you say is true. [37] Are they better than the people of Tubba' and those who came before them? We destroyed them, because they were guilty of sin.

[38] We did not idly create the heavens and the earth and all that lies between them;[a] [39] We did not create them save with a purpose, yet most people have no knowledge of this. [40] Truly, the Day of Decision is the appointed time for all of them, [41] the Day when no friend shall be of the least avail to another, nor shall any be helped,

---

a If one ponders over the system of heaven and earth—indeed, of the entire universe, it will become clear that its creation was effected with a definite purpose. Had this not been so, it would have been impossible in this world for man to build up glorious cultures.

Its entire functioning being meaningful is an indication that it will end also in a meaningful and purposeful way. It is unimaginable that its end could be otherwise. Its end, in reality, will herald the commencement of the life Hereafter. And belief in the Hereafter is but an extension of universal meaningfulness.

The present stage of the world is that of trial. So, everyone has his share in the meaningfulness of this world. But, in the Hereafter, only those who are actually deserving in the eyes of God, will have a share in the meaningfulness of the afterlife.

⁴² save those to whom God shows mercy. Surely, He is the Mighty, the Merciful One.a

⁴³ Surely the fruit of the Zaqqum tree ⁴⁴ shall be food for the sinners: ⁴⁵ like the dregs of oil, it shall boil in their bellies, ⁴⁶ like the boiling of hot water. ⁴⁷ [A voice will cry], 'Seize him and drag him into the midst of Hell. ⁴⁸ Then pour boiling water over his head as punishment. ⁴⁹ Taste this; you who considered yourself the mighty, the honourable! ⁵⁰ This is what you doubted?'

⁵¹ But those mindful of God will be in a safe place, ⁵² among gardens and springs, ⁵³ dressed in fine silk and in rich brocade, and they will face each other: ⁵⁴ so it will be. We shall wed them to maidens with large, dark eyes. ⁵⁵ They will call therein for every kind of fruit, in peace and security. ⁵⁶ They will not taste death therein, save the first death. God will save them from the torment of Hell ⁵⁷ as an act of grace. That will be the supreme triumph.

⁵⁸ We have made this Quran easy to understand—in your own language—so that they may take heed. ⁵⁹ Wait then; they too are waiting.

45. KNEELING (*AL-JATHIYAH*)

In the name of God, the Most Gracious, the Most Merciful

¹ *Ha Mim*

² This Scripture is sent down from God, the Mighty and Wise One. ³ There are signs in the heavens and the earth for those who believe: ⁴ in your own creation and all the creatures He has spread about, there are signs for people of sure faith; ⁵ and in the succession of night and day, and in the means of subsistence which God sends down from the skies, giving life thereby to the earth after it had been lifeless, and in the circulation of the winds: [in all this] there are signs for people who use their reason. ⁶ These are God's revelations, which We recite to you in all truth. But if they deny God and His revelations, in what message will they believe?

⁷ Woe to every sinful liar! ⁸ He hears God's revelations being

recited to him, yet persists in his arrogance as if he had never heard them. Forewarn him of a painful punishment. [9] When he learns something of Our revelations, he derides them: for such there will be humiliating torment. [10] In front of them is Hell; and of no profit to them is anything they may have earned, nor any protectors they may have taken to themselves besides God: for them there shall be a terrible punishment. [11] Such is Our guidance; those who reject their Lord's revelations shall suffer a woeful punishment.

[12] It is God who has subjected the sea to you so that you may sail thereon by His command, and so that you may seek His bounty, and so that you may be grateful. [13] He has subjected whatever is in heaven and on the earth to you; it is all from Him. In that are signs for those who ponder.

[14] Tell the believers to ignore those who do not believe in the coming of the days of God. He will requite people for what they have done. [15] Whoever does what is just and right, does so for his own good; and whoever does evil, does so to his own detriment, and you shall all return to your Lord.

[16] We gave Scriptures, wisdom and prophethood to the Children of Israel, and provided them with good things and favoured them over all other people. [17] We gave them clear arguments in matters [of religion]. It was only after knowledge came to them that they differed among themselves out of mutual rivalry. On the Day of Resurrection your Lord will judge between them regarding their differences. [18] Then We set you on a clear path [of religion]: so follow it, and do not yield to the desires of those who have no knowledge. [19] They can be of no avail to you against God. The wrongdoers are friends of one another, while the friend of the righteous is God. [20] This [Book] brings enlightenment and guidance to mankind, and is a blessing for those who have firm faith.

[21] Do those who commit evil deeds imagine that We shall deal with them in the same way as We deal with those who have attained to faith and do righteous deeds, that they will be alike in their living and their dying? How badly they judge! [22] God has created the heavens and the earth for a true purpose, so that every soul may be rewarded for whatever it has earned, and no one will be wronged.

²³ [Prophet], consider the one who has taken his own desire as a deity, whom God allows to stray in the face of knowledge, sealing his ears and heart and covering his eyes—who can guide such a person after God [has abandoned him]? Will you not take heed?

²⁴ They say, 'There is nothing but our life in this world: we die, we live, nothing but time destroys us.' They have no knowledge

of this; they only follow conjecture. ²⁵ Whenever Our clear revelations are recited to them, their only argument is to say, 'Bring back to us our forefathers, if what you say be true.' ²⁶ Say, 'God gives you life, then causes you to die, and then will gather you together for the Day of Resurrection, about which there is no doubt. But most people do not know it.'

²⁷ To God belongs the kingdom of the heavens and the earth; on the Day when the Hour comes, those who follow falsehood will be the losers. ²⁸ You will see every people on their knees, every people shall be summoned to its Record [and a voice will say], 'Today you will be requited for your deeds. ²⁹ This record of ours will declare the truth about you: We have been recording whatever you have been doing.'

³⁰ Those who believed and did good deeds will be admitted by their Lord into His mercy—that shall be the manifest triumph. ³¹ But those who rejected the truth [will be asked], 'When My revelations were recited to you, were you not arrogant and did you not persist in wicked deeds? ³² When it was said to you, "God's promise is true: there is no doubt about the Hour," did you not reply, "We do not know what the Hour is. We think it to be nothing but a conjecture, and we are not convinced"?'

³³ The evil of their actions will then become clear to them. The punishment they mocked will engulf them. ³⁴ It will be said to them, 'This Day We shall forget you, as you yourselves forgot that you would meet this Day. Your abode shall be the Fire,

and you shall have no helpers. ³⁵ That is because you made a mockery of God's revelations and were deluded by the life of this world.' Therefore, today they will not be brought out of the Fire, nor will they be allowed to make amends.

³⁶ Praise, then, be to God, Lord of the heavens, and Lord of the

earth, the Lord of all the worlds. ³⁷All greatness belongs to Him in the heavens and earth. He is the Almighty, the All Wise.

46. THE SAND DUNES (*AL-AHQAF*)

In the name of God, the Most Gracious, the Most Merciful

¹ *Ha Mim*.

² This Book is sent down from God, the Almighty, the Wise One. ³ We created the heavens and the earth and all that lies between them purely for just ends, and for a specific term, but those who reject Faith turn away from what they have been warned of.

⁴ Say, 'Have you thought about those you call upon apart from God? Show me what they have created on the earth. Or do they have a share in the heavens? Bring me a Book revealed before this or some other vestige of knowledge, if you are telling the truth.' ⁵ And who is more misguided than one who invokes, besides God, such as will not answer him until the Day of Resurrection, and who [in fact] are not even aware of his call, ⁶ and when mankind are gathered together, they will become their enemies, and will deny their worship?

⁷ And whenever Our clear revelations are recited to them and the Truth is brought to them, those who deny the truth say, 'This is plain magic.' ⁸ Do they mean to say that the Messenger himself has fabricated it? Say [O Muhammad], 'If I have fabricated it myself, you will not be able to do anything to save me from God. He knows quite well what talk you indulge in. He is enough as a witness between me and you; and He is the Forgiving, the Merciful One.'

⁹ Say, 'I am not the first of God's messengers, and I do not know what will be done with me or with you: I do not follow anything but what is revealed to me, and I am merely a plain warner.' ¹⁰ Say, 'Have you thought: what if this Quran really is from God and you reject it? What if one of the Children of Israel testifies to its similarity to earlier scripture and believes in it, and yet you are too arrogant to do the same? God certainly does not guide evil-doers.'

¹¹ Those who deny the truth say of the believers, 'If there were any good in this Quran, they would not have believed in it before we did.' And since they refuse to be guided by it, they say, 'This is an ancient fabrication.'

¹² Yet the scripture of Moses was revealed before it as a guide and a blessing; and this is a Book in the Arabic language, fulfilling [previous prophecies], to forewarn those who do evil and to bring good news to those who do good. ¹³ Surely those who say, 'Our Lord is God,' and remain firm [on that path] shall feel no fear, nor shall they grieve: ¹⁴ it is they who are the people of Paradise, they shall abide therein as a reward for all that they have done.

¹⁵ We have enjoined on man kindness to his parents: his mother bore him, in pain and in pain she gave birth to him, and his bearing and weaning takes thirty months. At length, when he reaches the age of full maturity and attains forty years, he says, 'O my Lord! Help me to be grateful for Your favours which You have bestowed upon me, and upon both my parents, and to do good deeds that will please You. Grant me righteousness in my offspring. Truly, I have turned to You and, truly, I submit to You.'ᵃ ¹⁶ We accept from such people the best of what they do and We overlook their bad deeds. They will be among the people of Paradise—this is a true promise that has been given to them.

¹⁷ But he who says to his parents, 'Shame upon you! Do you threaten me with being taken out of the grave after death while many a generation has passed away before me and none has risen from

---

a Human procreation takes place through a father and a mother who nurture their offspring through infancy to adulthood. This is, so to say, the natural system of man's training, which ensures that he develops a keen consciousness of rights and duties along with the feeling that he must acknowledge the grace of his Benefactor and discharge his duties towards Him. This feeling teaches a man two things: firstly, to honour his pledges towards other men and, secondly, to fulfil important obligations to God, the Creator and Lord.

Those who learn a lesson from Nature, the great teacher, who activate their sense of moral awareness to the extent that they properly identify and appropriately fulfil their duties towards all, ranging from their parents right up to God, are the ones who will be treated as deserving of the eternal Grace of God in the Hereafter.

among them?' The parents both cry for God's help and say to him, 'Believe! Alas for you! God's promise is true.' But he says, 'These are nothing but ancient fables.' ¹⁸ It is against such as these that the word of God has proved true, along with all the communities that went before them, jinns and humans: surely they are losers.

¹⁹ All will be ranked according to their deeds. We will requite them in full for their actions and they will not be wronged. ²⁰ On the Day when those who deny the truth are brought before the Fire, it will be said to them, 'You have had the good things of the life of this world, and you enjoyed them. Now this Day you shall be requited with humiliating punishment, because you were arrogant in the land without justification, and because you acted rebelliously.'

²¹ Tell of the brother of 'Ad; when he warned his people in the sand dunes—and indeed warners came and went before him and after him—saying, 'Worship none but God; surely I fear for you the punishment of an awful Day,' ²² but they said, 'Have you come to us to turn us away from our deities? Then bring down upon us what you threaten us with, if you are truthful.' ²³ He said, 'God alone knows when it will come, and I deliver to you the message with which I am sent, but I see you are a people who are ignorant.'

²⁴ So, when they saw it in the shape of a dense cloud approaching their valleys, they exclaimed, 'This is only a heavy cloud which will bring us [welcome] rain!' [But Hud said]: 'By no means! It is the very thing which you sought to hasten—a wind bearing grievous suffering ²⁵ which will destroy everything at its Lord's behest!' And in the morning there was nothing left to be seen save their [empty] dwellings: thus We repay the evil-doers.

²⁶ We had empowered them to an extent which We have not empowered you, [O people of later times]; and We had endowed them with hearing, and sight, and hearts: but neither their hearing, nor their sight, nor their hearts were of the least avail to them, since they went on rejecting God's revelations; and they were overwhelmed by the very thing which they had been wont to deride. ²⁷ We have also destroyed other towns that once [flourished] around you—We had given them various signs so that they might return [to the right path]—²⁸ so why did their gods not help them, those they set up as

gods besides God to bring them nearer to Him? No indeed! They failed them utterly: it was all a lie, a fabrication of their own making.

²⁹ Remember how We sent to you a band of jinn who wished to hear the Quran and as they listened to its recitation, they said to one another, 'Be silent and listen,' and, then when it was finished, they went back to their people, to give them warning.*ᵃ* ³⁰ They said, 'O our people, we have heard a Book, which has been sent down after Moses, fulfilling the predictions existing in previous scriptures; it guides to the truth, and to the right path. ³¹ Our people, respond to the one who calls you to God. Believe in him! God will forgive you your sins and protect you from a painful punishment. ³² But he who does not respond to God's calls can never elude [Him] on earth, nor can he have any protector against Him. Such people have clearly gone far astray.'

³³ Have they not seen that God, who created the heavens and the earth and was not wearied by their creation, has the power to bring the dead back to life? Yes, indeed, He has power over all things. ³⁴ On the Day when those who deny the truth will be brought before the Fire, they shall be asked, 'Is this not the truth?' They will reply, 'Yes, by our Lord.' He will say, 'Then taste the punishment, because of your denial of the truth.'

³⁵ Have patience, then, as had the steadfast Messengers before you; and be in no haste about them. On the Day when they see what they are threatened with, it will appear to them as though they had not tarried longer than an hour of a day. [Your responsibility is] to deliver the message: and none but the disobedient shall be destroyed.

---

a In the tenth year of Muhammad's prophethood in Makkah, the life and work of the Prophet were becoming seriously jeopardized. At that time he went from Makkah to Taif in the hope that he might find some supporters there. But the people there received him rudely. While returning, he stayed at a place called Nakhla to spend the night. Here he was reciting the Quran while offering prayers, when a group of jinn heard the Quran and became believers in it. One group rejected the Quran. But, at that very moment, another group accepted it and did so with such eagerness that it became its missionary.

47. MUHAMMAD

In the name of God, the Most Gracious, the Most Merciful

¹ God will bring to naught all the good deeds of those who are bent on denying the truth and bar [others] from the path of God. ² As for those who believe and do good deeds and believe in what has been revealed to Muhammad—and it is the truth from their Lord—God will remove their sins from them and set their condition right. ³ That is because the ones who deny the truth follow falsehood, while those who believe follow the Truth from their Lord. Thus God sets forth comparisons for mankind.

⁴ When you meet those who deny the truth in battle, strike them in the neck,ᵃ and once they are defeated, make [them] prisoners, and afterwards either set them free as an act of grace, or let them ransom [themselves] until the war is finally over. Thus you shall do; and if God had pleased, He would certainly have exacted retribution from them, but His purpose is to test some of you by means of others. As for those who are killed in God's cause, He will never let their deeds be in vain; ⁵ He will guide them and improve their condition; ⁶ He will admit them into the Garden He has already made known to them.

⁷ Believers! If you succour God, He will succour you and make your footsteps firm. ⁸ But as for those who are bent on denying the truth, destruction will be their lot, and [God] will make their deeds come to nothing. ⁹ It is because they are averse to what God has revealed that He has rendered their deeds futile. ¹⁰ Have they not travelled the earth and seen how those before them met their end? God destroyed them utterly: a similar fate awaits those who deny the truth. ¹¹ That is because God is the protector of the believers, and those who deny the truth have no protector at all.

¹² God will admit those who believe and do good deeds to Gardens through which rivers flow. Those who deny the truth may take their fill of pleasure in this world, and eat as cattle do, but the Fire will

---

ᵃ See note to 2:191.

be their ultimate abode. ¹³ How many towns We have destroyed, greater in strength than your city which has driven you out, and there was no one to help them.

¹⁴ Can then he who takes his stand on clear evidence from his God be likened to those for whom the evil that they do is made to look beautiful, and who follow their own desires? ¹⁵ Here is a description of the Garden promised to the righteous: therein are rivers of water which is forever pure; and rivers of milk of which the taste never changes; and rivers of wine, a delight to those who drink it, and rivers of pure honey. And in it they will have all kinds of fruit, and will receive forgiveness from their Lord. Can those who enjoy such bliss be like those who abide in the Fire and who are given boiling water to drink so that it tears their bowels?

¹⁶ Among them are those who listen to you, but then, when they leave your presence, say to those who have been given knowledge [Scripture], "What was that he just said?" Such are those whose hearts God has sealed, and who follow their own base desires. ¹⁷ But as for those who follow guidance, He adds to their guidance, and shows them the way to righteousness.

¹⁸ Are they awaiting the Hour of Doom to come upon them suddenly? Its signs have already come. But of what avail will their admonition be to them when it has actually come upon them? ¹⁹ Know then that there is no god except God. Ask forgiveness for your wrongdoing, and for the men and women who believe. God knows both your movements and your lodging.

²⁰ Those who believe ask why no chapter [about fighting] has been sent down. Yet when a decisive chapter that mentions fighting is sent down, you can see the sick of heart looking at you [Prophet] as if they were under the shadow of death. Therefore, woe to them! ²¹ Obedience and saying what is just would become them more; when the decision is taken, it would be better for them if they acted sincerely towards God. ²² Then if you turn away, you are likely to spread corruption on the earth and sever your ties of kinship. ²³ Such are those whom God has rejected, making their ears deaf and their eyes blind.

²⁴ Will they not, then, ponder over this Quran? Or are there locks

upon their hearts? ²⁵ Surely, those who turn their backs [on this message] after guidance has been shown to them, [do it because] Satan has embellished their fancies and God gives them respite; ²⁶ because they say to those who abhor what God has revealed, 'We will obey you in some matters.' God knows their secrets. ²⁷ Then how will it be when the angels take their souls, beating them on their faces and their backs, ²⁸ because they followed the way that made God wrathful, and hated to adopt the way of His pleasure? So He made their actions come to nothing.

²⁹ Do the sick at heart imagine that God will not bring to light their malice? ³⁰ Now had We so willed, We could have shown them clearly to you, and then you could have identified them by their marks, but surely you will know them by the tone of their speech! God knows all that you do.

³¹ Most certainly We will try you until We have discovered those among you who strive their hardest, and those who are steadfast, and will test your record. ³² Surely, they who are bent on denying the truth and on barring [others] from the path of God, and oppose the Messenger when they have been shown guidance, cannot harm God in any way. He will cause all their deeds to come to nothing.

³³ Believers, obey God and obey the Messenger: do not let your deeds go to waste—³⁴ surely those who reject the truth and bar others from the path of God, then die as deniers of the truth, will not be granted forgiveness by God. ³⁵ So do not lose heart or appeal for peace when you have gained the upper hand. God is with you and will never let your works go to waste.

³⁶ The life of this world is only a game, a pastime, but if you believe and are mindful of God, He will recompense you and will not ask you for your wealth. ³⁷ If He were to ask it [wealth] of you, and continued to press you, you would be niggardly, and this would show your ill-will. ³⁸ Behold! You are those who are called upon to spend for God's cause, but among you are those who are niggardly, and whoever stints does so against his own self. Indeed, God is self-sufficient, but you stand in need [of Him], and if you turn back, He will bring in your place another people, who will not be like you.

48. VICTORY (*AL-FATH*)

In the name of God, the Most Gracious, the Most Merciful

¹ Truly, We have granted you a clear victory ² so that God may forgive you your past and future sins and complete His favour to you and guide you to a straight path, ³ and so that God might bestow on you His mighty help.

⁴ It was He who sent down tranquillity into the hearts of the believers, to add faith to their faith—the forces of the heavens and earth belong to Him; He is all knowing and all wise—⁵ and so that He might admit the believers, men and women, into Gardens through which rivers flow, to dwell therein forever, and so that He may remove their evils from them—that is, indeed, a supreme triumph in God's eyes—⁶ and so that He might punish hypocritical men and women as well as the polytheists men and women who think evil thoughts about God; an evil turn of fortune will fall upon them, for God has become angry with them, and has rejected them and prepared Hell for them. How evil is such a destination. ⁷ The forces of heavens and earth belong to God; He is almighty and all wise.

⁸ We have sent you forth as a witness*a* and a bearer of good tidings and a warner, ⁹ so that you may believe in God and His Messenger, and may help him, and honour him, and so that you may glorify God morning and evening. ¹⁰ Behold, all who pledge their allegiance to you indeed pledge their allegiance to God: the hand of God is over

---

a The real work of the Prophet is to be an exponent of the truth ('shahid ', as translated by Shah Waliullah). He should clearly show who will be entitled to God's Grace and who will deserve punishment from God in the eternal life after death.

The rising of such a 'shahid ' or witness of Truth poses the greatest trial for his addressees. They have to hear God's voice in the voice of a human being. They have to see a representative of God in the shape of human being. While giving their hand into the hands of a man, they have to think that they are giving their hand into the hands of God. For those who prove to have this superior insight, God has great rewards in store, but to those who fail in this test, God will mete out the most severe punishment.

their hands. Hence, he who breaks his oath, breaks it only to his own loss. Whereas he who remains true to what he has pledged to God, shall have a great reward bestowed upon him by God.

¹¹ Those desert Arabs who remained behind will say to you, 'Our belongings and our families kept us occupied, so ask forgiveness for us.' They will say with their tongues what is not in their hearts. Say, 'Who then has any power at all [to intervene] on your behalf with God, if His will is to do you harm, or if He intends to do you good? Indeed, God is well aware of all that you do.' ¹² No. You thought that the Messenger and the believers would never return to their families; this prospect seemed pleasing to your hearts, and you conceived evil thoughts, and thus were doomed to perish. ¹³ For those who deny the truth, who do not believe in God and His Messenger, We have prepared a blazing Fire. ¹⁴ To God belongs the kingdom of the heavens and the earth. He forgives whom He pleases, and punishes whom He pleases. And God is most forgiving and merciful.

¹⁵ When you [believers] set off to gather the spoils, those that stayed behind will say, 'Let us come with you.' They want to change God's word, but tell them, 'You shall not follow us. God has declared this beforehand.' Then they will say, 'You are jealous of us.' But how little they understand!

¹⁶ Say to the desert Arabs who stayed behind, 'You shall be called against a mighty people; then shall you fight, unless they submit.*ᵃ* Then if you prove obedient, God will grant you a good reward, but if You turn back as you did before, He will inflict on you a painful punishment—¹⁷ the blind, the lame, and the sick will not be blamed.' God will admit anyone who obeys Him and His Messenger to Gardens through which rivers flow. But whoever turns back shall be severely punished by Him.

¹⁸ God was pleased with the believers when they swore allegiance to you [Prophet] under the tree: He knew what was in their hearts and so He sent tranquillity down to them and rewarded them with a victory near at hand ¹⁹ and with many future gains—God is mighty

---

a See note to 2:191.

and wise. ²⁰ God has promised you many future gains, and He has given you these in advance; and He has restrained the hands of men from harming you, so that it may be a sign for the believers, and so that He may guide you to a straight path. ²¹ And there are yet other [gains] which are still beyond your grasp, [but] which God has already encompassed [for you]: for God has power over all things.

²² If those who deny the truth were to fight you, they would certainly turn their backs; then they would find neither protector nor helper: ²³ such was the law of God in the past; and you shall find no change in the law of God. ²⁴ It is He who withheld their hands from you, and your hands from them in the valley of Makkah, after giving you victory over them. God sees what you do.

²⁵ It was they who were bent on denying the truth, and who debarred you from the Sacred Mosque and who prevented your offering from reaching its place of sacrifice. And had it not been for the believing men and believing women [in Makkah] whom you might unwittingly have trampled underfoot, and on whose account you might have, unknowingly, become guilty, [God would have commanded you to fight it out with them; but He ordained it thus] so that He may bring whoever He will into His mercy. If they [the believers] had been clearly separated, We would have punished those who were bent on denying the truth with a painful punishment.

²⁶ While those who deny the truth made it a prestige issue [in their hearts]—the bigotry of the days of ignorance—God sent His tranquillity down on to His Messenger and believers and firmly established in them the principle of righteousness, for they were indeed better entitled to it and more worthy of it. God has full knowledge of all things.

²⁷ God has in all truth shown His Messenger a true vision in which He said, 'God willing, you will most certainly enter the Sacred Mosque in safety and without fear, shaven-headed or with hair cut short'—God knew what you did not; and has given you a victory beforehand.

²⁸ He is the One who has sent His Messenger with guidance and the true religion, so that He may have it prevail over all [other] religions. God suffices as a witness!

[29] Muhammad is the Messenger of God.[a] Those who are with him are firm and unyielding towards those who deny the truth, but compassionate towards one another. You see them bowing and prostrating themselves, seeking the grace of God and His good will. Their marks are on their faces, the traces of their prostrations; they are described in the Torah and in the Gospel as being like a seed which sends forth its shoot, then makes it strong; it then becomes thick, and it stands firm on its own stem, delighting the sowers. He seeks to enrage the disbelievers through them. God has promised forgiveness and a great reward to those of them who believe and do good works.

49. THE APARTMENTS (*AL-HUJURAT*)

In the name of God, the Most Gracious, the Most Merciful

[1] Believers, do not push yourselves forward in the presence of God and His Messenger. Fear God—God hears all and knows all.

[2] Believers, do not raise your voices above the voice of the Prophet, and do not speak as loudly when speaking to him as you do when speaking to one another, lest your actions come to nothing without your realizing it. [3] Those who lower their voices in the presence of God's Messenger are men whose hearts God has tested for piety— they shall have forgiveness and a great reward—[4] those who call out to you from outside your apartments are lacking in understanding.

---

[a] The Prophet Muhammad had to perform a historic role which is referred to in the Quran as making religion predominant. For this he needed a group of men of high calibre. Such men were available to him thanks to Ishmael, their progenitor, having been settled in the Arabian desert two thousand five hundred years before. With such ancestry it was the most vibrant group of history. When their full potential was tapped, thanks to Quranic instruction, the Arabs, according to Prof. Margoliath 'turned into a nation of heroes.' The importance of this group was so great in the eyes of God that He informed the prophets about them in advance. In the Torah their individual qualities were mentioned while, in the Bible, their collective qualities were emphasized.

⁵ If they waited patiently until you came out to see them, it would be better for them. But God is forgiving and merciful.

⁶ Believers, if an evil-doer brings you news, ascertain the correctness of the report fully, lest you unwittingly harm others, and then regret what you have done,⁷ and know that the Messenger of God is among you. If he were to obey you in many things, you would suffer for it. However, God has endeared the faith to you, and beautified it in your hearts, and has made denial of the truth, wickedness, and disobedience hateful to you. People such as these are rightly guided ⁸ through God's bounty and favour; God is all knowing, and wise.

⁹ If two parties of believers fight against each other, make peace between them; then if after that one of them transgresses against the other, fight the party that transgresses until it submits to the command of God. Then if it complies, make peace between them with equity, and act justly. Truly, God loves the just. ¹⁰ Surely all believers are brothers. So make peace between your brothers, and fear God, so that mercy may be shown to you.

¹¹ Believers, let not some men among you ridicule others: it may be that the latter are better than the former: nor should some women laugh at others: it may be that the latter are better than the former: do not defame or be sarcastic to each other, or call each other by [offensive] nicknames. How bad it is to earn an evil reputation after accepting the faith! Those who do not repent are evil-doers.*a*

---

a From birth, there is hidden in every man an instinct to be 'great'. That is why, if a man finds some weakness in another man, he makes a point of highlighting it, so that in this way he may prove himself to be great and the other small. He ridicules the other person, finds fault with him and calls him by insulting nicknames, in order to satisfy his instinct for self-aggrandisement.

But the criterion of goodness or badness is not that which an individual himself decides upon. One is really good who is good in the eyes of God and one is bad if he is adjudged bad in the eyes of God. If a man really develops these feelings in himself, he will lose the desire to be known as 'great'. Ridiculing others, finding fault with others, giving nicknames to others will all become meaningless to him, because he will come to know that a man's true status and position are actually going to be determined by God. He will then ponder over the fact that if he considers anyone as small in this world and if later, in the real world of Hereafter, he [the latter] is treated as worthy of respect, his way of

¹² Believers, avoid much suspicion. Indeed some suspicion is a sin. And do not spy on one another and do not backbite. Would any of you like to eat his dead brother's flesh? No, you would hate it. Fear God, God is ever forgiving and most merciful.

¹³ Mankind! We have created you from a male and female, and made you into peoples and tribes, so that you might come to know each other. The noblest of you in God's sight is the one who fears God most. God is all knowing and all-aware.

¹⁴ The Arabs of the desert say, 'We have believed.' Say to them, 'You have not believed yet; say rather, "We have submitted," for faith has not yet entered into your hearts. But if you will obey God and His Messenger, He will not detract anything from your good deeds. God is most forgiving and ever merciful.' ¹⁵ The believers are only those who have faith in God and His Messenger and then doubt not, but strive, hard with their wealth and their persons for the cause of God. Such are the truthful ones.

¹⁶ Say, 'Do you presume to teach God your religion when God knows everything in the heavens and earth? God has knowledge of all things.' ¹⁷ They think they have done you a favour by becoming Muslims! Say, 'Do not consider your Islam a favour to me. No indeed! It is God who bestowed a favour on you by guiding you to the true faith. [Admit this], if you are telling the truth.' ¹⁸ God knows the unseen things of the heavens and the earth. God sees all that you do.

50. QAF

In the name of God, the Most Gracious, the Most Merciful

¹ *Qaf*

By the glorious Quran! ² Indeed, they are astonished that a warner should have come to them from among themselves. So these deniers of the truth say, 'This is indeed a strange thing, ³ to come back to

---

thinking will be absolutely meaningless.

life after we have died and become dust? That is most improbable!'
⁴ We know very well what the earth takes away from them: We hold a book which records all things. ⁵ But they denied the truth when it came to them, so they are in a state of confusion.

⁶ Have they not observed the sky above them and marked how We have built it and adorned it, leaving no flaws in it; ⁷ We spread out the earth and set upon it solid mountains and We brought forth from it all kinds of delightful plants, ⁸ as a lesson and reminder for every human being who turns to God; ⁹ and We have sent down from the sky blessed water with which We have brought forth gardens and grain to be harvested, ¹⁰ and tall palm-trees with their thickly-clustered dates, ¹¹ as a provision for human beings; and by [all] this We bring dead land to life. Such shall be the Resurrection.*a*

¹² Before them, the people of Noah and the people of Rass denied this truth; and so did the people of Thamud. ¹³ And the tribe of 'Ad, and Pharaoh, and the brethren of Lot, ¹⁴ and the dwellers of the Wood, and the people of Tubba': every one denied their messengers, and so My warning came true. ¹⁵ Were We then worn out by the first creation? Yet they are in doubt about a second creation.

¹⁶ We created man—We know the promptings of his soul, and are closer to him than his jugular vein—¹⁷ and the two recording angels are recording, sitting on the right and the left: ¹⁸ each word he utters shall be noted down by a vigilant guardian.*b*

---

a The meaningfulness of the universe, its creative wisdom, its being free of shortcomings, and its being consistent with human needs compel every thinking and rational man to accept the sublimity of creation, and one who gives serious consideration to the system of the universe, will find the Creator in His creations. He will see a glimpse of the other world (the Hereafter) in this world, because, in fact, the world of the Hereafter is essentially another, more superior form of the present world.

b The study of this world shows that there is an unerring system of 'recording' in operation here. Man's thoughts are impressed on the membrane of his brain. Every utterance a man makes is permanently preserved in the shape of sound waves in the air. Man's actions are preserved in the external world by means of heat waves in such a way that they can be repeated at any time. All these are known facts of today, and these known facts are what make the Quran's claim credible that man's intentions, his utterances and his actions,

¹⁹ The trance of death will come revealing the truth: that is what you were trying to escape. ²⁰ The trumpet will be sounded. This is the Day [you were] warned of. ²¹ Each person will arrive attended by an [angel] to drive him on and another to bear witness. ²² You were heedless of this, but now We have removed your veil, so your sight today is sharp. ²³ His companion attendant will say, 'I have here his record ready.' ²⁴ 'Cast into Hell every ungrateful, rebellious one, ²⁵ hinderer of good, transgressor, causing others to doubt, ²⁶ who has set up another god besides God: cast him into severe punishment'—²⁷ and his associate [Satan] will say, 'Lord, I did not make him transgress, he had already gone far astray himself.' ²⁸ God will say, 'Do not quarrel in My presence. I gave you the warning beforehand ²⁹ and My word shall not be changed, nor am I unjust to My servants.'

³⁰ On that Day, We shall ask Hell, 'Are you now full?' Hell will answer, 'Are there any more?' ³¹ Paradise will be brought near to the righteous and will no longer be far away. ³² This is what you were promised—this is for everyone who often turned to God and kept Him in mind, ³³ who fears the Compassionate One, though He is unseen, and comes to Him with a penitent heart; ³⁴ so enter it in peace. This is the Day of everlasting life. ³⁵ There they shall have all that they desire, and there is even more with Us.

³⁶ How many a generation, far greater in prowess, have We destroyed before them! They searched the entire land: but could they find a refuge? ³⁷ There is truly a reminder in this for whoever has a heart, whoever listens attentively.

³⁸ We created the heavens, the earth, and everything between them in six days [periods] nor were We ever wearied. ³⁹ So bear with patience what they say, and glorify your Lord with His praise, before the rising and before the setting of the sun; ⁴⁰ proclaim His praise in the night and at the end of every prayer.*ᵃ*

---

are all in the knowledge of his Creator. All affairs of all human beings are entered in the registers of the angels.

a The creation of the heavens and the earth in six days, in other words in six stages, indicates that God's method of doing things is a gradual one. When

⁴¹ Hearken! The Day when the caller will call from near. ⁴² The Day when men will hear the fateful cry, they will rise up [from their graves]. ⁴³ Truly, it is We who give life and cause death, and to Us shall all return ⁴⁴ on the Day the earth will be rent asunder over them, and from it they shall emerge in haste. To assemble them all is easy enough for Us.

⁴⁵ We know best what those who deny the truth say. You are not there to force them: so remind, with this Quran, those who fear My warning.

51. SCATTERING WINDS (*AL-DHARIYAT*)

In the name of God, the Most Gracious, the Most Merciful

¹ By the winds that scatter the dust, ² and those that bear the burden [of the rain], ³ and those speeding along with ease, ⁴ and distributing the command of God at His behest!*a* ⁵ What you are promised is certainly true: ⁶ the Judgement will surely come to pass—⁷ by the heaven full of tracks, ⁸ surely you are deeply at variance [as to what to believe]— ⁹ he is turned away from [the truth] who is destined to be so turned away.

¹⁰ May the conjecturers perish, ¹¹ who flounder in the depths of ignorance. ¹² They ask, 'When will the Day of Judgement come?'

God, in spite of being the possessor of all Powers, brings things into existence gradually on a long-term basis, man should also desist from making undue haste, but rather try to reach his goals through action marked by patience.

Preaching, from beginning to end, is an act of patience. In this process one has to put up with the bitterness evinced by others, and persevere in one's task in spite of there being no favourable results in sight. This patience-trying process can be pursued only by one whose days and nights are spent in remembrance of God, who reposes all hope not in human beings but in God and who does not fall a prey to a feeling of frustration, in spite of having lost everything.

a There are countless stars in the sky. All of them are revolving in their respective orbits. If a collective picture is drawn of these, it will resemble a network. This wonderful system indicates a deep, inherent meaningfulness. Those who exercise their mental powers will find a lesson in it. But for those who do not, it will be a meaningless charade.

[13] It will be the Day when they are tormented at the Fire. [14] 'Taste your trial. This is what you sought to hasten.' [15] Surely the God-fearing will find themselves in the midst of gardens and springs. [16] They shall receive what their Lord will bestow on them. They have done good works in the past, [17] sleeping little in the night-time, [18] praying at dawn for God's pardon, [19] and sharing their possessions with the beggars and the deprived.

[20] On the earth, and in yourselves, [21] there are signs for firm believers. Do you not see then? [22] In heaven is your sustenance, and also that which you are promised. [23] By the Lord of the heaven and the earth, it is certainly the truth. It is as true as your ability to speak.

[24] Have you heard the story of Abraham's honoured guests? [25] When they came to him they said, 'Peace!' He answered, 'Peace!' [saying to himself]. 'They are strangers.' [26] Then he turned quickly to his household, and brought a fatted calf, [27] and placed it before them. 'Will you not eat?' he said, [28] beginning to be afraid of them. But they said, 'Don't be afraid'; and they gave him the good news of a son who would be endowed with knowledge. [29] Then his wife came forward, crying and beating her brow. She said, 'I am surely a barren, old woman.' [30] 'Such is the will of your Lord,' they replied. 'He is the Wise, the All Knowing.'

[31] Abraham asked, 'What is your errand, O messengers?' [32] They replied, 'We have been sent to a sinful people, [33] so that we may bring down upon them a shower of stones of clay, [34] which are marked by your Lord for the punishment of those guilty of excesses.' [35] We saved all the faithful in the town. [36] We found in it only one household of true believers—[37] and We left therein a sign for those who fear a painful punishment.

[38] There is another sign in Moses: We sent him to Pharaoh with clear authority. [39] But he turned his back, he and his courtiers, and said, 'This is a sorcerer or a madman.' [40] Then We seized him and his army and cast them all into the sea: he himself [Pharaoh] was to blame. [41] There is another sign in the [tribe of] 'Ad; when We sent against them a life-destroying wind [42] and it destroyed everything over which it passed and reduced it to dust. [43] In the Thamud [there was another sign], when they were told, 'Make the most of your

lives for a while.' [44] But they rebelled against the command of their Lord. So the thunderbolt overtook them while they looked on: [45] they could not stand up again, nor could they defend themselves. [46] [We destroyed] the people of Noah before them. They were certainly a sinful people.

[47] We built the universe with Our might, giving it its vast expanse. [48] We have spread out the earth—how well We have spread it out— [49] and We created pairs of all things so that you might reflect. [50] Therefore hasten to God; truly, I am sent by Him to give you clear warning. [51] Do not set up another god, along with God. I come from Him to warn you plainly.

[52] Likewise, there came no messenger to those before them, but they said, 'He is a sorcerer or a madman.' [53] Have they handed this down to one another? They are certainly a people who exceed all bounds, [54] so ignore them—you are not to blame—[55] but keep on exhorting them, for exhortation benefits the believers.

[56] I created the jinn and mankind only so that they might worship Me:[a] [57] I seek no sustenance from them, nor do I want them to feed Me—[58] it is God who is the great Sustainer, the Mighty One, the Invincible. [59] The wrongdoers will meet the same fate as their predecessors—let them not ask Me to hasten on [the punishment]—[60] woe, then, to those who are bent on denying the truth, when the Day arrives which they have been promised.

---

[a] God Himself possesses all kinds of powers. However, He has created the angels to effect the administration of His vast domain. But, the case of human beings is different. Human beings were not created to fulfil any administrative or other need of God. The sole purpose of their creation was their devotion and servitude (*'ibadah*) to God. This implies bowing down without any reservation before God completely and dedicating oneself entirely to Him.

The substance of this devotion is deep inner realisation of God (*ma'rifah*) (*Tafsir ibn Kathir*). In other words, it is required of man that God should be a discovery for him. He should recognise God without seeing him. This is essential to *ma'rifah*. The shape which the life of a man takes as a result of this ma'rifah is one of devotion and subservience.

52. MOUNT SINAI (*AL-TUR*)

In the name of God, the Most Gracious, the Most Merciful

¹ By the Mount Sinai, ² and by the Scripture penned ³ on unrolled parchment, ⁴ by the much-visited House, ⁵ and by the lofty vault of the sky, ⁶ and by the swelling sea, ⁷ the punishment of your Lord shall certainly come to pass*ᵃ*— ⁸ there is no one who could avert it— ⁹ on the Day when the skies are convulsed, ¹⁰ and the mountains shudder and shake. ¹¹ Woe on that Day to those who deny the truth, ¹² who divert themselves with idle chatter: ¹³ on that Day they shall be ruthlessly thrust into the Fire of Hell. ¹⁴ This is the fire which you used to deny. ¹⁵ Is this magic or do you not see? ¹⁶ Now enter it. Whether you behave patiently or impatiently will make no difference: you are only being repaid for what you have done.*ᵇ*

¹⁷ Truly, the God-fearing will dwell [on that Day] in gardens and in bliss, ¹⁸ rejoicing in whatever their Lord has given them. Their Lord has saved them from the torment of the Fire, ¹⁹ 'Eat and drink with good cheer as a reward for your good deeds,' ²⁰ reclining on couches arranged in rows. And We shall wed them to fair maidens with large beautiful eyes.

²¹ To those who have attained to faith We shall unite their offspring who have also followed them in faith, and We shall not let any of

---

a Mount Tur is that mountain in the desert of Sinai where Moses was awarded prophethood. The Scripture penned on unrolled parchment or the written Book (*kitabun mastur*) here means the Torah. The much-visited House or the Kabah (*al-bayt al-ma'mur*) means the earth. The lofty vaults of the sky or high roof (*al-saqf al-marfu'*) means the sky. The swelling sea (*al-bahr al-masjur*) means a sea with waves. All these things bear testimony that the Day of seizure by God is certain to come. Almighty God has repeatedly given these very tidings through the prophets. This has also been mentioned in ancient holy scriptures. Heaven and earth announce this in their silent language. The waves of the sea relate this story to every listener.

b Man will have to face the result of his actions. This the prophecy of today. The negligence and arrogance of those who do not come to their senses now with the forewarning, will ultimately suffer grievous punishment. When they try to run away from this, they will find no refuge anywhere.

their good deeds go unrewarded; every human being is a pledge for whatever he has earned. [22] We shall provide them in abundance with such fruit and meat as they desire. [23] There, they shall pass from hand to hand a cup which does not lead to any idle talk or sin. [24] They will be waited upon by immortal youths, like pearls hidden in their shells. [25] They will converse with one another, putting questions to each other, [26] 'Before this, when we were among our families, we were full of fear of God's displeasure—[27] God has been gracious to us and has saved us from the torment of Hell's intense heat—[28] before this, we used to pray to Him. Surely, He is the Beneficent, the Merciful.'

[29] Therefore continue to give warning, for by the grace of your Lord, you are not a soothsayer or a madman. [30] If they say, 'He is but a poet; we are waiting for some misfortune to befall him,' [31] say [to them], ''Wait then: I too am waiting along with you!'— [32] is it their minds that prompt them [to say] this, or are they merely insolent people? [33] Or do they say, 'He has invented it himself'? Indeed, they are not willing to believe. [34] Let them produce a scripture like it, if what they say is true.

[35] Were they created out of nothing, or are they their own creators? [36] Did they create the heavens and the earth? No! They have no faith. [37] Do they own the treasures of your Lord, or have they been given charge of them? [38] Have they a ladder up to heaven by means of which they can overhear? Then let their listeners bring a clear proof. [39] Does God have daughters while you have sons?

[40] Or do you ask them for a reward, so that they are over-burdened by debt? [41] Do they possess knowledge of the unseen, so that they can write it down? [42] Do they want to hatch some plot? Those who deny the truth will be the victims of the plot. [43] Or have they a god other than God? Exalted be God over what they ascribe as partners [to Him]!

[44] If they should see a part of the heavens falling down, they would say, 'A mass of clouds,' [45] so leave them alone till they face the Day on which they will be struck dumb, [46] the Day when none of their scheming will be of the least avail to them, and they will receive

no succour. [47] Truly, for those who do wrong there is a punishment besides that, though most of them do not know it.

[48] So wait patiently for the Judgement of your Lord—you are certainly under Our watchful eye. And glorify and celebrate the praises of your Lord when you rise up [from your sleep]. [49] Extol His glory at night, and at the setting of the stars.

53. THE SETTING STAR (*AL-NAJM*)

In the name of God, the Most Gracious, the Most Merciful

[1] By the setting star, [2] your companion has neither strayed nor is he misguided, [3] nor does he speak out of his own desire. [4] It [the Quran] is nothing but revelation sent down to him. [5] He was taught by [an angel] who is mighty in power, [6] and endowed with wisdom; who in time manifested himself; [7] standing poised at the highest point on the horizon, [8] then came down close [9] until he was two bow-lengths away or even closer [10] and revealed to God's servant what he revealed. [11] The heart [of the Prophet] did not misconstrue what he saw. [12] Will you then dispute with him as to what he saw? [13] And certainly he saw him[a] descend a second time: [14] by the lote-tree of the farthest limit, beyond which none may pass [15] by the Garden of [Eternal] Repose, [16] when the lote tree was covered in mystic splendour. [17] His sight did not waver nor was it unduly bold. [18] He saw some of the greatest signs of his Lord.

[19] Have you really considered al-Lat and al-'Uzza, [20] and the third one, Manat?[b]—[21] 'What! For you the males and for Him the females?' [22] That indeed is an unfair division—[23] these are nothing but names which you yourselves have devised, you and your forefathers. God has sent down no authority for them. They follow nothing but conjecture and what their own selves desire, even though guidance has already come to them from their Lord! [24] Shall man

---

a Gabriel.
b Al-Lat, al-'Uzza and Manat were the deities of ancient Arabia.

have whatever he craves? ²⁵ But it is to God that the Hereafter and this world belong.

²⁶ There may be countless angels in heaven, but their intercession will be of no avail until God has given permission to those whom he chooses and accepts. ²⁷ Those who do not believe in the life to come call the angels by female names. ²⁸ They have no knowledge to base this on. They merely indulge in guess-work which can never replace the truth. ²⁹ So ignore those who turn away from Our revelation and seek nothing but the life of this world. ³⁰ That is the ultimate extent of their knowledge. Surely your Lord knows best those who stray from His path and He knows best those who follow His guidance.

³¹ Everything in the heavens and on the earth belongs to God and so He will requite those who do evil in accordance with their deeds and will reward those left with that which is best, for those who do good. ³² As for those who refrain from committing grave sins and indecent acts, though they may commit minor offences, your Lord is unstinting in His forgiveness.^{*a*} He knows you when He brings you out of the earth, and when you were embryos in the wombs of your mothers; so do not make claims to be pure. He knows best who is truly righteous.

³³ Have you [Prophet] considered the man who turned away, ³⁴ who at first gave a little, then later held back? ³⁵ Has he knowledge of the unseen, so that he sees? ³⁶ Has he not been made acquainted with what was written in the scriptures of Moses? ³⁷ And with Abraham who kept his word: ³⁸ that no soul shall bear the burden of another; ³⁹ and that man shall have only that for which he strives; ⁴⁰ and that [the fruit of] his striving shall soon be seen; ⁴¹ and in the end he will be repaid for it in full; ⁴² that all things in the end shall return to God;^{*b*} ⁴³ that it is He who brings laughter and tears; ⁴⁴ that it is

---

a Man has been created with human weaknesses. So, it is not required that he be as pure as the angels. Almighty God has given full guidance to man as to what he should do and what he should not. However, man may be pardoned in the case of lesser offences (*lamam*), i.e. indulging in some mischief because of fleeting emotion, on the condition that he should immediately realise his lapse and, being ashamed of it, seek pardon of his Lord.

b The sum and substance of the reality revealed by Almighty God through

He who causes death and gives life; [45] and that He Himself created the two sexes: male and female, [46] from an ejected drop of sperm; [47] and that He will bring about the Second Creation; [48] that it is He who gives wealth and possessions; [49] that He is the Lord of Sirius.[a]

[50] It was He who totally destroyed the former 'Ad [51] and Thamud tribes, [52] and before them the people of Noah who were even more unjust and insolent; [53] and He overthrew the subverted cities [of Sodom and Gomorrah] [54] and then covered them from sight forever. [55] On which then of your Lord's signs do you cast doubt?

[56] This is a warning just like those of former times. [57] The Hour that was to come draws ever nearer. [58] None but God can avert it. [59] Do you then find these tidings strange? [60] Why do you laugh rather than weep? [61] Will you remain proudly heedless? [62] Prostrate yourselves before God, and worship Him alone!

54. THE MOON (*AL-QAMAR*)

In the name of God, the Most Gracious, the Most Merciful

[1] The Last Hour draws near and the moon is split asunder. [2] Yet, when they see a sign they [who deny the truth] turn their backs and say, 'The same old sorcery!' [3] They deny the truth and follow their own whims—every matter has its appointed time—[4] there has come to them many a tiding wherein there are warnings, [5] profound in wisdom, but all warnings have been of no avail: [6] so ignore them. On the Day when the Crier will call out about a horrible event, [7] with downcast eyes they shall come out of their graves, as if they were locusts milling about [8] hastening towards the Crier. Those who deny the truth will cry, 'This is such a hard day!'

[9] The people of Noah denied [the truth] before them. They belied

---

His prophets is that every man has to receive the reward befitting his deeds. Nobody can save himself from the fate attending his deeds and nobody else can be his saviour. There is nobody more foolish in this world of God than those who are not affected by this prophetic warning.

a The Dog-Star, worshipped by the pagan Arabs.

Our messenger saying, 'He is mad!' He was rebuffed, [10] so he cried out to his Lord, saying, 'I am overcome, so help me!' [11] So We opened the gates of the sky with water pouring down in torrents, [12] and We caused the earth to burst with gushing springs: so that the waters met for a purpose which had been decreed. [13] We bore him on an [ark] which, made of planks and nails, [14] floated on under Our eyes: a vindication of him who had been rejected. [15] We have left this as a sign: but will anyone take heed? [16] How terrible then was My punishment and My warning. [17] We have made it easy to learn lessons from the Quran. Is there anyone who would receive admonition?

[18] The people of 'Ad too rejected the truth. How terrible was My punishment and My warning. [19] We sent a raging wind against them on a day of continuous calamity. [20] It swept people away as if they were trunks of uprooted palm trees. [21] How [dreadful] was My punishment and My warning! [22] We have made it easy to learn lessons from the Quran: is there anyone who would receive admonition?

[23] The tribe of Thamud also rejected Our warnings: [24] they said, 'Are we to follow a man from amongst ourselves? We would surely then fall into error and madness. [25] Has the [Divine] message been revealed to him alone of all of us? No, he is a boastful liar.' [26] [We said to him] 'Tomorrow they shall know who is the boastful liar, [27] for We are [going to] send the she-camel as a trial for them, so watch them and be patient. [28] And tell them that the water [of the well] is to be divided between them, and that each one should drink in turn.' [29] But they called their companion who took a sword and hamstrung her. [30] How [terrible] were My punishment and My warnings! [31] Then We sent a single blast against them and they became like dry stubble which has been trampled upon. [32] Indeed, We have made the Quran easy to learn lessons from. Is there anyone who would receive admonition?

[33] The people of Lot rejected Our warnings. [34] We sent a sandstorm against them which destroyed them all, except the family of Lot, whom We saved at the break of dawn, [35] as a blessing from Us: this is how We reward the thankful. [36] Lot warned them of Our punishment, but they disputed the warnings—[37] they even wanted

to seduce his guests—but We blinded them, and said, 'Taste My punishment now that you have scorned My warnings!'—[38] and early in the morning the punishment decreed overtook them—[39] 'Taste My punishment now that you have scorned My warnings!' [40] We have made it easy indeed to learn lessons from the Quran. Is there anyone who would receive admonition?

[41] Surely warners came to the people of Pharaoh. [42] They, too, rejected all Our signs. So We seized them with the seizure of One Mighty, Omnipotent.

[43] Are your people who deny the truth better than those? Or have you been given immunity in the Scriptures? [44] Or do they say, 'We are a united group, and we are bound to prevail'? [45] The hosts shall soon be routed and they shall be put to flight. [46] Indeed, the Hour of Doom is their appointed time, and the Last Hour will be the most severe, and the most bitter. [47] The evil-doers are indeed sunk in error and folly—[48] on the Day when they are dragged into the fire on their faces, it will be said to them, 'Now feel the touch of Hell!'

[49] We have created everything in due measure; [50] We command but once: Our will is done in the twinkling of an eye; [51] We have indeed destroyed many a people like you. Is there anyone who would receive admonition? [52] All their deeds are recorded in their books: [53] every action, small or great, is noted down. [54] The God-conscious will find themselves in gardens and rivers, [55] in the seat of truth with an all-powerful sovereign.[a]

---

a The present world is a world of trial. Here everybody has full freedom. So, in this world it is possible for a man to gain prominence, even if he lives a life of falsehood in order to obtain respect and status. But nothing of this sort will be possible in the Hereafter. In the Hereafter, the manifestation of the perfect authority of God will guarantee that standing on any ground except that of Truth will be of no avail to anybody.

55. THE MERCIFUL (*AL-RAHMAN*)

In the name of God, the Most Gracious, the Most Merciful

¹ The Merciful ² who taught the Quran—³ He created man ⁴ and He taught him speech. ⁵ The sun and the moon move according to a fixed reckoning; ⁶ the stars and the trees bend in prostration. ⁷ He raised the heavens and set up the measure, ⁸ so that you should not transgress the measure. ⁹ Always measure with justice and do not give short measure.*a*

¹⁰ He has laid out the earth for His creatures. ¹¹ On it are fruits and palm-trees with sheathed clusters [of dates], ¹² and grains with their husk and fragrant plants. ¹³ Which of your Lord's wonders would you deny? ¹⁴ He has created man, from dry ringing clay, like the potter's, ¹⁵ and He created the jinns from a flame of fire. ¹⁶ Which of your Lord's wonders would you deny? ¹⁷ He is the Lord of the two easts and the Lord of the two wests. ¹⁸ Which of your Lord's wonders would you deny? ¹⁹ He has set the two oceans in motion, converging together. ²⁰ Between them is a barrier, which they do not overrun. ²¹ Which of your Lord's wonders would you deny? ²² Pearls and corals come forth from both of them. ²³ Which of your Lord's wonders would you deny? ²⁴ His are the lofty ships, that rear aloft on the sea like mountains. ²⁵ Which of your Lord's wonders would you deny?

²⁶ All that is on the earth is doomed to perish, ²⁷ while your Lord's own Self will remain full of majesty and glory. ²⁸ Which of your

---

a Almighty God created human beings. He granted them the unique power of speech—a power not bestowed upon any other creature or anything else in the whole known universe. Then, there is the practical example of the role of justice and fair play which He wants human beings to fulfil in this world at His behest. The whole world surrounding the human being is based on this principle of balance and justice, which Almighty God wants human beings to follow; and this balance and justice are clearly set forth in the Quran. The Quran is the verbal expression of this Divine justice and the universe is its practical expression. It is imperative that the subjects of God weigh their words and deeds in this balance. They should not be unjust in either giving or taking.

Lord's wonders would you deny? [29] Everyone in the heavens and on the earth entreats Him. Every day He manifests Himself in a new state. [30] Which of your Lord's wonders would you deny?

[31] Soon We shall attend to you—two big groups [of jinn and mankind]. [32] Which of your Lord's wonders would you deny? [33] O company of jinn and men! If you have the power to go beyond the realms of the heavens and the earth, pass beyond them: you cannot pass out but with [Our] authority. [34] Which of your Lord's wonders would you deny? [35] Flames of fire and molten brass shall be sent against both of you, and you will not be able to defend yourselves. [36] Which of your Lord's wonders would you deny?[a]

[37] When the sky is rent asunder, and becomes red like red leather, [38] which of your Lord's wonders would you deny? [39] For, on that Day, neither man nor jinn will be questioned about his sins. [40] Which of your Lord's wonders would you deny? [41] The guilty shall be recognized by their marks so they shall be seized by their forelocks and their feet. [42] Which of your Lord's wonders would you deny? [43] This is the Hell which the guilty called a lie. [44] They will go round between its flames and boiling water. [45] Which of your Lord's wonders would you deny?

[46] There are two gardens for one who fears standing before his Lord. [47] Which of your Lord's wonders would you deny? [48] [There will be two gardens with] spreading branches. [49] Which of your Lord's wonders would you deny? [50] In both of them, there are two springs flowing. [51] Which of your Lord's wonders would you deny? [52] In both of them, there will be two kinds of every fruit. [53] Which of your Lord's wonders would you deny? [54] They will recline upon carpets lined with rich brocade; and the fruits of both these gardens will be within easy reach. [55] Which of your Lord's wonders would you deny? [56] Therein are maidens of modest gaze, whom neither

---

a The present world is a place of trial. So long as the period of testing lasts, everybody has the opportunity to be as arrogant as he pleases. But, in spite of this complete freedom, no jinn or human being has the power to go beyond the limits of the universe. This fact itself is enough to prove that man is completely in the grip of God. On the expiry of the test period, when He starts seizing hold of people, it will not be possible for anybody to save himself.

a man nor a jinn had ever touched before them. ⁵⁷ Which of your Lord's wonders would you deny? ⁵⁸ [There will be] maidens as fair as corals and rubies. ⁵⁹ Which of your Lord's wonders would you deny? ⁶⁰ The reward of goodness shall be nothing but goodness. ⁶¹ Which of your Lord's wonders would you deny?

⁶² Besides those two there shall be two other gardens. ⁶³ Which of your Lord's wonders would you deny? ⁶⁴ Both [gardens] of the darkest green. ⁶⁵ Which of your Lord's wonders would you deny? ⁶⁶ In both of them live springs gush forth. ⁶⁷ Which of your Lord's wonders would you deny? ⁶⁸ In both of them there will be fruit trees and date-palms and pomegranates. ⁶⁹ Which of your Lord's wonders would you deny? ⁷⁰ Therein will be maidens chaste and beautiful. ⁷¹ Which of your Lord's wonders would you deny? ⁷² [There the blessed will live with their] pure companions sheltered in pavilions. ⁷³ Which of your Lord's wonders would you deny? ⁷⁴ Whom neither a man or jinn had ever touched before them. ⁷⁵ Which of your Lord's wonders would you deny? ⁷⁶ [They will live in such a paradise] reclining upon green cushions and the finest carpets. ⁷⁷ Which of your Lord's wonders would you deny? ⁷⁸ Blessed be your Lord's name, full of glory and majesty!

56. THE INEVITABLE EVENT
(*AL-WAQI'AH*)

In the name of God, the Most Gracious, the Most Merciful

¹ When the inevitable event takes place, ² and there can be no denying its happening, ³ some shall be abased and others exalted. ⁴ When the earth is shaken violently, ⁵ and the mountains are totally shattered and crumble to pieces ⁶ and become like scattered dust particles, ⁷ [on that Day] you shall be divided into three groups.^a

---

a In the present world, man observes that he is free to do whatever he likes. So the question of retribution in the Hereafter makes no impact on his mind. But the formation of the 'other world' is just as possible as the formation of the present world. When that time comes, the whole system will be reversed. Those

8 Those on the Right—how blessed are those on the Right![a]
9 Those on the Left—how unlucky are those on the Left! 10 The third to the fore shall be the foremost. 11 They shall be the nearest to God. 12 They will dwell in the Gardens of Bliss: 13 a large group of the early believers, 14 and a lesser number from the later generations. 15 Seated on couches wrought in gold and encrusted with precious stones, 16 reclining on them facing each other; 17 they will be waited on by ageless youths 18 carrying goblets and ewers and cups filled with the purest wine, 19 neither causing headaches, nor intoxication; 20 along with fruits of their choice; 21 and the meat of any bird that they may desire; 22 and fair maidens with large, lustrous eyes 23 like the pearls in their shells: 24 shall be their recompense for their deeds. 25 They will not hear therein any vain or sinful talk, 26 only the words of peace and tranquillity.

27 Those on the Right, how fortunate are those on the Right![b] 28 They shall recline on high amidst lote trees without thorns 29 and clustered bananas, 30 and spreading shade 31 and flowing water, 32 and fruits in abundance, 33 never-ending and unrestricted, 34 on

---

people who were higher in position will go down and those who were lower in position will be seen up above. At that time human beings will be divided into three groups, forward group (*al-sabiqun*), people of the Right (*ashab al-yamin*) and people of the Left (*ashab al-shimal*).

a The people of forward group (*al-sabiqun*) are those who, when Truth appears before them, immediately accept it and surrender themselves to Truth without hesitation. According to the Prophet's wife, 'A'ishah, the Prophet said, 'Do you know, on the Day of Judgement, who will be the first to find a place in the protective shade of God?' People said that God and His Prophet knew best. Then he said, 'It will be those to whom Truth was presented and they accepted it. When Truth was demanded of them, they gave it. They gave the same decision with regard to others as they did with regard to themselves.' (*Tafsir ibn Kathir*).

b 'Those on the Right' (*ashab al-yamin*) means the ordinary people of paradise. This category includes all those people who, according to their belief and character, were pious. As regards faith, they were not in possession of a high degree of consciousness. However, they were sincere about God and His prophet, and they maintained themselves on the path of justice and went in fear of God throughout their lives. In this category there will be a fair number of persons from the earlier period and a considerable number from the later period.

raised couches. [35] We have created maidens perfectly [36] and made them virgins, [37] loving companions, matching in age, [38] for those on the Right, [39] a large group of the earlier people [40] and a large group of those of later times.

[41] Those on the Left: how unfortunate are those on the Left![a] [42] They will find themselves in scorching wind and scalding water, [43] and under the shadow of black smoke, [44] neither cool nor refreshing. [45] They had been affluent before, [46] and they persisted obstinately in awful sin, [47] and they used to say, 'What! After we have died and become dust and bones, shall we indeed be raised up again? [48] And also our forefathers?' [49] Say, 'Indeed, the earlier ones and the later ones [50] will indeed be gathered together at a fixed time on an appointed Day. [51] Then you, you misguided ones, who deny the truth, [52] shall eat the fruit of the tree of Zaqqum, [53] and fill your bellies with it, [54] and shall drink boiling water on top of that. [55] You shall drink it as the thirsty camels drink.' [56] This shall be their entertainment on the Day of Judgement.

[57] We have created you: why then do you not accept the truth? [58] Have you thought about [the semen] that you discharge—[59] did you create it or did We?[b] [60] It is We who have ordained death for all of you; and We cannot be prevented [61] from replacing you by others like yourselves or changing your forms and re-creating you in forms that you know nothing of. [62] You have certainly known the first creation. Why, then, do you not take heed? [63] Have you thought about what crops you plant? [64] Is it you who cause them to grow or do We? [65] If We so pleased, We could turn your harvest into chaff.

---

a 'Those on the Left' (*ashab al-shimal*) means those to whom it will be decided to mete out punishment. They were deceived by the amenities they had in this world. They had made things other than God the centre of their attention, and this is the greatest crime on the part of a man. They had made themselves so forgetful of the Hereafter, it was as if it was not to become a reality at all. Such people will receive severe punishment on the Day of Judgement.

b The birth of a human being from the womb of his mother, the growing of crops from the earth, falling of rain water, the availability of fire from fuel—all these things come directly from God. They should be treated as gifts of God, for which man should be grateful, and not as the results of human effort.

Then you would start lamenting, [66] 'We are ruined, [67] nay, we are deprived [altogether].' [68] Have you considered the water that you drink? [69] Is it you who cause it to descend from the clouds, or do We? [70] If We so pleased, We certainly could make it salty. Why, then, are you not grateful? [71] Have you thought about the fire that you kindle. [72] Did you produce the tree that serves as fuel or do We? [73] We have made it to be a reminder and a benefit for the wayfarers. [74] So glorify the name of your Lord, the Supreme.

[75] Nay, I swear by the setting of the stars—[76] and, indeed, that is a most mighty oath, if you only knew—[77] that this is indeed a noble Quran, [78] in a well-guarded preserved Book, [79] which none can touch except the purified. [80] It is a revelation sent down from the Lord of the worlds. [81] How can you regard this discourse with disdain? [82] Do you make its denial your means of livelihood?

[83] Why, then, when the soul of the dying man reaches the throat, [84] and you are [at that moment] looking on [helplessly]—[85] and We are nearer to him than you, although you cannot see Us—[86] why, then, if you are not subject to Our command, [87] do you not cause the soul to return to him if you are truthful in your claim? [88] But if he [the dying person] is one of those brought near to God, [89] then for him there shall be comfort and plenty and a Garden of Bliss; [90] and if he is of those who are on the Right, [91] he will be greeted with, 'Peace be to you,' by those on the Right. [92] But if he is one of those who rejected [the truth] and went astray, [93] he will be welcomed with boiling water. [94] He will burn in Hell. [95] This is indeed the indubitable truth. [96] So glorify the name of your Lord, the Supreme.

57. IRON (*AL-HADID*)

In the name of God, the Most Gracious, the Most Merciful

[1] Everything in the heavens and earth glorifies God—He is the Mighty, the Wise One. [2] He has sovereign control over the heavens and the earth. He gives life and brings death. He has power over all things. [3] He is the First and the Last, the Outward and the Inward. He has knowledge of all things. [4] It was He who created the heavens and

earth in six Days [periods] and then ascended the throne. He knows what enters the earth and what comes out of it; what descends from the sky and what ascends to it. He is with you wherever you are; He sees all that you do; ⁵ He has sovereignty over the heavens and the earth. All affairs will return to God. ⁶ He causes the night to pass into the day and the day to pass into the night. And He knows all that is in the hearts of men.

⁷ Have faith in God and His Messenger and spend in charity from that of which He has made you trustees: those of you who believe and give alms shall be richly rewarded.ᵃ ⁸ What could be your reason for not believing in God, when the Messenger calls on you to have faith in your Lord and He has already made a covenant with you, if indeed you are true believers? ⁹ It is He who sends down to His Servant clear revelations, so that He may lead you out of darkness into light. God is indeed compassionate and merciful to you. ¹⁰ Why should you not spend for the cause of God, when God alone holds the heritage of the heavens and the earth? Those of you who spent and fought before the victory will be higher in rank than those who spent and fought afterwards.a Yet God has promised you all a good reward. He is aware of all that you do.ᵇ

¹¹ Who will offer God a generous loan? He will double it for him and give him a rich reward. ¹² On the Day, you [Prophet] shall see the faithful, both men and women, with their light streaming out before them and on their right hands, [and you shall hear a voice saying to them:] 'Glad tidings for you today! You shall enter gardens with rivers flowing through them wherein you shall forever dwell. That is the supreme triumph.' ¹³ On that Day, the hypocrites, both men and women, will say to the faithful, 'Wait a while for us, so that we may have some of your light.' They will be told, 'Turn back

---

a The universe, in its silent language, sings the praises of and describes the attributes of its Creator. In the Quran, those same attributes have been put into words. When a thing comes into being here, it has manifestly been brought into existence by the Supreme Being. Its end itself announces its termination by the Supreme Being. The fact is the universe is the vehicle of God's praises, while the Quran is their verbal recitation.

b See note to 2:191.

and look for a light elsewhere.' A wall will then be raised between them. It will have a gate on the inside of which will be grace and mercy and on the outside of which will be punishment. [14] The hypocrites will call out to the faithful: 'Were we not on your side?' They will reply, 'Yes, but you gave in to temptation, you wavered and doubted and were deceived by your wishful thinking until God's will was done; then the Deceiver [Satan] misled you about God.' [15] So this Day no ransom can be taken from you nor from those who were bent on denying the truth. Your home is the fire; that is your companion, and a hapless journey's end.

[16] Has the time not come for the faithful when their hearts in all humility should engage in the remembrance of God and of the revelation of truth, so that they should not become like those who were given the Book before them, whose hearts with the passage of time became hardened and many of whom were disobedient? [17] Remember that God brings the earth back to life after its death. We have made Our signs clear to you, so that you may fully understand.

[18] Alms-givers, both men and women, who give a generous loan to God, shall have it multiplied and shall have an honourable reward. [19] Those who believe in God and His messengers are the truthful ones and the witnesses in the sight of their Lord. They shall have their reward and their light. But those who are bent on denying the truth and reject Our signs shall be destined for Hell.

[20] Never forget that the life of this world is only a game and a passing delight, a show, and mutual boasting and trying to outrival each other in riches and children. It is like the growth of vegetation after the rain, which delights the planter, but which then withers away, turns yellow and becomes worthless stubble. In the life to come there will be a terrible punishment, or God's forgiveness and approval: the life of this world is nothing but means of deception. [21] Vie with one another for your Lord's forgiveness and for a Paradise as vast as heaven and earth, which has been made ready for those who believe in God and His messengers. Such is God's

grace. He bestows it upon whoever He pleases. There is no limit to God's bounty.[a]

[22] No misfortune can affect the earth or your own selves without its first having been recorded in a book, before We bring it into being. That is easy for God to do; [23] so that you may not grieve for what has escaped you, nor be exultant over what you have gained. God loves neither the conceited nor the boastful, [24] nor those who, being miserly themselves, urge others to be miserly. He who turns his back should remember that God alone is self-sufficient and worthy of all praise.[b]

[25] We sent Our messengers with evidence and, with them, We sent down the Book and the Scales of Justice, so that men might act in all fairness. We sent down iron with its great inherent strength and its many benefits for mankind, so that God might know who would stand up for God, though unseen, and His messengers. God is powerful, and almighty.

[26] We sent forth Noah and Abraham and bestowed upon their offspring prophethood and the Book. Some of them were rightly guided, but many others were transgressors. [27] Then, in their wake, We followed them up with [others of] Our messengers and after them Jesus, son of Mary. We gave him the Gospel and imbued the hearts of those who followed him with compassion and mercy. But

---

a God has created examples of the Hereafter in this world. One of these examples is that of a field. When, after receiving water, the crops ripen, their greenery looks very attractive for a few days. But soon hot winds blow and they begin to wither away. Then, the crops are reaped and threshed.

Similarly, the glamour of this world is also temporary. It lasts but a few days. After coming into possession of it, man becomes misled. He starts thinking that it is his everything. But, afterwards, when he is taken back to God, it will be evident to him that the glories of the world were valueless.

b The receiving of things in the world or the losing of them is purely for the purpose of putting man to the test. Almighty God has settled in advance what shape man's test-paper should take. A man should pay real attention not to what he has received or what has been taken away from him, but to how he reacted on each of these occasions. The correct and required reaction is that a man should not be disheartened if he suffers some loss, nor should he develop feelings of pride and vanity if he gains something.

We did not prescribe monasticism for them: that was their own innovation by which they sought to please God. But then, they did not observe it in the way that it should have been observed. So We rewarded only those who were truly faithful, for many of them were disobedient.

²⁸ Believers, fear God and believe in His messenger. He will show you mercy in double measure and will provide a light for you to walk in. God will grant you forgiveness. He is forgiving and merciful. ²⁹ The People of the Book should know that they have no power whatsoever over God's grace. His grace is entirely in His hand and He bestows it upon whoever He wills. God is truly infinite in His bounty.

58. THE PLEADING (*AL-MUJADALAH*)

In the name of God, the Most Gracious, the Most Merciful

¹ God has indeed heard the words of the woman who pleads with you about her husband and lays her complaint before God: God hears what the two of you have to say. God is all hearing, all seeing.
² Those who separate themselves from their wives by pronouncing, 'To me you are like my mother's back,'ᵃ must concede that they are not their mothers; none are their mothers except those who gave birth to them—surely they utter an evil word and a lie. God is pardoning, forgiving. ³ Those who put away their wives by equating them with their mothers, and then wish to go back on what they have said, must set free a slave before the couple may touch one another again. This is what you are exhorted to do. God is fully aware of what you do, ⁴ and anyone who does not have the means must fast for two consecutive months before they touch each other, and who is not able to do that must feed sixty needy people. That is to affirm

---

a Before Islam, it was the custom in Arabia that if a man said to his wife, 'To me you are like my mother's back' she was for ever forbidden for that man. This was called *zihar*.

your faith in God and His messenger. These are the limits set by God. Those who deny the truth shall have a painful punishment.

⁵ Those who oppose God and His Messenger will be humiliated, as were their predecessors. We have sent down clear revelations. A humiliating punishment awaits those who deny the truth. ⁶ On the day God raises them all up from the dead, He will make them understand what they have done. God has taken everything into account, even though they have forgotten, for God is a witness to all things.

⁷ Do you not see that God knows all that is in the heavens and on the earth? There is not a secret consultation between three, but He makes the fourth among them—nor between five but He makes the sixth—nor between fewer nor more, but He is in their midst, wherever they may be: in the end He will tell them the truth about their conduct, on the Day of Judgement. For God has full knowledge of all things.*a* ⁸ Have you not seen how those who were forbidden to hold secret counsels yet revert to that which they were forbidden to do? And they conspire to indulge in wrongdoing, aggressive behaviour and disobedience to the Messenger. When they come to you, they greet you, but not in the words God would use, and inwardly they wonder, 'Why does God not punish us for what we say?' Hell will be a fitting punishment for them: they will burn in its flames—a wretched fate!

⁹ Believers, when you confer together in private, do not confer in support of sin and transgression and disobedience to the Messenger, but confer for the promotion of virtue and righteousness. Fear God, before whom you shall all be gathered. ¹⁰ Conspiracy for evil purposes is the work of Satan, by which he means to bring grief to believers. But he cannot harm them in the least, unless it be by God's leave. Let the believers put their trust in God.

---

a The universe with its complex system bears testimony to the fact that it is under the careful watch of a Higher Power. The evidence of this vigilance over the universe proves that man is also constantly under the eyes of his Creator. In view of this, indulging in secret activities against Truth is the act of blind people who are unable to read the attributes of God either in the expressly worded Quran directly, or in the unworded message of the universe indirectly.

[11] Believers, if you are told to make room for one another in your assemblies, then do so, and God will make room for you, and if you are told to rise up, do so: God will raise in rank those of you who believe and those who have been given knowledge: He is fully aware of all that you do.

[12] Believers, when you come to consult the Messenger privately, give something in charity beforehand. That is best for you and most conducive to purity. But if you cannot find anything to give, know that God is Forgiving and Merciful. [13] Do you fear that you will not [be able to] give in charity before your consultation? Then if you are unable to do so, [know that] God has turned to you in His mercy; then observe your prayers and pay the prescribed alms and obey God and His Messenger. God is aware of all that you do.

[14] Do you not see those who have befriended a people who have brought down upon themselves the wrath of God? They are neither with you nor with them and they wittingly swear to falsehood. [15] God has prepared a severe punishment for them; surely what they have done is evil. [16] They have used their oaths to cover up their misdeeds and have thus turned others away from the path of God. A humiliating punishment awaits them.

[17] Neither their wealth nor their children will be of the least avail [in protecting them] against God—they are the inheritors of Hell, and there they shall remain forever. [18] On the day God raises them all up from the dead, they will swear to Him just as they have sworn to you, thinking that they are on firm ground. But surely they are liars. [19] Satan has got the better of them and has caused them to forget the remembrance of God. They have gone over to the side of the devil, and it is as the devil's partisans that they shall be the losers: [20] those who oppose God and His Messenger will [on Judgement Day] be among the most abased. [21] God has decreed, 'I and My messengers shall most certainly prevail.' Truly God is Powerful and Almighty.

[22] You will find no believers in God and the Last Day consorting with those who oppose God and His Messenger, even though they be their fathers, their sons, their brothers or their close relatives. He has engraved faith on their very hearts and has strengthened them with a spirit of His own. He will usher them into Gardens

through which rivers flow where they shall dwell forever. God is well-pleased with them and they are well pleased with Him. They are God's party. God's party shall surely enter into a state of bliss.

59. BANISHMENT (*AL-HASHR*)

In the name of God, the Most Gracious, the Most Merciful

[1] Everything in the heavens and on the earth glorifies God. He is the Almighty, the All Wise. [2] It was He who turned those People of the Book who denied the truth out of their homes in the first banishment. You never thought they would go, and they thought their strongholds would protect them against God. But God came upon them from where they least expected and cast such terror into their hearts that their houses were pulled down by their own hands as well as by the hands of the believers. Learn a lesson, then, you who are endowed with insight.

[3] If God had not prescribed exile for them, He would surely have punished them in this world. But they shall have the torment of Fire in the Hereafter, [4] because they set themselves against God and His Messenger: God is stern in His punishment of anyone who sets himself against Him. [5] Whatever palm trees you cut down or left standing on their roots, it was by God's leave, so that He might disgrace the transgressors.

[6] Whatever God has given to His Messenger as spoils from them is by His grace; you spurred neither horse nor camel for them, but God gives power to His messengers over anyone He wills. God has power over all things—[7] whatever gains God has assigned to His Messenger from the inhabitants of the town is for God and for the Messenger and for his kinsfolk and for orphans and the needy and the wayfarer, so that they may not become the property of those of you who are rich. Whatever the Messenger gives you, take it; and whatever he forbids you, abstain from it. Fear God; surely, God is severe in retribution. [8] It is for the poor refugees who were driven from their homes and possessions, desiring the favour and

the pleasure of God and supporting God and His Messenger. Such people are the truthful.

⁹ Those who were already settled in the city [Madinah] and firmly rooted in faith, love those who migrated to them for refuge, and harbour no desire in their hearts for what has been given to the [latter]. They give them preference over themselves, even if they too are needy: those who are saved from their own souls' greed are truly successful.

¹⁰ Those who came [into the faith] after them say, 'Our Lord, forgive us and our brothers who preceded us in the faith and leave no malice in our hearts towards those who believe. Lord, You are indeed compassionate and merciful.'

¹¹ Have you not seen those who act hypocritically? They say to their disbelieving companions from among the People of the Book, 'If you are driven out we shall surely go out with you, and we shall never listen to anyone against you, and if war is waged against you, we shall help you.' God bears witness that they are indeed liars. ¹² If they are driven out, they will not go with them, nor, if they are attacked, will they help them. Indeed, if they go to their help, they will turn their backs in flight, and then they will not be helped.

¹³ They are more in dread of you than of God, because they are people devoid of understanding. ¹⁴ They will never fight against you in a body except from within fortified strongholds or from behind walls. There is much hostility between them. You think they are united, but their hearts are divided, because they are a people devoid of reason.

¹⁵ Like those who went just before them, they have tasted the evil consequences of their doings. And they shall have a painful punishment. ¹⁶ They are like Satan, who says to man, 'Deny the truth!' but when man denied the truth, said, 'I disown you; I fear God, the Lord of the Universe.' ¹⁷ Thus, in the end, both will find themselves in the Fire, therein to abide: that is the reward of evil-doers.

¹⁸ Believers! Fear God, and let every soul look to what it lays up for the future. Fear God: God is aware of what you do. ¹⁹ Do not be like those who forgot God, so that He caused them to forget their own souls [their own true interests]. It is they who are the rebellious

ones. ²⁰ The people of the Fire and the people of Paradise are not equal. The people of Paradise are the victorious ones.

²¹ Had We sent down this Quran on a mountain, you would certainly have seen it falling down and splitting asunder, because of the fear of God. We set forth these parables to men so that they may reflect.*ᵃ* ²² He is God: there is no deity save Him. He knows the unseen and the visible. He is the Compassionate, the Merciful. ²³ He is God, there is no deity save Him, the Sovereign, the Most Pure, the Source of Peace, the Granter of Security, the Protector, the Mighty, the Subduer, the Supreme, Glory be to God, who is far above what they associate with Him. ²⁴ He is God—the Creator, the Originator, the Giver of Form. His are the most excellent names. Everything in the heavens and earth declares His glory. He is the Mighty, the Wise One.*ᵇ*

60. SHE WHO IS TESTED
(*AL-MUMTAHANAH*)

In the name of God, the Most Gracious, the Most Merciful

¹ Believers! Do not offer friendship to those who are enemies of Mine and of yours. Would you show them affection when they have rejected the truth you have received; when they have driven you

---

a The Quran is a declaration of the vital fact that man is not free, but is answerable for all his deeds to God who is all-powerful and who keeps a close watch on everybody's actions. This fact is of such grave import that it is enough to make even mountains tremble. But man is so negligent, forgetful and insensitive that, even after knowing this awesome fact, he is not perturbed.

b The names of God mentioned here are, on the one hand, an introduction to God's Being. On the other hand, they show how Great is that Being who is the Creator of human beings and who keeps a constant watch over them. If an individual actually realises this, he will be completely engrossed in reciting and singing the praises of God.

The universe, by virtue of its creative meaningfulness, mirrors the attributes of God. It is itself wholly taken up with reciting and singing the praises of God and urges human beings to follow suit.

and the Messenger out [simply] because you believe in God, your Lord. If you have left your homes to strive for My cause and out of a desire to seek My goodwill, how can you secretly offer them friendship? I know all that you conceal and all that you reveal. Whoever of you does this will surely stray from the right path. [2] If they gain ascendancy over you, they will behave towards you as enemies and stretch out their hands as well as their tongues with evil intent; they long for you to renounce your faith. [3] Neither your relatives nor your children will be of any help to you on the Day of Resurrection. He will judge between you, and God sees all that you do.

[4] Indeed you have an excellent example in Abraham and those who followed him, when they said to their people, 'We disown you and whatever you worship besides God. We renounce you. Enmity and hatred shall endure between us and you, until you believe in the one God.' [The exception was] when Abraham said to his father, 'I shall indeed pray for [God's] forgiveness for you; although I do not have it in my power to obtain anything from God on your behalf.' They prayed, 'O our Lord, in You we have placed our trust and to You we turn in repentance and to You is the final return. [5] Our Lord, do not make us a prey for those who deny the truth, and forgive us our Lord. For You alone are the Mighty, the Wise One.' [6] Surely, there is a good example in them for you; for those who place their hopes in God and the Last Day. Whoever turns away will surely learn that God is self-sufficient and worthy of all praise. [7] It may well be that God will create goodwill between you and those of them with whom you are now at enmity—for God is all powerful, most forgiving and merciful.

[8] He does not forbid you to deal kindly and justly with anyone who has not fought you on account of your faith or driven you out of your homes: God loves the just. [9] God only forbids you to make friends with those who have fought against you on account of your faith and driven you out of your homes or helped others to do so. Any of you who turn towards them in friendship will truly be transgressors.

[10] Believers! When believing women come to you as refugees,

submit them to a test. Their faith is best known to God. Then if you find them to be true believers, do not send them back to those who deny the truth. These [women] are not lawful for them, nor are those who deny the truth lawful for these women. But hand back to those who deny the truth the dowers they gave them; nor is it an offence for you to marry such women, provided you give them their dowers. Do not maintain your marriages with those women who deny the truth: demand repayment of the dowers you have given them and let the disbelievers ask for the return of what they have spent. Such is God's judgement; He judges with justice between you. God is all knowing and all wise. [11] If any of your wives desert you to go over to the disbelievers, and you subsequently have your turn, [by the coming over of a woman from the other side] give to those who have been deserted by their wives the equivalent of the dowers they gave them. Fear God in whom you believe.

[12] O Prophet! When believing women come to you and pledge themselves not to associate in worship any other thing with God, not to steal or commit adultery or kill their children or indulge in slander, intentionally inventing falsehoods, and not to disobey you in that which is right, then accept their pledge of allegiance and pray to God to forgive them their sins, for God is forgiving and merciful.

[13] Believers! Do not make friends with those who have incurred the wrath of God. Such men are indeed bereft of all hope of a life to come, just as those who deny the truth lying in their graves are bereft of all hopes.

61. RANKS (*AL-SAFF*)

In the name of God, the Most Gracious, the Most Merciful

[1] Everything in the heavens and earth glorifies God—He is the Almighty, the Wise. [2] Believers! Why do you say one thing and do another. [3] It is most hateful to God that you do not practise what you preach; [4] surely, God loves those who fight for His cause in ranks, as if they were a solid cemented structure.

[5] Remember when Moses said to his people, 'O my people, why

do you cause me grief when you know that I am God's Messenger to you?' When they wavered, God let their hearts waver too. God does not guide transgressors.

⁶ Remember when Jesus, son of Mary, said, 'O Children of Israel, I am sent to you by God, confirming the Torah that came before me and bringing good news of a messenger to follow me, whose name will be Ahmad.' Yet when he came to them with clear signs, they said, 'This is merely sorcery.' ⁷ Who could be more wicked than one who invents lies about God when called to submit to Him? God does not guide the wrongdoers: ⁸ they wish to put His light out with their mouths. But He will perfect His light, much as those who deny the truth may dislike it; ⁹ it is He who has sent His Messenger with guidance and the true religion, so that He may cause it to prevail over all religions, however much the polytheists may dislike it.

¹⁰ Believers! Shall I guide you to a profitable course that will save you from a painful punishment? ¹¹ You should believe in God and His Messenger, and strive for God's cause with your possessions and your lives. That will be better for you, if you only knew— ¹² and He will forgive you your sins and admit you into Gardens with rivers flowing under them. He will lodge you in fine dwellings in the Gardens of Eternity; that is indeed the supreme achievement. ¹³ He will give you another blessing which you desire: help from God and imminent victory. Give good tidings [O Muhammad] to believers!

¹⁴ Believers, be God's helpers,ᵃ as Jesus, son of Mary, said to the disciples, 'Who will be my helpers in the cause of God?' The disciples said, 'We shall be God's helpers.' Some of the Children

---

a 'Be God's helpers' here means calling people to God (*dawat ilal'lah*). Since it is a task which is seen as desirable by God Himself and is performed by servants of God, it is, therefore, called 'helping God'. This is an exceptional honour which is granted only to a true believer.

What is the meaning of helping God or being the helpers of God in this verse? It means giving oneself wholeheartedly to the divine *dawah* mission. It means joining oneself with the divine plan whole-heartedly in both word and deed, so that mankind might have no argument against God on the Day of Judgement.

of Israel believed in him and some denied the truth; We supported the believers against their enemies and they triumphed over them.

62. THE DAY OF CONGREGATION
(*AL-JUMU'AH*)

In the name of God, the Most Gracious, the Most Merciful

[1] Whatever is in the heavens and on the earth glorifies God, the Sovereign Lord, the Holy One, the Mighty, the Wise. [2] It is He who has raised among the unlettered people a messenger from among themselves who recites His revelations to them, and purifies them, and teaches them the Book and wisdom, for they had formerly been clearly misguided—[3] and to others also, from among them, who have not yet joined them. He is the Mighty, the Wise One. [4] That is God's grace; He bestows it on whom He pleases; for God is limitless in His grace.

[5] Those who were charged with bearing the Torah, but did not do so are like an ass carrying a load of books. How unfortunate are those who belie the sign of God. God does not guide the wrongdoers. [6] Say, 'You who are Jews, if you claim that you are favoured by God out of all people, then long for death, if you are truthful.' [7] They will never wish for it, because of what their hands have sent forward. God has full knowledge of evil-doers. [8] So say, 'The death you run away from will certainly meet you, and thereafter you will be brought back to the Knower of the unseen and the seen, and He will declare to you what you have done.'

[9] Believers! When the call to prayer is made on the day of congregation, hasten to the remembrance of God, and leave all worldly commerce: this is for your own good, if you but knew it. [10] When the prayer is ended, disperse in the land and seek to obtain [something] of God's bounty; and remember God much, so that you may prosper. [11] Yet when they see some merchandise or entertainment, they break away to go to it and leave you standing.

Say, 'That which God has in store is far better than any merchandise or entertainment.' God is the most munificent Giver.[a]

63. THE HYPOCRITES (*AL-MUNAFIQUN*)

In the name of God, the Most Gracious, the Most Merciful

[1] When the hypocrites[b] come to you, they say, 'We bear witness that you are indeed the Messenger of God.' God knows that you are indeed His Messenger, but God bears witness that the hypocrites are surely liars—[2] they use their oaths as a cover and thus they bar others from God's way: what they have been doing is truly evil—[3] that is because they believed and then rejected their faith: their hearts are sealed up, so that they are devoid of understanding.

[4] When you see them, their outward appearance pleases you; when they speak, you listen to what they say. But they are like propped up blocks of timber. They think that every shout is directed against them. They are the [real] enemies, so beware of them. The curse of God be upon them! How they turn away! [5] When they are told, 'Come! The Messenger of God will ask forgiveness for you!' they turn their heads away and you see them walking away arrogantly.

---

a Once in Madinah, during the sermon of the Friday prayers, some people left the mosque and went to the market. These verses were revealed in that connection. These injunctions are directly in connection with the Friday prayers but, indirectly, they apply to every religious task. Whenever people have been called upon and are assembled for some special religious purpose, it will be highly inappropriate to leave the place without the permission of the Imam (leader of the gathering).

b A hypocrite protects his interests by his compromising and self-interested approach. He does not involve himself in considerations of right or wrong. Consequently, he maintains good relations with everybody. His life is free of sorrow. When he speaks he takes into account the nature of his hearers. Therefore, everybody finds something of interest in his conversation. But these apparently 'fresh green trees' consist in reality of 'dry sticks'. In the hypocrite's eyes, worldly interest is much more important than any religious interest. Such people, in spite of being vociferous claimants of Faith, are totally deprived of God's guidance.

⁶ It makes no difference whether you ask forgiveness for them or not. God will not forgive them: God does not guide such rebellious people.

⁷ They are the ones who say, 'Give nothing to those who follow God's Messenger, until they abandon him;' but the treasures of the heavens and the earth belong to God, though the hypocrites do not understand this ⁸ [and] they say, 'Indeed, when we return to Madinah, [we] the ones most worthy of honour, will surely drive out from there the contemptible ones!' [referring to poor Muslims]. However, all honour belongs to God, and to His Messenger and those who believe [in God]: but of this the hypocrites are not aware.

⁹ O believers! Do not let your wealth or your children distract you from remembrance of God. Those who do so will be the losers. ¹⁰ And spend out of what We have provided you with before death comes to one of you and he says, 'My Lord! If only You would grant me respite for a little while, then I would give alms and be among the righteous.' ¹¹ But God will not grant a reprieve to a soul when its appointed time has come; God is well-aware of what you do.ᵃ

64. LOSS AND GAIN (*AL-TAGHABUN*)

In the name of God, the Most Gracious, the Most Merciful

¹ All that is in the heavens and on the earth extols the glory of God. To Him belongs the Kingdom and to Him all praise is due. He has power over all things. ² It was He who created you; and some of you are those who deny this truth, and some who believe [in it]. God sees everything you do. ³ He created the heavens and the earth for a purpose. He formed you and gave you the best of forms. To Him

---

a The biggest problem for a man is the inevitability of the Hereafter. But the consideration of riches and children make a man unmindful of it. Man should know that riches and children are not the final goal but the blessings which are given to him so that he may utilise them for God's work. He should therefore use them to improve his life in the Hereafter. But man, in his stupidity, takes them to be his goal. When such people come face to face with their eventual final fate, they will experience only frustration and regret.

you shall all return. [4] He knows whatever is in the heavens and the earth. He knows all that you conceal and all that you reveal. God is aware of what is in your hearts.

[5] Have you not heard about those who denied the truth before you and tasted the evil consequences of their conduct? They will have a painful punishment. [6] That was because their messengers came to them with clear signs, but they replied, 'Shall mortals be our guides?' And so they rejected the truth and turned away. God has no need of such people; God is self-sufficient and worthy of all praise.

[7] Those who deny the truth claim that they will never be raised up again. Say, 'By my Lord, most surely you will be raised up again and then you will be told of all that you have done; and that is easy enough for God.' [8] Believe then in God and His Messenger, and in the light which We have sent down. God is fully aware of all that you do. [9] When He shall gather you all for the Day of Gathering, that will be the Day of loss and gain; and whoever believes in God and does good deeds shall be forgiven their sins and admitted to Gardens through which rivers flow, where they shall dwell forever. That is the supreme triumph. [10] But those who denied the truth and rejected Our signs shall be the inmates of the Fire, there to remain—what an evil destination!

[11] No affliction can befall man but by God's permission—He guides the hearts of those who believe in Him: God has knowledge of all things—[12] obey God and obey the Messenger; but if you turn away, remember that Our Messenger is only responsible for clearly conveying the message. [13] God! There is no god but He, so let the faithful put their trust in Him.

[14] Believers! [Even] among your wives and your children you have enemies: so beware of them. But if you overlook their offences and forgive and pardon them, then surely, God is most forgiving and merciful. [15] Your wealth and your children are only a trial; God's reward is great: [16] so be mindful of God as best as you can; and listen, and obey; and spend in charity: it is for your own good.[a]

---

a People take the world to be a place of winning or losing (*taghabun*). One who is successful here becomes very happy, but one who meets with failure is

Those who guard themselves against their own greed will surely prosper: ¹⁷ if you give a good loan to God, He will multiply it for you and forgive you, for God is appreciative and forbearing; ¹⁸ God is the Knower of the unseen and the seen: He is the Almighty, the Wise One.

65. DIVORCE (*AL-TALAQ*)

In the name of God, the Most Gracious, the Most Merciful

¹ O Prophet! When any of you divorce your wives, divorce them during their period of purity and calculate the period carefully: be mindful of God, your Lord.[a] Do not drive them out of their homes—nor should they themselves leave—unless they become openly guilty of immoral conduct. These are the bounds set by God. He who transgresses God's bounds wrongs his own soul. You never know, after that, God may well bring about some new situation. ² And when their waiting term is ended, either keep them honourably or part with them in honour. Call to witness two reliable men from

---

looked upon with contempt. In this world, however, success is as valueless as failure is. The place of true success or failure is the Hereafter. One is a failure if he fails in the Hereafter and successful if he is successful in the Hereafter, and the criterion of success or failure there is entirely different from that of this world, where it is based on outward materialism: success or failure in the Hereafter will be on the basis of Divine moral values. At that time, people will be surprised to see that the whole complexion of things has completely changed. Gaining, which was considered as such will actually turn out to be losing, while what was considered as losing will turn out to be gaining in the real sense. Failure on that Day is real failure and success on that Day will be real success.

a Divorce is permitted in Islam in exceptional situations and a procedure has been prescribed for it which must be completed within a specific period. In this way the process of divorce has been subjected to certain conditions. The purpose of these limitations is that, till the last moment, the parties should have the opportunity for rapprochement, and the divorce should not create any disturbance in the family or society. Divorce is endorsed by Islam provided that, during the process, a God-fearing spirit is prevalent throughout.

among you and bear true witness for God. This is an admonishment for those who believe in God and the Last Day. To one who fears God, He will grant a way out [of his difficulties], ³ and God will provide for him from an unexpected source; God suffices for anyone who puts his trust in Him. God will surely bring about what He decrees. He has set a measure for all things.

⁴ In the case of those of your wives who have passed the age of menstruation, if you have any doubt, know that their waiting period is three months; and that will apply likewise to those who have not yet menstruated; the waiting period of those who are pregnant will be until they deliver their burden [give birth]. God makes things easy for those who are mindful of Him. ⁵ Such is the commandment which God has revealed to you. He who fears God shall be forgiven his sins and richly rewarded.

⁶ Let the women [who are undergoing a waiting period] live in the same manner as you live yourselves, in accordance with your means; and do not harass them in order to make their lives difficult. If they are pregnant, maintain them until they give birth; if they suckle your infants, pay them for it; discuss things among yourselves in all decency—if you cannot bear with each other, let another woman suckle for you—⁷ let the man of means spend in accordance with his means; and let him whose resources are restricted, spend in accordance with what God has given him. God does not burden any person with more than He has given him. God will soon bring about ease after hardship.

⁸ How many a town rebelled against the commands of its Lord and His messengers and We called them sternly to account and punished them severely, ⁹ so they tasted the evil consequences of their conduct and the result of their conduct was ruin. ¹⁰ God has prepared a severe punishment for them. So, fear God, O men of understanding, who have believed. God has sent down to you a Reminder ¹¹ and a messenger who conveys to you God's clear messages, so that he might lead those, who believe and do good deeds, out of darkness into light. God will admit those who believe in Him and do good deeds into Gardens with rivers flowing through them, where they will remain forever. God has indeed made excellent provision for them.

¹² It is God who created the seven heavens and the same number of earths. His commandment descends among them, so that you may know that God has power over all things; and that He encompasses all things with His knowledge.

66. PROHIBITION (*AL-TAHRIM*)

In the name of God, the Most Gracious, the Most Merciful

¹ Prophet, why in your desire to please your wives, do you impose a ban on what God has made lawful to you? God is forgiving and merciful. ² God has already ordained that you be absolved of such oaths. God is your patron. He is the All Knowing, the Wise One.

³ The Prophet once told one of his wives something in confidence. She did not keep it secret and God informed him of this; he made known a part of it, and avoided [mentioning] part of it. When he spoke to his wife of this, she asked him who had told him about it. He replied, 'The All Knowing, the All Aware One.' ⁴ If only both of you would turn to God in repentance—and your hearts are already so inclined. But if you uphold each other against him, then surely God is his protector, and Gabriel and the righteous among the believers; and the angels too are his helpers. ⁵ Were he to divorce you, his Lord might well replace you with better wives—submissive [to God], believing, pious, penitent, devout in worship, given to fasting—previously married and virgins.

⁶ Believers, safeguard yourselves and your families from a Fire fuelled by people and stones, and watched over by angels, stern and strong: angels who never disobey God's commands to them, but promptly do as they are commanded. ⁷ You who are bent on denying the truth, make no excuses today: you are only being rewarded according to your deeds.

⁸ Believers, turn to God in sincere repentance. Your Lord may well forgive your bad deeds and admit you into gardens watered by running streams, on a Day when God will not abase the Prophet and those who have believed with him. Their light will shine out

ahead of them and on their right, and they will say: 'Lord perfect our light for us, and forgive us; You have power over all things.'[a]

⁹ Prophet, exert yourself to the utmost against those who deny the truth and the hypocrites. Deal severely with them. Hell will be their abode—a vile destination. ¹⁰ As an example to those who are bent on denying the truth, God cited the wife of Noah and the wife of Lot, who were married to two of Our righteous servants, but who betrayed them. So they could not help them against God, and they were told, 'Enter the Fire along with all the others.'

¹¹ To the believers God has given the example of Pharaoh's wife who said: 'My Lord, build me a house in nearness to You in Paradise and save me from Pharaoh and his misdeeds. Save me from all evil-doers.' ¹² [God gave another example in the story of] Mary, 'Imran's daughter, who preserved her chastity and We breathed Our spirit into her; she testified to the words of her Lord and His Scriptures, and was truly devout.

67. THE KINGDOM (*AL-MULK*)

In the name of God, the Most Gracious, the Most Merciful

¹ Blessed is He in whose hand is the Kingdom: He has power over all things; ² He created death and life so that He might test you, and find out which of you is best in conduct. He is the Mighty, the Most

---

a In the present world man has been kept in trial conditions and as such he is liable to commit errors. In compensation for this, he must turn towards God in repentance. In essence, true repentance comes from a sense of shame. If a man fully realises his mistake, he will feel ashamed, and this sense of shame will compel him not to indulge in such action in future. That is why a hadith says, 'Being ashamed is repentance.' A companion of the Prophet Muhammad said, 'True repentance is a man turning towards God and then not repeating that action.'

Repentance has to be borne out by actions. It is not just the repetition of some words. 'Ali ibn Abi Talib saw an individual who, after making a mistake, was simply repeating the words '*tawbah, tawbah*'. 'Ali said that this was repentance of liars. True *tawbah* is the light of the Hereafter and false *tawbah* is the darkness of the Hereafter.

Forgiving One. ³ He created seven heavens one above the other in layers. You will not find any flaw in the creation of the Gracious One. Then look once again: can you see any flaw? ⁴ Then look again and again. Your gaze will come back to you confused and exhausted.

⁵ We have adorned the lowest heaven with lamps, and We have made them for driving away devils. For them We have prepared the punishment of the blazing Fire. ⁶ Those who are bent on blaspheming against their Lord will have the punishment of Hell: an evil destination. ⁷ When they are cast into it, they will hear its roaring as it boils up, ⁸ as though bursting with rage. Each time a group is cast into it, its keepers will ask them, 'Did no warner come to you?' ⁹ They will say, 'Of course, a warner did come to us, but we belied him and we said, "God has revealed nothing; you are in gross error".' ¹⁰ They will say, 'If we had only listened or understood, we should not now be among the inmates of Hell,' ¹¹ and thus they will confess their sin; far from God's mercy are the inmates of Hell.ᵃ

¹² As for those who fear their Lord in the unseen will have forgiveness and a rich reward. ¹³ Whether you speak in secret or aloud, He knows what is in every heart. ¹⁴ How could He who created not know His own creation, when He alone is the Most Subtle in His wisdom and the All Aware?

¹⁵ It is He who has made the earth subservient to you, so traverse its regions and eat its provisions. To Him you shall all be resurrected. ¹⁶ Do you feel secure that He who is in heaven will not cause the earth to sink beneath you and then begin to quake? ¹⁷ Do you feel secure that the One in heaven will not send against you a whirlwind to pelt you with stones, so that you will know how [true] My warning was? ¹⁸ Those who went before them belied [the truth]: then how great was My rejection of them.ᵇ

---

a At various places in the Quran, the picture of hell has been drawn. Though this hell is not observable today by man, it can be seen indirectly and imagined through the meaningfulness of the universe. The fact is that if there were to be no reckoning of the evil people brought to account in the Hereafter, the entire meaningfulness of the universe would become inexplicable.

b Everything on earth is extremely well-balanced. It is this balance which has made the earth habitable for human beings. Should the slightest disturbance

¹⁹ Do they not see the birds above them spreading and closing their wings? None save the Merciful sustains them. Surely, He observes all things. ²⁰ Who is there to defend you like an army, besides the Lord of Mercy? Those who deny the truth are in deception. ²¹ Who can provide for you, if He withholds His provision? Yet they obstinately persist in rebellion and avoidance of the truth.*ᵃ*

²² Is he who walks grovelling upon his face better guided, or he who walks upright upon a straight path? ²³ Say, 'It is He who brought you into being, and made ears and eyes and hearts for you, yet you are seldom grateful.' ²⁴ Say, 'It is He who has scattered you on the earth; and it is to Him that you shall all be gathered [on the Day of Resurrection].'

²⁵ They ask, 'When will this promise be fulfilled, if you are truthful?' ²⁶ Say, 'God alone has knowledge of that; and I am only a plain warner.' ²⁷ But when they see it drawing near, the faces of those who deny the truth will turn gloomy and they will be told, 'This is what you were calling for.' ²⁸ Say, 'Have you thought: if God destroys me and those who are with me, or treats us mercifully, then who will protect those who deny the truth from a painful chastisement?' ²⁹ Say, 'He is the Most Gracious: we believe in Him and we put our trust in Him. You will soon come to know who is in evident error.' ³⁰ Say, 'Have you considered if your water were to sink into the ground, who could then bring you flowing water?'*ᵇ*

---

ever occur in this balance, man's life would be destroyed. We should be grateful to God for the balanced world provided to us and seek His gracious help against any destructive conditions that may develop as a result of the world's equilibrium being upset.

a Birds flying in the air, the emergence of man's sustenance from the soil and similar events are most wonderful. If one gives serious consideration to such things, one will become caught up in the realisation of God. But man is so forgetful that he indulges in arrogance in a world in which the natural phenomena visible all around him ought to teach him the lesson of obedience to God.

b When the addressee of a missionary call is not convinced by reasoning, the missionary repeats his utterances of firm faith and thus stirs his inner self into awakening. Even if there is the slightest sensitivity in a man, these last utterances are enough to make him feel the urge to reform himself. But one

68. THE PEN (*AL-QALAM*)

In the name of God, the Most Gracious, the Most Merciful

¹ *Nun*

By the pen, and all that they write! ² By the grace of your Lord, you are not a mad man. ³ Most surely, you will have a never ending reward. ⁴ For you are truly of a sublime character.*ᵃ* ⁵ Soon you will see, as will they, ⁶ which of you is a prey to madness. ⁷ Your Lord knows best who has fallen by the wayside, and who has remained on the true path.

⁸ Do not give in to the deniers of truth. ⁹ They want you to make concessions to them and then they will reciprocate. ¹⁰ Do not yield to any contemptible swearer of oaths, ¹¹ or to any defamer or one who spreads slander, ¹² or to one who places obstacles in the way of good being done or to the wicked transgressor, ¹³ who is ignoble and besides all that, base-born; ¹⁴ just because he has wealth and sons, ¹⁵ when Our revelations are recited to him, he says, 'These are just ancient fables.' ¹⁶ Soon We will brand him on the nose.

¹⁷ We have tried them as we tried the owners of a certain orchard, who vowed to harvest all its fruits the next morning, ¹⁸ and made no allowance [for the will of God]. ¹⁹ A calamity from your Lord befell the orchard as they slept. ²⁰ And by morning it lay as if it had already been harvested, a barren land. ²¹ So they called out to each other at the break of dawn, ²² saying, 'Be quick to reach your orchard, if

---

whose conscience has been completely extinguished, can never be awakened by any device. He appreciates the value of water only when he is deprived of it and cast out into a desert.

a Having a sublime character means rising above others' behaviour. It should not be his way that he deals badly with those who are not good to him, while giving fair treatment to those who are good to him. On the contrary, he should do good to everybody, even though others may not do the same for him. The character of the Prophet was of the latter type, which proves that he was a man of principle. He was not a product of circumstances, but of his own high principles. His sublime character was consistent with his claim to be a prophet.

you want to gather all your fruits.' [23] So they went off, whispering to one another, [24] 'Be sure to stop any poor person from entering the orchard today.' [25] They set out early in the morning, thinking they had the power to prevent. [26] But when they saw it, they said, 'We must have lost our way. [27] Indeed, we are utterly ruined!'[a] [28] The more upright of the two said, 'Did I not bid you to glorify God?' [29] They said, 'Glory be to God, our Lord. We have surely done wrong.' [30] Then they began to heap reproaches on each other. [31] They said, 'Alas for us, our behaviour was beyond the pale. [32] May be our Lord will give us a better orchard in its stead; we turn to Him.' [33] Such was their punishment, [in this life]. But the punishment of the life to come is much more severe, if only they knew it!

[34] Those who are mindful of their Lord will be rewarded with gardens of bliss. [35] Should We treat the true believers and the wrongdoers alike? [36] What ails you? How ill you judge! [37] Have you a Scripture that tells you

[38] that you will be granted whatever you choose? [39] Or do you have Our solemn oaths, binding upon Us till the Day of Resurrection, that you shall have whatever you yourselves decide? [40] Ask them, which of them will vouch for that! [41] Or have they other partners [besides God]? Let them bring forth their other partners, if what they say be true.

[42] On the Day when the truth shall be laid bare, they will be called upon to prostrate themselves, but they will not be able to do so. [43] Their eyes will be cast down and they will be covered in shame; they were bidden to prostrate themselves, when they were safe and sound [but they did not obey].[b] [44] So leave to Me those

---

a Whatever a man earns in this world is apparently from farming or industry or other such pursuits. But, in fact, it is all given to him by the grace of God. If one considers it a gift from God and sets apart a portion of it for other subjects of God, Almighty God will bless his earnings. On the contrary, if one who considers his earnings the result purely of his own talents and is not, therefore, prepared to give others their dues, his earnings will be of no avail. This is a strict law of God. In some cases, it manifests itself in this world, but in the Hereafter it will manifest itself for all.

b On the Day of Judgement when God will reveal Himself, the true

who reject this message. We shall lead them step by step to their ruin, in ways beyond their ken. ⁴⁵ I shall grant them some respite, for My plan is powerful.

⁴⁶ Do you demand some recompense from them that would weigh them down with debt? ⁴⁷ Is the unseen within their grasp so that they write it down? ⁴⁸ Wait patiently for your Lord's judgement; do not be like the man who, having been swallowed by a whale, called out in distress. ⁴⁹ Had his Lord's grace not been bestowed upon him, he would have been cast away in disgrace upon that desolate shore. ⁵⁰ But his Lord chose him for His own and made him one of the righteous. ⁵¹ When those who deny the truth hear the admonition, they would almost cause you to stumble with their evil eyes; and they say, 'He is certainly mad.' ⁵² Yet it is purely an admonition to mankind.

69. THE INEVITABLE HOUR
(*AL-HAQQAH*)

In the name of God, the Most Gracious, the Most Merciful

¹ The Inevitable Hour! ² What is the Inevitable Hour? ³ And what will make you realize what the Inevitable Hour is? ⁴ The tribes of Thamud and 'Ad denied that disaster would strike them: ⁵ the Thamud were destroyed by a terrible storm of thunder and lightning; ⁶ and the 'Ad were destroyed by a furious wind ⁷ which God let loose

---

believers will fall prostrate before their Lord, just as they bowed down before Him in their previous life. But, on the occasion when God reveals himself, it will be the true believers who will be inspired to prostrate themselves (*sajdah*). The backs of the people who offered 'false prostration' in this world, will grow stiff just as they virtually were in this world. Such people will want to prostrate themselves at that time of realisation, but they will not be able to do so. It will be the greatest sign of God's appreciation of sincere people of Faith that He Himself should appear and accept their offering of *sajdah*. On the contrary, it will be the moment of the greatest humiliation for those making false claims of Faith; in spite of their Creator and Lord being right before them, they will not be able to do obeisance to Him.

against them for seven nights and eight days unremittingly, so that you could have seen its people lying prostrate as though they were the hollow trunks of palm-trees which had fallen down. ⁸ Do you see any vestige left of them now? ⁹ Pharoah and those before him and the inhabitants of the overthrown cities persistently committed grave sins. ¹⁰ They defied their Lord's messenger, so He seized them with an ever-tightening grip. ¹¹ But We bore you away in the Ark, when the waters rose high, ¹² so that We might make it a reminder for you and so that attentive ears might retain it.

¹³ When a single blast is blown on the trumpet, ¹⁴ and the earth and the mountains are lifted up and then crushed with a single blow, ¹⁵ on that Day the Great Event will come to pass. ¹⁶ And the sky will be rent asunder, for on that Day it will be so frail. ¹⁷ The angels will appear by its sides and, on that Day, eight [angels] will bear your Lord's throne above them. ¹⁸ On that Day you will be brought to judgement and none of your secrets will remain hidden.*a*

¹⁹ Then he who is given his record in his right hand will exclaim, 'Here is my record, read it. ²⁰ Surely, I knew that I should meet my reckoning,' ²¹ so he will live in a state of Bliss ²² in a lofty garden, ²³ with clusters of fruit within easy reach. ²⁴ We shall say to him, 'Eat and drink joyfully as a reward for the good deeds you did in days gone by.' ²⁵ But he who is given his record in his left hand will say, 'If only I had never been given my Record ²⁶ and knew nothing of my reckoning. ²⁷ How I wish my death had ended all. ²⁸ My wealth has been of no use to me. ²⁹ I am bereft of power.' ³⁰ Seize him and fetter him, ³¹ and then let him enter Hell. ³² Then fasten him with a chain seventy cubits long: ³³ for he did not believe in Almighty God, ³⁴ nor did he feel any urge to feed the needy, ³⁵ so today he has no friend here, ³⁶ and the only food he has is filth ³⁷ which no one will eat except the sinners.

---

a The present world has been made with a view to putting human beings to the test. When the period of testing is over, this world will be demolished and a new world fashioned to meet new requirements will be made. The majesty of God at present reveals itself indirectly, but at that time the Majesty of God will be directly manifested.

³⁸ But nay, I swear by all that you can see ³⁹ as well as all that you cannot see: ⁴⁰ most surely, this is the word brought by a noble messenger, ⁴¹ it is not the word of a poet—how little you believe!—⁴² Nor is it the word of a soothsayer—how little you reflect! ⁴³ It is a revelation sent down by the Sustainer of the Universe: ⁴⁴ if he had invented any lies about Us, ⁴⁵ We would indeed have seized him by his right hand ⁴⁶ and would indeed have cut his life-vein, ⁴⁷ and none of you could have held Us off from him. ⁴⁸ And surely it is an admonition to the God-fearing. ⁴⁹ We know very well that there are some among you who reject Our signs—⁵⁰ it will be a source of bitter regret for those who deny the truth—⁵¹ it is the indubitable truth. ⁵² So glorify the name of your Lord, the Almighty.

70. THE ASCENDING STAIRWAYS
(*AL-MA'ARIJ*)

In the name of God, the Most Gracious, the Most Merciful

¹ A doubter once demanded that punishment be immediately meted out, ² to those who deny the truth. No power can hinder God ³ from punishing them. He is the Lord of the Ascending Stairways, ⁴ by which the angels and the Spirit will ascend to Him in one Day which will last for fifty thousand years. ⁵ Therefore, [O believers] behave with seemly patience. ⁶ They see it [the Day of Judgement] to be far off, ⁷ but We see it near at hand. ⁸ On that Day the heavens shall become like molten brass, ⁹ and the mountains will become like tufts of wool, ¹⁰ and no friend will ask about his friend, ¹¹ though they shall be within sight of each other. The guilty one will gladly ransom himself from the torment of that Day by sacrificing his own children, ¹² his wife, his brother, ¹³ and his kinsfolk who gave him shelter, ¹⁴ and all the people of the earth, if that could deliver him.

¹⁵ But no! There is a raging blaze ¹⁶ stripping away his skin, ¹⁷ and it will claim all those who turned their backs [on the true faith] and turned away [from the truth], ¹⁸ and amassed wealth and hoarded it. ¹⁹ Indeed, man is born impatient: ²⁰ when misfortune touches him he starts lamenting, ²¹ and whenever good fortune comes to him, he

grows niggardly. ²² But not so the worshippers ²³ who are steadfast in prayer; ²⁴ those who give a due share of their wealth ²⁵ to those who ask [for help] and to the destitute; ²⁶ and those who believe in the Day of Judgement ²⁷ and are fearful of the punishment of their Lord; ²⁸ for none may ever feel secure from the punishment of their Lord; ²⁹ those who preserve their chastity ³⁰ except from their spouses and those whom they rightfully possess [through wedlock], for which they incur no blame—³¹ but those who go beyond that limit are transgressors; ³² and those who are faithful to their trusts and to their pledges; ³³ and those who stand by their testimony ³⁴ and are steadfast in their prayers. ³⁵ They will be honoured in the Gardens of Bliss.

³⁶ But what is the matter with those who deny the truth, that they come hastening towards you ³⁷ from the right and from the left, in crowds? ³⁸ Does every one of them aspire to be admitted into a Garden of Delight?*a* ³⁹ Certainly not! They know quite well out of what We created them.

⁴⁰ But nay! I call to witness the Lord of the Easts and the Wests, that We have the power ⁴¹ to replace them with others better than them: nothing can prevent Us from doing this, ⁴² so leave them to indulge in vain idle talk and amuse themselves, until they face the Day which they have been promised, ⁴³ the Day when they shall come out of their graves in haste, as if they were racing to a goal, ⁴⁴ with downcast eyes and faces distorted in shame; such is the Day which they are promised.

71. NOAH (*NUH*)

In the name of God, the Most Gracious, the Most Merciful

¹ We sent Noah forth to his people, saying, 'Warn your people before there comes upon them a grievous punishment.' ² [Noah] said, 'My

---

a These verses give a brief description of the qualities of two types of human beings: those who will be treated as entitled to enter Paradise and those whose deeds will cause them to be thrown into Hell on Doomsday.

people! I am but a plain warner to you, ³ that you should worship God [alone] and be conscious of Him. Pay heed to me. ⁴ He will forgive your sins and will grant you respite till an appointed time. When the time appointed by God arrives, it cannot be postponed, if you only knew.' ⁵ He said, 'My Lord! I have called my people night and day ⁶ but my pleas have only increased their aversion. ⁷ Every time I have called to them, so that You might forgive them, they have only thrust their fingers into their ears, covered themselves up with their garments, grown obstinate, and given themselves up to arrogance. ⁸ Then I called them openly, ⁹ and spoke to them in public and in private.' ¹⁰ Then I said, 'Ask forgiveness of your Lord. Surely He is the most forgiving. ¹¹ He will send down abundant rain from the sky for you, ¹² increase your wealth and sons; and grant you gardens and waterways. ¹³ What is the matter with you that you deny the greatness of God,*a* ¹⁴ when He has created you through different stages of existence? ¹⁵ Do you not see how God has created the seven heavens one above another, ¹⁶ and made the moon therein a light, and made the sun a lamp, ¹⁷ how God has produced you from the earth and caused you to grow, ¹⁸ how He will then return you to it and bring you forth again, ¹⁹ how God has spread the earth out for you ²⁰ so that you may walk along its spacious paths?'

²¹ Noah supplicated, 'Lord, they have disobeyed me, and followed those whose wealth and children have only added to their ruin; ²² and they have hatched a mighty plot, ²³ and they said [to their followers], "Do not ever abandon your deities: abandon neither Wadd, nor Suwa', and neither Yaghuth, nor Yauq nor Nasr!"*b* ²⁴ They have

---

a Literally 'Why do you deny the greatness of God?' This has been explained by 'Abdullah ibn 'Abbas thus, 'You do not accept the Majesty of God as it should be accepted.' This shows that Noah's people did accept God, but the consciousness of His Majesty had not gained mastery over them as it should have done. The fact is that this acceptance of God's greatness is the real standard of God-worship. One who is living in the knowledge of the Majesty of God is a real God-worshipper, while one whose heart is not immersed in God's greatness is not a true believer.

b The opponents of Noah devised many great schemes against him. One of

led many astray; so lead the wrongdoers to further error.' 25 They were drowned and sent to Hell for their misdeeds; they found no one to help them against God.

26 Noah prayed, 'O my Lord! Do not leave on earth a single one of those who deny the truth— 27 if You leave any, they will misguide Your servants, and they will beget none but sinners and deniers of truth—28 Lord! Forgive me and my parents and every true believer who enters my house, forgive all the believing men and believing women; and bestow no increase upon the wrongdoers except in ruin.'

72. THE JINN (*AL-JINN*)

In the name of God, the Most Gracious, the Most Merciful

1 Say, 'It has been revealed to me that a band of the jinn listened [to the Quran] and they said, "We have heard a really wonderful recital, 2 which guides to the right path; so we have believed in it and we will not associate anyone with our Lord— 3 and exalted is the majesty of our Lord—He has taken neither a wife nor a son. 4 And [now we know] that the foolish among us have been saying outrageous things about God. 5 We had supposed that men and jinn would never utter a lie against God. 6 Some men used to seek refuge with the jinn in the past, but that only increased their insolence. 7 They thought, as you did, that God would never raise up anyone from the dead. 8 We sought to reach heaven, but found it filled with strong guards and flames—9 we used to take up a position to listen, but whoever listens now finds a flaming fire lying in wait for him—10 we cannot tell if this bodes evil to those who dwell on earth or whether their Lord intends to guide them. 11 Some of us are

---

these was to spread it about that Noah was against their great ones of old, viz., Wadd, Suwa', Yauq, Yaghuth and Nasr. All of them had been of great piety in ancient times. Gradually they became sanctified and ultimately people started worshipping them. It was easy to turn the people against Noah in the name of these men. So, they made Noah's mission look dubious to the people by saying that he was treading a new path, straying from the path of their revered forebears.

righteous, while others are not; we follow divergent paths. [12] We have realized that we could never thwart God on earth and that we would never be able to thwart Him by flight. [13] When we heard the call to guidance, we believed in it. He who believes in his Lord has no fear of loss or of injustice. [14] Some of us are obedient while others are wrongdoers; it is the obedient who have found the right path, [15] but those who are wrongdoers will become the fuel of Hell." [a]

[16] If they had followed the right path, We would have provided them with abundant rain—[17] so that We may test them by it—whoever turns away from the remembrance of his Lord shall be sternly punished. [18] The mosques are for God's worship—so do not invoke anyone else along with God—[19] when God's servant stood up to pray to Him, they pressed close to him in great numbers, almost stifling him. [20] Say, 'I call only upon my Lord and do not associate anyone else with Him.' [21] Say, 'It is not in my power to cause you either harm or good?' [22] Say, 'Surely no one can protect me against God, nor can I find besides Him any place of refuge. [23] My duty is only to convey that which I receive from Him and His messages.' For those who disobey God and His Messenger there is the fire of hell, wherein they will abide forever.[b]

[24] When they are confronted by what they have been promised, they will realize who is weaker in helpers and fewer in numbers. [25] Say, 'I do not know whether what you are promised is imminent, or whether my Lord has set for it a far-off day.' [26] He alone has knowledge of what is hidden. He reveals this to none, [27] except the messenger whom He has chosen. He sends down guardians

---

a The jinn who heard the Quran not only accepted it immediately, but also became its propagators. This shows that whenever a true discourse reaches the ears of living people, it creates a two-fold effect—first, an open-hearted admission of its truth and second, a willingness to propagate its teachings.

b The entire system of the present world has been formulated with the aim of putting human beings to the test. Therefore reality is revealed here solely to the extent of conveying the divine message. Had there been no human trial to be considered, and had the concealing veils been removed, the people would have seen that, from the angels to the righteous among the jinn, all acknowledge the god-head of God and the whole universe testifies to this.

who walk before them and behind them, ²⁸ so that He may know that the messengers have delivered the messages of their Lord. He encompasses all that is with them and He keeps count of all things.

73. THE WRAPPED ONE (*AL-MUZZAMMIL*)

In the name of God, the Most Gracious, the Most Merciful

¹ O you who are wrapped up in your mantle, ² stand up to pray for much of the night. ³ It may be half the night or a little less than that ⁴ or a little more, but recite the Quran slowly and distinctly.ᵃ ⁵ For We are about to send down to you a message of considerable gravity.

⁶ Surely, getting up at night [for worship] is the most potent means of subduing the self and most suitable for the word [of prayer]. ⁷ You have by day prolonged occupations [with *Dawah* work]. ⁸ Remember the name of your Lord, and devote yourself to Him wholeheartedly. ⁹ He is the Lord of the east and the west, there is no deity but Him, so take Him as your Guardian. ¹⁰ Bear patiently with what they say, and ignore them politely. ¹¹ Leave it to Me to deal with the deniers, who live a life of comfort, and bear with them a little longer. ¹² We have in store for them heavy fetters and a blazing Fire, ¹³ food that chokes and painful punishment ¹⁴ on the Day the earth and mountains shall shake and the mountains crumble into shifting sand dunes.

¹⁵ We have sent a messenger who is a witness over you, just as

---

a Literally 'recite the Quran in slow, measured rhythmic tones'. This means 'recite, paying full attention to the import of the content'. When recited like this, a two-way process between Quran and its reciter comes into play. For him, the Quran is an address or speech by God and his heart starts answering this address at every verse. In the Quran where there is any mention of God's majesty, the reciter's entire existence is strongly affected by his realisation of His greatness. When God's blessings are enumerated in the Quran, the reciter's heart overflows with gratitude; when God's retribution is described in the Quran, the reciter trembles on reading it; when an order is laid down in Quran, the feeling becomes intensified in the reciter that he should become the obedient subject of his Lord by carrying out that order.

We sent a messenger to Pharaoh before you. ¹⁶ But Pharaoh rebelled against the messenger, so We seized him with a strong, crushing grip. ¹⁷ If you persist in denying the truth how will you escape the Day that will turn the children's hair grey. ¹⁸ The Day when the heavens will be rent asunder and God's promise shall be fulfilled. ¹⁹ This, surely, is an admonition. So let him who will, take the right path to his Lord.

²⁰ Your Lord knows that you stand up praying for nearly two-thirds of the night, or one-half of it and sometimes one third of it, as do others among your followers.ᵃ God determines the measure of night and day. He knows that you will not be able to do it, so He has turned to you in mercy. Recite, then, as much of the Quran as is easy for you. He knows that there will be some among you who may be sick and others who will be travelling throughout the land seeking God's bounty, and yet others who may be fighting for the cause of God. So, recite, then as much of it as you are able, and be constant in prayer, and spend in charity, and give to God a goodly loan. For whatever good deed you send on before you for your souls, you will find it with God. It will be improved and richly rewarded by Him. Seek God's forgiveness, He is most forgiving, most merciful.

---

a The compulsory duties in religion have been set forth in terms of the common man's capabilities. But these duties indicate only the minimum of compulsory limits. Beyond these limits there are certain requirements, but these are of a voluntary nature, for example, the offering of the post-midnight prayer (*tahajjud*) in addition to the five compulsory prayers (*fard salat*) said at different times throughout the day, or charity in addition to the prescribed alms-giving (*zakat*), etc. This is the test of a man's devoutness to see how many more good deeds he performs, thus making himself eligible for greater rewards.

74. WRAPPED IN HIS CLOAK
(AL-MUDDATHTHIR)

In the name of God, the Most Gracious, the Most Merciful

¹ O, you, wrapped in your cloak, ² arise and give warning!*ᵃ* ³ Proclaim the glory of your Lord; ⁴ purify your garments; ⁵ shun uncleanness; ⁶ do not bestow a favour in the expectation of receiving more in return; ⁷ and for the sake of your Lord, be patient.

⁸ When the Trumpet is sounded, ⁹ that Day will be a hard and distressing Day. ¹⁰ It will not be easy for those who deny the truth. ¹¹ Leave Me alone [to deal] with him whom I have created alone, ¹² and to whom I have granted resources in abundance, ¹³ and sons to be by his side, ¹⁴ and whom I have provided with every resource, ¹⁵ and yet, he greedily desires that I give him even more! ¹⁶ By no means! He has been stubbornly hostile to Our revelation: ¹⁷ I shall force him to endure a painful uphill climb!

¹⁸ For he thought and he plotted—¹⁹ and woe to him; how he plotted! ²⁰ Let him be destroyed. How he calculated! ²¹ Then he looked round; ²² then he frowned and scowled, ²³ and he turned his back and behaved arrogantly ²⁴ and said, 'This is nothing but sorcery from the ancients. ²⁵ This is nothing but the word of a mortal!'

²⁶ Soon I will cast him into hell. ²⁷ What could make you conceive what hell-fire is? ²⁸ It does not allow anyone to live, and neither does it leave anyone to die; ²⁹ it scorches the skin; ³⁰ there are nineteen [angels] in charge of it—³¹ We have appointed only angels to be wardens of the Fire. We have specified their number only as a trial for those who are bent on denying the truth, so that those who were given the Book might gain in certainty, and those who believe might

---

a The real work of a prophet is warning the people, i.e. informing them of the serious nature of the events which will unfold in the Hereafter. This task can be performed only by one whose heart is overflowing with the realisation of God's Majesty, who possesses a noble character, who shuns all evil, who does good without aspiring to any recompense, who can be unilaterally tolerant and exercise patience in the face of trouble created by others.

increase in faith—and so that neither those who have been given the Scripture nor the believers might have any doubts, and that those sick at heart and those who deny the truth might ask, 'What does God mean by this parable?' In this way, God lets go astray whom He wills, and guides whom He wills. And none knows the forces of your Lord but He. This is but a Reminder for man.

³² No, by the moon! ³³ By the night when it departs. ³⁴ By the dawn when it lightens! ³⁵ Surely, it is one of the gravest things, ³⁶ it is a warning to man, ³⁷ alike to every one of you, who want to go forward or hang back. ³⁸ Every soul is held in pledge against its own deeds, ³⁹ except those of the right hand ⁴⁰ who in their gardens will be enquiring ⁴¹ about the sinners. ⁴² 'What has brought you into the Fire of Hell ?' ⁴³ and they shall reply, 'We were not among those who prayed; ⁴⁴ and we did not feed the poor; ⁴⁵ we indulged in vain arguments along with those who indulged in them; ⁴⁶ and we denied the Day of Judgement ⁴⁷ until the Inevitable End [death] overtook us.' ⁴⁸ So no intercession will avail them.

⁴⁹ Then what is wrong with them that they turn away from admonition, ⁵⁰ like frightened donkeys ⁵¹ fleeing from a lion? ⁵² Indeed, everyone of them desires to have sheets of revelations unfolded before them—⁵³ No! They do not fear the Hereafter—⁵⁴ but this is truly a reminder. ⁵⁵ Let him who will take heed: ⁵⁶ they will only take heed if God so wills: He is the Lord who is worthy to be feared: the Lord of forgiveness.

75. THE DAY OF RESURRECTION
(*AL-QIYAMAH*)

In the name of God, the Most Gracious, the Most Merciful

¹ By the Day of Resurrection, ² and by the self-reproaching soul! ³ Does man think that We cannot [resurrect him and] bring his bones together again? ⁴ Indeed, We have the power to restore his very finger tips! ⁵ Yet man wants to deny what is ahead of him: ⁶ he asks, 'When is this Day of Resurrection to be?' ⁷ But [on that Day], when mortal sight is confounded, ⁸ and the moon is eclipsed,

⁹ when the sun and the moon are brought together, ¹⁰ on that Day man will ask, 'Where can I escape?' ¹¹ But there is nowhere to take refuge: ¹² on that Day, to your Lord alone is the recourse. ¹³ On that Day, man will be told of all that he has sent before and what he has left behind. ¹⁴ Indeed, man shall be a witness against himself, ¹⁵ in spite of all the excuses he may offer.*a*

¹⁶ [Prophet], do not move your tongue too fast in your attempt to learn this revelation: ¹⁷ We Ourself shall see to its collection and recital. ¹⁸ When We have recited it, follow its words attentively; ¹⁹ and then, it will be for Us to make its meaning clear.

²⁰ Truly, you love immediate gain ²¹ and neglect the Hereafter. ²² Some faces will be radiant on that Day, ²³ looking towards their Lord; ²⁴ and some faces will on that Day be gloomy, ²⁵ dreading some great affliction. ²⁶ But when [man's soul] reaches the throat, ²⁷ and when it is asked: 'Could any magician save him now?'; ²⁸ and he knows that it is the time of parting; ²⁹ when his legs are brought together [when affliction is combined with affliction]; ³⁰ on that Day he will be driven towards your Lord!*b*

³¹ He neither believed nor prayed, ³² but rejected the Truth and turned away! ³³ Then he went off to his people, swaggering. ³⁴ Woe to you, [O man!], yes, woe to you. ³⁵ Again, woe to you, [O man!], yes, woe to you! ³⁶ Does man, then, think that he is to be left to

---

a Man has the innate capacity to distinguish between good and evil. By his very nature he wants anyone indulging in evil to be punished and anyone doing righteous deeds to be rewarded. It is this consciousness which is called in the Quran the self-reproaching soul or *al-nafs al-lawwamah*. This faculty bears testimony to the reality of the world of the Hereafter. If, in spite of this inner testimony, an individual does not live up to the highest moral standards, it means that he negates his previously accepted ideals.

b There is only one reason for neglect of the Hereafter and that is the desire to obtain an immediate reward for all one's striving (*kalla bal tuhibbuna'l 'ajilah*). In relation to the Hereafter, the result of one's actions seems infinitely remote. Therefore, man disregards it. But in relation to this world, instant gratification appears to be a distinct possibility, so man rushes towards it. It is obvious that ultimately death overtakes every human being and nullifies all successes. Yet nobody learns a lesson from this, until he himself faces death—which takes away all opportunities for learning lessons.

himself, to go about at will? ³⁷ Was he not once a drop of ejaculated semen, ³⁸ which then became a leech-like clot; then God shaped and fashioned him in due proportion, ³⁹ fashioning out of him the two sexes, the male and the female? ⁴⁰ Then is He not able to bring the dead back to life?

76. MAN (AL-INSAN)

In the name of God, the Most Gracious, the Most Merciful

¹ Was there not a period of time when man was nothing worth mentioning? ² We created man from a drop of mingled fluid so that We might try him; We gave him hearing and sight; ³ We showed him the way, whether he be grateful or ungrateful.ᵃ

⁴ [Now,] behold, for those who deny the truth, We have prepared chains, iron collars and a blazing fire, but ⁵ the righteous shall drink from a cup mixed with the coolness of *kafur*,ᵇ ⁶ a spring from which God's servants will drink, making it gush forth in branches. ⁷ They keep their vows and fear a day the woe of which will spread far and wide; ⁸ they give food, despite their love for it, to the poor and orphans and captives, ⁹ saying, 'We feed you for the sake of God alone, we seek neither recompense nor thanks from you. ¹⁰ Truly, we fear from our Lord a woefully grim Day.' ¹¹ Therefore, God will ward off from them the woes of that Day, and make them find brightness and joy, ¹² and their reward for being patient will

---

a The Quran was revealed in the seventh century A.D. At that time nobody in the whole world knew that the formation of a human being in the mother's womb started with a drop or clot. It was only in the twentieth century that man came to know that a human being's (as well as an animal's) initial creative clot was formed by a combination of two parts—the ovum of a woman and the sperm of a man. When these two microscopic elements combined, that living thing started forming in the mother's womb which finally took the shape of a human being. The occurrence of the expression, 'a drop of mingled fluid' (*min nutfatin amshajin*) in the Quran one thousand five hundred years ago proves that the Quran is the Book of God.

b Camphor—a sweet smelling herb.

be a Garden and silk [clothing]. ¹³ Reclining upon couches, they will find therein neither the heat of the sun nor bitter, biting cold, ¹⁴ the shading branches of trees will come down low over them, and their clusters of fruit, will hang down where they are the easiest to reach. ¹⁵ Vessels of silver and goblets of pure crystal will be passed round among them ¹⁶ and gleaming silver goblets which have been filled to the exact measure, ¹⁷ and they will be given a cup to drink flavoured with ginger, ¹⁸ from a flowing spring called *Salsabil*. ¹⁹ They will be attended by youths who will not age—when you see them you will think them to be like sprinkled pearls—²⁰ wherever you look, you will see bliss and a great kingdom: ²¹ they will wear green garments of fine silk and rich brocade. They will be adorned with silver bracelets. And their Lord will give them a pure drink. ²² This is your reward. Your endeavour is fully acknowledged.*a*

²³ Truly, it is We who have revealed to you the Quran, a gradual revelation. ²⁴ So wait patiently for the command of your Lord, and do not yield to anyone among them who is sinful or ungrateful; ²⁵ and glorify your Lord morning and evening; ²⁶ and during the night prostrate yourself before Him, and extol His glory for a long part of the night. ²⁷ Those people [who are unmindful of God] aspire for immediate gains, and put behind them a Heavy Day. ²⁸ It was We who created them and made their constitution strong, but if We wish we can replace them with others like them. ²⁹ This is a reminder. Let whoever wishes, take the right path to his Lord. ³⁰ But you cannot will it unless God wills [to show you that way]—God is indeed all-knowing and wise—³¹ He admits whoever He will into His grace and has prepared a painful punishment for the evil doers.

---

a This is the description of a higher plane of Paradise where people of a higher level of faith will be settled. Royal bounties will fall to the lot of the inhabitants of this Paradise.

77. THOSE THAT ARE SENT FORTH
(*AL-MURSALAT*)

In the name of God, the Most Gracious, the Most Merciful

¹ By the winds sent forth in swift succession, ² and then storming on with a tempest's force, ³ and the rain-spreading winds, ⁴ separating one from another, ⁵ by those who bring down the reminder, ⁶ to excuse some and warn others: ⁷ that which you have been promised shall be fulfilled.

⁸ When the stars lose their light, ⁹ and when the sky is rent asunder, ¹⁰ and when the mountains crumble into dust ¹¹ and when the messengers are brought together at the appointed time—¹² for what Day has this been appointed? ¹³ For the Day of Decision. ¹⁴ What will explain to you what the Day of Judgement is? ¹⁵ Woe on that Day to those who reject the truth. ¹⁶ Did We not destroy the earlier peoples? ¹⁷ We will now cause the later ones to follow them: ¹⁸ thus do We deal with the culprits. ¹⁹ Woe on that Day to those who reject the truth!

²⁰ Did We not create you from a humble fluid, ²¹ then placed it in a secure repository [the womb], ²² for an appointed term? ²³ Thus We have determined the stages of development and Our power to determine is excellent indeed. ²⁴ Woe on that Day to those who reject the truth! ²⁵ Have We not made the earth a receptacle, ²⁶ for the living and the dead? ²⁷ Have We not placed high mountains upon it and given you fresh water to drink? ²⁸ Woe on that Day to those who reject the truth!

²⁹ Proceed to that which you denied. ³⁰ Proceed to a shadow rising in three columns: ³¹ affording neither shade, nor protection from the flames, ³² and throwing up sparks as huge as towers ³³ and as bright as a herd of yellow camels. ³⁴ Woe on that Day to those who reject the truth! ³⁵ On that Day they will be speechless, ³⁶ nor shall they be permitted to offer excuses. ³⁷ Woe on that Day to those who reject the truth! ³⁸ This is the Day of Judgement. We have assembled you

all together with past generations. ³⁹ If now you have any strategy, use it against Me. ⁴⁰ Woe on that Day to those who reject the truth!ᵃ

⁴¹ The righteous shall dwell amidst cool shades and fountains, ⁴² and shall have fruits such as they desire; ⁴³ [They will be told], 'Eat and drink with relish in return for what you did [in life]: ⁴⁴ this is how We reward those who do good.' ⁴⁵ [But] woe on that Day to those who reject the truth! ⁴⁶ Eat [your fill] and enjoy your life for a little while, O you who are lost in sin. ⁴⁷ Woe on that Day to those who reject the truth! ⁴⁸ When they are bidden to bow down, they do not bow down. ⁴⁹ Woe on that Day to those who reject the truth! ⁵⁰ In which word then, after this, will they believe?ᵇ

78. THE TIDINGS (*AL-NABA'*)

In the name of God, the Most Gracious, the Most Merciful

¹ What are they asking each other about? ² About the awesome tidings [of resurrection] ³ concerning which they are in disagreement! ⁴ But they will soon come to know. ⁵ Surely, they will soon find out the truth! ⁶ Have We not spread the earth like a bed, ⁷ and raised the mountains like supporting poles? ⁸ We created you in pairs, ⁹ and gave you repose in sleep, ¹⁰ and the night as a cover, ¹¹ and made the day for earning a livelihood. ¹² We have built above you seven mighty heavens, ¹³ and We have set therein a glowing lamp. ¹⁴ From the rain clouds We send waters pouring down in abundance,

---

a When a man is confronted with the horrors of the Hereafter, he will find himself helpless. At that time, those who were wont to speak as if their vocabulary was inexhaustible, will be rendered speechless.

b God's bounties exist in the present world for the purpose of putting human beings to the test and only for a limited period of time. God's bounties will appear in the Hereafter in an ideal form and will be eternal. Today, everybody shares those bounties. But the bounties of the Hereafter will be shared only by those who were obedient when they had freedom, who bowed down when they were not compelled to do so. Those who accept the Truth purely on the strength of arguments, and as a matter of faith, deserve Paradise, while those who submit to the divine will only after experiencing the wrath of God will be cast into Hell.

¹⁵ so that We may bring forth thereby grain and a variety of plants, ¹⁶ and gardens dense with foliage. ¹⁷ Surely, the Day of Judgement has an appointed time.

¹⁸ On that Day when the trumpet shall be sounded, you shall come in droves, ¹⁹ and the heaven shall be opened, and become gates, ²⁰ and the mountains shall be made to vanish, as if they had been a mirage. ²¹ Surely, Hell lies in wait, ²² a home for the transgressors, ²³ where they shall remain for ages, ²⁴ and where they will taste neither coolness nor any drink ²⁵ save boiling water and a stinking fluid—²⁶ a fitting requital, ²⁷ for they never expected to be called to account, ²⁸ and they rejected outright Our signs; ²⁹ but We have recorded everything in a Book. ³⁰ [So We shall say], 'Taste, then, [the fruit of your evil doings,] for now We shall bestow on you nothing but more and more suffering!'

³¹ As for those who are mindful of God, they shall surely triumph: ³² theirs shall be gardens and vineyards, ³³ and young maidens of equal age, ³⁴ and overflowing cups. ³⁵ There they shall not hear any idle talk, or any untruth: ³⁶ all this will be a recompense, a gift, that will suffice them, from your Lord,[a] ³⁷ the Sustainer of the heavens and the earth and all that lies between them, the most Gracious [and] none shall have it in their power to raise their voices to Him. ³⁸ On the Day when the Spirit and the angels stand in ranks, no one will speak, except for those to whom the Lord of Mercy gives permission, and who will say only what is right. ³⁹ That Day is sure to come, so whoever wishes to, let him take the path that leads towards his Lord. ⁴⁰ We have warned you of a chastisement which is near at hand, on the Day when man shall [clearly] see what his hands have sent ahead, and when he who has denied the truth shall say, 'Oh, would that I were dust!'

---

a The atmosphere of Paradise will be free of all vain talk and falsehood. Therefore, only those who can prove that they have the inclination to live their lives in this world without indulging in trivialities and deceit, will be chosen to inhabit the pure and sublime atmosphere of Paradise.

79. THE PLUCKERS (*AL-NAZI'AT*)

In the name of God, the Most Gracious, the Most Merciful

¹ By [the winds] that pluck out vehemently ² and those that blow gently, ³ and by [the clouds] that swim serenely and ⁴ by those that outstrip them suddenly, ⁵ and by those who regulate events. ⁶ On the Day when a violent convulsion will convulse [the world], ⁷ to be followed by further [convulsions], ⁸ hearts will be throbbing, ⁹ while eyes will be downcast. ¹⁰ They say, 'What? shall we be brought back to life, ¹¹ even after we have turned into decayed bones?' ¹² and they say, 'That indeed would be a losing return.' ¹³ But all it will take is a single blast, ¹⁴ and behold! They will all come out in the open.*ᵃ*

¹⁵ Have you heard the story of Moses? ¹⁶ His Lord called out to him by the sacred valley of Tuwa: ¹⁷ [saying], 'Go to Pharaoh, he has exceeded all bounds, ¹⁸ and say, "Will you reform yourself? ¹⁹ Do you want me to guide you to your Lord, so that you should fear Him?"' ²⁰ Moses showed him the great sign, ²¹ but he denied it and refused [the faith]. ²² Then he quickly turned his back. ²³ And he summoned all his people, ²⁴ and proclaimed, 'I am your supreme Lord,' ²⁵ but God seized him and meted out to him the chastisement of both the next world and the present: ²⁶ surely there is in this a lesson for the God-fearing.

²⁷ [O Men!] Are you more difficult to create than the heaven which He has built, ²⁸ by raising its vault high and fashioning it flawlessly, ²⁹ and making its night dark and bringing forth its morning light, ³⁰ and the earth which He spread out, ³¹ after that bringing forth from it its water and its pasture land, ³² and making the mountains firm: ³³ [all this] as a means of sustenance for you and your animals?*ᵇ*

---

a Every year we experience periods of calm weather followed by gales bringing clouds and rainstorms. Soon it is clearly visible that where the land was desolate, a new world has sprung up. This event of nature indicates the possibility of the Hereafter. This shows in symbolical fashion that the emergence of the Hereafter from the present world is just as possible as the emergence of lush green foliage from dry barren land.

b The magnificent phenomenon before us in the shape of the universe is so

³⁴ When the great over-whelming event arrives, ³⁵ on the Day that man remembers what he strove for ³⁶ and Hell is there for all to see, ³⁷ anyone who has acted arrogantly ³⁸ and prefers the life of this world, ³⁹ will find himself in Hell; ⁴⁰ but one who fears to stand before his Lord and restrained himself from base desires, ⁴¹ shall dwell in Paradise. ⁴² They will ask you [Prophet] about the Hour, saying, 'When it will come to pass?', ⁴³ what have you to do with the mentioning of it? ⁴⁴ Your Lord alone knows when it will come; ⁴⁵ you are but a warner for those who fear it. ⁴⁶ On the Day when they see it, they will feel as if they had tarried in this world for only one evening or one morning.

80. HE FROWNED (*'ABASA*)

In the name of God, the Most Gracious, the Most Merciful

¹ He frowned and turned away ² when the blind man approached him,ᵃ ³ for how can you know that he might seek to purify himself, ⁴ or take heed and derive benefit from [Our] warning? ⁵ As for him who was indifferent, ⁶ you eagerly attended to him—⁷ though you are not to be blamed if he would not purify himself—⁸ but as for one who comes to you, eagerly ⁹ and in awe of God ¹⁰ you pay him

---

great that all other things are small in comparison to it. So, in the world when the occurrence of a big event is possible, why should the occurrence of a small event not be possible? There are already many factors in existence on a large scale which explain the Quran's declaration that man shall one Day have to face resurrection.

a The Prophet Muhammad was once preaching to the chiefs of the Quraysh in Makkah, when a blind man, 'Abdullah ibn Umm al-Maktum, arrived at the gathering and said, 'O, Prophet of God ! Please teach me something of what God has taught you.' The arrival of a blind person at this juncture displeased the Prophet. These verses were revealed on that occasion. In these verses the apparent addressee is the Prophet Muhammad, but actually it has been clarified with reference to this incident that, in the eyes of God, those prominent people who have turned away from religion have no value. Before God, the valued person is the one who is imbued with the God-fearing spirit, though apparently he may be a 'blind' person.

no heed. [11] Indeed, this [Quran] is an admonition. [12] Let him who will, pay heed to it. [13] It is set down on honoured pages, [14] exalted and purified, [15] by the hands of scribes,

[16] exalted and purified. [17] Woe to man! How ungrateful he is! [18] Of what [stuff] has He created him? [19] Out of a drop of sperm! He creates and proportions him, [20] He makes his path easy for him. [21] Then He causes him to die and be buried. [22] Then when He pleases, He will bring him back to life. [23] Yet man declines to do His bidding. [24] Let man reflect on the food he eats. [25] We let the rain pour down in torrents [26] and then We cleaved the earth asunder. [27] We make the grain grow out of it, [28] and grape vines and vegetables, [29] and olive trees and date palms [30] and burgeoning enclosed gardens [31] and fruits and fodder [32] as provision for you and for your cattle to enjoy.

[33] But when the deafening blast is sounded, [34] on that Day a man shall flee from his own brother, [35] his mother, his father, [36] his wife and his sons: [37] on that Day every man among them will have enough concern of his own— [38] on that Day some faces will be beaming, [39] laughing, and rejoicing, [40] but some faces will be covered with dust [41] and overcast with gloom: [42] those will be ones who denied the truth and were immersed in iniquity.

81. FOLDING UP (*AL-TAKWIR*)

In the name of God, the Most Gracious, the Most Merciful

[1] When the sun is folded up, [2] and when the stars lose their light, [3] and when the mountains are moved, [4] when ten-month pregnant camels are left untended, [5] and when all beasts are gathered together, [6] and when the seas are set on fire, [7] when the souls are divided into different classes, [8] and when the female infant buried alive is asked [9] for what sin she was killed, [10] when the records of men's deeds are laid open, [11] when the sky is unveiled, [12] and when Hell is set ablaze, [13] when Paradise is brought close: [14] [then] each soul shall know what it has put forward.[a]

---

[a] The scenes of Doomsday, or the Day of Judgement, have been described

¹⁵ I swear by the receding stars, ¹⁶ the planets that run their course and set, ¹⁷ and the night that falls, ¹⁸ and the first breath of morning. ¹⁹ Truly, this is the word brought by a noble messenger, ²⁰ endowed with power and held in honour by the Lord of the Throne—²¹ who is obeyed there and is worthy of trust. ²² Your companion is not one possessed: ²³ he truly beheld him [the angel] on the clear horizon. ²⁴ He is not avid of the Unseen. ²⁵ Nor is this the word of an outcast devil. ²⁶ So where are you going? ²⁷ This is merely a reminder to all mankind; ²⁸ to every one of you who wishes to tread the straight path. ²⁹ But you cannot will it unless God, the Lord of the Universe, so wills it [to show you that way].

82. THE CLEAVING ASUNDER
(*AL-INFITAR*)

In the name of God, the Most Gracious, the Most Merciful

¹ When the sky is cleft asunder; ² and when the stars are scattered; ³ when the seas overflow; ⁴ and when the graves are laid open: ⁵ then everyone will know what he has sent ahead, and what he has left behind. ⁶ O man! What is it that lures you away from your bountiful Sustainer, ⁷ who created you, fashioned you and proportioned you, ⁸ in whatever form He pleased? ⁹ Yet you deny the Last Judgement. ¹⁰ Surely, there are guardians watching over you, ¹¹ noble recorders, ¹² who know all that you do:*ᵃ* ¹³ the virtuous will dwell in bliss,

---

at various points in the Quran. When Doomsday arrives, the present balance of the world will break down, and man will feel himself helpless. On that Day, all things except good deeds will lose their value. Then the oppressed person will have the right to take his revenge upon his oppressor in whatever manner he likes.

a The Quran informs us that the Day of Judgement will finally come: all of humanity will be assembled on that Day and will be rewarded or punished according to their deeds. These tidings are absolutely consistent with the present condition of the world. Indeed, the meaningful creation of the human being has its justification in this announcement. Moreover, a system exists in the present world for the recording of the words and deeds of man. That becomes

¹⁴ whereas the wicked will be in Hell; ¹⁵ which they shall enter on the Day of Judgement, ¹⁶ and from which they will find no escape. ¹⁷ What will make you realize what the Day of Judgement will be? ¹⁸ Again: what will make you realize what the Day of Judgement will be? ¹⁹ It will be a Day when no human being shall be of the least avail to any other human being, God [alone] will hold command on that Day.

83. THOSE WHO GIVE SHORT MEASURE (*AL-MUTAFFIFIN*)

In the name of God, the Most Gracious, the Most Merciful

¹ Woe to those who give short measure, ² who demand of other people full measure for themselves, ³ but when they give by measurement or weight to others,*ª* they give them less.*ᵇ* ⁴ Do such people not realize that they will be raised up, ⁵ on a fateful Day. ⁶ The Day when mankind will stand before the Lord of the Universe? ⁷ Indeed! The record of the wicked is in the *Sijjin*— ⁸ and what could make you understand what the *Sijjin* is?—⁹ it is a written record. ¹⁰ Woe, on that Day, to those who reject, ¹¹ those who deny the Day of Judgement. ¹² No one denies it except for the evil aggressor.

---

understandable in the light of what the Quran tells us. (For details regarding the recording of words and deeds, see the translator's book titled: *God Arises*).

a Literally 'when they give by measure to others, or weigh out to them'.

b Every human being wants to have his dues paid in full. But it is only right and proper that, if he is an individual of character, he should also take care to give to others their full and rightful dues. He should want for others whatever he wants for himself. Those who take full measure for themselves and give less to others, will reach the Hereafter in such an ill state of grace that they will be doomed to eternal perdition.

One who tries to ensure full measure for himself knows that everyone should receive his just deserts. In this context, if he gives less while giving to others, he lessens his realization of or sensitivity to the rights of others. If a man repeats this sort of misdeed again and again, a time will finally come when he will completely lose his sensitivity to others' rights. His heart will be completely corroded by his sinful actions.

¹³ When Our revelations are conveyed to him, he says, 'Fables of the ancients!' ¹⁴ No! Their own deeds have cast a veil over their hearts. ¹⁵ Indeed! On that Day a barrier will be set between them and their Lord, ¹⁶ then they shall enter the Fire of Hell, ¹⁷ and they will be told, 'This is what you were wont to belie.'

¹⁸ But, the record of the righteous is [preserved] in the '*Illiyyin*— ¹⁹ and what will make you understand what the '*Illiyyin* is?—²⁰ a written record, ²¹ which those angels closest to God will bear witness to. ²² The virtuous will surely be in bliss, ²³ seated on couches and gazing around in wonder. ²⁴ You will find in their faces the brightness of bliss. ²⁵ They will be given a drink of pure wine, sealed, ²⁶ its seal will be of musk—for this let the aspirants aspire—²⁷ a wine tempered with the waters of Tasnim, ²⁸ a spring at which those drawn close to God will drink. ²⁹ The wicked used to laugh at the believers— ³⁰ when they passed by them, they would wink at one another; ³¹ and when they returned to their own people, they would speak of them jestingly; ³² and when they saw them, they said [scornfully], 'These men have surely gone astray,' ³³ though they were not sent to be their keepers—³⁴ so today those who believe shall [be able to] laugh at those who denied the truth ³⁵ as they sit on couches, gazing around. ³⁶ Have those who deny the truth [not] been paid back for their deeds?

84. THE BURSTING OPEN
(*AL-INSHIQAQ*)

In the name of God, the Most Gracious, the Most Merciful

¹ When the sky bursts open, ² and obeys its Lord as it must, ³ when the earth flattens out, ⁴ and casts out all that is within it and becomes empty; ⁵ and obeys its Lord as it must,ᵃ ⁶ O man, having

---

a Whatever is related here about Doomsday refers apparently to an unknown world. However, such evidence exists as points to its veracity. An example of this is the present world itself. The very existence of the world proves that another similar or different world may come into existence. Furthermore,

striven hard towards your Lord, you shall meet Him: [7] he who is given his record in his right hand [8] shall have an easy reckoning [9] and he shall return to his people, joyfully, [10] but as for him whose record shall be given to him from behind his back, [11] he will pray for utter destruction [12] and he will enter the blazing flame. [13] He used to be happy with his own people; [14] for he never thought that he would have to return [to God]. [15] But he will indeed! His Lord was ever watching him. [16] I swear by the glow of sunset, [17] by the night and what it covers, [18] and the moon when it grows full, [19] you will progress from stage to stage. [20] What is wrong with them that they do not believe? [21] When the Quran is read to them, why do they not fall to their knees? [22] Indeed, those who are bent on denying the truth reject it— [23] God is quite aware of what they are storing in their hearts. [24] Therefore, give them the news of a painful punishment.[a] [25] But for those who believe and do good works; for them there shall be a never-ending reward.

85. THE CONSTELLATIONS (*AL-BURUJ*)

In the name of God, the Most Gracious, the Most Merciful

[1] By the sky with its constellations, [2] and by the promised Day, [3] by the Witness and the witnessed, [4] destroyed were the people of the trench, [5] the makers of the fuel-stoked fire! [6] They sat by it [7] to watch what they were doing to the believers, [8] whom they hated for no other reason than that they believed in God, the Almighty, the Praiseworthy, [9] to whom belongs the kingdom of the heavens and the earth. God is witness over all things. [10] Those who persecute the believing men and believing women, and then do not repent, will

---

certain extraordinary aspects of the Quran prove that it is the Book of God. (For details see The Quran: An Abiding Wonder by the translator).

a In spite of such clear indications, there are those who do not believe in the Hereafter and live out their lives without ever taking it into account. Such individuals are certainly committing a crime which is deserving of the punishment mentioned above.

surely suffer the punishment of Hell, and the torment of burning. [11] But those who believe and do good deeds shall be rewarded with gardens watered by flowing rivers. That is the supreme triumph.[a] [12] The grip of your Lord is indeed severe—[13] it is He who begins and repeats [His creation]—[14] and He is the Forgiving and Loving One. [15] The Lord of the Glorious Throne, [16] Executor of His own will. [17] Have you not heard the story of the hosts [18] of Pharaoh and Thamud? [19] Yet those who deny the truth persist in denial. [20] God encompasses them from all sides. [21] It is indeed a glorious Quran, [22] written on a preserved Tablet.

86. THAT WHICH COMES IN THE NIGHT (*AL-TARIQ*)

In the name of God, the Most Gracious, the Most Merciful

[1] By the heavens and that which comes in the night—[2] and what could make you know what it is that comes in the night? [3] It is the shining star[b]—[4] [for] no human being has been left unguarded. [5] Let man reflect on what he was created from. [6] He was created from spurting fluid, [7] issuing from between the backbone and the breastbone: [8] He certainly has the power to bring him back to life.

---

a The perfect organisation of the system of the universe ensures that the Day of Final Judgement will come. Tidings of this very Day have been given by all the prophets and their true deputies. In spite of this, those who do not accept the Truth and even become the enemies of the preachers of the Truth, indulge in such aggressiveness and arrogance that they cannot save themselves from the dreadful consequences. However, those who give a positive response to the call for the acceptance of Truth, in spite of different kinds of difficulties, will receive the greatest possible reward from Merciful God.

b It is quite evident that there is planning in the creation of man and the world. This planning strongly implies that there must be some purpose behind this creation. And indeed, this purpose has been revealed to man through divine revelation. However, only that individual learns a lesson from revelation who is of a receptive nature. Such people will be introduced to the eternal bounties of God. But those whose arrogance prevents them from accepting guidance, will be doomed to being cast into the flames of the eternal fire.

⁹ On the Day when secrets are disclosed, ¹⁰ [man] will have no power, and no helper. ¹¹ By the heavens, ever-revolving, ¹² by the earth cracking open with new growth. ¹³ It is surely a decisive utterance; ¹⁴ and is not to be taken lightly. ¹⁵ They are planning a scheme, ¹⁶ and so am I: ¹⁷ so bear with those who deny the truth, and let them be for a little while.

87. THE MOST HIGH (*AL-A'LA*)

In the name of God, the Most Gracious, the Most Merciful

¹ Glorify the name of your Lord, the Most High, ² who created all things and gave them due proportions, ³ who determines the nature [of all that exists], and guided it accordingly;ᵃ ⁴ who brings forth green pasture, ⁵ then turns it into black stubble. ⁶ [O Prophet!] We shall make you recite the Quran so that you will not forget any of it—⁷ except whatever God wills; He knows both what is manifest and what is hidden—⁸ We shall facilitate for you the Easy Way. ⁹ Remind, if the reminder can be of benefit. ¹⁰ He who fears [God] will heed the reminder, ¹¹ but it will be ignored by the most unfortunate, ¹² who will enter the Great Fire, ¹³ where he will neither die nor live. ¹⁴ He who purifies himself, ¹⁵ who remembers the name of his Lord and prays, shall indeed be successful. ¹⁶ But you prefer the life of this world, ¹⁷ although the Hereafter is better and more lasting. ¹⁸ This indeed is what is taught in the former scriptures— ¹⁹ the scriptures of Abraham and Moses.

---

a It is quite evident that there is planning in the creation of man and the world. This planning strongly implies that there must be some purpose behind this creation. And indeed, this purpose has been revealed to man through divine revelation. However, only that individual learns a lesson from revelation who is of a receptive nature. Such people will be introduced to the eternal bounties of God. But those whose arrogance prevents them from accepting guidance, will be doomed to being cast into the flames of the eternal fire.

88. THE OVERWHELMING EVENT
(*AL-GHASHIYAH*)

In the name of God, the Most Gracious, the Most Merciful

¹ Have you heard about the Overwhelming Event? ² On that Day, there shall be downcast faces, ³ labouring, weary, ⁴ they shall enter a burning Fire ⁵ and will be made to drink from a boiling spring, ⁶ they shall have no food but thorns, ⁷ which will neither nourish nor satisfy hunger. ⁸ Some faces on that Day will be radiant, ⁹ well pleased with the result of their striving, ¹⁰ in a sublime garden, ¹¹ where they will hear no idle talk, ¹² with a flowing spring,¹³ raised couches, ¹⁴ and goblets set at hand, ¹⁵ cushions ranged, ¹⁶ and carpets spread out. ¹⁷ Do they never reflect on the camels and how they were created, ¹⁸ and on the sky, how it is raised aloft, ¹⁹ and on the mountains, how they are firmly set up, ²⁰ and on the earth, how it is spread out?*ᵃ* ²¹ So, [O Prophet] exhort them: your task is only to exhort, ²² you are not their keeper. ²³ But whoever turns back and denies the truth, ²⁴ will be punished by God with the greatest punishment. ²⁵ Certainly, it is to Us that they will return. ²⁶ Then, surely, it is for Us to call them to account.

---

a Man observes that a serviceable animal like the camel is obedient to him. The sky in all its majesty is well disposed towards him. The earth, without any effort on our part, is subservient to our interests. All these phenomena remind a thoughtful man of God and the Hereafter. Those who derive the nourishment of remembrance from these arrangements of the world have established their entitlement to God's eternal bounties, while those who have remained lost in forgetfulness and neglect, have proved that they deserve to be deprived of every kind of bounty—forever.

89. THE DAWN (*AL-FAJR*)

In the name of God, the Most Gracious, the Most Merciful

¹ By the Dawn, ² by the Ten Nights, ³ by the even and the odd, ⁴ and by the passing night, ⁵ is there not in this strong evidence for a man of sense? ⁶ Have you not heard of how your Lord dealt with the tribe of 'Ad, ⁷ the people of Iram, the city of many pillars, ⁸ the like of which has never been created in the land, ⁹ and with the Thamud, who cut out [huge] rocks in the valley, ¹⁰ and with Pharaoh of the stakes? ¹¹ All of them committed excesses in their lands, ¹² and caused much corruption in them: ¹³ so your Lord unleashed on them the scourge of punishment: ¹⁴ for, indeed, your Sustainer is ever on the watch! ¹⁵ As for man, when his Lord tests him, through honour and blessings, he says, 'My Lord has honoured me,' ¹⁶ but when He tests him by straitening his means of livelihood, he says, 'My Lord has disgraced me.' ¹⁷ No indeed, but you show no kindness to the orphan, ¹⁸ nor do you urge one another to feed the poor, ¹⁹ and you greedily devour the inheritance of the weak, ²⁰ and you have a love of wealth which can never be satisfied. ²¹ No indeed! When the earth is crushed and ground to dust, ²² when your Lord comes down with the angels, rank upon rank, ²³ and Hell is made to appear on that Day, then man will be mindful, but what will being mindful then avail him? ²⁴ He will say, 'Oh, would that I had provided beforehand for my life!' ²⁵ On that Day no one will punish as He punishes, ²⁶ and none can bind with bonds like His! ²⁷ [But to the righteous, God will say], 'O soul at peace, ²⁸ return to your Lord, well-pleased, well-pleasing. ²⁹ Join My servants. ³⁰ Enter My Paradise.'

90. THE CITY (*AL-BALAD*)

In the name of God, the Most Gracious, the Most Merciful

¹ I swear by this city—² and you are dwelling in this city—³ and by parent and offspring, ⁴ that We have created man into a life of toil

and trial.[a] [5] Does he think then that no one has power over him? [6] He says, 'I have spent enormous wealth.' [7] Does he then think that no one sees him? [8] Have We not given him two eyes, [9] and a tongue, and a pair of lips, [10] and shown him the two paths?[b] [11] But he has not attempted the ascent. [12] What will explain to you what the ascent is? [13] It is the freeing of a slave; [14] or the feeding in times of famine [15] of an orphaned relative [16] or some needy person in distress, [17] and to be one of those who believe and urge one another to steadfastness and compassion. [18] Those who do so are the people of the right hand, [19] and [as for] those who are bent on denying the truth of Our revelations, they are the people of the left hand, [20] and the Fire will close in on them.

91. THE SUN (*AL-SHAMS*)

In the name of God, the Most Gracious, the Most Merciful

[1] By the sun and its rising brightness [2] and by the moon as it follows it, [3] and by the day as it reveals its glory [4] and by the night when it draws a veil over it, [5] by the sky and how He built it [6] and by the earth and how He spread it, [7] by the soul and how He formed it, [8] then inspired it to understand what was right and wrong for it. [9] He who purifies it will indeed be successful, [10] and he who corrupts it is sure to fail.[c] [11] The Thamud tribe rejected the truth because of

---

a Man has never been able to free himself from hardship. This shows that he is subordinate to some Superior Power. Similarly, man's eyes show that there is also a Superior Eye which is watching him. His power of speech indicates that there is One capable of speech over and above him, who has bestowed upon him the power of speech and showed him the right path. If a man realizes himself in the true sense, then he will certainly recognise God.

b God has commanded man to scale two heights—one is to treat others with justice, and help them in their hour of need. The other is to have firm faith in God. When such belief enters the inner depths of a human being, it does not remain confined to his own thinking but rather makes him become communicative. He then attempts to lead others along the path of Truth which he himself has adopted.

c Almighty God has made threefold arrangements for the guidance of

their arrogance, [12] when the most wicked man among them rose up. [13] Then the messenger of God said to them, 'This is God's she-camel. Let her drink.' [14] But they gave him the lie, and hamstrung the she-camel. So their Lord destroyed them for their crime and razed their city to the ground. [15] He did not fear the consequences.

92. NIGHT (AL-LAYL)

In the name of God, the Most Gracious, the Most Merciful

[1] By the night as it veils [the earth] in darkness, [2] and by the day as it appears radiantly, [3] and by the creation of the male and the female.[a] [4] O men, you truly strive towards the most diverse ends! [5] As for one who gives [to others] and fears [God], [6] and believes in the truth of what is right, [7] We will pave his way to ease. [8] But as for one who is miserly and unheeding, [9] and rejects what is right, [10] We shall pave his way to hardship, [11] nor will his wealth profit him when he falls [into the pit]. [12] Surely, it is for Us to provide guidance— [13] and to Us belongs the Hereafter as well as the present world— [14] I have warned you then about a raging Fire: [15] none shall enter it but the most wicked, [16] who denied [the truth], and turned away. [17] One who fears God shall be kept away from it— [18] one who gives his wealth to become purified, [19] and owes no favour

---

man. On the one hand, the universe has been so constructed that it has become the practical manifestation of God's will. On the other hand, the human psyche has been infused with an intuitive consciousness of good and bad. Thereafter, it was arranged that Truth and falsehood, justice and injustice be revealed clearly through the prophets in a language understandable to the people. Even after this, if people do not adopt the right path, they are undoubtedly transgressors.

a All things in this world are in pairs—male and female; night and day; positive and negative particles, matter and anti-matter. Everything in this world joins its pair and fulfils its purpose. This is a clear proof of the fact that this universe is purposeful. In such a purposeful universe it is impossible for both the good deeds and the bad deeds performed in it to have the same final consequences. This would not be consistent with the image of the Creator presented by the universe.

to anyone, which is to be repaid, ²⁰ acting only for the sake of his Lord the Most High—²¹ and before long he will be well satisfied.

93. THE GLORIOUS MORNING LIGHT (*AL-DUHA*)

In the name of God, the Most Gracious, the Most Merciful

¹ By the glorious morning light; ² and by the night when it darkens, ³ your Lord has not forsaken you, nor is He displeased with you, ⁴ and the Hereafter will indeed be better for you than the present life;*a* ⁵ soon you will be gratified with what your Lord will give you. ⁶ Did He not find you orphaned and shelter you?*b* ⁷ Did He not find you wandering, and give you guidance? ⁸ Did He not find you in want, and make you free from want? ⁹ Therefore do not treat the orphan with harshness,*c* ¹⁰ and do not chide the one who asks for help; ¹¹ but proclaim the blessings of your Lord.

---

a The system of this world has been so formulated that here the day dawns and night also falls. Only with the occurrence of both is the system perfect. Similarly, for the proper development of a man, it is necessary that he should have hardship as well as easy circumstances. In this world, hardship befalls the servant of God in order to activate his latent capabilities. Impediments are put in his way so that he may strive to make his future brighter than his present.

b The Prophet Muhammad was born an orphan. Then God provided him with the best of guardians. He went eagerly in search of the Truth. Then God opened the door of Truth for him. He was apparently without wealth. Then God made him prosperous through his wife, Khadijah. These are historical examples which show how Almighty God helps His subjects.

c Man should help the weak so that he may be entitled to God's grace. His words should be full of the expression of God's grace, so that God may confer His blessings upon him.

94. COMFORT (*AL-SHARH*)

In the name of God, the Most Gracious, the Most Merciful

[1] Have We not lifted up your heart,[a] [2] and removed your burden [3] that weighed so heavily on your back, and [4] have We not given you high renown? [5] So, surely with every hardship there is ease; [6] surely, with every hardship there is ease. [7] So, when you are free, strive hard, [8] and to your Lord turn [all] your attention.

95. THE FIG (*AL-TIN*)

In the name of God, the Most Gracious, the Most Merciful

[1] By the Fig and the Olive, [2] and by Mount Sinai, [3] and by this secure land,[b] [4] We have indeed created man in the best of mould, [5] then We cast him down as the lowest of the low, [6] except for those who believe and do good deeds—theirs shall be an unending reward![c]

---

a The Prophet Muhammad went tirelessly in quest of knowledge about reality and Truth. Almighty God blessed him with this knowledge, to culminate opening his heart to the deep realisation of Truth (*ma'rifah*). Then he started preaching the oneness of God in Makkah, where he had to face stiff opposition, but it was thanks to this opposition, that he became known throughout the country.

This is God's law in the present world. Hence, a man has to face difficult conditions (*'usr*) in the beginning, but if he perseveres with patience, this *'usr* or hardship becomes a stepping stone to new and easy circumstances (*yusr*). Therefore, a man should always look towards God and continue to struggle according to his capacity.

b Fig (*Tin*) and Olive (*Zaytun*) are the names of two hills in the vicinity of Jerusalem where Jesus's field of action was situated. Mount Sinai (*Tur Sinin*) refers to that hill where God made His revelation to Moses. The 'secure land' (*al-Baladu'l Amin*) refers to Makkah where the Prophet Muhammad was born.

c Almighty God has created the human being with superior capabilities. These capabilities have been given to man so that he should be able to recognise the Truth revealed to him through the prophets, and to shape his life in accordance with it. Those who do so, will reach a high position of honour, which will be theirs for all eternity. On the contrary, those who do not make

[7] What then after this, can make you deny the Last Judgement? [8] Is not God the greatest of the judges?

96. THE CLOT (*AL-'ALAQ*)

In the name of God, the Most Gracious, the Most Merciful

[1] Read! In the name of your Lord, who created:[a] [2] created man from a clot [of blood]. [3] Read! Your Lord is the Most Bountiful One [4] who taught by the pen, [5] taught man what he did not know.[b] [6] Yet man behaves arrogantly, [7] because he thinks himself self-sufficient: [8] truly, all will return to your Lord. [9] Have you seen one who prevents [10] a worshipper from praying? [11] Do you think he is rightly guided, [12] or enjoins true piety? [13] Do you see how he has denied the truth and turned away from it? [14] Does he not know that God observes all things? [15] Let him beware! If he does not desist, We will drag him by the forelock—[16] his lying, sinful forelock. [17] Then let him call his associates; [18] We shall summon the guards of Hell. [19] No indeed! Do not obey him, but prostrate yourself and come closer to God.

---

their God-given capabilities subservient to God's will, will have even the existing blessings taken away and they will have no place to take refuge. Their lot will be total deprivation. The raising of prophets and the end-results of their mission, bear testimony to the veracity of this fact.

a The first five verses of this chapter were the very first verses which were revealed to the Prophet Muhammad. Almighty God created man out of ordinary material elements. Then He blessed him with the rare capacity to read and to understand the import of what he read. Then, man was given the additional capacity to use the pen and thus systematise and preserve his knowledge. While the capacity to read enables a man to acquire knowledge, the pen makes him capable of spreading this knowledge to others on a large scale.

b The 'pen' is a symbol of knowledge. In other words, through written words the believers are enjoined to acquire and spread the knowledge of the truth, wisdom and beauty of Islam. Today, spreading the words of God will be done by means of printed material and through other means of communication which includes internet and the multimedia. Translations of the Quran in various languages, Islamic books and other printed material on Islam should be distributed as a part of *dawah* work on a large scale, so that the message of Islam may be communicated to everyone.

97. THE NIGHT OF DESTINY
(*AL-QADR*)

In the name of God, the Most Gracious, the Most Merciful

¹ We sent it [Quran] down on the Night of Destiny. ² And what will make you comprehend what the Night of Destiny is?*ᵃ* ³ The Night of Destiny is better than a thousand months; ⁴ on that night, the angels and the Spirit*ᵇ* come down by the permission of their Lord with His decrees for all matters; ⁵ it is all peace till the break of dawn.

98. THE CLEAR EVIDENCE
(*AL-BAYYINAH*)

In the name of God, the Most Gracious, the Most Merciful

¹ The deniers of truth from among the People of the Book and the polytheists would not desist from disbelief until they received clear evidence—² a messenger from God, reciting to them pure scriptures, ³ containing upright precepts. ⁴ Those who were given the Book did

---

a A particular night of the year (perhaps some night in the last days of the month of Ramadan) is the night of decisions by God. Certain tasks have to be performed in the course of the year in connection with the administration of the world, and the angels descend to the earth to arrange for them to be carried out. On a similar particular night, the revelation of the Quran began.

It seems that on that night there is an abundance of angels on the earth. Those who are spiritually aroused are influenced by this atmosphere and, as a result, they become imbued with a spirituality which enhances the value of their religious deeds at that time, as compared to such deeds as are performed in ordinary circumstances.

For this reason, as the month draws towards the last ten days, the worshippers give more time to prayers, give more in charity and read as much as possible from the Quran, beseeching their Lord for His mercy and forgiveness. When the Prophet was asked by his wife, 'A'ishah, what one's prayer should be if one finds the Night of Destiny or *Lailatul Qadr*, he taught her this simple prayer: O God, You are forgiving, You love forgiveness, so forgive me.

b This refers to the Angel Gabriel.

not become divided except after clear evidence was given to them.
[5] They were commanded only to worship God, offering Him sincere devotion, to be sincere in their faith, to pray regularly; and to give alms, for that is the right religion.[a] [6] Those of the deniers of truth among the People of the Book and the polytheists will dwell forever in Hell-fire. They are the worst of creatures. [7] Truly, those who believe and do good works are the best of creatures. [8] God has a reward in store for them: Gardens of eternity, through which rivers flow; they will dwell therein forever. God is well pleased with them and they are well pleased with Him. Thus shall the God-fearing be rewarded.

99. THE EARTHQUAKE (*AL-ZALZALAH*)

In the name of God, the Most Gracious, the Most Merciful

[1] When the earth is shaken with its violent shaking, [2] when the earth shakes off her burdens, [3] when man asks, 'What is happening to her?'; [4] on that Day it will narrate its account, [5] for your Lord has so directed it. [6] On that Day people will come forward in separate groups to be shown their deeds: [7] whoever has done the smallest particle of good will see it; [8] while whoever has done the smallest particle of evil will see it.[b]

---

a The true religion of God is that according to which man should pray to and worship the one and only God; he should love and admire God from the bottom of his heart; he should consistently say his prayers and pay *zakat*. This is the real religion which comes from God. The best of all are those who adopt this correct religion and the worst are those who do not do so, or who devise another religion instead of the proper one and call the new religion the true religion.

b The earthquake on Doomsday will be the announcement of the end of the testing period for man. This would mean that the freedom which was theirs on account of their being on trial, has now been snatched away from them. Now the time has come when human beings will be recompensed for their deeds. Today, God's world is silent, but when conditions change, everything found here will start talking. The inventions of the present day have proved that lifeless or inanimate things also have the capacity to 'talk' .A performance in a studio is fully reproduced by video film and records. Similarly, the present world is, so to say, a big 'studio' of God. Whatever a man does or says or

100. THE SNORTING HORSES
(AL-'ADIYAT)

In the name of God, the Most Gracious, the Most Merciful

[1] By the snorting, panting horses, [2] striking sparks of fire with their hooves, [3] as they gallop to make raids at dawn, [4] and raising clouds of dust, [5] forcing their way into the midst of the enemy, [6] surely, man is ungrateful to his Lord. [7] He himself bears witness to that. [8] Surely, he is ardent in his love of wealth. [9] Is he not aware of the time when the contents of the graves will be brought out? [10] And the hearts' contents shall be brought into the open? [11] Surely, on that Day, they will know that their Lord had full knowledge of them all.[a]

101. THE CLATTERER (AL-QARI'AH)

In the name of God, the Most Gracious, the Most Merciful

[1] The Clatterer! [2] What is the Clatterer? [3] Would that you knew what the Clatterer is! [4] [It is] a Day when mankind shall be like scattered moths [5] and the mountains like tufts of carded wool. [6] Then, the one whose good deeds weigh heavy on the scales, [7] will have a most pleasing life. [8] But as for him whose deeds are light

---

even thinks, everything is being recorded at every moment. And when the time comes, this world will repeat everybody's story in such a way that not a thing, great or small, will be left out.

a In this world, the animal is grateful to his master, but man is not grateful to his Lord. Here an animal knows his obligations towards his master, but man does not know his obligations towards his Lord. Here an animal is totally obedient to his master, but man is not totally obedient to his Lord.

Man appreciates any animal which is loyal to him. Then, how is it possible that he does not comprehend that, in the eyes of God, only that individual is worthy of appreciation who is loyal to Him? It is the love of wealth that blinds him. He is unable to learn the truth even from his own experiences.

on the scales, ⁹ the Abyss shall be his home. ¹⁰ What will convey to you what this is like? ¹¹ It is a blazing fire.*a*

102. GREED FOR MORE AND MORE (*AL-TAKATHUR*)

In the name of God, the Most Gracious, the Most Merciful

¹ Greed for more and more distracted you [from God] ² till you reached the grave. ³ But you will soon come to know. ⁴ But you will soon come to know. ⁵ Indeed, were you to know the truth with certainty, ⁶ you would see the fire of Hell. ⁷ You would see it with the eye of certainty. ⁸ Then on that Day you shall be questioned about your worldly favours.*b*

---

a The turmoil of Doomsday will smash everything. People will completely lose their bearings. Thereafter a new world will come into existence where only Truth will carry weight. All falsity will be set at naught. In the present world, the approval of the people prevails. Here things carry weight according to the likes and dislikes of human beings. The world of the Hereafter is the world of God. There, according to God's will, one thing will carry weight while another may carry no weight at all.

In the world the deeds performed are judged according to their appearance. In the Hereafter deeds will be judged according to their inner reality. The more sincere a man's deeds are the more importance they will be given. The deed which is devoid of sincerity will carry absolutely no weight in the Hereafter, however significant it might have seemed to the superficial people of the present world.

b Man wants to earn more and more so that he may accumulate more and more material things. He is totally immersed in that thought till the day he dies. At that time he comes to know that whatever was worth accumulating was one thing while what he was bent on accumulating was something else.

Any increase in worldly goods increases a man's accountability. But man, in his foolishness, thinks that he is adding to his success.

103. THE PASSAGE OF TIME (*AL-'ASR*)

In the name of God, the Most Gracious, the Most Merciful

[1] I swear by the passage of time, [2] that man is surely in a state of loss, [3] except for those who believe and do good deeds and exhort one another to hold fast to the Truth, and who exhort one another to stead-fastness.*a*

104. THE BACKBITER (*AL-HUMAZAH*)

In the name of God, the Most Gracious, the Most Merciful

[1] Woe to every fault-finding back-biter, [2] who amasses wealth, counting it over, [3] thinking that his wealth will make him live forever. [4] By no means! He shall surely be cast into the crushing torment. [5] Would that you understood what that crushing torment is like. [6] It is a Fire kindled by God. [7] Reaching right into the hearts of men, [8] it closes in on them from every side [9] in towering columns.*b*

---

a At every moment man is advancing towards his death. This means that if a man does not make the best of the time still available to him, he will finally face total destruction. In order to be successful, a man has to exert himself, while for failure he has to do nothing. It is itself rushing towards him.

A venerable gentleman tells us that he understood the meaning of this chapter of the Quran from an ice vendor who was shouting in market, 'O, people! Have mercy on one whose assets are melting away.' On hearing this shout, the gentleman said to himself that just as the ice melts and reduces, similarly the lifespan given to man is fast passing away. If the existing opportunity is lost in inaction or in evil action, this is man's loss. (Imam Razi, *Tafsir Kabir*).

One who utilises his time properly is one who adopts three courses in the present world. One is that of Faith (*al-ladina a'manu*), i.e. consciousness of Truth or reality and its acceptance. Secondly that of virtuous deeds (*wa a'milu al-salihat*), i.e. doing that which is required to be done as a matter of religious duty and abstaining from what is sinful. Thirdly that of advising people about Truth and forbearance. This follows upon such a deep realisation of Truth that the concerned person becomes its preacher and missionary.

b If a man has a difference with another, he can settle it by argument. But

105. THE ELEPHANT (*AL-FIL*)

In the name of God, the Most Gracious, the Most Merciful

[1] Have you not seen how your Lord dealt with the people of the elephant? [2] Did He not foil their strategy [3] and send against them flocks of birds, [4] which pelted them with clay stones? [5] Thus He made them like stubble cropped by cattle?[a]

106. QURAYSH (*QURAYSH*)

In the name of God, the Most Gracious, the Most Merciful

[1] For the security of the Quraysh: [2] their security in their winter and summer journeys. [3] So let them worship the Lord of this House,

---

it is not proper for him to denigrate the other person, defame him and make him the target of allegations. While the first course of action is legitimate, the second is not.

Those who resort to calumny, do so because they see that their worldly position is safe and strong. They think that they are not going to lose anything if they level baseless allegations against another. But this is mere foolishness. The fact is that their doing so amounts to jumping into a pit of fire—a pit of fire from which there will be no escape.

a Abraha was a Christian ruler of Yemen in southern Arabia in the sixth century A.D. Out of religious fanaticism, he attacked Makkah in the year 570 A.D. with a view to destroying the Ka'bah by demolishing it. He had with him an army of sixty thousand soldiers and about a dozen elephants. That is why they were called 'the People of the elephant'. As these people approached Makkah, the elephants refused to move ahead. Besides that, flocks of birds flew over them carrying pebbles in their beaks and claws. They showered these pebbles on Abraha's army and the whole army was afflicted by a strange disease. The army was terrified and took flight. But many of its soldiers, including Abraha died on the way.

This event took place in the very year in which the Prophet Muhammad was born. this was Almighty God's way of showing that the Prophet was associated with domination. Whoever clashed with him or his religion would be vanquished.

⁴ who provided them with food lest they go hungry and saved them from fear.*[a]*

107. SMALL THINGS (*AL-MA'UN*)

In the name of God, the Most Gracious, the Most Merciful

¹ Have you seen one who denies the Day of Judgement? ² Who turns away the orphan, ³ and who does not urge the feeding of the poor? ⁴ So woe to those who pray ⁵ but whose hearts are not in their prayer. ⁶ Those who do things only to be seen by others. ⁷ Who are uncharitable even over very small things.*[b]*

---

a The Quraysh was a trading community. During the summer their traders' caravans used to go to Syria and Palestine and in winter they would trade with Yemen. Their economy was dependent upon these trading activities. In ancient times, when the robbing of traders was common, the caravans of the Quraysh went unscathed. The reason for this was their connection with the Ka'bah of which the Quraysh were the servants and trustees. Since respect for the Ka'bah dominated the minds of the people, they used to respect its servants and trustees also, and on account of this they did not rob their caravans.

Here, in connection with the call for the acceptance of the Truth, the Quraysh have been reminded of this circumstance and called to Islam. They are told that it would be highly ungrateful to enjoy the worldly benefits of the House of God—the Ka'bah, while shirking the religious responsibility incumbent upon them. They are enjoined to worship only God who conferred all material benefits upon them.

b Belief in the reckoning of the Hereafter makes a man pious. One who does not believe in this will be devoid of all goodness; he will be neglectful of prayer to God; he will not be ashamed of pushing over a weak person; he will not think it necessary to discharge the dues and rights of the poor; he will not even give to others such things as will cause him no substantial loss—even if it be only matchsticks or his good wishes.

108. ABUNDANCE (*AL-KAWTHAR*)

In the name of God, the Most Gracious, the Most Merciful

¹ We have given you abundance. ² Pray to your Lord and sacrifice to Him alone. ³ It is the one who hates you who has been cut off.*ᵃ*

109. THOSE WHO DENY THE TRUTH (*AL-KAFIRUN*)

In the name of God, the Most Gracious, the Most Merciful

¹ Say, 'You who deny the Truth,*ᵇ* ² I do not worship what you worship. ³ You do not worship what I worship. ⁴ I will never worship what you worship. ⁵ You will never worship what I worship. ⁶ You have your religion and I have mine.'*ᶜ*

---

a The Prophet Muhammad had arisen with the pure mission of calling all men to the Truth. In the present world this is the most difficult task. So for the sake of this mission he had to forego his all. He was isolated from his community. His economic position was ruined. The future of his children became dark. Nobody except a few supported him. But under these very discouraging conditions, he was told by Almighty God, 'We have given you abundance' i.e. the highest success of every kind. This prediction of the Quran was fulfilled to the letter in later years.

This very promise is also applicable in various degrees to the followers of the Prophet. For them also there was an 'abundance of good things' provided they rose in the cause of the pure religion for which the Prophet and his companions had risen. This 'abundance' extends from this world up to the Hereafter. It is never-ending.

b This chapter of the Quran was revealed in the last days of the Makkan period. In the beginning the Prophet used to address the people as 'O my people' or 'O my community'. But when, in spite of completion of the arguments, the people did not accept him, he addressed them as 'You who deny the Truth'. At this stage, in fact, this is a statement of repudiation and not the utterance of a missionary call.

c 'You have your religion and I have mine'—this is an expression of mutual understanding meaning, 'follow one and respect all'.

You follow your religion and I shall follow mine, but at the same time both of us should respect each other's faiths.

110. HELP (*AL-NASR*)

In the name of God, the Most Gracious, the Most Merciful

¹ When God's help and victory come, ² and you see people entering God's religion in multitudes, ³ then glorify your Lord with His praise and seek His forgiveness. He is always ready to accept repentance.[a]

111. TWISTED FIBRE (*AL-MASAD*)

In the name of God, the Most Gracious, the Most Merciful

¹ May the hands of Abu Lahab perish, may he be ruined. ² Neither his wealth nor his gains will avail him. ³ He shall soon enter a Blazing Fire, ⁴ and also his wife who carries the fuel, ⁵ with a rope of twisted fibre round her neck.[b]

---

a The help of God, which results in victory, always comes through dawah (the missionary call for the acceptance of Truth). Causing people to join the fold of Islam in great numbers in itself is the greatest help to God, and it is in this way that religious people will reach the destination of victory and domination. Accordingly, during the last days of the Prophet the position was that a larger number of people entered the Islamic fold, thus opening the door to further conquests.

For a believer, victory increases his feeling of humility. Even for his apparently right action, he seeks God's pardon. Even the success he achieves, seemingly by his own efforts, he attributes to the will of God.

b Abu Lahab, the name of an actual person, has come to denote a particular kind of character. 'Abu Lahab' has come to be a symbol of such an opponent of the call for the acceptance of Truth as will stoop in his hostility to meanness. Just as the Prophet had to face this character, similarly other missionaries among his followers (*ummah*) may have to face just such a character. However, if the missionary has become active for the sake of God in the real sense, then God's help will be given to him. The inimical efforts of people like Abu Lahab will, by God's grace, become ineffective and, in spite of all their means and resources, they will perish. They will themselves burn in the fire of their own jealousy and enmity. Their aim may have been wanting to drag the missionary of God to a miserable end, but they themselves will be the ones to suffer that everlasting fate.

112. ONENESS (*AL-IKHLAS*)

In the name of God, the Most Gracious, the Most Merciful

¹ Say, 'He is God, the One, ² God, the Self-sufficient One. ³ He does not give birth, nor was He born, ⁴ and there is nothing like Him.'ᵃ

113. DAYBREAK (*AL-FALAQ*)

In the name of God, the Most Gracious, the Most Merciful

¹ Say, 'I seek refuge in the Lord of the daybreak ² from the evil of what He has created, ³ from the evil of darkness as it descends, ⁴ from the evil of those who blow on knots ⁵ and from the evil of the envier when he envies.'ᵇ

---

a This chapter of the Quran is about the oneness of God. The concept of God has been presented here in its purest form, ridding it of all polluting associations which people of every age have brought to it. There is no plurality of gods. There is only one God. All are dependent upon Him, but He is not dependent on anybody. He Himself has power over everything. He is far above being the progeny of anybody or having any offspring. He is such a unique being that there is nobody like Him or equal to Him in any manner whatsoever.

b God—the One who rends the darkness of night and brings out from it the light of dawn. It is this God who can remove the dark clouds of trouble overshadowing a man and bring him into the sunshine of well-being.

The present world has been made with a view to putting human beings to the test. So, here there is evil along with good. The only way for man to be safe from the ill effects of evil is to seek refuge in God against it. Evil is of different kinds. For example, the mischief indulged in by evil-hearted people in the dead of the night, and the practitioners of witchcraft. Similarly, there are individuals who, seeing others living prosperously, become jealous and make the latter the victims of their jealousy-inspired actions. A believer should seek refuge in God from the mischief of all such people, and undoubtedly it is God alone who has the power to protect man from all kinds of evil.

114. PEOPLE (*AL-NAS*)

In the name of God, the Most Gracious, the Most Merciful

[1] Say, 'I seek refuge in the Lord of people, [2] the King of people, [3] the God of people, [4] from the mischief of every sneaking whisperer, [5] who whispers into the hearts of people, [6] from jinn and men.'[a]

---

[a] Man is a humble creature. He essentially needs protection. But this cannot be given to him by anybody except the one and only God. It is God who is the Lord and Sustainer of all human beings. It is He who is their King. It is He alone who is worth worshipping. Indeed, who except God can become the support of believers in their trials and tribulations?

The most dangerous mischief against which man should seek God's refuge is that of Satan. He is most dangerous because he always hides his real position. He misleads people by his deceitful ways. So, only one who is extremely alert can save himself from the machinations of Satan. He is one to whom God has given the capacity to distinguish between Truth and Untruth; who can understand what is reality and what is falsity. Evil-inspirers are not only the known Satans. Even among human beings there are certain Satan-like people who present themselves in artificial guises and, by means of deceitful words, brain-wash others and put them on the path of misguidance.

Seeking refuge in God from mischief is a two-sided action. On the one hand, it entails obtaining God's grace. On the other hand, its purpose is to awaken one's awareness of mischief so that one may become capable of countering it more consciously.

INDEX

ABOUT THE TRANSLATORS AND THE PUBLISHERS

MAULANA WAHIDUDDIN KHAN, born in [1925] in India, is an Islamic spiritual scholar who is well versed in both classical Islamic learning and modern science. Ever the idealist, he has from the outset made his life's mission the establishment of world-wide peace. To this end, he has consistently striven for the development of a complete Quran-based ideology of peace and non-violence. Moreover, having come to the conclusion that the need of the hour was to present Islamic teachings in the style and language of the present day, the Maulana has written over [200] books on Islam. These include a commentary on the Quran entitled, *The Quran: English Translation, Commentary and Parallel Arabic Text,* the Arabic version of which was published by Darel Wafa, Cairo, as *al-Tadhkir al-Qawim fi Tafsir al-Quran al-Hakim.* To cater to the needs of inquisitive minds and of the spiritually inclined, the Maulana established at New Delhi in [2001] the Centre for Peace and Spirituality. His most recent publication are *The Seeker's Guide, Discovering God, Leading A Spiritual Life* and *The Prophet of Peace: The Teachings of the Prophet Muhammad.*

PROF. FARIDA KHANAM, the daughter of Maulana Wahiduddin Khan, holds a Ph.D. in Islamic Studies. She was the professor at Jamia Millia Islamia University at New Delhi. She has written and translated a number of books on Islam.

GOODWORD BOOKS is a publishing house with a splendid range of Islamic books and children's products. It also publishes a wide range of the Quran in various languages. Goodword is also involved in many dawah projects, such as free distribution of the Quran in English and introductory booklets on Islam. To see our complete range of products and online shopping visit: www.goodwordbooks.com.

CPS INTERNATIONAL is an organization, which aims to promote and reinforce the culture of peace and spirituality. CPS is also distributing free copies of the Quran and dawah material worldwide, to spread the peaceful message of Islam. For more details or to get involved with our mission, please visit our website: www.cpsglobal.org.